THE CHRISTIAN RENAISSANCE

THE
CHRISTIAN RENAISSANCE

A HISTORY OF THE
"DEVOTIO MODERNA"

BY

ALBERT HYMA

76051

SECOND EDITION

ARCHON BOOKS
HAMDEN, CONNECTICUT
1965

Library of Congress Catalog Card Number: 65-17070
Printed in the United States of America

PREFACE TO THE SECOND EDITION

Forty-two years ago the present writer composed a history of a powerful religious movement known as the Devotio Moderna. At that time the historians of Europe and America evinced little interest in this phase of late medieval culture. As a result it was difficult to locate the original sources and to evaluate the contributions of those men and women who participated in the work begun by Gerard Groote and his associates. The founders of the Devotio Moderna had so long been treated with indifference that the greatest of Dutch historians ignored to a large extent their institutions and literary productions. In Great Britain and Germany the general public also was ignorant of the atmosphere in which such influential writers as Thomas à Kempis and Erasmus labored.

But during the past thirty years a large number of scholars have turned their attention to the Devotio Moderna, with the result that thousands of manuscripts have been carefully examined and their contents made known. The outstanding mystics, reformers, and humanists who were connected with the movement are now much better understood by us than they once were. For this reason a second edition can now make its appearance which presents a clearer delineation than was possible before. The leading figures together with their books and their constitutions have become more familiar to us all, and the author can speak with greater confidence than he did in the days of pioneering.

Albert Hyma

ACKNOWLEDGMENTS

The author gratefully acknowledges his debt to the following for permission to reprint and use material first published by them.

William B. Eerdmans Publishing Co., Grand Rapids, Michigan, for quotations from *The Brethren of Common Life*.

Martinus Nijhoff, The Hague, for quotations from two articles, "Super Modo Vivendi" and "The Influence of the 'Devotio Moderna'", appearing respectively in volumes 16 and 19 of *Nederlandscn Archiefvoor Kerkgeschiedenis*.

The University of Colorado, Boulder, Colorado, for quotations from "Erasmus and the Reformation in Germany," appearing in volume 8 of *Medievalia et Humanistica*.

PUBLISHER'S NOTE

The second edition of *The Christian Renaissance* consists of a facsimile of the first edition, with five additional chapters containing new material placed at the end of the original book.

CONTENTS OF SECOND EDITION

THE CHRISTIAN RENAISSANCE
Part I

PREFACE

In this book I have sought to tell the story of a great religious movement named "Devotio Moderna", or "Christian Renaissance". Early in the year 1917 my attention was called to this movement and in particular to the Brethren of the Common Life by Professor Leonard Ch. Van Noppen of Columbia University. As literary representative of the "Board of the Queen Wilhelmina Lectureship, Columbia University", he not only gave me much valuable information, but also enabled me to secure financial assistance from the board he represented. Among the members of this board were Professor G. Kalff, of the University of Leiden; J. Heldring, of Heldring and Pierson, Bankers, the Hague; J. W. Yzerman, President of the Royal Netherland Geographical Society at Amsterdam; Wouter Nijhoff, President of the Dutch Publishers' Association; and Dr. H. J. Kiewiet de Jonge, President of the General Dutch Alliance. To these gentlemen, therefore, I wish to express my thanks, both for their willingness to support an unknown American student, and for the way in which they allowed him to carry on his research work in various foreign countries. Consul Jacob Steketee and Mrs. H. Hulst of Grand Rapids, Michigan, who are their representatives in Michigan, also deserve my gratitude. However, I feel just as greatly indebted to the Graduate Council of the University of Michigan for enabling me to devote one whole year exclusively to research work, before going abroad.

In Holland I received many helpful suggestions from Professor A. Eekhof, Leiden; Professor W. J. Kühler,

Amsterdam; and Professor J. Lindeboom, Groningen. Many other scholars, and several librarians, and archivists in Holland contributed to make this book possible. I had delightful visits with Dr. K. Löffler, librarian at Cologne; Dr. A. Bömer, librarian at Münster (University Library); Professor L. Schmitz-Kallenberg, Münster; Mgr. W. E. Schwarz, "Kammerherr" of the pope, Münster; and Dr. Paul Hagen, Lübeck. Besides, I am also greatly indebted to librarians and archivists of other libraries and archives where I conducted researches, as at Düsseldorf, Berlin, Nuremberg, Munich, Brussels, Liège, Vienna, Innsbruck, Rome, Paris, and London.

Special mention must be made here of the painstaking labors of Dr. R. Flatscher, of the University Library at Innsbruck. He copied several medieval writings for me; without his work the composition of this book would have been greatly delayed. Professor A. Eekhof of Leiden, as one of the editors of the "Nederlandsch Archief voor Kerkgeschiedenis", helped revise one article for me, which appeared in that magazine: and a year later another one was accepted. I also felt greatly encouraged by the response made by Dr. J. de Jong, of the Episcopal Seminary at Driebergen in Holland, who is editor of the "Archief voor de Geschiedenis van het Aartsbisdom Utrecht", a Roman Catholic periodical. He immediately accepted a series of articles on Gerard Groote and Gerard Zerbolt, which meant that the present volume could appear in print sooner than had been anticipated. By far the greatest debt I owe is to Professor E. W. Dow of the University of Michigan. His ripe experience as scholar and teacher, his sane judgment, his prudence and moderation, are all alike reflected on almost every page of this book.

TABLE OF CONTENTS

INTRODUCTION

CHAPTER I

GERARD GROOTE

CHAPTER II

THE RISE OF THE CHRISTIAN RENAISSANCE

INTRODUCTION.

CHAPTER IV

THE CONGREGATION OF WINDESHEIM

CHAPTER V
THE "IMITATION OF CHRIST"

INTRODUCTION.

CHAPTER VI
WESSEL GANSFORT

CHAPTER VII

THE CHRISTIAN RENAISSANCE IN FRANCE

CHAPTER VIII

THE CHRISTIAN RENAISSANCE

INTRODUCTION.

INTRODUCTION

Somewhere among the wooded hills of Westphalia the little river known as Oude (or Old) Yssel takes its source. Descending through forest, heath, and meadow, on a northwestward course, it soon crosses the borders of Holland. Here both it and its neighbor the Rhine come up against the plateau Veluwe, or "Barren Meadow". Confronted by this plateau, the Oude Yssel turns northward, and for the rest of its course is called simply Yssel; while the Rhine turns mostly westward, but discharges about a ninth of the water with which it enters Holland into the Zuiderzee by way of the Yssel.

Once on a northward course, the river changes greatly in character. Slowly it winds past thriving cities — no longer an obscure little river, but a dignified stream whose quiet waters have nearly finished a long journey. The valley through which it now flows is very attractive, and is made doubly attractive by the striking contrast between the verdant meadows along the gentle waters and the dusty heaths of the Veluwe. Down in the valley are fertile banks with green pastures and smiling grain fields; on the plateau are stunted pines and barren sand-dunes. Below, the busy hand of man has planted willows and elms, has transformed the monotonous green into the radiant colors of flowers and shrubbery, and has built a multitude of homes; on the solitary heaths of the Veluwe few fragrant garden spots are found, few riversides, and few prosperous homes.

Four or five centuries ago, the contrast between the valley of the Yssel and its nearer environment was even stronger than now. For at that time the Veluwe, to the westward, was far more weird and forsaken. In spring and autumn, when the Rhine, Yssel, and Grebbe[1] overflowed their banks, it would appear like a huge sand heap, devoid of human and animal life. On stormy days the wind would shriek among the tops of the lonely pines and the sand would swirl through the air. This spectacle was in itself sufficient to frighten away most invaders. East of the Yssel the landscape was almost equally desolate. Three different zones could be distinguished there, parallel with the river. First came the fertile strip of land bordering the stream; then the sand hills with their extensive forests of oaks and pines, but not wholly without cultivation, particularly along the little brooks which had their source in the higher land farther to the east. The third zone was nothing but a waste of heaths, forests, and moors, showing but very few signs of human habitation[2].

In this valley were situated the cities of Deventer, Zutphen, and Kampen, with Zwolle close by. Deventer was near the centre. Bordered on both sides by lonely expanses of heath and fen, Deventer was only to a relatively small degree subjected to the influence of international commerce. True, it was a prosperous town, but not a mighty port like Bruges or Antwerp; nor was it exposed so much to foreign influences as were the cities of Utrecht, Leiden, Amsterdam, and Dordrecht. Did the green pastures and the silent waters encircling the town perhaps foster in religious men of Deventer that spirit of mysticism which attracted a Thomas à Kempis and impelled him to leave his home at distant Kempen for the Yssel country?

Great mystics have always loved to seek communion with God on the banks of quiet rivers, in forests and deserts. It was of such a country that David wrote: "The Lord is my shepherd; I shall not want. He maketh me to lie down in green pastures; he leadeth me beside the still waters. He restoreth my soul".

However this may be, the valley of the Yssel became the centre of a great religious movement,—the "Devotio Moderna", or "New Devotion", which developed the institution of the Brethren of the Common Life. It was in this valley that the "Imitation of Christ", next to the Bible the most widely read book in Europe, was composed. Here the "Spiritual Ascensions" was written by Gerard Zerbolt of Zutphen, as well as the "Rosary of Spiritual Exercises" by John Mombaer or Mauburn, which two works later had a profound influence on Ignatius Loyola. Not only did Loyola use Zerbolt's work as the pattern for his "Spiritual Exercises", but Luther gave it the highest praise, as will appear. In this valley also Gerlach Peters composed his "Soliloquy", which became the mystical text-book of the Port Royalists or Jansenists in France. Here John Cele lived, the first teacher to introduce the study of the Bible into the elementary schools. And here Gansfort and Erasmus acquired the ideals of reformation which they in turn passed on to Luther, Zwingli, and Calvin.

The "New Devotion" succeeded another religious movement, which had found its most perfect expression in the works of Bernard of Clairvaux, and Francis of Assisi; and in the cathedrals of Amiens, Rouen, Reims, Paris, Brussels, and Cologne. This movement had led to far-reaching monastic reforms; it had touched the hearts of the masses, inspiring them to rise to higher ideals than the worship of self, and the amassing of material riches, honor, and fame among mortals. Learning had flourished in those days, and philosophy had been a living force. France had been the chief centre of this older movement; its monks had brought monastic reforms to the Low Countries and Germany; and its literature had served as a model; beautiful Gothic houses of worship had been erected, seldom if ever surpassed in grandeur and ennobling simplicity.

But the thirteenth century had been followed by the fourteenth, a century notable for its spirit of strife and discontent. National and dynastic wars had brought misery to Western Europe, and no country had suffered more than France. With the loss of economic strength came the gradual eclipse of France as a dominating force in the realms of learning, literature, and art[3]. And England was scarcely in a better position than its neighbor across the Channel[4]. The same can be said of the German Empire, where many disintegrating forces were gradually undermining the prosperity of the people[5]. And what of the Church? Was it not growing from bad to worse as time went on, the more the clergy neglected their duties? Everywhere a decline in moral standards was noticeable, and everywhere a reform was badly needed.

What Europe of the fourteenth century apparently lacked was some great Apostle, a man able to organize a lasting movement for reform; a man who could preach, write, and draw thousands of others behind him, who in their turn would preach, write, and found schools where the rising generation might learn the ideals of the great leader himself. It was the fortune of the Yssel valley to produce such a man; for Gerard Groote, the founder of the Brotherhood of the Common Life, not only preached and wrote, but induced thousands of others to follow his example. He was the spiritual ancestor of Thomas à Kempis, Wessel Gansfort, Hegius, and Erasmus; the inaugurator of the "New Devotion", or Christian Renaissance. Through his influence the schools of Deventer and Zwolle were to become the seats of a revival of learning that was soon to spread all over Western Europe and be carried into the New World.

How did it happen that Groote and the movement he inaugurated became devoted to the reform of the schools as well as of the Church? Why did the "New Devotion", which, as has been said, was a religious movement, extend its influence to the realm of education, and why should one call it the "Christian Renaissance"? The word Renaissance means literally *rebirth,* and the term Christian Renaissance, therefore, should refer to a great rebirth of Christianity. At the same time it should denote some movement which, like the Italian Renaissance, produced a revival of learning. This was exactly the scope of the "New Devotion". Thus far it has been commonly believed that the revival of learning North of the Alps was a product of the Italian Renaissance. We shall consider whether this actually was the case; whether the reform of the schools at Deventer and Zwolle, and of those reformed after their pattern grew out of the Italian Renaissance; and whether Groote and Cele in 1374 were inspired by the Italians, or originated their own ideas.

Perhaps the physical geography of the Yssel valley had something to do with the twofold reform instituted by Groote and his followers. The cities in the Yssel country, though surrounded by immense heaths and moors, and situated somewhat apart from the busiest thoroughfares in the West, were nevertheless commercial centres and shared in the prosperity of Bruges, Ghent, and Antwerp. They formed a part of the Low Countries, where from the days of Charlemagne until the end of the fifteenth century the currents of Western thought met and intermingled[6]. Through this middle region French monastic reforms, epics, and chivalry passed into Germany; and whatever ideas came from Germany to France traveled mostly by way of the Low Countries[7].

It was here that intellectual as well as religious and commercial currents met and mingled; and from here they issued forth. The Flemish towns were the first in Transalpine Europe to supplant the monasteries as chief seats of learning and art[8]. Under the rule of the dukes of Burgundy, Bruges and Ghent became the wealthiest cities North of the Alps, not excepting Paris and London. In the middle of the fifteenth century the court at Bruges outshone even the court at Paris[9]. Then followed the rise of Antwerp and Brussels, which brought more wealth, more leisure, and consequently more learning to the Low Countries. Never before had the world seen such a port as Antwerp, since in this city for more than half of the sixteenth century nearly all the great routes of commerce converged,—something which has never happened before nor since in any other port[10]. The Low Countries, therefore, shared with Italy the honor of being the most opulent districts in Europe at the very time that the "New Devotion", or Christian Renaissance made its influence felt throughout the West.

Just as France bought wares of Italy in the Low Countries, so did Paris receive many of the best fruits of the Italian Renaissance by way of the Low Countries. The same can to a large extent be said of Germany, Switzerland, England, and Scandinavia. How this "New Devotion", or Christian Renaissance, between 1380 and

1520, absorbed the wisdom of the ancients, the essence of Christ's teachings, the mystic religion of the Fathers and the saints of medieval Europe, as well as the learning of the Italian humanists; how it assimilated all these ingredients and presented them in a new dress to the old world and the new, will be shown in the following pages.

CHAPTER I
GERARD GROOTE
I

Gerard Groote[1] was born at Deventer in the year 1340[2], the son of Werner Groote, a prominent "schepen", or magistrate[3], and Heylwig van der Basselen[4]. At an early age he was sent to the parochial school in his native city, then to Aachen, and later to Cologne[5]. In 1355 he matriculated in the University of Paris, where he stayed three years, studying philosophy, medicine, Canon Law, and logic[6]. He also studied magic at that time, a fact which caused him much regret in later years[7]. In 1358 he obtained the degree of Master of Arts[8], but remained some time at Paris after having secured the degree[9]. At Prague also he sought to improve his knowledge. How much time he spent there, however, the sources do not reveal. They merely inform us that he soon returned to Deventer[10], where he won great distinction, as the magistrates asked him to represent them at the papal court at Avignon, to negotiate with Pope Urban V on a question of tolls and other dues[11]. The mission proved successful. Not long after this he was living at Cologne in the enjoyment of the return from two prebends[12]. Heedless of the masses, and without eyes for the many forms of corruption ruining the Church, he "walked in the ways of the world", according to Thomas à Kempis[13].

One day, however, a mystic stopped Groote on the street and pointed out to him the wickedness of indulging in selfish delights. "Why do you stand here", he asked, "intent upon empty things? You ought to become another

man". The appeal made some impression on him, but not sufficient to alter his mode of life[14].

A second warning came to him in his native city, where next we meet him. He was now living with his uncle, as his father had died some time before. There he fell very ill. Nevertheless, the pastor of his uncle's parish church refused to administer the sacrament of communion to him, for he refused to give up the study of astrology and magic. The illness grew worse until finally Groote thought his end was near. Suddenly he realized how many years he had spent in quest of self-aggrandizement. At Cologne in particular he had wasted his opportunities. Experience had taught him how great was the need of reform in every part and office of the Church. But he had paid no heed to the deplorable state of affairs among the clergy, especially in the higher ranks. Just as a drowning man in one brief moment reviews all the events of his past life, so did Groote on his sick-bed at Deventer go over the days of his lost youth. He had much reason to condemn himself. He ordered his books on magic to be burned, and it seemed as if he was henceforth to be a changed man. But no, as soon as the disease left him, his good resolutions vanished also. We may safely conclude, however, that the warnings he had received at Cologne and at Deventer prepared the way for his final conversion, which took place shortly after the illness at Deventer[15].

In 1374 Groote and an old friend, named Henry of Calcar, met at Utrecht. They had both been students at Paris, where an intimate friendship had knitted their souls with ties of common ideals and aspirations. But Henry had already yielded to the warning voice of conscience, while Gerard still hesitated. After a long talk Groote was convinced of the necessity of amending his

life. This third and last appeal had struck home; it resulted in a complete conversion[16]. Firmly resolved to amend
his ways, he returned to Deventer once more. First he
gave up his two prebends[17]; next he ceded the use of his
house to a few poor women[18], keeping only two small
rooms for his own use[19]; then he entered upon the task
of mastering his lower self. A terrific struggle, indeed!
Yet Groote did not fail. The greater the load of his former wrongs seemed to him, the greater his desire became
to root up the last vestiges of his sin, and to replace the
conquered vices by virtues.

Thus he battled for five long years[20], the last two of
which he spent in the Carthusian monastery of Monnikhuizen near Arnhem, where his friend Henry of Calcar
was then prior[21]. At Monnikhuizen Groote became an
ascetic. Spurred on by the example of the other monks,
he began to mortify the flesh, hoping thereby to overcome
his sinful nature more rapidly and completely. His life at
Monnikhuizen has been described by Thomas à Kempis:
"Dressing in a long and coarse garment of hair-cloth,
totally abstaining from the use of flesh and other lawful
things, and passing a considerable portion of his nights
in watching and prayer, he forced his feeble body into
complete subservience to the spirit"[22]. The Carthusian
monks were delighted with their enthusiastic disciple.
Groote was never able thereafter wholly to escape from
their influence, although his writings and his acts after
1379 reveal a changed attitude, which was further
developed by his disciples after he had passed away.

There was one other person who exerted a considerable
influence upon Groote during the period of his spiritual
struggles. This was John Ruysbroeck, prior of Groenendaal, the Augustinian monastery in the forest of Soignies,
near Brussels[23]. Spending most of his time out of doors,

a friend of birds and flowers, a lover of the contemplative
life, he had tried to solve the mysteries of the universe,
and had learned much. "Before I saw you", he told
Groote, "I knew you were coming". He found a responsive listener in Groote, but the latter was unable to
follow Ruysbroeck's theories of the kingdom of heaven,
the secret of love, the union of the human soul or spirit
with God, the various stages of the active and the contemplative life, the hierarchy of angels, and kindred sub-·
jects. Groote had not yet made much progress in mysticism as an abstract system of thought. And Ruysbroeck
knew that. Therefore he said to Groote: "Some day you
will understand"[24].

The first visit by Groote to Groenendaal must have
taken place in the year 1375 or 1376. Groote had brought
one of his most intimate friends with him, named John
Cele, rector of the school at Zwolle[25], the teacher who was
to inaugurate the reformation of the schools in the
Netherlands and Western Germany. We know much
about Groote's friendship with Cele and shall see his
influence in Cele's work.

In 1379 Groote's years of preparation were at an end.
The Carthusian monks of Monnikhuizen, astonished at
his gifts of argumentation and persuasion, told him that
so great a light of religious ardor as he possessed should
no longer remain beneath the roof of their little monastery, and advised him to go out among the people and
preach[26]. This advice Groote gladly followed. But he had
too much reverence for the priesthood to don the garb of
such an exalted calling[27], and thought the rank of deacon
good enough for him. Consequently he was ordained deacon shortly before the first of January, 1380, by the
Bishop of Utrecht[28].

Beginning with the cities near the Yssel, he preached

the gospel of repentance at Deventer, Zwolle, Kampen, Zutphen, Amersfoort, Amsterdam, Haarlem, Leiden, Utrecht, Gouda, Delft, Ghent, and many smaller places[29]. He labored in the spirit of John the Baptist, says Thomas à Kempis, laying the axe to the root of the tree. His magnetic personality, burning zeal to win souls, and power of conviction carried their message straight to the heart. The people came for miles to hear him, many of them leaving their work unfinished and their meals untouched. The huge churches in the larger cities did not have enough room to hold the surging crowds[30]. Remembering his own experiences, he warned the people of a future which might bring bitter regret and severe punishment. He addressed the clergy in Latin, the masses in the vernacular[31].

One day Groote addressed a considerable group of clerical dignitaries at Utrecht, and reproved them severely for their most flagrant sins: immorality, simony, and laziness mental and physical[32]. He had himself seen the evils that were undermining the Church, for he had been a monk himself, and before that had held two prebends, so was quite familiar with the state of affairs in his day. He had personal acquaintance with a great many priests, and fully realized how widely hypocrisy, immorality, greed, and self-indulgence were rampant among all ranks of the hierarchy. Many were wolves in the form of shepherds, as he knew, and said that he knew!

But Groote was equally concerned about the people, the wandering sheep, who were roaming about without the guiding help of their spiritual guardians, and exhorted them to be directed by their own consciences. For they possessed the reflex image of divinity within their breasts. He preached to them about Christ's commandments, and urged them to imitate the life of Christ, as he, Groote, himself was trying to do. To love God above all things, and one's neighbors as one-self, those were the two commandments, he said. We should try to eradicate vice and supplant it with newly acquired virtues, for we human beings, having been endowed with a spark of divinity, are not totally depraved. We should purge the impure flesh in which the soul condescends to dwell until our body's death. Our soul should be allowed no longer to remain obscured by the dense mists of sin woven around it by evil thoughts, words, and deeds. Man has fallen low, but he does not have to remain in the dust. Let him realize the tremendous possibilities of future glory or future punishment. He must choose, and is free to choose, though all his acts have been predestined from eternity.

With this appeal to all classes of men and women Groote aimed to teach others what he had already experienced himself. Instinctively the people felt that a new prophet had appeared, a man of extraordinary experience and power. As he went from town to town, he sent one of his disciples ahead to post the announcement of his intended address on the church door[33]. Then the people would come and look, tell their neighbors about the great news, and make the necessary preparations to hear the sermon. The farmer would hear of it, and take his family to town, leaving his crops to take care of themselves; shops were closed, almost everybody came.

Wherever Groote came to preach, a group of men and women, aroused from apathy, changed their lives and continued his work in their locality by personal example and appeal, and by lending religious books to their neighbors[34]. This was the beginning of the great religious movement, named "Devotio Moderna", or New Devotion, which will be the subject of our study. In Deventer, Zwolle, Kampen, Zutphen, Doesburg; also in Arnhem,

Utrecht, Amsterdam, Haarlem, Leiden, and Delft the fires of devotion were kept burning brightly after Groote had passed on. He himself gathered about him a band of twelve disciples at Deventer[35]. Among this number was a young man of about thirty, named Florentius Radewijns, who had given up his prebend at Utrecht to be in closer touch with Groote[36]. In Deventer he was vicar of the altar of St. Paul in the church of St. Lebwin[37], and soon it became a custom for Groote's followers to hold meetings in the vicar's house. A few of them came to live with him[38], while others followed Groote on his journeys[39], or remained at home[40]. These meetings in the house of Radewijns were the earliest visible beginnings of the society or congregation of the Brethren of the Common Life[41].

Groote continued his labors as itinerary preacher till the year 1383. His success had been great, but he had made many enemies among the mendicants and the secular clergy, by pointing out the evils among them. They were the more exasperated because with his great learning and his pure, unselfish mode of life he had easily confounded their wits. Their temporary defeat engendered a jealous, spiteful hatred for the man who had so boldly attacked them[42]. They went to the Bishop of Utrecht and made their complaint; they told him that Groote had attacked and denounced them; and that he had tried to lead the masses away from the folds of the Church. Now the sheep were leaving their true shepherds, they said, in order to follow after a man who was not even a priest. Should not such a person be commanded to stop preaching entirely? The bishop listened and assented. No deacon was henceforth to preach in public; Groote was silenced[43].

But Groote, though he obeyed the edict, decided not to sit idle in the future. His friends appealed to the pope[44].

In the meantime Groote continued to write. The end of his mortal life was near, but this last year at Deventer may perhaps be considered the most important one in the history of the great religious revival which he inaugurated. He now had more time to reflect upon his past, to instruct his followers, and to speak oftener with the teachers and pupils of the cathedral school. Several boys and young men were employed by him to copy books. Whenever he had a chance, he talked to them about some religious subject, trying to win them for the kingdom of God. They were the material most needed, he thought, for the reform of the Church[45]. Religion and learning must go hand in hand. The clergy ought to receive a liberal education before assuming the leadership of the people. Teachers, on the other hand, would do well to include religious instruction among the other subjects taught by them. These boys, said Groote to himself, will some day be leaders among men. Some of them will enter monasteries, others will teach; one or two among them are likely to become merchants or magistrates, while a few others may rise to the priesthood, or even higher. While their characters are still pliable, the ardor of youth in their veins, it is time to fill their minds with noble ambitions. Hence Groote gladly devoted a considerable share of his energy to the religious training of school boys. He was assisted in this undertaking by his followers, both at Deventer[46], and at Zwolle[47]. Thus the foundations were laid for the great revival of learning which was started and supervised by the Brethren of the Common Life.

In 1383 Groote entered also upon a new task. It was not enough, he said, that the clergy be educated. The people too must read and decide for themselves. Religion should be personal for all men and women. What good does it do, he reasoned, for a layman merely to go to church? Will that cure his spiritual ills? Certainly not. He must do more than listen to his preacher; he must read and think for himself. And in order to make this possible, he began to translate portions of the Bible and a great many church hymns into the vernacular, at the same time providing these translations with glosses and other explanations[48].

A pestilence broke out at Deventer in the summer of the year 1384. One of Groote's followers, named Lambert Stuerman, caught the disease. Groote felt it incumbent upon him to visit his beloved friend and became infected himself. There was no hope of recovery; on the 20th of August he passed away[49]. But his ideals and his plans did not die with him, as will appear.

II

Groote had gleaned part of his knowledge from the Bible, the writings of Albert Magnus, Ambrose, Anselm, Antony, Apuleius, Aristotle, Augustine, Bede, Bernard of Clairvaux, Boethius, Bonaventura, Cassianus, Cato, Chrysostom, Cicero, Climacus, Cyprian, Demosthenes, Dionysius, Eusebius, Fabricius, Francis of Assisi, Gregory, Gregory of Nianza, Henry of Ghent, Hippocrates, Isidor, Jerome, Juvenal, Lucan, Lyra, Nepos, Permenianus Donatista, Peter of Damiani, Plato, Pliny, Seneca, Socrates, Suetonius, Suso, Theophrastus, Thomas Aquinas, Valerius, Vegetius, Virgil, and the Canon Law with its commentaries[50].

Another field of knowledge was the contact with his friends, of whom John Ruysbroeck was one. It was he who had initiated Groote into the mysterious realm of the contemplative life: " 'The creature is in Brahma and Brahma is in the creature; they are ever distinct yet ever united', says the Indian mystic. Were it translated into Christian language, it is probable that this thought — which does not involve pantheism — would have been found acceptable by Ruysbroeck, for the interpenetration yet eternal distinction of the human and divine spirits is the central fact of his universe. Man, he thinks, is already related in a three-fold manner to his Infinite Source, for we have our being in him, as the Father, we contemplate him as does the Son, we ceaselessly tend to return to him as does the Spirit. So the Superessential Life is the simple, the synthetic life, in which man actualises at last all the resources of his complex being. The active life of response to the Temporal Order, the contemplative life of response to the Transcendent Order are united, firmly held together, by that eternal fixation of the spirit, the perpetual willed dwelling of the being of man within the Incomprehensible Abyss of the Being of God, *qui est per omnia saecula benedictus.* 'To this divine vision but few men can attain, because of their own un-fitness and because of the darkness of that Light where-by we see, and therefore no one shall thoroughly under-stand this perception by means of any scholarship, or by own acuteness of comprehension. For all words, and all that men may learn and understand in a creaturely fashion, is foreign to this and far below the truth that I mean' ''[51].

Groote, also, became a mystic. His mysticism, how-ever, differed considerably from that of his aged friend. In spite of his great reverence for Ruysbroeck[52], he could never persuade himself to adopt those views which the church of Rome considered heretical[53]. From the day of his conversion at Utrecht in 1374 Groote saw very little value in abstract thinking. He never became more than a distant admirer of Ruysbroeck, and similarly

refused to subscribe to the views of the scholastic philosophers. He was not a Thomist, though he has been
thought one[54]. In his opinion Thomas Aquinas wasted
a great deal of time on topics of no practical value whatsoever. There is but one work of Groote left in which
he enunciates purely philosophical views. This is the
"Sermon, or Treatise, on the Birth of Christ", which
in all probability he addressed to a learned body of clerics.
In this sermon he most explicitly disapproves of scholastic
philosophy[55], and does not mention the name of Thomas
Aquinas, while in many of his other works he only refers
to this philosopher as an authority on theological or moral
questions, never as a philosopher whose views he admires.
At least two subsequent leaders of the "New Devotion"
likewise warned their followers against the writings of
Aquinas. One of these was John Vos of Heusden, a
disciple and intimate friend of Groote's.

The theology and philosophy of Gerard Groote was
based chiefly upon the New Testament, and the Fathers;
in a lesser degree also upon the works of Greek, Roman,
and medieval philosophers. If we are to compare his
ideas with those of any other philosopher, we might say
that his works betray the exceedingly powerful influence
of Augustine. And if we are to give a name to Groote's
philosophy, we might safely call it Augustinian.

With Adam the whole human race fell, says Groote[56].
There have been wise men like Solomon, humble men
like David, strong men like Samson, yet every one of
these was but a shadow of what he might have been[57].
Man, created in the image of God, has fallen low, un-
speakably low. Once enjoying the pure reflex light of
divinity, he now is no longer able to fathom the mysteries
of life. His fall was the inevitable result of disobedience
to the "Lex Dei", the immutable law of God. When-

ever man disobeys that law, he sins, for sin is disobedience[58]. And since the "Lex Dei" is the highest of all laws, one should never obey the command of any man, be he the pope himself, if such a command should oppose God's law; for is not the pope also subject to the "Lex Dei"[59]? Before the Fall, man had this law engraved in his heart, but since that time his intellect has grown dim, and the more he sins, the further he is removed from the "suprema ratio", or supreme source of wisdom[60]. God is the Alpha and the Omega, from whom all things develop, and to whom they all return, either in a natural way or through grace[61]. Sin obscures the intellect, evil enfeebles the will; slowly the light of wisdom vanishes as the obstinate sinner turns farther and farther away from the supreme Law-giver, who offers peace and joy through humble obedience.

But man is not wholly depraved. He still possesses a small spark of divinity within his breast, a radiant gleam of light, which may be fanned into a bright flame[62]. God is a spirit, and all who worship him must obey the voice of their spirits. We should aim to cultivate the inner life, for the kingdom of heaven is within us, as Christ said; here in the innermost depths of our hearts we may find the voice of God[63]. Similarly, the kingdom of evil is also within us, for from the corrupt heart of man come forth all sinful thoughts. He who cannot control his inner life will never succeed in governing his outward acts[64]. Let us therefore endeavor to silence the forces of evil, and listen to the Father's voice. It is God alone who can convert the sinful heart[65]. Happy the man that has decided to make room within his heart for Christ, who is continually knocking at the door, patiently waiting for a response. And if the door is once opened, when Christ enters with his sweet conversation, then the wisdom from heaven will fill that human temple with the peace which passes all understanding[66]. "When I read the psalms", said Groote to his friend, John Brinckerinck, "hidden manna is flowing into my inner self, so that I experience no fatigue in reading, but sweet rapture instead"[67]. Groote constantly urged his disciples to seek communion with God the Father, a spiritual communion with a spiritual God. For God is the "summum bonum"; if we have him, we have all goodness; if we lose him, nothing but evil is left unto us. And why? Because that part of us which is divine cannot exist without the life-giving contact with him who alone can sustain life and nourish our inner selves[68].

Hence the need Groote felt in common with all other mystics to remain in touch with God. As a Christian mystic he sought this contact through Christ[69]. He made it a point to attend mass every day. "Let me first seek the kingdom", he thought, "and then I shall so much the better be able to serve my neighbor". Consequently he would stay till the end of the mass as often as pos-sible to partake of the communion[70]. It was also his habit to withdraw himself several times a day from the busy life of the outer world for prayer, surrendering himself wholly to God, saying: "Here I am Lord; teach me to do thy will, make mine conform to thine"[71]. As a mystic Groote maintained that the reading of good books should at all times be supplemented by meditation and prayer, for contact with God himself he considered the only way of obtaining the highest wisdom[72]. Whenever he was conscious of this contact between himself and God, his "soul would leap with joy". Songs of thanks-giving would escape from his fervent lips, for at such moments "that wonderful peace promised by Christ would settle upon him"[73].

And what is the tie which unites man with his maker? Groote held that it is love, and love only. "Try to love", he said, "for in loving you shall find the kingdom of heaven[74]. If once you have found this kingdom, you will enjoy righteousness, peace, and joy in the Holy Ghost. Without these three gifts all outward show of piety, such as fasting, and mortification of the flesh, will be of no avail"[75]. But how is one to show one's love for God? By sitting in one's cell, aloof from the outside world? Not at all, for he who really loves God, loves all of God's creatures. "Although one should avoid too much idle conversation with 'worldly people'[67], one ought never to shun their presence, but work among them, trying to make them also participants of the joys celestial, far superior as they are to any delights bestowed by our bodily senses"[77]. Groote had tasted the supreme felicity love brings to all those who cheerfully lay their dearest treasures upon the altar of self-sacrifice[78]. Thomas à Kempis tells that "when Groote felt the force of love in his heart, his soul would sing with joy, and his spirit, as a flame, was borne upward to God"[79]. Groote constantly exhorted his disciples to cast out jealousy for sympathy, spite for charity, rancor for love. "Close your eyes to your neighbor's defects", he would say, "and try to discover his good qualities, which are always worth considering; nay more than that, they are the only side of his character it is well for you to dwell upon[80]. For our soul's health can only be sustained by thoughts of love.   And strange to say, the more love we spend, the more we receive, together with much joy in the spirit. We must also fight melancholy, despondency, dejectedness: these are the enemies of our spiritual existence"[81]. Groote found it quite easy to love even his enemies, after once having tasted the heavenly bliss which attends every act of whole-hearted forgiveness[82]. "The health of his soul", says Thomas à Kempis, "gave to his food a savor beyond that of any pleasant meat...... He sent away his guests joyful in the Lord"[83].

Groote was more than a philosopher, more than a mere mystic. He carried on an active campaign against the dying scholasticism of his day. "Why should we indulge in those endless disputes", he would say, "such as are held at the universities, and that about subjects of no moral value whatsoever"? "Do not therefore attend court", he advised, "and if you are asked to go, send a substitute"[84]. When he referred to the works of philosophers, he always singled out those passages which had practical value. Among the philosophers of ancient Greece and Rome he preferred men like Plato, Socrates, and Seneca, who had endeavored to solve certain moral problems for the benefit of their fellow-men. "Words merely serve to convey our thoughts to others", he wrote one day; "they are the servants, not the masters of sense and expression"[85].

The same spirit which impelled Groote to attack the decadent scholasticism of his time induced him also to combat indolence, physical as well as mental. He wanted no women to live in his house at Deventer, for example, who did not want to gain their own livelihood with their own hands. "At present", he wrote in a certain letter, "I am firmly resolved to accept no one who is able to work, but wants to beg for her meals somewhere in the city. All those shall work who are in a condition to do so, and if the time should come when they cannot perform manual labor any longer, then it will be early enough for them to accept alms. This I say, because labor is necessary for the well-being of mankind. In trying to avoid physical exertion, these women fall into the danger of idleness, thereby forgetting the study of their own inner selves, and wander from house to house, inquisitive and restless, prying into other people's affairs, ignoring their own duties"[86]. On the ground of indolence Groote also attacked the mendicant friars, who in return showed him and his followers after him no small amount of hostility[87].

What Groote wanted was more Christianity, plain and simple. To follow in the footsteps of Christ, to bear his cross in humble submission, that was Groote's aim[88]. For that reason he gave up his prebends, ceded his house to some devout women, and compassed land and sea to tell others about Christ's message; he tried to return good for evil, to treat the obstinate with patience, the suffering with sympathy, the impudent with forbearance. Thus he labored for three years and a half, loved by the masses, and followed by thousands of grateful disciples. He was not a profound scholar, not a great philosopher. The subtle arguments of the learned doctors at Paris, Cologne, and Prague he regarded as foolishness. He sought nothing but the conversion of sinners, the formation of a harmoniously developed character on the part of his disciples, and the extension of God's kingdom on earth. Groote was neither Thomist, nor Scotist; he did not imitate Ruysbroeck as a lover of solitary nooks in forest or monastery, but preferred a life of action among men. He wanted to be a Christian, and the movement he set on foot was a Christian Renaissance.

III

Groote was deeply concerned about the Church. Indeed, among the reformers of the fourteenth and fifteenth centuries he occupies a leading position. Few men were so well acquainted with the decline in moral stan-

dards among all ranks of the clergy as he, and very few, if
any, so bitterly lamented the impending collapse of the
Church. Instead of ignoring the dangers which were
threatening the Church from within, he sought to stay
the evil by attacking those who were the cause of the
wide-spread demoralization : monks, priests, and bishops,
as well as common people. He tried to rouse them all
from their mental and spiritual lethargy.

In the first place he endeavored to extend the meaning
of the word "religio", which in his time was not the
equivalent of the English word *religion,* but served to
distinguish the monks, or regular clergy, from other
people. He protested against the wrong interpretation
of the word "religio". "If devout women", he wrote,
"separate themselves from the world, and try to serve God
in the privacy of their homes, without taking monastic
vows, they are just as religious as the nuns in their convents. To love God and worship him is religion, not
the taking of special vows. For the cause and purpose
of things give them their names and forms. If it is,
therefore, one's aim to live a religious life, his way of
living becomes religious in God's opinion, and according
to the judgment of our consciences"[89]. On another
occasion he said: "Truly religious men are not confined
by place, time, or manner of men"[90]. "All these", he
continued, "who live aloof from the world to serve God,
who despise temporal honors; leading chaste lives. obedient and poor : they are religious people"[91].

"No one may found a new religious order", continues
Groote, "without the pope's permission, but it is not
wrong, I believe, for two or more persons to live together
in observance of certain established rules, or the rule of
all rules, namely, the blessed Gospel; that is not forbidden,
I think. The mere name 'religio' signifies but little;

it is not the name which determines the nature of a thing.
Names are conventional. Therefore, the 'Horologium'[92]
is right in saying: 'Many so-called religious people go
about in cowls and wear other outward garbs of religio,
but within they are lions, bears,—terrible beasts'. There
are many who are not protected by the name 'religio',
and yet they may be more religious than those whom
the Church calls religious'[93].

In the year 1379 Groote left the monastery, and never
returned to it. Did he afterwards perhaps cherish so
much reverence for the monastic life that he never dared
to enter a monastery again[94]? We know that he had
great respect for a pious monk who left his friends and
relatives for the sole purpose of worshiping God more
perfectly. Whenever he made acquaintance with persons
who showed a burning desire to come into closer relation
to God, and seemed to be eminently fitted for the monastic state, he did not hesitate to praise and recommend
monasticism[95]. To others, who had taken monastic
vows, he was accustomed to write frequently, reminding
them of the reason why they entered the monastery.
Since they had decided to serve God in comparative se-
clusion, they should no longer indulge in gossip, but
should close their ears to rumors, quarrels, wars, and
festivals; they should live soberly, and perform their daily
tasks with alacrity[96]. Many other examples might be
adduced to show that Groote approved of monasticism[97],
though his approval was not unqualified. Some people
seemed to be particularly well fitted for the monastic life,
but not he, nor those among his disciples whose ability to
instruct the young, to preach to the masses, to remind
the clergy of their shortcomings, or to comfort the poor
and the afflicted, impelled them to employ their talents in
the service of their neighbors, instead of burying them in

the solitude of a lonely cell. Hence we find him writing to one of his followers: "I dare not advise you to enter a monastery, though it is not for me to judge, being ignorant of God's ways. My desire is that you remain in the world, and be not of the world"[98]. When John Cele, rector of the school at Zwolle, wanted to discontinue his work as teacher and become a monk, Groote urged him to remain at Zwolle, where he was doing such splendid work, not only among the school boys, but also as a preacher[99]. Though Groote perfectly understood and never failed to appreciate the merits of monasticism, he was by no means blind to the laxity of discipline noticeable in nearly all monasteries. Monks were not less prone to sin than other men[100]. Hence he vigorously attacked the greatest monastic evils: immorality, simony, and indolence[101].

Groote's attitude towards the secular clergy and the Church in general was that of a reformer, not that of a revolutionist. He did not engage in negative criticism alone, as many of the humanists did, but supplemented his criticism with constructive plans. He was not satisfied with conditions as he had himself seen them at Deventer, Aachen, Cologne, Paris, Utrecht, and Avignon, for he loved the Church too much not to be grieved at its dangerous condition. However, he did not attack the doctrines or dogma of the Church. "Everything I have preached is in complete accordance with the teachings of the Church", he wrote; "wherever I have been wrong I shall gladly retract. I submit myself to the authority (judgment) of the Church"[102].

The Church, in Groote's opinion, was a divine institution; its teachings were promulgated by servants of God, who had been inspired by the Holy Ghost. In the realm of dogma or doctrine, therefore, the Church was

supreme, and its teachings infallible. Although he drew
a careful distinction between the Bible and other religious
writings, he did not go so far as later reformers and say:
"I submit myself only to the authority of the Scriptures",
for he was firmly convinced that since Christ had promised to remain with his church until the end, it would
be preposterous for him to lay claim to a better knowledge
of the Bible than the Church Fathers and the medieval
saints possessed[103].

Groote never dreamed of calling the Church supreme
in the realm of morals, however, for he said: "There are
some men to-day who exalt the judgments of the Church,
because to them they are better known than the commandments of God, or the laws of nature, since they are
ignorant of these laws, due to the darkness of their hearts;
they are disposed, as were the Scribes and Pharisees, to
transgress the law for the sake of human traditions, or
the regulations of the Elders, for the instructions of the
Church are more familiar to them than the laws of nature, or the commandments of God"[104]. Far from wishing
to break the Church, he deplored the schism within the
Church and exclaimed: "I wish that both popes with all
their cardinals would sing a 'Gloria in excelsis' in heaven,
and that a true Eliakim would bring peace and harmony
upon earth[105]. This schism cannot be healed without
some terrible blow to the Church, which has long been in
a position of decrepitude, ready to fall to pieces, and now
the head itself is in a sad condition"[106].

The most exalted office a man could fill on earth, in
Groote's eyes, was the cure of souls, and even the pope
was a greater man as priest than as head of the
Church[107]. Consequently the worst form of simony
was that of accepting or dispensing such a benefice for
money. The cure of souls should be a thing quite

spiritual, quite divine[109]. And it should be a bishop's duty to appoint for these spiritual tasks only men who had been endowed with a clear mind, whose hearts were pure, and whose aims were unselfish. If a bishop could not find trustworthy shepherds for his sheep, he had better resign his office, in spite of all the regulations found in the Canon Law and all the laws enacted by the Church[109].

Groote's views on the sacraments are closely allied with his opinion regarding the duties of the clergy. "If the pope should command you", he says to the lower clergy, "or a bishop, or any other superior, under whatever form of penalty, even that of excommunication, suspension, deposition, or privation, to administer the Holy Supper, and you have not repented of certain mortal sins, no human law of obedience can compel you to do it; on the other hand, you should refuse to administer the sacrament in question, heedless of all temporal loss or calumny[110]. For the laws and regulations of the Church are on the same level with those enacted by all human agencies"[111]. "The sacraments", continues Groote, "have power independent of the priest who administers them, and his sins have no effect on the nature of the sacrament; all one's pollutions are taken away by one's faith in Christ, nor can any sinner pollute the divine sacraments"[112].

As for the sacrament of penance, no priest, says Groote, has the right to forgive any sins of any person who has not confessed all his evil deeds and decided never, if possible, to repeat them again. For if the sinner intends no repentance, absolution is idle; in such cases the priest must repeal his pronouncement of forgiveness. The sole condition required in this transaction is the sinner's repentance. All the priest can do is to act when the sinner is sincere in his confession and has resolved to amend his evil ways[113]. Great caution is required of him, for suppose he forgives sins which God as yet cannot forgive, what benefit will the sinner receive? The priest presents the sinner to the Church as absolved from his load of sin, whereas the Church Triumphant or the Immaculate Church, that is, the inner circle of true believers terrestial as well as celestial, refuses to accept him. He is introduced at the outer gate, but is repelled by those within the enclosure[114]. The priest's chief aim should be to convert sinners, for the conversion of sinners is a greater work than the creation of the world. "I believe", said Groote, "that prayer is more beneficial than mechanical rules and transactions; admonition is better than absolution, for after all it is God alone who can convert sinners[115]. Suppose somebody takes his neighbor's property, and is unrepentant, then all his confessions are of no avail, and every one who absolves him is simply a servant of the devil"[116].

Groote was here taking a stand that later made Luther famous. It should be noted that Groote had no desire to break away from the Church. He even tried to silence four "heretics". In one of his letters we find him addressing a certain "Brother John", who had preached against him at Zutphen, Zwolle, and Kampen. "Your words were full of idle boasting and blasphemy", he tells him; "thus far I have suffered you to continue, but now I can stand it no longer. You shall retract, else I shall take you before the Roman Curia. Beware, if you still persevere in your obstinate course, after these friendly warnings"[117]. John probably heeded Groote's warning, but the other three men Groote attacked publicly. One of them was Bartholomew, an Augustinian friar from Dordrecht, a friend and to a great extent a follower of a curious sect, known as the "Free Spirits"[118], who preached the following doctrines: "God is neither life, nor light, nor nature. The divine essence is my essence, and my essence is divine essence. Just as man cannot exist without God, God is unable to live without man's aid. Divinity is dependent on man. Man is perfect God. Man from eternity is God in God. Man is never born, but has existed from eternity. The aim of every man should be to lose himself in the Nothingness of the Godhead; then he will be like Christ, both God and man. Every man, therefore, is saved through the immanence of the Holy Ghost, not through Christ's sacrifice. There is only one sin: to remain under the law of good works, rewards, and punishment; consequently there is but one virtue: to free oneself from these. And again, there is no evil in such imaginary sins as lust, pride, theft, hatred"[119]. Groote wanted to silence preachers who taught such doctrines. "Bartholomew enters inns", he wrote, "and gets many friends there, for he finds fault with no one. Nothing is so dangerous as to preach about God and perfection, and not to point out the way which leads to perfection. Penitence is hardly necessary in his opinion; tell him that if he is to preach any longer, he must show the people the way to heaven through Christ by following in his footsteps, not by ignoring the imperfection of man, and the existence of sin. I mean to listen to him in secret with a notary public, catch him at his game, and make it impossible for him to continue his present work as servant of the devil"[120]. After some delay he finally succeeded in having Bartholomew silenced by the Bishop of Utrecht[121].

From the day of Groote's conversion he never was a friend of the mendicant monks, for he hated indolence. "It is well for a true Christian", he would say. "to cede his possessions to the poor. This will compel him to work for his daily bread[122]. Poverty without begging is a boon to the pilgrim, for he should be freed from all temporal encumbrances[123]. Man is only a steward here on earth, wherefore it is his duty to confine his expenditures to a small minimum[124]. Why should one be jealous of one's neighbor who is leading a life of luxury"[125]? Groote himself had spent all his possessions for the extension of God's kingdom upon earth. So little, in fact, he had reserved that sometimes he had to ask one of his friends for a small loan[126]. In his poverty he aimed to imitate Christ. "O Lord of all riches", he exclaimed, "why didst thou elect such humble garments? Why didst thou choose to sit on an ass which was found tied to a gate near a public road, upon which even the humblest man was free to ride, and worse, on a colt upon whose back no man had ever sat, as it had thus far been used for the meanest sorts of employment? Rejoice, ye poor ones, for this seeming poverty is but a guise, since he, though poor in earthly goods, was master of all, magnificent, royal, divine! Follow in his footsteps, ascend the road which leads from ignominy to glory, from toil and strife to peace and rest, to heights sublime"[127].

All obstacles should be removed which might in any way obstruct his path, wherefore he deemed it best for men such as he not to marry or to be at all familiar with women. He shunned them himself: to the women in his house he never spoke except through a closed and curtained window[128]. Basing his views upon certain passages found in the New Testament and in the writings of St. Augustine[129], he exhorted the lower clergy who wished to serve God above all things not to marry[130]: "Marriage is a hindrance to him who intends to develop his spiritual nature, for it brings sorrows of its own, as well as joys, cares, and much worldly thought. There are many men who have had to give up their career as scholar or philosopher, as the inevitable result of their friendships with women"[131].

To those for whom he thought marriage fitting, he also offered serious counsel. His disciples should choose devout wives, — chaste, virtuous, and true, — and one must not assume that he can draw an ungodly woman to God[132]. The marriage tie is sacred, for marriage is a symbol of the eventual union between Christ and his church. Therefore it is a man's duty to love his wife as much as the church is loved by Christ; he has no right to frequent inns and loaf about town at night. Christ does indeed love his church, and readily forgives the sins of his beloved, as husbands and wives should remember, cover each other's defects, avoid quarrels and ill-feeling. For perfect love hides all the faults of its object[133].

It would not be right to call Groote a pessimist. He thought that it was always best to dwell more upon the hope of eternal glory rather than upon the pains of hell[134]. As for the theory of good works, he wrote: "Christ would rather see a wife obedient to her husband and quietly performing her daily tasks than any ascetic doing penitence, and not obedient, or kind-hearted"[135]. "Asceticism", he writes on another occasion, "is often very harmful, for the devil will frequently use it as a tool, telling the person in question that it is a very helpful method for the religious student, and yet all this watching, praying, and fasting will often cause mental diseases, anger, or pride. Man is prone to think that he can do good on his own initiative, thus taking too much pride in his own work, which if really good, is not his work, but that of God. Hence there are many people who pray much and inflict physical hardships upon themselves, while within they are unrighteous and avaricious"[136].

Groote himself did not lead a gloomy life, for he felt he had lived in that peace which passeth all understanding, and all temporal delights. The happiness enjoyed by him when conscious of this blessed peace was plainly visible upon his features[137]. The reading of the Scriptures gave him great joy[138]. When his friend Cele was depressed and worried about his shortcomings and his weakness amidst the many temptations he had to encounter, Groote wrote him an encouraging letter: "Be happy in the Lord, for nothing is so helpful in temptation as mental happiness and confidence in God"[139]. "It is our duty", he says, "to make ourselves worthy habitations, where Christ will be pleased to dwell[140]. The Holy Ghost will readily assist us in acquiring virtue, for virtues are indeed gifts of the Holy Ghost. Far above the sacraments, above miracles and prophecies stand virtue and love[141]. All virtues are to be employed as tools wherewith we can increase love; through love they unite us with God the Father, and the Holy Ghost. Just as many twigs sprout from one common root, so are many virtues shaped by one force—namely, love[142]. Our enemy Satan knows very well that all external works and all spiritual exercises without love and faith are valueless. He persuades many to perform good works, telling them that thereby they will obtain salvation. Thus by devoting all their attention to these 'good works', they neglect their inner selves, where salvation and the kingdom of heaven may be found"[143].

The greatest of all virtues was humility. "The more we realize our own imperfections", says Groote, "the nearer we approach perfection"[144]. "Before all things", he continues, "and in all things study specially to become humble inwardly. For it is far better to do but little good out of obedience to God's will than to do a great deal more on one's own account, since the lesser becomes the greater before God[145]. 'Good will' means to acquiesce in God's will, for everything that occurs is an act of God's will. God speaks to us through his acts. Blessed is he who obeys God's voice and bears in mind that everything which befalls him is predestined by God, even the wrongs done by others. False accusations and slander he ought to bear in peace, for God knows best[146]. Let him say to his Creator: 'Lord, all that is mine and my own self I surrender to thee; I renounce my will for thy sake. This is the greatest thing I have been able to do in this world' "[147].

IV

Groote also was deeply interested in education. He never became a teacher himself, nor did he expect much of mere formal study as an aim in itself. Such subjects as geometry, arithmetic, rhetoric, logic, grammar, poetry, and astronomy, he thought, were of very little use to him. "Whatsoever doth not make thee a better Christian", he once said, "is harmful". He asserted that for him it was really a waste of time to get a degree in medicine, for such a degree would bring no practical results. The same was true of a degree in civil and canon law[148]. Yet he was by no means opposed to learning, as his writings plainly show.

Groote loved books. He never had enough of them, and eagerly acquired each new addition to his library. Sometimes five copyists were kept busy writing manuscripts for him[149]. His friends bought books or lent them to him[150]. So much he thought of his library that he

arranged for a committee of three men to be in charge
of his books after his death. These three men are called
"guardians of Groote's books" in the documents of that
time[151]. Groote not only read books whenever he had a
chance, he simply devoured them, says one of his biographers[152]. There were times when he would wonder
whether it really was right for him to love those books
so passionately, but when he reproached himself for
this "thirst of his after mere book-learning"[153], he very
soon would dismiss his misgivings.

He devoted himself to encourage learning in school
boys, often inviting them to his house, where he had
them copy books for him and talked with them about
their work at school, their aims and ideals. As they
opened their hearts to him, he formed plans to help the
boys who had no home and practically no friends at
Deventer. If they needed good food and clothing he
provided it, and he arranged for them to lodge with
kind matrons who treated them as their own children[154].
Furthermore, he reasoned that the boys needed capable
teachers, men of sound learning, and of character, men
who would try to win their love, and refrain from any
kind of punishment until their friendly admonition had
failed utterly[155]. They should be university men, if
possible. Hence we find Groote busy at work in the
Yssel valley, trying to secure comfortable quarters for
the homeless, and capable teachers for all. At Deventer,
Zwolle, and Kampen he cultivated the friendship of both
teachers and their employers[156]. The most intimate
friend he seems ever to have had was John Cele, the
teacher at Zwolle from 1374 or 1375 to 1417. "These
two men were one heart and one soul", says Thomas
à Kempis[157]. Partly through Groote's influence Cele
obtained his position as rector of the city school at

Zwolle. At first he had not been inclined to teach, but Groote showed him the crying need of education for all classes of men and women, particularly for the clergy[158]. "How are these men to instruct the masses", he would often remark, "if they have no knowledge to give, their brains being empty and void of all sound learning"[159]? Cele's business was to teach. When after some time he decided to enter a monastery, where life would be much easier for him, Groote did not rest till he had persuaded him to continue teaching[160]. He urged him to go to Prague, to study at the university, while at the same time he found a substitute for him at Zwolle[161]. The reforms introduced into the schools of Zwolle and Deventer were therefore the direct outcome of Groote's educational activities. Their history will be treated further in the following chapter.

* *

* * * *

We have followed Groote's activities as student, scholar, reformer, and educator. His career as the accomplished son of a wealthy magistrate, his experiences as a holder of two prebends, the conversion which came to him in 1374, these and other factors we have endeavored to place in their proper light. He made a great impression on the men and women of his time, as the following eulogies show.

William de Sarvarvilla, cantor of the University of Paris, wrote in a letter addressed to Pope Urban VI, which induced the latter to grant Groote a license to preach, shortly before he died: "Truly he was 'The Great', for in his knowledge of all the liberal sciences, both natural and moral, of civil law, canon law, and of theology, he was second to no one in the world, and all these branches of learning were united in him. He was a man of such saintliness and gave so good an example of the mortification of the flesh, his contempt for the world, his brotherly love for all, his zeal for the salvation of souls, his effectual preaching, his reprobation and hatred of wickedness, his withstanding of heretics, his enforcement of the canon law against those that broke the vow of chastity, his conversion to the spiritual life of divers men and women who had formerly lived according to the world, and his loyalty to our Lord Urban VI, — in all those things I say he gave so good an example, that many thousands of men testify to the belief that is in them that he was not less great in these virtues than he was in the aforesaid sciences"[162]. William Vornken, prior of Windesheim, calls Groote the "Fountain of the Devotio Moderna", and adds: "The fathers of the former congregation say, Through what act of grace or miracle came it to pass that as master Gerard Groote was preaching and sowing the seed everywhere, there were added to him so suddenly and unexpectedly men of such kind and so great, for these were of one mind with him, and every one of them in each city and place burned with the zeal with which he also burned to exhort and convert a people that was stiff-necked. O happy day on which that great Gerard was born amongst us, for he was the fount and source whence flowed the waters of salvation to our land, so that what before his time had been parched became a pool, and the thirsty land, springs of water"[163]. Thomas à Kempis claims that Groote "illuminated the whole country with his life, words, ways, and doctrine"[164].

In 1424 John Vos of Heudsen, prior of Windesheim, and leader of the "New Devotion", said on his death-bed

to the monks of his monastery and the Brethren of the
Common Life from Deventer, Zwolle, and Hulsbergen
(near Hattem, also in the Yssel country) : "Groote was
the first father of this our reformation, the source and
origin of the New Devotion; he was an apostle in this
country who kindled fires of religious fervor in the
cold hearts of men, and drew them to God"[165]. John
Busch, who had been sent from the Yssel valley to
Erfurt, Magdeburg, Hildesheim, and other cities of
central Germany, where he helped to reform many a
monastery, also called Groote the fountain-head of the
"Devotio Moderna", or "New Devotion"[166]. This same
opinion was expressed by Ruysbroeck's biographer at
Groenendaal[167]. Then we have the series of biographies
written in Dutch, which describe the lives of Groote and
his followers at Deventer. In the chapter devoted to
Groote it is set down: "All religious fervor in this
country for one hundred miles around was caused by
master Gerard"[168]. And when the news of Groote's
death reached the convent of Weesp near Amsterdam,
a devout sister wrote the following notice in her manuscript: "Gerard Groote, with his holy life and example,
has enlightened the whole bishopric of Utrecht"[169].

It is obvious that the men and women of the late
fourteenth and early fifteenth centuries who were of
the "New Devotion", or Christian Renaissance, considered Gerard Groote their spiritual father. He was
in fact the founder of the Brotherhood of the Common
Life and the Windesheim Congregation, which instituted
the only lasting reforms of the whole fifteenth century,
corrected the Vulgate, translated parts of the Bible, sent
thousands upon thousands of religious books throughout
Western Europe, reformed schools and text-books,
comforted the sick, consoled the afflicted, fed the poor,

lodged the homeless, and composed that well-nigh perfect fruit of Christian mysticism: "De Imitatione Christi", or "Imitation of Christ".

To conclude, Gerard Groote, as founder of the Christian Renaissance, became the spiritual father of all the men educated by the Brethren of the Common Life and by their pupils, such as Thomas à Kempis, Gansfort, Erasmus, Dringenberg, Hegius, Murmellius, Agricola, Beatus Rhenanus, Wimpheling, Luther, Zwingli, Bucer, Calvin, and Loyola, as we shall see in the following chapters.

CHAPTER II

THE RISE OF THE CHRISTIAN RENAISSANCE

Among Groote's followers at Deventer and elsewhere three groups or classes may be distinguished. They all had decided to change their lives, but many among them preferred to remain at home, where they could live just as religious a life, they said, as in a monastery or as members of a definitely organized society or brother-hood. To this class belonged the pious women who lodged so many poor school boys at Deventer, Zwolle, and several other places. But soon we lose sight of these unorganized little bands. Many of them became affiliated later with the Brethren and Sisters of the Common Life, who constituted the second class of Groote's disciples; or they joined the third class, namely the Augustinian Canons and Canonesses Regular of the Windesheim Congregation. It is to the last two groups, accordingly, that the following pages are devoted.

I

On the 21st of September, 1374, Groote ceded the use of his house to some poor women[1]. Five years later he drew up a constitution for the little society[2], in which he clearly set forth the reason why he had asked these women to live in his house. Not to found a new monastic order, he wrote, had they come to live here, or a beguin-age, but simply to find a place where they might worship God in peace. Only those could secure admittance who were not bound by monastic vows; nor were they expected to take such vows on entering the house. They should all be free to leave if they chose, though they could not re-enter, after once having taken their departure. All the inmates of the house would remain members of the local parish church, just as all other laymen. Their clothes should in no respect be different from those of the other women in the city, for they were neither nuns nor beguines. One might even be a member of the society without living in the "Meester-Geertshuis", or Master Gerard's house, at all. At first they had one matron, later two[3]. The matrons were to act as treasurers of the house, and would have authority to make all the members perform manual labor. Their orders were expected to be promptly obeyed. In case of ill-behavior the matrons would consult with two other sisters as to the form of punishment for breach of discipline. The offender would in most cases lose her share in the common savings. But if more serious offences were committed, such as theft, stubbornness, or too great a familiarity with men, the guilty person would have to be expelled[4]. After Groote's death the city council of Deventer would be asked to deal with such cases[5]. During the first few years, when the new society counted but a limited number of members, the two matrons took care of all the business transactions, such as buying supplies, matters of discipline, and supervision of the sisters' daily tasks. Later a division of labor was created. A provisor was chosen, and in 1383 Groote appointed John van den Gronde as the first rector. A procurator was appointed in 1435 and the various tasks of the sisters were also supervised after Groote's death by members specifically directed by the superiors[6].

The constitution of the "House of Master Gerard" further stated that the members were to live soberly, wear simple clothes, avoid familiar intercourse with men, and restrict their visits to a limit of eight days and a distance of not more than ten miles. No one would be expected to cede her property, on entering the house; the sisters would all work in common and share the expenses together, while the income would be equally divided. Every member of the house who was able to work would be expected to contribute her share of manual labor[7], for Groote did not want the sisters to beg under any circumstances[8]. Each member, however, was to perform those tasks for which she was specially fitted by nature. Soon the sisters became great adepts in agricultural pursuits; they had a flourishing dairy business, and many of them earned neat little sums through their skill in sewing, knitting, weaving, spinning, and similar purely feminine employments[9].

In composing this constitution for the Sisters of the Common Life, Groote prepared the way for a mightier organization, known later as the Brethren of the Common Life. Shortly after he left the Carthusian monastery of Monnikhuizen near Arnhem, he had succeeded in recruiting a number of devout followers. In 1380 a man joined them who was destined to become the leader of the "New Devotion". This man was called Florentius Radewijns. Born at Leerdam[10] in the year 1350[11], he had gone to Prague in 1374[12], and received a master's degree in 1378[13]. Thereupon he had gone home to Gorinchem[14], where he lived with his parents till the news of Groote's fame as preacher reached him[15]. This must have happened in the year 1380, for Groote had not yet left the Yssel valley[16]. So much impressed was he by Groote's imposing personality that he decided to imitate him in all things[17]. One of the first things he did was to give up his prebend at Utrecht, in order to be nearer to Groote. At Deventer he became vicar of the altar of St. Paul in St. Lebwin's Church[18].

It was in Radewijns' vicarage that Groote's twelve disciples used to meet, though not all of them actually lived in this house[19]. When did these disciples begin to live the common life? One writer thinks in 1372[20]; that is, two years before Groote's conversion. Another one sets down a later date: 1381 or 1382[21]. Still another one places the date several years after Groote's death[22]; while the latest "authority" on the Brethren of the Common Life claims that the brothers did not even have a rector until thirty or forty years after the organization was firmly established[23].

The sources, however, show plainly that Groote, shortly after his return from the monastery of Monnik-huizen near Arnhem, began to preach in the cities along the Yssel. Among his numerous followers there were twelve who clung quite faithfully to the master, except one of them, called a backslider, and traitor[24]. Groote advised some of them to live together in one house, where they could exhort each other, work and pray together — in short, serve God with greater chance of success[25]. We also read that Groote had several boys and young men copy books for him. The boys were often invited to his house. He purposely paid them a little each time so that they would have to come quite often and have a talk with him. It was not these boys whom Groote urged to live together in one house. And not only Groote invited school boys to his house, but also some of his followers at Zwolle and Deventer, most of whom were soon to become known as Brethren of the Common Life. Hence the founders of the new organization were not those school boys who were asked to Groote's house from time to time. The fact is, there were also girls among the young people entertained by Groote's friends[26]. Moreover, the sources do not at all tell us that these boys and girls who were given financial or other assistance by Groote and his followers founded the congregation or brotherhood, called Brethren of the Common Life[27]. It is only some modern critics who make that assertion, and wrongly so.

Among the twelve disciples at Deventer there were several copyists, who made their living by copying books, and some of them, we saw, were living in Radewijns' vicarage. Now these copyists wanted to join their funds. Accordingly, Radewijns came to Groote one day and said to him: "Master, what harm should there be in our uniting our weekly earnings, and living the common life"? "Unite your funds"? Groote exclaimed in surprise. "Impossible, for the mendicant monks would surely attack us for trying to found a new monastic order"[28]. But as Radewijns would not give up his plan so readily, Groote finally answered that in case they would in the near future lead the common life, he would gladly be their leader and instructor[29].

Should one call Florentius Radewijns then the founder of the Brethren of the Common Life? For did not he suggest to Groote the idea of uniting the funds? It should be remembered, however, that Groote had composed the constitution for the Sisters of the Common Life before Radewijns had ever heard of him. And it was Groote himself who had stipulated that the sisters should combine their wages and share the common expenses. For this reason the mendicants had already attacked him.

He had even found it necessary to defend them in a sermon at Deventer, together with the beguines, who also united their earnings[30]. When the men in Rade-

wijns' house wanted to lead a life similar to that of the
Sisters of the Common Life, he naturally hesitated, and
pointed out to them the great danger of attack from his
enemies, the mendicant monks, who were living a life of
indolence and hated Groote for his love of poverty and
manual labor. But his hesitation did not last long, for
he knew well that the Canon Law would protect them.
He mapped out their future mode of life, drew up a
schedule for their daily tasks and their religious exercises[31], and would undoubtedly have made further
arrangements, if the hand of death had not suddenly
intervened, as it did on the twentieth of August, 1384.
Groote was indeed the founder of the new brotherhood,
though his plans were only materialized after his
death[32].

II

On the afternoon of the twentieth of August, 1384, a
pathetic scene was enacted at Deventer. In one of the
houses on the Bagynestraat a group of men were stand-
ing around Groote's bed. Their beloved master was
dying. They saw his life ebbing fast and trembled. And
he himself was conscious of their dismay. There was
a long silence. But at last he opened his eyes and spoke:
"My friends", he said, "do not fear, and let not your
hearts be troubled. You will not have to give up your
present mode of life. In order that you may protect
your temporal possessions I advise you to build a
monastery, where those among you best fit for the
monastic life may find shelter and perform their work
in peace, while at the same time it will protect the others
who prefer to remain in the world". "But which order
shall we join"? they asked. "The Augustinian", he

answered, "for their rules are not so harsh as those of the Carthusians and Cistercians"[33].

Groote also gave a last message to the Sisters of the Common Life. He had regretted the fact that only middle-aged women were willing to join the little society. But better times would come, he thought. "When I shall have departed hence", was his final remark, "I shall send some little flowers from above, benignant spirits, which will swell your numbers"[34].

Thus we are told by John Busch and Thomas a Kempis, the two most reliable historians of the Windesheim circle. Their narratives do in no respect contradict each other, as some writers have thought, who failed to read Thomas à Kempis very carefully[35]. On the contrary, they are supported by other trustworthy sources. It was not John Busch, for seven years the pupil and assistant of John Cele at Zwolle, who indulged in flights of the imagination, but those modern scholars who insist on overthrowing the best sources we have. Groote, it appears, had openly attacked Bartholomew of Dordrecht, a mendicant monk, and the clergy at Utrecht besides. They were furious. Moreover, Groote, as founder of the Sisters of the Common Life, had instituted a semi-monastic organization which was looked upon by the mendicant monks as a hostile rival of their order. He was also translating parts of the Bible into the vernacular, preached against indolence, abhorred all forms of begging, and bitterly denounced those monks and priests who failed to perform their duty. Last but not least, he had a group of disciples who were holding regular meetings in the vicarage of Radewijns. One half of these disciples were actually living with the vicar. They copied books for Groote and for others, and were surely going to live the common life. Perhaps they had already given

up their private property. At any rate, they were founding a monastic order, it seemed, without taking the
customary vows, or asking the pope for his sanction.

Whenever these copyists were seen on the streets, they
were addressed as Beghards and Lollards, hooted at,
and commended to burn in hell, or some other suitable
place of torture. The common people, and those among
the lower classes who frequented inns or lounged about
the streets all day, were instigated by some monks to
slander Groote's disciples. These monks composed songs
in which Groote was mocked and ridiculed[36]. Then there
were many laymen as well as clergymen who had attended Groote's sermons, and had felt some compunction
about their evil ways, but finally had decided to ignore
Groote's appeals. They gradually moved away farther
and farther from the path so persistently pointed out to
them by Groote. Finally the clergy resented his attacks.
For it seemed to them as if he had singled them out for
reproval. Groote had advised them to give a large share
of their possessions to the poor, to visit the sick and
afflicted, to take care of the homeless, and to shun all
forms of indolence, intemperance, and immorality. The
man was insane, they said to each other. And look at
those copyists: always writing books on religion, and
never ready to visit us in the tavern and the dance-hall.
Do you think we would lead such miserable lives as
those wretched copyists are doing? Thus they argued,
glad to find support among other members of the clergy,
both secular and regular.

Groote was aware of these things. He had already
told Radewijns to act with caution. As the people grew
bolder each day, and the mendicants increased their
attacks, the situation began to look serious. The brethren,
not being protected by monastic vows, were uneasy and

held daily consultations in Radewijns' vicarage. Finally
they came to the conclusion that a monastery should be
built where a part of them could live and by their
example lead and protect the others. They were to join
the Augustinian Canons Regular[37].

But Groote's end was near, as we have seen. Though
he must be considered the founder both of the Brethren
of the Common Life and the Windesheim Congregation,
he left his work unfinished. Would he also leave his
disciples without a leader? Great was their affliction in
having to lose so kind and so learned a master. But as
he looked up for the last time at his faithful followers,
now only eleven in number, his eyes rested upon the one
he loved best. "I will not leave you defenseless", he
said, "I appoint Florentius as your new leader. He will
instruct you, and help you, as I have tried to do". And
then he departed.

III

So highly in fact did Groote respect his faithful friend
that he had urged him to become a priest[38]. As for
himself, we know, he thought he was too great a sinner
to join the ranks of the priesthood. But Radewijns was
endowed with special gifts of devotion. No one was
kinder than he to the poor, the sick, and the afflicted. He
often went to visit the suffering. Many a meal he was
wont to send to certain famishing families in the slums
of Deventer. A list was kept by him of all the sick people
in the city[39]. The feeble-bodied and all others who
through no fault of their own were in need of material
assistance, he supplied with food and clothing, and the
poorer class of school boys with pens, ink, and paper.
One lenten season there was great scarcity of food and
of work, so that an unusually large number of poor

people came to Radewijns for help; whereupon he, finding himself unable to give assistance to so many at once, persuaded his friends and followers to add one hour a day to their work for the period of one week. The extra money thus saved he handed over to the "Overseer of the Poor" at Deventer. During the month of May he was accustomed to gather herbs for the sick. He would invite all those people to his house who were afflicted with ulcers, sores, and other skin diseases. They were then given a bath in warm water, perfumed with aromatic herbs. A clean bed was also prepared for each patient, where they were told to rest themselves, after first having received a cup of wine[40].

Radewijns did not even shrink from lepers, and to the maimed and deformed he was particularly kind. "I once knew a leper", says Thomas à Kempis, "who used to abide outside the walls of the city. Florentius would often sit beside him and talk to him". "I have seen", he continues, "one blind of an eye, and one lame of one foot, who were both converted by him". At times he was consulted by so many people that he had no time even to go to church[41]. And who was there who could comfort the people as did Radewijns? Involuntarily their hearts were filled with new hope and happiness at one touch of his hand, or a single glance from those starry eyes which bespoke tender sympathy. The moment one approached him, one's troubles and anxieties would suddenly subside. What was there in this singularly attractive person to shed about him as it were a halo of almost celestial felicity? Was he so great an orator? Did he perhaps cast the hypnotic spell of fiery eloquence upon the fascinated crowds?

Among all the men Thomas à Kempis had met before he wrote the "Imitation", Radewijns, he thought, was

the one who had taught him most about the Cross of
Christ. We should learn of him, Christ had said, by
imitating him[42]. And how could we imitate him best?
By taking his yoke upon us, the yoke of humility, and
charity. One should try to sympathize with the poor
and afflicted, visit the sick, comfort orphans and widows,
and be ready to perform the most humble tasks at
home[43]. We should never seek our own good, Radewijns
used to say, but rather consider only our neighbor's
welfare. Thus one might become a Christian, in his
opinion. And Radewijns was wont to practise what he
preached. He was always ready to take an active share
in his neighbor's sorrows. Naturally, his feeling of pity
was instinctively felt by all who came near him[44]. Thomas
à Kempis himself had often experienced a thrill of
rapture simply in being near his teacher and master. A
few words from Radewijns' lips would comfort all.
"This", says Thomas à Kempis, "I have often tried
and experienced myself"[45]. Is it any wonder that
Thomas à Kempis, who had spent several years in
Radewijns' presence, often used to look upon his stay
at Deventer with a feeling of reverence and intense
gratitude? Florentius Radewijns was a man who lived
the ideals of the "Imitation of Christ". Whether he
formulated those ideals we shall consider later.

But Radewijns was also a famous preacher. From
far and near the people used to come to his house, where
he or one of his followers addressed them in their own
language[46]. These sermons were held in the open air,
and particularly on holidays the crowds that assembled
in the garden of the vicarage were quite large. Gradually
it became a custom among the people to write down
parts of Radewijns' discourses, for they were so easy
to understand and so practical[47]. He spoke to them in

their own dialect, unadorned with pompous foreign quotations. Had not Christ done the same in his day? Had he preached in a foreign language? Why should Radewijns then employ Latin or fine speeches in reminding the people of Christ's message to his followers? Plain speech, simple words he used. And these were kept alive in the shops, the mills, and the farm-houses.

Though fully aware of his duties as a member of society, Radewijns loved the contemplative life. "I often used to look at him in the choir", says Thomas à Kempis, "and whenever I saw him, I was careful not to chatter, so impressed I was by his great religious fervor. When he was walking on the street, he seldom would notice the greetings of his friends, being engrossed in meditation. Scarcely five or six words would he speak at our supper-table. But when he was alone, then his mind became illuminated with so pure a light of divine radiance that whether he was reading the Old Testament or the New Testament, always some mystic interpretation of every passage came to him"[48].

As a faithful follower of Christ, Radewijns loved the simple life, wearing plain garments even after he had been ordained priest, avoiding dainty food, and reading only such books as might aid him in improving his character. His followers he exhorted to do the same. Novices and other inexperienced people should avoid the study of subtle questions, he used to say[49]. But in one respect he failed to grasp the true meaning of Christ's teachings. "He did not consider with due care the weakness of his body", Thomas à Kempis wisely remarks[50]. As a result of his excessive fasting, he ruined his digestive organs, losing all taste for different foods, mistaking wine for oil or beer[51]. Often his friend Everard Eza of Almelo, one of Gerard Groote's most influential disciples, would warn him of his folly, and cure him for the time being[52]. Fortunately Everard induced him to take more rest and to work more often in the open air[53]. He had to admit, however, that if it had not been for Radewijns' prayers and the grace of God, he must have died long before his time[54].

In spite of his weak body Radewijns had an imposing personality. His presence in the choir was sufficient to banish all jesting[55]. Thomas à Kempis himself did not stir when he was near. Says Thomas: "Even though he were not looking at me, yet I did not dare to talk in the choir, so I feared and respected his presence. Once he came up to me, to sing with me out of my book. I stood as if rooted to the ground and did not dare to move"[56]. There were people who fearlessly insulted Groote's disciples after his death, but not those living in Radewijns' house; and although a few condemned the habits of Brethren of the Common Life at Deventer, they nevertheless all agreed in praising Radewijns[57].

His knowledge of human nature was remarkable. Each one of his followers he treated in such manner as to stimulate his heart and mind. When reproach was needed he would freely employ it, but if one could be won through gentleness, praise, or jest, he was glad to employ those means also[58]. He was not weak in his kindness, or proud in his coolness. Great talents he had none, nor was there any particular virtue or vice observable in his character. The man's whole personality had undergone a harmonious development. Thoughtful and prudent, painstaking, calm, persevering, free from violent passions, and devoid of special talents, he was always composed, a perfect master of his lower self, harsh to his own nature, but filled with love and sympathy for his neighbor. Such was the man appointed by Groote as the leader of the "New Devotion", according to his biographers.

The works he wrote himself enable us to give a few more particulars. Radewijns was neither a scholar nor a great author in our sense of the word. Many paragraphs in his writings appear to have been copied from the Fathers and the works of medieval mystics. One of his writings, called "Omnes inquit artes", is merely a collection of excerpts; and the only real composition from his hand, known as the "Tractatulus de Spiritualibus Excercitiis", or "Treatise on Spiritual Exercises", contains many a sentence copied verbally from Bonaventura, Cassianus, and other writers. But they do show us what sort of a thinker Radewijns was; they reflect his theological and philosophical views.

Our aim and final destination, Radewijns writes, is the kingdom of God. The road which leads to that goal is purity of heart[59]. All our labors, our watching, fasting, meditation, prayer, and reading of the Scriptures are only means employed by us to eradicate vice, ere we ascend toward the plane of perfect love[60]. And as we advance on our road we shall be able to resuscitate the slumbering memories of the spirit — memories of a glorious past and of a still more glorious future. In keeping steadily before our eyes the destination at the end of our road, we shall continue to exercise our spiritual nature, lest our first ardor should cool. These spiritual exercises will finally enable our weary souls to enter the harbors of rest and peace, after a long voyage across the seas of time[61]. We, as pilgrims, wandering aimlessly in the desert of time, should seek the joys of heaven upon earth[62], which can be done most effectively by checking the desires of our mortal bodies, for the way of the spirit is life, and the way of the flesh is death[63].

As the pilgrim advances upon the high-way of this mortal life, faint memories come to him of a lost heritage. Sometimes, when he pauses on his way to look about him, he catches feeble glimpses of his happy past before the fall of man. At such moments it is the voice of the spirit which urges him to turn his steps homeward once more, by purifying his heart from the stains made by sin. For the purer his heart, the clearer his memory will become; he will then regain that marvelous secret of immortal life: love. The two chief ends of all religious or spiritual exercises, therefore, are the purging of our heart from sin, and the cultivation of love[64]. Perfect love is never acquired by any one, except he first has cleansed his heart from vice and supplanted evil by virtue[65]. Consequently the more successful we are in purging our hearts, the greater our love will become[66]. Our final aim, therefore, is love; everything else is but a means to reach that end[67]. Through the Fall our mind or reason has become blind to the truth, our will perverted, our memories unstable[68]. Man is a depraved being, but through Christ's sacrifice he is not hopelessly lost, nay he may gain a better fate than those spirits which are not allowed to enter mortal bodies[69]. But he must act, although his soul has already been saved through faith. For Christ's sacrifice, supplemented by our personal faith, does not purify our heart nor reform our mind.

All virtue, says Radewijns, is contained in love[70]. He compares man with a musical instrument; man in his present state is out of tune with the Infinite[71]. When one is converted, one's improper and imperfect affections or emotions are changed into pure love; one will then love God for God's own sake[72]. All our reading, meditations, and prayers should be concentrated chiefly upon the abolition of sin, thus making room for love[73]. Love, we must remember, is worth more than the negative attitude of fighting vice; it is the end, the crown of human existence. Nothing but love can lead us to the heavenly country[74]. Love for God in the first place, then love for our neighbor. We must strive to promote mutual friendships, practise modesty, suppress hatred, jealousy, and spite, and be careful in admonishing others. Obedience is the greatest virtue: it perfects our humility. It is in fact very sinful to seek one's own welfare rather than that of one's neighbor[75].

Radewijns urges his readers to exercise themselves in the acquisition of brotherly love[76], to read the Bible, to pray often, to confess their sins, to perform their daily tasks with alacrity, and to cultivate a healthful discipline of mind and morals[77]. Manual labor should be performed by all[78], but not all forms of manual labor were fitted in his opinion to favor the practice of spiritual exercises; those which resembled the spiritual exercises in kind were preferable, such as copying religious writings[79]. No one should study to acquire knowledge for its own sake, for there is no true learning except that which teaches us to acquire love through the conquest of evil[80]. The whole Bible was written for one end only; if one succeeds, and remains steadfast, one will not need to read the Bible any longer[81]. There surely can be no use in studying difficult passages in the Bible, according to Radewijns[82]. He thought no human brain could grasp the meaning of those passages, unless one were aided by the Spirit.

Somewhere within our inner selves a mysterious force resides, called conscience. It should be our daily care to stimulate this force into action. Usually it suffers from neglect, grows feebler and feebler till its voice is but faintly distinguished. Know thyself, Socrates had said, and Radewijns repeated this message. Examine your inner nature, he wrote, and arouse your conscience from its long slumber[83]. Pray, watch, and work, lest the force of habit overwhelm you. One should meditate frequently on the ultimate approach of death[84], the sufferings of Christ, and the final judgment[85]. He also gives directions for fighting various vices, which he copied largely from the works of Cassianus[86]. We should also seek the blessings of solitude and silence, for when human voices are absent, God will come to talk with us. Especially should we seek a few moments of this conversation with God shortly before retiring at night[87].

Virtue, says Radewijns, can only be acquired through grace. We of our own selves can never overcome evil, so low have we fallen. Even our good works are not wholly good, but mixed with imperfections of various kinds[88]. If we humiliate ourselves, however, as Christ once did, this grace will come to us in abundant measure. And how can we best cultivate this virtue of humility? By frankly admitting how depraved we have become since the fall of man, how prone to evil, how powerless in fighting vice; by patiently bearing with accusations, insults, and calumnies heaped upon us by slanderous tongues, and by giving all the credit to God, if perchance we should succeed in overcoming vice[89]. Thus we shall find love, the greatest of all blessings[90]. Love will bring peace, and much inward joy, though not unalloyed with grief about our continued shortcomings[91]. When once this love has come to us, we shall seek to draw more souls to Christ, which we can do most successfully on holy days, when people have more leisure and are in a better position to listen to our appeals[92].

After the purgative way comes the illuminative way. Man will then begin to understand God's tenderness to him[93], and will fathom the mystery of the fall of man and of his redemption through Christ. Christ's sacrifice on the cross is in fact the greatest event in the history of the human race[94]. No one can realize this more perfectly than he who has felt the load of sin gradually being lifted from his weary back and shoulders. With tears of joy he will look upon that central cross at Golgotha, where all at once the whole guilt of humanity was paid for, where the redemption of all souls was bought at a terrific price. Christ our savior and example, the chief factor in every man's life, should therefore have the chief and best place in every man's life[95]. Thus wrote he who for sixteen years was the leader of the "New Devotion", or Christian Renaissance.

IV

In the year of Groote's death the religious revival inaugurated by him had gained a foot-hold in those places where he himself had preached, or where his followers had begun to continue his work, namely at Deventer, Zwolle, Doesburg, Zutphen, Kampen, Almelo, Utrecht, Amsterdam, Haarlem, Leiden, etc. But among all these cities and villages only those situated nearest to the Yssel valley succeeded in retaining the master's best thoughts. Naturally it was Deventer and Zwolle which at once assumed a leading position in the history of the "New Devotion", and kept the fires of religious zeal burning, when all the others gradually lost their first ardor.

During Groote's life-time the question of the common life had been brought up for discussion. Groote had assured his followers that he would gladly become their

leader and protector, in case they should decide to follow
the mode of life practised by the women in his own
house at Deventer. Some of them were to build a
monastery, he had said, while the others would remain
at Deventer. The monastery was not built at once, however. Two years elapsed before the brethren felt the
need of seeking protection there. For they had not yet
begun to lead the common life, wherefore the mendicant
monks left them comparatively at ease, seeing that their
society did not resemble a monastic organization. The
brethren used to meet in a very informal way. Some of
them were living with Radewijns in the vicarage, but
not a few merely came to visit at stated times. Not long
after Groote's death an important event took place.
Radewijns had been accustomed to keep charge of the
money earned by the men living in his house. When he
noticed their indifference to merely temporal advantages.
such as wealth, fame, and honor, he decided to unite
their wages, and make of them one common fund[96].
From that day they were Brethren of the Common Life.
The exact date of this is not clear; it naturally must
have happened between Groote's death and the foundation of the new monastery. For they built that monastery
because they had offended their rivals, the mendicant
monks, by founding a semi-monastic organization, having united their funds and shared their expenses in
common. It had now become a vital necessity for them
to build the monastery, where some could live and all
would find protection[97]. Since Groote died on August
20, 1384, and the monastery was founded in 1386, we
may assume that the common life was begun before
1387, and probably during the fall of 1384 or the year
1385, inasmuch as Groote had drawn up definite rules
in August or July, 1384.

There were at this time ten men living in the vicarage with Radewijns at Deventer[98]. An important character was John of Huxaria or Höxter. The brethren were so impressed by this man's religious fervor that for a time they were uncertain whether they should elect him as their first rector or Radewijns, the acknowledged leader of the "New Devotion"; finally they chose Radewijns[99]. According to the obituary of the Brethren of the Common Life at Deventer[100], John of Höxter died on the 7th of January, 1387[101]. Consequently the brethren must have chosen their choice before this date[102].

The next event of importance took place in the year 1391, when the "House of Florentius" was founded, the first real house of the Brethren of the Common Life, and named after the first rector, Florentius Radewijns. Till 1391 the brethren had been living in the vicarage with Radewijns. As their number increased from year to year, they finally decided to move to more comfortable quarters. There was a devout lady, called Zwedera of Runen, the wife of a nobleman, who had heard of their plight. She offered them a house and lot, situated in the Pontsteeg, in exchange for two small buildings in the Enghe Straat. This house in the Pontsteeg was torn down and replaced by a fine new building, the "House of Florentius". Most of the brethren now moved from the vicarage to the "House of Florentius", taking their books and furniture with them[103].

Still another house was founded during the life of Radewijns: the "Nova Domus", "Domus Pauperum", or the new house for poor clerks. It was built in 1398[104], and intended for the poorer class of pupils attending the cathedral school[105]. For the Brethren of the Common Life faithfully continued Groote's policy in helping poor boys and girls to get an education. Radewijns and his followers often invited them to their house, providing them with material and spiritual sustenance[106]. "Behold", Radewijns wrote in 1398, "we take these youths into our house, inexperienced as they are, changeable, having as yet no definite aims or exerting much will power, but they are tractable and pliable. Oh what would happen, if one, or two, or three of us would persuade these boys to work, and teach them discipline, and humility"[107]? Many devout burghers at Deventer would take an interest in the younger boys, due to Radewijns' influence[108]. One Lambert van Galen always had eight of them in his house[109], and a certain Bye van Dunen also took care of eight boys[110]. These boys were all consigned to the people by the brethren in the "House of Florentius"[111]. For only after 1400 did the Brethren of the Common Life take in boys who had not yet finished their work at the cathedral school[112].

Upon the whole we may say that the brethren during the rectorate of Florentius Radewijns conscientiously tried to imitate the lives of the Apostles as set forth in the New Testament[113]. It was the simple life they led[114], a life of work and devotional exercises[115]. Says Badius Ascensius, the celebrated humanist and printer, who had received his early education from the Brethren of the Common Life at Ghent:

> "All were to approach as near as possible the life of the Apostles and of the primitive church of Christ, so that in the whole congregation there should be one heart, and that no one should consider or call anything his own. No one should seek outside the house the cure of souls, ecclesiastical benefices, or worldly occupations for the sake of gain; but clerics who should be found worthy would be promoted to cures that were

not too lucrative. All should dwell together in chastity and poverty, and should be clad in that manner of dress which Gerard Groote had approved. No one should beg from door to door; and in order that they might not be driven to this by want, all should avoid idleness, and according to their abilities should transcribe books, or instruct children. They were to take care that they themselves and all whom they should teach, should venerate and worship God with the deepest piety. They should love their neighbor with due charity, and should assist the poor with alms, according to their means. All should observe brotherly love. To their superior or spiritual Father in all lawful and just concerns they should yield unquestioning obedience, considering that their highest merit consisted in charity and submission. All earnings accruing from their labor in common or in private they should, according to the apostolic rule, lay at the feet of the Superior, and if perchance they left the Brotherhood, they should carry nothing with them"[116].

When Thomas a Kempis lived in the house of Radewijns (1398-1399) there were about twenty inmates, three of whom were laymen[117]. And in a document of the year 1396 we read that there should be at least four priests and eight clerics, that is, twelve members belonging to the clergy; the number of laymen was not specified[118]. Gradually their number increased, for their fame soon spread, even into distant countries. Many priests, says one biographer, attracted by the rumor of Radewijns' virtues and those of his followers, came to Deventer and submitted themselves to Radewijns' rule, laying open to him their hearts. Particularly from Westphalia they came in great numbers[119]. It was not long before the mendicant monks and their friends heard of the growing repute of the Brethren of the Common Life. Groote's fear had not been ill-founded. In spite of the new monastery they had built, the men at Deventer who now remained behind, were not sufficiently protected, having taken no monastic vows. One of their friends and protectors, named John ter Poorten, a prominent member of the city council, was publicly attacked as "Pope of the Lollards"[120].

Not satisfied with instigating the people and inventing sundry unofficial attacks, the Dominicans began to look for other ways of harming the brethren. They carefully studied the Canon Law and its commentaries, thereby hoping to prove that the Brethren of the Common Life had no right of existence. To live the common life without taking monastic vows was a crime, they said. No one had a right to found a new religious order without the pope's consent. And here were those upstarts at Deventer who had never asked for the pope's consent. They had a rector whom they had decided to obey, yet they took no vows of obedience. They earned their daily bread with their own hands, had definite rules and regulations, read sacred writings in the vernacular, and even held addresses to the people in their own language. All this they did without waiting for any one's permission. Surely, so strange and newfangled an institution was an offense to the Church!

The attacks grew fiercer, as time went on, for the jealousy of the mendicant and other monks increased in correspondence with the rising power of the new brotherhood. The Augustinian Canons Regular of Windesheim heard of these attacks. In 1395 they drew up a document in which they defended their friends at Deventer. The Brethren of the Common Life were virtuous men, they wrote. They taught no heresy of any kind, represented no secret societies or lodges, did not preach outside of the churches, had assumed no rules, no new monastic garments, had taken no new vows, and their whole mode of life had been approved by Gregory XI[121].

This document was not sufficient, however, to stop the enemy's assaults. What was worse, in 1398 another enemy appeared in the form of a terrible pestilence. William of Vianen first caught the disease. Ten brothers were infected and died. They were nursed by John Ketel, their pious cook, but he also passed away in 1398[122]. Then the remaining brethren, led by Radewijns, decided to leave the city and go to Amersfoort across the Veluwe, leaving a few members behind to take care of their property at Deventer[123]. At Amersfoort the brethren continued their work with new energy. They had taken several school boys with them, for whom they found suitable quarters among Groote's disciples at Amersfoort[124], where the first brethren-house west of the Yssel had been founded in 1395[125]. Here the men from Deventer copied books, and preached to the people in the vernacular, especially on holidays[126], "instructing them by example and doctrine"[127]. But it was not a happy time for them. They were now staying far away from the home they had built with their own hands and means. The attacks of their enemies continued, and the pestilence was sweeping one after another to the grave in Deventer. True, they were living with friends who were hospitable and kind, but still these friends were comparative strangers to them.

A spirit of sadness pervades the letters written by the fugitives at Amersfoort to the men at Deventer. "Let us go and die with them", says Gerard Zerbolt of Zutphen, one of the brethren who had gone to Amersfoort, "or else let them come and die with us, though we are able to die here and you to live there. What will life be worth to me, after they have passed away"[128]? And when they were told that one of their beloved friends at home had followed the others to the grave in their absence, they were almost overwhelmed with grief[129]. Their next three letters also breathe anguish. The brethren appeared to have lost all interest in life, so down-cast they were[180]. But in their last letter the dawn of a new hope breaks. They are expecting to return to Deventer soon! "Just as the members of one body all suffer together and console each other", they now write, "so do they also exult in each other's good fortune. The expectation of our return home is a great source of joy to us. Florentius is going to Amsterdam soon and when he returns, we hope to go back home to you"[131].

And what of their other enemies, the mendicant monks? Suddenly their attacks were rendered forceless by a scholar, who came to their aid at the right moment. This new defender of the brethren was Gerard Zerbolt of Zutphen, a man of considerable learning and sharp insight into all questions pertaining to law and tradition. A much greater scholar than Radewijns himself, he was more successful in affairs. With a sort of prophetic vision he perceived the dangers encircling the new brotherhood on all sides, when the brothers themselves were scarcely aware of impending trouble. They had written a great deal about the sorrows of separation, but the dangers from without they could not perceive.

The crisis came in 1398. Radewijns had been at Utrecht and at Amsterdam. The brethren at Deventer and Amersfoort were sure of his success in obtaining privileges from Frederick van Blankenheim, Bishop of

Utrecht. But Radewijns had to write home from Amersfoort: "The business of the Lord has made no progress; wherever we turn we meet with obstacles"[132]. That was all he could say. He now was home-sick. He had resolved to leave Amersfoort for Deventer in secret. His first attempt was a failure, but finally he succeeded in fleeing. Strange though it seems, Radewijns, the first rector of the Brethren of the Common Life, forsook his followers in the thick of the fight. He had been unequal to his task. How fortunate therefore that now his work could be continued by his more vigorous disciple. The name of this disciple we seldom read in the documents of that time, and the chronicles devote only a few pages to the story of his life. He loved to sit in his lonely cell, unknown to the world about him. But by uniting the best thoughts of Radewijns with the scholarly labors of Groote, he became the representative of both types of devotion or mysticism: the simple and the worldly-wise, the practical and the theoretical, the active and the passive.

V

Gerard Zerbolt was born at Zutphen in the year 1367[133]. After attending school in his native city he went to a university, probably that of Prague, where he studied hard from early dawn till late at night. But he does not seem to have stayed there very long, for in 1384 we find him at Deventer. Radewijns persuaded him to become a member of the brotherhood at Deventer[134]. A born student, he passed nearly all his time in his room at the "House of Florentius", reading "sacred writings", that is, the Bible, the Fathers, the Canon Law, and similar works[135]. He used to be so occupied with his work that he would forget the whole world about him, perfectly oblivious to any changes in the weather for example. Even at the dinner-table he was wont to continue his meditations. As soon as the meal was over, however, and the Bible was brought forward, he was all attention[136]. This book-worm, the other brothers reasoned, should be appointed librarian of their house. And Zerbolt, once in possession of Groote's books, together with his learned discourses which might be manipulated as a key to the books themselves, soon became the foremost scholar among the Brethren of the Common Life. Thomas à Kempis was a member of the house at that time. Says Thomas: "Many clerics used to come to him for advice, asking him to solve difficult problems for them. Radewijns often called for him when business transactions had to be undertaken for the house, and particularly when questions of law came up for discussion. Whenever Zerbolt was confronted with problems too difficult for him to solve, he would write them down and keep them in mind till he would meet some learned doctor. The scholars and great writers praised him highly for his learning"[137]. Thus Zerbolt gradually prepared himself for the struggle in which he was to bear the brunt. The struggle lasted from 1384-1419, but it was decided in favor of the brethren, when Zerbolt collected his arguments in their defense — which he used in soliciting the protection of important church officials — and arranged them in the shape of a treatise, called "On the Common Life"[138].

It was prohibited to found a new monastic order, Zerbolt admitted[139], but to live in private houses and share one's expenses with others was quite permissible, as it had been customary in the past; it had been recommended by the saints of old, and approved by the

pope[140]. Those chapters in the Canon Law, Zerbolt
continued, which were directed against the founders of
new monastic orders, were in no way opposed to the
common life as such[141]. What did the words "religious"
and "religion" imply, he asked, and who might be said
to be founding new monastic orders in contravention
of the Canon Law? Surely, the way in which the
Brethren of the Common Life conducted themselves
was irreproachable[142]. There were six ways of possessing temporal goods, some of which were far from
commendable[143], but to live outside of monasteries and
still to have no property of one's own, was highly
praiseworthy[144]. In the first place, it would be in complete accordance with Christ's wish as found in the
Gospel of St. Matthew, ch. XVIII [ch. XIX, verse 21] :
"If thou wilt be perfect, go and sell that thou hast"[145].
Secondly, man's natural mind or reason impels him to
live a simple life, that is, the common life, though man
has sinned against his natural mind or reason[146], wherefore the common life appears more difficult now. Again,
many saints and doctors recommend the cession of one's
private property for the benefit of the whole society or
family, such as Egidius, Thomas Aquinas, and Bede[147].
Where love reigns supreme, no one will want to have
possessions of his own, and friendship is promoted by
the common life, as has so well been said by Seneca[148].
Furthermore, in the primitive, the Apostolic Church,
all goods had been in common, and was not the early
church the best one[149]? We are taught by nature to
lead the common life, for man is indeed a social animal,
as Aristotle justly remarked. Hence the Stoics used to
say that man was born to assist other men, which saying
is supported by Genesis II[150]. This is what Plato also
asserted in the myth of Timaeus[151]. Paul preached the

same doctrine in the twelfth chapter of his Epistle to the Romans, and Ambrose in the first book of the "De Officiis", ch. CXXVIII, while there are several chapters found in the Canon Law which exhort all clerics to lead the common life[152]. Augustine also recommended the common life on several occasions[153].

But now it happens, says Zerbolt, that in our day we are told that the common life is only to be lived by monks, and that all the references in the "sacred writings" which approve the common life apply solely to the monastic state. For this reason one very rarely meets with men or women living the common life except in monasteries, though it was not that way in the days of the primitive church and long thereafter. For the same reason it may perhaps seem justifiable to all those monks who have lost all traces of religious fervor, and are filled with iniquity, gradually to do away with the common life altogether. Similarly many evangelical precepts are no longer obeyed, although they are most beneficial to all those who still follow them[154].

Here Zerbolt exposes the secret of the great decline in morals among the clergy, secular as well as regular. At first it was customary for all to follow Christ and obey every one of his commandments in so far as humanly possible. As the first ardor cooled, only the spiritual leaders were expected to do what in preceding centuries had been performed by all. And in Zerbolt's time many members of the clergy had relinquished all hopes and desires of becoming imitators of Christ and his apostles. Zerbolt knew quite well where they failed. Even when the most experienced members of his house at Deventer built a monastery which was generally regarded as a model of piety, Zerbolt remained in the "House of Florentius", as Radewijns, his teacher, did.

One could practise religion just as well in private homes, he thought, and for many years it was his highest ambition to prove this to the outside world.

Zerbolt had by no means exhausted his evidence in favor of the Brethren of the Common Life. Augustine advises us, he continues, in cases of doubt to refer to the older laws, writings, or customs of the Church. We should not hesitate to search among the works of the Ancients. What do we find regarding the theory of the common life? Not only was it practised by the apostolic church, but even long before the coming of Christ. The common life was begun in Paradise[155]. And if man had not fallen, this mode of living would still be universal among men. After the state of innocence man was placed under the law of nature, or the natural laws. Even in this state the common life was continued among religious men, and it flourished where love and friendship were cultivated[156]. Many philosophers, although they lived without the guidance of the Scriptures, were taught by the "Law of nature" and the "natural light" that the common life would promote friendship and love. Consequently they also lived the common life[157]. Of the Pythagoreans we read that all the disciples of Pythagoras laid all their money in their midst, and among them was great friendship. For Pythagoras had taught them to make one out of many. That was true friendship, he said[158]. On the question of the common life the philosophers of old almost completely agreed with the theologians, hence there was no need of giving other quotations from philosophical writings[159].

Again, the common life flourished under the régime of the Mosaic law, particularly among the wisest and most virtuous men. There were namely three sects among the Jews, the Pharisees, Sadducees, and Essenes, and of these three the Essenes were the noblest, for according to Josephus they lived in many respects the apostolic life and had all goods in common. This mode of life was reinstated therefore by Christ, observed by the Apostles and their disciples, and continued afterwards. But in the state of glory, when God will be all in all, and the joys of us all the joys of each, and the joys of each the joys of all, then this common life is to be perfected and universally applied. For where all things shall be in common, there will be no discord, but perfect love and unity. And the more sincerely we practise this common life and this love for God and our neighbor, the more rapidly we shall approach this state of glory[160].

In the last part of the third chapter Zerbolt shows that the dwelling together of pious men in private homes does not necessarily institute an officially recognized "collegium", for these men hold no offices in the Church, and if some of them do, it is certainly not on account of their office that they were admitted as members of their society[161]. The fourth chapter of the "Treatise on the Common Life" deals with the subject of secret societies. Three kinds of such societies are prohibited, Zerbolt writes, namely the assemblies of conspirators, of heretics, and of the seditious. But the Brethren of the Common Life are a quite different sort; they are pious, loyal, orderly[162]. The fifth chapter is devoted to the question of preaching in private houses. This is forbidden, Zerbolt admits, but the members of a group may address and exhort one another, correct each other's faults, and even deliver speeches to the whole group in the house, as long as no one speaks to the common people, which may only be done by the prelates[163]. The same subject is continued in the next chapter, where

it is explained that the Brotherhood of the Common
Life is quite distinct from all secret societies[164].

The seventh chapter is perhaps the most interesting
one of the whole treatise. It has been printed twice in
the original since 1889, and once in the Dutch translation[165]. As early as the year 1400 it had been translated by a monk in Brabant[166], and not long after this
date it spread across all of Germany, being copied in
great numbers[167]. In the table of contents this chapter
is entitled: "It is permitted to read and have Dutch
(Germanic) books; what Dutch (Germanic) books are
dangerous for laymen and what are prohibited"[168]. We
have seen that Groote shortly before his death translated
parts of the Bible and a great many church hymns. If
he had lived several years longer, he would undoubtedly
have translated a great deal more into the Dutch vernacular. Now Zerbolt regarded it his duty to continue in
part the work left unfinished by Groote. Each disciple
performed his fitting share. Cele took over Groote's
interest in educational reforms; John Brinckerinck became a leader among the Sisters of the Common Life;
Radewijns was the appointed guide of the whole body
of Groote's disciples, — the great physician of the men-
tally and spiritually diseased, the friend of the poor, the
sorrowful, and the homeless; but Zerbolt inherited the
master's love for books, and for learning; it was he who
had to defend the new brotherhood with weapons too
heavy and cumbersome for Radewijns' use; it was he
who became the only distinguished scholar in the house
at Deventer, and its most influential author till the days
of Hegius, Murmellius, and Erasmus.

To read the "sacred writings", as long as they contain
no heresy or errors, particularly, if they are easy to
understand, and in so far as they do not disagree with

the canonical writings in style or subject matter, is per
missible and praiseworthy, claims Zerbolt. This can be
proved in the following manner. If laymen are not
allowed to read such books, it will be necessary to state
why, that is, because they are laymen and unlearned,
and for such it is not fit to read or study religious
writings; or, although it is not prohibited for laymen
to read them, nevertheless they shall not be permitted
to read them in their native tongue. But it would be
wrong to make such an assertion. For in the first place,
laymen are not forbidden to read such works on account
of being laymen, as is plainly inferred from several
decisions found in the Canon Law[169]. Augustine even
reprehends laymen for being unwilling to read religious
writings. Chrysostom does the same. Jerome exhorts
even women to study the Scriptures, as is done also
by Gregory[170]. There are many laymen to-day, Zerbolt
remarks, who spend a great deal of their time in reading
wholly impractical and useless stories and fables about
knights errant, the war of Troy, and similar subjects.
Would it not be far better for them to study the Scriptures instead[171]? And what does the Bible have to say
about this matter? The New Testament commands us
more frequently to study God's precepts than does the
Old Testament, but in the latter many commandments
are given to read and study the Scriptures, as for
example in Deuteronomy, ch. VI and ch. XI, and in
many other places. In Deuteronomy, ch. XI, we read:
"Therefore shall ye lay up these my words in your heart
and in your soul, and bind them for a sign upon your
hand, that they may be as frontlets between your eyes.
And ye shall teach them your children, speaking of them
when thou sittest in thine house, and when thou walkest
by the way, when thou liest down, and when thou risest

up. And thou shalt write them upon the door post of thine house, and upon thy gates". That such commandments were not addressed to the clergy only is very plain indeed. From these and many other proofs which might be given, it clearly appears that laymen are not prohibited from reading religious writings, simply because they are laymen[172].

Now we still have to prove that it is not forbidden to read religious writings in the vernacular. Much evidence can be brought forward to establish this point also. In the first place, we may say that the greater part of the Old Testament was written for the Hebrews in Hebrew, which was the vernacular for them. Similarly, the New Testament was drawn up in the Greek vernacular with the exception of the Gospel of Matthew, and Paul's Epistle to the Hebrews, which were directed to Hebrews, hence written in their vernacular. Some say that Paul wrote his Epistle to the Romans in Latin. At any rate, the whole or nearly the whole of the Bible was written in another language than Latin.

In the second place, we find that many a missionary translated parts of the Bible into the language of the people he tried to convert. Dorotheus writes that Bartholomew, when he came to India, translated the Gospel of St. Mark into the language used there. This he surely would not have done, had he thought it wrong for any one to read the Bible in the vernacular. The sole reason why the Bible is now read in Latin, is on account of this language being so widely used[173]. The Hebrews read the Old Testament in Hebrew, the Greeks had Greek Bibles, the Chaldeans had the Scriptures in their own language. In the days of old the Syrians and the Arabs read the Bible in the vernacular. Ulfilas translated it into Gothic. The Bible has been translated for the Egyptians, the Slavs, the Armenians, and if one were to search further he might find a translation of parts of the Bible in every language under the sun[174]! For when the Holy Ghost descended upon the Apostles on that great day of Pentecost, many devout men were present and each heard the Apostles speak in his native tongue, for a sign that the gospel of Christ was to be preached in every language on the globe. Yes, in all languages except the Dutch or Teutonic? Would not that be a curious, a ridiculous thing? Impossible. Why should not they, the Brethren of the Common Life, who counted many laymen among their members, be allowed to read the Bible in the vernacular? Every one endowed with an infinitesimal spark of intelligence would at once admit that they were permitted to study the Bible in Dutch. Not only permissible it was, but meritorious and quite praiseworthy[175].

But it would not be wise to read all books indiscriminately; laymen are not allowed to read heretical works for example. They should study those writings which plainly and openly discuss simple doctrines, as was indicated by Paul in his first Epistle to the Corinthians, the third chapter, and in the fourth chapter of the Epistle to the Hebrews. Augustine gives us similar instructions, and Chrysostom also. There are certain parts of the Bible which are more or less obscure, as the Revelation by St. John. Such books ought to be explained and properly interpreted for laymen to comprehend their hidden meaning. What benefit could one derive from the study of books one could never hope to understand? Hugo of St. Victor and Augustine have taken great pains to explain this matter. One should also avoid those books which use profane and abusive language in dealing with the most sacred subjects. There are such Teutonic

works in existence, like certain sermons by Eckhardt.
And finally, laymen should read no religious works in
the vernacular that deviate from the doctrines promulgated by the acknowledged leaders in the Church[176].

Chapter VIII of the "Treatise on the Common Life"
is devoted to the subject of obedience. The Brethren
of the Common Life had taken no vows, for they did
not intend to form a monastic organization. Consequently they could not bestow so great authority upon
their superior or rector as was the case with the regular
clergy. Not a single member of their house was obliged
or compelled to obey the instructions of the rector. They
did not promise to obey any office-holder in such manner.
No matter how humble and how ignorant one might be,
no one, however virtuous, talented or noble, could
threaten him with punishment, for no one expected him
to render homage to any superior in that way. For
they had decided to obey Christ only, and to imitate
the Apostles. If one were to find the kingdom of
heaven, Christ had said, one should become like unto
a little child. The greatest men in God's kingdom were
those who not only obeyed their superiors, but also their
equals, and even their inferiors. In the apostolic church
all members had been considered each other's superiors
and equals, — all as members of one body.

These and similar questions Zerbolt discussed in chapter eight of his treatise. All men were expected to
render obedience to their superiors, he began, laymen
as well as the clergy. For this reason the Church has
condemned that sect which claims that man may attain
to such perfection in this life that he no longer has to
obey any law or commandment issued either by temporal
or ecclesiastical powers. But in houses like the one in
which Zerbolt was living one found oneself transported

into a wholly different atmosphere. Here all men were considered equal[177].

Yet no society can exist without law and order. It is as with a family, where the father is like a king in his kingdom. The children and the domestics all obey the master of the house, and he takes care of the whole family[178]. Yet there is a great difference also between the house of the brethren and a family. In a family we find inferiors obeying a superior. In the brethren-house one finds equals correcting and admonishing each other as equals, not as a father treats his children[179]. Is such kind of obedience permissible? It is, according to Peter, Augustine, Bernard, and Thomas Aquinas[180]. The fact is, there could not be harmony or peace in such a house without this sort of obedience[181]. It is permissible then for the Brethren of the Common Life to have a rector to take care of the house, and to obey each other's wishes, in order to promote peace and harmony.

Is it also permissible for them to confess their sins to each other? Some declare they should not do this, but these people are wrong, says Zerbolt in chapter nine. One may confess one's sins to laymen. In case of necessity one may even confess one's mortal sins to a laymen[182]. And as for venial sins, one is permitted to confess them at any time. For in the sixth chapter of James we read: "Confess your faults one to another"[183]. And although the learned doctors and theologians are not agreed on this subject, nevertheless we are permitted to confess our sins to laymen. But it seems best to confess to priests whenever possible. To-day the custom of confessing sins to one another is scarcely ever practised. Perhaps because we have so many priests, or because many doctors are opposed to the practice[184].

It certainly is permissible, Zerbolt continues, to confess daily shortcomings to each other. For such a humble confession almost in itself brings one forgiveness of the sins committed[185]. In the second place, this kind of confession will teach us more clearly the nature of sin, the difference between vice and virtue, and the various remedies for each vice[186]. It is easily understood that for this kind of confessions we do not so much need a person who has the keys of authority, as one with experience in spiritual affairs, who can teach us to fight temptations and the devil's attacks[187]. When somebody reproved Arsenius for confessing his sins to an unlearned farmer who knew a great deal about spiritual exercises, he answered: "I have learned Latin and Greek, but the alphabet of this farmer I have thus far failed to decipher". Thirdly, if one is accustomed sincerely to reveal his shortcomings, he finally becomes ashamed of having to admit the repeated yielding to the same temptation, and firmly resolves to defeat the enemy who sent that temptation. Confession also frees us more quickly from the snares of the tempter[188].

This non-sacramental confession, Zerbolt argues, was once very common among virtuous men and highly praised, but now it is not common and some consider it wrong[189]. Here we have the secret of the institution founded by Groote: a protest against the formalism of the Church in the fourteenth century. One by one the commandments of Christ had been disregarded as too difficult to follow. Even the clergy generally were disregarding them, and what was infinitely worse, the men who wanted to return to the customs of the apostolic church were attacked by the very leaders in Christendom. The Brethren of the Common Life were called heretics, — they were attacked for trying to obey, where their enemies refused to obey. They were not to live the common life, nor to have a rector, nor to read religious books in the vernacular. To confess their sins to each other was said to be prohibited, though James had plainly commanded all Christians to practise it frequently.

What else was wrong about the new brotherhood? Groote had prepared a schedule for the men who had decided to live the common life, according to which they were to regulate their daily tasks[190]. The brethren had chosen a rector soon after Groote's death[191], and now they had a procurator besides[192], while some or all of the members practised a certain course of spiritual exercises. Although it is impossible to tell exactly what sort of a constitution they had in Zerbolt's day, inasmuch as the original written constitution was drawn up after 1413[193], certain it is that they were following definite rules. That was wrong, their enemies said. Hence the tenth chapter of the treatise is intended by Zerbolt to defend this feature of the brotherhood's organization[194]. The same subject is continued in the eleventh or last chapter. To perform manual labor at stated times, and to read books, to fast, pray, and meditate regularly is permitted, says Zerbolt, not only to monks but to all virtuous men[195]. For even the simplest laborers eat, work, rest, and sleep at stated times[196]. Therefore the Brethren of the Common Life too are allowed to have their rules or regulations. And here the treatise ends.

Zerbolt's theological views are most clearly set forth in his "Spiritual Ascensions", the work which exercised such a profound influence on Catholic Europe of the fifteenth and sixteenth centuries, particularly on Ignace Loyola. Based on and partly copied after the "Treatise on Spiritual Exercises" by Radewijns, Zerbolt's book

on the spiritual ascensions repeats the views set forth
by Radewijns, which views are supplemented by certain
chapters found in the "Reformation of the Faculties
of the Soul", — also written by Zerbolt. They form
a course of spiritual exercises, which were practised by
thousands, worked over by Mauburn (or Mombaer),
and finally incorporated, though changed to some extent,
by Loyola in his "Spiritual Exercises", as we shall have
occasion to observe in another chapter[197].

Man fell from his privileged state of innocence in
paradise. This was the first fall[198]; the second fall of
man is due to his sins on earth[199]. "If one wishes to
find the kingdom of heaven", says Zerbolt, "one must
steadily keep in view whence he originally came, —
what he was before the fall, in order that he may know
how to regain his lost estate, for it is useless to strive
after perfection, if one knows not what such perfection
implies. Man must in all his spiritual exercises remember his final end: purity of heart and love[200]. To purify
the heart is to extinguish evil desire, which we may also
call the reformation of the soul or the mind[201]. For
Oh man, thy mind, which is more exalted than all mortal
creatures, becomes defiled in subjecting itself through
improper affection to temporal objects[202]. Explore your
sinful nature, strive to realize the extent of your fall,
and carefully examine your evil deeds each day[203]. For
there is also a third fall, which for example happened
to the prodigal son, when he went among the swine[204].
In this condition man continually commits mortal sins.

Since we can distinguish three falls or descents, there
must also be three ascents, each divided into several
steps or stages. As man ascends the steps, he gradually
reforms his intellect, his will, and his memory, for these
are the three faculties of the soul[205]. During the first

ascent he leaves the ways of the godless, as the prodigal left the swine[206]. He begins to confess his sins and to show repentance[207]. During the second ascent his repentance is sufficient to bring forgiveness, but that is not enough[208]. Three things are needed before he reaches the third ascent, namely: fear of the Lord, hope, and love. Zerbolt begins with fear, for often he had read this text: "The fear of the Lord is the beginning of wisdom". In the first place, this holy fear plainly exposes the evil fruits of sin[209]. One also should reflect often on the approach of death[210], the last judgment[211], and the pains in hell[212]. The second step of the second ascent is hope, the hope of future joy[213]. Then follows the third step, where the active life begins. Here one learns to love, after having purified the heart. And here one commences the real exercises.

Zerbolt asks, How are we to purge ourselves from sin, and acquire perfect love? Only through Christ, who is our model and example. For Christ said that no one could come to the Father but through him. It should be our aim to become his companions, his followers[214]. Secondly, we should love and adore Christ both as God and man, and thirdly, through the example of Christ's humanity, we could rise to great heights of spiritual perfection, while, in looking upon his divinity as our mirror, we ourselves might obtain knowledge of and love for things divine[215]. Just as Radewijns had devoted a considerable part of his "Omnes inquit artes" to the life of Christ[216], and as Thomas à Kempis, who was now collecting the material for the "Imitation of Christ", was soon to follow Radewijns, so Zerbolt also reserved thirteen chapters for this same subject[217].

The third ascent is directed against the evil consequences of the first fall or descent, commonly called

original sin. Zerbolt holds that it is our duty to cleanse
our hearts in so far as we are able, humanly speaking,
from the tares introduced into our blood by Adam's sin
with Eve[218]. The first thing to do is to extinguish vice,
as Radewijns also had said[219]. Then follow about a
dozen other chapters, some of which remind us forcibly
of certain passages in the "Treatise on the Common
Life"[220], but they contain nothing new.

Zerbolt wrote his two mystical works shortly before
his death, which occurred in 1398. In November, 1398,
the Brethren of the Common Life of Deventer had
returned from Amersfoort[221]. Radewijns was ill, wherefore Zerbolt was sent to an old friend north of Deventer.
On his return he caught an infectious disease and died
on the 4th of December[222]. With him the house at
Deventer lost its scholar, author, and defense. Radewijns, heart-broken as he was, passed away on the 25th
of March, 1400, and the centre of the "New Devotion"
shifted northward to Windesheim and Zwolle.

VI

The monastery of Windesheim had been founded in
the year 1386 by Groote's followers at Deventer, who
wished to materialize his plans. They wanted a per-
manent place of refuge for those among their number
who preferred the monastic life, and a place that might
afford a temporary shelter to the brethren left behind
at Deventer, in case of need[223]. "For this reason did
they decide to build a monastery", says Rudolph Dier,
"because they, living the simple, common life, were
afraid of further persecutions by rivals, and thus, if
some of their members would be actually living in a

monastery, the others would be protected by them"[224].
The brethren in Radewijns' vicarage had felt no need of
such protection until they had introduced the common
life. In 1386, however, we find them looking for a site
for their new monastery. They found one near Hattem
on the Veluwe, about three miles south-west of Zwolle.
After having secured permission from the Duke of
Gelderland to erect some buildings there, they went to
their ecclesiastical lord, the Bishop of Utrecht. Radewijns and six other men were sent to tell the bishop
about their plans. "Do not build that monastery in
Gelderland", the bishop told them, "but somewhere in
my territory east of the Yssel". Now it happened that
one of the men, a certain Berthold ten Hove, owned
some property there, wherefore the brethren agreed to
build on his land, which was situated at Windesheim in
the Yssel valley, three miles south-east of Zwolle[225].

First one man was sent to make the necessary preparations; later five others were added, and one was appointed procurator[226]. They began to work at once. The
site was found to be a lonely tract of land with some
few willows on it[227], but no buildings of any kind to
house the men[228]. A small elevation was selected for
the buildings. This spot, they were told, had never been
flooded by the Yssel[229]. Soon gifts came pouring in:
Lambert Stuerman, of whom Groote had caught the
pest, as they thought, but who had recovered, gave 100
French crowns; some one else gave 200, and a third one
136. Henry of Wilsen, one of the six men sent to inspect the grounds, sold all he had, and handed the money
over to the brethren at Deventer. Many among his
relatives and acquaintances contributed, so that the
amount required for the erection of the buildings was
soon raised. Encouraged by this the men at Windes-

heim worked with redoubled energy. In October of the year 1387 the monastery proper, with its church, had been finished[230]. All was now ready for the dedication. The six brethren were to take the vows of chastity, poverty, and obedience. But, although they had been instructed by Groote and Radewijns in the essentials of the Christian religion, they knew practically nothing about the monastic life and its ceremonies. They decided to spend a few days at the Augustinian monastery of Eemsteyn near Dordrecht, where some of Groote's best friends were now practising the rules of the Augustinian Canons Regular with the ardor of new devotion[231]. Here they were kindly accepted and initiated into the rituals of the Augustinian order, which the monks of Eemsteyn had learned from those of Groenendaal, Ruysbroeck's monastery[232]. On the 17th of October the dedication took place. The brethren went through the customary ceremonies, and each of them read from a strip of parchment the vows of obedience, poverty, and chastity. Just those and no others. No vows of obedience to the bishop of Utrecht, no promises of allegiance to any party or power, and no submission to any rules except those they were to formulate themselves. What was the cause of this independent attitude? Perhaps it was, as Acquoy suggests, the inborn love for personal liberty so characteristic of the Frisians and the Saxons[233].

There stood the little monastery with its thatched roofs among the willows planted beside the still waters. Who would have thought in 1387 that this humble convent would soon be sending its missionaries all over the Low Countries and thence into the farthest outpost of the German Empire; that it would bring about the only lasting monastic reform in fifteenth century Europe, and incorporate within its fold some of the most famous monasteries in the West? Though its men were first taught by the monks of Eemsteyn near Dordrecht, Groenendaal near Brussels, and St. Victor at Paris, not long thereafter it surpassed them all in moral force and religious zeal.

This apparently marvelous success may not seem strange, however, to one who has noted how the founders of Windesheim spent their lives. Under the leadership of Henry of Höxter (17 October 1386–17 October 1387) and that of William Keynkanp (October 1387–November 1391) the works of love and faith were plentiful[234]. Particularly during the priorate of John Vos of Heusden (1391–1424) Windesheim was the pride of Groote's followers, and from 1400–1424 it was the centre of the "New Devotion". So great was the love among the Brethren of the Common Life at Deventer and their friends at Windesheim in those early years that all their possessions were considered almost as one common fund, placed at the disposal of the one who needed them most[235]: In 1392 Deventer and Windesheim founded the monastery of Mariendaal near Arnhem. John Ketel, the pious cook at Deventer, who possessed 1300 florins, gave the whole sum to the founders, and Radewijns also gave some money[236].

John Vos of Heusden was in fact the greatest prior Windesheim ever had. Born at Heusden in 1363, he had come to Deventer to receive instruction in the cathedral school of St. Lebwin[237]. Radewijns had introduced him to Groote one day. The first meeting had been decisive. Groote had looked at him with one of those penetrative glances of his, which seemed to pierce one's very soul, and said: "This is the man I have sought; with him I will do something worth while on earth"[238]. Till 1388 he had remained with the other brothers in Radewijns' vicarage. But the monastery called him[239], and in 1391 he was elected prior[240].

The first thirty years were a time of great moral strength and rapid growth. Of the forty brethren invested before 1424, one half became rectors or priors of monasteries built or reformed under their supervision[241]. For there were other great reformers in those early days besides John Vos of Heusden. There was John à Kempis, a disciple of Groote and later of Radewijns[242]. At Deventer and Windesheim he was a model of piety, and later he became rector and prior of several monasteries in succession[243]. Then there was Arnold of Calcar, sub-prior at Windesheim for 35 years[244], and Henry Wilde, one of the six founders, who was sent to St. Victor at Paris to study the rules of the Augustinian order[245]; Henry Wilsem, once a prominent magistrate at Kampen, and a convert of Groote[246], Berthold ten Hove, also converted by Groote[247], John Scuutken, another disciple of Groote[248], and Albert Wijnberghen[249].

It should be noted, however, that whatever Windesheim possessed before the year 1400 was a gift from the Brethren of the Common Life and their friends at Deventer. And similarly, when a monastery was built for the Augustinian Canonesses Regular, it was founded by the Sisters of the Common Life of Deventer.

In 1383 the sisters had secured a rector and confessor in the person of John van den Gronde[250]. When Groote was about to die, he had promised to send "little flowers" from heaven[251]. But for several years his promise remained unfulfilled. The rector was getting old, and could devote but a small part of his time to their care, as he often went out preaching, or to hear confessions of the sisters at Zwolle, or the brethren at Mount St. Agnes, three miles north-east of Zwolle[252]. Left without proper guidance, the Sisters of the Common Life at Deventer gradually neglected Groote's instructions; discipline relaxed, and the blessings of manual labor were ignored. When Van den Gronde died[253], a reform was at once instituted by his capable successor, named John Brinckerinck. This brother was one of the most ardent followers Groote ever had, for he had attended the master on nearly all his trips. He became as close a friend of Groote as John Cele had been[254]. Not being able to find a single monastery in or near the Yssel valley where Christ was imitated, he had joined the Brethren of the Common Life at Deventer[255]. In 1392 he left their house for the "House of Master Gerard", — Groote's ancestral home, — this being the year in which Van den Gronde passed away.

Brinckerinck has rightly been called the second founder of the "House of Master Gerard"[256]. The moment he entered the building, the sisters felt that their life of ease was ended. They were told to lead the common life again, to work with their own hands and to discontinue begging for alms. "You must either work or leave the house", was his command. But they stayed, for he at once won both their love and respect[257]. It was said that rays of holiness radiated from him[258]. Soon his fame spread beyond the walls of Deventer. From Zeeland, Friesland, Münster, and Cologne all sorts of persons came to the "House of Master Gerard" for counsel and religious instruction[259]. And the sisters, inspired by his saintliness, were full of religious fervor[260]. Soon the old home of Groote was found altogether too small. Four other houses were founded at Deventer during Brinckerinck's life-time[261]. Says one early biographer: "So great a fire of the Holy Ghost was kindled among those saintly sisters in the House of Master Gerard that the whole country around here grew warm with it, and all this as the result of the doctrine and instruction of their father, John Brinckerinck"[262].

Meanwhile some of the clergy were not pleased. Others were filled with holy anger, because the poor women read books in the vernacular, which was considered reprehensible by certain members of the clergy at that time. The sisters should immediately stop this evil practice, they said, and when they saw that their orders were disregarded, they attacked the sisters publicly. At last Brinckerinck found it necessary to defend them in church, where he held a lengthy discourse on the subject of reading books in the vernacular. The arguments used on this occasion he had gleaned from a book he had read in the library of the brethren-house[263], which probably had been composed by Zerbolt.

There were other reasons why the Sisters of the Common Life were attacked in those early days, — the same reasons which caused the Brethren of the Common Life to seek protection in a monastery. Many a time Brinckerinck had to ascend the pulpit in the church of St. Mary at Deventer to defend the sisters. It should not surprise us to learn that they too wanted to found a convent, for the times were so different from what they are to-day. On the seventeenth of June, 1400, Brinckerink called the sisters together to draw up the necessary plans. They possessed a piece of land near the Yssel, three miles north of Deventer[264]. Here they decided to build their home. But it was a lonely tract of land they had selected, — marshy and unattractive. Ditches had to be dug, stumps rooted up, holes filled with sand; in most places the surface of the soil had to be raised six feet. Undaunted by hardship, fatigue, and discomfiture, the women did the work, assisted by the brethren of the "House of Florentius" and later by hired laborers. Before that year was over, the first buildings, made of wood, were finished[265]. In 1401 the sisters bought some more land, in 1406 still more; they built a barn also, and soon they had become prosperous farmers, possessing a fine herd of sheep, cows, pigs, and who knows what else? The monotonous brown of the murky soil had been replaced by soft green grass[266]. And soon the wooden cloister buildings were exchanged for a fine brick convent, — the convent of Diepenveen[267].

VII

After Zerbolt's death the centre of the "New Devotion" had traveled northward from Deventer to Windesheim and Diepenveen. It was to shift still farther to the north, for in the city of Zwolle a flourishing brethren-house had attracted many devout from Flanders, Brabant, Friesland, Westphalia, and other districts. Soon it opened its doors to a Wessel Gansfort, an Alexander Hegius, and a Rudolph von Langen, and before long it began to send out missionaries to several other cities, such as Groningen, 's-Hertogenbosch, and Doesburg, where daughter-houses were founded. The reform of the school at Zwolle was the beginning of a mighty revival of learning. And although this intellectual revival found its most perfect expression in the labors of Hegius at Deventer, Murmellius at Münster, and Dringenberg at Schlettstadt, Zwolle was the place which provided the source material, and gave the movement its impetus.

Among Groote's first and most influential disciples was Henry Foppens of Gouda. Anxious to imitate his master as friend of poor school boys, he bought a house at Zwolle, where he intended to lodge some of them[268].

Also as preacher and leader of the Sisters of the Common
Life at Zwolle he became a worthy follower of Groote[269].
Then there was Reynold of Drenen, pastor at Zwolle[270],
and blind John Ummen, a very pious man, who together
with two other laymen, named Jacob Wittecoep and
Wychmannus Ruerinck, bought a lot next to Foppen's
house. On this lot a house was built, where the three
laymen in question lived the common life, acting upon
Groote's advice[271]. We might therefore call them the
first Brethren of the Common Life, for they had kept
no private property of their own[272]. On the 5th of July,
1384, the house was sold to Groote, lest the heirs might
claim it some day[273]. "These three men", says Jacob
Voecht of Utrecht, "were therefore the first Brethren
of the Common Life at Zwolle, to which number many
others were added later, among whom blind John
Ummen was foremost; he became their rector and
procurator. Together they moved to Mount St. Agnes,
where Groote showed them the site for their new
house"[274].

The first brethren-house at Zwolle was not a success,
for the men who had founded it moved to a lonely hill,
three miles away from the city, where but few people
were found to give them employment, and few boys
to be cared for. A better fate was reserved for the
second institution. On April 4, 1393, Frederick van
Wevelinkhoven, Bishop of Utrecht, died. His successor,
named Frederick van Blankenheim, was a friend of
Groote's disciples. The brethren at Zwolle, as soon as
they were made aware of the new bishop's friendly
attitude, decided once more to found a house, hoping
that this time they would not be compelled to seek protection and rest in a solitary place[275]. There was a certain Meynoldus of Windesheim, a disciple of Groote,

who had sold his property and had come to Zwolle, where in a humble dwelling he lived with a few poor school boys[276]. Encouraged by the success of the Brethren of the Common Life at Deventer, he wanted to found a house where priests and clerics might live the common life. A suitable site was secured, and a fine building erected, called "House of St. Gregory". This happened in the year 1396[277].

Who was to be elected rector of the second institution at Zwolle? Meynoldus of Windesheim, the real founder, felt himself unfit for so exalted a task. It was not for him, he said, to become the spiritual guide of the men and boys living with him in his house. One day he came to Florentius Radewijns, rector at Deventer. "Can you lend me one of your clerics"? he asked of Radewijns. "Yes", was the answer, "take this youth with you; his name is Gerard Scadde of Calcar". At the expiration of one year Meynoldus returned to Deventer with Gerard. "The young man should at once be ordained priest", he said to Radewijns, "in order that he may become our rector". Radewijns gladly assented[278]. In 1396, then, the Brethren of the Common Life at Zwolle obtained both a new house and a capable rector. They were instructed in the ways and means practised at Deventer; the rules of Deventer, as yet unwritten, became theirs also[279]. And with these rules they acquired religious fervor in great measure, surpassing their friends at Deventer for a time, as will be shown in the following chapter.

Thus far we have but casually mentioned the name of Zwolle's great teacher, John Cele. A native of Zwolle, he received a master's degree at some university, — Prague perhaps. Through Groote's friendship he seems to have obtained his position as rector of the city school at Zwolle, in or shortly after the year 1374[280]. The fact that Groote selected him as his trusted companion on his visit to Ruysbroeck is significant. Groote often corresponded with him in later years[281], and also often came to visit him[282]. In almost every respect Cele tried to imitate his beloved friend. Not only did he, as Groote had done, refuse to become a priest, declaring that a priest's responsibilities were greater than those of the angels[283], but he also stayed a short time (1381–1382) at Monnikhuizen[284], the Carthusian monastery near Arnhem, where Groote also had spent two years. And, as had been the case with Groote, he found but little satisfaction there[285]. Duty, he thought, had called him back to Zwolle: "his light should no longer be hid beneath a bushel".

Cele brought about the reform of the city school at Zwolle, and succeeded in attracting as many as 1200 boys at a time from districts far removed from the Yssel valley. He became the founder and originator of what we now call the secondary schools, and it was his school that served as model for those of Dringen-berg, Hegius, Murmellius, Melanchton, Sturm, Calvin, the Jesuits, and all their followers. There were several causes which contributed to his success. In the first place, after having been taught by Groote to make a careful distinction between the form and the inner essence of things, he pruned away from his curriculum all dead formalism, at least as far as he was able. Of what use was the study of Canon Law, medicine, and astronomy to the average school boy, he used to ask, consciously in imitation of Groote's standpoint[286]. And as for the study of religion and the harmonious development of one's mental and spiritual self, the Gospels, the Epistles of the New Testament, and other biblical works, together

with the Fathers, were a more fruitful source of instruction than the subtle and wholly impractical scholastic
disputes engaged in by the learned doctors of Paris and
Cologne. Scholasticism was as good as any other system
of philosophy, but there were different kinds of scholasticism: the living and the dead, the practical and the
formal, as there were different kinds of religion or faith,
such as the theoretical and the personal, such as the
religion of Christ versus that of the Pharisees.

John Cele did this thing, which was new. Three times
a day (on holidays at least) he read and explained to
his pupils selections from the Bible: from the Epistles
in the morning, the Gospels in the afternoon, and from
some other book in the evening[287]. He exhorted his
pupils to write down those parts of his addresses which
seemed most useful to them. The life of Christ was
continually referred to as the only reliable pattern we
could find on earth. To imitate him was Cele's chief
aim; it should be theirs also, he said. "Cele himself",
says Busch, "as a true imitator of Christ, never taught
us anything which he had not previously practised, in
order that he might be our example"[288]. The pupils
were taught to pray both in Latin and in Dutch; Busch
gives us both versions of a prayer taught by Cele[289]. He
never undertook anything without commending it first
to God in prayer[290], for at all times he felt himself in
the presence of God[291]. The one chief cause of his fame,
says Schoengen, the archivist at Zwolle, was his maxim:
"The kingdom of heaven consisteth not in knowledge
and speech, but in work and virtue"[292]. Cele was not at
all opposed to book-learning. He asserted that God's
will or testament was expressed in "sacred writings",
and that the Church would long have perished had it
not been for the reading of good books[293]. Here he was

trying to break away from the official stand-point of
the Church, according to which a virtuous man had no
need of reading the Bible any longer. Cele and Zerbolt
proved themselves in this respect at least closer to
Groote's principles than Radewijns, who stressed the
importance of intuition or inspiration more than the
scholarly Groote had done. Zerbolt, we remember, had
followed Groote's view in realizing the needs of the
masses. The farmers and the burghers should read the
Bible for themselves, he had argued, and since most of
them could not read Latin, they ought to be given an
opportunity of reading the Bible in their own tongue.
Cele, in following these same views, invited all the inhabitants of Zwolle to attend his discourses, thus giving
them a chance to gain a better understanding of the
passages he advised them to study[294].

But there were a great many other books to be studied
besides the Bible and the Fathers, in Cele's opinion.
Not a single subject was scrapped by him from the
curriculum then in vogue. It was wise to examine everything, he thought, but one should learn to select the best,
the useful, the practical. There was no harm in the
study of geometry, astronomy, logic, and medicine, as
long as one used those subjects as a means of reaching
a certain end. If one was to become a priest some day,
he would not need to know so very much about geometry,
for example, nor would the future merchant or farmer
have much occasion to study medicine, or astronomy.
The Bible should be studied by everybody, for all men
were created in God's image; they all should strive to
regain a part of their lost heritage. Virtue and love
were essentials, character a necessity, if one wished to
build up a society where peace and order would reign.
One should also develop one's intellect, however. The

priest ought to know a great deal about literature and philosophy. The teacher, so long as he avoided as much as possible the merely theoretical, or formal side of things, would be justified in retaining all subjects taught in the schools thus far[295]. Cele, therefore, retained the exercises in scholasticism, grammar, logic, ethics, and philosophy[296]. "But although he took great pains in teaching these subjects with effect", says Busch, "nevertheless he did not thereby diminish his interest, — nay, he even increased his zeal in instructing his pupils in the sacred writings, good manners, a saintly and Christian life, and the fear and love of God. For in the morning he would explain an Epistle, and in the evening some other part of the Scriptures, addressing the whole school"[297].

Cele was a practical teacher. He saw that no two boys were exactly alike, nor were they equally well supplied with funds. With the Brethren of the Common Life at Zwolle he made arrangements to house them in a suitable manner[298]. Those who could afford it were expected to pay the brothers for their room and board, while Cele asked a certain sum as tuition fee. The poorer class of boys, of whom there were a great number, instead of being compelled to beg for alms, were kindly taken care of by the brethren, and Cele even gave them money for the books, ink, and paper they needed in school[299]. In order to take care of each pupil's individual needs, he divided his school into eight classes. This arrangement may seem quite simple and natural to us to-day. We should remember, however, that this phase of Cele's reform was an innovation, a pedagogical discovery, we might say[300]. And this discovery, or invention, led to other discoveries. The "quadrivium" was included in the curriculum, and last but not least, in

the two highest classes special studies were taught by
specialists[301]. As the inevitable result of Cele's reforms,
his pupils generally made more rapid progress at the
universities than most other students[302].

Another factor which may partly explain Cele's fame
was his way of keeping order in the school-room. The
teachers of that time resorted to various forms of
punishment, which in spite of, or rather as a result of,
their harshness failed to bring about better discipline.
Cele rightly reasoned that a teacher's personality was
the great factor in the matter of order and discipline.
He took a personal interest in every one of his pupils;
as far as he was able, naturally. As to punishment, every
form was too severe, if one had not first exhausted all
the ways of correction taught him by sympathy and
love[303].

If he was right in asserting that the Church would
have perished centuries ago without the use of books,
then the clergy in particular, but all laymen also, should
read much. Groote had held the same, and so had
Zerbolt. And since there never could be too many good
books in the world, Cele taught his students the elements
of rhetoric. One feature of his method was the
"rapiarium", or collection of excerpts, which every pupil
of his had to make. From the Gospels and other books
of the New Testament he selected the plainest and most
helpful sayings. These he dictated in a loud voice to
the whole school. "For he wanted his pupils to have
the leading events and the most striking passages found
in the Epistles and the Gospels collected in one copy-
book, a theological excerpt-book, in which the most
useful thoughts found in the sacred writings were
gathered in brief extracts. This would enable them more
easily to commit such passages to memory"[304].

The influence exerted by him on the Europe of the fifteenth century is incalculable. Students, attracted by his fame, flocked to Zwolle from the bishoprics or principalities of Cologne, Trier, Louvain, Utrecht, Brabant, Flanders, Westphalia, Holland, Saxony, Cleves, Gelderland, and Frisia. Among the thousands of boys who between the years 1374 and 1417 were educated at Zwolle, a considerable number entered monasteries, where they helped to introduce better discipline, and more love for sound learning. "Paris, Cologne, Erfurt, and the Roman Curia testify how many learned men Cele's school sent out", is Busch's complacent remark. The whole population of Zwolle was changed for the better as a result of Cele's educational work. Among the prominent magistrates were found several of his pupils, from which we may infer that many a burgher of Zwolle, if not converted by Groote himself, became through Cele's influence a defender of the principles advocated by the "Devotio Moderna", or Christian Renaissance. "It is now more than forty years ago", Busch wrote in 1459, "that he migrated hence, and still his name is upon the lips of those who were fortunate enough to be instructed by him"[305].

Although he was very generous in helping his poorer pupils, Cele made a great deal of money with his school. With this money he constructed a fine library in the church of St. Michael at Zwolle. There he placed a large collection of codices on theology, philosophy, and literature, to which all devout citizens were freely admitted. Furthermore, many of Cele's followers imitated his noble example by collecting books and lending them to others[306]. By this also the city of Zwolle became a centre of popular learning. The clergy in particular were woefully lacking in sound learning. And if the

Church was to be regenerated, if a lasting religious revival, so sadly needed, was to take place, the clergy would have to be instructed first of all, the laymen should be taught to exert themselves, and school teachers must break with the empty formalism and the dying scholasticism which were injuring both the Church and society. This had been Groote's message to the men and women of his day. Radewijns, Zerbolt, Vos of Heusden, Brinckerinck, and Cele each took over a part of Groote's work, repeating his message in their own way. Thus began that mighty religious and intellectual revival, the "New Devotion", or Christian Renaissance. Soon it succeeded in permeating the lives of the men and women living in the Yssel valley, then it spread in ever-widening circles across the continent. This was made possible by the strong organization built by the Brethren of the Common Life, which will be treated in the following chapter.

CHAPTER III
THE BRETHREN OF THE COMMON LIFE
I

From the year in which the "House of Florentius"[1] was built till the death of Radewijns in 1400 the brothers at Deventer led a very quiet and uneventful life. Radewijns was succeeded as rector by Amilius van Buren, an intimate friend of Thomas à Kempis, as will appear in a later chapter[2]. It was his constant aim to preserve mutual love and harmony among the men. Often he would say to them: "There is one thing which we must all adhere to and observe: our status as Brethren of the Common Life; for although the monastic state is preferable in the opinion of the Church, nevertheless he who lives a saintly life outside of a monastery will receive the reward of saintliness"[3].

Amilius carefully guarded the rules of the house, and during his rectorate large numbers of school boys flocked to Deventer, many of whom acquired the habit of visiting the brethren-house, where they were regularly instructed in the essentials of the Christian faith[4].

It naturally followed that the brethren received most of their recruits from these boys[5]. In 1400 the community counted so many members that forty of them were sent to found other houses[6]. One young man went to Münster, where in the same year he induced a small number of followers to lead with him the common life[7]; a few others moved to Delft, also to found a house[8]. The rectorate of Amilius was therefore compared with the reign of Solomon, while Radewijns' rule was thought to correspond to that of David[9].

But Amilius van Buren did not reign so long as Solomon. During the first week in June, 1404, he felt the end of his life approaching. Calling all the members of the community together, he addressed them in a lengthy speech. "John of Haarlem shall be my successor", he concluded; "obey him, and let no one say to himself that John is still so young, or that you have read much more and know a great deal more than he does. It is our duty to love our fellow-men, and obey them all in order that we may properly humiliate ourselves". On June 10 Van Buren, the second rector of the Brethren of the Common Life at Deventer, passed away[10].

John of Haarlem ruled the brethren for six years. In 1410 he was succeeded by Godfried Toorn, who was rector for forty years. Although he had to sustain a great deal of hatred and opposition from the enemies of the new brotherhood, his temper always remained serene. The sources also say that he knew how to search the inner recesses of the heart and to delve into the rich mines of theology and jurisprudence. Always looking beneath the surface of form and outward appearances, he was not satisfied with mere style. The brethren were encouraged by him to read as many books as possible, and to select those first which contained the most practical religious and moral teachings. "Father John Vos of Heusden", he used to remark, "was wont to restrain his men from reading Thomas Aquinas and other modern scholastics of his type on obedience and kindred subjects, hoping that they might thus retain their simplicity"[11]. There were two virtues he never ceased to extol: friendship and chastity. "Brethren", he once exclaimed, "we have left all our relatives and acquaintan-

res, our native country and other ties behind; we have
come here to dwell together in this house that we might
serve the Lord through the common life. If we, therefore, are querulous, impatient, or in any way unkind to
each other, we shall become the most miserable among
men. You will indeed kill me, if discord should arise
among you"[12].

The man who uttered these words was by no means
devoid of talent. He had been a teacher at Deventer[13],
and it was during his rectorate that the Brethren of the
Common Life drew up their first written constitution.
Before 1413 they had failed to secure official recognition from the papal see. True, the monks of Windesheim had defended them in 1395, the alumni of the
University of Cologne had approved their mode of life,
and Frederick van Blankenheim, bishop of Utrecht, had
proved to be their faithful supporter; but the brethren
wanted still more. In 1413 Cardinal Pierre d'Ailly came
to the Yssel valley as papal legate for the Germanic
peoples. He gave the brethren and sisters at Deventer
several privileges, amongst them a document in which
he officially confirmed the approbations signed by the
Cologne jurists in 1398. Whether the cardinal personally
requested or suggested that the brethren draw up a written constitution, we do not know. At any rate, it appears
from the preamble to their first written constitution that
the cardinal's official support had encouraged them to
write down these rules which had been in vogue among
them, lest their successors should forget their own constitution[14].

In September, 1450, Godfried Toorn's health began to
fail. His successor was elected by the brethren before
he died. Six weeks later his death occurred, namely,
on the 3rd of November[15]. The new rector was called

Egbert ter Beek (1450-1483). During the first year of his rectorate Cusa, the famous cardinal, mathematician, and reformer, came to Deventer. He must have enjoyed himself there, as in this very same city, supported by these very same brethren, he is said to have received part of his early education[16]. Quite naturally he offered them a great many privileges in the form of prebends, and similar things. But the rector flatly refused to accept them, being unwilling to depart from the ways of simplicity and humility taught by the first members of his brotherhood[17].

Egbert ter Beek distinguished himself for his zeal in upholding the status of the Brethren of the Common Life. Many a day he spent in visiting the daughter-institutions in Flanders, Brabant, Holland, and West-phalia; anxiously watching, lest the encroaching armies of monasticism overwhelm the brotherhood. One day he heard that the rector of the local institution at Does-burg on the Yssel had invited the prior of Windesheim to change his house into a monastery of the Augustinian Canons Regular. He immediately hurried to the scene of operations. Yes, the prior was already there, having begun to invest the brethren. "What on earth are you doing here"? he exclaimed, addressing the brethren. "And what business brings you here"? was his remark to the prior of Windesheim. "Well", answered the prior in question, "have I done any wrong in advancing the brethren to the monastic state, which, as you must admit, is superior to yours"? "I make no objection", was Egbert's reply, "if you merely seek to induce laymen or secular clergy to enter monasteries, but you ought not to usurp our houses. This house has always been ours, and it shall remain ours. It was given to our brethren, in order that they might live the common life, and if any of them should wish to become monks, they would be free to leave the house". Whereupon the bewildered prior, according to our chronicle, quickly left the place[18].

It was during Ter Beek's rectorate that John Brugman, perhaps the most popular preacher the Low Countries ever produced, was changed from a Saul into a Paul. Even to-day the people throughout the Netherlands, who as a rule have not the slightest idea who Brugman was, or where he lived, still make him a proverb, often remarking after having listened to an unusually eloquent preacher: "He preaches like a Brugman"[19]. Like many a monk of his day, he had for a time been very bitter against the Brethren of the Common Life, who, as conscience but too plainly told him, were living more saintly and Christ-like lives without the protection of the monastic vows than most so-called religious people. After his "reformation" he suddenly changed his attitude, and thenceforth praised the brethren very highly in his sermons, letters, and treatises[20].

On the sixteenth day of April, 1483, Egbert ter Beek followed the other four rectors to the grave[21]. A few days later his body was solemnly carried to the churchyard by the mourning brethren. Future leaders of the German Renaissance were among those who attended the funeral, for in that year Alexander Hegius was called to Deventer as rector of the school of St. Lebwin's and Erasmus was one of the boys who had been given religious instruction by the brethren for several years past. From Zwolle the great revival of learning inaugurated by Groote and Cele had come traveling southward again, selecting Deventer as its centre till the death of Hegius. After 1483, the rectors of the brethren-house fade away into comparative oblivion[22].

As for the different buildings used by the brothers at

Deventer, a few remarks will suffice. Radewijns' vicarage was later referred to as the "Antiqua Domus", or the "Ancient House", in distinction from the "Nova Domus", or the "New House", which was founded about the year 1398 for the school boys of the cathedral school[23]. The house built in 1391 for the use of the members themselves, was called "Domus Domini Florentii", or "Heer Florenshuis", or "House of Master Florentius". Several plots of ground were added to their property from time to time, and additional buildings were erected for various purposes[24]. The chief building occupied by the brethren at Deventer during the days of Erasmus was erected in 1441[25]. And finally, those boys who could find no room in the "Nova Domus", or "Domus pauperum" ("New House", or "House for Poor Boys") were sent to two other houses: the "Hieronymushuis" ("House of Jerome") and the "Jufferenhuis", or "Juffer Wibbenhuis" ("House of Lady Wibben")[26].

II

In 1410 the brothers at Zwolle elected Theodore Herxen as their second rector — the man who for a period of thirty-three years was to become the acknowledged leader of the "New Devotion". Born in 1381, he had received his early education at Deventer. He was one of those devout school boys who were so kindly treated by the brethren of the House of Florentius. As a faithful follower of Gerard Groote, he wanted to train his inner self somewhere in a Carthusian monastery. One day he came to John Vos, prior at Windesheim, and asked him for advice. The prior saw at once how easily this pious youth could be persuaded to enter his monastery. Furthermore, he was rich in earthly possess-

iono, which Windesheim would be able to use to
advantage. True, the young man had thus far hesitated
to become a monk, inasmuch as his desire to win other
souls for Christ had been urging him to remain in the
world among people. The monastic state, however, was
at that time considered by most religious folk as vastly
superior to that of a preacher who had not taken the
three vows. Now it happened that in those days the
doctrine of self-denial still remained indelibly engraved
in the hearts of Groote's disciples. Accordingly, the prior
of Windesheim told the young man: "Do not enter this
or any other monastery, but go to Gerard Scadde of
Calcar, rector of the brethren at Zwolle, and ask him for
admission into their house"[27].

On the 23rd of December, 1409, Gerard Scadde of
Calcar died. Although Theodore Herxen was only
twenty-nine, the brethren, struck by his great religious
fervor, and aware of the superiority of his talents as
educator, preacher, and scholar, elected him rector in
Gerard's place[28]. Herxen was at once a zealous preacher,
a skillful teacher, and a versatile writer. How one could
most successfully win children and youths for Christ's
kingdom he set forth in three of his works, called: "A
Book showing how to draw the Little Ones to Christ",
"A Treatise concerning the Drawing of Youths to
Christ", and "A Book concerning the Praiseworthy Efforts of the Brethren in drawing the Little Ones to
Christ"[29]. The Brethren of the Common Life were
conscientiously imitating Groote in trying to secure
recruits from the boys and girls (though chiefly boys)
for God's army on earth. Theodore himself undoubtedly spent many an hour giving these boys religious
instruction. Later he wrote down the results of his
experiences, in the three above-named treatises.

As preacher and author he won great fame, for he preached to the people in their own language. Two big books were composed by him for laymen, which the brethren used to read from to the people on holidays. Among the many other works he wrote was a book called "Devout Exercises", which was read a great deal in his time. From far and near people came to him for advice and instruction[30], and the brethren themselves stood in such awe of him that a mere look of his would send them qualing with fear to their respective rooms. All devout men and women of Zwolle and its environment revered this pious leader of the "New Devotion". It was whispered among them that he held daily converse with angels[31].

His influence must have been great upon some few at least among the many boys who came to him, as their custom was, to confess their sins. The sources tell of a very wayward son of a magistrate at Woudrichem, how his father had sent him to a monastery, whence he had returned home in a short time. Shortly after that he had been sent to Zwolle to attend school. Here he comported himself in a most disgraceful manner. The gravest misdemeanors were but trifles to him. One day he came to Herxen to tell what he had done and ask for absolution. "My dear boy", the rector replied, "no human being can absolve you from your sins, not on account of their great number, but of your state of mind. Not until you have utterly annihilated that evil force within you which prevents you from doing penance, not until you have firmly resolved to commit no one of these offenses any longer, can I absolve you from the guilt which now weighs down upon your soul. Go, and I will pray for you; try to sin no more, and I will struggle with you; and then return unto me once more. Then we shall rejoice together and praise the Lord for his grace, for I must wait till God himself forgives you, ere I can absolve you from sin". The young reprobate went away, vaguely wondering why he, the well-favored son of a prominent magistrate, should be treated thus. But the rector of the brethren did not forget him, for he had been reminded by this youthful sinner of certain parables mentioned in the Gospels, which speak of the great joy in heaven caused by the sincere repentance of truly humble sinners. Finally, through love and sympathy, Herxen gained his end. The boy returned and was absolved[32].

A man like this was bound to make enemies. Groote had preached the same views about repentance; he too had drawn a careful distinction between the true Church, consisting of a small group of devout believers, and the outer court, where many clergymen were dwelling. Groote, the first leader of the "New Devotion", had ruthlessly torn down the idols of indolence, self-indulgence, and mammon worship. His example was now being followed by Theodore Herxen, the fourth and last universally recognized leader of the same movement. And since Groote had been persecuted, Herxen could hardly escape the same fate.

There was a certain Liefard, rector of the Sisters of the Common Life in one of their six houses at Zwolle, who had failed to perform his duties as rector and confessor. As Liefard had many rich friends at Zwolle, Herxen was unable to remove him from his office. In the meantime the news of Liefard's scandalous behavior reached the bishop of Utrecht, and the man was imprisoned. Shortly before the imprisonment Liefard's friend, Theodore Henso, pastor at Zwolle, together with the cathedral chapter of St. Lebwin at Deventer had begun to compel the Sisters of the Common Life at

Zwolle to confess to the chaplains of his parish. This
had grieved Herxen very much, for evidently the chaplains in question did not take life so seriously as one
might expect of servants of Christ. Herxen went to
Cologne, but the archiepiscopal curia of that city was
bribed by his enemies at Deventer and Zwolle, wherefore
he was now threatened with excommunication. One day
the kind, old rector was hissed out of the church by a
shouting mob, who, instigated by their spiritual father,
cried: "Throw the Beghard into the water". The pastor
even prohibited Herxen from hearing confessions of the
school boys, although one of his predecessors had given
Herxen this privilege, while it had been confirmed by
Frederick van Blankenheim, bishop of Utrecht[33].

Herxen was followed by Albert Paep of Calcar
(1457–1482). Thinking to divert for a time at least
the dangers of attack from the various office-holders in
the church of St. Michael, he invited the city council
and the vicars of the local parish to supper one day.
The magistrates were very sociable, but the vicars
adopted a haughty attitude toward the humble brethren.
"We discovered", says the chronicler, "that we had made
no progress, for the vicars did not want to be corrected
by us"[34]. Although he does not tell us what the brethren
wished to discuss with the vicars, we can easily guess
their intention. It had long been the custom among the
Brethren of the Common Life to confess their own
faults to each other, as Zerbolt had pointed out in his
"On the Common Life". Christ had warned his disciples
never to speak evil of any one, except to the person who
committed the evil in question. That there was a great
deal amiss with the Church during the closing years of
the fifteenth century must have been apparent to all
honest men and women. It had been one of Groote's

chief tasks to point out the existing evils, but it was to
the clergy themselves in his "Sermon against the Immoral
Clergy". When he addressed the clergy, he spoke of
their many faults, and the people's shortcomings were
exposed in the people's presence. Such had been Groote's
method in trying to reform the Church. His reformation
had been continued by the Brethren of the Common Life.
But exactly where he had met with the strongest resistance, they also were opposed. Hence Albert Paep, the
third rector at Zwolle, had to cancel those suppers with
the vicars of the local parish.

Albert Paep was in turn followed by other rectors,
whose names need not be mentioned here[35]; and, as was
the case with the house at Deventer, a few brief remarks
about the buildings belonging to the society will suffice.
Mention has been made of the chief building, the "House
of Gregory", where the brethren themselves lived[36].
Several other buildings were used to house the great
crowds of school boys from Frisia, Flanders, Brabant,
Westphalia, Trier, Cologne, Liège, and Holland. There
was the "Domus divitum scolarium" ("House for Rich
Boys") for boys with means[37]; the "Domus vicina"
("House next door"), or "Parva domus" ("Small
House"), also for those whose expenses were paid by
their parents or guardians[38]; the "Domus pro medio-
cribus" ("House for the Middle Classes"), where boys
were lodged who paid part of their expenses[39]; and the
"Domus pauperum scolarium" ("House for Poor Students")[40]. As for the property donated to the Brethren
of the Common Life at Zwolle, a long list of documents
has been published by Dr. Schoengen, which shows that
the brethren had other sources of income besides the
copying of books[41].

III

The brethren-houses of Deventer and Zwolle until the year 1520 were the two chief centres of the "New Devotion" outside of the monasteries. By these two all the other houses of the new brotherhood were founded, either directly or indirectly. As early as the year 1395 Radewijns, the first rector of the brethren at Deventer, was asked to found a congregation at Amersfoort. Three clerks were sent by him in the same year[42]. The next place in the Netherlands to ask for a few missionaries of the common life, was the city of Delft, where the magistrates, having heard of the rising fame and the good works of the brethren at Deventer, were anxious to secure a similar society of copyists and teachers. The procurator of the "Nova Domus" together with other members of the house at Deventer were sent to Delft. This seems to have occurred in the year 1403[43]. There also was a house at Hoorn for a few years[44], which must be looked upon as a daughter-institution of the house at Deventer.

The first house founded by the men of Zwolle was that of Albergen, in eastern Overyssel. Its foundation took place in the year 1406[45]. The next house was founded in 1407 at Hulsbergen near Hattem, a short distance west of the Yssel[46], and the one after that in 1424 at 's-Hertogenbosch[47]. In 1425 the brethren at Zwolle were compelled to leave their house on account of an interdict[48]. They moved to Doesburg, where a new community was established in 1426[49]. The house at Groningen was founded between 1426 and 1432[50], that of Harderwijk on the Zuiderzee in 1441[51], also by the brethren of Zwolle, the one at Gouda in 1445 by the brethren at Delft[52], at Utrecht in 1474, also by the house at Delft[53], and at Nijmegen in 1469 or 1470, by the brethren of 's-Hertogenbosch[54]. The Brethren of the Common Life also had a house at Berlikum in Friesland[55], but at present we know very little about its history. The same is true of those other houses which may have existed without leaving us any records of their history. For as long as the minutes of the annual meetings held by the Brethren of the Common Life of the above-named houses at Zwolle have not been discovered, we shall know very little about the less important houses.

In Germany, the brethren had many houses. There was a congregation at Münster from the year 1400, founded by Henry of Ahaus, a missionary of the Deventer house[56]. The same Henry of Ahaus instituted a society at Cologne in the year 1417 or earlier[57]. There was a congregation at Osterberg near Osnabrück as early as the year 1410[58], and one at Osnabrück from 1415[59], at Herford from 1428[60], at Wesel from 1436[61], and at Hildesheim since 1440[62]. The brethren at Cologne founded the houses at Wiesbaden, Butzbach near Mainz, Königstein on the Taunus, and Wolf on the Moselle[63]. There were important houses at Rostock[64], Magdeburg[65], Marburg[66], Cassel[67], and Emmerich[68], and less important ones in Wurtemberg[69]; also one at Kempen[70], and at Culm in Poland[71].

In the Southern Low Countries houses of the Brethren of the Common Life were founded at Ghent[72], Antwerp[73], Brussels[74], Grammont[75], Mechlin[76], Cambray[77], Liège[78], Louvain[79], and Wynoksberg[80].

The Sisters of the Common Life also succeeded in founding a large number of houses, particularly in the Yssel valley. At Deventer they had five houses[81-85]. At Zwolle there were six[86]. There were three houses at Zutphen, two at Doesburg, Kampen and Lochem, two at

Utrecht, one at Arnhem, Doetinchem, Gorinchem, and a host of other places[87]. The "House of Master Gerard" at Deventer, the first institution, founded a community at Sonsbeke, Xanten, Essen, and Cologne[88], and reformed the houses at Neuss[89], Calcar[90], and Emmerich[91]. The house of the brethren at Zwolle had charge of nineteen sister-houses[92].

Not all of the houses founded by the brethren or sisters of Deventer and Zwolle were equally prosperous, however. We have seen how the first institution of the brothers at Zwolle was a failure, inasmuch as the men had left the city for a community where only a few people were found to give them employment and still fewer school boys[93]. Nearly all the brethren at Amersfoort joined the Fransiscans in 1399[94]. Between 1399 and 1405 the house regained part of its former strength, but in 1405 the majority of its members entered the monastery of St. Andriescamp[95], and in 1415 became Augustinian Canons Regular of the Windesheim Congregation[96]. Two years afterwards, however, they left the monastery[97], and from that time the success of the house at Amersfoort was assured. At Delft the brothers were compelled by circumstances to exchange their rules for those of the third rule of St. Francis. In 1433 they joined the Augustinians Regular[98]. Before 1436 the house was again occupied by Brethren of the Common Life, who remained there as such until Delft became Calvinistic[99]. The house at Hoorn perished without leaving records of perceptible influence, which may also be said of the house at Berlikum. As for the institution founded at Albergen in 1406, it was changed into a monastery of the Windesheim Congregation in the year 1447[100]. Albergen evidently was too small a place to support a brethren-house. After the year 1447 it became the policy of the brothers at Deventer and Zwolle to recognize no houses founded in small towns. When the institution at Gouda for example asked for such official recognition, it was refused, as Gouda was said to be too small and too poor a place[101]. Not until 1456, that is, eleven years after the foundation of the house at Gouda, was it accepted as a member of the organization[102].

At Culm in Poland (Culm became a part of Poland in 1466), near the frontier of Prussia, the brethren were confronted with difficulties of an entirely different nature. They had been invited by a certain Balthasar, a native of East Prussia, who, attracted by the fame of the school at Zwolle, had left his home in search of western culture. It was no small matter to migrate to so distant a country; nevertheless the brethren readily had granted Balthasar's request. Three men were sent in 1472. The country around Culm was not so pleasant a sight as the green pastures along the Yssel, or the smiling fields near Zwolle. The town itself contained but a few inhabitants, and not a single carpenter among them. A little hut was given to the brethren, — very shabby, and unfurnished, but it was love which prompted the owners to give it to them. Others there were, how-ever, who vaguely wondered what those three foreigners wanted in lonely Culm. The brethren responded: "We have come here to instruct your children in the 'sciences' and virtues, as we are doing in the bishopric of Utrecht". Indescribable were the hardships which the brethren underwent. It was not long before the mendicant monks began to attack them, who themselves were not even keeping their own vows. Other monks there were not. The three brethren remained there for two years; then they could hold out no longer. Two of the three, to-gether with the rector of the school they had founded at Culm, returned to Zwolle, but not in despair. The harvest was great, they said, and the laborers few. They should send some experienced brethren together with a few students, and liberally provide them with funds. After some deliberation the request was granted. Several brethren were sent from time to time, and large sums of money. A flourishing school was founded, which in cooperation with the labors of the brethren finally resulted in the moral and intellectual uplift of a considerable part of East Prussia and Poland[103].

Great as were the difficulties which the Brethren of the Common Life had to face, the sisters were as a rule still more hardly pressed. We must never lose sight of the fact that they were living in an age when the superiority of the monastic state was almost universally recognized. As long as those disciples of Groote upon whom part of the master's spirit seemed to have descended, remained near them, they were able to hold their own. But about the year 1400 the majority of the communities were compelled to adopt the third rule of St. Francis, particularly those so far removed from the Yssel valley that they lost contact with the houses at Deventer and Zwolle[104]. Although the Brethren and Sisters of the Common Life were not hostile to monasticism, they were always and everywhere fighting the battle of self-preservation against the various monastic orders. A great many of the noblest monks in the Low Countries, Germany, and Northern France had proceeded from the ranks of the new brotherhood, and yet the whole institution was a living protest against the decadent monasticism of the fifteenth century. Groote's brotherhood was one of the chief causes of that phase of the Reformation which in certain regions involved the disappearance of monasticism, and everywhere in the West produced a growing desire for more personal faith, more religion in the schools, more knowledge of the Bible, a saner method of discipline, and a reaction against all manner of empty formalism, including the return to the use of the people's language, be it Dutch, German, French, or English.

IV

How did the Brethren of the Common Life usually pass their time, and what were the most characteristic features of their organization? Their constitutions, which were practically uniform in Germany, and nearly so in the Low Countries, together with a number of chronicles, treatises, and biographies, enable us to gain a fairly accurate knowledge of their daily work, habits, and ideals.

"Our house was founded", the brethren of Deventer and Zwolle wrote, "with the intention that priests and clerics might live there, supported by their own manual labor, namely, the copying of books, and the returns from certain estates; attend church with devotion, obey the prelates, wear simple clothing, preserve the canons and decrees of the saints, practise religious exercises, and lead not only irreproachable, but exemplary lives, in order that they may serve God and perchance induce others to seek salvation. Since the final end of religion consists in purity of heart, without which we shall seek perfection in vain, let it be our daily aim to purge our poisoned hearts from sin, so that in the first place we may learn to know ourselves, pass judgment upon the vices and passions of our minds, and endeavor with all our strength to eradicate them; despise temporal gain, crush selfish desires, aid others in overcoming sin, and concentrate our energy on the acquisition of true virtues, such as humility, love, chastity, patience, and obedience. Toward this end we must direct all our spiritual exercises: prayer, meditation, reading, manual labor, watching, fasting, — in short, the harmonious development of our internal and external powers"[105].

"Whereas the fear of the Lord is necessary to those who wish to overcome evil, it is expedient for each of us to meditate on such subjects as induce man to fear the Lord, like sin, death, judgment, and hell. But lest continued fear might engender dejection and despair, we shall have to add more hopeful subject matter for meditation, such as the kingdom of heaven, the blessings of God, the life of Jesus Christ, and his passion. These subjects we shall arrange in such a way that on Saturdays we shall meditate on sin, Sundays on the kingdom of heaven, Mondays on death, Tuesdays on the blessings of God, Wednesdays on the final judgment, Thursdays on the pains of hell, and Fridays on the passion of Christ"[106].

The constitutions further state that the brethren were to rise between three and four o'clock in the morning (later shortly before five), preparing themselves at once for prayer and the reading of certain prescribed selections[107]. All the members of the house were expected to attend the daily mass, and were exhorted to free their mind from all distractions, "thus preparing themselves, as it were, for a spiritual communion"[108].

Since it was considered most beneficial for all men to perform some manual labor every day, the brethren would be expected to spend several hours a day in copying religious books, or else in performing other tasks. But lest the spirit suffer from neglect, they should occasionally utter short prayers, called "ejaculations"[109].

The brethren were to consume their meals in silence, in order that they might pay proper attention to the reading of a selection from the Bible[110]. After supper they could do as they pleased in their own rooms till eight o'clock. At eight all guests would have to leave the house. The doors were shut fast, and silence was observed till half past eight, when they went to bed[111].

On Sundays and holidays certain passages in the Scriptures were read and explained; and in this connection there was opportunity for general discussion, when each member of the house could freely express his opinions, as long as he did not indulge in impractical disputes and argumentations. The school boys and other people were invited to attend the discussions which were held in the vernacular[112]. The influence thus exerted upon the common people by the brethren is incalculable. For not only were there a great many among them whose fame as orators brought people long distances to hear them, but it was their combined, their continued efforts, which must have brought tangible results, considering the great number of holy days they observed. Not one of them was as famous as a Brugman, Wycliff, Hus, or Savonarola, but they formed a vast organization. Their voices were seldom heard on the streets, for they wished to avoid publicity. Nevertheless, their influence, though not always manifested visibly, reached the minds of thousands, while the books they circulated reached still larger numbers. They continued their labors in an orderly way. Like the persistent drops of water, which in the course of time even form impressions on the most solid rocks, so did the efforts of the Brethren of the Common Life affect the most perverse sinners. One could always rely on their addresses. The brethren were always ready to help the sick and comfort the afflicted. And the school boys could always get a room in their dormitories, no matter whether they were able to pay for them or not. By avoiding notoriety and scandal, by preaching reform to all men and women without stressing unduly the faults of the clergy, the brethren labored, — unnoticed by those historians who record only the interruptions against the course of nature, against peaceful reform and bloodless revolution, thereby ignoring the great movement which throughout the fifteenth and sixteenth centuries helped to change the medieval mind into the modern mind.

The most interesting feature about the brethren's labors as preachers was their informal addresses. On Sundays and holy days the people were accustomed to assemble in the room designated for this purpose. A chapter of the Bible was read in the people's language which contained some practical advice or instruction. Those passages in particular were selected which in very plain words taught the people how to "extinguish vice, acquire virtue, despise worldly things, and fear the Lord". Thereupon all members of the house, in so far as they were gifted by nature to act as spiritual guides of the masses, would be expected to exhort the people, either separately in their respective rooms, or in addressing the whole assembly in turns. But they were not to preach, the constitutions[113] state, — merely to exhort and instruct. Confession of sins, and mutual correction were looked upon by the brethren as very helpful means of combatting evil[114].

As time went on the Brethren of the Common Life found it necessary to appoint rectors, procurators, librarians, and several other office-holders. In the constitutions of the houses at Deventer and Zwolle the duties of the rector[115], procurator[116], librarian[117], tailor[118], and nurse[119]

were carefully outlined; several other offices were treated
together in one chapter[120], though later they were more
elaborately discussed in the constitutions used by the
German houses, belonging to the "Colloquium of
Münster"[121].

The houses of the Brethren of the Common Life in
the Low Countries used to send representatives to their
annual meeting, called "Colloquium Zwollense". Another
means of preserving discipline and unity were the annual
visitations by two rectors, preferably those of Zwolle
and Deventer[122]. The houses in Germany, of which the
one at Münster was the chief, also were visited in the
same manner[123]. There also were held monthly meetings
in each house, where divers matters relating to discipline,
religious exercises, or manual labor could be discussed[124].

Each house should, if possible, have four priests and
some other members of the clergy. If somebody applied
for admission, the brethren were required to examine
his physical condition, and his mental equipment; he
should be asked from which country he had come. He
would be asked, also, whether he could write, and loved
to read books. In case he was found to be in good health
and of sound mind and habits, he would be allowed to
remain in the house for two or three months, whereupon
he might be promoted to a further trial of ten or twelve
months. After this lapse of time he might become a
Brother of the Common Life, having first sworn before
a notary public and in the presence of some witnesses
that he renounced all claim to any property of his own[125].
Members could be expelled in case of ill-behavior[126]. The
brethren were exhorted to preserve mutual love, peace,
and harmony[127], and although none of them would be
expected to take the vows of chastity and obedience,
nevertheless they all should strive to cultivate these

virtues[128]. The virtue of humility in particular was highly extolled by the brethren at Deventer and Zwolle[129]. No member of the brotherhood was to have any property of his own, as it had been ceded by him to the house on being admitted as a member there. They were to spend a part of their income to meet current expenses, and the remainder for the relief of the poor[130]. As for the other regulations found in the various constitutions, they need not be commented upon here[131].

The Brethren and Sisters of the Common Life may well be called practical mystics, in distinction from such men as John Ruysbroeck. Love for their neighbor impelled them to work among the people in the cities. Their highest aim was the reformation of the Church, which could most effectively be done, they thought, by educating the youths of the land, and by instructing the common people in the essentials of the Christian religion. They paid much attention to their "spiritual natures", or their "inner selves". Formed in the image of God, as they believed, and assured by Christ that the kingdom of heaven is found within the human heart, they continually strove to explore their inner lives, to unite their inner selves with God or Christ, and thus regain their lost heritage[132]. They were also much given to meditation[133].

As Christian mystics they constantly aimed to imitate the lives of Christ, and the apostles. They loved to seek parallels between Christ's life and their own[134], for their religion was one of action, of deeds. Groote had instructed them to read the Gospels and the lives of the Church Fathers in preference to other books, as the former contained biographies[135]. Paul's Epistles and the various books of the Old Testament were by no means neglected by them, however[136]. As they read the Acts of the Apostles, the thought must often have struck

them that it was not at all necessary for a good Christian
to seek refuge in a monastery. At any rate, their desire
to win ever more souls for Christ kept them in the cities.
"We have decided", the Brethren of the Common Life
at Zwolle wrote in 1415, "to live in cities, in order that
we may be able to give advice and instruction to clerics
and other persons who wish to serve the Lord"[137]. One
of the most successful ways by which the brothers at
Deventer won the hearts of young men, was the church
drama[138]. Theodore Herxen, as we saw above[139], devoted
several treatises to the "art of drawing boys to God".
Both the Brethren and the Sisters of the Common Life
were particularly fond of finding practical lessons in
the selections read from the Scriptures at their meals.
These lessons they tried to remember for the purpose
of applying them on specific occasions, and for the sake
of mutual exhortation[140]. Another feature of their practical mysticism was the collection of excerpts from writings perused by them.   These were called "good points"
or "rapiaria"[141]. Special notebooks or slips of paper
were at all times kept in readiness in order to improve
their knowledge[142].

The Brethren and Sisters of the Common Life, in
conscientiously following Christ, gloried in self-denial,
poverty, humility, and obedience[143], but if we bear in
mind the circumstances under which they had founded
and sought to develop their institution, we may say that
their outlook upon life was quite free from excessive
asceticism. True, they lived very soberly: their meals
were extremely simple[144], their clothing at first scarcely
respectable[145]. But whatever may have been their worst
form of mortifying the flesh, their asceticism was of a
mild nature[146]. And as time went on, experience taught
them that stinting the body does in no way enhance the

beauty of the soul, or the dignity of the spirit. Consequently, we find that after the year 1400 they dressed
more properly[147], used more wholesome meals[148], reduced
the number of hours devoted to copying books[149], took
more exercises in the open air[150], lived less estranged
from "worldly" people[151], and also acquired more respect
for learning as a final end[152].

V

It has often been asserted by scholars of late that the
Brethren of the Common Life paid little or no attention
to education[153]. On the other hand one also frequently
reads statements to the effect that they even made their
living by teaching[154]. Once again the sources should be
consulted, rather than the conflicting opinions of modern
scholars. In the first place, then, let it be understood that
the brothers at Deventer never had a real school of their
own there, nor did any of their members teach in the
cathedral school of that city until several years after the
death of Radewijns[155]. There were two schools at
Deventer during the days of Groote and Radewijns[156].
From 1378 till 1381 they were both supervised by
William Vroede, Groote's friend, who upon Groote's
advice brought about certain reforms in these two
schools[157]. As rector of the cathedral school he was
succeeded by John Lubberts (1381–1385)[158], and not by
Florentius Radewijns, as some writers believe.

At Zwolle John Cele was rector of the city school
from 1375 till 1417[159]. His educational labors, which
were imitated at Deventer, together with the assistance
freely accorded to the school boys by the Brethren of
the Common Life and the other disciples of Groote at
Deventer and Zwolle, were causes which made the schools

of Zwolle and Deventer famous long before the days of Hegius. It will be remembered that under the administration of Cele the attendance at the school at Zwolle rose to 1200. The hearty welcome extended by those pious matrons and the kind-hearted brethren must have acted as a very powerful magnet for the boys who had come from Poland, the interior of Germany, the upper Rhine valley, and the distant shores of Flanders, where on their return they extended the influence of the school. The brothers themselves received their interest in education from Groote and Cele. Groote had always laid stress on the importance of offering a better education to future pastors. Hence his friendship with the teachers at Deventer and Zwolle. The brethren, in inheriting most of Groote's ideals, soon shared his views on the need of a better education, particularly for those boys who intended some day to join the ranks of the clergy. Groote's chief aim had been the reform of the Church; the surest and quickest way to reach that happy end in his opinion was the training of young men. This training should by no means exclude the study of literature, pagan or classic as well as Christian; while grammar, rhetoric, logic, mathematics, and philosophy were to retain their places in the curriculum. Cele materialized Groote's plans at Zwolle, aided as he was by the brethren in that city. Not long after his death the reform inaugurated by him spread to Deventer and many other places where Groote's disciples had founded brethren-houses.

At Amersfoort the brethren never had a school of their own, and for more than a century after the foundation of their home, none of them seem to have taught in that city. We find, however, that in 1529 one of the brothers was forbidden to teach school by the city council, at least until the quarrel between him and the rector of

the city school was settled. During the years 1530 and
1531 the magistrates were trying to secure a new rector
for their school, and asked the brothers to pay his salary,
"as had been the custom before"[160]. The brethren, therefore, appear to have been interested in the local school.
At Cassel they taught school in their own house[161]. At
Culm the brethren, as was indicated above[162], founded
a splendid new school, which helped to introduce the
best fruits of Western education into East Prussia and
Poland. At Delft twelve poor boys were usually provided
by the brethren with food, clothing, and lodging. Whereas during the first period of their history in Delft they
sent these boys to the public school for instruction[163],
later on the latter were taught by the brethren themselves[164]. A boarding school was founded at Doesburg[165],
while at Gouda[166], Ghent[167], and Grammont[168] they had
schools of their own, as well as at Groningen[169], 's-Hertogenbosch[170], Liège[171], Magdeburg[172], Marburg[173], Nijmegen[174], Rostock[175], and Utrecht[176]. At Mechlin they
formed part of the local school-board[177]. Doubtless the
brethren in other cities conducted a like work[178].

The most important schools were found at Deventer,
Zwolle, and Münster, where also the most influential
brethren-houses had been established. A complete proof
of the excellence of these schools was given by John
Sturm, the celebrated rector at Strasbourg, when he
outlined the plans of his "gymnasium" to the magistrates
of the Alsatian metropolis[179]. He did not recommend
the schools of Cologne, of Louvain, and of Trier, and
preferred Deventer to Utrecht. Nor was Sturm the only
teacher who acknowledged the debt he owed to Cele's
followers, as will be seen later.

John Cele was succeeded as rector of the town school
at Zwolle by Livinius of Middelburg, one of Groote's

followers[180], and he in turn by Herman Keistken[181]. About the year 1432 John van Dalen was appointed rector[182]; he helped to usher in a second period of prosperity enjoyed by the public school at Zwolle, aided as he was by the Brethren of the Common Life[183]. Again several hundred boys came flocking to Zwolle from all directions[184]. Several buildings had to be erected by the brothers to lodge them, but even these did not suffice. Many kind mothers were induced to open their doors to one or more of them. Their own mothers and aunts had done so in the days of John Cele, when they themselves had often asked where all those strangers had come from; and many a pious father had once gone to that same school, where he had been taught so well that for many years the maxims of Zwolle's learned teacher were upon his lips, when friends of his youth would come to visit him[185]!

It is no wonder that among all those boys at least a few great minds were found. And where Groote's ideas were acted upon with so much tender devotion, where so much love was lavished upon responsive hearts, and such ideals were expounded as the "Imitation of Christ" contained, the school at Zwolle could not fail to send out once more a host of religious youths. The names of most of these boys have been lost to memory, and of the others only a few can be mentioned here. Naturally one turns first to him who became the most famous educator in Transalpine Europe, — to Alexander Hegius.

Hegius was born near the village of Heek in Westphalia in 1433[186]. He was teacher at Wesel in 1474, and from 1475–1483 taught school at Emmerich[187], no doubt supported in the usual way by Brethren of the Common Life, who had a house in each of these two places, while at Emmerich they had founded two dormitories for the pupils of the local school[188]. In 1483 Hegius was appointed rector of the school attached to St. Lebwin's at Deventer[189], where he remained until his death in 1498[190]. When teaching school at Emmerich he had become acquainted with Agricola, of whom he learned Greek[191]. Gansfort also was an intimate friend of his, as appears from one of his letters[192]. Anxious to promote the study of the classics, he encouraged his pupils to learn both Latin and Greek. He himself had been taught Greek too late to master that language so well as some of his contemporaries[193]. But he was always eager to learn more, and diligently read the classics and the Fathers[194].

Alexander Hegius, though he may be called one of the leading humanists of the late fifteenth century, as he showed a great interest in the study of the Ancients, was nevertheless too closely associated with the Brethren of the Common Life to despise the use of the vernacular, as so many scholars of his time were doing[195]. As poet, he became the forerunner of the "younger humanists", and, although he lacked real poetic enthusiasm, his labors in this direction are nevertheless of historical significance[196].

His school at Deventer grew to 2200 pupils. This was due in part to the assistance given him by the brethren At Zwolle he had been instructed in what might be called the rudiments of Christian education. The ideals of the Christian Renaissance were never opposed to art or learning, as many a manuscript will show us to-day, written and illuminated as they were by the Augustinian Canons Regular and the Brethren of the Common Life. Before Hegius began the study of Greek, he had managed to attract fifteen hundred pupils to his school at Emmerich. In 1475 he was not yet a humanist in the proper sense of the word. Still his fame had reached the cities of Trier, Cologne, Strasbourg, Liège, Magdeburg, and other centres of learning. His love of poetry, of the Greek language, and of ancient letters in general were not the causes of his early fame. The secret of his success lay deeper than that. It was the favorable circumstances attending the presence of the brothers at Wesel and Emmerich, Hegius' early instruction at Zwolle, and the peculiar bent of his nature which enabled him to become Cele's truest successor. Hegius was not a Petrarch nor a wandering humanist like Agricola or Hermann von dem Busche, to name some of the best types of the true humanists, but he was the greatest educator of Transalpine Europe in the fifteenth century, and the marvelous success he enjoyed as teacher from 1474 till 1498 he owed mainly to the work of two men: Gerard Groote, founder of the Brethren of the Common Life, and John Cele, who inaugurated upon Groote's advice, the reform which turned into the revival of learning in Northern Europe. This revival till 1455 developed wholly independently of the Italian Renaissance and later added the best thoughts of the classics, in so far as they were discovered by Italian humanists, to its great storehouse of medieval learning. Hegius, in continuing Cele's work, advocated a reform in the text-books. The "Medulla" was not worth being read any longer, he said[197]. On the last page of his "Invectiva" he gives a list of grammars which should be altered. Throughout this whole essay, in fact, he indicates the need of better text-books. As for style, he asserted in his "Farrago" that one should appropriate the diction of Cicero, Virgil, and Sallust, and imitate the Italian humanists. The "Disciplina Scholarium", the "Gemma Gemmarum", and the Lexica of Hugutio Brito and John Januensis, should be cast aside as no longer worthy of study[198]. Here he does not speak as a true medievalist, but appears to have absorbed some of the ideas of the Italian Renaissance.

A striking portrait of Hegius was drawn by Butzbach, one of his last pupils[199]. It shows him not only a scholar and teacher. As a true child of the "New Devotion", he directed much of his attention to the relief of the poor, the sick, and the afflicted, a practice in which he differed from humanists of the Italian type. When death claimed him[200], he was followed to the grave by a mourning crowd of grateful men, women, and children, who loved and revered him. All his possessions he had spent in "helping to extend God's kingdom on earth"[202]. Other humanists have received greater praise from Erasmus and others[203], but where some of his contemporaries were greater scholars, his influence upon the several thousand pupils sent out by him to reform the Church in the Low Countries, Germany, and France, was greater than that of a mere scholar. For instance, Agricola and Mutian Rufus did not leave thousands of students behind who eagerly and unitedly carried out their plans for reform in school, church, and monastery. They were not constructive, though great critics. Butzbach rightly pointed out the difference between the thorough reform instituted by Hegius and the ineffective work of the shifting, homeless humanists of the Erfurt type. "Nowadays", he says, "one only has to give presents in order to get a degree. Knowledge is no longer the first essential"[204].

It was easy enough for the wandering Bohemians of learning in the early sixteenth century to poke fun at existing conditions. All negative criticism is easy. When it came to actual reform, however, it was the school at Deventer which furnished the required missionaries. Thus it had been in the early years of the fifteenth cen-

tury, and so it remained throughout the whole life-time
of Hegius. The priors were always glad to get recruits
from Deventer[205]. While certain contemporaries of his,
like the celebrated Anton Vrye, or Liber, were soon forgotten after their death, Hegius continued to be a living
force in the hamlets and cities of the Yssel valley and
beyond[206].

During the rectorate of Hegius, then, Deventer was
one of the chief centres of the movement usually referred
to as the German Renaissance. The best thoughts of the
Italian Renaissance were absorbed at Deventer and
Zwolle, and from there they entered Germany, now transformed by the "New Devotion", or Christian Renaissance, which had now become an intellectual movement,
though its chief aim remained the restoration of the
Church in all its members[207]. An index of how strong
an intellectual movement this was, is the fact that many
classics were issued from the presses at Deventer before
1500: more than four hundred and fifty works[208].

One of the best known humanists of the Yssel valley
type was Ortwin Gratius, a man of great learning, and
sound judgment. Few of his contemporaries were such
warm advocates of the revival of ancient learning as he;
not many equalled his scholarly equipment; his poems
were unusually fine, his Latin quite praiseworthy. Few
men have ever been so shamefully and so unjustly attacked as he, not only by his contemporaries but also by later
writers. The investigations of three modern historians,
however, have vindicated his claim to the title of Christian humanist, scholar, poet, and educator[209].

Much might be written about other pupils of the
Brethren of the Common Life, some of whom taught
school while they were members of the celebrated brotherhood. Thus the schools at Deventer and Zwolle not only

served as a means of improving intellectual standards
among the clergy, but offered preparatory courses for
students intending to enter the universities, and also
sent out a great number of teachers to other cities. So
great was their number that in the Netherlands scarcely
a school could be found during the opening years of the
sixteenth century, where there was not felt at least some
connection with the Yssel valley "gymnasia"[210]. In Germany at that time, and throughout the preceding century,
if one were to study the origins of each of the early
secondary schools throughout the North and West, he
would undoubtedly be able to trace the influence of
Deventer and Zwolle. Mention can only be made here
of the two chief centres of the German Renaissance, that
is, the two schools which contributed most largely to the
dissemination of learning in Germany from 1450 till
1520, — the schools of Schlettstadt and Münster.

For several centuries Strasbourg had been the ecclesiastical and intellectual metropolis of Alsace. With Trier,
Cologne, Liège, Aachen, and Utrecht it had possessed
a sort of educational monopoly in the regions which once
had separated Germany from France. But conditions did
not always remain thus. Cologne and Trier began to
send their most promising sons to little Zwolle, which
was only an insignificant parish in the diocese of Utrecht,
but the town of Cele's school. It was not long before
Alsace developed a similar situation.

A Westphalian teacher, named Louis Dringenberg,
who had been trained at Deventer[211], came to Schlettstadt
in 1441. Here, for a period of 36 years, he was rector
of the public or town school[212]. There were no Brethren
of the Common Life in Schlettstadt, which may account
for the fact that he was unable to draw such vast
numbers of pupils to his school as Cele had done to

Zwolle, but this school at Schlettstadt eventually surpassed that at Strasbourg. The reason was given by
Charles Schmidt, the author of the "Histoire littéraire de
l'Alsace": "While thus Strasbourg and most other cities
lagged behind, Schlettstadt already possessed a flourishing school. Founded about the middle of the fifteenth
century and supervised by the magistrates, its rector was
the Westphalian Louis Dringenberg, who had carried
hither the spirit and method of the Brethren of the
Common Life"[213]. More to the point is the following
statement by G. C. Knod, another Alsatian scholar of
note: "This spirit of pedagogical skill and pious wisdom,
as it prevailed in the schools of the Brethren of the
Common Life, had also asserted itself in the town school
of Schlettstadt....... It was the first school conducted
by laymen in South-German regions which, in conscious
deviation from the clerical institutions, outlined its scope
and method after the humanistic fashion"[214].

In several cities the Brethren of the Common Life had
schools of their own, as at Rostock, Ghent, Liège, and
Utrecht, while in almost every city where they had a
house, one or more of the members of the brotherhood
became school teachers, particularly after the year 1450,
when, as time went on, the printed type made it unnecessary for them to continue their work as copyists.
If one takes these facts into consideration, one can form
a better opinion of the way in which Dringenberg brought
this new "pedagogical spirit of the Brethren of the
Common Life" from Deventer to Schlettstadt. He
doubtless adopted much of the course he had followed
at Deventer, where the teachers used Cele's method of
combining sound religious instruction with a well-selected
list of studies, took due care of the pupils' individual
needs, preferred kind warnings to harsh punishment,

sought to inculcate a love for individual research by
letting pupils delve among the classics rather than confine
themselves to text-books, and taught the boys the use of
their vernacular as well. This method Dringenberg introduced at Schlettstadt. His successors continued his
method in general[215-220].

At Münster the Brethren of the Common Life founded
a house as early as the year 1400[221]. They did not found
a school at that time, but aroused an interest in learning,
which was very great during the second half of the
fifteenth century[222-223]. This fact has been established
by the research of Dr. Bömer, the librarian of the
university at Münster[224]. Münster in the fifteenth century became the great gate-way through which the religious and educational reforms of Groote's followers
entered Germany, passing Almelo, Frenswegen, Schüttorf,
and Coesveld to Münster, and beyond, to Rostock,
Hildesheim, Magdeburg, and even to Cologne and the
Upper Rhine valley[225].

Now it happened, as we saw, that both at Zwolle and
at Deventer the schools were reformed and rendered
famous mostly by men who were connected with the
brotherhood. At Münster, when eventually the cathedral
school was reformed, it was by Rudolph von Langen,
who had attended school at Zwolle with Alexander
Hegius.

Impressed by the fame of Deventer's school, Von
Langen believed that the school of the ancient and
celebrated cathedral of his own city should at least equal
St. Lebwin's at Deventer in luster. To secure a good
rector, it has been said that he asked his old friend Hegius
to come, but the sources leave the question undecided[226].
Von Langen appointed Timan Kemener, a pupil of
Hegius[227], and in the year 1500 a thorough-going reform

of Münster's cathedral school began. His successor, John Murmellius, a native of Roermond, continued the work of educational reform. He had studied at Deventer and Cologne[228], and in 1500 we find him teaching school at Münster under the direction of Timan Kemener. In the cathedral school at Münster he taught till 1507, in the school of St. Martin, from 1507 till 1512, and from 1512 till 1513 again in the cathedral school[229].

Few men so faithfully followed the policy outlined by Gerard Groote, and first practised by John Cele at Zwolle, Hegius at Emmerich and Deventer, and Dringenberg at Schlettstadt, as Murmellius. He cared little for mere style and mere eloquence. Education would be a complete failure, he taught, if one concentrated all his energy on oratory and style[230]. He freely criticized the lives of bad priests and monks[231], as Groote also had done, and in his attack on the decadent forms of scholasticism so prevalent in his day, he simply repeated what Groote had said. He did not direct his assaults against philosophy, but against empty phrases, devoid of practical contents. To roam about the continent in search of fame and honor, as many mere humanists were doing, was a vocation not suited to his character. Not the love of self, he said, but the glory and honor of God should be the final aim of all instruction; all knowledge was useless without the acquisition of virtue[232]. Whereas many leaders of the Italian Renaissance studied the classics for style only, the men of Deventer, Zwolle, Schlettstadt, and Münster delved into the same mine and found there fine phrases, but greater treasures in wisdom. When they wrote, they proved themselves good stylists too. Murmellius, though he died at thirty-seven, published fifty works in fifteen years, some of which were wonderful store-houses of pedagogical, literary, philosophical, and

historical value[233]. Considering his distinguished career
as a teacher, it is astonishing how he contrived to produce so much. His text-books were popular in Germany
for several generations; one of them passed through
seventy-seven editions, and was used in the schools till
1800[234]. His "Pappa Puerorum" was published thirty-
two times in less than sixty years. In editing both classic
and Christian writers he became a mighty force in the
realm of revived learning[235]. In laying proper stress on
physical and moral improvement, on grammatical constructions, the proper study of art and literature, he
aimed at that harmonious development of character which
was possessed by the Greeks of old[236]. His commentary
on Boethius shows how well he was acquainted with the
classics. One remarkable feature about his works is the
simple, clear style, the absence of pompous expressions.
Better than most scholars of his time he knew how to
compress brilliant thoughts into brief sentences[237], — a
rare quality in a humanist of the early sixteenth century.
And though he indulged in the use of satire, as was usual
at that time, his language remained remarkably free from
revengeful or spiteful sarcasm[238], as was unusual.

Murmellius was assisted and followed at Münster by
other noteworthy teachers, such as John Pering, a former
pupil of Hegius; Joseph Horlenius, a pupil of Pering;
and Jacob Montanus, later a member of the Brethren of
the Common Life at Herford, and a friend of Luther[239].

The fact is, Münster and Deventer sent out so vast a
host of really great scholars and teachers that it is quite
impossible to enumerate them. Under their leadership
practically all the larger schools in Western Germany
were reorganized and reformed. Through them the
benevolent influence of Cele's work found its way into
many a city where no Brethren of the Common Life

were found, such as Attendorn, Dortmund, Düsseldorf, Eisleben, Essen, Lübeck, Lüneburg, and Minden[240]. And as the pupils of these teachers in their turn continued Cele's work, the literary productions and the educational reforms of Groote's followers were diffused throughout the land, entering shop and farm-house, chapel and monastery, kitchen and workshop, appealing to the hearts of high and low, of rich and poor, of old and young. Who can calculate or describe the influence which thus radiated from the Yssel valley schools in all directions? Such influence never dies, and readers must have been impressed by the fact that modern education perpetuates the best features of the reformed education of Groote, and Cele, and the Brethren of the Common Life.

CHAPTER IV
THE CONGREGATION OF WINDESHEIM
I

Simultaneously with the development of the Brother-hood of the Common Life came the rise of the Con-gregation of Windesheim, the centre from which pro-ceeded monastic reform, and from which many books were distributed. The Brethren-house at Deventer kept on sending recruits to the new monastery at Windesheim, until Radewijns, the rector of the brethren in Deventer, became somewhat alarmed. At last he sent a letter to John Vos, prior of Windesheim: "Beloved father John in Windesheim, I note that many are inclined to enter a monastery, and only a few come to our brethren-house. And though some at first prefer the brethren-house, where they are contented for some time, sooner or later, having become acquainted with your calm lives and saintly conversation, they are easily impelled to admire you, as happened with John Brinckerinck, who wanted very badly to be invested there"[1]. One feels in perusing the whole of this letter that Radewijns, in common with most men of his day, regarded the monastic state as something more saintly than any other. Brinckerinck had twice wanted to leave the brethren-house for a monastery[2]. John Vos himself had been one of the mem-bers of the brethren-house, before he had gone to Win-desheim. The monastery, it should be remembered, was erected in order to provide a place of shelter for the brethren in times of need. Here, amidst those dignified

rows of elms and willows and surrounded by smiling
pastures, one would be three miles from the nearest city,
and beside the silent waters. Here one could lead a life
of rest and contemplation, undisturbed by school children
and the bustle of busy streets. No wonder that so many
members of the brethren-house were eager to go to
Windesheim! And no wonder that Radewijns himself
would have liked to leave Deventer, if such a course of
action had seemed proper to him, for he writes on one
occasion: "If it is convenient to you, I shall be glad to
visit you, for the last days I have been ill.   I would
rather be ill there with you, as one of you, and die there,
than at Deventer"[3]. Only duty kept him "in the world".

For several years the brethren at Deventer and Windesheim acted as if they were all members of one house.
Thus, when in 1392 it was thought expedient to erect
another monastery, the men at Deventer again sent the
required funds. John Brinckerinck was still a member
of their house at that time. His skill as carpenter was
well known among the brethren, for in the previous year
he had helped to build the new brethren-house. Now he
was equally ready to exert himself[4]. John Busch preserved the following letter by Radewijns to prior John
Vos: "John Brinckerinck arrived yesterday from the
monastery of Marienborn [Mary's Fountain] near Arnhem. And Henry Wilde and Henry Wilsem would like
to know whether the house should have a roof of stone
or not. John Brinckerinck says that if lack of funds
compels us to cover it with straw, it will only last eight
years. We have 392 florins with which to finance the
construction, and no more than that. We can arrange
that John Ketel, our cook, give his thousand florins to
Marienborn and three hundred of his mother's money.
This money we could use to great advantage ourselves,

but charity weighs more with us, though our means are small"[5].

The history of the brethren-house at Deventer and the monastery of Windesheim, until the year 1424, may be compared to two streams from one source, which often unite, and usually flow side by side[6]. Shortly after the founding of Marienborn, came that of "New Light" near Hoorn by the same men, aided by two other disciples of Gerard Groote[7]. Deventer and Windesheim also had common interests at Eemsteyn near Dordrecht, founded in 1382, and protected till 1384 by Groote[8]. This monastery must have joined the other three about the year 1393[9]. Together they formed the Congregation of Windesheim in 1394 or 1395[10], favored with privileges from both the pope and the Bishop of Utrecht[11].

Once secure of its position, the new chapter rapidly extended its sway, adding new members at the average rate of one a year[12]. In 1395 or later a monastery near Amsterdam joined[13]. In 1398 Mount St. Agnes, near Zwolle, became a member[14], followed by Frenswegen in Bentheim, east of Overijssel, in 1400[15]; Leyderdorp, near Leiden, in 1403[16]; Briel in 1406[17]; Haarlem[18], Thabor, in Friesland[19], and Zalt-Bommel, in Gelderland[20], in 1407. Then came the incorporation of the celebrated chapter of Groenendaal, in 1413, comprising seven monasteries, of which the monastery of Groenendaal, near Brussels, was the chief[21]. The spiritual force of Windesheim was sweeping across the Low Countries, absorbing and overpowering even the most ancient houses. Soon the Augustinian monasteries in many parts of Germany began to swell the tide. First a few single monasteries joined, then a whole chapter, namely that of Neuss, consisting of thirteen monasteries, of which however the one at Bethlehem near Doetinchem hesitated

till 1441[22]. About the same time several other monasteries joined the Windesheim circle, such as Wittenburg,
near Hildesheim[23]; Ludingakerke, in Friesland[24]; Sion,
in Beverwijk[25]; Richenberg, near Goslar[26]; Sacravallis,
near Dalfsen, in Overijssel (which joined in 1430)[27].
Also, another monastery belonging to the chapter of
Neuss, namely the one at Reimerswaal, in Zeeland, joined
in 1430[28].

A large number of other communities followed in due
time. The story of their reform or their foundation is
partly found in the "Chronicle of Windesheim" and
partly in Acquoy's work on Windesheim, while several
articles which have appeared since 1880 in various historical magazines in Holland and Germany give further
particulars. Suffice it to say here that in the year 1464
the entire congregation counted more than 84 members
and about the year 1500 it had more than 100[29]. One
wonders how it was possible for these two apparently
obscure and certainly not wealthy convents of Windesheim and Diepenveen to cause so great a veneration in
the minds of contemporaries. Why did Eemsteyn, where
the founders of Windesheim had been instructed, apply
for admission, and why did the monks of Groenendaal
so gladly submit to the rules of the Windesheim Congregation? Why did the instructed absorb the instructors?

Now the most striking fact about the history of the
"New Devotion" is the way in which from humble, poor
beginnings mighty forces developed. Not brain-power
or money only caused the movement from Deventer and
Windesheim to become a world-force in religion and
education. Nor did the privileges given to Groote's
followers by bishops and popes have so very much to
do with their rapid growth. There were other orders
and congregations highly favored by the Church, many

of which were swiftly approaching collapse or utter ruin. No, the protection of the Church, though helpful to some extent, was not responsible for the power of Windesheim. When its missionaries journeyed from city to city they carried no papal bulls with them, and they seldom spoke of their privileges. Their mission was to waken a new religious ardor and personal faith, a faith accompanied with "good works".

One of the most interesting examples of this monastic reform is that introduced at Frenswegen in Bentheim, near the Dutch frontier. This monastery had been founded by Henry Crul and Everard of Eza, assisted by the count of Bentheim[30]. Everard of Eza was a learned scholar. When the fame of Groote's preaching had attracted his attention, he had almost immediately left for Deventer to hear the new preacher. With the intention of catching Groote in some lapse, he posted himself out of sight and listened, expecting to come forward and confute him. But instead of silencing Groote, who had not without reason been considered one of the brightest stars at Paris, he was completely won by the master's spirit and powerful arguments. Not long thereafter Groote passed away, and now Everard wanted to join the brethren at Deventer; but at that time these brethren were attacked by many enemies, and Everard was considered one of them. When he opened the door of the vicarage the brethren ran away into their rooms for fear. Only after some lengthy deliberations he was finally accepted as a member. It was he who warned Radewijns and his followers against the folly of neglecting their bodily needs, and persuaded them to take physical exercises in the open air. Thus he was useful to them in his own way. But soon he left Deventer for Almelo, where he invited some priests and clerics to live the common life with him. Finally he decided to found a monastery for them, which led to the erection of Frenswegen[31]. But what happened? The men who had so hopefully started upon their new life needed the guiding hand of a monk from the Yssel country. They were reduced to the direst poverty; and when a pestilence came, despair seized upon the remaining few. Windesheim heard of it, and ordered Eemsteyn to send one of their inmates[32]. In 1400 Frenswegen was incorporated into the Windesheim Congregation. Now for a time all went well, but soon want once more troubled the small community, and the men seemed unable to go on. Finally they lost their new rector and for the second time turned to Windesheim for aid. This time the brethren sent one of their own men, named Henry Loeder, who had spent eleven years with them. For twenty-one years (1415–1436) Loeder was prior at Frenswegen, raising this monastery to a position of prominence in Northwestern Germany, for he carried to Frenswegen the ideals of John Vos, the practical mysticism of Groote, and the enthusiasm he had himself absorbed in the Yssel country during his long stay. Poverty and manual labor did not seem a hardship any more to the monks at Frenswegen. They worked, read, and loved each other as brothers till the glory of their mutual loves shed its radiant beams across Westphalia, Saxony, Friesland, and the Rhine provinces. Sixteen missionaries were sent out to various monasteries, of whom twelve became priors of as many houses. From far and near people came to seek admission at Frenswegen, and more than one hundred men were invested during Loeder's priorate. He himself was wont to travel from community to community, reviving relaxed discipline and stimulating despondent or negligent hearts into new activity. He was rightly called the Apostle of the Westphalians, Saxons, and Frisians[33].

Another missionary sent from Windesheim was John Busch, author of the "Chronicon Windeshemense", in whose life it is evident how the Christian Renaissance spread from Windesheim. Born at Zwolle in 1399[34], he was for several years a pupil and later an assistant of John Cele, the famous teacher[35]. Busch was a brilliant student, wherefore his parents wanted him to go to Erfurt. "No", said he, "I wish to do some work for God — to reform monasteries". Gerard Calcar, rector of the brethren-house at Zwolle, accordingly sent him to Windesheim, where he was invested in 1419[36]. Here he labored hard to master his lower self. For a time the enemy seemed too strong for him, till one day (the 21st of January, 1421) he thought he heard Jesus say to him: "Now thou art mine, and I am thine". "From that day", says Busch, "my enemy could trouble me no more"[37]. In 1424 he was sent as missionary to the monastery of Bödingen[38]; in January, 1429, to Ludingakerke, in Friesland[39]; in August of the same year to Sion, at Beverwijk[40]. From 1431–1434 he lived at Bronopia, near Kampen[41], whence he went to Windesheim once more. In 1436, or 1437, he was sent to the monastery of Wittenburg, situated about ten miles west of Hildesheim[42]; in 1439 he went to Sülte, near Hildesheim, where in 1440 he became prior[43]. Here he labored with considerable success till, in 1447, he was called to the celebrated monastery of Neuwerk near Halle[44], where he resided till 1454[45].

This monastery of Neuwerk was one of the richest in all German lands. Its domains extended over an area of eleven square miles, with a population of twenty thousand inhabitants. When Busch first arrived upon the scene, he found the monks living dissolute lives, having lost all sense of propriety[46]. These monks certainly had not left the outside world in order to serve God more perfectly! They were the kind of persons who deserved the lash of derisive scorn applied by men like Erasmus. Busch was outspoken in condemnation. He was not satisfied with mere criticism, either. To the much needed negative criticism he added constructive suggestions and ideals. John Busch told those monks what Groote had said to the monks of his day. One feels while perusing the account left by Busch himself that he did not possess that warmth and freshness of newly-born religious ardor so characteristic of the founders of Windesheim; but he was sincere, and steadfast. He loathed wantonness, selfishness, pride, and indolence. The ideals of Groote's earliest disciples he carried with him wherever he went, and usually he succeeded in his task. That he had to meet with much opposition cannot be doubted, for men are not prone to exchange a life of ease and luxury for one of self-abnegation. Busch made enemies everywhere, just as Groote had done before him, and every other earnest reformer does. But he persevered, and won. Pope Nicholas V heard of his work, and sent Cardinal Cusa to Magdeburg in 1451, instructed to appoint Busch to supervise the reform of all the monasteries of the Augustinian Canons Regular in Saxony, Meissen, and Thuringia[47].

Cusa at once ordained that the monastery of Neuwerk should be the head of a number of other monasteries, which together were to be called the Chapter of Neuwerk. This chapter was then to join the Chapter of Windesheim, as had been the case with Groenendaal, near Brussels, and Neuss, on the Rhine[48]. Consequently Busch was sent to Windesheim to obtain the required permission. But when the men at Windesheim considered the enormous estates possessed by Neuwerk, and contrasted the luxurious living of its wealthy inmates with their own spare living, they felt that such monasteries as Neuwerk were not fit places for servants of Christ. Their own lives, though not marred by excessive asceticism, embodied the ideals of their predecessors. They told Busch all this. For wealth and fame they did not care, they said; no matter what the pope would think, or Cardinal Cusa. Only monasteries could join their congregation whose inmates were willing to cast aside the idols of material advancement. Thus Neuwerk had to remain outside the Windesheim circle, but so great was the moral and spiritual influence of Windesheim that this rich and powerful chapter of Neuwerk gave up its own ancient rules and accepted those of the Windesheim Congregation[49].

In 1454 Busch resigned his position at Neuwerk[50]; in 1455 we find him in the monastery of Wittenburg, near Hildesheim. From this centre he reformed four monasteries[51]. Then he went to Windesheim once more[52]; from Windesheim to Diepenveen (1456)[53]; and thence to Bronopia, near Kampen[54]. Not long thereafter Germany called him back. He accepted the call and went to the monastery of Sülte, near Hildesheim, where he spent twenty years (1459–1479), and reformed twenty monasteries[55].

Windesheim was transforming not only the Augustinian Canons Regular, however, for we read of the reform of Benedictine monasteries conducted by the missionaries of Windesheim[56], and of the reform of Cistercian[57] and Premonstratensian monasteries[58]. From Windesheim the movement spread to other congregations, such as that of Bursfeld, which was Benedictine, for John Dederoth, usually called John von Minden, abbot at Clus near Gandersheim, in the diocese of Hildesheim, had become acquainted with John Vos, the prior of Windesheim, at the Council of Constance. Inspired by the religious ardor of Vos, Von Minden sought with the help of prior Rembert of Wittenburg to reform his own monastery. He continued his work at Bursfeld, where he became abbot in 1433. Thus the new devotion of the Augustinian Canons Regular passed to the Benedictine order[59].

Much worthy reform was also accomplished by the monastery of Böddiken in Westphalia ("Kreis" of Büren), which like Frenswegen and Bursfeld also became a great centre of renewed religious life[60], but these examples must suffice here. Böddiken, as a member of the Windesheim Congregation, shone merely as the reflex of the greater light, and the labors of its monks resembled those of their friends at Frenswegen to so great an extent that they need not be recounted.

The work of the sisters of Diepenveen was more than a reflection of that of Windesheim. This convent was founded by the Sisters of the Common Life of Deventer. It was Deventer and not Windesheim which gave Diepenveen its best thoughts and its best leaders. From Diepenveen convents were founded and reorganized, as monasteries were from Windesheim. To its missionaries, therefore, our attention will now turn.

II

The convent of Diepenveen, founded as it had been by the Sisters of the Common Life, always kept in close touch with the sister-houses. Together with the "House of Master Gerard" at Deventer, it continually strove to improve conditions in the existing houses, and to found new ones. With the message of self-renunciation, preached by Groote's disciples, fresh upon their minds

and hearts, the leaders at Diepenveen always sent out
their most devout sisters as missionaries, for well they
knew that these might never return[61].

One of these missionaries was Fije van Reeden, who
had first spent some time in the "House of Master
Gerard", from where she had been transferred to Diepenveen by Brinckerinck. Before she had lived there long
enough to be invested, her convent was asked to found
a new house of the Sisters of the Common Life at
Xanten on the Rhine. Fije was chosen as the person
best fitted for this task. As matron of the new institution she performed her duties so well that she won the
respect of all the sisters and of their friends outside the
house, and she was so successful that Brinckerinck called
her the Apostle of Cleves. Xanten was located in the
duchy of Cleves.

But the activities of the Brethren and Sisters of the
Common Life were watched by many clerics with feelings of unmistakable hostility. Groote had been persecuted by them, Zerbolt had been impelled to write his
"Treatise on the Common Life", and Brinckerinck had
often found it necessary to defend the brethren and
sisters at Deventer[62]. At Xanten some clerics bitterly
attacked the Sisters of the Common Life as heretics.
Here no great leaders of the "New Devotion" were
found, and Fije van Reeden accordingly had to appear
before the inquisitors at Cologne. The poor woman was
frightened beyond measure. She tried to persuade a
pious cleric to accompany her to Cologne, but she
appealed in vain. No one was found who dared to meet
the inquisitors in her company. She therefore appeared
all alone before the papal inquisitors, many of whom,
filled with "holy anger" against the Brethren and Sisters
of the Common Life, for reasons not difficult to divine,

maligned and slandered her, saying that she deserved the stake. But in spite of all their efforts they failed to convict her of heresy. Then they tried another plan: they accused her of immorality, but the charges brought against her were not proved, and the end of the whole matter was that she went home vindicated. In 1429 she died at Xanten[63].

There were also some houses of the Sisters of the Common Life which had been founded by Diepenveen and which at a later date were changed into convents. As examples might be named the house at Tienen, in Brabant, and that of St. Truyen, near Tienen[64]. Then there were several convents founded or reformed by the sisters of Diepenveen — probably fourteen or fifteen in all[65]. The story of one of these reforms is interesting and instructive enough to be related here. It is that of the Benedictine convent of Hilwartshausen on the Weser, between Bursfeld and Minden.

Tradition told that in the days of Charlemagne a pious hermit, named Hilwert, lived in a large forest near the place where the Fulda and Werre join. Here the son of a king was killed one day by a wild beast, and shortly afterwards his sister erected a convent on the spot where he had been killed. It was named Hilwartshausen, or Hilwert's house, after Hilwert, the hermit. At first only kings' daughters lived here, later on daughters of dukes and counts were accepted; still later, those of rich nobles were taken in. As time went on discipline relaxed. The nuns had broken all the rules of obedience and restraint, went out hunting and gambling, and sometimes danced all night with monks from neighboring monasteries. At last the scandal reached the ears of their parents and nearest relatives, who with the aid of dukes, counts, and priors endeavored to enforce discipline. For forty years no advance was made. Finally the nuns were compelled to dress in the white garments of the Augustinian order. But what happened? The women ran about the house, frantically exclaiming: "We can not distinguish one from the other any more. They have dressed us as if we were to be buried".

A short time afterwards John Busch came to Hilwartshausen. He was accustomed to see his work crowned with almost immediate results. But although he remained here for eight days, he failed absolutely to improve conditions. What was now to be done? The countess on whose estates the monastery was situated appealed to the prior of Böddiken, which, as has been said, was a member of the Windesheim Congregation. He appointed a pious nun from Fritzlar as prioress, while two other sisters from the same convent were sent to assist her. It soon appeared that he had not made the right choice. The new sisters found it impossible to remain there long. When they left, the inmates of the convent joyfully ran to the windows, crying: "Thank God that we got rid of those devils"!

The prior of Böddiken now decided to try a safer scheme. He went to Windesheim to ask for two or three sisters from Diepenveen. His request was granted only when he promised that the persons entrusted to him were to be returned "without injury either to body or soul". Three sisters were sent, named Stijne des Grooten, Dayken Dyerkens, and Aleid ter Maat. They arrived at Hilwartshausen about the year 1460. As soon as the nuns were aware of their arrival they screamed: "The devils have come". They made such a noise that it was not thought safe to let the reformers enter the building. Only the prioress came to meet them. She led Stijne des Grooten, the leader of the little party, through the build-

ing, but could not prevent the sisters from making all
sorts of hostile grimaces. One of the nuns, in seeing
them approaching, threw herself upon the floor and
sought to indicate her feelings of disapproval by gro-
tesque movements of her limbs. This astonished Stijne
not a little, but she was unaware of the meaning of the
strange spectacle. "What ails this sister"? she asked the
prioress in surprise. The latter, not knowing what to
say, answered with a forced laugh, whereupon the new-
comer, believing the other sister to be troubled by some
physical disease, said in a very soft and kind voice to
the prioress: "Dear mother, give her some wine to drink;
perhaps she will improve then". Thus in her innocence
and tenderness of heart she softened the animosity of
one of her enemies. A short time afterwards Stijne was
appointed sub-prioress. With the greatest circumspection
she went to work. First one should try kindness, she
reasoned, later, severity. Besides, she knew what it was
to love one's neighbors as dearly as oneself; Groote,
Radewijns, and Thomas à Kempis had said that one
should even strive to be kinder to them than to one's
own nature. Stijne had often meditated upon these
teachings at Deventer and Diepenveen — now the time
had come for her to practise them. Gradually she won
the love and respect of the sisters, and they would come
to her for help rather than go to their own prioress.
Especially the younger ones soon learned to love her as
a mother or a dear friend, though still she insisted that
they all should perform their proper duties with alacrity.
When the hour had come for spinning, she would say:
"Come, dear children, let us now do a little spinning.
Now you know that we are not allowed to talk, but we
may laugh". Then the sisters would group themselves
about her and begin working in silence. All of a sudden

Stijne would start to smile. The younger sisters, encouraged by her example, would all respond with hearty laughs, "so that for a long period a loud noise was heard in the room, though none of them spoke a word". Thus she gradually taught them that manual labor and even enforced silence did not necessarily imply hardship or misery.

The other two sisters from Diepenveen contributed their share to the reform of Hilwartshausen. Dayken Dyerkens practised each day this well-known maxim of Groote's disciples: "Be harsh to yourself and kind to others". Whenever injustice had been done to her or an act of unkindness, she always sought to repay it with some form of what one might call true Christian service. How much those little deeds of love must have cost her can only be felt by those who have also gone through such experiences. In a very short time she bad broken down all barriers of resistance. And her success must appear the more remarkable because she combined the strictest discipline with her unselfish love. One evening she had left the younger sisters alone for a few moments. Now the time had come, they thought, to have a little fun. Accordingly they began to dance, for the moment completely oblivious to the newly introduced monastic reform. But woe to them, when Dayken came back! There was no end to the penances, and never again did they venture to dance when Dayken was out of sight.

The most lovable of the three reformers from Diepenveen was Aleid ter Maat, who was assigned a humbler post than the other two sisters. All day long she was busy in the kitchen, but in the evening she would visit the sick, or else some of the sisters would come and spend a few sweet moments of confidential talk with her. There was no harshness about Aleid. To her they could freely open their hearts, and confess their secret wishes and their sorrows. She reminds us of John Ketel, the pious cook at Deventer, and of Florentius Radewijns. "One suspects", says Dr. Kühler of Amsterdam, "that it was largely due to her lovable character that the monastic reform attempted by the sisters of Diepenveen was so complete a success, though the sources are silent on this point"[66].

Several uneventful years passed before it was found expedient to let the three sisters return to Diepenveen. Not that they had forgotten their "earthly paradise", as they called it. Far from it. Often Dayken Dyerkens would sigh: "Oh, that I might once more see the gates of Diepenveen opened to me, and that I might enter there — how happy I would be"! Finally, after the lapse of six years, her wish was granted. Great was the joy of the three reformers, but equally great the sorrow of the nuns they were to leave. For a good while the new religious fervor at Hilwartshausen was a living force — just as long as the remembrance of the kind words and deeds of the departed sisters remained impressed on the minds of the nuns. But gradually these impressions were weakened, and supplanted by entirely different ones. Discipline relaxed once more[67]. The nuns of Hilwartshausen were not in touch with that great spiritual force which Groote's disciples in the Yssel country successfully maintained. Far away from the Yssel valley, no matter how brightly the new fires of devotion had at first lighted up the whole atmosphere in brethren-house or monastery, the principles of the "New Devotion" were less effectually assimilated. Well might the more pious nuns at Hilwartshausen exclaim: "If only we had kept those sisters from Diepenveen with us, we would have kept up our first love"[68].

III

The monasteries of Windesheim and Diepenveen have often been called the "model convents" of the fifteenth century[69]. The reforms introduced by them were the chief cause which for a time at least halted the downfall of monasticism in north central Europe. To Windesheim and Diepenveen the pious abbots, priors, bishops, and princes looked for help, when indolence, greed, and vice threatened to ruin the lives of the monks and nuns. Many an ambitious prior took a journey to the Yssel valley to watch those men and women who so steadfastly clung to Groote's ideals of piety, and as a rule they returned with one or more assistants, filled with new hope. Thus Windesheim and Diepenveen helped to reform several hundred monasteries in the Low Countries, Germany, and France. Nearly one hundred of these actually joined the far-famed Congregation of Windesheim, humbly obeying the instructions of the prior superior, and devoutly following the Windesheim rules embodied in the constitution drawn up during the closing years of the fourteenth century — a very remarkable document. Before 1387 the founders of the new monastery had cared little about monastic life in general, or about the rules of the Augustinian order, but in 1394 they decided to form a chapter and to prepare the foundation of a constitution. John Vos and Henry Wilde went to the celebrated monasteries of St. Victor and Ste. Geneviève at Paris to study the rules followed there, but instead of slavishly copying those rules, they studied many others, and finally drew up a constitution which contained elements selected with great care from those used in various monasteries[70]. In 1395 Pope Boniface officially approved of their work. This encouraged the men of Windesheim to compose an "Ordinarius", a "Kalendrium", and a "Manuale". Shortly after that a committee was appointed to draw up the Windesheim missales, evangelaria, epistolaria, lectionaria, capitularia, and collectaria, all agreeing to a letter. The brethren must have had great will-power, for nothing so complete had ever been attempted before[71].

The constitution they adopted prescribed the way they and their successors were henceforth to spend their time. Their lives were not very different from those of the Brethren of the Common Life, while the theological views they entertained coincided absolutely with those of their friends at Deventer, at least during the life of Florentius Radewijns. But as time went on monastic conditions differentiated them from their brethren. The men at Windesheim had left the "world" behind them in order to explore their inner selves in a life of comparative solitude, and this silence and meditation did not fail to react upon their minds. Jealously the monks at Windesheim, and in all of the monasteries belonging to their chapter, clung to their old ideals. They began with Groote's enthusiasm fresh upon their responsive hearts and minds; their early acts clearly personified that living faith which abounds in "good works", as James had commanded in his Epistle. Windesheim passed through a golden age, a silver age, and a period of decline[72]. By the opening years of the sixteenth century one would look in vain for great theologians and great scholars at Windesheim.

After studying the works of Groote, Radewijns, Mande, and Peters (the last two were the best writers Windesheim produced), one can picture the sort of life the men at Windesheim led. They loved to read the Bible and the Fathers, and they devoted much of their time to manual labor of some sort. Their clothes and meals were quite simple. Certainly there was much real piety to be found at Windesheim. Not only were the "sacred writings" copied there with zest[73], but the monks conscientiously strove to follow in the foot-steps of Christ. They believed in the blessings of manual labor and of poverty[74]; and their meals, taken but twice a day, were plain, though wholesome and fairly plentiful[75]. Most of the monks had at one time been members of the Brethren of the Common Life, and the clothes they wore differed but little from those used by their friends at Deventer[76]. They too were ascetics to a certain extent. Not that they starved or mutilated their bodies[77], but they distrusted sensuous pleasures as their enemy, and to be free from all external things was their ideal, perhaps also their secret motive in "fleeing the world". Some of the monks even thought it wrong to have a hearty talk with their own mothers[78].

One can easily imagine that it was not the braver, the more active sort of men that left the brethren-house for the monastery. There were some great minds among the early inhabitants at Windesheim, and some splendid men like John Vos of Heusden, but many were timorous[79], or carried away by excessive humility and self-abasement[80].

There was much about the lives of the monks at Windesheim that deserves respect. It seems that the loving heart of Radewijns had inspired the men who founded the new monastery under his supervision, — inspired them to emulate his numerous deeds of charity. Seldom if ever did the poor ask Windesheim in vain for material assistance. Many a lonely wanderer, after having crossed the weird outskirts of the Veluwe or the vast heaths of Overijssel, would hopefully knock at the gate of Windesheim to ask refuge for the night. Windesheim became famous for its charity[81].

And Windesheim became famous also as a centre of literature and art. The monks belonging to this congregation often spoke about the inner life, but that did not always signify little regard for learning. There were many scholars in the monasteries[82], and splendid libraries[83]. Though at first the monks at Windesheim copied books chiefly for their own use[84], they began about the year 1500 to edit works for export to foreign countries[85].

One of the most remarkable achievements Windesheim could boast of was the correction of the Vulgate. The monks had made up their minds that the Latin Bibles then in use differed too much from each other to be all correct. Consequently they wanted to get a version which should form the standard for all further copies. They had one sent from Paris, one from the monastery of Bethlehem near Doetinchem, and one from the monastery of St. Jansdal near Harderwijk. For several years they compared and copied until finally their standard-copy was completed[86]. So well did they perform their task that their copy, according to Hirsche and other authorities, became the basis for the Vulgate adopted officially by the Church at the close of the fifteenth century[87]. In a similar way they brought out editions of the Fathers[88].

Furthermore, the Windesheim circle not only produced a great mass of manuscripts, but illuminated them beautifully[89]. Many capable artists were developed in these monasteries, both sculptors[90], and painters. Thus the monastery of Rooklooster in Brabant produced Hugo van der Goes, one of the greatest painters North of the Alps during the second half of the fifteenth century[91].

Dr. Acquoy says that if one takes a general view of

the Windesheim group, he must come to the conclusion that the remarkable moderation displayed by the monks and nuns of this chapter in all their ways of living, and of expressing their thoughts, is highly commendable and truly amazing. The chapter of Windesheim, he continues, was indeed one of the greatest and perhaps the most influential in the whole history of Western monasticism[92]. Several hundred monasteries had for a time at least basked in the gentle warmth of the newly awakened religious life, that was proceeding in all directions from Windesheim and Diepenveen. The missionaries from the Yssel valley had journeyed from place to place, carrying with them the best thoughts of Gerard Groote, the founder, and of Radewijns and Zerbolt, the two first leaders of the Brethren of the Common Life. No new theories had been expounded by them, nor had they at any time hinted at a need of revolutionary changes in church, home, or monastery. A mild form of asceticism clung to the followers of Groote at Deventer and Windesheim until the opening years of the sixteenth century. Windesheim broke with no hallowed traditions; it made much of Mary, the mother of Christ, and believed in indulgences and in the invocation of saints[93].

But the Windesheim Congregation, in pointing out the uselessness of mere form, and in stressing the need of a personal, living faith, helped unconsciously to prepare the way for a great religious upheaval. For a time it tended to stay the onward march of demoralization among the regular and secular clergy. Its missionaries scattered the works of Groote, Radewijns, Zerbolt, Peters, and Thomas à Kempis across the Continent, so that even to-day one finds copies of them in libraries and book-stores in most of the larger European cities. Thus the principles of the "New Devotion" became the spiritual food of many thousands of devout men and women beyond the Low Countries, in Germany, France, and Spain, and would later, as we shall see, be crystallized in the lives of great reformers, like Luther, Calvin, Zwingli, and Loyola.

CHAPTER V

THE "IMITATION OF CHRIST"

For more than three centuries a multitude of writers have written books and articles on the authorship of the "Imitation of Christ". So vast is the amount of printed material devoted to this subject that no human being will ever be able to read it all. In the fifteenth century the "Imitation" appeared in print at Augsburg, Cologne, Nuremberg, Paris, Lyons, Rouen, and Venice, ascribed respectively to St. Bernard, Gerson, and Thomas à Kempis. Now that the dispute is about to be terminated, thanks to the discovery of a number of manuscripts at Lübeck, which once belonged to the Sisters of the Common Life in that city, we are able to manipulate properly the material at hand, and note how essential it is to study the lives and writings of Groote, Radewijns, Zerbolt, and their followers, before one can understand how the "Imitation of Christ" was composed and how it became the Gospel of the "New Devotion", or Christian Renaissance.

I

"After the Gospel, the 'Imitation' undoubtedly is the book that reflects with the greatest perfection the light which Jesus Christ brought us down from heaven. It eminently contains the Christian philosophy.......... Nowhere else do we find the same doctrine inculcated with a more persuasive eloquence and simplicity than in the unpretending little volume that all of us have a hundred times perused". Thus reads the verdict of a notable Catholic author in America[1]. His view is supported by that of thousands upon thousands of other writers in all countries, and belonging to every religious denomination. For rich and poor, high and low, learned and simple — all who for the time being are weary of external, formal observances, or dissatisfied with the dry bones of dogma held out to them by many preachers may find the advice and instruction they need in turning over even the first few leaves of the "Imitation of Christ". Nobody knows through how many thousands of editions the little book has passed since the close of the fifteenth century, or into just how many languages and dialects it has been translated[2]. Not a single year passes without adding a score of new editions to the many already existing. Together with the Bible it has found its way into the remotest regions, eagerly devoured by Christian and pagan, by civilized and barbarian. Who knows how many millions of stubborn hearts it has softened, how many aches it has healed, how much hatred it has melted as the sun melts the snow in spring?

In analyzing the teachings of the "Imitation", one is reminded immediately of Groote's theological and sociological views, which are repeated in the works of Radewijns, Zerbolt, and Peters. The great underlying thought of the "Imitation", as Hirsche says[3], is the fact that man is a pilgrim here, an exile. According to Groote and his disciples, man is a sort of prisoner on earth, his prison, the flesh, which besets him on every turn with obstacles, blocking his way back home to the happy state before the fall. Man has to cleanse his blood from poison, his mind from sin, his heart from vice. First vice must be extinguished, ere virtue and love can find room in the human heart.

The "Imitation" therefore distinctly teaches the depravity of human nature: "O how great is human frailty, which is always prone to evil. There is no man that is altogether free from temptations whilst he liveth on earth: for in ourselves is the root thereof, being born with inclination to evil. For through Adam the first man, Nature being fallen and corrupted by sin, the penalty of this stain hath descended upon all mankind"[4] It is man's duty to extirpate sin, to cleanse his blood from poison, his heart and mind from vice: " 'Hope in the Lord, and do good', saith the Prophet, 'and inhabit the land, and thou shalt be fed in the riches thereof' ". A great many pages are devoted to the problem of fighting various sins: Radewijns, it should be remembered, had made excerpts from Cassianus about the principal sins and their remedies; Zerbolt had copied after Radewijns' "rapiarium", when drawing up his "Spiritual Ascensions"; in the "Imitation" also the reader is exhorted to study his daily shortcomings. He is urged to "resist the blood", and to conquer his lower self: "This ought to be our daily endeavour, to conquer ourselves. Who hath a greater combat than he that laboureth to overcome himself? Thou must be lord and master of thine own actions, and not be a slave or a hireling. The perfect victory is to triumph over ourselves". Groote and his disciples carefully explored the inner self. "Know thyself", was one of their maxims; hence we read in the "Imitation": "The highest and most profitable reading is the true knowledge and consideration of ourselves"[5].

The "Imitation" urges us to fight our passions, and repeatedly elaborates upon the nature and effects of temptation[6]. This also is in accordance with Groote's and

Radewijns' writings. On several occasions Groote had been obliged to give counsel to those among his disciples who were dejected on account of their inability to get the better of their temptations, and all the inmates of Radewijns' vicarage had considered the conquest of sin as man's prime duty. They searched every day in religious books for practical help in their constant struggle against evil, writing down the most helpful excerpts they could find in their "rapiaria". In the "Imitation" we meet with many of these excerpts: "O, if men bestowed as much labor in the rooting out of vices, and planting of virtues, as they do in the moving of questions, neither would there so much hurt be done, nor so great scandal be given in the world, nor so much looseness be practised in religious houses (monasteries). Examine diligently thy conscience, and to the utmost of thy power purify and make it clear....... Think with displeasure of all thy sins in general, and more particularly bewail and lament thy daily transgressions". There are many shortcomings singled out for a more detailed study, such as the love of "worldly things", and too much familiarity with human beings, especially with women[7]. Gossip is a great evil, so is curiosity. The opinions of others are not to be given undue regard: "He enjoyeth great tranquility of heart that careth neither for the praises nor dispraises of men". Fame, therefore, is absolutely worthless, as also are honors, and material possessions. And if one looks for comfort from human beings, one is certain to be disappointed sooner or later[8]. Since man is a pilgrim and exile here on earth, he must not give himself to mirth; he has much more occasion for tears than for laughter, though dejection is not desirable[9]. The flesh, man's greatest enemy perhaps, should be made subject to the mind or spirit: "The more the flesh is wasted by affliction, so much the more is the spirit strengthened by inward grace. Know for certain, that thou oughtest to lead a dying life. And the more any man dieth to himself, so much the more doth he begin to live unto God"[10].

"O, if men bestowed more labor in the rooting out of vices, and planting of virtues". The more one's vices disappear, the more room there will be for new virtues; this is the view set forth by Radewijns (d. 1400) in his "Omnes inquit artes", where he elaborates upon the eight principal vices, and their "remedies". These "remedies" are the new virtues to be introduced into the mind and heart. Zerbolt (d. 1398) used the "rapiarium" of Radewijns in composing his "Reformation of the Faculties of the Soul" and his "Spiritual Ascensions"[11]. The "Imitation" follows these in devoting much space to the "rooting out of vices, and planting of virtues". Above all other virtues rank humility[12] and obedience[13], which are the "remedies" against pride[14]. Self-renunciation and resignation are ranked high among virtues[15]. The reader is taught that only through suffering[16], by carrying his cross with him every day, in imitation of Christ, can he reach the heavenly country. One must keep one's eye single, one's attention concentrated upon the final goal: Heaven[17]. It is advisable to avoid society as much as possible, to devote much time to contemplation, to read the "sacred writings" with one's mind freed from temporal cares, and with devotion. Traveling is to be avoided as much as possible, but manual labor is recommended, and poverty deemed essential[18]. On every page of the "Imitation", it will be seen, one meets with thoughts expressed before by Zerbolt, Radewijns, and Groote.

When the mind becomes clear, and the heart pure, one receives the highest gift from heaven: love. Thus Groote had thaught his disciples. Love is more than virtue, and more than the mere absence of vice, wherefore the men and women of Deventer could find no words fit to describe the value of love. The "Imitation" in turn makes much of love; in the first place, the love the creature owes to the Creator[19], and to Christ his savior[20]; in the second place, love for his neighbor[21]. But the love and worship of self is looked upon as an abomination in God's sight[22].

Groote and his disciples were all mystics. Much of Groote's mysticism found its way into the "Imitation": " 'The Kingdom of God is within you', saith the Lord. Learn to despise outward things, and to give thyself to things inward, and thou shalt perceive the Kingdom of God to come in thee. Christ will come unto thee, and show thee his own consolation, if thou prepare for him a worthy mansion within thee. Let not Moses speak unto me, nor any one of the prophets, but rather do thou speak, O Lord God, Inspirer and Enlightener of all the prophets; for thou alone without them canst perfectly instruct me, but they without thee can profit nothing. They indeed may sound forth words, but cannot give the Spirit. Unless thou help me, and inwardly inform me, I become altogether lukewarm and ready to fall to pieces. He to whom all things are one, he who reduceth all things to one, and seeth all things in one, may enjoy a quiet mind, and remain peaceable in God. O God, make me one with thee"[23]. As mystics, Groote's disciples placed the acquisition of virtue above that of learning, as is indicated in passages like the following: "Be studious for the mortification of thy sins; for this will profit thee more than the knowledge of many difficult questions". But the "Imitation" does not disparage the value of book-learning: "Yet learning is not to be blamed, nor the mere knowledge of any thing whatsoever to be disliked, it being good in itself, and ordained by God". Empty phrases, mere style, and scholastic disputes, however, are considered worthless[24].

As for the views about God and man expressed in the "Imitation", not a single statement can be found deviating from those taught by Gerard Groote. The Brethren of the Common Life at Deventer built their views upon the teachings contained in the New Testament and the Fathers. Perhaps they failed to grasp the meaning of certain phrases in the Gospels and in the Epistles by Paul, Peter, and James. If they did, they only repeated the errors made by men like Augustine, Jerome, Ambrose, Bernard, Bonaventura, Cassianus, and Thomas Aquinas. One important theological question is the salvation of man, and closely connected with it, the conception of heaven and hell, of man's depravity, the value of faith and "good works", and the nature of "grace". That Groote's disciples implicity believed in the depravity of human nature has been repeatedly indicated above[25]. But Groote had taught that man remained in touch with his Creator, for Groote was a mystic[26]. The tie which united man with God, according to the "Imitation", is the Holy Ghost, the Comforter, divine love, or grace[27]. Man has fallen so low that he cannot rise any more without divine help. But since he was created in God's image, something divine remains in his sinful heart: "For the small power which remaineth is as it were a spark lying hid in the ashes"[28]. Grace can fan this spark beneath the ashes into a bright flame, if man wishes. This inner light will then purge away vice and finally make room for love, until the inner self is transformed into a mansion for Christ to inhabit. Thus human nature is sanctified, and the small spark of divinity augmented into a flame of pure love. Such was Groote's view, and such was the view of those who composed the "Imitation".

Paul and the Church Fathers held that through the transgression of one man the whole human race fell, and that through the sacrifice of one man the gift of salvation was offered to every human being, so Groote based his belief upon this teaching. He did not come to the conclusion that all men were saved through Christ's sacrifice, for the simple reason that the Church Fathers had not done so. The doctrine of universal restoration was very little known in Groote's day. Hence the Brethren of the Common Life believed, in common with most Catholics and Protestants since, that only those souls were to be saved that accepted Christ as their Savior. One could be saved by becoming one of Christ's followers, for which faith was the only requirement, though not faith as defined afterwards by Luther. Groote's disciples held that there could not be such a thing as an empty faith, a faith without works. They took to heart the warning of James: "What doth it profit my brethren, though a man say he hath faith, and have not works? can faith save him? Thou believest that there is one God, thou doest well: the devils also believe, and tremble. But wilt thou know, O vain man, that faith without works is dead"[29]? The brethren were always dwelling on the following themes: prepare yourself for heaven; remember the Beatitudes, for every vice eradicated, and every newly acquired virtue, is a step nearer the final goal, wherefore we read in the "Imitation": "And I [God] daily read two lessons to them [Mine elect], one in reproving their vices, another in exhorting them to the increase of all virtues"[30].

II

The compiler of the "Imitation of Christ" was Thomas à Kempis, or rather, Thomas Hemerken of Kempen. He was born in the town of Kempen in the diocese of Cologne. The date of his birth is not certain. Some writers claim it must be placed in the year 1379 or 1380[31]; others, in the year 1380 or 1381[32]. His father was called John Hemerken, or John with the little hammer, for he earned his living with his hammer[33], though he also owned a tract of land[34]. That both Thomas and his brother John à Kempis were not mere phantoms invented by chronicle writers, is shown by a document written at Kempen in the year 1402, in which the sale of their father's home is attested[35].

In 1392 the fame of Deventer's cathedral school had reached the duchy of Guelders, in which Kempen was situated. Whether it was due to the presence of the Brethren of the Common Life or to the reforms initiated on Groote's advice, certain it is that many parents were anxious to have their boys educated at Deventer. In Thomas' case there was an additional reason for his going there. His brother John had been an inmate of Radewijns' vicarage, and was now living at Windesheim[36]. In 1392 Thomas arrived at Deventer[37]. "When I came to study at Deventer", he wrote afterwards, "I went to Windesheim, where my brother was living. He told me to visit Florentius Radewijns"[38]. Eager to follow John's advice, for John knew the vicar well, Thomas came to Radewijns. He was not a wealthy boy; he could not even pay for his board and lodging. Radewijns took compassion on him, and invited him to stay at his house[39]. Thus fortune smiled upon him from the first day.

Not only did Radewijns provide him with lodging, but he gave him books and paid his tuition at the school of St. Lebwin's. His teacher at that time was a certain John Boheme. One day Thomas brought him the tuition fee. "Who gave it to you"? the teacher asked. "Radewijns", was the boy's reply. "Then take it back to your kind master", said the teacher[40]. It takes very little imagination to see how much the friendship of a man like Radewijns meant to the boys then attending the cathedral school. Thomas must have told his parents about it, and the other boys. His parents in turn probably mentioned his experiences to other parents. In this way even before the close of the fourteenth century the influence of Gerard Groote was being felt in homes far beyond the Yssel valley.

But the brethren-house at Deventer was too small to lodge school boys. Radewijns, therefore, looked around for some other quarters, and sent Thomas to a certain devout woman, doubtless one of Groote's disciples[41]. How long the boy stayed with her we do not know. It seems that after a few years he lived with the brethren again, for he tells of experiences in the brethren-house: "All I earned", he writes, "I gave to the community; the rest I needed was given by Florentius[42]. Here I learned to read and write the Holy Scriptures and books on moral subjects, but it was chiefly through the sweet conversation of the Brethren that I was inspired yet more strongly to despise the world[43]. I took pleasure in their godly conduct. Never before could I recollect to have seen such men, so devout and fervent"[44].

What Florentius Radewijns did reminds us of Groote's work among the school boys at Deventer. He also had often invited them to come to his house, and had given them work to do. Some of these boys became Brethren

of the Common Life, though at the time they visited
Groote they were living still in private homes. Thomas
à Kempis too was first lodged with a pious woman, as
soon as Radewijns found a place for him. Later he was
asked to become a real inmate of the brethren-house.
Perhaps Thomas lived only one year with the brethren
at Deventer, as his own remarks seem to prove[45], but
the influence of Radewijns had been shaping his young
mind before he re-entered the brethren-house. Later he
wrote: "During seven years of my life [1392-1399] I
experienced the wonderful compassions of Florentius
Radewijns"[46]. Add to this that his own brother John
had lived with Radewijns, Brinckerinck, and Vos in the
first brethren-house at Deventer, and the conclusion is
justified that when Thomas began to preach and write,
he repeated the maxims of Groote and Radewijns, the
two founders of the new brotherhood, the two men who
inaugurated the "New Devotion", or Christian Renaissance[47].

Thomas was one of the many young men sent out by
the Brethren of the Common Life to erect or reform
monasteries. We have already seen how John Vos of
Heusden, Henry Mande, and Gerlach Peters carried the
thoughts of Groote, Radewijns, and Zerbolt to the
monastery of Windesheim. John Brinckerinck had done
the same thing to Diepenveen. Thomas à Kempis was
to follow their example at Mount St. Agnes, three miles
north-east of Zwolle[48]. He probably carried some manuscripts also with him from Deventer to the new monastery; certain it is that manuscripts were brought there
from Deventer, for Thomas à Kempis was the person
who preserved and edited a great many sayings of Groote
and Radewijns, which he incorporated into his well-
known biographies of Groote and his disciples. The

friendship between Radewijns and Thomas must have
been very intimate; says Thomas: "I often made ready
his table at his request and brought from the pantry the
things he needed"[49]. Radewijns often sent him to the
Sisters of the Common Life living in Deventer, and
whenever Radewijns was ill Thomas had to ask them to
pray for him[50]. It is not surprising that Thomas wrote
the best biographies of Groote, Radewijns, and Zerbolt,
the three founders of the brotherhood. The significance
of this fact is seldom appreciated. If writers interested
in the authorship of the "Imitation of Christ" had
properly reflected upon this point before they decided to
add another work to the many hundreds already composed, and if those French, Italian, German, and English
authors who thought they were solving the problem
without reading any one of the works by Groote or his
disciples had first spent a few years in the Hague,
Utrecht, Liège, and Cologne, carefully investigating the
mystical productions of the Brethren of the Common Life
at Deventer, they would have dropped the matter entirely
or concluded that the "Imitation of Christ" must have
proceeded from the pen of one or more of Groote's
followers[51].

The world has long waited for a history of the whole
movement inaugurated by Gerard Groote, in which the
services of each predominent personality are clearly
pictured, their productions carefully measured, and
properly balanced. The moment one fails to grasp the
significance of any one of the leaders of Deventer, he
cannot understand the others. Hence the only thing to
be done is to study Thomas à Kempis in his spiritual
heredity and environment.

It must have been near the close of the year 1399 that
Thomas à Kempis went to the monastery of Mount St.

Agnes[52]. The spot may have seemed sacred to him for the reason that Gerard Groote had visited the place in the summer of the 1384, pointing out to his disciples this site for their first brethren-house. Here the pious John Ummen had lived, the blind leader of the Brethren of the Common Life of Zwolle, and now a monastery had been erected on this hill of St. Agnes, or "Agnietenberg".

In 1412 or 1413 Thomas à Kempis was ordained priest[53], and shortly after this began his career as editor, writer, and copyist. In 1425 he was elected sub-prior[54], for soon the other monks had been impressed by his great religious fervor. Says Tolensis, who spent many years at Mount St. Agnes: "In the church and in the performances of ecclesiastical ceremonies, it is difficult to describe his rapt intention, and I might say inspiration. While he chanted the psalms, his eyes were ever raised towards heaven, and he appeared to be filled with a divine enthusiasm, captivated and carried away by the unutterable sweetness of the holy psalmody: so that he never stood with his heels resting upon the ground; that is to say, as he meditated, the tips of his toes alone touched the floor, the rest of his body was lifted heavenwards, whither his soul tended with all its desires"[55]. When in 1471 he passed away, it was his name which had made the monastery of Mount St. Agnes celebrated above many ancient convents. Even the greatest among the great, like a Wessel Gansfort, had not deemed it below their dignity to have a few moments of conversation with this venerable mystic. He had written thirty-eight works, among which the "Soliloquy of the Soul", the "Garden of Roses", and the "Valley of Lilies" are excellent[56].

III

Thomas à Kempis never could have chosen a better time to "learn to read and write the sacred writings" than in the year 1398–1399. It was in the summer of 1398 that the two institutions of Gerard Groote at Deventer passed through the greatest crisis that ever was to threaten their existence. In the brethren-house at Deventer the men had lived a semi-monastic life, undisturbed by quarrels, feuds, and hostile attacks. Then came the terrible pestilence in June, taking the lives of nearly all the experienced members. First in the vicarage of Radewijns, and later in the "House of Florentius", or the real brethren-house, they had for more than fourteen years tried to do what they believed Christ had commanded in the Beatitudes. They had conscientiously endeavored to "despise the world", to "remain unknown", to "offer themselves to God", and to "subdue the flesh".

Let us in imagination visit Deventer. It is early in the month of June that the pestilence has made its appearance in the brethren-house. More than half of the inmates have the disease, while most of the others have hurriedly fled across the Veluwe to Amersfoort, taking many school boys with them. Thomas à Kempis remains at Deventer, where for six years he has followed in the footsteps of his beloved Radewijns. The pious cook in the brethren-house and all the older members have died. Heart-rending letters have been passing between Amersfoort and Deventer. In the brethren-house Thomas has found the spiritual exercises of John Ketel, the cook, and of Lubbert ten Bossche, besides those of the other dead brothers. Zerbolt has just left for Amersfoort, and Thomas finds himself practically the sole possessor of the jealously guarded treasures in the library[57]. Most precious to him seem the "devout exercises" of Groote and Radewijns, of which a few excerpts are given below:

"Likewise after the example of Bernard, utter no word by which thou mayest seem to be very religious, or endowed with knowledge. Resolve to avoid and abhor all public disputations which are but wranglings for success in argument, or the appearance thereof (such as the disputations of graduates in Theology at Paris), and take no part therein......... So also I will never argue with anyone in private unless it is certain that some good end shall follow......... My first resolution is to desire no further preferment..... According to the rule of the primitive church thou canst not hold several benefices......... Let there be a daily fast which doth consist in not wholly satisfying the appetite......... All philosophers advise this, specially Seneca and Aristotle....... Likewise Gerard said a man ought not to be disturbed about any affair of this world...... Before all things study specially to be humble inwardly. The knowledge of all knowledge is for a man to know that he knoweth nothing. The more a man is assured that he is far from perfection, the nearer he is thereto. The beginning of vainglory is to be pleasing to oneself......... With whatsoever thoughts a man doth fall asleep, with such doth he awaken; at these times it is well to pray or read some psalms.

"Before all things know thy vices and thy passions. Be watchful against temptation and the promptings of thy passions......... Reply humbly to them that ask of thee. Avoid women, and beware of looking upon them. It is an ill example to the world to keep no guard over the eyes......... Thou oughtest not to speak evil of any, unless it can profit thee or him......... I think that the thoughts and promptings which come into our hearts are not under our control, but it is in our power to plant good in the heart by reading, prayer, and meditation until these promptings to what is unlawful are overcome and yield, and by the grace of God do cease......... We ought to raise our heart to heaven without ceasing, and to turn again and again to the Holy Scripture......... By too great haste devotion is lost. Therefore avoid mere repetitions, and do all things with attention and thought, not from habit only......... Worldly knowledge is very alluring; therefore let a man beware that he be not too much attracted thereto; let him earnestly desire to pass over to God by means of such knowledge, and not be satisfied therewith as an end in itself......... A man ought to direct all his exercises and studies to the conquest of his passions and weaknesses, for otherwise he doth profit little thereby. In the hours of common labor stand ever on thy guard, and be careful of much speaking......... Never be idle, but be busied with some occupation".

Thomas also copied the letter sent by Amilius van Buren to the brethren at Amersfoort, where Radewijns was then staying. In this letter Amilius told the absent rector about the death of Lubbert ten Bossche, or Lubbert Berner, as Thomas calls him. Thomas adds that Van Buren was sitting beside the dying man: "He [Amilius] carefully kept account of all the edifying words which he heard fall from his lips; and after Lubbert's death he faithfully made record of them, writing them in order in a letter......and this letter I have determined to insert

here". Not satisfied with that, Thomas also copied the
letter composed by Lubbert shortly before his death, together with the answer from Radewijns to the brethren
at Deventer. The story of Lubbert's decease is very impressive: "And he answered me, as it were in great
amazement: 'Wonderful, wonderful, marvelous, marvelous, yea great and marvelous are the things which I saw
when I sat up'. And then he added: 'Call the brethren,
call the brethren'; and when I called them, immediately
he breathed his last". What is still more remarkable,
Thomas copied èxcerpts from the "devout exercises" of
this pious brother. He began with the following sentence:
"Thy task shall be to labor to uproot thy vices and to
gain virtue".

This is not all. Thomas was the trusted friend of
Amilius van Buren, rector of the brethren at Deventer
during Radewijns' absence in the summer of the year
1398. Amilius had watched by the bed-side of the dying
Lubbert ten Bossche. From his mouth Thomas "received
many of those good things concerning the virtues of the
brethren", which he wrote down in his "Lives of Gerard
Groote, Florentius Radewijns, and their Disciples".
Who knows how much more Thomas might have told us,
and how many more brief sayings he might have preserved which now are lost? He shows how well he was
acquainted with the kind cook: "He made the kitchen a
house of prayer, for he knew that God is everywhere....
He passed no time unfruitfully, nor for a moment
neglected his spiritual exercises". Thomas copied the
cook's "devout exercises", most likely from the original
itself, so that we owe to his busy hand the preservation
of this literary production, together with those of Groote,
Radewijns, Ten Bossche, and some other men.

Early in 1398 Thomas à Kempis was living in the

old vicarage of Radewijns, and not in the new brethren-house, which was called "House of Florentius". "At that time", writes Thomas, "there was no small number of clerks living in the several houses under the rule and discipline of that most devout Father, and following the holy commandments of their Lord, his counsels and precepts, and also at set times toiling at the work of copy-ing books for the schools......... At this time by the aid and counsel of Florentius I also took up my abode in this house and continued in the community for about one year, having Arnold as my companion. Here indeed I learned to write, to read the Holy Scriptures and books on moral subjects, and to hear devout discourses....... All I was then able to earn I gave for the expenses of the community......... As he [Arnold] sat with the boys in school he noted not their childish clamor, but as the master delivered his lecture he wrote the same on paper and afterwards read it over to himeslf or with a comrade......... At this time the disciples and most devout pupils of our beloved father Florentius, whose lives I have written above, were still in the flesh, namely, Lubbert, Henry [Brune], Gerard [Zerbolt], Amilius, James [of Vianen], and John Ketel, and there were with them some others who had been amongst the first mem-bers of the community", in other words, among the Twelve of Groote himself[58].

What was more stimulating still, Radewijns, whom Thomas had now known for six years, felt that he was about to die. Many a time he sent Thomas to the Sisters in Groote's old home to ask them to pray for him, and Thomas also served as his personal attendant in other ways. Although Radewijns did not die till 1400, often it seemed as if death would snatch him away long before the close of the year 1399. How often must not Thomas

have been called to the bed-side of the sick rector. And
the latter, more intent than ever on things spiritual, cannot have refrained from filling his pupil's mind with
spiritual thoughts. It is no wonder that to Thomas à
Kempis we owe the best biographies of Groote, Radewijns, and Zerbolt. Moreover, the words of a dying
man, or of one who believes he is dying, are always
doubly impressive; they are always retained longest. On
the works of Zerbolt and Ketel the breath of newly departed spirits lay fresh and magnetic; here the books of
Groote, the founder, were passed from hand to hand;
here Thomas found all the "rapiaria", or excerpt-books,
of the leaders, who had lived and labored in the brethren-
house. In this house Thomas also found the Latin book
composed by some one whose name the sources do not
reveal, at least not in connection with the piece itself,
for it seems to have disappeared very soon. This unknown work, very probably drawn up at Deventer by one
or more brethren living in the vicarage of Radewijns,
we know that Thomas à Kempis copied at Mount St.
Agnes between 1416 and 1420, adding some chapters
himself; and that it was copied almost immediately in
many other monasteries and brethren-houses. Soon it
became widely known as the "De Imitatione Christi", or
"Imitation of Christ".

IV

If two hundred or one hundred years ago a work had
appeared in which the lives of Groote and his followers
had been clearly portrayed and their literary productions
carefully analyzed, probably but few books and articles
would have been written on the authorship of the "Imitation of Christ", for those who are well acquainted with

the labors of Groote's disciples at Deventer cannot support the views of authors like Wolfsgruber, Puyol, and Renan. Fortunately, however, the long-disputed question has caused many a writer to discover evidence which otherwise would not have been found. Thus a vast amount of material has been made accessible to a relatively large number of students. And although this material in itself has failed to convince thinkers that the "Imitation" was composed or put together in the Yssel country, nevertheless it will greatly lighten our task of showing that it was produced there.

"In the first place", writes Sir Francis Cruise, "I may state, with what I am satisfied is incontrovertible certainty, that no manuscript of the 'Imitation of Christ' has ever been produced of an age antecedent to the mature manhood of Thomas à Kempis — that is to say, the first third of the fifteenth century"[59]. How much paper has been wasted on this point alone! All the efforts of those who wanted to produce a copy written before 1410 have failed. Loth, for example, found the first book of the "Imitation" in a manuscript at Paris which he believed to have been written in 1406[60]. Hence, he concludes, the work must have been produced before this date[61]. A few years afterwards Becker carefully examined the manuscript in question and found that it contained a collection of treatises written in many different hands. If one piece in it had been copied in 1406 or 1410, that by no means implied that all the others were of the same date[62].

About four hundred manuscripts are still in existence containing one or more books of the "Imitation", most of which are undated. The oldest dated one written in France is from the year 1456; Italy can boast of no earlier dated copy than that of 1464. About 20 were written in Italy, 25 in France, 15 in England, 240 in Germany, 50 in Belgium, and 45 in Holland[63]. It is exceedingly difficult to estimate the exact age of an undated manuscript, for very often a copyist would write with exactly the same hand at the age of sixty as he had employed forty years earlier. Consequently one must always leave a margin of at least fifty years, wherefore even those copies written in an Italian Renaissance hand, such as the one found in the British Museum at London[64], may very well have been written fifty years later than some people imagine[65].

As for the copies bearing a date, or provided with a note of some sort from which the correct date can be deduced, the earliest copy known containing all four books is the one found in the "Codex of Gaesdonck", written in the Augustinian monastery of Bethlehem near Doetinchem, a house of the chapter of Neuss, which joined the Windesheim Congregation in 1430. This was written in the year 1426[66]. At Brussels, however, a manuscript is found in the Royal Library (no. 10137) which has the first three books, written in the year 1425[67] in the monastery of Windesheim for the monastery of Bödingen[68]. One year earlier, book I was copied in the house of the Brethren of the Common Life at Hulsbergen, near Zwolle[69], and in 1420 or 1421 the Dutch translation of book I at Windesheim[70]. Then there is the so-called "Mölk codex", or "Codex Mellicensis I", containing also book I of the "Imitation", which may have been written in 1421, for the codex bears the number XXI (although this number does not follow after this book I, but after the "Contemplatio S. Bernardi de passione Domini", wherefore the former piece may have been written much later). In this case it was very probably given by the representatives of Windesheim to those of the monastery of Mölk when they met each other at the Council of Constance[71]. Next in order comes the "Codex Noviomagensis", written at Nijmegen in 1427, also in a monastery of the Windesheim Congregation[72]. But there seems to be another copy, produced in 1426 at Ewick, another house of the Windesheim circle, according to Spitzen[73]. Then there is the "Codex Osnabrugensis", written in 1429 by the Brethren of the Common Life at Osnabrück[74], and then the "Codex Thevenot" at Paris, written about the year 1430 in the brethren-house at Hulsbergen near Zwolle[75]. The "Codex Roolf" was written in 1431, in the monastery of Bethlehem near Louvain, a monastery of the Congregation of Windesheim[76]. It appears, therefore, that all or nearly all the earliest dated copies of the "Imitation" were written by the followers of Gerard Groote. Moreover, the first German translation of the "Imitation" was made by the Brethren of the Common Life at Cologne in the year 1434[77]. The Brethren of the Common Life and the monks belonging to the Windesheim Congregation were at first solely responsible for the rapid spread of this remarkable work[78].

As for the verdict of the contemporary witnesses, this also points to Thomas à Kempis as the author, or editor, for those writers who in the fifteenth century regarded Gerson as the author, did not know who had first ascribed it to him and why. John Busch says that Thomas à Kempis wrote the "De Imitatione Christi"[79]. True, even his opinion is sometimes disregarded; and more than that, one German writer uses it as evidence against the supporters of Thomas à Kempis, but with arguments that carry little weight[80]. There is, too, the testimony of a certain Herman Rijd, who had talked with Thomas à Kempis himself[81]; also of a great many others[82]. That so many contemporaries are silent on this question need not surprise us, for it was not customary for the Brethren of the Common Life at Deventer to add the names of the authors or the dates to the works they were copying. Moreover, they had all been taught the "ama nesciri", or "love to remain unknown" by Groote and Radewijns, their spiritual ancestors[83]. And furthermore, they all regarded Thomas à Kempis as the author of the "Imitation"; only, they would have been more exact if they had called him the compiler.

That Gerson, the famous chancellor of the University of Paris, could not have written the "Imitation" is a well-established fact to-day[84]. But several writers in France, Italy, and England still favor the conclusion that the "Imitation of Christ" must have been written in Italy about the middle of the thirteenth century. These authors as a rule know very little about the mystical productions of Groote, Radewijns, Zerbolt, Peters, and Mande. They write a great deal about a phantom invented by them, called John Gersen, abbot of a Benedictine monastery in Lombardy, who, they claim, composed the "Imitation". In some mysterious way this work reached the Yssel valley about the year 1400 or 1410 Thomas à Kempis, they continue, found it there, copied it, and placed it at the head of his other works. They admit that the Brethren of the Common Life and the monks of Windesheim were the first to appreciate its inestimable worth. They argue (1) that only after they had made it known to the world did other people read and copy it, (2) that the thirteenth century was the golden age of monasticism, and that the Cistercians and Carthusians, who are mentioned in the "Imitation", were true to their vows only in that century, so that no monk after the year 1400 could have pointed to those orders and say: "Observe the Carthusians, the Cistercians, and the monks and solitaries of various orders, how they do every night rise to sing Psalms to the Lord"[85]. Furthermore, (3) that the fifteenth century was a time of strife, of civil war, and of disorder, in which a work like the "Imitation" could never have been composed; and (4) that, since it contains no references to Thomas Aquinas or any other scholastics of note, it must have been written before their time[86].

To these arguments we reply (1) that John Gerson and John Gersen are one and the same person. Both names refer to the chancellor of the University of Paris, who defended the Brethren of the Common Life at the Council of Constance, but was not the sort of mystic to write a book like the "De Imitatione Christi". His name was usually spelled "Gerson", though it is also quite often spelled "Gersen" in fifteenth century manuscripts or incunabula. (2) And how could a work like the "Imitation", written about the year 1250, have remained absolutely unknown until the year 1415? If Thomas à Kempis discovered it on its mysterious and hypothetical journey from the plains of Lombardy to Deventer, he must have received it from Groote's disciples, who gave him books to read, but who never referred to the "Imitation" until he himself had copied it. That Thomas à Kempis copied it is beyond question, for his autograph copy, finished in 1441, is still in existence[87]; and that Groote's disciples were the first to distribute it is now admitted. As to the argument about the Carthusians, Groote and his disciples respected that order very highly. (3) Also, they paid very little attention to civil wars. (4) That they refrained from quoting Thomas Aquinas in the "Imitation" is exactly what one should expect[88].

But Thomas à Kempis was not the author of the whole

"Imitation", if we use the term in the modern sense. The first Dutch translation of book I appeared in 1420 or 1421 at Windesheim, as we have said; books I–III, found in the "Kirchheim Codex", "were copied from the autograph of Thomas à Kempis in the bishopric of Utrecht [at Windesheim] in 1425"; and the "Gaesdonck Codex" contains all the four books, copied in 1425, 1426, or 1427. Then we have the autograph copy of Thomas à Kempis at Brussels, with book I–IV, but book IV placed before book III, and followed by eight other works of Thomas himself, with a note at the end to the effect that this manuscript was written by him, and finished in the year 1441. Spitzen asserts that Thomas wrote the whole work in this codex before 1425, since the "Gaesdonck Codex" already has all the four books. He rightly concludes that Thomas must have written the original between 1416 and 1420[89]. Book I–III appeared in 1416 or 1417, and book IV in 1418 or 1419[90]. This view is supported by Paul Hagen of Lübeck[91], who discovered a Low German translation of parts of books II–IV in the "Stadt-bibliothek" of Lübeck. Bishop F. J. van Vree of Haarlem found a Dutch translation of two chapters of book IV in a manuscript left by the Sisters of the Common Life at Deventer[92]. Van Vree thought it possible that Thomas à Kempis borrowed these two chapters from some work composed by one or more disciples of Groote[93]. He and other writers, like Malou[94], Spitzen[95], Becker[96], and Bonet-Maury[97] have made an extended list of extracts from the works of Groote, Radewijns, and their followers which they compared with corresponding passages in the "Imitation". A few years later Becker, in a series of articles, endeavored to show the futility of all such work. He concluded that all one can prove, is a similarity in thought and construction[98]; and he now holds that the "Imitation" is an original work, composed in the monastery of Mount St. Agnes near Zwolle.

Thus matters stood when a short time ago Hagen published an article in the "Beiaard", called "De Navolging van Christus en Thomas van Kempen"[99], which is the Dutch translation of an article intended for a German periodical[100]. Hagen briefly commented here on the interesting discoveries he had made, and also gave the present writer some valuable information, explaining to him how he had conducted his researches.

Among the numerous manuscripts in the City Library at Lübeck which originally belonged to the Sisters of the Common Life of that city, there are two which contain a treatise in Low German called "Admonitions tending to Things Internal"[101]. Also, there is a manuscript in the same library in which chapters VI–IX of the fourth book of the "Imitation" are found, all in the same Low German dialect apparently in use at Lübeck in the fifteenth century[102]. This was not left by the Sisters of the Common Life living in the convent of Michael[103], but by the beguines in the "Johanneshof", a house situated near that of the Sisters of the Common Life[104]. There can be no doubt that these beguines got this literary material from their friends across the street, and that the latter, in turn, had received it from one of the sister-houses of Deventer or Westphalia, for it was the Low Countries that provided those pious women at Lübeck with religious productions of various kinds[105]. Just as Thomas à Kempis was only one of the many boys who received the teachings of Groote's followers at Deventer, and just as the works he wrote had been preceded by a great many others, so did the sixty-four chapters of the "Imitation", translated at Deventer and

adapted for the use of the sisters at Lübeck, form merely
a small portion of the writings produced originally at
Deventer and spread abroad by the disciples of Gerard
Groote.

What conclusions are we justified in drawing? Those
sixty-four chapters in the Low German dialect, which we
shall call L, were put together by Thomas à Kempis
when he was still living at Deventer, and must be looked
upon as the work of Radewijns, Zerbolt, or one of their
followers. Now, L differs so much from the other
chapters of book III and IV that they must have been
written by two different personalities and at different
times, even though the whole work seems after all to
have been compiled by Thomas à Kempis, as will be
shown presently. We find, for example, that in the first
twelve chapters in L the word "O" occurs but once, while
in the very few fragments found in book II of the
"Imitation" (which, as we know, consists of twelve
chapters), and which are lacking in L, it occurs 25 times.
In the first sixty chapters of L we find it but 9 times;
but in the few passages missing here and found in the
complete "Imitation", it occurs 30 times. It is well
known that Thomas à Kempis in his later life was in the
habit of using this interjection. The almost complete
absence of the interjection in the L chapters proves that
these were written during the last year spent by Thomas
at Deventer, where he was so strongly influenced by the
lives and ideals of Radewijns, Zerbolt, Ketel, and Ten
Bossche. The interjections used by Thomas à Kempis
are often followed by rhetorical questions. Such questions rarely occur in L. Thus we read in chapter XXI
of book III of the "Imitation" proper: "O when shall
it be fully granted me, to consider in quietness of mind
and see how sweet thou art, my Lord God"? And in

chapter XXXIV: "O when will that blessed and desired hour come"? In chapter XLVIII no fewer than ten such questions succeed each other, of which the first and last start with "O when", and the others with "When". Rhetorical questions are very often repeated in other works by Thomas à Kempis, as, in the "Valley of Lilies", where, in chapter XXVI, eight similar questions are found with the word "O" in six, and the word "when" in eight. Rhetorical repetitions are also characteristic of Thomas à Kempis' own style. When the writer of the L chapters repeats a word as he repeats "in the cross" nine times in chapter XII of the second book of the "Imitation", it is because this is strictly necessary; when Thomas à Kempis repeats, as in using "many" in book III, chapter XLVIII, he does so rhetorically. A second example of this sort of repetition, which the L chapters do not have, can be found in book III, chapter XXI, where "above all" occurs eighteen times, and in addition the word "thou" is used seven times, the word "alone" six times. Here eleven superlatives are employed. Again, that part of book III, chapter LVIII which has the word "I" sixteen times, in a series, is not a part of the L chapters.

The difference in style between the L chapters and those added by Thomas à Kempis is further illustrated by the manner in which God is invoked. While L has only nine comparatively short titles by which to invoke God, the whole "Imitation" has forty-one, some of which are quite elaborate and rhetorical[106]. It is worth noting also that every one of the titles found in the "Imitation", but absent in L, repeatedly occurs in the other writings of Thomas à Kempis. He undoubtedly was the person who worked over the Latin equivalent of L, adding the customary interjections, questions, and exclamations, so characteristic of his own works. The material he found at Deventer in the year 1398–1399 is simpler in style, and far more powerful than the paragraphs which he added on Mount St. Agnes.

One can also prove that the matter which was added to L was added by a young monk. In 1416 Thomas à Kempis was a young monk. He was *the* young monk who wrote that "the life of a good monk is a cross", and that once having proceeded, it will not do for him to look behind him. The author of L, on the contrary, must have been a man of ripe experience outside of a monastery. Apparently he had not been a monk in his previous life, or at least not for a long period. Thomas himself wrote especially for monks, as the contents of book III, chapter X plainly indicate, whereas L was not addressed to monks only, but to all Christians generally. He who wrote L, even if he was a monk, which appears very doubtful, nowhere so enthusiastically praises monasticism as Thomas à Kempis does. Thomas writes in chapter X of book III: "For it is not granted all to forsake all, to renounce the world, and to undertake a life of religious [monastic] retiredness......... O sacred state of religious [monastic] servitude"......... In chapter LVI we read: "Truly the life of a good monk is a cross"; this same sentence is also found in Vol. IV of his "Opera", p. 249.

In the use of dialogue the writer of L far surpasses Thomas à Kempis. In L the Lord is the principal speaker, and he is not interrupted by approbation, whereas, in those chapters of book II not found in L, the author, who is Thomas à Kempis himself, often breaks into the dialogue, and in a wholly unwarranted and inartistic fashion, just as he does in Vol. V of his "Opera", on pp. 146–150. There he at first addresses Christ, and then speaks to Jesus, Pilate, the reader, and humanity in general, after which he turns to Christ once more. In L the Lord affirms the words of his Son with a short "It is so, my Son" (chapter XII of book III); whereas in the "Imitation" we read: "O Lord, it is true", in which the 'author injects his own personality (book III, chapter IV, of which this part is lacking in L), and: "O Lord, what thou sayest is true" (in: book III, chapter XVII; also lacking in L). In a similar way Thomas throws in some remarks of his own, thus interrupting the Lord, in book III, chapter XXIII: "O Lord, do as thou sayest, for this is delightful for me to hear", just as he does in Vol. I of his "Opera", on p. 4: "Thou hast well said, Lord", and in Vol. IV, on p. 199: "O Lord, it is true what thou sayest: all that thou sayest pleases me".

When one comes to analyze the subject matter of L, one sees that chapters I–XII, XIII–LX, and LXI–LXIV form three independent and original treatises. They are not dependent on the chapters which follow them in the "Imitation" proper. Chapters I–XII of L correspond to book II of the "Imitation", which Thomas himself treated as a separate piece of work with a title of its own. Chapters XIII–LX are like forty-eight chapters of book III, and the way in which they close proves that here the original treatise, called: "Of Internal Consolation", ends. In L chapters I–LX appear like one treatise, beginning with the celebrated saying of Christ: "The kingdom of heaven is within you". They close with the following sentence: "Give me a happy departure from this world, and lead me straight-way into the kingdom. Amen". They begin and finish with "the kingdom of heaven". Thomas spoiled this fitting end by adding some material of his own, and by changing the order of some of the chapters. The same can be said of chapters LXI–LXIV of L, which also form an independent treatise with a title and a fitting close. They constitute the best part of book IV of the "Imitation"; in form and contents they can be easily distinguished from the preceding and following chapters of book IV. Their title is: "A Short and Fitting Exercise for the Communion Service", which "exercise" forcibly reminds us of the religious exercises, or "devota exercitia", of the men at Deventer who left Thomas à Kempis in possession of their literary productions.

The chapters discovered in Lübeck (the L chapters) enable us to restore the original text of the whole "Imitation". In doing this one can correct mistakes made by Thomas à Kempis in copying the treasures he brought from Deventer. In book II, chapter X of the "Imitation" we read for example: "Semper enim debetur gratia digne gratias referenti: et auferetur ab elato quod dari solet humili". The word "debetur" cannot possibly be correct. The disciples of Groote at Deventer, in common with most theologians in Europe at that time, believed that "grace" was always freely bestowed, and never earned by any mortal being. No one of them would ever have said that grace ought to be given to anybody, as if God was obliged to give it as a sort of payment. When Thomas came to this place he probably found the word in question in an abbreviated form, as very many words were abbreviated in his day. The original certainly did not have "debetur", but "dabitur". Thus we read in Matthew XIII, 12: "Quia enim habet, dabitur ei, et abundabit: qui autem non habet, et quod habet auferetur ab eo". What does L have here? For "debetur" we find "wet gheven", or "it will be given", which is the equivalent of the Latin "dabitur".

In book IV, chapter IX we read: "Offero quoque tibi

omnia pia desideria devotorum: necessitates parentum, amicorum, fratrum, sororum, omniumque carorum meorum". The word "amicorum" cannot be in its right place here, for who would ever think of saying: "My parents, friends, brothers, sisters, and all my dear ones (friends)"? The author must have said: "My parents, brothers, sisters, and all my friends (or dear ones, which means friends)". Hence we read in L: "My parents, brothers, sisters, and all my dear friends". Thomas mistook the word "meorum" for "amicorum", and the original must have been: "necessitates parentum meorum, fratrum, sororum, omniumque carorum meorum". Two copies of the "Imitation" have already been found which have "meorum" instead of "amicorum", and more will doubtless be produced later on. It can also be proved that most of the chapters in book IV of the "Imitation" were composed by Thomas à Kempis, that he must have found one other short treatise corresponding to chapters X, XII, XV, and XVIII of this book, and still another which was transformed into book I, but lack of space forbids further discussion here.

Once more then we must ask why the "Imitation" at once acquired such world-wide circulation, leaving the other productions by Thomas à Kempis far, far behind? He did indeed place it at the head of his other works, thereby showing that he regarded it as his own work. And John Busch called Thomas its author. The "Imitation" in its present form, therefore, may be termed the work of Thomas à Kempis, using this term in its early sense, for he composed a considerable portion of the work himself, and worked over into it the "devout exercises" of Radewijns, Zerbolt, Ketel, and Ten Bossche, which he later adopted for the use of novices at Mount St. Agnes. It should be noted in particular that Florentius Radewijns, rector of the brethren at Deventer, and the acknowledged head of the "New Devotion", was a poor copyist. Before he fell sick in 1398 it was his custom merely to bind and to draw lines in the manuscripts which the brothers needed for their writing. During his illness, when Thomas à Kempis waited on him, he probably dictated letters and other compositions to Thomas.

Radewijns was the only person whom Groote considered fit for the priesthood. A halo of sanctity surrounded his beloved personality. Thousands of people had come to him for advice and help. The sick, the poor, and the afflicted—all had been comforted by him. Though not a brilliant author, he composed some treatises from which Gerard Zerbolt had partially copied his two mystical works. No one had composed "religious exercises" which resemble the L chapters so closely as those which flowed from his pen. It is he, therefore, who should be considered as the real author of those L chapters, and of book I of the "Imitation" — in other words, of that part of the "Imitation of Christ" which made it, next to the Bible, the most popular book in Europe.

CHAPTER VI

WESSEL GANSFORT

"Behold"! wrote Luther one day in surprise, "a Wessel has appeared, whom they call Basil, a Frisian from Groningen, a man of remarkable ability and of rare and great spirit; and it is evident that he has been truly taught of the Lord, even as Esaias prophesied the Christians would be........ If I had read his works earlier, my enemies might think that Luther had absorbed everything from Wessel: his spirit is so in accord with mine. But now my joy and courage begin to increase, and I have not the slightest doubt that I have been teaching the truth, since he, living at so different a time, under another sky, in another land, and under such diverse circumstances, is so consistently in accord with me in all things, not only as to substance, but in the use of almost the same words"[1]. It was in the year 1522 that Luther made this remarkable statement about Wessel Gansfort. What could have induced the victorious Reformer to draw such a sweeping conclusion as to that "most Christian author", as Luther called Gansfort a little later? Why had Gansfort remained so little known, and how did his writings resemble those of Martin Luther so closely?

I

Wessel Gansfort was born at Groningen in the year 1419 or 1420. His parents were poor and intended to make him go to work at a tender age, after they had let him go to school for a few years. But a kind woman, Oda Jarges, enabled him to stay in school. The sources do not inform us which school the boy's friend selected for him. Probably he went at first to the old school attached to St. Martin's, the leading church in Groningen. Certain it is, however, that in 1432 or soon thereafter he was sent to Zwolle, which at that time was the centre of the "New Devotion". Here John Cele had taught for more than forty years, making his school so famous that both John Sturm and John Calvin would later make it their model for their "gymnasia" at Strasbourg and Geneva respectively.

Wessel remained seventeen years at Zwolle. A good many if not all of those seventeen years he spent in the "Parva Domus", the dormitory erected by the Brethren of the Common Life at Zwolle for boys attending the city school[2]. In this dormitory there was an assembly room for the students, as was customary in many other houses of these pious brethren. After Wessel had passed through the eight grades of the town school, he became a teacher there. He also taught in the dormitory from 1440 till 1449[3]. Very soon an intimate friendship sprang up between Wessel and the "Procurator" of this dormitory. Whenever of an evening the latter held his address to the inmates of the building, Wessel would stand by his side, thus "inspiring the boys to love virtue and to hate vice"[4], — again, that characteristic stress on the fight against defects in character, or in other words, against sin. And again, that insistence on the increase in virtue and eradication of vice!

In the room next to Wessel's a young boy was staying, who could communicate with his brilliant neighbor through a small window. They would have long talks with each other, Wessel imparting learning, the other,

the "fear and love of God"[5]. What a significant phrase
for our chronicler to use: "the fear and love of God"!
Groote's disciples often would muse upon this text: "The
fear of the Lord is the beginning of wisdom". Radewijns had repeatedly pointed out that the last vestiges of
sin should be removed, before perfect love could find an
abiding place in the human heart, — again that contrast
between vice and virtue, unrest and peace, punishment
and reward, preached and lived by the Brethren of the
Common Life.

One wonders what kind of instruction was given in
the school-room of the "Parva domus". Much of it must
have been purely religious, for the city school provided
the pupils with the best instruction of other kinds that
could be desired. The boys undoubtedly received a
splendid opportunity to rehearse their lessons in the
dormitory. This was one of the reasons why the schools
of Zwolle, Deventer, Liège, and Wesel became so
popular. It is probable that a great deal of time in the
school-room of Wessel's dormitory was devoted to the
art of writing, illuminating, and binding of manuscripts,
by which the Brethren of the Common Life themselves
largely made their living. Many of the boys living in the
dormitory sooner or later became members of this
brotherhood; in fact it was from such ranks that most
of the new members were generally taken. In the preceding chapter we saw that a considerable number of
manuscripts at Liège, Cologne, and Düsseldorf were
produced in the dormitories erected by the brethren at
Deventer and Zwolle, so that the presumption is that
much of the work connected with the production of
manuscripts was performed, or at least learned by the
boys living in those dormitories.

And what were the writings that the boys at Zwolle

and Deventer were instructed to copy? Included among them were not only the works of Groote, Radewijns, and Zerbolt, but also the Bible and the Fathers, together with some mystical productions of certain saints like Bernard, Francis of Assisi, and Bonaventura. A large number of copies of the "Imitation of Christ" must have been turned out by them, too. But as for the leading scholastic writings of the thirteenth and early fourteenth centuries, the Brethren of the Common Life said of them that they were lacking in personal religion[6]. Thomas à Kempis expressed the same view when he wrote: "Tell me now, where are all those Doctors and Masters, with whom thou wast well acquainted whilst they lived and flourished in learning? In their lifetime they seemed something, but now they are not spoken of.......... What availeth it to cavil [and dispute] much about dark and hidden things? It is a great folly to neglect the things that are profitable and necessary, and give our minds to that which is curious and hurtful. And what have we to do with *genus* and *species* (the dry notions of logicians)"[7]? The chronicler thought he could say no better thing about Wessel Gansfort than that he was wont to go to the procurator's evening address as one of the least among the boys, and that he inspired them to improve their characters.

Only three miles north-east of Zwolle was situated the humble monastery of Mount St. Agnes, where still lived Thomas Hemerken of Kempen, known as the author of the "Imitation of Christ", and loved for his childlike piety. Wessel soon made it a habit to take a walk to "Agnietenberg", as the hill and its monastery were called, in order to have a talk with the venerable recluse. With feelings of boundless reverence he would approach his beloved friend. Thomas à Kempis and he had both been instructed by the Brethren of the Common Life. The only difference between these two followers of Groote was the divergence in their outlook on life's duties. Thomas had felt the call of the monastery and obeyed it; Wessel believed duty should keep him outside. There are writers who do not themselves see any good in monasticism, and who have invented stories to the effect that Wessel was "shocked" by the "superstitious" views of Thomas à Kempis on monasticism and also on the veneration of Mary. As a matter of fact, Wessel's views on these points were identical with those of Thomas à Kempis, as appears from statements of his which seem to have been overlooked by these biographers[8].

As we have seen, nobody was unduly urged by the Brethren of the Common Life to enter a monastery. Gerard Groote himself had never after 1380 wanted to re-enter one. If the brethren at Deventer and Zwolle had actually believed that the monastic state embodied all that was most noble and perfect in religion, they themselves would not have remained outside the walls of a monastery. That Gansfort appreciated the value of silence and rest cannot be doubted, but his was a work to be done outside of the monasteries. When time came at last for him to part with his friends at Zwolle and Mount St. Agnes, he did not act against their wishes, and later was to return and finish his work among them.

In the fall of the year 1449 Gansfort matriculated as a student in the department of "arts" at the University of Cologne. He was fortunate to secure a place in an endowed dormitory, where he made good progress. In 1450 he obtained an A. B. degree, in 1452 the degree of Master of Arts. In December, 1452, he seems to have left Cologne for Louvain, where he probably stayed until August, 1453. In 1454 and 1455 he was at Paris, which place he left in the summer of 1455, having accepted an appointment as professor in the University of Cologne. The next year he departed for Heidelberg, where he taught for one year. Then we meet him again among the Brethren of the Common Life at Zwolle[9].

The year 1458 closes the first period of Gansfort's absence from his native country. He had been connected with several universities of note, but had felt no inclination to remain long in any definite place. Why he so suddenly returned to Zwolle we do not know. Certain it is, however, that this time the Yssel country could not hold him, for in the same year, 1458, he arrived at Paris once more, now to stay longer. Paris was the city where Groote had received his university training, and for one in search of higher learning it seemed about the best place in Europe. At any rate, Gansfort liked it there. With the exception of a short trip to Angers about the year 1461, concerning which but little is known, he remained at Paris from 1458 till 1469.

What was the reason why Gansfort grew to like Paris so well that for a number of years he gave up his travels? It was not on account of some advantageous position, since he occupied no official post of any kind, nor was it for any mercenary reasons, since he cared little for money and still less for fame. He found here a group of thinkers, the followers of Occam in philosophy, and of Ailly and Gerson in theology. Gansfort enthusiastically supported the Occamists, but not because he was of their particular system of philosophy. One reason why he joined the Occamists at Paris was because he considered their views in harmony with the teachings promulgated by the Church Fathers[10]. Another and more potent reason was the fact that Ailly and Gerson had also been Occamists, as well as most other prominent leaders in the

Church who strove to fight the many abuses among the clergy. He knew that Ailly and Gerson had supported the Brethren of the Common Life, and that they revered Hugo of St. Victor, abbot of the celebrated Augustinian monastery near Paris, whence the founders of Windesheim had obtained a goodly share of their theology[11]. Many people at Paris were now reading the works of Gerard Zerbolt and Thomas à Kempis, and here Gansfort felt himself among friends.

In 1469 Gansfort decided to make a trip to Rome, for he had heard much about the artists and scholars of the "eternal city", and many people from the Netherlands were making pilgrimages to Rome. He soon became acquainted with several members of the papal court, and tells of an occasion when he held a dispute with two of them in the presence of some other person, all three being graduates of the University of Paris. The subject under debate was indulgences, and Gansfort challenged them to put forward any bit of evidence or any argument. His own arguments were based entirely on the Holy Scriptures. One of the group, John of Picardy, had just come from Paris, where he had heard Gansfort dispute before, and he advised him to keep his views to himself in Rome.

Of very great significance is Gansfort's friendship with Francesco della Rovere, who afterwards became Pope Sixtus IV, and with Bessarion. These two men he seems to have met first at Rome in 1470. By this time he was personally acquainted with many leaders in the Church throughout Europe.

In 1470 Gansfort returned to Paris, where he met John Reuchlin, the German humanist. Melanchton relates that Reuchlin used to regard his learned friend from Groningen with feelings of affection and veneration.

Gansfort had now become a man of considerable note among the greatest scholars in France. Very curious stories are told by contemporary writers about his doings at Paris in 1473. Melanchton says that he was expelled from Paris for having attacked the superstitious views of certain dignitaries in the Church; another writer remarks that Gansfort had this time been called to France by King Louis XI on account of his extraordinary learning, in order that he might be a sort of pillar to sustain the tottering university. Still another writer speaks of him as "Wessel of Groningen, the restorer of the University of Paris under Louis XI". Several other accounts to the same effect as the last two, all from the pens of leading scholars, impress one with the fact that Gansfort occupied a place of great distinction at Paris[12]. Afterwards, when almost too old to teach, he was invited once more by the French king to come to Paris.

But while it is evident that Gansfort was enjoying the appreciation of the most distinguished men at Paris, he had made many enemies in his various attempts to reform the Church. In February, 1473, he received the following letter from the bishop of Utrecht:

"Beloved Son, Wessel:

We command our blessing to abide ever upon you. We would have you know that we need you here in person at this time to give good counsel to our soul. I have many about me who esteem you greatly for your learning and character; but I do not hear them teach the truths that long ago you were accustomed to declare so faithfully.

I have long been aware of your brilliancy as a teacher and yet I know that there are many who are seeking to destroy you. This shall never be so long as I am alive

to protect you. But come tó me as quickly as possible,
that I may talk everything over with you, and may have
with me one in whom I delight my soul.

    Farewell,

                I am the unworthy Bishop

Vollenhove,   David.

    On the eve of the feast of Pontian (Jan. 13), in
the year of our Lord, 1473[13].

Gansfort did not leave immediately for the Netherlands, however, for he wanted to visit Italy again, to
seek audience with his former friend Francesco, now
Pope Sixtus IV. On meeting him, the pope exclaimed:
"My son, ask me what you wish; I will refuse you nothing that is in keeping with my esteem for you and with
your circumstances". To which Gansfort promptly replied: "Most holy Father, my kind and just patron,
there is nothing with which I would greatly burden your
Holiness. I have never sought great honors, as you
know; but since you now sustain the character of the
Supreme Priest and Shepherd upon earth, I pray that
your reputation may correspond with your name; and
that you may so administer your high office that when
the great Shepherd of the sheep, whose chief servant on
earth you are, shall come, he may say, 'Well done, good
and faithful servant; enter thou into the joy of thy
Lord' ". Then Sixtus replied: "This shall be my concern;
do you ask something for yourself". "Well then", said
Gansfort, "I beg you to give me a Greek and a Hebrew
Bible from the Vatican library". "These shall be given
to you", Sixtus answered. "But, you foolish man, why
do you not ask for a bishopric or something similar?"
"Because I do not need it", was Gansfort's final reply[14].

    In some respects Gansfort must have been disappointed

in Rome. He had come from cities where the lives of
Florentius Radewijns and Theodore Herxen, rectors of
the Brethren of the Common Life at Deventer and
Zwolle, had been shining lights to guide their followers,
of whom he was one. There the "Spiritual Ascensions"
and the "Imitation of Christ" had been composed, un-
equaled by anything else in the religious world. One
would have expected such men and such books from
Rome rather than from Deventer and Zwolle, for here
lived the leaders of the whole Church, here lived the pope!
But the lives and the writings of these leaders did not
embody the purest fruits of Christian thinking in Gansfort's eyes. Rome did not keep him longer than a few
months; then he started north again, toward the Yssel
country.

On his way he visited Florence, then the world-famous
home of the Platonic Academy of Lorenzo de' Medici
and Marsilius Ficinus. However magnificent the city,
however witty and polished its inhabitants, and learned
its scholars, Florence also did not attract Gansfort. If
Augustine had lived there at that time, or Bernard, surrounded by a circle of admirers, such as were now
flocking around Ficinus, Gansfort might have lingered
for years. As it was, the simple men of Zwolle attracted
him more, he said, than the humanists at Florence[15];
wherefore he did not tarry there. From Florence he
seems to have gone to Venice, for he visited that city in
1474; Melanchton mentions his stay at Basel, where he
was said to have taught Greek and Hebrew for a few
months. Then, traveling down the Rhine, he finally
arrived in the Yssel country once more[16].

What were the impressions he had received of the
university men at Paris and Cologne, and what did he
have to say about his friends in Rome? Shortly after

arriving at Zwolle, Gansfort wrote a treatise, called "On the Sacrament of Penance", in which he set down some of his views regarding the leading scholars of his time. Says he: "Knowledge is the interpreter of truth; wisdom is concerned with our welfare. Hence knowledge may be useless and vain. Such is all knowledge which follows truth out of curiosity. Just as the garrulousness of women is foolish because it seeks satisfaction in mere talk, so knowledge seeks merely the truth. But wisdom seeks the benefit from the truth...... There is a strong and weighty argument against universities to be drawn from the fact that Paul secured but little fruit at Athens; accomplishing more in the neighboring city of Corinth and in Thessaly, which was then almost barbarous, than in the Attic city, at that time the fountain of Greek philosophy. It goes to show that liberal studies are not very pleasing to God. In fact what I saw when I lived in Cologne and Paris is certainly hateful to God, — not the study of sacred literature, but the moral corruption existing in the midst of such studies........ 'Many publicans and sinners sat down with Jesus; for there were many, and they followed him'. This word points to the great corruption of the Pharisees and scribes of that time. For although from childhood they had received holy training in the Law, they practised it for gain rather than for piety, and they neither heeded nor followed piety, even when it displayed itself incarnate. Instead they scoffed, they mocked, they persecuted........ To-day, we have good reason to fear that there is a still worse plague in the corruption of our preachers and pastors. Publicans and harlots will be converted to right-eousness more easily in the great day of the Lord than men of this sort, who know the will of God and yet scoff at it"[17].

One would almost think that he heard Groote again. Groote also had studied at Paris, had observed the clergy at Cologne, and the papal court at Avignon, and also had returned to the Yssel valley, if not with feelings of regret for some of his past experiences, at least with the knowledge that the clergy of his day were not always good servants of Christ, though they were expected to be. He also had been accustomed to draw a distinction between mere knowledge and wisdom, or the correct use of knowledge. Groote and his followers also had regarded knowledge as a tool, no more and no less, as a tool that might be put to good or harmful uses. They were by no means opposed to the acquisition of knowledge, for how could they themselves work without tools, and why should they have wanted to work without them?

This time Gansfort had come to the Low Countries to stay. For fame and wealth, for honor and distinction he did not care. His desire was to associate himself with men who were sincere and true to their word. He knew that Zwolle and Groningen possessed an extraordinarily large number of such men. And, though Thomas à Kempis had died in 1471, there were still many other sincere men in the monastery of Mount St. Agnes. Then there was the monastery of Adwert, five miles north-west of Groningen, where several men of his kind used to meet. In these four places, accordingly, Zwolle, Mount St. Agnes, Adwert, and Groningen, Gansfort chose to spend the remainder of his life, first residing chiefly at Zwolle and Mount St. Agnes, after 1482 more generally at Adwert and Groningen[18].

At Zwolle, Gansfort must have been warmly welcomed by the Brethren of the Common Life, for they might rightly regard him as one of themselves. One incident is told which proves their regard for him. In April, 1482

he was asked to cure Albert of Calcar, the rector, of a
serious illness. About his life on Mount St. Agnes we
have little information; he seems to have been there a
great deal between 1475 and 1482, but often was called
away by the bishop of Utrecht, who usually resided in
the little town of Vollenhove on the Zuiderzee. Gansfort
acted as the bishop's physician, and was treated as a
trusted companion[19].

We are pretty well acquainted with Gansfort's experiences in the Cistercian monastery of Adwert, where
the chief humanists in German lands used to gather for
exchange of views, always cordially invited by the learned abbot Henry van Rees. Rudolph von Langen was
often found there, and Alexander Hegius, as well as
Gansfort's compatriot, Rudolph Agricola. One day a
learned professor from Paris came, too. Gansfort invited
him to have a discussion. After they had touched upon a
considerable number of topics, the professor from Paris
suddenly threw off his doctor's cap, and exclaimed in admiration: "You are either a second Alanus [de Insulis],
or an angel from heaven, or something I shan't name.
Praise the Lord, I have not been deceived in my expecta-
tions. I have not sought you in vain. Not without reason
did the scholars at the Sorbonne call you the 'Master of
contradictions', and admire and hate you for it"[20].

At Adwert Gansfort passed much of his time in conversation with the monks. He would often read Hebrew
to them. To the younger monks he would explain the
Psalms, and remark frequently that the Latin Vulgate
was not very clear in places; whereupon some one would
quickly fetch him the Hebrew text. After a few years,
Gansfort's eyes became so weak that he would often
blunder in his reading. This amused the monks greatly,
which may perhaps account for the fact that Gansfort

now preferred to make his home in Groningen, where he was taken in by the nuns of a small convent, called the "Convent of the Spiritual Virgins". He probably lived there before 1484, for it appears from various sources that he and Agricola used to visit each other a great deal. In one of his letters Agricola writes: "I am often invited to his table and live on very intimate terms with him". Melanchton also relates that the two men were united by ties of the deepest friendship. Gansfort was visited also by John Oostendorp and Herman Torrentinus, pupils of Hegius and of the Brethren of the Common Life. Besides, he was in active correspondence with many prominent men. He should now have stopped studying, for his health began to fail rapidly, but he kept on reading and writing. Shortly before his death he had a period of doubt as to the doctrines of the Church, but it did not last long. "Now I know nothing else", he faltered, "than Jesus Christ and him crucified". With this confession he passed away, on the fourth of October, 1489[21].

II

"An humble knowledge of thyself is a surer way to God than a deep search after learning; yet learning is not to be blamed, nor the mere knowledge of any thing whatsoever to be disliked, it being good in itself, and ordained by God. But because many endeavor rather to get knowledge than to live well, therefore they are often deceived". Thus reads the third chapter of the "Imitation of Christ". Gansfort must often have read this chapter with approbation, for he always listened attentively to his teachers and friends at Zwolle and Mount St. Agnes. At Cologne, at Paris, and in Italy he had constantly sharpened the tools of his mind with which nature had generously equipped him. Long before Erasmus was born, and at a time when probably few other natives of Transalpine Europe knew Greek, Gansfort had mastered this language, together with the rudiments of Hebrew. Logic, argumentation, and scholastic philosophy had been studied carefully by him, but empty words and arguments used only for argument's sake were valueless in his opinion. Thus he condemned equally those doctors at Paris and Cologne who would argue for hours on questions which were wholly lacking in practical value, and the theologians of his day who were speaking and writing on momentous questions without having taken pains to master the elements at least of sound scholasticism. We find him making the following remark in one of his letters concerning John of Wesel, a contemporary scholar: "You have heard of the peril of that venerable man, Master John of Wesel. Now, although— as you have heard me say repeatedly—I do not like his absurdities, which deviate from the truth and are a stumbling block to the people; yet his learning and unusually keen faculties are such that I cannot help loving the man and sympathizing with him in his misfortune. Oh, what an advantage it would have been to him, as I often said *inter nos* at Paris, if he had first been trained thoroughly, as we were, in the studies both of the Realists and the Formalists! For in that case he would not have been incautious and off his guard, but as if from a citadel and watch-tower he would have foreseen the coming assault........ I have often feared his inconsiderate and rash manner of speech. For although his teaching had some scholastic subtlety and possibly at times contained some catholic truth, yet to make such statements as he did to the unlearned crowd and to those who were incapable of understanding them caused serious scandal to simple-minded people and was altogether odious"[22].

Few men of Gansfort's day were so eager as he to acquire knowledge. It is a credit to him that about the year 1455 he had mastered the elements of the Greek and Hebrew tongues, without the aid of any text-books[23], and at a time when no instruction in these languages was given in Northern Europe. Of course, one must not ascribe to him an extensive knowledge of either Greek or Hebrew, but he was able at least to read several books in the Greek and Hebrew original[24]. To him also belongs the credit for having first employed the word Jehovah in lands beyond the Alps[25]. He was now able to read the Bible in the original, except a very small part, and there is no doubt that he had time and again perused all of its books. The Talmud and the Koran were not quite so familiar to him, but he refers in one place to their contents. Among the ancient writers he quotes from Homer, Plato, Aristotle, Theophrastus, Demosthenes, Cicero, Seneca, Plutarch, Procul, Themistius, Virgil, Valerius Maximus, and Aulus Gellius; among Church Fathers from: Augustine, Jerome, Chrysostom, Ambrose, Origen, Gregory of Nazianze, Athanasius; and he also quotes from: Dionysius the Areopagite, Gregory the Great, Bernard, Bonaventura, Thomas Aquinas, Hugo of St. Victor, Gerson, Ailly, Occam, and a few others of lesser note[26].

Having lived with the Brethren of the Common Life from his twelfth till his twenty-ninth year, Gansfort owed much to these followers of Gerard Groote, and, notwithstanding his very striking independence of mind, he remained always true to their teachings. For example, he learned from them how to make a "rapiarium", or collection of excerpts from diverse authors. The present writer, as was said above, had the good fortune to find two copies of such "rapiaria"[27], called "farrago", a term which Gansfort employed in naming his best known work, the "Farrago Rerum Theologicarum"[28]. A considerable portion of his "rapiarium" must have been filled with extracts from Augustine and Bernard, which two writers were loved most by Groote's followers. Hence one may safely conclude that Gansfort was introduced to Augustine and Bernard by the Brethren of the Common Life. Moreover, his repeated visits to the Augustinian monastery of Mount St. Agnes and his intimate friendship with Thomas à Kempis left many indelible impressions upon his mind, both at the time of his early stay at Zwolle and between the years 1475 and 1482.

Gansfort's acquaintance with Alexander Hegius, the celebrated rector at Deventer, was fruitful, as is shown by the following remark found in a letter addressed to Wessel by Hegius: "You ask to be informed about my tutoring. I have followed your counsel. For all learning is pernicious that is attended with loss of honesty"[29]. Considering the fact that the monks at Windesheim had been busily engaged in improving the "Vulgate" and texts of the Church Fathers, one sees why Gansfort studied Greek and Hebrew shortly after his departure from Zwolle: in order that he might interpret correctly the meaning of certain dark passages in the translations. His disapproval of certain phases of scholasticism he probably had acquired also at Zwolle, inasmuch as the rector of the brethren had been very outspoken on this point. As might be expected of a mystic, he often preferred Plato to Aristotle. Says Gansfort: "Now if my opinion, as opposed to Aristotle's concerning the active intellect is true, — an opinion which is confirmed by many passages of Holy Writ, ... we conclude that since it is always best to reduce things to their simplest elements, it is not necessary to superadd some natural power to the intellect[30]. One of his admirers wrote not long after his death: "Since Wessel greatly admired the teaching of Plato as being more divine and nearer to Christianity, and at times inveighed against Aristotle more sharply than the tender ears of scholastic doctors could bear, some called him 'Master of contradictions' "[31].

Gansfort was about the same sort of mystic that Groote and Zerbolt had been, which will chiefly explain his preference for Plato. He writes in one place: "Therefore what Aristotle calls the active intellect I call the light of God's countenance. What he says concerning conscience and reason pleading for the best things, I ascribe, not to any power of the soul or to the natural state of the soul, but rather to the breath of life breathed into man by divine power, and to divine assistance not only for the will but also for intelligence". Consequently Gansfort agreed with Groote's followers that "when it is said that man was made in the image and likeness of God, this applies only to the inward man........ The image of God, the likeness of God, is not perfected unless perfect union is attained, so that the soul holding fast to its prototype, the living God, becomes one in spirit with him"[32].

But Gansfort was a profound thinker, and built his theories upon the fundamental religious principles taught him by the Brethren of the Common Life. One of his new theories concerned purgatory, or the state of spirits after their departure from the body. He says: "The first human beings, Adam and Eve, who were placed in paradise, were far removed from the union of angels.

It was necessary for them to attain it by progressive steps, clinging to and loving God. In order that our first parents might of necessity hasten to this end they had— written in their hearts—the first commandment, on which hangs all the Law and the Prophets. They were as far removed from the image and likeness of God as they were unable to keep this commandment. I do not believe that if [Mary] Magdalene, loving the Lord Jesus as she did, had received a commandment from him not to taste of the tree of the knowledge of good and evil as Eve and Adam did from the Lord God, she could have been enticed to disobey the command by any subtlety of the serpent". Hence, in Gansfort's opinion, Adam and Eve in paradise were in need of improvement, even before the fall; paradise, for them, was purgatory, or a place where their sinful minds were to be purged or purified. It follows, then, that purgatory is paradise, and for this reason Christ said to the murderer on the cross: "To-day thou shalt be with me in paradise"[33].

This peculiar view of Gansfort would seem to be in conflict with the doctrine of the universal fall of mankind caused by the sin of Adam and Eve. Not in Gansfort's opinion, however, and if he had been convicted of a deviation from the doctrine of the Church, he would immediately have relinquished his private opinions. It would have been difficult to prove that he was guilty of renouncing some of Groote's personal beliefs. He did not fight monasticism, believing that many monks were leading useful lives; those who were a disgrace to monasticism had no right to be monks. And although he said a great deal more about the sacrament of communion than Groote, still his ideas differed but little from those of Groote. He seems to contradict himself sometimes, however, for he makes the following statement: "Necessarily it must be admitted that when he says, 'Except ye eat the flesh of the Son of man and drink his blood', we are to understand that it is an inward eating and drinking, that is, of the inner man........ He who thus eats already has the benefit of outward sacramental eating, just as Paul, the first hermit, and very many after him had it even without the outward sacramental eating. To eat therefore is to remember, to esteem, to love". But a few pages further he writes: "This opinion of mine, in which I maintain that in commemorating Christ we not only have him present with us in the body to strengthen us, but that we even corporeally eat of him, is strongly confirmed by the words of Ambrose in his 'De Verbis Dei' "[34]. What Gansfort was trying to say seems to be this: If Christ made a certain statement, it has to be believed. "Except ye eat the flesh of the Son of man and drink of his blood", was Christ's own word, "ye have not life in yourselves". "But", Gansfort reasoned, "to one who remembers his name, the Lord Jesus is truly present, not only in his deity, but also in his flesh and blood and entire humanity"[35]. Only the inner man can eat of Christ's body, which is his spirit, and the spirit cannot eat corporeally. Therefore, though still clinging to the generally accepted view, Gansfort was half spiritualizing the sacrament of communion. His view closely approached that held later by the Calvinists, namely, that of Christ being present only in a spiritual way. And quite naturally some one among his followers, a pupil of the Brethren of the Common Life in the Netherlands, would adopt that view, as will be seen presently.

On the question of predestination and of justification by faith Gansfort was true to the brethren's teachings, but here also apparently contradicted himself, as in his view on the Lord's Supper. He believed "with Plato that

nature is nothing else than the will of God acting with
regularity, while a miracle is an extraordinary operation
of the divine will"[36]. He agreed with Groote that every
man has a part of divinity within his breast, and that this
spark of divinity unites him with God and may induce
God to act on and with it, thus causing man to believe
in Christ, his savior. Groote and Gansfort believed in a
complete system of predestination, which to them appeared to be perfectly in harmony with the Scriptures:
"Are not five sparrows sold for two farthings", quotes
Gansfort from the Gospels, "and not one of them is
forgotten before your Father in heaven"? "Indeed, not
a leaf falls from a tree without his will!"[37], he continues.
"Therefore in the greater works of salvation believers
cooperate with God in his operations. In this life by
believing, fixing our gaze upon him, loving him, we may
truly cooperate with God. And in this God makes us
cooperate, because without him we can do nothing; but
we can do all things in him, that strengthens us. For
through him it is given us both to will and to do. In that
cooperation on our part lies our sin or our piety"[38].

Is there then any difference between the faith without
works referred to by Paul and the works without which
faith is dead, as mentioned by James? Not at all, in
Gansfort's opinion[39]. As for the reward of good works,
Christ taught in the Beatitudes that every act of Christian
service would bring its reward, which promise was repeated by him in the parable of the last judgment, where
even a cup of cold water having been presented in love
to some needy Christian is promised its reward. Not
mere faith, therefore, but love would be required; a love
without which faith could not exist[40].

Gansfort, accordingly, writes: "For when he bade us
be pure, perfect, holy and worthy of God, what else does

he seem to promise to the sinner who turns to him in
faith but that, if he has but the desire to acquire virtue,
all these blessed commands will be completely fulfilled,—
if not in this life of trouble and misery, at any rate,
sometime in the land of the living? Spiritual weakness
is sin, because we are enjoined to be brave in faith and
resist the lion that goeth about, roaring, seeking whom
he may devour. For it is a lifelong war to which God
has appointed all who are in flesh, and not a mere
battle, which is occasional and is only for the hour. All
weakness, however, such as folly, ignorance, lack of wisdom, is sin. These compel one to go defenseless into
battle. Hence it is to some degree clear why we 'ought
always to pray and not faint, to watch and be sober, to
withstand stedfast in our faith'......... Faith is not
the cause of our justification, but its proof.........
'The just shall live by faith'......... Hence in unbelievers, their unbelief separates them from life. But 'he
that believeth on him hath eternal life'. Therefore our
good works nourish and strengthen our faith, but do
not make it alive, yet they strengthen the bond of life,
namely our faith. For only Christ and the Spirit quicken
us, and Christ's sacrifice sanctifies us, and we are more
strongly bound to this life by the stronger bond of our
faith. But nothing strengthens this bond more than love;
for love is strong as death. When indeed faith works
through love, it is firm and the beginning of our confidence is firm......... By the works of the law shall
no flesh be justified before him; even if one fulfil the
chief commandment by his work, he will not because of
this be righteous in God's sight......... Hence it is
not our faith—whether it be in Christ or in God who
delivered Christ over to be a sacrifice—nor is it the
sacrifice of Christ that constitutes our righteousness;

but it is the purpose of God, who accepteth the sacrifice of Christ, and who through Christ accepteth the sacrifice of Christians"[41]. Here then we have the doctrine of predestination in as clear and as logical a form, as closely allied to the teachings of Christ and the Apostles as any Calvinist could have made it. And as for the doctrine of justification by faith only, Gansfort was as much in harmony with Paul as Luther was in 1522, or any Protestant after him.

Gansfort's views on confession of sins and penance are also noteworthy. He admitted that "Peter and all the apostles had the power of binding and loosing on earth". As was customary for all in those days, he called Peter the first pope, that is the first chief shepherd of Christ's followers, and reasoned that, since Christ had placed the keys to heaven in Peter's hands, these keys undoubtedly were the best ever possessed by mortal men. It had been generally asserted in Christendom that those keys had been handed down from Peter to the first bishop of Rome, from him again to the second bishop of Rome; then to the third, fourth, and fifth, and so on. These bishops of Rome, as history teaches us, came in due time to be recognized as the chiefs of all other bishops. Then those bishops of Rome were called popes, and Peter was counted the first of them, as he had died at Rome, and had received the appointment of principal shepherd from Christ.

What was Gansfort's interpretation of these facts? It was in agreement with the views mentioned above, completely in accord with Groote's teachings, and sometimes even phrased almost literally in Groote's own words. He writes: "I do not believe that Peter possessed the right either to loose whomsoever he pleased from the bond of Satan or to bind him therewith. For just as there is but one that baptizes in the Holy Spirit, so there is but one that binds and looses,—binds, I say, and looses with authority. For with what authority can the pope loose, when he does not know whether the person he has loosed has been loosed from the bond of Satan or not"[42]? This is exactly what Groote used to remark. Speaking about the duties of a priest in connection with the forgiveness of sins, Groote had said: "Of what use will it be to introduce an unworthy sinner to the inner circle of true believers, if this group of believers closes their doors upon him"[43]? Gansfort argues in one of his letters: "You, therefore, cautiously take refuge behind a *condition* as though behind an impregnable wall, declaring that only that will stand unshaken which the pope in matters of this sort shall decide, *'if his key is not in error and Christ does not reject it'*. What, I ask, is the meaning of this indispensable condition, 'if his key is not in error'? What is this key of the kingdom of heaven? And what is the error of this key? You are obviously assuming a key that may err and at the same time be the effectual and lawful key of the kingdom of heaven. O dreadful kingdom, if its gates, bars, bolts, and keys are such that through them error, falsehood, and ignorance can creep stealthily within! The key, as Augustine explains, is love diffused through the Holy Spirit in the hearts of the children of the kingdom. The Lord Jesus before his resurrection promised these two keys to Peter when he said: 'I will give unto thee the keys of the kingdom of heaven: and whatsoever thou salt loose on earth shall be loosed in heaven'. In like manner he presented these keys after the resurrection—not to one—but to all unitedly, when he breathed on them, saying: 'Receive ye the Holy Spirit: whose soever sins ye forgive, they are forgiven unto them; whose soever sins ye

retain, they are retained'. These two keys, in Augustine's
opinion, are never rejected by Christ, nor does it ever
happen that they are in error. For he defines the keys
of the kingdom as being: (1) love diffused through the
Holy Spirit in the hearts of the children of God, and
(2) the Holy Spirit. And he says that to loose and to
bind is to receive into fellowship because of the similitude
of love or to exclude from fellowship because of dissimilitude....... When the Lord Jesus promised Peter
the keys of the kingdom of heaven so that whatsoever
he bound on earth would be bound in heaven, he promised
nothing else than the Holy Spirit, and through the Holy
Spirit the diffusion of love in the heart of Peter"[44].

Gansfort proceeds as follows: "Indulgences and excommunications are on the same plane with the authority
or power of the keys. The pope has no more power in
reconciling souls to God than in alienating them from
him. Indeed in excommunicating he has no power except,
through an ecclesiastical court, publicly to exclude a person from the privileges of the Church. Similarly, in
indulgences he can only free a person from the bond of
the canons and from censure......... In absolution
before a court of penance, special considerations must be
given to the fact that it is not the priest that binds the
chain by which the sinner is held. For it is sin alone
that separates the sinner from God. Nevertheless by
this I do not mean that confession ought not to be made
when it can be done to advantage, that is, so that those
who are quickened and see may have a wider vision"[45].
In all this Gansfort is again reiterating the doctrines of
his teachers, adding from time to time his own interpretation. He agrees with Groote that the sacrament of
confession and penance was merely instituted to aid believers in their struggle against sin. Zerbolt had clearly

expressed the views of his friends in his "Treatise on the Common Life", where he insisted that the Brethren of the Common Life had a perfect right to confess their sins to each other. One could also confess his sins to a priest; that was confessing sacramentally, Groote and Zerbolt had explained. But all the priest could do was to state that the person in question had sinned, was determined to sin no more, and that for this reason his sins were forgiven. He could merely preach, exhort, and be a witness that the Holy Spirit, working in his heart, also was operating in the sinner's inner self[46].

Even Groote's views on the authority of the pope and of the clergy are repeated in Gansfort's writings. The pope was bound to have his convictions, Gansfort reasoned, just as all Christians had theirs. If the pope found the belief of some other man to be more in harmony with the gospel than his own, he should concur in the former. "So when Peter did not walk uprightly according to the truth of the gospel, he was obliged to believe Paul, not because it was Paul, but because Paul walked more uprightly according to the truth of the gospel". Laymen and the lower clergy only had to obey their superiors in the Church under certain conditions, that is, when these superiors were more faithfully obeying Christ's commandments than they themselves. The more responsible the position one was occupying in the Church, the better follower of Christ one ought to be. To deny that would be so blasphemous, says Gansfort, "that it is actually more pernicious than any heresy whatever". Peter was allowed by God to err, he continues, in order that people may know "what to do with salt that has lost its savor"[47].

Gansfort, following Groote's example, compared the impious clergy of his time with the Pharisees of old, who used to ask why Christ allowed his disciples to transgress the laws of the elders. Gansfort, in accord with this, protested against the sale of benefices by the higher clergy for personal gain, and for other reasons: "Nor may even the pope give them away or sell them. And when he commits God's interests in remote provinces to mere fortune as it were — as if he had no concern for them — then alas, what evils ensue, — as one cannot but see about him"[48]! No wonder that when Gansfort had been arguing one day with a certain Rabineus at Angers, the latter had to admit: "If these things are so, our entire foundation is false"[49]. And that is exactly what many scholars and clerics must have said about Groote's views. The state of affairs witnessed by Groote and Gansfort was leading to a general catastrophe. A reformation was needed; and the Yssel country was demanding one, but Rome paid no heed; no one among Groote's followers had ever broken openly with Rome.

III

Luther was wondering in 1522 why Gansfort had remained so little known. "Possibly", he mused, "it was because he lived free from blood and war, in which particular alone he differs from me"[50]. There is a great deal of truth in this remark of Luther's. He had himself challenged Rome to a fight out in the open, in full gaze of the public. That challenge had focused the attention of all Christendom upon his activities. Gansfort, on the other hand, although he had often debated with noted scholars at Paris and elsewhere about the leading issues in their time, always avoided the clash of battle. Also, he had been protected by the bishop of Utrecht, who stood ready to shield him from any unpleasant attack, for he needed Gansfort's services as physician. Again,

his extraordinary learning enabled him to silence every
one who dared to argue with him. As appears from one
of his letters, when he dreaded an assault from the papal
inquisitors, he would prepare himself so thoroughly for
their approach that he would "pass through their persecutions as over a shallow ford and with light step"[51].

Gansfort loved the quiet and privacy of his study. He
does speak of the abuses in the Church, and he calls the
sale of indulgences an abuse[52]; but we never hear of his
addressing a crowd of common people to awaken them
to the need of a reformation; we never find him giving
them books to read, translating parts of the Scriptures
for them, or instructing their boys, except for a short
time at Zwolle. Though he was ready to suffer for the
faith, as he said, he never called the clergy together at
Utrecht, as Groote had done, to tell them their shortcomings. He bewailed the sad state of affairs in the
Church, but spoke of it only in private circles. How
different it had been with Groote, Cele, and Zerbolt, and
how different it was to be with Luther, Melanchton, and
Calvin!

That was a significant comparison Luther made between his beliefs and those of the "learned Frisian from
Groningen". How had he become acquainted with the
writings of Wessel Gansfort? It had happened that some
of Gansfort's writings had been given in charge of a
certain Cornelius Henrixs Hoen, a former pupil of the
school conducted by the Brethren of the Common Life
at Utrecht. Hoen had been greatly impressed by Gans-.
fort's treatise on the sacrament of communion, or the
eucharist. He noticed how far Gansfort had gone in
spiritualizing the eating of Christ's flesh, and drew the
conclusion that the word *is*, in "This is my body",
should be interpreted as *signifies*; just as it is interpreted

in "I am the door, the vine, the way". He discussed this point with Hinne Rode, rector of the school of the brethren at Utrecht. Rode fully agreed with him, and it was decided that he (Rode) should show Gansfort's work to Luther, together with a treatise prepared by Hoen on the eucharist. Early in the year 1521 Rode appeared in Wittenberg. Luther read Gansfort's works with whole-hearted approval, but did not approve of Hoen's treatise. Rode also asked the great Reformer to have Gansfort's works printed. What reply he got is not known, but Luther could not have attended to their publication, as he had to leave for Worms and later for the Wartburg. In August, 1522, however, an edition appeared of some of Gansfort's letters with Luther's letter of approbation as a sort of preface. In the same year these same letters were published at Basel, together with Gansfort's "Farrago", and introduced again with Luther's letter, written on the thirtieth of July, 1522, very probably after Luther had familiarized himself with the contents of the "Farrago"[53].

Now the question rises, What did Luther mean in saying that if he had read Wessel sooner, his enemies might have accused him of having copied from Gansfort? The two latest authorities on Gansfort[54] suggest that Luther was feeling lonesome at that time in his singular position, and a little afraid of the terrible consequences of his drastic step, so that he was glad to discover one eminent scholar at least who had entertained views similar to his. These two authorities also bring forward a number of questions on which Gansfort and Luther disagreed.

A problem of this kind should lead scholars to study very carefully the formation of Luther's views from, say, 1495 till 1522. The question is not what Luther believed in 1525 or 1530, but what was in his mind when he sat down to read Gansfort's works. Luther speaks of the fact that Gansfort and he express the same thoughts almost in the same words, referring to the works he had written between 1517 and 1521. The question now shifts to this: Where had he found the ideas for those works? Were they all his own, or did he owe them to former writers? Luther says himself that at Magdeburg he "went to school with the Brethren of the Common Life"[55]. In many places, as at Deventer, Zwolle, and Münster, the Brethren of the Common Life did not conduct schools of their own, for there they found good schools already in existence, or schools that could easily be reformed. As time went on, they became more and more interested in education, and supplied more and more teachers. In Utrecht, Groningen, and Liège they even founded schools of their own; also at Rostock, Cassel, Ghent, and Nijmegen. According to Luther, they did the same at Magdeburg, where he lived in 1497. Through this school he came in contact with the ideas and the ideals of Groote, Radewijns, and Zerbolt, which had helped to mould the mind of Gansfort also.

It is likely that Luther read some works of Gerard Groote, in manuscript form, many of which can still be found in practically all large European libraries, even distant ones like those at Rome, Vienna, and Innsbruck[56]. The National Library at Berlin now has a copy of some of Groote's works which formerly belonged to a monastery at Erfurt[57]. In 1515 or 1516 Luther himself makes the enlightening remark: "Nowhere have I found such a clear explanation of original sin as in the treatise of Gerard Groote, 'Blessed is the man' "[58]. It is probable that Luther became acquainted with some monks who lived in the many monasteries in Saxony reformed by

the missionaries from Windesheim, for these monks were
spreading broadcast the mystical productions of the men
of Deventer and Windesheim. Besides, after 1498 Luther
can hardly have failed to meet some of the boys who had
been taught with him at Magdeburg and to discuss
ideas that they had absorbed in this school from the
Brethren of the Common Life. The brethren were
accustomed to preach to the people on holidays and Sundays. Had Luther heard some of their sermons?
Might he not, like Thomas à Kempis and Wessel Gansfort, have become the personal friend of at least one
member of Groote's new brotherhood? Is it likely that
Luther had not read the "Imitation of Christ" before
1522? He had read Zerbolt's "Spiritual Ascensions"
before 1516[59], also the "Rosary of Spiritual Exercises"
by John Mombaer, a monk of the monastery on Mount
St. Agnes near Zwolle[60]. Hence the "Imitation", the
most popular book of the time, cannot have escaped his
attention.

Now there are certain classes of people who cannot see
any similarity in thought between the Luther of the year
1520 and the ideals of Groote's followers, just as many
others cannot understand how Luther ever dared to
appeal to the Scriptures, he having deviated so far from
their precepts, as they claim. The same is true of many
Catholics and Protestants who keep on arguing about
Wessel Gansfort, neither being able or willing to understand the man's ideas; wherefore an American author
wrote a few years ago: "The contrary conclusions reached
by modern Catholic and Protestant scholars as to the
proper classification of Wessel indicate how much more
influential partisan prejudice is than the much vaunted
'scientific method' claimed by both parties"[61].

We begin now to see what Luther meant when he made

that much disputed statement about Gansfort, that if he had read him sooner, his enemies might accuse him of having copied from Gansfort. In 1522 Luther was fighting the sale of indulgences, which both he and Gansfort called an abuse. He was also discussing the question of the authority of the Scriptures as compared with that of all popes and other members of the hierarchy of the Church, and now he saw that on this question also he agreed with Gansfort. Says Gansfort: "You admonish me in matters of this sort to regard the authority of the pope, not merely as a substitute for reason, but as superior to it! What, I ask, am I to regard as reason in these matters? Is it not the Holy Scriptures? Do you wish to put the authority of the pope above the Holy Scriptures"[62]?

The familiar story of Luther's conversion shows another important point of agreement between him and Gansfort. Luther was struck by the thought, that "The just shall live by faith", but he was by no means the first to appreciate the significance of this text. Groote had already quoted it, not from Paul but from the Old Testament[63], and Gansfort quoted it from Paul. Gansfort had added this observation: "Whoever believes that he shall be justified by his own works does not know what righteousness is. For to be righteous is to give to everyone his due, but who has ever been able to render his full duty to God or indeed to man? A person who imagines that he has, possesses no conception of the magnitude of the blessedness of the future, to which no works of his can ever entitle him"[64]. When Luther read this passage in Gansfort's works, how could he have helped being reminded of the assertions that he had made himself? Any one reading carefully some of the chapters of the "Imitation of Christ" might easily have accepted the

same conclusion. "Without this [Grace]", reads chapter
LV of book III, "what am I but a withered piece of
wood, and an unprofitable branch only meet to be cast
away? Let thy Grace therefore, O Lord, always prevent
and follow me, and make me to be continually given to
good works, through thy Son Jesus Christ". Man cannot
accept Christ in pure faith of his own free will, but is
dependent on Grace, or the Holy Spirit, to give him
power. Then he will of necessity perform good works,
which are the visible fruits of faith.

Critics have said that Luther believed in predestination,
but Gansfort in the doctrine of "free will"[65]. This is
not true. Gansfort, Thomas à Kempis, and Luther all
believed in predestination, holding that man cannot perform one good work on his own initiative. The doctrine
of free will teaches that man can accept or reject Christ
as he pleases, and this was not taught by Groote's followers. They asked, Which human brain can comprehend
the powers of an omnipotent God? If not one hair fall
from one's head without God's will, how can anyone do
anything of his own will, although he seems to have a
free will? The answer to this puzzling question is thus
expressed in the "Imitation of Christ": "My son, beware
thou dispute not of high matters, nor of the secret judgments of God, why this man is so left, and that man
taken into such favor........ These things are beyond
all reach of man's faculties, neither is it in the power of
any reason or disputation to search out the judgments of
God"[66] And Gansfort remarks: "Shrouded in dense
darkness and hidden deep from the sight of all are the
judgments of God which are to be revealed in that clear
day of the last judgment". He adds: " 'He that believeth
on me, the works that I do shall he do also, and greater
works than these shall he do'. But he shall do them in

dependence upon God's action; for apart from him we can do nothing"[67].

One wonders, with Luther, why Gansfort and the movement he represented have remained so little known. The very name "Devotio Moderna" is practically unknown in France, England, and America. In Germany, where the name is sometimes mentioned, one hears much more about Hus and Wycliff, in connection with Luther's experiences from 1517–1521, than about the whole movement originated by Groote. The reason is not far to seek: as Luther himself intimated, none of Groote's followers were "men of blood and war". They were quite as anxious for a reform as he was, but led the clergy and the people to correct with love all the abuses in the Church. They seldom mentioned the sale of indulgences; they took no part in any abuses, but merely pointed to the life of Christ as a model. They cared not for fame or honor, and refused to discuss in public the motes in their neighbors' eyes. Desiring to remain unknown, they were left unknown, but that did not weaken their influence. If we compare their work with that of Hus and Wycliff, for example, we see that the latter attracted considerable attention during their lifetime, because they broke openly with Rome. And yet they had not said anything more revolutionary than Gansfort. Their teachings as such did not give them publicity. In discussing the influence of Wycliff and Hus, one naturally inquires what kind of organized society or group of followers they formed, and whether they founded an institution as Groote did; whether any of their disciples wrote a work like the "Imitation of Christ"; and whether their followers reformed schools or founded new ones, and reformed hundreds of monasteries, as did those of Groote and Cele.

As for the contact of Luther with the "New Devotion", we know that at Eisleben a school was reformed after the model of those at Deventer and Zwolle[68]. That was in Luther's native Saxony. We know also that Luther studied at Erfurt the text-books of Gabriel Biel, who is said to have been acquainted with Gansfort and later became rector of the Brethren of the Common Life at Butzbach near Mainz[69]. Last, but not least, we know that Luther himself spent nearly a year with the brethren at Magdeburg; so wherever he went he was surrounded by the invisible influences of the great movement from the Yssel country. At Erfurt, for example, all the monasteries needing reform had been placed in charge of John Busch, the missionary from Windesheim. Still most modern authors analyze the views Luther entertained between 1517 and 1521 as does one English writer who says: "On May 16, 1518, he can preach that the real communion of the Church is invisible, deducing the consequences that excommunication cannot cut one off from it, and nothing but sin can affect it. This idea of the Invisible Church boasts an honorable pedigree, running back to Hus, Wycliff, and to St. Austine [Augustine] himself"[70]. The fact is, that Luther did not read Hus until 1519!

Many writers do not know that when Luther read Gansfort he came upon the following: "How shall he [the pope] judge the faith of a man whose language he is not acquainted with? Hence we reach the conclusion that the Holy Spirit has kept for himself the task of encouraging, quickening, preserving, and increasing the unity of the Church. He has not left it to a Roman pontiff who often pays no attention to it. We ought to acknowledge one Catholic Church, yet to acknowledge its unity as the unity of the faith and of the Head, the unity of the corner-stone, not the unity of its director, Peter, or his successor. For what could Peter in Italy do for those in India endangered by temptation or persecution, except pray for them, even though he had greater power than his successors?........ Hence it is only the internal unity of its one essential Head that is implied in the words of the Apostles' Creed"[71]. Luther also read this: "There is a double priesthood: the one due to rank, and so sacramental; the other inherent in our rational nature, and so common to all men. The second is sufficient without the first. The first without the second involves guilt. The second imparts grace. Through the second Anthony ranked above many bishops, and a tanner above Anthony"[72].

This doctrine of the universal priesthood of all believers became one of the chief tenets of Luther and the Protestant faith, the other two being justification by faith and the supreme authority of the Scriptures. Luther may well have been surprised to find Gansfort so often voicing the same thoughts as he. If so, we should study Luther's relationship with the Brethren of the Common Life, — a relationship so complex and still so significant that it will have to be discussed more fully in a following chapter[73].

IV

Our acquaintance with Gansfort's life not only throws new light on some of Luther's views, but it may also assist us in understanding Erasmus' character, especially his attitude toward Luther from 1517–1522. Erasmus spent twelve years with the brethren, that is, nine years at Deventer, and three at 's-Hertogenbosch[74]. Hence the background for the mental life of Erasmus is not to be sought in the monastery of Adwert, as some writers think[75], but among the Brethren of the Common Life at Deventer and Zwolle. Adwert served merely as a sort of meeting-ground for the chief leaders of humanism in the Netherlands, and only for a short period. It did not send half a dozen boys in all to the universities[76], and none of its monks produced any writings worth noting. Gansfort even chided the monks of Adwert for reading books filled with falsehoods, whereupon they turned to more useful reading matter[77]. If it had not been for the congenial views of Abbot Henry van Rees, a great humanist, he would undoubtedly have visited the monastery very seldom. Adwert did not produce either great mystics or great humanists. At Zwolle and Deventer, on the other hand, were educated Rudolph von Langen, Alexander Hegius, Louis Dringenberg, Erasmus, Mutian Rufus, Herman von dem Busche, Herman Torrentinus, John Oostendorp, Gerard Listrius, and a host of other memorable scholars. During the closing years of the fifteenth century Deventer was the best and most famous town in Northern Europe for the pursuit of elementary and secondary education. In general the Brethren of the Common Life were, either directly or indirectly, the teachers of practically all the best scholars in German lands. How much France owed to them will be shown in the next chapter. They, more than any other discoverable agency, gave to the rise of the new learning North of the Alps its religious coloring.

Erasmus was a child of the "New Devotion", and could no more shake the ideals of Groote and Gansfort from his mind than he could change the color of his skin. Also there were times when he was not sorry that he had those ideas, although he probably never quite appreciated the source from which he had received them[78]. Like

Groote, he attacked energetically the bad monks of his time, and fought the abuses in the Church. He eagerly studied the Scriptures and the Fathers in the original texts, and corrected them. It is generally supposed that he received his ideals from Italy, but it is far more likely that he received it from Groote's followers. The monks at Windesheim had corrected the texts of the Bible and of the Fathers, and Gansfort had studied Greek and Hebrew for the purpose of getting a better understanding of them. Besides, the constitutions of the brethren-houses insisted on pure texts, "lest one's conscience might be hurt by some improper version"[79]. It was Gansfort who urged Agricola to study Hebrew, and it was he who persuaded this wandering Bohemian to devote a considerable share of his leisure time to the study of the Scriptures[80]. Now, Erasmus distinguished himself by his work on the Church Fathers. He was the first to find the pure humanity and the sublime divinity of the Ancients in Christianity. The love-ethics of the Gospel, especially of the Sermon on the Mount, loosed from ascetic idealism and from that sort of piety which flees the world, was to Erasmus the purest expression of the humanity expressed in the classics[81]. While many others were concentrating their whole attention on the classics of pagan Greece and Rome, Erasmus extended the services of humanism to a more liberal study of the Bible and the Fathers.

One English scholar says it was Colet who urged Erasmus in 1499 "to turn his attention to theology, and to help him in breaking through the web of dialectical sophistry that had been woven round it"[82]. Many other writers have shared this view, which they could not have done had they been acquainted with the history of the "New Devotion". When a boy, Erasmus loved Seneca

better than Cicero, because the Brethren of the Common
Life, his teachers at Deventer, had learned from Groote
to value practical advice on moral questions above mere
rhetoric[83]. It was the brethren, not Colet, who led him
to study Paul and Augustine, the authors whom they had
studied long before Colet appeared in the field. They
also aroused in him an interest in Jerome, to whom their
house at Deventer was dedicated, and it might be noted
here that in their original constitution the house was
dedicated to Paul, something which has thus far escaped
the attention of modern scholars. The brethren taught
him to regard the chief element in Christianity as faith
working through love, a return to the faith taught by
Christ himself. That Erasmus knew Gansfort is plain
from his own remark: "Doctor Wessel has much in
common with Luther, but how much more modestly and
like Christ did he propagate his ideas than most of those
[Lutherans] at Strasbourg"[84]. Erasmus' own thinking
was colored with the opinions of Wessel Gansfort: he
spiritualized the meaning of purgatory in imitation of
Gansfort[85], and he also spiritualized the Eucharist. It
was from him that Zwingli derived new views on
Christ's spiritual presence in the Eucharist, as Zwingli
told Melanchton afterwards[86].

Erasmus was likewise active in the monastic reforms
introduced into France by the Windesheim Congregation.
In 1497, or two years before he met Colet, he was intimately acquainted in Paris with John Mombaer, who
had come to France to introduce monastic reform among
the Augustinian monks in and near Paris[87]. Mombaer
had spent several years under the same roof with Thomas
à Kempis at Mount St. Agnes, and also wrote important
religious books. One of these is the "Rosary of Spiritual
Exercises", about which more will be said in the next

chapter. Erasmus undoubtedly read that mystical production. But Mombaer wrote another work, called
"Venatorium Sanctorum Ordinis Canonici", in which he
delineates the history and excellence of the Augustinian
order. A copy of this highly interesting work is still
extant, in Ms. no. 14662 of the "Bibliothèque Nationale"
at Paris. In this Mombaer tries to prove that the order
of the Canons Regular was instituted by the Apostles,
reformed by Pope Urban, reinstated by Augustine, and
protected by Gregory the Great[88]; and he gives a brief
account of the progress of the order from the seventh
till the fifteenth century[89]. "Then", he continues, "that
glorious Congregation of Windesheim was founded. It
began as a small flock, but soon gathered scores of
monasteries within its fold. As a result of this great
movement Pope Eugene IV reformed the monasteries in
Saxony through Nicholas Cusa, and Pope Martin V did
the same in Italy"[90].

There is one other fact about Erasmus' life that deserves our attention here. It is his very unusual spirit
of toleration and his constant efforts to preserve peace.
Although he instinctively felt that Luther was the direct
cause of his own downfall, he nevertheless sought to
befriend the German Reformer as long as he could. This
attitude seems natural in a follower of Gansfort. But
there was a limit beyond which the Brethren of the Common Life would not go. Groote silenced three different
theologians whom he considered heretics. Gansfort and
Erasmus would have judged them heretics also, for they
taught the doctrines of the Free Spirits, who attempted
to overthrow all moral laws and regulations. If they
had been allowed to spread in the Yssel country, they
would have increased vice a thousand fold. Groote was
so anxious to preserve the unity of the Church that he

had no rest till he had silenced those three men. Thereafter we hear no more of that sort of preachers endeavor-
ing to lead Groote's disciples astray. The "New Devotion" gained hundreds of new adherents each year, and
now the brethren seldom met with opposition from men
like the "Free Spirits". On the other hand, with the
rise of this new brotherhood, opposition arose in very
different quarters. The mendicants, particularly the
Dominicans, were jealous of the amazing growth of the
new institution. Here was a brotherhood very much like
a monastic order, but that exacted no vows. Its members
taught young and old alike, preached in the language of
the people, reformed schools directly and indirectly, and
even translated parts of the Bible into the vernacular.
Groote himself had found it necessary to defend them at
Deventer; Brinckerinck had done the same, and Zerbolt.
So did Gerson and Ailly at the Council of Constance.
Then there had been the constant menace of encroaching
monasticism. One day the rector of the house at Deventer even had to reprove the prior of Windesheim for
trying to tear one more house away from his fold. And
in various treatises the Brethren of the Common Life
explained their right to exist. One of these was the
"Treatise on the Common Life", by Gerard Zerbolt;
another was a treatise, though in a much more con-
densed form, by Gabriel Biel, rector of the house at
Butzbach near Mainz[91]. The brethren were always eager
to help reform monasteries, to keep all things as they
were, provided the abuses were done away with. Because
they had often been persecuted themselves, though in a
mild form, they had begun to look with sorrow on the
spirit of intolerance which was soon to overwhelm all
Christendom.

How then would one expect Gansfort and Erasmus

to regard this new wave of intolerance? Gansfort had
often been suspected of heresy, as he himself states; so
had Erasmus. Both resented and ridiculed the attacks
on their way of preaching reform. Gansfort had successfully maintained himself always; so would Erasmus,
though the Church supported him unwillingly. Gansfort
had a friend named John of Wesel, — a man strongly
influenced by Groote's teachings, who had been advocat-
ing the need of rèform in a very haphazard way, as one
gathers from the letter previously quoted[92]. Though he
had probably gone no farther than Gansfort, he was
prosecuted, and condemned to death. Erasmus had a
friend, named Martin Luther, a former pupil of the
Brethren of the Common Life, who had uttered opinions
much akin to those entertained by himself. Luther had
spoken a little rashly; he had cared more about telling
the truth than about the way he told it and about
the results of telling it, and naturally he was excommunicated.

Gansfort and Erasmus showed the same toleration
in these cases. Says Gansfort: "From my most faithful friends I learn that he has been convicted to
die by fire. I am not so much surprised at his being
condemned to the fire; but I think the methods pursued
by his judges ought to be laughed to scorn. . . . .
Besides, from the same friends I learn that as soon as
the inquisitor has disposed of him, he will descend with
an investigation upon me. And in this case, although I
do not fear the proceedings in the least, still I should
have to endure disquietude, suspicion, expense, trouble,
and — more than that — even calumny; especially from
the Abbot of the Old Mount and from some Doctors of
Cologne, whose hatred or rather whose envy you may
readily guess from your own misfortunes, — I speak

to one who has had experience with them.......... I am
looking for as speedy a reply as possible from you with
an account of what happened to you in a similar affair
and what you would advise me to do, for fear that some
sudden attack may confound me in my defenselessness
and ignorance of court trials. I do not fear anything
that I may have to undergo for the purity of the faith,
if only there be no calumny".

Erasmus wrote in 1518 that Luther ought to bring no
radical changes, that he should beware of sowing sedition,
and that moderation was needed, and much of it. On
the nineteenth of October, 1519, Erasmus still continued
in the same strain, commenting that Luther should not
"be suppressed, but rather brought to a right frame of
mind". Was not Luther right, he asked, in condemning
the sale of indulgences, and why should he not call
attention to the abuses at Rome? He admitted that Luther
had spoken rashly, and that rashness was a mistake, but
judged Luther right in protesting that the works of
Thomas Aquinas were wrongly placed above the Gospel.
"In former days", writes he, "a heretic was listened to
with respect; he was acquitted if he gave satisfaction,
he was convicted if he persisted. The severest punishment was not to be admitted to the communion of the
Catholic Church. Now the charge of heresy is quite
another thing, and yet on any frivolous pretext whatever
they have this charge ready on their lips, 'It is heresy'.
Formerly that man was considered a heretic who dis-
sented from Evangelical teaching and from the article
of faith, or from those which had equal authority with
them........ Whatever they do not like, whatever they
do not understand is heresy; to know Greek is heresy;
to do other than they is heresy"[93].

This letter reminds us of one by Gansfort in answer

to Dr. Jacob Hoeck, who had accused him of heresy: "To my mind the famous St. Jerome was as holy in argument and example as he was orthodox and catholic in his views. Yet, when he fell into a great and dangerous error that undermined the authority of all Canonical Scripture and was therefore worse than the error of Arius or Sabellius, he did not yield to the admonition of Augustine, but wrote a reply in defense of his opinion and in opposition to Augustine. Perhaps you will say it does not follow that there is any truce to be granted to-day. I do not dispute that. Nevertheless the precedent that was established is sufficient for my position. If indeed his scrupulous anxiety in searching into the truth, since he was sincere, defended St. Jerome from heresy, I do not believe that anyone is a heretic who with solicitude seeks the truth, and on finding it accepts it with equal promptness"[94]. By this Gansfort meant to say that anybody had a right to keep his own opinions so long as no one could prove them to be wrong to him; but as soon as he was convinced that they were false or incorrect, he would be obliged to relinquish them. No one was a heretic in Gansfort's opinion who, like Jerome in that one case, could not understand his opponent to be right and himself to be wrong. Jerome was wrong to be sure, and saw his mistake afterwards. But he was no heretic, for who would dare to call Jerome a heretic? Hence there were not quite so many heretics as most people supposed.

On April 14, 1519, Erasmus wrote of Luther: "No one has shown his error or refuted him, and yet they call him a heretic". Erasmus wanted him to be tried by competent and impartial judges. "Luther has admirable insight into the Gospel"[95], he asserted. He had asked for a discussion and only received insult; his thoughts were distorted, said Erasmus, and his writings falsified. On March 25, 1520, Erasmus wrote: "The Roman Church I know, which I think does not differ from the Catholic. Death will not part me from it unless the Church openly departs from Christ. I always abhor sedition, and I would that Luther and the Germans abhorred it equally....... I feared always that revolution would be the end, and I would have done more had I not been afraid that I might be found fighting against the Spirit of Christ"[96]. But Erasmus did not forsake the ideals of toleration. If he had, he would have received a bishopric. What did he say when he was asked to take a definite stand in November, 1520? "Luther is so great that I shall not write against him. He is so great that I do not understand him: his value is such that I derive more instruction from a single small page of his than from the whole of St. Thomas"[97]. He was exaggerating of course, but the attitude expressed in his reply is magnanimous. It is not the word of a coward, but it reveals a man who passionately abhorred the spirit of intolerance which was now breaking loose in its utmost fury. No wonder that Erasmus was abused and ridiculed by friend and foe alike. Is he understood even to-day?

CHAPTER VII

THE CHRISTIAN RENAISSANCE IN FRANCE

The character and history of the Christian Renaissance in France differs in many respects from that of the same movement in Germany. In Germany, both the Brethren of the Common Life and the Windesheim Congregation had a house, by 1400, that was destined in turn to found or reform several others. In France not a single brethren-house was ever erected, and the first missionary from the Windesheim Congregation arrived in 1496. In Germany one meets soon after 1400 with a large number of important institutions, whereas in France Paris became and remained the one chief centre of the Christian Renaissance. Two men only were to determine the character of this great movement in France: John Standonck and John Mombaer, or Mauburn, both natives of Brabant, in the present kingdom of Belgium. They arrived very late upon the stage of "prereform", that is, the reforms attempted before the Reformation. But in spite of their late arrival they were to play a larger part in the history of the Christian church in France than any apostle of the Christian Renaissance had ever played in Germany.

I

John Standonck was born at Mechlin about the year 1450. After attending school for a few years in his native town, he went to Gouda, in Holland, where the Brethren of the Common Life had founded a boarding school within their own building. Here the boy was given a scholarship. All his physical and mental needs were provided for by the pious brethren[1]. Standonck belonged to the "scolares pauperes", or poor school boys, who were educated entirely at the expense of the new brotherhood. Often the brethren received donations from friends to defray part of the expenses of their dormitories or boarding schools, as happened at Deventer[2]. This may also have been the case at Gouda. The sources inform us, however, that Gouda was but a comparatively small town, and that the brothers had very limited means of subsistence. Not until the year 1465 would the houses at Deventer and Zwolle recognize the one at Gouda officially as a member of the brotherhood[3]. The institution on the "Agnietenberg", or Mount St. Agnes, near Zwolle, had been a complete failure, for the brethren had found so few people there, and particularly few school boys[4]. Their business was to educate school boys in the "fear and love of the Lord", and to preach to the people. This they could not do in small towns. But the brothers at Gouda struggled along somehow, ignoring as much as possible their shabby clothes and empty stomachs. Some of the men were no doubt priding themselves on their poverty — not so much because it was any longer the habit among Groote's disciples to choose voluntary poverty and regard it a great blessing, for it simply was not[5], but they had to make the best of it.

At Gouda Standonck spent all his time with the Brethren of the Common Life. It would have been better for him perhaps could he have lived in one of the dormitories at Zwolle, as Gansfort did, for the brethren at Zwolle had much more money than their friends at Gouda. He undoubtedly had to suffer with the elder inmates of the house, and probably was taught to look upon poverty as a blessing in disguise. Soon he was taught to copy religious writings — the works of Groote and Zerbolt perhaps, and certainly those of Augustine and Bernard. He became one of the best students at Gouda, and the seeds of the "New Devotion" found a very fertile soil in his young heart[6]. They were destined to produce an abundant harvest at Paris.

On the 27th of November, 1469, Standonck matriculated at Louvain[7], and not long thereafter we find him at Paris. He had made his way to the Augustinian monastery of Ste. Geneviève, where he worked for his board. About the year 1475 he received a master's degree, and thereupon repaired to the ruined college of Montaigu to study theology. On May 30, 1483, the direction of the old college was entrusted to his care, while in 1485 Standonck occupied the office of rector of the university for a period of three months[8]. He was too faithful a student of the Brethren of the Common Life, as Renaudet puts it, to devote much of his time to the pursuit of poetry or scholastic disputes. Instead of writing learned commentaries on Peter Lombard or Aristotle, he spent his leisure time in preaching[9]. At Gouda the Brethren of the Common Life had been accustomed to preach to the people in their own language. Standonck must often have attended their addresses or sermons. Those poor wandering sheep ought to be taught something, the brethren had felt. Many a time they must have discussed in Standonck's presence the need of reform. One of the means they employed was the education of school boys, fashioned after Groote's model at Zwolle; the other, short addresses to the people on Sundays and holidays[10]. Standonck had caught something of Groote's message, for although Flemish was his mother tongue, he became one of the most famous preachers at Paris, as famous as

Oliver Maillard and John Raulin. The themes he dwelt
on most were the abuses in the Church and the need of
fighting sin for all the people, high and low, rich and
poor. He no doubt consciously imitated the Brethren of
the Common Life at Gouda[11].

But Standonck was in close contact with the Sorbonne,
the bulwark of conservative theology. For some time he
acted as librarian of the Sorbonne[12]. And what was of
still greater significance, he became very intimately
acquainted with Francis de Paule, one of the most influential mendicant friars in France, and founder of a
new monastic order. This man made a profound impression upon Standonck. His extraordinary humility,
love of poverty, and mortification of the flesh all
enhanced the magnetism of his personality[13]. Luther met
the same sort of a person at Magdeburg in 1497: also a
friar, whose wasted features haunted him for years[14].

"As a disciple of the Dutch mystics", writes Renaudet,
"of the theologians of the Sorbonne, and of Francis de
Paule, he fought until the day of his death for the reform
of the Church"[15]. Standonck conceived the idea of reforming the whole body of the clergy. In 1493 the
occasion was given him to present his plans, for in that
year Charles VIII, king of France, convoked an assembly
of prelates and doctors at Tours, where Standonck was
asked to read his report of proposed reform. He advised
that the secular clergy pay more attention to their duties
as pastors, that canons should come oftener to church,
that vicars ought to read the masses exactly as prescribed,
and curates and vicars who refused to administer the
sacraments except on payment of a fee should be severely
reprimanded. Above all, he advised that those who had
been appointed pastors of congregations be obliged to
reside among their people, instead of being allowed to

live at Paris. If altogether unable to absent themselves from Paris, they should provide assistants to take charge of the neglected flocks. Those who offered their prebends to the highest bidders should be deprived of these positions, or subjected to some other form of punishment. Standonck said little about the monks, or regular clergy, but plainly intimated that they should adhere strictly to monastic vows. No one should be allowed to ascend the pulpit whose ignorance or scandalous behavior might lead the people astray. Bishops and other officials were urged to tolerate no longer the sale of indulgences or the granting of absolutions whereby the people could be exploited. The synods of the dioceses would have to assemble every six months, the provincial councils once a year; the superiors of reformed monasteries should occupy a leading position among the attendants, and "diligent inquisition should be made regarding the excesses, crimes, abuses and defaults of the people of the church" (clergy). At intervals the bishops and archdeacons should inspect the activities of the priests.

The clergy were to meet all their obligations, to perform all their social functions. Standonck deplored the way in which "the clergy squandered the property of the Church in laying out grand estates, buying dogs and birds against God and reason". He wanted supervisors of the poor to be appointed; these men should then be ordered to support the needy with the revenues of the abbeys and cathedral chapters, for it was for the benefit of the poor that the clergy had received their material possessions. Hospitals should henceforth be left in charge of persons who did not nurse the sick for temporal gain. Delegates should be appointed by the provincial councils for the administration of the hospitals. At the same time the Church should not neglect its duties of correction and

justice. Many poor people were now being robbed by
certain clerics; innocent folk had been excommunicated;
the funds derived from the sacrament of penance were
divided among the bishops and the archdeacons; and,
certain of being able to purchase back again whatever
sort of a position they might occasionally lose, the
culpable rich, the blasphemers, usurers, and immoral
priests knew no scruples. All these scoundrels ought to
be subjected to corporal and public punishment!

But the restoration of the Church could never be accomplished unless prospective clerics were better educated.
No position of trust should be granted to "men without
virtue, without education, vicious, infamous, unknown,
or with titles unjustly conferred". The Benedictine prelates and the superior of the college of Marmoutier also
presented their projects of reform, but confined themselves largely to the monastic orders; Standonck proposed
a scheme which, if realized, might for a generation at
least have restored the Church in France. But before all
things it was absolutely necessary that the king prohibit
the pope from giving benefices to his favorites, and that
he cease selling these benefices to the highest bidder.
Standonck insisted that the Pragmatic Sanction should
be strictly applied. At Paris he gained a large circle of
friends and admirers, such as John Quentin, John Emery,
John Saulay, Nicholas de Hacqueville, Oliver Maillard,
John Clerée, Gilbert Fournier, Pierre Bourgeois, and
John Raulin[16].

It should be observed that Standonck's program was
that of Gerard Groote. Groote had asserted that the
coming reform would rest with the rising generation.
For that very reason he and John Cele, rector of the
school at Zwolle, became such intimate friends. Groote
had often invited poor boys to his house to copy books

for money. To these boys he gave religious instruction, and urged his followers to do the same. Gradually the school of Zwolle had attracted hundreds upon hundreds of boys; gradually also the brethren-houses had multiplied in the Low Countries and Germany. Groote also had wanted more than learning. He had spoken at length about those greedy Pharisees of his time, who put up everything for sale, robbed the poor, led immoral lives in spite of their long prayers, and left their flocks to take care of themselves. How sacred a task a priest had to perform, he had often said. No one could lead others before he had first overcome his own lower self. And years of study were needed ere one could ever hope to direct other souls with a chance of success. This preliminary study included mental as well as spiritual training. Bishops should beware of appointing ignorant, vicious, or indolent pastors.

Standonck was not influenced by Groote alone; many of the sentences he uttered had been copied from the rules of the council of Sens[17], and he mentioned some abuses which had been practically unknown in Groote's time, among them, the sale of indulgences. But Standonck's burning zeal for reform, and the kind of reform he was aiming at remind us very forcibly of Groote and the Brethren of the Common Life. And just as Groote had focused the attention of all the clergy in the Netherlands on his program for reform, when addressing their leaders at Utrecht, so Standonck now appealed to the whole body of the clergy in France.

John Standonck had been one of those poor boys who had been educated at the expense of Groote's new brotherhood. How many years he had lived with the brethren at Gouda we do not know; but no fewer than eight years, and perhaps as many as ten or twelve. He remained there long enough at any rate to be saturated with the ideas of the Christian Renaissance. Not only did he preach at Paris, and present his program for reform at Tours, but he founded a dormitory for poor students very much like those erected by the brethren at Deventer and Zwolle. In this dormitory Erasmus was to have a room some day, and also Calvin. Here also the master-pieces of Christian mysticism would be read and copied in untold numbers, among them the "Imitation", the "Spiritual Ascensions", and the "Rosary of Spiritual Exercises".

On the 17th of March, 1490, John Standonck bought a small house on the Rue des Sept-Voies, between the Rue Saint-Symphorien and the Rue de Reims, adjoining the garden of the Chateau-Festu, which belonged to the ruined college of Montaigu. Here he invited a small number of poor students to live with him, who attended the courses at Montaigu, but resided at Standonck's house, forming a sort of semi-monastic fraternity, in imitation of the "scolares pauperes", living in the dor-mitories of the Brethren of the Common Life. They confessed their sins to each other and often assembled to listen to addresses by their superior on the "rooting out of vices and the acquisition of virtues". Indolent inmates were punished[18]. Soon the odor of their piety spread abroad[19]. From Montaigu and several other colleges of the university students came asking for admission. In 1493 more than eighty of them were lodging with Standonck[20].

The house had become too small. Standonck was now obliged to look for more spacious quarters. He tried in vain to buy the building owned by the abbots of Vézelay, which was situated behind the college of Montaigu. But fortunately his acquaintance with some of the most in-

fluential men in the kingdom was to result in providing
him with a still better home. Shortly before the year
1492 he met Louis Malet de Graville, Admiral of France,
a man of large fortune as well as high office. He was
favorably impressed with Standonck's plans, and resolved
to repair the dilapidated buildings which constituted the
ancient college of Montaigu. The admiral commenced
by having a number of buildings on the corner torn
down, facing the monastery of Ste. Geneviève. After
this part of the program had been completed a new chapel
was built, and a new dormitory for poor students. In
the meantime another great personage had come forward
with further plans and additional means: John de Pont-
ville, of Rochechouart. Eighty-four men ought to inhabit
the place, it was decided, "representing the twelve
Apostles, the seventy-two select disciples of Jesus Christ",
together with two chaplains, who were to represent the
Savior and the blessed Virgin, making a total of eighty-
six. Early in the year 1495 the first eighty-six occupants
entered their new home.

The dormitory consisted of four stories. On the first
floor were the auditorium, two small rooms for the
chaplains, and the library, containing a very large number
of mystical writings. On the second floor the twelve
theologians were accommodated, on the third the seventy-
two students of arts. But this building was unfit for
those who needed airy and spacious quarters, consequently Standonck asked for permission to use the old Chateau-
Festu with its garden, adjoining the dormitory, which he
and his friends had at first occupied. His request was
granted in September, 1496. Moreover, Admiral de
Graville had the principal dormitory reconstructed, facing
the Rue des Sept-Voies. The whole group of buildings
was henceforth referred to as the college of Montaigu,

although the houses served quite a different purpose from
those which formerly had constituted the college of
Montaigu. Montaigu had been a sort of academy, a
boarding school for rather well-to-do students; Standonck added a dormitory for poor students. Of the first
he had been the principal ever since 1483; of the second
he was the founder[21]. Not satisfied with his two buildings and the garden at Paris, he secured in addition large
tracts of land in the Landes, some woods at Arcy, and
a farm at Wissous. These did not exactly belong to him,
but he drew rent from them, and the poor students could
work on the farm at Wissous in summer. In 1499
Standonck prepared a preliminary constitution for his
new dormitory[22], but soon he was interrupted in his
work, for Louis XII, the new king of France, expelled
him from the country.

What was the cause of the king's action? On the 24th
of June, 1497, Robert Briçonnet, archbishop of Reims,
and chancellor of France, had died. His brother William,
bishop of St. Malo, abbot of Grandmont and cardinal,
applied for the vacant position. He was recommended
by the king, supported by his son, the bishop of Lodève,
and by several other persons of note in the country. On
the cathedral chapter and the populace of Reims he now
exerted a scandalous pressure, bribing right and left, and
sparing neither menaces nor promises. Consequently he
received 67 votes out of 68. One canon, however, named
Biguet, did not let himself be coaxed or bribed. He came
to Paris, and was cordially received by the reformers. It
was agreed that Standonck should become a candidate,
in protest against the evil of plural benefices, for the
brother of the deceased archbishop ought to be content
with his bishopric, not to mention his position as abbot

and cardinal. All the formalities of the election were strictly observed: canon Biguet voted for Standonck.

Standonck's friends urged him to plead his cause before the Court. Never before had such a hopeless cause been tried, but John Raulin, the celebrated preacher, scorned all human prudence. "I feel", he wrote to Standonck, "that you have no confidence in the support of the king......... Take courage and assemble about you all those who mournfully bewail the troubles of the Church......... You are uneasy now and hesitate. I want you to hesitate no longer". This letter became known to outsiders. The abbot of Cluny demanded that he give an account of his action, whereupon he replied with his customary biblical eloquence: "I do not deny that I have encouraged Standonck......... Could I regard with dry eyes the desolation of my mother, the Church? How can I help weeping over the misery of the daughter of my people? You yourself, my father, I know you watch her with an anxious heart......... The bishop of Saint Malo should not be ignorant that a wise man prefers salutary bitterness to deadly sweetness......... The Savior did not give me light to be hidden under a bushel, but to declare war against those who are harming the Church of my Savior Jesus, to fight against the powers and authorities of darkness". Briçonnet proposed to let Standonck reform the abbey of Grandmont, and another one, if he would withdraw his candidature; but his friends persuaded him to persevere.

When the debates began at the end of July, 1498, it immediately became apparent that on the side of the reformers there was nothing to be hoped for. The king did not take the case seriously. Poulain, lawyer for the reformers, endeavored to prove that an election should be declared null and void when it was conducted under the pressure of secular powers in favour of an unlettered candidate, or carried on by men bribed with benefices. It was all in vain. Standonck was ordered to withdraw his application, and sentenced to pay a fine of two thousand pounds.

To complicate matters for Standonck, the king had won a divorce suit against his wife Jeanne of France by means of judges of the Church carefully selected by Pope Alexander VI, and was now about to marry Anna of Brittany. Standonck publicly condemned the act of the king. The Gospel of Mark, he asserted, forbade anyone to send away his wife except on the charge of adultery. Thomas Warnet, a pupil of Standonck, and one of his best friends among the missionaries from the Low Countries, thundered forth from the pulpit that text of John the Baptist addressed to Herod: "It is not lawful for thee to have her". To put it mildly, the king was considerably irritated; and the end of the whole matter was that Standonck was exiled from France. He entrusted the charge of Montaigu to Noël Béda, his pupil[23].

Standonck naturally turned his steps to his native country. First he stopped at Cambray, where he was the guest of Henry of Bergen, who had induced Erasmus to enter the college of Montaigu. Standonck and Henry of Bergen founded a college at Cambray, and agreed that it should follow the rules of Montaigu. From Cambray Standonck traveled to Valenciennes, where he founded a similar institution; next he stopped at Mechlin and Louvain, and founded two more colleges. In the latter place he left his work in charge of Adrian Floriszoon, the future Pope Adrian VI, who also had received a goodly share of his elementary and secondary education from the Brethren of the Common Life, and who acquitted himself so well of his task at Louvain that his college became the most flourishing of the four institutions. It even survived the college of Montaigu, for it existed till 1798[24].

In the meantime the friends of Standonck at Paris succeeded in getting the decree of exile repealed. Foremost among them were De Graville, the French admiral, Louis d'Amboise, bishop of Albi, and John Clerée, vicar general of the Congregation of the Holland Dominicans, a very powerful monastic organization founded in Holland in 1464. Standonck maintained very intimate relations with the Dominicans of the Holland Congregation, for they were burning with the zeal of reform and were inducing a large number of monasteries in the Low Countries and France to adopt their rules[25]. John Clerée, the vicar general of the Holland Dominicans, was confessor of Louis XII. Perhaps his influence may have swung the balance in favor of Standonck, who at once hurried back to Paris, arriving in July, 1500[26].

Immediately after his arrival at Paris, Standonck took the necessary steps for obtaining official recognition of the five new colleges[27]. He now drew up the final revision of the constitution of Montaigu, which was officially approved on the 30th of January, 1503. There were at this time more than 200 students living in the dormitory of Montaigu. The king was very much pleased with Standonck's work and in February, 1503, he granted the college 200 pounds a year. Though scarcely ten years old, the "congregation" had sent out three hundred men to reform monasteries, of whom the Dominicans and Franciscans had received the larger number. The Congregation of Montaigu therefore was practically nothing else than a preparatory school for the reformed monastic orders[28].

To what degree Montaigu resembled the institutions

of the Brethren of the Common Life may be learned from a comparison of their respective constitutions and other regulations. "The constitution of the Congregation of Montaigu was not made in a day", Godet rightly remarks. "It is probable", he continues, "that the first disciples, grouped about Standonck in his house on the Rue des Sept-Voies, received from him some oral precepts, borrowed directly by him from the methods of his first teachers, the Brethren of the Common Life. One might state, without making a great error, that the institution of Standonck at Paris was an offshoot of those of the brethren". Standonck remained continually in the closest touch with them; frequently he was their guest, and they eagerly supported his institutions in the Low Countries. When Noël Béda, who had become Standonck's successor shortly after his death in 1504, cut the ties which united the colleges in the Low Countries with the mother institution, the Brethren of the Common Life in Ghent took charge of the one at Cambray; throughout the whole of the sixteenth century they supported the college at Mechlin[29].

The rules of Montaigu owe much to those in use at Deventer and Zwolle, and therefore in use at Gouda[30]. The students residing in Standonck's dormitory were instructed to make a collection of excerpts, called "rapiarium". They had to confess their sins to each other, and were enjoined to correct each other's mistakes, shortcomings, and wrongdoings. The constitution also makes provision for the daily examination of one's conscience, and the performance of humble tasks for each member in turn. At Montaigu, as at Deventer, the novices and laymen wore grey clothes, the priests black ones[31]. But the dormitories of the Brethren of the Common Life were not preparatory schools for the mendicant orders, as one writer wrongly asserts[32]. It is also very doubtful whether the brethren at Deventer and Zwolle made much use of corporal punishments, or the rectors in the schools at Zwolle and later at Deventer, like Cele and Hegius. The Brethren of the Common Life were accustomed to be very harsh to themselves and use their neighbors gently. They also were much less ascetic than Standonck and his pupils. Standonck had in the first place been educated in a rather obscure and extremely poor brethren-house. If he really left Gouda directly for Louvain, as Godet thinks, he must have lived with the poor brethren at Gouda for at least ten years, for he was born shortly before the year 1450. In France he was influenced by the asceticism of Francis de Paule. His great liking for the friars should not be overlooked in this connection. He selected all the rigor and austerity of the rules followed by Groote's disciples, but added to these many ingredients of a severer type of mortification. He greatly increased the number of fasts, and made no provision for repose. In the middle of the night he and his followers rose to pray. Again, the spirit of the former college of Montaigu still pervaded the atmosphere, though the old buildings were gone. And there was the chapter of Notre-Dame with its exigences, and the various donators. All these elements combined to augment Standonck's asceticism, and were clearly reflected in his new constitution[33].

II

Six years after John Standonck had grouped his first followers about him in the house adjoining the forsaken college of Montaigu, the call came through him for some missionaries of the Windesheim Congregation. James d'Aubusson, abbot of Chateau-Landon, in the diocese of Sens, in 1496 conceived the project of re-establishing discipline in his monastery. He was advised to see Standonck, who wrote for him to the prior superior at Windesheim. Never before had the new congregation sent out reformers to districts where only French was spoken, but Tillman Stuermans, the prior of Windesheim, promised to send two monks, because he knew Standonck's zeal for reform. The two brethren were to visit Chateau-Landon, and render account of the situation in that monastery. They arrived at Paris in June. One of the two was called Reynier Koetken; the other's name we do not know. Koetken had entered the monastery of Mount St. Agnes in 1465[34], and had spent six years there under the direction of Thomas à Kempis. He must also have known Gansfort, for the latter was often a guest at Mount St. Agnes between 1475 and 1482. Standonck met Koetken, and wrote of him on June 28 in a letter addressed to the prior at Windesheim: "I rejoice to note that you have chosen him for planting your saintly reform in France — him, a man so worthy of veneration, so prudent, so virtuous". If they would send brethren like Reynier and one novice who could speak French, success would be assured[35].

Upon his return to the Netherlands, Koetken proposed that a mission be sent. A young monk of Groenendael, where Ruysbroeck had once lived, was entrusted with the preliminary negotiations. Shortly afterwards seven reformers appeared in France. The leader of the small party was John Mombaer, or John of Brussels, author of the "Rosetum Exercitiorum Spiritualium", or "Rosary of Spiritual Exercises". He had spent several years at Mount St. Agnes, and may have known Thomas à Kempis personally, whom he calls the author of the

"Imitation of Christ"[36]. Koetken was also in the party. The reformers were cordially welcomed by Standonck at Montaigu, and were conducted by him to the monastery of Chateau-Landon. Their pathway was not strewn with roses; the few they may have detected were studded with ugly thorns, for the monks of the abbey objected to the rigorous discipline now instituted. Two of them tore the boxes open where the archives were, and secreted the books of account; others took away the wine, and finally the stables were set on fire. The newcomers were deprived of their bread, wood, and clothes. For a moment Mombaer thought of returning to the Netherlands, but Standonck persuaded him to stay. It was only through the assistance of Admiral de Graville, John de Rély, archbishop of Sens, and some other friends of Standonck that the next year the reform at Chateau-Landon became a real success. Mombaer was made prior, and Standonck sent three young men from Montaigu to help him[37].

It was now decided to introduce the rule of Windesheim at the ancient monastery of St. Victor, in Paris. One by one the most famous Augustinian convents in the Low Countries and Germany had acknowledged the moral superiority of Windesheim; the time had now come, the French reformers believed, for St. Victor to follow their example. Once more a request for assistance was sent to the prior superior at Windesheim. Standonck and his pupils Noël Béda, Thomas Warnet, and John Goussard; the canons Nicholas of Hacqueville, du Refuge and Bailly; John Clerée the Dominican, and several other prominent reformers seconded the request. The Windesheim Congregation again sent two men to reconnoitre the situation. They met Standonck and some of his friends, and visited Chateau-Landon. Then they returned to Windesheim. Mombaer wrote a letter, saying: "I have received a letter in the name of the reverend bishop of Paris, of the presidents of the Parlement, the very celebrated company of doctors, stating that we must not hesitate. The archbishop of Sens, the bishop, the admiral, and all France address their prayers to you. A great work depends on you. It is not simply the question of reforming that once so famous abbey, but in its train, the whole Gallican Church. Of that I entertain profound and certain hopes. If the work is well conducted, it will be the beginning of an immense revival. For St. Victor we need learned and studious brethren, as they will have to show themselves in court and among the doctors"[38].

For the second time the Windesheim Congregation sent seven missionaries to France. The one among them best known to us is Cornelius Gerard, or Cornelius Aurelius of Gouda, a very intimate friend of Erasmus. He probably had been educated at Deventer, but in 1497 was living in a monastery near Leiden, a member of the Windesheim Congregation. For eight years he had been corresponding with Erasmus. Both friends were devoted readers of the Ancients, and both greatly admired the Italian humanists[39]. He was just about to visit Italy, when the order came from Windesheim for him to leave for Paris. The reformers entered Paris in October, 1497. Erasmus was glad to see them all. In spite of his unfortunate experiences as a monk at Stein in Holland, he still favored monasticism[40].

But Standonck had been too sanguine about the chances of success at St. Victor. From the very beginning the reformers were treated as intruders. They were refused admission to the rich library and had to borrow their books from elsewhere. Reynier Koetken, their leader, was lacking in tact, and none of them could speak

French. One can easily comprehend why nothing could be accomplished under such circumstances. On the 20th of December several influential persons visited the abbey, ordering the monks in the name of the king to restore discipline. The order was strictly obeyed. The reformers from the Windesheim Congregation, however, were not consulted. Still the monks acted as if it was all their work. The library was opened to them. Cornelius Gerard extolled the great abbey, and Erasmus joyfully told the story of his friends' success in a letter to the superior at Stein. Nevertheless, Hacqueville and John Emery were furious, and Standonck obtained a promise from Charles VIII of four commissioners charged to introduce a definitive reform. Unfortunately the king died on the 7th of April, 1498. During the following summer the reformers from the Netherlands became aware of their plight. Though Mombaer hesitated for months, he finally gave them permission to return to Windesheim[41].

The failure at St. Victor was quite a blow to the reformers. But John Raulin tried to comfort Standonck. He reminded him of the many mishaps of Paul and the other apostles, and Standonck remained steadfast. He decided to reform the monastery at Livry, situated a few miles north-east of Paris. Erasmus wrote Mombaer he would commemorate the affair, and took an active interest in it himself[42]. Mombaer finally appeared at Livry, followed by some of his friends, and in March, 1499, Standonck sent two pupils from Montaigu. One more monastery was reformed by them, namely, that of Cysoing in the diocese of Tournay. The prior superior at Windesheim refused to send any more men, wherefore the reform was left to Mombaer. And then still another monastery followed: Saint-Savior of Melun. But on the night of January 6, 1502, Hacqueville suddenly passed away, and in December of the same year Mombaer died. Still the reform instituted at Chateau-Landon, Livry, Cysoing, and Melun remained a success. They formed a chapter of their own, with a constitution modeled after that of Windesheim. As one after the other of the Dutch missionaries passed away, and no new ones from the Netherlands ever came to fill their places, the ties which united the four monasteries with the Windesheim Congregation gradually loosened[43].

More important than the monastic reform carried on under Mombaer's direction was the influence of his "Rosary of Spiritual Exercises". This work is the only well-known mystical production of the Windesheim Congregation written by a person who had not previously gathered the material in the house of the Brethren of the Common Life at Deventer. It bears unmistakable signs of having been copied after the "Treatise on Spiritual Exercises" of Radewijns and the "Spiritual Ascensions" by Zerbolt. As was to be expected, Mombaer began with the fall of man in Paradise. Man was created in the image of God, and fell. His prime duty now is to purge his flesh, his mind, and his heart from sin, or evil[44]. All the vices must be eradicated before virtues can enter the heart. Mombaer's whole method, and much of his terminology, he borrowed directly from Radewijns and Zerbolt. Man must by all means try to get back, but since he has fallen so low, it is impossible for him to return, except with the assistance of Grace or the Holy Spirit and religious exercises. Hence Mombaer believed in the doctrine of free will no more than did Gansfort.

Groote's followers made much of "Grace" and also much of "good works". Some theologians have thought

that the two exclude each other, just as many others have
stated that predestination leaves no room for even a
limited free will. Gansfort tried to solve the problem by
saying: "However faithfully and carefully a farmer may
sow his field, the sweat of his brow counts for nothing
unless God from heaven bless his work. But after the
seed is sown he does not expect a blessing from heaven
alone; he expects it because he has a fertile farm, because
he has the seed, the beasts of burden and agricultural
implements, because he has his limbs, and strength, and
willingness to endure. In a word, what he is and has is
altogether due to the beneficence of God; for in the last
analysis both we and all our possessions are from God.
But although God is the source of all things, still he
wishes the farmer to labor through these agencies, —
and this to such an extent that although God himself
does it all, no blessing, no fruit will attend a lazy, snoring
farmer"[45].

Gansfort and Mombaer were both children of the
"New Devotion", and both followers of Groote. Though
Mombaer wrote his "Rosary" more than a century after
Groote's death, he speaks of that great reformer as a
person well known to him and to his contemporaries.
"According to Gerard Groote", he writes, "two things
are to be avoided in our spiritual exercises, namely, too
great affliction and immoderate activity"[46]. Groote had
noticed that many among his disciples had become down-
hearted about their many shortcomings. They had tried
very hard, and still they had failed. Consequently Groote
wrote them time and again to cheer up. He also, as we
know, warned his followers against too great reliance
on external observances, like fasting, long prayers, and
keeping awake at night. Mombaer shows that Groote's
advice had not been forgotten and he admits the debt

he owes the founder of the new brotherhood at Deventer and Zwolle. Thus he called the attention of his readers in foreign lands to the teachings of Gerard Groote of Deventer. Luther, for example, read that statement in 1515, and Lefèvre, the great French scholar and reformer, read it even earlier[47].

It should be noted here that two previously unkown letters of Groote are found in Ms. no. 1250 of the new acquisitions of the "Bibliothèque Nationale" at Paris. One of the two is addressed to "somebody dearly loved by him in Christ and greatly tempted". "You must know", he writes, "that saintly and experienced men have often been beset by the gravest temptations, either through the lessening of divine grace in order to probe their faith, or through the influence of the enemy. The arrows of the devil do indeed more easily pierce the human heart when the shield of divine grace and truth appears to protect it less. In the Scriptures this withdrawal of grace is often called spiritual poverty. It is also likened to the cold of winter, to death, and the shadows of death; it has been called darkness, inferno, a desert, banishment, etc.". Then he quotes from a large number of psalms, often giving the wrong number. "Thus is man left alone", he continues, "in order that God may probe him and show him how much he will do for him. Wherefore Gregory says: 'Man will consider himself master of his lower self as long as he has not sensed the lack of faith, hope, and love in his mind'. We must firmly hope and believe that God will cause all things to work together for the good of his beloved, who according to his will are called saints, that is, predestined to eternal life. Hence we should humbly confess our guilt and negligence before God, as well as all our evil thoughts, and admit ourselves unworthy of

grace......... You should bear in mind that in temptations our aim must be to keep our intention right.......
Firmly endeavor to live your faith before God. Rise
above your grief and your fears, and above the
instigations of the enemy, who whispers: 'Where is
thy God'? When our faith is well founded, our life is
just. Hence Habakkuk says in his third chapter: 'The
just shall live by faith'. God secretly and invisibly
assists us in our inner selves......... Rejoice that you
are deemed worthy to suffer tribulation in Christ's
name, just as the apostles gloried in their calumnies......... And offer yourselves likewise to God,
saying: 'Let thy will be done'. Manual labor is very
helpful in freeing us from evil insinuations.........
The Apostle says God will not let us be tempted beyond
our strength.......... It is well to reflect often on
positive ideals, the kingdom of heaven, the articles of
faith, and the operations of virtue"[48].

Mombaer was familiar also with Zerbolt's "Spiritual
Ascensions" and prepared a course of spiritual exercises
which, if faithfully practised, would help the reader to
approach the final goal, the love of God and man. The
book is divided into titles, or articles. The first one is
called "Eruditiorium Exercitiorum", or "Of the more
learned (advanced) exercises", and covers six folios in
the Zwolle edition of 1494. It is divided into several
sub-divisions, which deal with a great multitude of
subjects, having little connection with each other. It
seems like a vast jungle of nouns and verbs, suggestive
of purity, fervor, moderation, advice, congruity; dignity,
doing, commanding, giving, promising, enemies, judgment, example, writing, evil, sin, pride, order, place,
time, etc.[49]. Probably this first title or article is intended
as a sort of introduction, or survey. Those following are

more to the point. Article II is called "Ordinarium vitae religiosae", or "The Arrangement of one's religious life", and deals with the attitude toward our superiors, equals or neighbors, and ourselves, and speaks of meditation, imitation, separation, emulation, etc.. In article III we find the real exercises, both for external and internal lives. We are told what to do when awaking early in the morning; if drowsy, we should shake up our minds, and utter a short prayer of thanksgiving. Next we are to consider the needs of the body: to take some physical exercises, and after that to prepare ourselves for the morning prayer. Next we are informed about the exercises of our inner lives. First, how we are to study: what to read, how to read, and why. Next, how we are to behave during and after the daily mass. Then comes dinner, and then the exercises after dinner. Once more we are referred to Magister Gerard Groote. "Groote teaches", says Mombaer, "that monks should not despise working on the farm and harvesting"[50].

Article IV is devoted to the subject of reading prayers. The following one is called "Chiropsalterium", and extols the method of singing hymns, "whereby one can accomplish more in one hour than else in a whole day". It also contains a list of subjects which are to be meditated on, — one subject for each day, most of the subjects dealing with the life and passion of Christ. Article VI discourses about the Holy Supper; articles VII, VIII, IX, X, and XI continue the discussion. Article XII contains a list of exercises, varying from day to day, and the following one elaborates upon the beneficial results of examining one's daily conduct every night, this closing the first part of the book. The other parts need not be analyzed here[51].

III

Mombaer's "Rosary of Spiritual Exercises" certainly is not a literary masterpiece. For although it exerted some influence on Lefèvre[52], and was assiduously studied by Standonck, Hacqueville, and most other leading reformers in France[53], the work lacked that freshness and fervor which had caused the fame of the "Imitation". Still it possesses historical significance.

The same may be said of Standonck's work. There is something fundamentally wrong about his gloomy asceticism; but his program for the reform of the Gallican Church and the constitution he composed for the Congregation of Montaigu contain many sound elements. And in focusing the attention of the whole kingdom on his plans and his work, Standonck played a very important part in the history of reform within the Church before the year 1520.

But he and Mombaer were not the only agents enlisted in sowing the seeds of the Christian Renaissance in France, though they were in charge of the visible organization conducted for this purpose. Long before their arrival in France, the "Imitation of Christ" and the best work of Zerbolt had been widely read. The situation before 1500 has been very ably summarized by a French writer who says, "From the houses of the Common Life and the convents of the Canons Regular, which were united by the same thought, had come forth innumerable and prolix works, inspired by the same intimate, contemplative, and still active piety, which was called 'New Devotion', and which shortly after the first two decades of the fifteenth century found in the 'Imitation' its most efficacious and human expression. Soon it spread across the

Occident, reached the University of Paris, imposed itself even upon those who at first, like John Gerson, combated the spiritual imprudences; exercised on the Christian world, through the 'Imitation', a gentle and strong influence; transmitted itself from generation to generation until the Reformation by driving a wedge between the exhausted scholasticism and the rising humanism, as a protest against the arid discipline of syllogism and the dogmatic dryness of the official theology, and consoled those who, submitted to the authority of the Church and tradition, had nevertheless preserved the need of thinking and living their faith"[54].

In a threefold way, then, the Christian Renaissance asserted itself in France. In the first place, it brought the mystical productions written or prepared in the brethren-house at Deventer. Secondly, it presented, through Standonck's work, its ideals of reform within the Church by means of the education of a better equipped and more pious clergy. In the third place, it scattered the germs of new religious fervor among the Augustinian Canons Regular. Even St. Victor in the end joined Livry, and the Dominicans of Holland were very successful in France. Thus the foundations were laid for the Counter-Reformation. For Standonck so changed the ideals of his teachers in the Netherlands that his successors at Paris were already provided with definite plans when in 1520, and after, the Church was disrupted.

It would be worth while to investigate to how great an extent James Lefèvre, the French reformer and humanist, absorbed the principles of the Christian Renaissance. That he was considerably influenced by the "Rosary" of Mombaer he attests himself. His first interest in mysticism, however, was probably aroused by the writings of Nicholas of Cues, with which he was acquainted as early as 1490"[55]. Nicholas Cusa, we must remember, had received the larger share of his elementary and secondary education at Deventer. In 1464, when he was about to die, he stipulated that a dormitory should be founded at Deventer with funds that he set aside for this purpose. The pupils in the new dormitory were to dress like the Brethren of the Common Life, and in every way they were to imitate their friends in the other dormitories at Deventer[56]. Cusa had officially aided the reforms launched by the Windesheim Congregation in Saxony, and had been the guest of the Brethren and Sisters of the Common Life at Deventer. He had enthusiastically commended the piety of the Augustinian Canons and Canonnesses Regular at Windesheim and Diepenveen[57].

We have often heard of Cusa as the forerunner of Leibnitz, and have seen his philosophy compared with that of Giordano Bruno, but if one reads Cusa's "Opera" carefully, he will find that Cusa was interested far more in the reformation of the Church than in philosophical questions. Suppose we examine the edition by Lefèvre. The first work is called "De Concordantia Catholica", and, as its tittle implies, deals with the unity of the Church. In the very first chapter Cusa says that there must be one head and many subjects. Christ is the head; his followers are all members of the body of the Church. The real head of the Church is Christ, not the pope. On folio 5 the name *Christ* meets us 14 times, and it is the only word written in large characters; this folio 5 is the first page of the first work edited by Lefèvre, whom we have every reason to call Cusa's pupil.

The same subject is continued in the following three chapters. Not a word is said about the pope, not one

stray thought enters deviating from the views of Groote.
Cusa speaks of predestination and faith in exactly the
same manner as did Groote. He also displays very
much the same interest in those subjects which were of
interest to Groote. Man can never judge, he says, who
really are the true members of the Church[58]. In
chapter V Cusa claims that the unity of the Church is
dependent on the attitude of the members. They should
hold similar, and, if possible identical, beliefs. Cusa and
Groote both speak of the militant and the triumphant
churches[59]. In chapter VI the leading topic again is
Christ, the head, the mystical head. The Church is the
mystical body of Christ: exactly as Groote taught. Cusa
also quotes from the same writers as did Groote and
his followers, chiefly from the Bible and the Fathers.
As for the powers of the pope, mentioned in chapters
XIV-XV, Cusa tells us nothing new. He admits there
had been many wicked popes, nevertheless the line of
succession had to be maintained, even as Christ was a
descendant of Adam[60]. Book II deals with the Church
Councils. What he says here about the papacy is not
quite so interesting as the views expressed by Gansfort.
Significant it is, however, that Cusa is seen to be more
interested in reform and theology than in anything else.

The following statement is worth noting: "But we
know that Peter did not receive any more power from
Christ than did the other apostles. And although Christ
had said, 'Thou art Peter and on this rock shall I
build my church', nevertheless this rock signifies Christ,
whom Peter confessed; and if Peter in this connection
is to be regarded as a rock upon which the Church was
founded, then the other apostles were likewise corner-
stones of the Church........ And if Christ said to
Peter: 'Feed my sheep', it is evident that this feeding

of the sheep is the spoken word and his example.......
Hence we may rightly say that all the apostles had
equal powers with Peter......... The pope is not a
bishop of the whole church, but the principal one among
all bishops"[61]. Many other instances could be adduced
showing how closely Cusa's mystic religion and plans of
reform resembled those of Groote's followers in the
Yssel country[62]. And as for the important question of
justification by faith, Cusa believed exactly what
Groote and Gansfort did. Said he: "Every sinner is the
servant of sin. The servant cannot liberate himself
from the bonds of sin. If the works of the law justified, he could bring about his own justification. This,
however, is impossible; hence, a contradiction"[63]. Such
were the views of the man who introduced Lefèvre to
the field of mystic religion.

Lefèvre greatly admired Cusa. For years he searched
for manuscripts containing Cusa's works, till finally
in 1514 he had them all published at Paris by Josse
Badius, or Badius Ascensius, a former pupil of the
brethren at Ghent. Lefèvre also induced Badius to
print the "Rosetum" of Mombaer in 1510[64], while in the
same year he was the guest of the Brethren of the
Common Life at Cologne[65]. The brethren seem to have
recommended several mystical productions to him, for
in 1511 he edited the "Opus Theologicum" of Richard
of St. Victor, and in 1512 the "De Ornatu Spiritualium
Nuptiarum" by Ruysbroeck[66]. It should be borne in
mind that the brethren at Cologne in 1434 had produced
the first German translation of the "Imitation of
Christ". Perhaps they told him about that work. He
was being reproved for editing a work of Ruysbroeck,
who had written all his works in the Flemish language.
Far from condemning Ruysbroeck, he held that even a

person well versed in Latin had a perfect right to write for the people in the vernacular. Renaudet suggests that Lefèvre formed this and similar ideas during or shortly after his visit at Cologne. "Already in that year", Renaudet continues, "he began to regret that the faithful ones could not understand the Latin prayers of the Catholic church services, the Gospel, or the Epistle, of which the priest, during the mass, recited the mysterious text"[67].

At Paris, where Lefèvre spent most of his time, the influence of the Christian Renaissance was strongly felt. Here, as well as in Western Germany, it changed considerably the character of the rising humanism. "The centre of French Humanism", writes Tilley, "was Paris, and this fact imparted what may be called a northern character to the movement. Gaguin himself was a Fleming by birth. So were his friends Pierre de Bur and the brothers Charles and Jean Fernand....... The result of this large northern element in northern Frenchman, Fleming, and Dutchman, was to impress upon the movement from the first a distinctive character, which clearly differentiated it from Italian Humanism. This character was theological, religious, moral, educational......... Another feature of French Humanism, though this it shared with Italian Humanism, was its recognition of the need for reform in education"[68].

The chief reformers in France were Lefèvre and Badius Ascensius[69]. A few words should be said here with regard to the life-work of the latter. He had attended the excellent school conducted by the Brethren of the Common Life at Ghent. The brethren had sent him to the University of Louvain, whence he had departed for Italy to study Greek. He became a better

equipped scholar than Gaquin. His work "fully sub-
stantiates his claim to be regarded as the chief promoter
of Latin studies in France during the reign of Louis
XII"[70]. The old medieval grammar called "Doctrinale"
was reformed by him, and his edition became very
popular. His press at Paris, set up in 1503, turned out
a huge mass of humanistic productions[71].

Badius Ascensius published the works of Thomas
à Kempis at Paris, together with a biography composed
by the humanist himself, in which he bears this witness
of the brethren: "All were to approach as near as
possible the life of the Apostles and of the primitive
church of Christ, so that in the whole congregation there
should be one heart, and that no one should consider
or call anything his own. No one should seek outside
the house the cure of souls, ecclesiastical benifices, or
worldy occupations for the sake of gain; but clerics
who should be found worthy, would be promoted to
cures that were not too lucrative........ No one
should beg from door to door, and in order that they
might not be driven to this by want, all should avoid
idleness, and according to their abilities should transcribe books, or instruct children. They were to take
care that they themselves, and all whom they should
teach, should venerate God with the deepest piety. They
should love their neighbor with due charity, and should
assist the poor with alms, according to their means"[72].

Of the school of the brethren at Ghent he wrote that
here "the youth of the land gathered to receive the
choicest literary instruction". And in 1500 he addressed
his teachers at Ghent in terms of the highest praise[73].

From Paris the chief literary productions of Groote's
followers spread throughout the whole kingdom, and
invaded Spain and Italy besides. It would be a very

complicated task to follow the trail of even the "Imitation" alone, on its journey from place to place, and often from home to home. One remarkable incident, however, should be recorded here. In the Benedictine monastery of Montserrat, near Barcelona, in Spain, lived a pious abbot, named Garcia of Cisneros, nephew of Cardinal Ximenes of Cisneros. He had heard the fame of the "Imitation", Gerard Zerbolt, and the brethren, wherefore he took a trip to France, and came back with a collection of mystical writings. In January, 1499, he set up a press at Montserrat. At once he began to print 800 copies of the "Spiritual Ascensions" of Gerard Zerbolt[74]. This work and the "Rosary" of Mombaer seem to have impressed him very much, for about this time he composed a work which he copied very largely after these two. He called it "Ejercitatorio de la vida expiritual", or "Spiritual Exercises". In 1500 he printed 1006 copies of this work, 800 in Spanish and 206 in the Latin translation. Several times it was reprinted in Latin, and both French and Italian translations were made[75].

The "Spiritual Exercises" of Garcia of Cisneros have been carefully analyzed by Watrigant, a Jesuit scholar. The result of his investigation shows that Garcia of Cisneros copied the general outline of his course of spiritual exercises from Zerbolt. The aim he pursues is the same as that sought by Zerbolt. Chapters XLIX— LII of the work are almost verbally reproduced from Chapters XXVII—XXX of the "Spiritual Ascensions" by Gerard Zerbolt of Zutphen[76]. His chief source was Zerbolt, but he also made use of the "Imitation", Mombaer's "Rosetum", Gerson, Richard of St. Victor, and Bonaventura. Garcia borrowed rather heavily from Mombaer. "Almost all the practical hints, and nearly everything relating to the general method simply are extracts from the 'Rosary' ''[77].

The Christian Renaissance had become a movement of consequence. Doubtless, many other men soon followed Garcia's example in Spain and Italy, and many students carried home with them from Paris works like the "Imitation" and the "Spiritual Ascensions". The main reason why the work of Garcia of Cisneros is mentioned here is that it had a great influence on the life of Ignatius Loyola, founder of the Jesuits.

Loyola was still a soldier when on the 21st of March, 1522, he knocked at the gate of the monastery of Montserrat, where Cisneros had died in 1510. Here he spent three days in a narrow cell, and confessed all his sins to Father Xanones. On March 24 he laid aside his armor for ever, put on a hair-cloth, and issued forth as a pilgrim and servant of God. He intended to go to Barcelona, but on his way he met some kind people who were going to the convent of St. Lucia at Manresa, situated only a few miles from Montserrat; there they secured a room for him. As the pestilence was raging at Barcelona, Loyola was obliged to remain at Manresa, and not only a few days, but nearly a whole year.

At Manresa, Loyola went through nearly the same experiences as hád Luther in the monastery at Erfurt. Tormented by the burden of sin and the fear of future punishment, he groaned, struggled, fasted, and prayed for forgiveness. He confessed his sins every day, but this very confession increased his fears, and then he would wrestle again, and again, till at last hope wiped the drops óf sweat from his weary brow. Luther fought from July, 1505, until October, 1512, while Loyola finished his battle in about half a year. There were several books that Loyola devoured at Manresa, chief

among which were the "Imitation", the "Life of Christ"
by Ludolph of Saxony (d. 1378), the "Flower of the
Saints", containing legendary accounts of martyrs, and
the "Spiritual Exercises" of Garcia of Cisneros. The
"Imitation" made such an overpowering impression upon
him that after reading it he cared little for any other
work. From day to day he read only in the "Gersoncito",
as he called the "Imitation"[78]. In fact, when he finished
his "Spiritual Exercises", in 1526, he placed the "Imitation" before the Gospel: "On the second day of the week
and thereafter, it will be very profitable to read a selection from the 'Imitation' or the Gospels, or the 'Lives
of the Saints' "[79]. Afterwards, when the official Latin
translation appeared, which was first printed in 1545,
this sentence was changed to read: "........ from the
Gospel or some other pious book, like the 'Imitation', or
the 'Life of the Saints' ". For Loyola did not mean to
say that the "Imitation" was a better work than the
Gospel. He probably meant that it was easier to understand[80]. But his extraordinary liking for this masterpiece of the Christian Renaissance linked him at once
with the other disciples of Gerard Groote. It has often
been intimated that what the Bible became for Luther,
the "Imitation" was for Loyola. The little work did
indeed to a very large extent mould his whole life and
all his plans[81].

Loyola loved the "Imitation". He just as anxiously
strove to circulate it as Luther did the Bible. Every one
whom he wished to honor he presented with a copy.
We involuntarily ask why this little mystical production
from the Yssel country appealed to him so soon and so
powerfully? It really contains nothing new, reasons
professor Böhmer of Marburg. Nevertheless, in some
way it changed Loyola's whole outlook upon life. Hence-

forth he no longer sought refuge in formal, external observances. He now tried to enrich his inner life. The mysticism of Groote's followers had gripped him, and it held him fast. Gradually his whole inner life became purified; his will, feelings, thoughts, prayers, and actions were simultaneously spiritualized; after that time he was a new man. It was then that he first thought of composing a course of religious exercises[82].

The "Spiritualia Exercitia" of Loyola may be termed one of the last fruits of the Christian Renaissance[83]. The method of contemplation and most of the material for the meditations Loyola borrowed from the "Life of Christ" by Ludolph of Saxony, who wrote his work before Groote's conversion. In some way, however, Loyola copied in an unmistakable manner after Zedbolt and Mombaer. He could not have read Zerbolt before 1526, for till then he only knew Spanish, but still he must have been acquainted with its contents. The pious folk at Manresa probably had received some copies of Zerbolt's "Spiritual Ascensions" from the neighboring town of Montserrat. However this may be, Loyola borrowed quite systematically from Zerbolt. No one can disguise the fact that there is a great analogy between the plan of the "Spiritual Ascensions" of Gerard and the general arrangement of the "Exercises" of Ignatius Loyola. And when one enters upon a more detailed comparison, he notices that the ascetic of Manresa resembles the Dutch author more closely than his compatriot of Montserrat. For in addition to the points which he has in common with both, he resembles Gerard only in several important particulars which Cisneros has left out. Striking examples of the instructions lacking in the "Exercitatorio", but which are found both in the "Spiritual Ascensions" and the "Exercises", relate to the examination of the conscience and the exact notion of true devotion. In the two masterpieces of Gerard of Zutphen and Ignatius we everywhere meet with a practical spirit which is not found to the same degree in the work of Garcia of Cisneros. This practical spirit expresses itself in the precise indication of the aim of the spiritual exercises: that one should regulate his manner of living in accordance with the divine plan. We also find this practical spirit in the objects of the exercises: our vices must be eradicated and new virtues acquired. Again, this same practical spirit is displayed in the method of procedure. Gerard of Zutphen and Ignatius employed it with greater discretion and moderation than did Mombaer[84].

Loyola finished his "Spiritual Exercises" in Paris, where he resided from 1528–1535. During his first year he attended the lectures at Montaigu. If he had not been able to become intimately acquainted with the works of Gerard Zerbolt at Manresa in Spain, he could now read them in Latin, for the library in the dormitory founded by Standonck contained chiefly the mystical productions read and composed by Zerbolt and by Groote's other followers[85]. Building upon the solid foundations of practical mysticism, and blending the views his own mind had evolved from past experiences and inspiration, and also from the perusal of the "Imitation", the "Life of Christ" of Ludolph of Saxony, and Zerbolt's "Spiritual Ascensions", Loyola drew up his final Latin version of his "Spiritual Exercises".

Loyola distinguished himself still further by founding a new brotherhood, just as Groote had done. This happened also in Paris, and also was in many respects a last fruit of the Christian Renaissance. That he must have enjoyed himself greatly in the library of the new dormitory cannot be doubted. If he found the works of Groote there, he must have read them with pleasure, and he would have been delighted with the "Treatise on Spiritual Exercises" by Radewijns, if he could have seen it, but this seems doubtful. Loyola cannot have failed to make acquaintance with Standonck's followers at Montaigu. Somebody must have told him about the four daughter-institutions in the Low Countries, two of which (those at Cambray and Mechlin) were now in charge of the Brethren of the Common Life. Thousands of little incidents must have linked him with the ideals of the Brethren of the Common Life. The Congregation of Montaigu became the stepping-stone, or rather, the intermediary between Groote's brotherhood and that of Ignatius Loyola[86].

At Montaigu, Loyola certainly had ample opportunity to study the constitution of Standonck's new dormitory. It was Standonck's burning desire to gain souls for God's service that had impelled him to group those poor students about him. This love of God and neighbor had ennobled his character and greatly improved the nature of his rules, in the opinion of a man like Loyola. A similar zeal to win souls had caused Groote's steps to hasten from city to city; it had induced him to assemble a small group of trusted followers. As time went on, these followers had won souls themselves. It had all been, they thought, for the glory of God and the reformation of the Church. Thus they had tried to do their work in God's vineyard. And every day spent at Montaigu brought Loyola closer to Groote's ideals. What he might have done if he had never seen the new dormitory with its poor students at Montaigu, we do not know. But his love of the "Imitation" proves him to be a child of the Christian Renaissance, — it suggests the measure of his appreciation of Standonck's life-work.

We may all the better understand Loyola's attitude, if we bear in mind how he manipulated the mystical text-books of the Christian Renaissance. Although Mombaer had built upon the "Spiritual Ascensions" of Zerbolt, and Garcia of Cisneros had succeeded him, Loyola, who used the latter's work, did not build upon Garcia's methods and theories, but turned to the simpler and more practical system of Zerbolt, adding to that system all those thoughts of Mombaer and Garcia which seemed most helpful to him. He acted in much the same way when he drew up the constitution for his new brotherhood. Standonck had unfortunately selected the most rigorous rules of his teachers at Gouda, adding many particulars himself. He believed strongly in the need of mortifying the flesh, interrupting his sleep, fasting more than was feasible, and dressing as shabbily as possible. Loyola saw the error in all this, and devoted a long chapter to the "preservation of bodily health". Still, his constitution resembles that of Standonck in a good many ways, for his aims as reformer coincided almost entirely with those of the Flemish educator.

What was the chief purpose of the Loyola's new Brotherhood? To educate prospective reformers, recruit the clergy, and rate learning less than character. Learning was to be employed merely as a tool. To win souls for Christ was Loyola's leading aim. All education should be saturated with Christian ideals. In order to stimulate their faith, and to preserve their piety, Loyola's followers were commanded to carry with them note-books, or "rapiaria", just as Groote's disciples had done. If possible they should commit all the contents of these excerpt-books to memory. Loyola wanted his associates to use correct editions of the Bible and the Fathers, as the Brethren of the Common Life had done before him[87].

The novices of Loyola's order had to be watched carefully wherever they were; very little freedom was allowed them. In all these particulars the constitutions of Standonck and Loyola agree[88].

There is an important resemblance between the aims of Loyola's followers and those of the Brethren of the Common Life. These men all saw the need for a thorough education and wanted good tools for their work. For them there was no such thing as too much knowledge; consequently they achieved much. Standonck's pupils, on the other hand, distrusted the rising humanism, wherefore they finally shrank behind the walls of their little world, — despised by almost all of the humanists. In this particular again Loyola agreed with the Brethren of the Common Life rather than with Standonck. It is of course very difficult to determine how far he consciously followed the men of Deventer and Zwolle. During the seven years he spent at Paris he must have met a great many persons who had either been educated in the schools of the brethren or taught by their pupils. From 1500 till 1550 few elementary or secondary schools could be found in the Low Countries which were not conducted by a teacher trained by pupils of men like Hegius. The same can be said of Westphalia and of part of the Rhineland. That many of these men were now Protestants does not matter. They had much in common with Loyola in 1530. If Luther praised the Brethren of the Common Life, the early Jesuits did exactly the same thing[89], and for nearly the same reasons. The brethren were reformers; so were Luther and Loyola. The brethren wanted to win souls for Christ, and to imitate him, so also did Luther and Loyola, wherefore the latter's disciples called themselves Jesuits. The Brethren of the Common Life labored hard between

1500 and 1520 to improve elementary and secondary education; after 1550 the Jesuits also did. Hence Miraeus, a Belgian Jesuit, wrote: "For does not the Society of Jesus, in imitation of the brethren, open schools throughout the whole world"[90]? Those writers who cling to the old belief that Loyola's new brotherhood was founded primarily to counteract the rising wave of Protestantism, are greatly mistaken[91], for both the Reformation on its religious side and the Counter-Reformation owed their origins in part to the same religious movement: the "New Devotion", or Christian Renaissance.

IV

Simultaneously with the rise of the Counter-Reformation a religious and educational movement developed in Alsace, which should also be treated in this chapter. For the Alsatians generally sided with the people in the Low Countries and France against Luther. The Christian Renaissance produced here a new theology, differing from both Catholicism and Lutheranism. This new theology has come to be called Calvinism, as Calvin placed upon it the stamp of his well-defined beliefs and made of it a systematic theology — something which Gansfort had not wished to evolve.

How did the Christian Renaissance reach the people in Alsace? We can trace its influence from the Yssel country to Alsace along three lines. The first runs directly from Deventer to Schlettstadt and thence to Strasbourg and Geneva. It was drawn by Louis Dringenberg, who brought the ideals of Groote, Cele, and the Brethren of the Common Life to the school of Schlettstadt[92]. The second line runs from Zwolle and Deventer through Liège and Paris to Strasbourg. The third one was made by the followers of Wessel Gansfort and Cornelius Hoen when they brought the latter's treatise on the Lord's Supper to Bucer, Oecolampadius, and Zwingli. This connects Alsace and Switzerland with Zwolle and Utrecht. But the main line runs through Paris. It was this line which united Alsace with the Low Countries and France in their rejection of Lutheranism.

One of the men at Paris who influenced John Calvin was Lefèvre. We have just seen him among the faithful sons of the Roman Catholic Church, but now we shall find him a precursor of the French Protestants. His Latin name is Faber Stapulensis, and his common name James Lefèvre of Etaples. The views promulgated by him and by his disciples are sometimes referred to as the "Fabrisian Protestantism"[93]. From 1507 till 1520 Lefèvre spent most of his time in the abbey of Saint-Germain des Prés, and it is here that the "Fabrisian Protestantism" originated. As early as the year 1509 Lefèvre wrote: "For a long time I had attached myself to human studies, and had scarcely tasted with my lips the divine studies: for they are sublime and ought not to be approached boldly. But already in the distance a light attracted my attention, ... a light so brilliant that the human doctrines seemed darkness to me in comparison with the divine studies; the latter appeared to exhale a fragrance the sweetness of which nothing on earth could equal"[94].

Three years afterwards (in 1512) appeared Lefèvre's commentary on the Epistles of Paul. In a way this book might be called the first Protestant book, according to Doumergue. The first thing that strikes one is the principle of the sovereign authority of God's Word. Says Lefèvre: "Do not follow the precepts and dogmas of men......... There are men nowadays who teach the people á foolish piety instead of the doctrine of Christ. Of what use will all those fasts be to me, and why should I commit myself to those formal prayers of which the author is unknown to me, and which cast aside the apostolic precepts? Why should I die in a monkish garb after having dressed myself all my life in secular clothes? Nothing like it has been ordained by Christ.......... The rest is perhaps more superstitious than religious......... Let us attach ourselves to Christ only and to the apostolic doctrine. For that suffices and is the first essential for obtaining salvation".

Then follows the second principle: justification by faith. Lefèvre is very clear on this point. "It is almost profane to speak of the merit of works, particularly when face to face with God. For merit does not seem to ask for grace but demands what is due to it.......... Let us not speak of the merit of our works, but extol the grace of God, which is everything". This does not signify that works are in vain. Lefèvre attempts to reconcile Paul with James. In failing to produce good works we lose the grace of justification. "The works which follow faith are the evidence of our living faith, as breath is the sign of our life". In reality, justification consists neither in faith nor in works. God alone justifies.

If we could find nothing else than this in Lefèvre's commentary, reasons Doumergue, we would still be justified in calling it the first Protestant book. But it contains three other Protestant views. Lefèvre holds that baptism brings no justification; it is merely the outward sign of our justification by faith in Christ. And what happens in the sacrament of the Eucharist, or Communion, is not a new sacrifice by Christ, a new sort of crucifixion, but merely a memorial service. Secondly,

Lefèvre reproves the clergy for their immorality, demands less frequent and less rigid fasts, and disapproves of the Latin prayers which the common people cannot understand. And thirdly, he expresses the hope that God may soon provide his Church with a more virtuous body of clerics. Therefore, concludes Doumergue, Lefèvre's commentary on St. Paul's Epistles, of the year 1512, is the first book of the "Fabrisian Protestantism"[95].

But he fails to tell us that two years before this work appeared Lefèvre visited the Brethren of the Common Life at Cologne[96], that in 1510 he induced Badius Ascensius to print Mombaer's "Rosary", and that in 1512 he edited a work of Ruysbroeck, in which two works some of his "Protestant" views are expressed. He is silent also on the response made by Lefèvre to those who reproved him for having recommended the works of Ruysbroeck, who had written everything in the vernacular. Lefèvre referred those men to that wonderful work, called "Gersonico", or the "Imitation". If that might be read in the vernacular, he reasoned, then Ruysbroeck's works also might be[97]. Doumergue does not mention the works of Cusa, which Lefèvre edited in 1514, nor the disputations of Gansfort, where all those "Protestant" views are maintained. Doumergue cannot of course have seen the treatise written by Zerbolt in 1398, which insists that laymen should read the Bible in the vernacular and say their prayers in the vernacular[98].

The so-called Protestant views of Lefèvre sound so much like some of the thoughts expressed in the "Imitation" and the works of Gansfort that one agrees with Renaudet that he must have acquired them during his visit in the brethren-house at Cologne. His friendship with Badius Ascensius and his love of Cusa's mysticism also link him with the pupils of the Brethren of the

Common Life. Of course his Commentary on the Epistle to the Romans was not the first Protestant book. Not one single view is expressed therein which cannot be found at least as plainly expressed in the "Imitation" and in Gansfort's writings. Lefèvre was a devout Catholic and much less of a Protestant than Gansfort had been, who died one year before the French reformer became interested in mystic religion (1489). He undoubtedly owed much to the "Imitation". Many a sentence in his Commentary seems almost to have been copied verbally from this work. And what did he do in the brethren-house at Cologne? Was it a mere accident that caused his Commentary to appear two years after his visit? He now wished to reconcile James with Paul, as the brethren had been trying to do for more than a century — had the brethren perhaps shown him the works of Gansfort, where a long list of quotations is given from this same Epistle to the Romans, all of which speak of justification by faith? They were sowing the seeds of reform and personal religion in the hearts of thousands, and had produced the most widely circulated text-books on mystic religion.

Lefèvre's work leads to the rise of Calvinism. In 1512 William Farel became Lefèvre's disciple, and in turn was to affect Calvin's religious views. In 1516 Lefèvre published his second edition of Paul's Epistle, and a treatise on Mary Magdalene, in which he displayed a very sound spirit of historical criticism. In 1523 appeared his French translation of the New Testament; in 1528 that of the Old Testament was completed. This work showed his desire to return to the Bible and circulate it among the people. He was unfortunately attacked by Béda, chief of the Sorbonne, principal of the College of Montaigu and Standonck's favorite pupil. In this and many other respects Béda was deviating from the principles of the Christian Renaissance, while Lefèvre was continuing Groote's work. "Long live the Bible"! cried the Evangelicals. "Burn it"! screamed the Sorbonne. Soon followed. horrible persecutions. In 1523 the first "heretic" was burned, in 1529, another. These "heretics" had not gone much further than Lefèvre, but had been less prudent[99].

Calvin arrived at Paris in 1523. At first he followed the courses in the College of La Marche, but remained here only a very short time. From La Marche he went to Montaigu, obtained a room in the dormitory for well-to-do students, and quietly obeyed his teachers until early in the year 1528, when he was ready to leave Paris. Just as he was about to depart, another student came to take a place in the lecture room at Montaigu. It was Ignatius Loyola[100].

From Paris Calvin moved to Orleans, where he remained about one year; from Orleans he went to Bourges, and in the year 1530–1531 we find him at Noyon, the city of his birth. In the year 1531–1532 he was at Paris again. About his movements after this we are not quite so well informed. On May 10 and June 11 of the year 1532 we meet him at Orleans, on August 23, at Noyon, and soon thereafter at Paris. Here he probably attended some sermons by Gerard Roussel, a pupil of Lefèvre, who was allowed to preach in public. During the course of the next year Calvin was "converted"[101].

What was this "conversion" of Calvin? How much did he change his convictions and beliefs between 1528 and 1534? The first changes are expressed in the speech of Nicholas Cop, the new rector of the university, which was delivered on the 1st of November, 1533, and which was prepared by Calvin. Here the Gospel was held to

be divinely inspired; God delivered up his only begotten
Son; in that act lies the sole hope of the forgiveness of
sins. It is true, the word "Ave" is still found here, but
Calvin had to leave it in as a sort of formality. He
wrote: "Ave gratia plena"; this is not even a prayer of
intercession, but a respectful greeting, which means:
"We salute you, Oh Grace", rather than: "We ask for
your intercession, Grace". And even Luther wrote as
late as the year 1522: "Ave Maria".

The text selected for the discourse was "Blessed are
the poor in spirit". The orator contrasted the old faith
with the new, the Law with the Gospel — the Law with
its precepts and menaces without pardon, the Gospel,
which does not constrain us by commandments and
teaches the "immense benevolence of God toward us".
He vehemently condemned those leaders of the blind
who were always disputing and quarreling with each
other and never spoke of faith, of the love of God, the
true good works. "Blessed are the poor in spirit, for
theirs is the kingdom of heaven". They shall inherit this
kingdom, just as a child will some day inherit its father's
property — not through any merit of its own, except for
the simple reason of heaving been docile and obedient.
Paul is very clear on this point in his Epistle to the
Romans. The Law does indeed mention God's mercy,
but insists on the fulfilment of all its commandments.
The Gospel, on the other hand, promises a gratuitous
forgiveness of sins, and justification. Every man who
doubts this promise is incapable of leading a pious life
and prepares himself for the punishment in hell. The
Savior grants a cure only to those who know they are
ill; only to those who believe is forgiveness of sins freely
given. If we doubt this pardon, we are the most miserable of all men........ We cannot adore God in a

doubtful frame of mind......... The most impious
state of mind for a Christian is doubt.

This certainty on the part of the believer, we are told,
is the foundation of the doctrine of predestination. It is
a corner-stone of Calvinism. Hence Calvin was a
Calvinist as early as in 1533. But he wrote something
bolder still. To the professors of the Sorbonne, who
were chafing with anger and violent passions, he addressed a message of peace and tranquillity: "Blessed are
those who bring peace and take away the dissensions in
the church". And then he reminded them of Christ's
denunciation of the Pharisees. "Those who sow dissension are not disciples of Christ but miserable Pharisees. Blessed are those who suffer persecution for the
sake of justice......... Rejoice, for great shall be your
reward in heaven"[102].

The speech is interesting, but if Calvin actually was a
Calvinist for having merely expressed the thoughts just
mentioned, we would be quite justified in calling practically all pious Catholics before him Calvinists. Groote,
for example, had said in one of his sermons: "The old
law was given by Moses, who promises temporal gain
to its observers. His disciples are those who seek material
advancement and riches. Therefore we find the blind
man asking the Jews in the Gospel of John: 'Do you also
wish to become his disciples'? Whereupon they answered:
'You are his disciple, but we are disciples of Moses'.
Alas, how many more disciples does Moses have than
Christ! For Christ taught humility and clemency, saying:
'Blessed are the poor in spirit. Learn of me, for I am
meek and lowly of heart' "[103]. Calvin also resembled
Gansfort, who had written: "No one, unless he is blind,
follows a foolish and blind leader. The Lord Jesus in-
timates not only that the Pharisees are leaders character-

ized by folly and blindness, but also that the very people that are led by them are like them. For he says: 'Foolish and blind leaders of the blind' "[104]. Gansfort had also written this: "Not as if infidelity alone was sin; for pride, envy, and falsehood, are so too. But this sin is spoken of, as if there were none but itself, because all other sins remain, so long as this remains, and all depart when this departs, so that when there is no more un-belief, all sins will be forgiven"[105].

We are told by one of the best biographers of Calvin that the latter had used only the Vulgate until 1533, wherefore the Bible was a closed book to him before that date[106]. Protestant writers have almost universally re-garded Calvin's residence at Montaigu as a dead loss of his time, but they are not justified in refusing to look for the Gospel and the Epistles of Paul in the Vulgate, which Calvin read there. We hear of the so-called Evangelicals preaching the Gospel. Does that signify that those who used the Vulgate did not preach the Gospel? Lefèvre prepared a translation of the Vulgate; those who composed the "Imitation" used the Vulgate, and so did the Brethren of the Common Life[107]. Calvin also read Augustine at Montaigu; every hour spent in Standonck's library brought him a little more closely in contact with Groote and his disciples. Here were the works of Zerbolt and Mombaer. Even if, as is not likely, he did not read here the treatise on the translation of the Bible by Zerbolt, and if he was never told by any one of Standonck's pupils about the Brethren and Sisters of the Common Life, he was nevertheless indirectly influenced by them. And though his "Institutes of the Christian Religion" appeared as late as the year 1535, Calvin must have taken several years to compose it, as Doumergue suggests[108]. At Montaigu he found at least some of the material for his "Institutes". It is now apparent that this remarkable work is at least in part one of the last fruits of the "New Devotion"[109].

It was in Alsace, however, that Calvin became a Calvinist and a great educator besides. He arrived at Strasbourg in 1538. In the year 1531–1532 he had attended in Paris the lectures of John Sturm; from 1539–1541 he taught with Sturm in the University of Strasbourg, which was connected with Sturm's celebrated "gymnasium". Here in his new environment he soon adopted those theological, philosophical, and sociological views which later were called Calvinistic. The Christian Renaissance had found a fertile soil in Alsace. First Louis Dringenberg had arrived from Deventer with the seeds of new religious ardor and advanced views on education[110]. From his school at Schlettstadt, which greatly surpassed the best one at Strasbourg, had gone forth a noble army of Christian humanists, who endeavored to improve the old methods, to educate both mind and soul, without hurting the body. Wimpheling, the most famous educator among these, was called the foremost teacher in German lands, long before Melanchton had begun his life-work. All, or nearly all of these men had displayed very liberal views. They were serious scholars, and honest teachers, reliable, patient, and steadfast.

The sixteenth century had brought other teachers and reformers from the Low Countries to Alsace. Among these, we meet again Hinne Rode, rector of the Brethren of the Common Life at Utrecht. In January, 1523, he had a talk with John Oecolampadius at Basel concerning the letter on the Eucharist by Cornelius Hoen, who has been mentioned above[111]. Hoen had denied the bodily presence of Christ in the bread and wine of the communion service. The way in which he had treated this subject had greatly impressed Oecolampadius[112]. In November, 1524, Rode also talked this matter over with Bucer, who was impressed with the new doctrine, and shortly afterwards praised Rode highly, saying that he did not know a single theologian who could equal the Dutch reformer, not excluding Luther. Although Rode considered Luther as his teacher in a certain way, he owed more to Wessel Gansfort's teachings. Bucer said that he was surprised that Rode and his friends did not give more attention to Gansfort. When Rode was his guest he had tried to defend Luther's views on the Holy Supper against that of Hoen and Rode, but he had soon become aware that he could not meet their arguments. Consequently he had relinquished Luther's view of the bodily presence of Christ in the sacrament of the Eucharist[113]. In 1525 Rode visited Zwingli. The Swiss reformer had already come to about the same view as that entertained by Hoen, owing partly to the influence of Erasmus, who in turn had been taught it by Gansfort[114]. But after Rode's explanation (Rode seems to have become a great authority on this subject) Zwingli became clear on this point. Before the month of October, 1525, he published Hoen's treatise at Zürich[115].

While Rode was "converting" Bucer and Oecolampadius, Calvin absorbed quite a different sort of theology from that of Rode and Bucer in his dormitory at Montaigu. He studied first of all the doctrines of the Fathers and the medieval saints, before he ventured to differ somewhat from them. The Christian Renaissance itself had gone through exactly the same experiences in the Netherlands, when from 1380 until 1450 Groote's followers had built their ideas solely upon the Bible and other works approved by the Church, without anxiously or tenaciously clinging to any doctrines of minor importance. When Gansfort evolved his new views on indulgences and purgatory, they by no means considered him a heretic. Gansfort's views on predestination, justification by faith, and the universal priesthood of all believers did not shock them at all. They employed Hinne Rode, and were highly extolled by Luther in 1532. After 1520 they lost their sense of unity; part of them joined the followers of Luther; others remained true to the doctrines of the Church, and still others were preparing a mixture of Lutheran and Calvinistic theology: Hinne Rode was more of a "Calvinist" in 1520 than Calvin was in 1535. Still, all of these brethren had studied the same Bible, the same Fathers, the same medieval saints and doctors. They had avoided writers like Eckhardt, and had built their mysticism chiefly on the works of French and Italian mystics — this was true, at least, of the brethren in the Low Countries and of the missionaries of the Windesheim Congregation in France. Calvin, for more than four years in succession, absorbed the very same kind of mysticism at Montaigu. Fortunately for him he had to use Standonck's books. He was fourteen when he came to Montaigu, and left at eighteen. He became a great reformer and the views expressed in his first edition of the "Institutes", in 1535, differ but very little from the tenets of Catholicism disseminated by the Christian Renaissance. They are certainly much less "Calvinistic" than the views entertained by Martin Bucer, whom he was soon to meet in Strasbourg.

Bucer, one of Schlettstadt's chief products, became the leading Protestant reformer in South Germany[116]. In Strasbourg he and his friend William Capito organized meetings to advance the cause of Protestantism[117]. Lang calls Bucer the pietist among the reformers[118]. He was the man who developed the two central ideas of Calvinism: the doctrines of predestination and that of justification by faith[119]. One of Bucer's pupils at Strasbourg was Farel[120], the first reformer in France to venture beyond Lefèvre's "Protestantism"[121]. In 1538 Calvin arrived at Strasbourg, to become John Sturm's assistant, and to follow Bucer's leadership[122].

Do these facts perhaps seem surprising? They are brought out fully in the works of Lang and Anrich. And among those acquainted with the history of the Christian Renaissance in general, and with the school of Dringenberg at Schlettstadt in particular, they excite no surprise. Schlettstadt, like Deventer, Zwolle, and Utrecht, had begun with the views of Groote, Cele, and Zerbolt. Like Zwolle, Deventer, and Utrecht, it finally became Calvinistic. When Calvin left Strasbourg, in 1541, he took with him the local views on the organization of the Church, on the use of the Psalms during the church services, on the officially recognized feasts, dropping most of those adhered to by the Roman Catholic Church; on the views on the relations between Church and State, on justification by faith, on the Lord's Supper, on predestination, and on the institution of elders and deacons in accordance with the custom of the primitive Church[123]. Most of these views were arrived at in the attempt to return to the practice of the Apostles. They are the logical outcome of the great underlying aim of the Brethren of the Common Life: a Christian Renaissance, a revival of the Apostolic Church. Suffice it to say here that Bucer had been born and educated at Schlettstadt, where for thirty-six years in succession Louis Dringenberg had taught the principles of the Christian Renaissance. Bucer had read Hoen's treatise on the Eucharist and the works of Wessel Gansfort; he even suggested

that Rode should study Gansfort more, and he considered himself a pupil of Gansfort. He went just one
step further than Rode, becoming what we should call a
Calvinist, and he made Calvin a Calvinist. Then Calvin,
with more profound mind and greater vital force, surpassed Bucer, his teacher, clarified Bucer's views, and
became the founder of the new church that bears his
name.

V

During the opening years of the sixteenth century the
study of the classics was introduced at Strasbourg. Here
Jacob Wimpheling, pupil of Louis Dringenberg[124],
founded a "gymnasium" in the year 1501. In 1507 the
cathedral school was reformed under the supervision of
Jerome Gebweiler, who had been one of Dringenberg's
successors at Schlettstadt. Wimpheling and his friend
Geiler of Kaisersberg directed the work[125]. Gradually
the methods introduced by Dringenberg and his pupils
at Schlettstadt were copied and partly improved upon at
Strasbourg. But not until the arrival of John Sturm did
the Alsatian metropolis attract international attention.
    Sturm had been born at Sleiden in the Eifel, a
mountain range situated between Cologne and Trier. At
an early age he was sent to the school of the Brethren of
the Common Life at Liège, where he remained till
1524[126]. This was the "Hieronymian gymnasium",
which he imitated in his school at Strasbourg in 1538[127].
From 1524 till 1527 Sturm studied in the "School of the
Three Languages" at Louvain, which had been founded
on Erasmus' advice in 1518. Here he taught Latin and
Greek from 1527–1529. Then he moved to Paris, where

he remained as long as possible, but having joined the Protestants, he left Paris early in the year 1537[128].

Sturm arrived at Strasbourg with a definite plan. The magistrates of this city had invited him to found a new school. Now that the church there had undergone a transformation, which they considered a reform, the city council decided to reform the schools as well. Already there were two Latin schools; one directed by John Sapidus, the former rector of the school at Schlettstadt, and the other by Otto Brunfels, who also taught by the method of Dringenberg and his pupils[129]. Both men had been trying for years to combine the acquisition of knowledge with improvement in character. John Sturm was expected to continue their policy. He addressed the magistrates in the following manner: "Unless the crowd of students is so large that they cannot be accommodated in one building, it is best to assemble them all in one place. At Liège, Deventer, Zwolle, and Wesel instruction is given in one building, with a number of classes. Hence better students are turned out by these schools than by others, called Academies. And it often happens that those who there have been ably and piously taught are spoiled in those other gymnasia......... When I was at Liège, dissension arose among the teachers, and some of them began to teach separately. If they had had their way, that Hieronymian gymnasium would have perished"[130].

Sturm advised the magistrates to get a school of the kind conducted at Liège, Deventer, Zwolle, and Wesel, where the Brethren of the Common Life were at that time in nearly sole charge of the management of the schools. After the year 1500 they had become more interested in education than in anything else, for the invention of printing seriously interfered with their

original purpose of trying to make their living chiefly
by copying religious writings. In 1530 there must have
been several hundred of their pupils attending the
universities of Paris, Louvain, Cologne, and Heidelberg,
where they were usually distinguished for their learning.
We have only mentioned a few of them here, but there
must have been many in the scholarly world from 1500
till 1530. Hegius alone had 2200 pupils at one time.
Cele had had 1000 nearly a century before him. If the
schools of the Brethren of the Common Life at Delft,
Utrecht, Groningen, Liège, Brussels, Ghent, Cambray,
Münster, Rostock, Culm, Marburg, Hulsbergen, Nyme-
gen, and Cassel, and the schools at Deventer, Zwolle,
Wesel, Emmerich, Magdeburg, Hildesheim, and Mechlin
together sent one hundred students (a very conservative
estimate) to the universities each year, and fifty teachers
to reform other schools; if we add to these the many
thousands of other students who received part of their
elementary and secondary education in these same places
between 1400 and 1500, and who were in touch with the
brethren; and if we add the multitude of pupils these
schools must have had, we may well wonder how any
student at Paris, Louvain, Cologne, Heidelberg, or Basel
could have escaped the ideas and the influence of the
Brethren of the Common Life.

And most of these men had a message. Sturm for
example must have talked a good deal about that "Hier-
onvmian Gymnasium" of Liège, when he was lecturing
at Paris; Badius Ascensius cannot always have refrained
from saying a word or two about the "Hieronymian
School" he had attended at Ghent; Standonck had his
followers; and so did Lefèvre, who had watched the
brethren at Cologne in 1510. Then, there was that institution founded on Erasmus' advice at Louvain, the

first one of its kind in Europe — probably Erasmus was inspired by Gansfort, who long before his birth had studied Latin, Greek, and Hebrew. King Francis I modeled the "College of France" after its pattern. We hear of Mathurin Cordier introducing reforms in the college of Sainte-Barbe[131], like Sturm, building his program upon the work of the Brethren of the Common Life[132]. It may well be that many similar reforms in the various colleges at Paris were merely the repercussion of the reforms instituted elsewhere, for wherever we find among humanists and educators a desire to employ learning as a tool only, and to stress the fundamental need of religious instruction, we can often trace this back to the principles of the Christian Renaissance.

Most of the elementary and secondary schools in Transalpine Europe needed a reform. Instruction in these schools was usually personal. In many of them the pupils of all the various grades were assembled in one room, and even where on account of larger numbers the pupils were divided into classes, they were for two or three hours a day grouped in one room again. Sometimes several grades were combined. There was often a considerable number of children belonging to no particular grade at all. Much time as a rule was devoted to the rehearsal of lessons that had never been explained. Not seldom were the pupils left to select the lessons themselves. Every day exactly the same subjects were taught as during the preceding day. Only in the afternoon a slight difference was made between summer and winter programs. The method of instruction was exceedingly monotonous. The pupils were kept busy from six in the morning till four in the afternoon, with an interval of one hour for dinner. Such was generally the method adhered to in the schools[133].

The schools conducted by the followers of Groote differed considerably from the ordinary kind. In the first place the school hours were shortened about one half. If Cele and his successors could teach the same subject matter in 3½ hours which was done in 9 hours by most other teachers, their method must indeed have caused much favorable comment. They realized that a child's mind cannot concentrate very long on any one subject. Then there were the dormitories of the Brethren of the Common Life, and the lodging of students in the homes of the female followers of Groote, some of whom lodged as many as eight boys at a time. From these admirable features one can partly deduce the reason why hundreds of boys flocked to Zwolle from Cologne, Trier, Liège, and Utrecht; from Flanders, Brabant, Holland, Westphalia, Saxony, Cleve, and Gelderland. Cele's success must not be underestimated, for the schools of Trier, Cologne, Liège, and Utrecht had been regarded for centuries as the best in the Rhineland and the Low Countries. Trier was the oldest city in Germany; Cologne had behind it a civilization introduced by the Romans; while the cathedral schools of Liège and Utrecht had always provided the best instruction given in their bishoprics. Here princes and bishops had received their education long before Zwolle became a town of importance. And now all of a sudden Zwolle surpassed in education the glory of these four ancient cities!

Discipline was maintained effectively. While in very many schools the parents of the pupils would often intervene, thus weakening the authority of the teacher, Cele and his successors were the sole masters. Absences and delinquencies were punished. The infliction of corporal punishment was not done away with, but the disciples of Groote were not cruel or harsh. With them the force of love came foremost in all the relations of life. The sources do not inform us how often or in what cases the pupils were punished, but they do tell us what sort of a man Cele was, and we are also quite well acquainted with the lives of Cele's friends at Deventer and Zwolle. Pupils who would not behave were simply sent away from school.

The whole school was divided into eight classes, and each class was subdivided into groups of eight or ten pupils. The six lower classes were each taught by one teacher during the whole day, while in the two highest grades each subject was taught by a separate teacher. The usual length of time needed to pass from one grade into the next was one year. Very capable students were advanced more rapidly; each teacher was authorized to examine every one of his pupils from time to time. The instruction given in the two lowest classes was entrusted to the best pupils found in the highest grades, or to those who had completed the whole course. Each subdivision of eight or ten pupils was in charge of one advanced student, who had to keep order.

Another remarkable innovation was the introduction of religious instruction, given in addition to the usual subjects, called "ethics, philosophy, grammar, and logic". Particularly on Sundays and on the very numerous holidays the pupils were "taught to love and fear God, to search the Scriptures, and to lead virtuous lives". Every one, therefore, of the thousands of school boys educated at Deventer and Zwolle, as well as in most of the other schools conducted by the brethren, was taught the fundamentals of the Christian Renaissance. On Sundays and holidays they were to listen for one hour in the morning to the reading and explanation of a definitely assigned portion of the Epistles of the New Testament. In the

afternoon an hour was devoted to a selection from the
Gospels, and in the evening another hour was given to
a selection from the Old or New Testament. The boys
were instructed to write down the most helpful thoughts
in their note-books. The text from the Gospels and the
Epistles formed the bases, to which were added the
comments and explanations of various Church Fathers.
Thus the boys obtained a select list of texts from the
Bible, grouped under various headings, and accompanied
with explanations. There would be, for example, the
subject of salvation. Under this heading the words of
Christ, the Apostles, and the prophets of the Old Testament would be grouped. Nothing like it had ever been
attempted in any medieval school.

In other schools, if any religious instruction was given
it was confined to the explanation of the Lord's Prayer,
the Ten Commandments, and the Apostles' Creed. In
Cele's school the Bible itself was studied, and not only
on Sundays, but also on week days. Again, the character
of men like Cele was such that even when they were
teaching ordinary subjects, their whole trend of thought
was directed to the divine. The subject matter was always
made subservient to the practical use it might have for
the pupil in the future. Cele also dictated prayers to the
student body, both in the Low Dutch vernacular and in
Latin. For about forty years he taught at Zwolle, sending
out hundreds of pupils, back to their homes again, or to
the universities or the monasteries[134].

One of the boys who was taught by this new method
was Desiderius Erasmus of Rotterdam. We might repeat
here that after he left Deventer he could no more shake
the ideals of Groote's followers out of his head than he
could change the color of his skin. Though he never
became a teacher, he was an influential educator. In his

"De Ratione Studii" he set forth very ably the views he
had partly received at Deventer. Erasmus proposed a
complete reform of the Latin schools. Greek literature
should be taught just as well as Latin. Care should be
taken that not too much time be devoted to the study
of grammar. The pupils should read the sources for
themselves. Particularly such writings should be selected
for perusal as would provide interesting reading for the
pupils. Many books of this kind contained valuable information. The works of Plato and Aristotle could be
used as text-books in ancient philosophy. Origen,
Chrysostom, and Basil would be excellent guides in the
field of Biblical learning. Geography could be taught by
Ptolemy or Pliny. In this way the pupils would also
learn something about history, natural sciences, music,
and architecture. The best way to teach rhetoric was to
let students write compositions on subjects in which they
were interested. Dialogues and little dramas were very
helpful. Some of the scenes in Homer, Virgil, and other
poets could be acted quite well by the boys. Erasmus
urged teachers to give practice and exercises as much as
possible. Whenever an occasion could be found to praise
or encourage the pupils, the teacher should never hesitate
to use it. Erasmus wrote here in a pious and kindly
fashion, as if inspired by the feeling of "good will toward
men". The most useful literary productions would thus
be studied. For centuries they had been buried under the
constantly accumulating dust of neglect. In one of Erasmus' best works he insists that moral training should not
be based on the works of Thomas Aquinas or other subtle
works of scholastic disputation, but chiefly on the Bible.
In the place of scholasticism he puts the Gospel. How
well he had digested the principles of the Christian
Renaissance appears from the little prayer-book he com-

posed for the benefit of Colet's school at London[135]
Erasmus certainly did not acquire his views from any
English reformers. The time has now come to inquire
how much the reformers at London and Oxford were
indebted to books like the "Imitation", and to educators
like Cele, Hegius, and Erasmus. This inquiry is bound
to be fruitful of results.

John Sturm undoubtedly read the "De Ratione Studii"
of Erasmus. He may have read it at Liège, for a very
handsome edition was printed by Froben at Basel in
1521[136]. In 1538 he drew up a new program for his new
"gymnasium" at Strasbourg, called "De Litterarum
Ludis, recte aperiendis". In this program he draws a
distinction between two periods in the student's life.
During the first period all his studies are obligatory, and
he attends the "gymnasium"; during the second period
he may select whatever subjects he likes best. The first
period lasts nine, the second five years. The pupils are
admitted to the "gymnasium" at the age of seven. The
"gymnasium" is divided into nine grades or classes.
Advancement depends chiefly on the pupils' ability and
diligence. Sturm suggests that poor school boys who
distinguish themselves should be given scholarships, as
was done with the pupils of Cele and the Brethren of the
Common Life. One may expect more of such boys, he
thinks, than of the sons of rich parents who see no need
of exerting themselves. Parents are urged to cooperate
with the teachers. The boys should be kept in good
health; their food should be wholesome and their clothes
neat. The virtue of modesty is extolled by Sturm. Pupils
must show due respect for parents, teachers, and aged
persons. As for the final aim of education, it is not so
much the acquisition of learning, as the practical use to
be derived therefrom. "The best school", writes Sturm,

"is that where equal care is bestowed on intellectual and on moral training......... If one's actions do not harmonize with his words, of what use is his learning"? The two final ends are personal religion (pietas), and wisdom (sapientia). But Sturm neglected Biblical training, though Bible stories were discussed. Catechism was taught on Saturdays, and on Sundays the teachers and pupils went to church together. Further than that Sturm did not go[137].

John Calvin founded a similar school at Geneva in 1559. From 1539 to 1541 he had given instruction in Sturm's school, and in 1556 he had once more visited Strasbourg. In the Geneva school there was a division, not into 9 classes, as Sturm had made, or into 8, which was Cele's number, but into 7. Then there were also examinations, or rather promotions of the pupils based on the progress they were making individually; also the subdivision into groups of ten each. But in several important particulars Calvin approached Cele's method much more closely than did Sturm. In the first place, Calvin opened school every morning with prayer. This prayer was found in the pupils' catechism, and was read by each one in turn. School closed with the Lord's Prayer and a short prayer of thanksgiving. At half past eleven the second period opened with the singing of a Psalm, and at the end of the third, three pupils recited the Lord's Prayer, the Apostles' Creed, and the Ten Commandments. Every Saturday morning was devoted to a repetition of what had been learned during the preceding five days. The followers of Groote and Cele made much of repetition; so did Calvin. During the last hour on Saturdays that part of the catechism was explained which was to be treated in church the following day. During the week preceding communion services one of the ministers exhorted the boys in the school room to "fear the Lord and preserve mutual love". In school the Latin and Greek writers received most attention, but the pupils in the sixth grade studied the Gospel of Luke every Saturday afternoon from three till four o'clock, and those in the highest grade studied an Epistle of the New Testament. To rhetoric much less time was devoted than other humanists insisted on. Prizes were awarded to the two best students of each class, as was done by the Brethren of the Common Life at Liège and by Sturm at Strasbourg[138].

One day John Sturm came to Dillingen, a small town situated in the Lower Rhine valley. It was twenty-two years after he had founded his school at Strasbourg. He investigated carefully a school in that place conducted by the Jesuits. The methods employed were wonderfully like his, he saw, and concluded that the Jesuits must have copied their school from his. This view has been entertained by many other educators after him. But no one has yet been able to prove it correct[139], and it is probable that during the first half of the sixteenth century the reforms introduced into the schools of both the Lutherans and the Calvinists, and also of the Jesuits were the continuation of Cele's work at Zwolle[140]. Loyola and Calvin had both studied at Montaigu. They were both familiar with Standonck's work, and with writings produced in the Yssel country. They and their friends knew well what had been going on in the Low Countries. Calvin married Idelette de Bure of Liège in 1540[141]. Loyola visited Antwerp several times, and probably knew some of the Brethren of the Common Life at Ghent. Thus Flanders, Brabant, and Liège, provinces of the present kingdom of Belgium, became the intermediary between the Yssel country and Paris, and from Paris the influence of the Christian Renaissance radiated in different directions, touching Alsace, Spain, and England. From England, Holland, and France it was to reach the shores of America. In short, we may safely conclude that the "New Devotion" or Christian Renaissance, though it lost its cohesive force shortly after the year 1520, still had enough strength left to mould the schools not only of the Protestants, but also of their opponents.

CHAPTER VIII

THE CHRISTIAN RENAISSANCE

"I dare not indulge in great wishes", wrote Luther in 1532 to the rector of the Brethren of the Common Life at Herford, "but if all other things were in as good a condition as the brethren-houses, the Church would be much too blessed even in this life. Your dress and other commendable usages do not injure the Gospel, but are rather of advantage to it, assailed as in these days it is by reckless and unbridled spirits who know only how to destroy, but not to build up".

And in the same year the German reformer addressed the magistrates of Herford in the following manner: "Inasmuch as the Brethren and Sisters were the first to begin the Gospel among you, lead a creditable life, have a decent and well-behaved congregation, and at the same time faithfully teach and hold the pure word, may I affectionately entreat your worships not to permit any dispeace or molestation to befall them, on account of their still wearing the religious dress, and observing old and laudable usages not contrary to the Gospel? For such monasteries and brethren-houses please me beyond measure. Would to God that all monastic institutions were like them! Clergymen, cities, and countries would then be better served, and more prosperous than they now are"[1].

These statements from the pens of Luther and Melanchton were written at a comparatively late date by men who led in the revolt from Rome. They seem to imply that Europe of the sixteenth century owed much to the Brethren of the Common Life, the exponents of the principles of the "New Devotion", or Christian Renaissance.

I

Far back into the past go the roots of the "New Devotion". From Plato and Aristotle, from Socrates and Seneca the deepest roots derived their nourishment; from the teachings of Christ and his disciples the movement obtained its profoundest principles, while the Church Fathers and the "saints" of medieval Europe provided most of the rest. The German mystics, on the other hand, contributed comparatively little: Groote had energetically warned his followers against the works of Eckhardt; he cared very little for Tauler, and Suso's "Horologium" he ascribed to Anselm. Groote's followers at Deventer, Zwolle, and Windesheim do not even mention the "German Theology", that famous text-book of mysticism, which Luther at one time ranked next to the Bible and Augustine. These are facts of the highest significance, for they help explain why in the sixteenth century a line of demarcation was drawn between the Protestants east and west of the Rhine.

Contemporaries of note realized much of Groote's greatness and left testimony of his influence. One of them says that Gerard Groote of Deventer was the "Fountain of the New Devotion", and "illuminated his whole country with his life, words, ways, and doctrine". "All religious fervor in this country", says one Netherlandish biographer, "for one hundred miles around was caused by master Gerard". And another wrote on the day of his death: "Gerard Groote, with his holy life and

example, has enlightened the whole bishopric of Utrecht".
William Vornken, prior of Windesheim, exclaimed: "Oh
happy day on which that great Gerard was born amongst
us, for he was the fount and source whence flowed the
waters of salvation to our land, so that what before his
time had been parched became a pool, and the thirsty
land, springs of water". And John Vos of Heusden,
greatest of Windesheim's priors, said on his death-bed:
"Groote was the first father of this our reformation, the
source and origin of the New Devotion; he was an
apostle in this country, who kindled fires of religious
fervor in the cold hearts of men, and drew them to
God".

These fifteenth century historians did not know how
great Groote's influence really was. However significant
and strong their statements may appear, they were only
thinking of that limited circle of Groote's disciples who
had come into personal contact with the reformer. Only
those can appreciate the influence of Groote who are in
a position to follow the labors of the Brethren of the
Common Life, of Cele and his pupils, and of writers
like Gansfort and Erasmus, through later history in the
Low Countries, Germany, and France. It is not enough
to follow Groote's career as preacher. One must study
the relations he had with Ruysbroeck, the friendship with
Cele, the way in which he attacked the clergy, the impression he made on the common people, the constitution
he prepared for the Sisters of the Common Life, and the
whole history of the Brotherhood of the Common Life
and the Windesheim Congregation. Even this will not
suffice. For there remains the work of men like Gansfort
and Erasmus; of teachers like Dringenberg at Schlettstadt, Hegius at Deventer, and Murmellius at Münster;
and of all those scholars and reformers who were directly

or indirectly influenced by the "New Devotion", such as Cusa, Luther, Zwingli, Sturm, Calvin, and Loyola.

In trying to define the "New Devotion", or Christian Renaissance, one must of course be very cautious not to ascribe any events or results to this movement which were caused by some other movement. Moreover, it is exceedingly difficult to determine exactly how it reacted on the religion, education, art, science, politics, and sociology of medieval Europe. For the minds of Groote's disciples were not all the same; some followers retained ideas almost intact, others transformed most of the impressions made on them. An intellectual movement cannot be treated as something individual with a personality of its own. But still, bearing all these facts in mind, we are quite able to distinguish the essence and course of the movement inaugurated by Groote.

The Christian Renaissance may be said to have had its birth in Groote's first sermons, preached early in 1380; and we make no great mistake in believing the movement to have lost its cohesive character after 1520. Groote had experienced his conversion in 1374. He gave up his prebends very soon after his conversion, and in the same year, 1374, ceded the use of his ancestral home to a small group of poor women. In 1375 or 1376 he made a trip to Ruysbroeck's monastery near Brussels, accompanied by Cele. These events may be called the preliminary activities, for in 1374 or 1377 Groote did not yet consider himself ready to preach the Gospel to the people at large. First he had to "overcome his lower self", which he did in the monastery of Monnikhuizen near Arnhem, where he spent a little over two years (1377–1379). Not that he felt he had then completely mastered "the flesh", but he thought that he ought not to spend more time in a monastery. Five years he had given to preparing for the task now before him. That was enough.

Groote knew more about the Church in 1380 than Luther did in 1517. He had traveled a great deal, and had been sent by the city of Deventer to Avignon to negotiate with the pope; he had studied at Paris, and had even taught there afterwards. He knew good and bad monks, and had held two prebends when living at Cologne. How he must have regretted his life at Cologne! Here, we remember, he spent large sums of money acquired from the people at Aachen and Utrecht, whose spiritual needs had left him unmoved.

Groote had tried to reform his own mode of life before he preached the message of reform to others. Now he could speak in public and with success, not as the Pharisees of old, but as an honest reformer. "Through his labors", we read in a letter addressed to the bishop of Utrecht, "there are many virgins set as flowers in the field of the Lord; lives of chaste widowhood and voluntary poverty, as an harvest therein; renunciation of the world, acts of restitution and many other fruits sprung from the seed of Ecclesiastical and Catholic doctrine, and the wickedness of usury and disordered lust have ceased from the land of Zeeland"[2].

No other province in Holland is so far removed from the Yssel country as Zeeland, and yet this eye-witness informs us that due to Groote's preaching "the wickedness of usury and disordered lust have ceased from Zeeland". It is no wonder that the "Pharisees" did not rest until Groote was commanded to stop preaching.

Now that Groote could not preach any more, he turned to education, the translation of the Bible and hymns, and the foundation of a new brotherhood. In imitation of Christ he selected twelve apostles, and was followed by a host of disciples. When he was about to die he appointed a "comforter". Florentius Radewijns certainly did comfort a great many poor people. Rarely in the annals of Christian charity do we meet with such a comforter! How significant that Thomas à Kempis[3] begins the first chapter of his biography of Radewijns with the following sentence: "Our Lord and Master Jesus Christ, the Flower of all virtue and of all knowledge, began in humility and meekness that rule of his life which he handed down to his disciples to be observed as their law and pattern, saying: 'Learn of me, for I am meek and lowly in heart, and ye shall find rest for your souls' ". A little further on we read the following passages: "He is called Florentius as one that gathered flowers together (Flores colligens), because he gathered together with him in his house many clerks and brethren who were in the flower of their age. These brethren Florentius ruled with such discipline and taught with such fervency of spirit that this house was a school of heavenly training, having therein a mirror of holiness, a garniture of moral virtues, a pattern of goodness, a door to admit the poor, a place of meeting for clerks, of instruction for lay folk, of refuge for the devout, and for the beginning and carrying forward of every good thing. In this house many honorable and learned men first conceived the spirit of devotion, and like bees laden with honey went far afield from the full hive to spread fertility in divers places......... Fitting enough is the name of Radewin as meaning 'The Divine Radiance', and by this name Christ is rightly signified, for he is the Brightness of the Father who doth illumine the world with the light of his wisdom......... He sent forth also his apostles like beams of the true Sun to preach his word in all the world and give a good example to all the faithful, saying to them: 'So let your light shine before men that they may see your good works and glorify your Father who is in Heaven' "[4].

Whatever one may think of the character of this new light, its beams were plainly visible in the Yssel country. "At this time", writes Rudolph Dier of Muiden, the librarian of the brethren at Deventer, "many burghers of Deventer and people from the neighboring country were wont to visit Florentius and his brethren, asking how they might save their souls, confessing their sins. Especially on holidays they would gather in the 'House of Florentius' to listen to the reading of the Scriptures, which was done and is still being done [1458] in the people's own language; also to hear the fervent addresses by the brethren......... And almost all the devout burghers had in their houses one poor school boy whom they supported for the Lord's sake. Lambertus van Galen always had at least eight boys in his home, sent by the brethren of the 'House of Florentius'. He constructed a special dining room for these boys. Still all he possessed was his house and the money earned with his hands. Besides these poor boys he received three or four others who paid him for his services. He was accustomed on holidays to discuss with his boys the nature of vices and virtues, and the brethren would often come to dine with them.

"At this time many priests, attracted by the goodly report of Florentius' virtues, came from far and near to submit themselves to his guidance. Particularly from Westphalia large numbers arrived, who opened their hearts. Not a few of these had formerly been excommunicated. ....One excommunicated priest from Westphalia was given a room in the old vicarage of Florentius, where, being excommunicated, he had to eat his meals all alone. Another priest from Westphalia lived with the brethren in the building behind the 'New House'. He often sent letters to his friends in Westphalia, urging them to despise the world.

"One day Wermbold, rector of the Sisters of the Common Life at Utrecht, came to visit the brethren. He said: 'I do not know a better way to please the Lord than the way of the common life'. In 1404 he visited again the brethren-house. Seating himself among us, he spoke as follows: 'Forty years ago I found less knowledge of God in Kampen, Deventer, and Zwolle than the least one among you now possesses. When I was a young man I desired to serve the Lord, but knew not which way to go. There was at that time a pastor from Schoonhoven in Holland, named John Goedman, canon at Deventer, who, in order to win souls gave up his prebend'. He told us once how little light there was then among men, and only very few good monasteries. In Amsterdam was Gysbert Dou, in Leiden Thomas or Damasus, who used to attend our meetings as one of our members; in Purmereinde was Nicholas, in Hoorn William of Putten . . . . and John Brinkerinck was in charge of the sisters at Zutphen"[5].

And what do the sources tell about Gerard Zerbolt of Zutphen? Thomas à Kempis says of him: "Although he lived but for a short time, yet he left us doctrinal treatises that are most acceptable, for he was a very diligent student of the Holy Scriptures, and from the dark sayings of the learned he extracted divers aromatic spices having virtue against the distempers of vice to heal the languors of the soul"[6]. These "aromatic spices" seem to have invigorated many languishing souls, if one is to judge by the way in which Zerbolt's works were devoured. Both Luther and Loyola at one time felt stimulated by them.

The art of extracting "spices" was quite common
among Groote's followers and Cele's pupils, and Thomas
à Kempis developed it to perfection. How he managed
to collect the "aromatic spices" found in the "Imitation
of Christ" is still a mystery to most scholars, — that
very remarkable work, whose influence can hardly be
exaggerated. We appreciate it justly when we take into
account the tribute paid to the "Imitation", not simply
by Roman Catholics, or even by Christians of other
denominations[7]. The book has been perused almost as
eagerly by Turks, Hindoes, and Chinese; and it is often
quoted with approbation by modern mystics who are
not affiliated with any church.

Who can estimate the influence of such a book? Here
we approach a large chapter in the history of mankind,
— a chapter as yet unwritten. From home to home the
"Imitation" traveled, unnoticed by historians. For we
cannot follow it with any instrument known to us, but
must in our imagination enter the homes of the countless
thousands of human beings who read the book and left
no record of what its messages of hope and consolation
meant to their languishing souls or their aching hearts.

Other works in which the principles of the Christian
Renaissance are expressed are those of Wessel Gansfort.
True, some of his individual views, like that on
purgatory, cannot be regarded as of the movement itself.
Wherever any one of Groote's followers differed from
all the others, his peculiar views are to be set aside as
something extraneous to the movement. It should be
observed, however, that when the fifteenth century drew
to a close, the Christian Renaissance had already undergone a change. And when finally Cornelius Hoen
appeared with his letter on the Eucharist in 1520, it was
resolved into other movements. The "Spiritual Exer-

elses" of Loyola, though written in 1526 and perfected
much later, the "Institutes" of Calvin, composed about
the year 1534, the educational reforms of Sturm at
Strasbourg, and some of Luther's best works, in
common with some by Erasmus, Melanchton, Zwingli,
Murmellius, Wimpheling, and Lefèvre, — all these must
be defined in part as fruits of the Christian Renaissance.

II

One naturally wishes to inquire first of all what ideas
the Christian Renaissance and the Reformation had in
common, and how much Luther was indebted to the
former movement. Denifle and Grisar have shown that
the turning point in Luther's religious life came as early
as the year 1515, when he was writing his lecture on
Paul's Epistle to the Romans[8]. For although the 95
theses against indulgences, posted on the Cathedral at
Wittenberg in 1517, were the chief cause of Luther's
fame, and although his "Address to the German Nobility" set forth views regarding benefices and other
burning topics of the day, and thereby greatly increased
his popularity, nevertheless his most remarkable work
of the period from 1517–1525 remains the treatise
"Concerning Christian Liberty"[9], and his most noteworthy doctrine that of the depravity of man or original
sin, which led to that of justification by faith alone.

This significant statement of Luther is found in his
Lecture on Paul's Epistle: "Nowhere have I found so
clear an explanation of original sin as in the little treatise
of Gerard Groote: 'Blessed is the man', where he speaks
as a sensible theologian, and not as a rash philosopher"[10],
the quotation making reference to the "Spiritual Ascensions" of Gerard Zerbolt, which begins with: "Blessed is

the man". Paul had written in the third chapter of his Epistle to the Romans: "Therefore we conclude that a man is justified by faith without the deeds of the law". What were the conclusions drawn by Luther? All our thoughts, and all our deeds are sinful. Even in our very noblest thoughts and our best works the stain of sin mars every effort we make to improve our character. Man can do nothing without grace; he is depraved, owing to the fall of Adam. "And what is original sin"? Luther asks. "According to the subtle arguments of the scholastic theologians, it is the absence of original justice...... According to the Apostle and the simple teachings of Jesus Christ, it is not merely the deprivation of a function in the will, not merely the withdrawal of light from the intellect, or power from the memory, but it is the loss of all rectitude and all efficacy in all our faculties, both of the body and the soul, of the interior and the whole of the exterior man. It is besides the inclination to do evil, the dislike of good, the aversion to light and wisdom, the love of error and darkness, the departure from and abomination of good works, and the approach to evil. Hence, as the Fathers have justly remarked, this original sin is the fuel itself of concupiscence, the law of the flesh, the law of the members, the disease of nature, the tyrant, the original disease........ Here you have that hydra with its many heads, that imperishable monster with which we here below are struggling till death. Here you have that untameable Cerberus, that invincible Antaeos. I have found no one to give such a clear explanation of original sin as Gerard Groote in his little treatise: 'Blessed is the man', where he does not speak as a rash philosopher, but as a sound theologian".

Luther can agree with only one earlier writer, and this writer Gerard Zerbolt of Zutphen, a Brother of the

Common Life at Deventer. His own words, then, prove how greatly he was indebted to Groote's brotherhood. And we can now understand in part at least the startling remarks of Luther respecting Gansfort's writings: "If I had read his works earlier, my enemies might think that Luther had absorbed everything from Wessel: his spirit is so in accord with mine......... I have not the slightest doubt that I have been teaching the truth, since he, living at so different a time, under another sky, in another land, and under such divers circumstances, is so consistently in accord with me in all things, not only as to substance, but in the use of almost the same words".

Luther was also a follower of Ailly, bishop of Cambray, who had written a letter in defense of the Brethren of the Common Life in the year 1413[11]. Ailly had come to Deventer in that year to protect the Sisters of the Common Life as well as the brethren[12], and so much did the good bishop encourage the brethren that they prepared their first written constitution, beginning with the prologue: "Since the mode of life of clerks and presbyters who are serving God by having no property of their own, in chastity and mutual friendship and by the labor of their hands, has been approved .... and confirmed by Peter d'Ailly, cardinal of Cambray, ... this mode of life is to be continued and its rules written down lest we or our successors may forget them".

Luther knew Ailly quite well. He writes in 1520: "Formerly, when I was imbibing the scholastic theology, my lord the Cardinal of Cambray gave me occasion for reflection, by arguing most acutely, in the fourth book of the 'Sentences', that it would be much more probable, and that fewer superfluous miracles would have to be introduced, if real bread and real wine, and not only their accidents, were understood to be upon the altar"[13]. Also,

Luther was a pupil of Gabriel Biel[14], who had become the rector of the Brethren of the Common Life at Butzbach near Mainz — a fact which cannot have escaped Luther's attention, the more so since he had been taught for a year by the Brethren of the Common Life at Magdeburg. Biel was an Occamist[15], like Gansfort. Gerson had also been an Occamist and Luther probably knew that chiefly due to Gerson's vigorous defense of the brethren against the Dominicans at the Council of Constance were they rescued from further oppression. The way he praises the brethren at Herford as late as in the year 1532, and also in 1534, would make us conclude that he always respected Groote's new brotherhood very highly.

Would it not have been useful for Gansfort's latest biographers to reflect duly on all these facts before they decided that Luther could not have meant what he said, when he asserted there was so much similarity between his views and those of Gansfort? Let us begin with indulgences, a problem uppermost in Luther's mind between 1517–1522. Luther wrote a number of theses on indulgences; so had Gansfort more than thirty years before, only he called them propositions, and did not nail them on any church door. Gansfort had seen no use in indulgences at all. He said: "On him who is returning, or who has returned, to God, nothing ought to be so strictly enjoined as to sin no more, but purely to love God. Purity of heart, therefore, is the only perfect penitence, and ought to be inculcated by instruction and admonition........ Plenary pardon of sin is the actual removal of every obstacle preventing the beatific vision; just as thorough repentance consists in true and sincere purity of heart. Both, however, come from God alone"[16]. And what did Luther himself say in 1520? "I wrote about indulgences two years ago, but now I extremely

regret having published that book. At that time I was
still involved in a great superstitious respect for the
tyranny of Rome, which led me to judge that indulgences
were not to be totally rejected, seeing them, as I did,
to be approved by so general a consent among men......
Afterwards I perceived that they were nothing but mere
impostures of the flatterers of Rome, whereby to make
away with the faith of God and the money of men"[17].
When shortly afterwards Luther found Gansfort calling
indulgences a pious fraud, an error, and a lie, this must
have pleased him greatly.

Another chief cause of Luther's fame was his attack
on the greedy and indolent clergy. Many of them
were drawing revenues from church lands or other
property; some of them grew wealthy by collecting the
contributions of several congregations, without doing
anything for them in return. Groote had had two prebends when living at Cologne, but in 1374 he had relinquished both. The Brotherhood of the Common Life
as an institution acted as a protest against the moral
decline of the clergy by trying to return to the customs
in vogue among the early Christians. Ailly and Gerson
no doubt had admired the brethren for this attitude.
What the brethren at Magdeburg taught Luther cannot
be stated with certainty. We do not know why his parents
sent him to Magdeburg. But as a boy of fourteen he
must have learned something there, although the brethren
did not urge him to become a mendicant monk. If it was
at Magdeburg that Luther's thoughts "first turned in the
direction of the monastic life", as some writers think[18],
the haunting picture of a friar he met there one day on
the street, "begging bread and carrying a sack like a
donkey", undoubtedly induced him to enter a monastery.
If the brethren had actually done what many modern

writers think they did, Luther certainly would have mentioned the fact later on. Instead of that he says in 1532:
"Such brother-houses and monasteries please me beyond
measure".

Gansfort's latest biographer, in summing up the differences between Luther's point of view and that of Gansfort, should have left out the question of manual labor
and monastic institutions[19], for the reference he gives to
one of Gansfort's letters proves nothing in favor of his
assumption. On the contrary, he quotes from a letter
which must have impelled Luther to commend Gansfort
very cordially for it to his friends. Part of this letter
reads as follows:

"Do not, my dearest sister, so misunderstand my words
regarding the pursuit of cleanness and purity of heart as
to think that you, in your own purity, can be found pure
in the sight of God, since all our righteousness is as
filthy rags in his sight. Do not therefore waste your
strength to no purpose. Your body is frail; you are of
the tender sex; do not undertake what of all of David's
warriors, the picked and stoutest men of Israel, could
not perform. No one shall be saved by his own merits
or his own righteousness. There is only one sacrifice of
the great High Priest, and only so far as we partake of
this we are sanctified and pure in heart.

"You will say to me, 'How shall I partake of this
sacrifice; we rarely go to communion, not oftener than
once a fortnight, or occasionally once a week'? It was
not so much this outward participation that I urged; but
rather that you should often bathe and wash and be
baptized in the blood of the Lamb, who was born for
you and given for your every necessity. At that time I
promised you only one thing, and now I repeat that I do
not merely assure you that as often as you pray the

Father through the sacrifice of his Son offered for your
sanctification you are sanctified......... If you think
and reflect on him often, you will be pure in heart. This
is the better part, which was chosen by that wise lover,
[Mary] Magdalene, who sitting at the feet of Jesus
listened to his words, intent in her longing and wearied
by no labor......... What then is the use of all this
needless hardship in trying to attain the impossible?
Through desire for Christ and pious meditation upon
him it is within our power to have righteousness and
purity of heart, if we but wish it......... There is no
necessity for severe fasts or the wearing of a rough
goat's-hair garment. The worthy fruit of repentance
requires no bodily severity, but only that which is
necessary for all, the piety that waiteth for all things.

"Be regular in the observance of your duties in your
cloister home, and that will suffice for bodily discipline.
In the matter of sleep and food and drink and clothing,
follow the common usage and be content......... In
your confessions, I advise you to do just as your faithful
Mother Superior and leader shall counsel. And you can
be content with the thought that you are ready to confess
orally, when it is expedient. For we are not bound to
confess except for our good, and for our progress in
salvation"[20].

This letter brings us to that celebrated doctrine of
justification by faith, the natural outcome of Luther's
doctrine on original sin and the universal depravity of
mankind. Here we attack the chief question of all
theology, wherefore we should duly consider the influence of Gerard Zerbolt upon Luther. And we also
shall have to bear in mind what Gansfort and the
"Imitation" said about this subject, for Luther approached Gansfort very closely, as was indicated in a preceding

chapter[21]. But Zerbolt, Thomas à Kempis, and Gansfort
had borrowed their ideas from Florentius Radewijns,
who had written in his "Treatise on Spiritual Exercises":
"In order that we may know what it means to purify
the heart and to acquire virtues we must consider that
to the first man faculties of the soul were given to seek
the good. For he possessed an intellect and emotion,
memory and other faculties, like love, fear, hatred, hope,
joy, etc., in order that he might know God through his
intellect, love him through his emotion or will, and have
rest in him through his memory; fear made him dread
to offend God and to be separated from him, hope made
him confide in the benevolence of God, love made him
love God above all things, and himself and his neighbor
for God's sake; joy had been given to him that he might
rejoice in God with felicity supreme. But in the fall
of the first man mankind incurred original sin; his
natural feelings were deformed so that they now are
prone to evil.

"For reason, blinded by sin, often accepts falsehood
for truth; the warped will takes evil for good; the unstable memory busies itself with those things which
cause it to grow restless and vacillating, as it no longer
concentrates on the highest good, where it might have
everything. Thus man now fears only temporal adversities, physical hardships, and loss of honor. Thus hope
has become deranged, for man now hopes for less or
for more than he ought to do"[22].

This was the doctrine of original sin that Luther
found in the "Spiritual Ascensions". Gansfort and
Thomas à Kempis were taught this same doctrine, though
they did not react on it in exactly the same way. It
may very well be that Luther was influenced more by
the "Imitation" than by Zerbolt, for this little work was

eagerly devoured at that time by men of his character. Luther often read it[23], wherefore we also wish to know what the "Imitation" says about the result of original sin. In chapters 31 and 55 of book III we read:

"I know not what it is, or by what spirit we are led, or what we pretend, we that seem to be called spiritual, that we take so much pains, and are so full of anxiety about transitory and mean things, while we scarcely at all, or but seldom, think of our own inward concernments, with full recollection of mind. We mind not where our affections lie, nor bewail the impurity that is in all our actions. For 'all flesh had corrupted his way', and therefore did the great deluge ensue. Since then our inward affection is much corrupted, our actions thence proceeding must needs be corrupted also, giving proof of the want of internal vigor.

"O Lord my God, who hast created me after thine own image and likeness, grant me this Grace, which thou hast shewed to be so great and so necessary to salvation; that I may overcome my most evil nature which draweth me to sin and to perdition. For I feel in my flesh the law of sin contradicting the law of my mind, and leading me captive to the obeying of sensuality in many things; neither can I resist the passions thereof, unless thy most holy Grace fervently infused into my heart do assist me. There is need of thy Grace, and of great degrees thereof, that Nature may be overcome, which is ever prone to evil from her youth. For through Adam the first man, Nature being fallen and corrupted by sin, the penalty of this stain hath descended upon all mankind, in such sort that 'Nature' itself, which by thee was created good and upright, is now taken for the sin and infirmity of corrupted nature, because the inclination thereof left unto itself draweth to evil and to inferior things".

Zerbolt is not quite so clear as Radewijns, or the "Imitation", but his view cannot be omitted here. Only it must not be forgotten that he copied from Radewijns. Says Zerbolt: "We have been contaminated by original sin, and wounded in all the powers and faculties of the soul. For through the loss of original justice as a result of our fall and the just judgment of God, these powers and feelings, having fallen from their proper status, have become deranged and diminished, though not completely destroyed. Hence, it happens that these powers and feelings deviate from their proper course, instituted by God; they are prone to evil. Again, our reason, rendered vacillating and obtuse, often accepts falsehood for truth, and frequently busies itself with useless and vain thoughts. The will has become warped; it often chooses degenerate objects, loves carnal, and detests spiritual and celestial things. Our desires are deformed: they are covetous, and have degenerated into carnal lusts. Our hope does not seek God, but wealth and fame, or something it has no right to ask for. We are grieved by loss of temporal riches, and of honor. Christ through his precious death does indeed redeem us from our original sin, so that this loss of soul powers or the law of the flesh is not guilt, in order that there be no condemnation for those who are in Jesus Christ, though he does not at once restore us to our original righteousness, nor does he reform the faculties of our soul, but left those to be reformed by us through saintly exercises"[24].

It appears that at the very moment when Luther evolved his view on justification by faith, he was profoundly influenced by the principles of the "New Devotion". In his "Lecture on the Epistle to the Romans" he indicated his contempt for scholastic philosophy, as we saw, and stated the need of referring to the words

of Paul and Christ, approving in one breath with this
the view of Gerard Zerbolt. Man was in a dreadful
condition, Zerbolt had asserted, in imitation of Radewijns. No one could help him but Christ through his
sacrifice on the cross. Man would obtain salvation as a
result of Christ's work, finished for him on Golgotha.
But he had to take many spiritual exercises, not for the
sake of regaining his lost heritage, which he could not
do anyhow, but to improve his character. Luther writes
in 1515: "Sin has remained behind in spiritually minded
persons as an exercise in the life of grace, in order to
humble pride, and restrain boldness"[25]. "Good works",
he continues, "do not please God because they bring
merit, but because God has predestined from eternity that
they shall please him. Consequently the good works do
not make us good, but our goodness or rather God's
goodness makes us and our works good; in themselves
they are not good, but God judges them good"[26]. This
reminds us of Gansfort, who wrote: "Do not think that
you in your purity can be found pure in the sight of
God, since all our righteousness is as filthy rags in his
sight"[27].

Luther, in common with Groote's followers, insists
however that man must exert himself. He wants us to
perform preparatory works, to "cultivate the soil".
Gansfort uses exactly the same simile, as we saw in the
preceding chapter. This must have struck the German
reformer in 1521. And as for the doctrine of free will,
neither of the two men believed in it at all. "Grace will
not be granted to man", says Luther, "if he neglects to
perform the agricultural work within himself". Man
must sigh for deliverance; he must hope for a change,
and believe in the Savior. Only in Christ lies our
justification. We must search our inner selves, and

bewail our multitudinous sins. God will elect us, though none of us can know whether God has done so. As yet he does not stress the phrase "by faith alone", and assurance of election is still lacking. Luther's theological views are not well defined in 1515 and 1516, but they plainly indicate the tendency of his thought[28].

In common with Groote and Gansfort, as well as with others not connected with the Christian Renaissance, he points out the abuses among the clergy as early as the years 1515 and 1516. The higher clergy he calls "seducers of the Christian people". Their love of wealth and luxury is crying to heaven for vengeance, he concludes. The common people are neglected, and even robbed. As for charity, what does the Church do? The clergy are building majestic structures, heaping up possessions, scrambling land and estates together.

In 1516 and 1517 Luther proceeded further on his way toward "heresy", as viewed by Catholics, or the "dawn of new light", as judged by men like Melanchton. "Now for the first time", Melanchton wrote afterwards, "the light of new theology appeared after a long, dark night. Luther showed the real difference between Law and Gospel; he refuted the Pharisaical errors which at that time ruled school and pulpit, as if man could earn forgiveness of sin through his own labors. He brought back the souls to the Son of God, and pointed out the lamb, which bore our guilt". And Mathesius praised Luther in the following manner: "Young Dr. Luther says he had solemnly sworn a true and public oath that he would abide by the Scriptures; it was better to appeal to the Scriptures in dealing with questions of belief or conscience than that one stake one's soul and conscience on the dark sayings of Scotus and Albert Magnus, the dubious Thomas Aquinas, the modern school or the

Occamists.......... He insisted on this before his attack on indulgences". Up with Augustine, cried Luther's followers early in 1517, and down with Aristotle, the heathen. Away with good works, was the refrain. "That horrible doctrine of predestination", adds Grisar, "was now formulated by them". "Faith alone justifies", Luther constantly repeated. Even Gabriel Biel was now rejected by him. Gradually he turned away from the teachers of his youth[29].

But before we investigate in what respects Luther deviated from the principles of the Christian Renaissance, we shall want to know what he had in common with Gansfort, Groote, and Thomas à Kempis in addition to the subjects discussed thus far. For Gansfort's latest biographers find fault with Ullmann for having considered Gansfort and Luther kindred spirits. Besides, we wish to extend our comparison between the Christian Renaissance and the Reformation. If Luther attacked the mendicant monks in 1520, he did not thereby oppose Gansfort's views on monasticism or on manual labor. Many of Gansfort's writings had been burned by the Dominicans, and the mendicants had repeatedly attacked the Brethren of the Common Life. Luther said this about monasteries in 1520: "It would be, I think, necessary, especially in these perilous times, that foundations and convents should again be organized as they were in the time of the Apostles and a long time after". And this: "Let no more mendicant monasteries be built"[30].

Luther and Gansfort also agreed on the absolute necessity of faith. Luther wrote in 1520: "The highest worship of God is to ascribe to him truth, righteousness, and whatever qualities we must ascribe to one in whom we believe......... On the other hand, what greater rebellion, impiety, or insult to God can there be than not to believe his promises? .... What then can works, done in such a state of impiety, profit us, were they even angelic or apostolic works"[31]? Gansfort had written thus: "Not as if infidelity alone was sin; for pride, envy, and falsehood, are so too. But this sin is spoken of, as if there were none but itself, because all other sins remain so long as this remains, and all depart when this departs, so that when there is no more unbelief, all sins will be forgiven"[32].

There is one thing about the Protestants of the third and fourth decades of the sixteenth century that should be noted here. They very generally consider themselves to have been emancipated from a realm of darkness. They often mention the Gospel as having transplanted the Law, and Luther and Calvin as the prophets of enlightenment, teaching the misguided people the uselessness of good works, but what had Gansfort said? "The Law, both that which was given by Moses and that which is written in the hearts of all men, merely vexed. It vexed, I say, but it did not justify. There was therefore need for some law which was not vexatious, some paternal law, some sweet law of love which justified, and by which the sons became obedient and inherited the kingdom. Such is the law of the Gospel, which gives no temporal promises, and hence was published after the fulness of time, in order to admonish us to lift our eye above time, and point our hopes to eternity"[33].

As for the doctrines of the universal priesthood of all believers and the authority of the Scriptures, these were mentioned in a preceding chapter. Even though Augustine had on one occasion asserted that one should believe in the Gospel because the Church did, Gansfort does not hesitate to state: "It is for God's sake that we

believe the Gospel, and for the Gospel's sake that we
believe the Church and the pope; we do not believe the
Gospel for the Church's sake"[34]. Luther deserves credit
for having admitted the similarity between his views and
those of Wessel Gansfort. And Melanchton rightly
asserted: "On most of the main articles of the Evangelical creed, Wessel's views had been the same that are
taught now and if at present particular points by God's
help are more fully inculcated, the cause is that sentiments of different parties are enlivened and developed
in their contact with each other, — an advantage of
which Wessel was destitute in his isolated position"[35].

There can be no doubt that when Luther first read
Gansfort's works, he must have been reminded of statements he had made himself. He had accused the papacy
of hiding behind three walls, while Gansfort speaks of
the pope's friends seeking shelter behind one wall[36]. Both
reformers attacked the evil of simony[37]; and insisted on
reduction of formal observances[38] and on reform of
the universities, where they both had been shocked by
the dissolute lives led by most students[39].

Why then should any one ask in surprise how Luther
could have approved of Gansfort's writings so warmly[40]?
Why lay so much stress on differences between the views
of Gansfort and Luther of which Luther himself was
not aware? One of them has just been discussed; it is
the question of manual labor and monasticism[41]. The
second point is the fact that Gansfort never thought of
leaving the Church; the same can be said of Luther
before 1522, as he had not thought of leaving. His
opponents gave him no chance to argue his views; he
was forced out. The third point deals with the papacy
as instituted by God; that will pass, though we should
bear in mind that almost all that Gansfort said about

the papacy must have pleased Luther greatly. The little
power he ascribed to the pope was negligible. Fourthly
we are told that Gansfort believed the sacraments work
"ex opere operato", that is, they have power in themselves to bring forgiveness of sins. This point is
badly taken, for Gansfort says: "The effects of the
sacraments are dependent upon the inclination of the
partaker, and upon an inclination requisite for the intention. But the requisite inclination for the efficacy of
this sacrament [Eucharist] is a hungering and thirsting
for the life-giving food and drink. Hence the less one
hungers and thirsts for it, the less also will be the effect
he receives......... It follows that a sacrifice renders
satisfaction only so far as he, for whom the sacrifice
is made, is fit for the gift......... If the whole world
were offered for one who disdains it, little satisfaction
or none at all were made......... It is true that baptism
and the sacrament of penance take away all sin, and that
too entirely. But this truth is to be accepted as dealing
with those sins which one has committed before baptism
and before penance. For since those sins are past and
no longer in his power, if he believes in God and respects
and holds fast to him as his great priest and sacrifice,
they are altogether cleansed away by faith. If, however,
some impurity is intermingled with the cleansing,......
since this is in his power and is his fault, it is not the
result of any defect in the sacrament that he rises from
baptism alive and not yet pure, even if he be baptized
by Peter or Paul"[42]. In other words, faith alone brings
forgiveness of sins, which is exactly what Luther taught.
Fifthly, Christ is truly present in the Eucharist, wherefore one must worship the Host, Gansfort is supposed
to have taught. This would be a good point, if the first
part were left out, for Luther also believed in the presence

of Christ in the Host. Moreover, Gansfort did not say that one should worship the Host, but Christ in the Host, where Luther agreed with him. Sixthly, only priests may consecrate the sacraments, according to Gansfort. This would have become another good point, if distinction had been made between the views entertained by Luther before and after 1522, for Luther very soon had to change his view. He began with the universal priesthood of believers, but as soon as he and his followers built up a church organization themselves, they could not maintain this doctrine. Seventhly, it is not necessary to accept both the wine and the bread, according to Gansfort. This is true, for Gansfort lays very little stress on external observances. And yet it is quite likely that Luther was favorably impressed by Gansfort's dislike of formalism. Next, the Eucharist is a sacrifice in Gansfort's opinion. If such is the case, Gansfort made very little of it, for he stresses the phrase: "Do this in remembrance of me". Point ten is a poor one. The priest has the power in administering the sacrament of penance to forgive sins. Gansfort never said such a thing at all, as was indicated above[43]. Then follow about a dozen other points, none of which could have made much of an impression on Luther for the simple reason that he was overwhelmed by the many important views of Gansfort on which he completely agreed with the "Frisian" reformer.

We can understand perfectly well Luther's gratification in reading Gansfort's works for the first time. His friends had been lauding him as the herald of enlightenment. They were hailing what they considered the aurora of better Evangelical teachings. Impenetrable was the darkness of the past, and the first beams of light had been cruelly extinguished. But here was Wessel, a learned

Frisian from Groningen, who had not retracted, who
had not been persecuted, and yet, how many of his ideas
exactly resembled those of the great reformer himself!
Luther's "heresy" was therefore no innovation. Gansfort was introduced to him by two men from the Netherlands who enthusiastically embraced the teachings of
Luther's party. They felt Gansfort and he had much in
common, and thus that eulogy of Martin Luther on
Gansfort's works flowed very naturally from his pen.

III

There is one marked difference, however, between the
theology of the Christian Renaissance as a whole and
that of the Lutherans. Luther reasoned this way: "A
Christian, like Christ his head, being full and in
abundance through his faith, ought to be content with
this form of God obtained through faith, except that he
ought to increase this faith till it is perfected. For this
faith is his life, justification, and salvation.........
Thus from faith flow forth love and joy in the Lord,
and from love a cheerful, willing, free spirit, disposed
to serve our neighbor voluntarily, without taking any
account of gratitude or ingratitude, praise or blame, gain
or loss"[44]. Luther does speak about love, but as the result
of faith. He begins with faith in God and ends with
love for his neighbor. The Christian Renaissance on the
other hand (and the Roman Catholic church as well)
teaches that love is supreme and that faith is generated
by it. Groote, Radewijns, Zerbolt, and the "Imitation"
do not consider perfect faith the highest good, but perfect
love. They pay less attention to faith, for in cultivating
love they added faith to the virtues they hoped to acquire.
Luther mentions the word faith oftener than the word

love, and Paul as often as Christ. In doing this he deviated somewhat from the teachings of the Christian Renaissance[45].

Luther differed further from the principal tenets of the Christian Renaissance by ignoring, and even scorning, the remarks made by the Apostle James on the confession of sins, and on faith without works being absolutely worthless.

Most of Luther's followers also, who proudly called themselves "Evangelicals", reflected just as much on the justification by faith taught by Paul as on the Sermon on the Mount. They often spoke of the Gospel in connection with the faults of their predecessors and opponents, thereby meaning to imply that they themselves were following its instructions more faithfully than the former. Nevertheless, they not seldom showed a deplorable lack of charity and forbearance. "Away with the pope", they cried, "away with all the monks, priests, and bishops; down with intolerance and persecution"! Shortly afterwards they organized a church government themselves, and persecuted their opponents wherever feasible, which afterwards could also be said of many Calvinists and Jesuits. Groote's followers, on the other hand, had insisted on moderation, and brotherly love, and the Brethren of the Common Life, as far as we know, never showed much inclination before 1520 to interfere with anybody's religious aspirations, or to harm their opponents in any way. After 1520 they were generally molested and soon were disbanded almost everywhere, after having preached the message of reform to clergy and laymen alike. Erasmus, who for about twelve years had been their pupil, in 1528 voiced their views in writing:

"Some persons emphasize the confessional too much, others on the contrary want to do away with it altogether, though there might be a mean between the two extremes. Likewise certain persons have carried the Mass so far that it almost becomes with unlearned and sordid priests, or rather sacrificers, a source of profit and ground of confidence for evil-living men; others again would totally abrogate it. But here, too, there is room for moderation whereby we might have a more holy and pure Mass, and yet avoid having none at all. In a similar way certain persons in their extreme and superstitious worship of spirit almost obscure the worship of Christ. Some persons strive utterly to overthrow all the status of the monks; others on the contrary lay too much emphasis on their constitutions, ceremonies, titles, and kinds of vesture. In these and all other matters it might be brought about by prudent moderation that we might hold the dogma of faith more certainly and better; that the confession might be improved and made less irksome; the Mass might be more sacred and more venerated; we might have priests and monks, if fewer in number, yet certainly better........ That would be more easy to accomplish if private reasonings were laid aside and we were all to look to one great objective, that is, the glory of Christ. At present most persons look after their own interests, and so it happens that it is not well with us either in private or public"[46].

The same views are expressed in a letter addressed in 1528 to Martin Bucer, the Alsatian reformer: "Those who have given up the recital of the canonical hours do not now pray at all; many who have laid aside the pharisaical dress are really worse than before........ The first thing that makes me draw back from this company is that I see so many among this troop becoming altogether estranged from the purity of the Gospel". To Lefèvre he had written in 1526: "We see with what kind of literature the Lutherans fill the world. Nor are those documents a whit more sane which are written on the other side by certain theologians. From the collision of such books, what else arises except conflagration? The same result happens from the meetings and speeches of both parties; so they wildly abuse one another and the rope of contention is strained"[47].

These letters remind us of Erasmus' remark about Gansfort: "Wessel and Luther have much in common, but how much more modestly and like Christ did he propagate his teachings than those Lutherans at Strasbourg"! Gansfort's followers generally saw little use in radical changes, in blood and strife. For that reason perhaps they did not create so great a stir as men like Luther, who did not always owe their celebrity to exalted views or great learning, but chiefly to their break with the Church. It is indeed very doubtful whether Luther was a greater theologian than Gansfort. He may not even have had so much influence as the latter, for real influence is exerted in various invisible and intangible ways, and usually is not recorded correctly in the pages of history. Many of Gansfort's followers came to regard the universal religious quarrels about them as sad mistakes. For that they have as yet received but little recognition. Nevertheless, their action will be viewed in a different light in future days when passion has given place to caution and moderation. Then perhaps the scholarly world may change its views on the influences of peaceful compared with revolutionary reforms.

IV

A few moments should now be devoted to the line of demarcation which between 1520 and 1570, roughly speaking, was drawn between the Protestants east and west of the Rhine. One doctrine has been held chiefly responsible for the rift in the harmony between the Protestants. It was the new doctrine regarding the presence of Christ's body in the Holy Supper, or Host. The doctrine of "transubstantiation", held by the Roman Catholic church, teaches that the bread and wine is changed into Christ's flesh and blood; that of "consubstantiation", held by the Lutherans, compares the presence of Christ's body in the bread and wine with the immanence of fire in red-hot iron; while the corresponding doctrine of the Reformed churches in Holland, France, and Switzerland, the Anglican or Episcopal church, the Presbyterians, Methodists, Baptists, and most other Protestants, rejects the bodily presence of Christ in the bread and wine of the communion service. We have in the preceding chapter considered Hoen's startling view, written down by him in the year 1520. On account of its historical significance, part of Hoen's letter should be quoted here:

"Christ has instituted the Holy Supper in order that the soul may firmly believe that she really has a Bridegroom of her own, who gave himself for her, and shed for her his precious blood. By this means she is induced to avert her affections from the objects she formerly loved, to fix them on Christ alone, and to make him her chief good. This means, as the Savior says (John VI), to feed upon Christ and to drink his blood; and whoever partakes of the Lord's Supper, without such faith, feeds rather upon the manna of the Jews than upon Christ. Of this quickening faith the schoolmen of the Romish church knew nothing. They inculcated a dead faith, which, being merely historical, could not save. They imagined it sufficient to assert, and artificially, but without Scriptural proof, to show that the bread after consecration is the true body of Christ. In this belief they paid to it divine honor, which if God be not in the bread differs little from the reverence paid by the heathen to stocks and stones. They allege indeed that they have the word of God which says: 'This is my body'. Yes, they have the word of God, that same word which they have used to uphold the Romish tyranny in the text: 'Whatsoever thou shalt bind on earth', etc.. All depends, however, upon how the word is understood. The Lord has forbidden us to believe those who say: 'Lo, here is Christ, or lo there'. Consequently I ought not to believe them who tell us that Christ is in the bread. If I do not listen to the Lord's warning I cannot excuse myself as being the victim of deception, for these are the perilous times he foretold. The apostles spoke in a different way of this sacrament. They broke bread and called it bread, and all observe the most perfect silence about that which Rome believes. Nor does Paul object, as in I Cor. X he speaks of the bread of communion of the body of Christ [verse 16: 'The bread which we break, is it not the communion of the body of Christ'?]. He does not say: 'The bread is the body of Christ'. It is rather evident that in this passage 'is' must be taken for 'signifies', which may be clearly inferred from the comparison between the bread and the sacrifice to idols [verses 17–21]. Something of which he does not aver that it is transmuted *is* yet to him, that is, *signifies* to him a fellowship with the devil to whom it is offered.

"That Christ was once to become man was foretold by the prophets, demonstrated as a fact by himself, and preached as such by the apostles; but that he was daily to become bread under the hands of every sacrificing priest, was foretold neither by prophets nor apostles, but is founded upon the single expression: 'This is my body'. But it is strange that they do not also assert that John the Baptist was transmuted into Elijah, seeing that Christ says of him: 'This *is* Elijah', or the evangelist John into Christ, seeing that the Lord upon the cross said to his mother respecting him: 'Behold thy son'. I know that custom is to blame for the alarm felt at an interpretation of the words of the institution which elsewhere is adopted without scruple, but I cannot find any good ground for the difference. Many other texts might be adduced, in which Christ calls himself a door, a way, and a corner-stone; or says: 'I am the vine', etc.; yet no one cleaves so stoutly to the letter as to maintain that Christ is a real and natural vine. At least I am aware of no other ground why we are so straitened in interpreting the words of the institution, but the authority of the pope"[48]

That these views of Hoen were the natural sequence of Gansfort's teachings was firmly believed by Hoen himself as well as by Rode, rector of the brethren at Utrecht, and his friend Sagarus. Rode and Sagarus discussed Hoen's treatise with Martin Bucer, who shortly afterwards praised Wessel Gansfort and Rode as the greatest thinkers among all the Reformers, including Luther. The following theses from Gansfort's treatise on the sacrament of the Eucharist prepared the way for the view entertained by Hoen, Rode, Sagarus, Bucer, Oecolampadius, Zwingli, and Calvin: " 'He that eateth my flesh and drinketh my blood abideth in me and I in him'. But he that saith he abideth in Christ ought also to walk even as he walked. Thus did [Mary] Magdalene eat, when she sat at the feet of Jesus; when at first she loved much, and when in anointing him she wrought a good work. She was scourged with his stripes,

she was reproached with his reproaches; nay, more than
if she had been reproached herself. She was crucified
with his wounds. In his death she died with him from
bitter grief. She rejoiced with him in his victory over
death, and exulted in his triumph. In all this she ate
the flesh of the Son of man and drank his blood, and
therefore lives indeed for ever"[49].

At the moment when Oecolampadius and Bucer were
hesitating, when Zwingli had not yet formulated a definite
view on this subject, the rector of the Brethren of the
Common Life from Utrecht brought certainty and conviction. He and his friend knew their favorite arguments
so well that neither the Swiss nor the Alsatian reformers
had any doubt left on this matter after the year 1522.
In 1522 and 1523 Gansfort's letters and his "Farrago"
were printed by Adam Petri at Basel. In 1523
Petri wrote to his friend Conrad Faber, Professor at
Küsnacht:

"Behold, most learned sir, what an author has been
removed out of the way, and by what sort of men, and
for what cause[50]! In what other, excepting only the Bible,
have you ever seen the whole work of Christ and the
contents of Scripture set forth with clearer arguments,
or those imposters and enemies of God combated with
stronger ones? In what other have you found the traditions of men more effectually shaken and obscured?
.... I hope that he will now influence the minds
of all, if they would but read him, for he teaches not
as they do, but as one that hath authority. I could wish
also that he were read by those who, destitute of charity
and puffed up with knowledge, give offence to the weak
in Christ......... And therefore it is, that, although
yourself adorned with all theological gifts, you have not
scrupled to call him 'The great Theologian' "[51].

One characteristic feature of the principles of the Christian Renaissance was the aversion to formal, lifeless observances. Groote's disciples generally stressed the inner essence of things. Thus Groote, in addressing a simple "beguine", or sister, told her that the three monastic vows had very little significance. To serve God with pure devotion was religion, he claimed, not the taking of vows. There probably was no organized group of men and women in the Europe of the fifteenth and early sixteenth centuries who so consistently sought to return to the ideals and customs of the apostolic church as did the Brethren and Sisters of the Common Life. They were always dressed in simple garments, avoided all forms of luxury and self-indulgence, humbly served one another, — superior, equal, or inferior, all alike; when they saw others go wrong they ignored it as much as possible; the mendicant monks, who often slandered and openly attacked them, they did not malign in abusive terms, nor did they seek revenge in any other way. The money earned by them was given in return for useful books, or for practical instruction imparted to their pupils. If perchance they earned more than they needed, this extra money was not spent in adorning their buildings, but as a rule the brethren used it for charitable purposes of various kinds. During the rectorate of Radewijns at Deventer, for example, they lodged poor school boys, healed the sick, and supplied the poor with alms. What was their incentive in doing all this? They wanted to be Christ's disciples. At no other time and in no other place could Thomas à Kempis have gathered the material for the "Imitation of Christ" but at Deventer between 1384 and 1400. Christ had always remained poor in earthly goods, the brethren reasoned, wherefore they too wished to have no property of their own. He

had spent almost all his time in serving others; hence
the brethren, if they wanted to be his disciples, were
bound to do the same. As long as sick and hungry
people remained among them they had no right to erect
costly churches, they thought.

This love of simplicity, poverty, and service had found
expression in the literary masterpieces of Groote's disciples. As the sixteenth century dawned, some of their
ideas would of necessity develop into others. Thus we
proceed from the works of Groote to those of Gansfort
and from Gansfort's works to those of Cornelius Hoen,
who had received his elementary education in the school
of the Brethren of the Common Life at Utrecht. For
the Christian Renaissance did not influence all men alike.
Even its own inner essence was subject to change. Hence
we are quite prepared to hear Hoen say: "If God is
believed to be in the bread, then must the worship paid
to him also be external. Hence the costly monstrance,
the splendid temple with all its decorations, the lamps
and tapers, the sacred garments interwoven with silk and
gold, the choral chant of the monks, the unction and
celibacy of the priests, the withdrawal of a part of the
sacrament from the laity"[52].

This desire to return to the pristine simplicity of the
apostolic church we find personified in the deeds of the
Swiss reformers and the Calvinists in the Low Countries.
We cannot with absolute certainty conclude that Zwingli
and Calvin, together with their followers in the Low
Countries, followed the same impulse in sweeping away
all the "idolatrous" emblems in their churches that
impelled Hoen to reject the rites of the Catholic church.
One American scholar reasons that the Swiss were the
most democratic people in Europe, wherefore their Reformation was "radical and thorough". For the Luther-

ans retained the crosses, altars, pictures, and emblems, while the Swiss whitewashed the walls in their churches, and took the crosses away[58]. There may be some truth in this view. Nevertheless, we should not confine ourselves to the Swiss, for the Calvinists in France and the Low Countries also whitewashed the walls of their churches. The whole trend of the Christian Renaissance had been away from external observations. Hoen's letter was written as early as the year 1520, and its author may have entertained some of the views expressed therein several years before that date. Once more therefore we should bear in mind the extremely powerful influence of the Brethren of the Common Life and of the "Imitation".

Some scholars will undoubtedly object to this interpretation of the Christian Renaissance. Roman Catholic writers may at first be inclined to hold that the movement adhered strictly to the faith of their church, not only during the whole of the fifteenth century, but later as well. The lives of Bucer, Sturm, and Zwingli seem to prove, however, that the religious movement inaugurated by Gerard Groote did not confine its influence to Roman Catholic reformers. Nor did the Yssel country remain overwhelmingly Catholic. Among others, the old church of St. Lebwin's at Deventer had its walls whitewashed; and it has retained the whitewash until the present day, as also has the church of St. Michael at Zwolle, where Cele had his library. There is but one building left of the monastery of Windesheim; it was transformed into a church by Calvinists, and to-day it is still a Reformed church building. The brethren-house at Groningen was situated near the venerable pile of St. Martin's, which also is now a Reformed church building. The same can be said of the prominent old Catholic churches at Utrecht, Delft, and a great many other cities in the Netherlands. We should indeed be making a great mistake in saying that the noblest ideas of the Christian Renaissance were entirely absorbed by the Roman Catholics of the sixteenth century and after. On the other hand, we should be just as greatly mistaken in going to the other extreme by seeing nothing but Protestant ideas in the writings of Groote's school.

The Calvinistic doctrine of predestination also may partly be considered a product of the new revival. It differed slightly from Luther's doctrine, which had been built in part upon Zerbolt's exposition on original sin. Whether Calvin was chiefly influenced by Luther, Lefèvre, or Bucer, he ultimately received something from the Christian Renaissance. "Principally", said Calvin, "I have wished to follow Bucer, man of holy memory"[54]. And Bucer, a native of Schlettstadt, and an ardent admirer of Gansfort, was intimately in touch with the teachings of Groote's disciples. Gansfort may very well be called a precursor of Calvinism in this respect. He and Bucer both differed somewhat from Luther. For the latter, though absolutely certain of his salvation, confided in the revelation of God through Jesus Christ. God could never be expected, Luther reasoned, to refuse the gift of salvation to any one trusting him and believing in him. Calvin on the other hand connected the doctrine of predestination with that of divine providence, as Gansfort had done.

The doctrine of predestination taught by Gansfort and Calvin is of course very different from what a great many people suppose it to be. Calvin by no means teaches that it is useless for man to act, though all of man's actions are dependent on God's will. All good works, says Calvin, are gifts of the spirit of God; while Gansfort wrote: "God is the real agent in all things, and the only creative agent, that is, he so operates in every outward action of his creatures that, whether secondary causes cooperate or not, whenever he efficaciously wills that something be done, the effect always follows. And if he does not thus exert his will, nothing will result, no matter how great the natural force and zeal exerted by other powers. And therefore, though secondary causes may be true causes, still in comparison with the first cause they are to be regarded as mere occasions, so that indeed all our care and thought may fittingly and wisely be cast on him"[55].

There is something sublime about the thought that, whenever we lift up our hand, it is God who assists us in doing it, — he the master and controlling power of the world, the planets, and all the stars. Wherefore Motley bears this witness: "The doctrine of predestination, the consciousness of being chosen soldiers of Christ, inspired those Puritans who founded the commonwealths of England, of Holland, and of America with a contempt of toil, danger, and death which enabled them to accomplish things almost supernatural. No uncouthness of phraseology, no unlovely austerity of deportment, could, except to vulgar minds, make that sublime enthusiasm ridiculous, which on either side of the ocean ever confronted tyranny with dauntless front, and welcomed death on battlefield, scaffold, or rack with perfect composure. The early Puritan at least believed. The very intensity of his belief made him, all unconsciously to himself and narrowed as was his view of his position, the great instrument by which the widest human liberty was to be gained for all mankind"[56].

V

One important question still remains to be considered, namely the influence exerted by the Christian Renaissance on the revival of learning North of the Alps. We found that the Yssel country, where the movement originated, and the cities of Deventer and Zwolle in particular, were closely in touch with the prosperous cities in Flanders, and we noted that the Christian Renaissance, though essentially a religious movement, partook not a little of the aid that wealth and leisure gave to the cultivation of learning and art in Flanders. In Deventer and Zwolle the schools were founded which became the two main fountain-heads of the Transalpine Renaissance — in Deventer and Zwolle, and not at Windesheim or Mount St. Agnes. Groote's followers, though they were not aware of it themselves, were driven by an unseen but exceedingly powerful force to advance the cause of learning. This force or impulse was not generated by the Italian Renaissance, but by a combination of circumstances very much like those which in Italy had given birth to a great revival of learning. Groote and his disciples said a great deal about despising the "world". At the same time, however, they, more perhaps than any other organized group of men and women in Transalpine Europe, wrought to make this world a better place in which to live. Beset on all sides by the powers of monasticism, asceticism, and decadent scholasticism, they gradually moved away from these very forces.

Shortly after Groote's death hundreds of boys gathered in the school of John Cele at Zwolle. From every direction they came, and not only from obscure little villages or hamlets, but from Trier, Cologne, Liège, and Utrecht, the cathedral cities, famous for centuries as the

seats of the best schools in their dioceses. About half
a century afterwards Wessel Gansfort left Zwolle in
search of more learning, as untold numbers of other
youths had done. He had not been trapped in a monastery. Nothing of the kind. At Cologne he met a Greek
who probably was one of the fugitives from Constantinople. Of this man he learned Greek, and from a Jew
he learned Hebrew. He now knew the three ancient
languages, and could delve into the rich stores of ancient
literatures. A decade afterwards Nicholas of Cusa, one
of the greatest scientists and philosophers of his time,
bequeathed a large sum of money for the purpose of
founding a dormitory for poor school boys at Deventer.
Why did he not want one at Trier, the oldest city in
Germany, and near his parental home? Why should that
dormitory be built in distant Deventer? Is not this
question worth asking?

Then there was the work of Dringenberg at Schlettstadt in Alsace. He had been educated at Deventer.
Somehow his pedagogical reforms produced such startling results that from his school went forth Beatus
Rhenanus, Wimpheling, Sapidus, and Bucer. The school
at Schlettstadt became a training school for prospective
teachers, who in their turn trained hundreds of others.
And what school in all Europe could equal the fame of
the one attended by Erasmus? What teacher could boast
of successes like those achieved by Hegius? Moreover,
it was Münster which became the chief centre of humanism in Western Germany early in the sixteenth century;
and it was Murmellius who attracted huge crowds of
ambitious students from distant Silesia, from districts
along the Baltic Sea, and from the Rhineland. Who can
estimate the number of teachers that received their training at Münster? In Herford and Minden labored Möller,

in Lübeck Bonnus, in Emmerich Aelius, Bredenbach, and Uranius, in Düsseldorf Monheim, — the schools at Emmerich and Düsseldorf under the rectorate of Bredenbach and Monheim are said to have counted 2000 pupils, — in Attendorn Mülle, in Warendorf Scheve, in Osnabrück Scheibing, in Lüneburg Tulichius, — who formulated the famous 'rules of Tulichius' or 'leges Tulichianae', — in Borken Gildeshues and Dickmann. Many of these men were great scholars, poets, and reformers[57]. If we add the number of teachers trained at Wesel, Rostock, Cassel, Marburg, Groningen, Utrecht, Nijmegen, Amersfoort, 's-Hertogenbosch, Liège, and Ghent, we get a formidable total indeed.

The German Renaissance was partly a product of the Christian Renaissance. Even Mutian Rufus, Erfurt's glory, had received his elementary and secondary education at Deventer. None of the humanists in central Germany before 1520 could surpass Gansfort and Wimpheling. And who was called the German Petrarch, if not Rudolph Agricola, the pupil of the brethren at Groningen? Erasmus rightly said of him that he could have become the leader among the most learned humanists in Italy itself; for he had baffled the greatest wits at Ferrara, — he, the only native of Transalpine Europe who before 1500 could meet all their requirements[58]. And Erasmus, what a power he wielded during the first three decades of the sixteenth century!

In France, also, new life was introduced by the Christian Renaissance. This movement received in many respects a more appreciative welcome in France than in Germany. Gansfort and Erasmus consistently avoided Erfurt and Leipzig. Groote had shunned the writings of Eckhardt; his followers paid very little attention to the works of Tauler and the "German Theology". Standonck gained a larger following among the men of power in France than any apostle of the Christian Renaissance ever had in German lands. And when the rift deepened between the Protestants east and west of the Rhine, it became perfectly clear how powerful was the grip of the "New Devotion" on Calvinism. The school at Liège became the pattern after which the best schools in France were modeled, like the one of Gouvea at Bordeaux and Baduelle at Nîmes[59].

It is interesting to note how many historians have assumed that Wittenberg in Germany was the one great centre of reform early in the sixteenth century[60]. Luther was the magnetic force whose overwhelming influence no Protestant could escape. Yet we find Zwingli confessing his indebtedness to Erasmus, and denying any connection with Luther before 1518 at least. He had explained the gospels for two years before he ever had heard about Luther, was his answer to those who called him a Lutheran. The first change came to Zwingli when he visited Erasmus in 1516. Immediately after this he began his career as reformer, which career he pursued for at least two years independently of Luther. In 1521 Rode and Sagarus came from the Netherlands with Hoen's letter and Gansfort's writings. Bucer, Calvin's teacher, extolled Rode above Luther, and praised Gansfort no less. Zwingli published Hoen's letter in 1525, and used Hoen's best arguments himself. Nowhere were Gansfort's works appreciated as they were in Switzerland and the Netherlands, if one may judge by their circulation. Few men understood Wessel Gansfort so well as Huldrich Zwingli. Gansfort and Erasmus exerted perhaps more influence on Zwingli than did Luther. Henceforth the Protestants in the Low Countries and Switzerland were to join hands in a common cause. They were to whitewash their churches, resist tyranny and persecution, and oppose both Roman Catholics and Lutherans. But the Netherlands remained the leaders. As the sixteenth century advanced and finally gave place to the seventeenth, the Dutch Republic became a mighty force in the realms of theology, science, art, and literature. Leiden, not Zürich, or even Wittenberg, was for more than a century to be the foremost centre of learning in Protestant Europe.

VI

It is by no means an easy task to estimate the influence of the Christian Renaissance. In England, for example, it was exerted in various ways ; chiefly at first through the circulation of the "Imitation of Christ", which soon was translated into English, and was almost as widely read as the Bible itself. During the sixteenth century the teachings of the new religious movement were disseminated everywhere in England through the writings of Englishmen, Dutchmen, and Flemings.

The Catholics in England owe much to the Christian Renaissance. This is apparent from the edition of the "Chronicle of the English Augustinian Canonesses Regular at St. Monica's in Louvain", by Hamilton[61]. The chronicle relates that "towards the close of the reign of Elizabeth, and in the earlier years of James I, a large number of English ladies, whose families had remained loyal to the ancient Faith, despairing of being able to enjoy the happiness of religious life in their own country, betook themselves to the communities established on the Continent........ These communities weathered the storms of war and revolution in their continental homes, and the greater part of them have, during the nineteenth

century, returned to England". Two of these communities belonged to the Augustinian Canonesses Regular,
one of which was founded at Louvain in 1609, and the
other at Bruges in 1629. The latter is still in existence,
while the former was transplanted to England. Many
ladies of high rank joined them from time to time, and
their experiences form an important chapter in the
history of English Catholicism. Hamilton adds this
remark: "A nun of that Congregation [Windesheim]
was placed at the head of St. Ursula's community [at
Louvain] and the spirit of such saintly men as Gerard
Groot and Thomas à Kempis, with the largeness of
mind, the simplicity and austerity, and the noble traditions of Windesem, formed the spirit of the infant
community of St. Ursula's, which, in 1515, finally embraced the Windesem rule. The Congregation of Windesem . . . . survives in spirit and discipline among
our English nuns through their descent from the sisters
of St. Ursula's of Louvain"[62].

It may be noted here that the English convent at
Bruges still observes the rules of the Congregation of
Windesheim, while St. Ursula's at Louvain was founded
by seven sisters from the convent of Diepenveen. They
arrived at Louvain in 1415, where for a period of five
years (1415–1420) they lived in a house on the Halve-
straat as Sisters of the Common Life. Their prioress
was Margareth Scherpings, formerly a member of the
first sister-house at Deventer: the "House of Master
Gerard"[63]. Thus not only the spirit of Windesheim
survives among the nuns in England to-day, but also
that of the old home of Gerard Groote, the inaugurator
of the "New Devotion". These nuns can point to their
spiritual descent from the very first Sisters of the Common Life who owed their home to the great master
himself.

Catholicism in England also is greatly indebted to the labors of the Jesuits. They were descendants of the Brethren of the Common Life, were intimately connected with the life-work of Groote and Cele through the influence of Standonck, Béda, and Loyola, and carried with them wherever they went the gospel of the "New Devotion": the "Imitation of Christ".

More important is the history of the Church of England, also known as the Anglican or Episcopal Church. This church, like the Reformed churches, adopted at first the chief tenets of the Calvinistic faith, but has always differed from the latter on the question of rites and church government. It owed much to Wicliff, who, long before the days of the Reformers, had insisted on the general use of the sacrament of the Eucharist. He had also preached against the abuses in the Church, though this activity he merely had in common with many continental reformers of his time. Many of the other principles of English Protestantism were the products of the Christian Renaissance. This Protestantism greatly resembled that of Hoen, Bucer, Zwingli, and Calvin. Moreover, the researches of Burrage[64] have clearly demonstrated that the beginnings of independency, or Congregationalism, are not to be traced to the Brownists or Barrowists, but to the Congregational Puritanism advocated by Henry Jacob and William Bradshaw about 1604 and 1605, and later put in practice by various Puritan congregations in Holland, whence it was brought to America and back into England. "Puritan Congregationalism accordingly did not have its source in separatism, nor was it separatist in spirit, but was constantly declared by its upholders as involving a separation only from the world, and not from the Church of England"[65]. Hence the following statement by John Robinson, pastor of the Pilgrim Fathers at Leiden, about the time when the larger part of his congregation departed for America:

"To conclude, I believe with my heart before God, and profess with my tongue, and have before the world that I have one and the same faith, hope, spirit, baptism, and Lord which I had in the Church of England and none other; that I esteem so many in that church, of what state or order soever, as are truly partakers of that faith (as I account many thousand to be) for my Christian brethren, and myself a fellow-member with them of that one mystical body of Christ scattered far and wide throughout the world: that I have always in spirit and affection all Christian fellowship and communion with them, and am most ready in all outward actions and exercises of Religion lawful and lawfully done to express the same"[66].

We should not therefore be surprised to hear the following remark made by John Paget in "An Arrow against Separation", printed at Amsterdam in 1618: "Seeing Mr. Robinson and his people do now (as divers of themselves confess) receive the members of the Church of England into their congregation, and this without any renunciation of the Church of England, without any repentance for the idolatries committed in the Church of England: how can you hold them to be a true church and communion with them lawful"[67]? Once more we have to listen to a tale of dissatisfaction, of the need of separation, of a sort of escape from the realm of darkness; and yet how little did the Separatists differ from their "idolatrous" friends! A large percentage of them for a time at least joined some Classis of the Reformed churches in Holland. Many Puritan ministers went to Holland in search of greater religious freedom than England offered them. Nevertheless, the church

they separated from was almost as purely Calvinistic as
the Dutch Reformed church. For the same man who
had taught Calvin the essence of Calvinism formulated
for the Church of England a goodly share of its new
theology[68]. This man was Martin Bucer of Schlettstadt,
the admirer of Hoen and Rode, and in many respects the
follower of Wessel Gansfort. To Gansfort, through the
labors of Bucer, Calvin, Zwingli, and their disciples, the
Anglican church owed much of its Protestantism, just
as the Calvinists in Holland did[69].

Those who are interested in the rise of the Baptist
church will approve the following quotation from Burrage,
after having become acquainted with the history of the
"New Devotion": "It may be more than a coincidence,
therefore, that later, when the Barrowists had for the
most part emigrated to Campen in Holland [Kampen on
the Yssel], the prevalence of Anabaptist views of a Continental type became quickly manifest in the congregation, and resulted in the formation of the earliest group
of English Anabaptists of whom we at present have any
definite knowledge"[70].

It would no doubt be a mistake to say that the
Reformation was the outgrowth of the Italian Renaissance, or that it began with the labors of Martin Luther.
The term itself was wrongly chosen; it misrepresents the
true state of affairs, as also does the word Counter-
Reformation. There was but one reformation, and it
included the so-called Counter-Reformation. This the
history of the "New Devotion" very plainly shows,
though many other causes contributed.

Thus it must become apparent to every one that few
religious movements deserve more study than the "New
Devotion". This movement inspired men and women
of all ranks and of many nationalities to increase their

religious fervor, to follow Christ's instructions more faithfully, and to imitate the apostolic church more earnestly. The study of its influence opens up a very attractive field of largely unexplored history. The "New Devotion" reached down to the people, and welled up from the people; it entered the kitchen, the farm-house, and the workshop, as well as the school house, the pulpit, the office, and the palace; where the great humanists refused to go it readily came, and where they were forbidden to enter, it approached unhindered. Selecting noble and helpful sayings from the literatures of the Ancients, and combining these with the wisdom of philosophers and saints of later periods, the followers of Groote and Gansfort interpreted all learning in the light of Christ's teachings. Whatever was pure and saintly in the religion of the Church they aimed to preserve or perfect, and the abuses that had crept in among clergy and people they sought to do away with or hide under the cover of love.

Henceforth the "New Devotion" or Christian Renaissance should occupy a prominent place in the history of religion and modern education, of English, German, and French literatures, and of modern philosophy. To those not interested in religion, philosophy, or education it nevertheless ought not to remain an unknown force or a negligible quantity, for the greatest wars of the sixteenth and early seventeenth centuries were to a very large degree the outcome of the changes in religious views, owing partly to the influence of this movement. For once the so-called civilized nations of Europe did not fight for material possessions, as now religion and theology engaged most of their attention. The period from 1520 till 1650, therefore, is unique in the history of mankind. It was shortly before and during this period that the Christian Renaissance helped to shape the destinies of England, Holland, Spain, Germany, and France. Even to-day it still sways the minds of multitudes, and it will continue to exert much influence as long as the "Imitation of Christ" is read, and the views of Gansfort, Erasmus, Luther, Bucer, Zwingli, Calvin, and Loyola are upheld.

To conclude, the greatest leaders of the Reformation — both Protestant and Roman Catholic — appear, at least as we have known them, like the visible portions of huge icebergs above the surface of the sea of the old history. We have looked at these men as sailors in polar seas see the small visible parts of icebergs, thinking little about the vast masses of ice below the surface, which in turn were once parts of a still greater mass. The farther these icebergs travel, the farther they move apart. Yet they all have come from the same place. So it was with the men who in the age of the Reformation founded great churches. We seldom remember the sources from where they received most of their so-called new views. One of the greatest of these sources was the movement we have just studied, — the Christian Renaissance.

NOTES TO INTRODUCTION

1. The Grebbe is a small river to the west of the Veluwe.

2. W. L. Bouwmeester, De ontwikkeling van Nederlands landschappen, The Hague 1911, p. 334.

3. Ch. Petit-Dutaillis, Charles VII, Louis XI et les premières années de Charles VIII (1422-1492), in: E. Lavisse, Histoire de France, vol. IV², Paris 1902, pp. 115, 147.

4. W. Denton, England in the fifteenth century, London 1888, pp. 118-123.

5. K. Lamprecht, Deutsche Geschichte, vol. IV, Berlin 1896, pp. 435-488.

6. H. Pirenne, Histoire de Belgique, vol. I, Brussels 1902, pp. VIII-IX, 27, 30, 32, 156-158, 161-169, 244-245; vol. II, Brussels 1903, pp. 178-180, 380-383, 394-395.

7. H. Pirenne, Hist. de Belgique, vol. I, pp. 326-327, 336. — K. Lamprecht, Deutsche Geschichte, vol. III, Berlin 1895, pp. 310-312.

8. H. Pirenne, Hist. de Belgique, vol. I, pp. 156-161.

9. Ch. Petit-Dutaillis, l. c., p. 170: "La cour la plus brillante de l'Europe, au milieu du XVe siècle, était celle de Phillippe le Bon, duc de Bourgogne. Aucune région en effet n'était aussi riche que les Pays-Bas, qui lui appartenaient, et Phillippe était le plus prodigue des hommes. Il passa son règne dans un long éblouissement. Sa cour, comme plus tard celle des rois de France, fut le rendez-vous des seigneurs de ses immenses domaines; ils imitaient ses vices et dissipaient leur patrimoine en dépenses extravagantes. .... Sa cour fut vraiment une préfiguration de la cour de Versailles. Tout y était réglé pour relever la majesté du prince. C'est là que fut inventée ou tout au moins développée l'étiquette des monarchies chrétiennes".

10. H. Pirenne, Hist. de Belgique, vol. III, pp. 266-267.

NOTES TO CHAPTER I

1. In the biographies and other sources I have used, his name appears as Gerardus Magnus, Gerardus Groot, Gerardus Groet, Gerardus Groit, Gheryt (de) Grote, Gherit (de) Groete, Gherd or Gheerd (de) Groote, etc. I have decided to call him Groote instead of De Groote, simply because he is better known by that name. In the documents his name usually appears as De Groote, but most manuscripts have the name Groot, Groet, or Groit without the article, and nearly all modern writers have called him Groote, and not De Groote.

2. J. Badius Ascensius, Vita Thomae Malleoli a Campis, ch. VIII, based on: Th. à Kempis, Vita Gerardi Magni, ch. XVIII, § 4.

3. J. de Hullu, De statuten van het Meester-Geertshuis te Deventer, p. 74. — R. Dier de Muiden, Scriptum, p. 11.

4. J. de Hullu, De statuten van het Meester-Geertshuis, p. 74.

5. P. Horn, Vita Gerardi Magni, pp. 333-334.

6. H. Denifle, Cartularium Universitatis Parisiensis, vol. III, pp. 92-93. — R. Dier de Muiden, Scriptum, pp. 1-2.

7. P. Horn, Vita Gerardi Magni, pp. 355-356.

8. H. Denifle, Cartularium Universitatis Parisiensis, vol. III, p. 92, note 31.

9. J. Badius Ascensius, Vita Thom. Malleoli, ch. VIII.

10. P. Horn, Vita Gerardi Magni, p. 334.

11. J. D. Van Doornink, Kamerrekeningen van Deventer, vol. III, part 1, nos. 339, 541, 615, 625, 636.

12. One at Aachen (see: G. Dumbar, Kerkelyk en wereltlyk Deventer, vol. I, p. 548. — R. Dier de Muiden, Scriptum, p. 3), and one at Utrecht (see: R. Dier de Muiden, Scriptum, p. 3. — Thomas à Kempis, Vita Gerardi Magni, ch. II, § 2).

13. Thomas à Kempis, Vita Gerardi Magni, ch. XI, § 7. — R. Dier de Muiden, Scriptum, p. 2. — P. Horn, Vita Gerardi Magni, p. 333.

14. Thomas à Kempis, Vita Gerardi Magni, ch. III, § 2.

15. R. Dier de Muiden, Scriptum, p. 2.

16. Thomas à Kempis, Vita Gerardi Magni, ch. IV, § 2. — R. Dier de Muiden, Scriptum, p. 3.

NOTES

17. J. G. R. Acquoy, Gerardi Magni epistolae XIV, p. 62.
18. G. Dumbar, Kerkelyk en Wereltlyk Deventei, vol. I, pp. 507-510, 549-550. — J. de Hullu, De statuten van het Meester-Geertshuis te Deventer, pp. 63, 75. — J. G. R. Acquoy, Gerardi Magni epistolae XIV, p. 63.
19. J. de Hullu, De statuten van het Meester-Geertshuis, p. 71.
20. R. Dier de Muiden, Scriptum, p. 5.
21. W. Moll, Kerkgeschiedenis van Nederland vóór de Hervorming, vol. II, part II, pp. 119-120. — J. G. R. Acquoy, Het Klooster te Windesheim, vol. I, pp. 27-28.
22. Thomas à Kempis, Vita Gerardi Magni, ch. VII, § 1-2. See also: ch. VI, § 1 of this same work, and D. A. Brinkerink, Biographieën van beroemde mannen uit den Deventer-kring (1901), p. 413.
23. The following works may be recommended for a study of the life and writings of this remarkable mystic: J. v. Ruusbroec, Werken, ed. J. B. David, Ghent 1856-1869. — J. Ruysbroeck, Alle de werken in nieuwere taal overgezet, ed. H. W. E. Moller, Bussum 1914. — Henricus ex Pomerio (Bogaerts), De origine monasterii Viridis Vallis et de gestis patrum et fratrum in primordiali fervore ibidem degentium, in: Analecta Bollandia, vol. IV, pp. 263-333, and in particular: pp. 283-308. — A. A. van Otterloo, Johannes Ruysbroeck, Amsterdam 1874, The Hague 1896. — W. de Vreese, Het leven en de werken van Jan van Ruusbroec, Ghent 1895-1896. — A. Auger, Étude sur les mystiques des Pays-Bas au Moyen-Age, in: Mémoires couronnés et autres mémoires de l'Acad. Royale de Belgique, Brussels 1902, pp. 157-264. — The best work in English is: E. Underhill, Ruysbroeck, London 1915.
24. H. Pomerius, De origine monasterii Viridis Vallis, p. 289.
25. A. Auger, Étude sur les mystiques des Pays-Bas au Moyen-Age, p. 171. Cele did not commence his teaching career in 1377, but about the year 1374. See: M. Schoengen, Jacobus Traiecti alias de Voecht narratio de inchoatione domus clericorum in Zwollis, p. 6, note 3.
26. Thomas à Kempis, Vita Gerardi Magni, ch. VIII, § 1.
27. R. Dier de Muiden, Scriptum, p. 5.
28. M. Schoengen, Jacobus Traiecti alias de Voecht narratio, p. 5, note 2. Thomas à Kempis, Vita Gerardi Magni, ch. XV, § 1. — Thomas à Kempis, Vita Florentii, ch. VI, § 2. — J. Busch, Chronicon Windeshemense, p. 252.

29. Thomas à Kempis, Vita Gerardi Magni, ch. VIII, § 2; ch. XV, § 1.

30. J. Busch, Chronicon Windeshemense, p. 252. — D. A. Brinkerink, Vita venerabilis Ioannis Brinckerinck, p. 259. — Thomas à Kempis, Vita Gerardi Magni, ch. XV, § 1. — Thomas à Kempis, Chronicon canonicorum regularium Montis Sanctae Agnetis, ch. I. — Thomas à Kempis, Vita Flor., ch. VI, § 1. — P. Horn, Vita Gerardi Magni, pp. 341-342.

31. Thomas à Kempis, Vita Gerardi Magni, ch. XV, § 1.

32. The sermon preached by Groote on that day has been preserved in several manuscripts; it was called Sermo contra Focaristas, and has been printed by A. Clarisse and his son J. Clarisse, in: Archief voor Nederlandsche Kerkgeschiedenis, vol. I, Leiden 1829, pp. 364-379; vol. II, Leiden 1830, pp. 307-395; vol. VIII, Leiden 1837, pp. 5-107. For the date when this sermon was preached see: A. and J. Clarisse, Over den geest en de denkwijze van Geert Groete, in: Archief voor Ned. Kerkgesch., vol. I, p. 385, note 6. As for its celebrity see: K. Grube, Gerhard Groote und seine Stiftungen, pp. 35, 96.

33. D. A. Brinkerink, De vita venerabilis Ioannis Brinckerinck, p. 324. — D. A. Brinkerink, Biographieën van beroemde mannen uit den Deventer-kring, 1901, p. 417. — Frensweger manuscript, p. 7.

34. P. Horn, Vita Gerardi Magni, p. 342: "Fecit igitur egregius iste predicator signa et prodigia magna in populo, non autem in despicabili et mortifera carne, sed revera in ipsius interioris hominis adorande Trinitatis ymagine, videlicet mortuos suscitando". — Thomas à Kempis, Vita Florentii, ch. VI, § 1: "Vita vox magistri praedicantis tanto fortius valuit in cordibus audientium, quanto perfectius caeteros praeibat in via virtutum". Many examples of conversions are related by the biographers. See: W. J. Kühler, Johannes Brinckerinck en zijn klooster te Diepenveen, pp. 135-136.

35. D. A. Brinkerink, Biographieën van beroemde mannen uit den Deventer-kring, 1902, p. 24. — D. A. Brinkerink, De vita venerabilis Ioannis Brinckerinck, p. 324.

36. Thomas à Kempis, Vita Florentii, ch. XI, § 1. — D. A Brinkerink, Vita venerabilis Ioannis Brinckerinck, p. 324.

37. Thomas à Kempis, Vita Flor., ch. XI, § 1. The church of St. Lebwin at Deventer was named after Lebwin, an English missionary who had tried to convert the Saxons and Frisians

north and east of the Yssel. For the history of this church see: G. Dumbar, Kerkelyk en Wereltlyk Deventer, vol. I, pp. 235-441.

38. D. A. Brinkerink, Vita venerabilis Ioannis Brinckerinck, p. 324.

39. One of the men who accompanied Groote as a rule was John Brinckerinck; see p. 87.

40. D. A. Brinkerink, Biographieën van beroemde mannen uit den Deventer-kring, 1902, p. 24.

41. See p. 44.

42. See p. 13.

43. Thomas à Kempis, Vita Gerardi Magni, ch. VIII, § 3. — D. A. Brinkerink, Biographieën, 1901, p. 417. — P. Horn, Vita Gerardi Magni, p. 348. The edict was promulgated between August and October 21, 1383; see: W. J. Kühler, De prediking van Geert Groote, p. 224.

44. D. A. Brinkerink, Biographieën, 1901, p. 417. A letter by William de Salvarvilla to Pope Urban VI, asking for a license from the pope for Groote is found in the Opera of Thomas à Kempis, behind the Vita Gerardi Magni. This letter was written on the 21st of October, 1383.

45. D. A. Brinkerink, Biographieën, 1901, p. 417. — Th. à Kempis, Vita Gerardi Magni, ch. IX, § 2. — M. Schoengen, Jacobus Traiecti alias de Voecht narratio, p. 15, note 1.

46. D. A. Brinkerink, Biographieën, 1901, p. 418.

47. M. Schoengen, Jacobus Traiecti alias de Voecht narratio, pp. 6, 17. — J. H. Gerretsen, Florentius Radewijns, p. 66, note 3.

48. He translated the seven penitential psalms (Psalm 6, 32, 38, 51, 102, 130, 143), and 63 other psalms. See: R. Dier de Muiden, Scriptum, p. 6. — P. Horn, Vita Gerardi Magni, p. 349. — W. Moll, Geert Groote's dietsche vertalingen, pp. 2-77, 107-112, 113-148, 149-180, 181-220. For the glosses see: W. Moll, Geert Groote's dietsche vertalingen, pp. 42-44, 55-59, 62-67.

49. R. Dier de Muiden, Scriptum, p. 10. — Th. à Kempis, Vita Gerardi Magni, ch. XVI, § 4. For the history of his bones see: G. Dumbar, Kerkelyk en Wereltlyk Deventer, vol. I, pp. 507-510. — J. G. R. Acquoy, Het klooster te Windesheim, vol. I, p. 57.

50. See: Appendix A.

51. E. Underhill, Ruysbroeck, pp. 66-67, 184, 88.

52. G. Groote, Epistolae, ed. W. Preger, p. 30: "Venerabilibus patris meis et dominis universaliter intime commendari intimius

desidero, precipue capitibus prepostiti et priori [Ruysbroeck], cuius scabellum pedum tam in hac vita quam in futura, quia sibi anima mea pre cunctis mortalibus amore et reverencia conglutinata est, fieri concupisco".

53. Ibid., p. 30, p. 51.

54. See: J. H. Gerretsen, Florentius Radewijns, pp. 1-42.

55. G. Groote, Sermo de nativitate Domini, fol. 122^b-123^a.

56. G. Groote, Tractatus de matrimonio, p. 171: Adam, undique bene formatus divinis manibus, suasu mulieris, cum toto genere humano cecidit.

57. Ibid., p. 171.

58. Ibid., p. 181: "Inde namque omnes malitiae cupiditatum nostrarum originem sumunt, quia supremae rationi sensitivae vires ea caro non obediunt. Quae ei ideo non obediunt, quia ipsa ratio Deo non obedit nec subjicitur". See also p. 161 and p. 233 of this same treatise.

59. G. Groote, Sermo contra focaristas, 3rd part, p. 13: "Et ante et post ibidem pulcerrime probat [Bernard in the seventh epistle to Adam Monachus], nec Papam posse dare licentiam, ut scandala fiant; et si Papa praeceperit, vel licentiaverit, illicite sibi quis obedit".

60. Ibid., p. 65: "Rursus inde est, quod quidam adeo magnificant Ecclesiae judicia et ab ipsa judicanda, quia sunt notiora eis quam Dei mandata, vel praecepta divina aut jura naturae, propter cordis tenebras nescientes vim legum et institutionum Ecclesiasticarum". — Tractatus de matrimonio, p. 207: "Imo et homo interior non in propriam, nec in Dei imaginem, sed in bestiam et diabolicum monstrum transformatur".

61. G. Groote, Epistolae, ed. J. G. R. Acquoy, p. 91.

62. G. Groote, Epistolae, ed. G. Bonet-Maury, p. 99: "Quam fraternitatem si relinqueremus, necesse esset principem relinquere et divinum exemplare. Quem in secreto animo, in interiore homine, divinos complexus noscendo, concepimus". — Tractatus de matrimonio, p. 181: "Omnis ergo tentationis diabolicae et traditionis Satanae et cujuslibet cupiditatis origo est delicto supremae rationis, Dei capacis, sed se Deo non unientis, Deum cognoscere non curantis". — P. 193: "Nam resistentia est in suprema ratione, ubi major hominis consistit libertas, quam in inferiore sensitiva, in qua est concupiscentia carnalis, cui saepe, sive velit, sive nolit, in suo objecto delectabili complacet".

63. G. Groote, Epistolae, ed. G. Bonet-Maury, p. 99.

64. G. Groote, Tractatus de matrimonio, p. 198: "Nam ignorantia illa est Legis Dei et naturalis, et conscientiae propriae, et lapsus humani, et est ex neglecta sui ipsius custodia et notitia. Ex quibus ignoratis et neglectis omnia mala oriuntur et sequuntur; nam omnis contumelia filiae Diaboli, sicut gloria filiae Regis, ab intus est. Qui intus se non custodit, exterius vane laborat".

65. G. Groote, Epistolae, ed. X. de Ram, p. 94.

66. G. Groote, Sermo de paupertate, p. 438: "O efficacis paupertatis dies, que est dies spiritualis Iherusalem, interne visionis et pacis! O dies aggressus Domini in templum suum vivum!"

67. D. A. Brinkerink, Biographieën, 1901, p. 419: "My invloyen alsoe vele verborgenre synne uytten psalmen, die mij inwert trecken, alsoe dat ic gene zwaerheit en voele in den leesen, mer ic heb der grote gnoechte in".

68. G. Groote, Epistolae, ed. G. Bonet-Maury, p. 100: "Cave ne Deum derelinquas. Si ipsum reliqueris, qui omne bonum est ipse, quid restabit tibi nisi omne malum?"

69. G. Groote, De locatione ecclesiarum, p. 130: "Regimen animarum mundat conscientiam et aperit homini Ecclesiam triumphantem et coelum, et unit hominem corpori Christi mystico". See p. 34, note 140.

70. Th. à Kempis, Vita Gerardi Magni, ch. XII, §§ 4, 13.

71. R. Rier de Muiden, Scriptum, pp. 6-7. — W. J. Kühler, Johannes Brinckerinck, p. 184.

72. P. Horn, Vita Gerardi Magni, p. 365: "Omnes lectiones, quas didicistis, reputabuntur vobis sicut oracio dominicalis propter piam intencionem, quam ad Deum in studendo habuistis". See also: G. Groote, Epistolae, ed. X. de Ram, pp. 83-84.

73. P. Horn, Vita Gerardi Magni, p. 358.

74. G. Groote, Sermo de nativitate Christi, fol. 109a-b: "Ut finis precepti et omnis exercitacionis nostre caritas sit et fiat de corde puriori, consciencia meliori et fide minus ficta, ut quia simus quasi os Domini, preciosum secundum prophetam a vili separentes"; fol. 117b: "Quod si sic non est caritas de corde puro et fide non ficta que finis est precepti". — Epistolae, ed. X. de Ram, p. 109. — J. Busch, Chronicon Windeshemense, p. 264.

75. G. Bonet-Maury, Gérard de Groote, p. 96.

76. G. Groote, Sermo contra focaristas, 3rd part, p. 97:

358 NOTES

"Vicesimum quintum dictum meum est, quod adhuc exeundum et recedendum est ab omni amicitia carnali et mundana omnium carnaliter et seculariter viventium".

77. Ibid., p. 100: "Verum omnes etiam, tam malos quam bonos, spiritualiter amare debemus et spirituali jungi amicitia, et, si necesse vel congruum fuerit, etiam societate corporali conjungi; maxime, si fortes fuerimus, ne, si debiles sumus, cum alios ad nos spiritualiter trahere nitimur, nos ipsos carnaliter tractos sentiamus.

78. Th. à Kempis, Vita Gerardi Magni, ch. XIV.

79. Ibid., ch. XII, § 1.

80. G. Groote, Epistolae, ed. X. de Ram, p. 81.

81. G. Groote, Epistolae, ed. X. de Ram, p. 73: "Ante omnia videtur mihi vobis congruum, ut sitis laetus spiritualiter; nam tristitia et pusillanimitas et solitudo, si ad multum veniunt, melancolicum faciunt". — P. 90: "Tristitia, quae nocet cordi...".

82. Th. à Kempis, Vita Gerardi Magni, ch. XVIII, § 10.

83. Ibid., ch. XI, §§ 1-2.

84. Ibid., ch. XVIII, § 8.

85. G. Groote, Prologue to his translation of certain church hymns, in: W. Moll, Geert Groote's Dietsche vertalingen, p. 53: "Want die woerde sijn ende dienen omme die sinne, ende die sinne niet omme die woerde".

86. G. Groote, Epistolae, ed. W. Preger, p. 33; ed. X. de Ram, p. 74.

87. See pp. 47-48, 63-65.

88. G. Groote, Epistolae, ed, X. de Ram, p. 87. — Sermo de nativ. Domini, fol. 108a-b.

89. G. Groote, De Simonia, p. 5.

90. G. Groote, Epistolae, ed. J. G. R. Acquoy, pp. 77-78.

91. G. Groote, De Simonia, p. 30.

92. The Horologium was written by Suso, a German mystic.

93. G. Groote, De Simonia, pp. 32-33.

94. W. Moll, Geert Groote's sermoen over de vrijwillige armoede, p. 430: "Dat hij om dergelijke reden ook ongezind was monnik te worden, meen ik voor zeker te moeten aannemen".

95. G. Groote, Epistolae, ed. X. de Ram, pp. 91-92: "In nomine Domini ingredere monasterium hoc ea intentione et proposito tanquam in eo eligens et assumens totius tuae vitae statum Deo magis beneplacitum et meliorem et securiorem inter omnes status, quos in hac vita invenire potes, qui tibi de

praesenti possunt contingere". For other examples, where Groote advises some of his followers to enter a monastery, see: J. G. R. Acquoy, Gerardi Magni Epistolae XIV., p. 77.

96. G. Groote, Raadgevingen aan eene Kluizenaarster, pp. 434-437.

97. For eight other examples see: G. Groote, Epistolae, ed. J. G. R. Acquoy, p. 77.

98. See p. 22. — G. Groote, Epistolae, ed. J. G. R. Acquoy, p. 77: "Etiam, secundum meum videre, non auderem vobis consulere quod intraretis religionem, licet non confidam nec confidendum sit mihi, quia ignorans viam Dei. Desiderium meum est secundum cor meum, ut maneatis in mundo et non sitis de mundo".

99. G. Groote, Epistolae, ed. W. Preger, pp. 46-47: "Nescitis, quia tenemini reddere testimonia iure divino? Et nescitis, quod maximum et fidei negocium vertitur?........ Quid? Est vobis dies posita, in qua sanabimini, quam, si preteritis, vos negligitis? Quid est, si modicum absens fueris, quod vobis decrescet? Vos non solum testis esse deberetis, sed consolator, sed promotor pro vestris fratribus Zwollensibus, quos scitis, qualiter sunt turbati........ Cavete, ne videamini fugere, qui stare debetis in acie. Numquid pro vobis et vestris pugnamus? Numquid decet et vos compugnare? Magnus promissor magni sit solutor. Non dicatur amicus gaudii sed necessitatis".

100. G. Groote, Tractatus de matrimonio, p. 221: "Omnia cedunt pecuniae. Nummus vincit, Christus repellitur: praecipue in congregationibus".

101. G. Groote, De Simonia, p. 3; Epistolae, ed. X. de Ram, p. 96-97; Raadgev. aan eene kluiz., p. 436.

102. G. Groote, Protestatio de veridica Evangelii praedicatione, ed. Th. à Kempis, Opera, ed. Somm., p. 782.

103. Groote divides all sources of the Christian religion of his time into four classes: (1) The Bible, which is infallible; (2) the writings of the recognized leaders of the Christian church. who had been inspired by the Holy Ghost; (3) the determinations of the doctors; (4) visions of various kinds. G. Groote, Sermo de nativitate Christi, fol. 109b-110a: "In primo ordine sunt que de Christi nativitate, vita vel morte in canonica scriptura, quibus contrarium sentire fas non est, continentur. In secundo ordine sunt que sanctis aliquibus de eisdem sunt vel dicuntur postea revelata. Tercio que assercioni doctorum vel

verisimili coniecture, vel probabili argumento, vel rationi triumphanti innituntur, ut secundum hec tria vel verisimilia vel probabilia vel rationabilia vocentur. In quarto autem ordine multa secundum et ad nostre parvitatis amminiculum ymaginata et ficta modo inferius annotando assumuntur".

104. G. Groote, Sermo contra focaristas, part 3, p. 65.

105. G. Groote, Epistolae (Hague Manuscript), fol. 230ª: "Sic suggessit mens, que valde unitatem desiderat; que vellet quod ambo pontifices cum omnibus cardinalibus cantarent in celi empirio 'gloria in excelsis' et alius verus Eliachim poneret pacem et unitatem in terris .... sed hec est hora et potestas tenebrarum".

106. G. Groote, Epistolae, ed. W. Preger, p. 53: "Estimacio mea est, quod scisma hoc sine ciatrice aut, ut magis opinor, sine fistula profunda non sanabitur aut consuetur. Diu dispositum est corpus ad lapsum, sed iam caput vehementer dolemus".

107. G. Groote, De locatione ecclesiarum, p. 129: "Unde ista est spiritualissima negociatio. Nam solvendo aperit Presbyter coelum, et repellendo claudit. .... Et est etiam magna potestas celebrandi, unde a pluribus dicitur, quod Papa est potentior, quia Presbyter est, quam quia Papa".

108. Ibid., pp. 120-121.

109. G. Groote, Sermo contra focaristas, 3rd part, pp. 71-73.

110. G. Groote, Sermo contra focaristas, 3rd part, p. 61: "Si tibi Papa vel Episcopus, vel Superior, sub quaecunque poena praeciperet, etiam sub poena excommunicationis, suspensionis, depositionis, vel privationis, ut rem sacram tangas, velut minister Ecclesiae, ved sacrum officium ut minister Ecclesiae peragas, te non contrito in mortali existente, nulla et obedientis humana debet ad hoc compellere".

111. Ibid., pp. 64-65, 73.

112. Ibid., pp. 68-69, 106, 82, 69, 90, 70, 54, 62.

113. G. Groote, Epistolae, ed. J. G. R. Acquoy, p. 86.

114. Ibid., p. 83: "Quid est hoc, quod presbyter eum absolvit in terris, qui non absolvitur in coelis? Ostendit eum ecclesiae absolutum, quem mater ecclesia immaculata non suscepit. Intromittitur ad extra per presbyterum, sed repellitur ab intra, quem tamen ad intus admissum presbyter, interiora ejus perscrutatus, ostendit vel dissimulat. Dicit verbo: 'Absolvo te'; dicit sibi ipsi mente contrarium".

115. Ibid., p. 831 "Credo orationem pro eis magis utilem quam regimen; item praedicationem et monitionem quam absolutionem"; p. 85: "Ergo omnino primo laborandum est ad eorum conversionem et precibus et monitionibus, imo et poenitentiarum injunctionibus, antequam ad eorum absolutionem procedatur". — Cautele confessorum circa magnos peccatores adhibendi, fol. 126ᵇ.

116. G. Groote, Epistolae, ed. G. Bonet-Maury, p. 97.

117. G. Groote, Epistolae, ed. J. G. R. Acquoy, pp. 21-23.

118. G. Groote, Epistolae, ed. J. G. R. Acquoy, p. 28.

119. W. Preger, Beiträge zur Geschichte der religiösen Bewegung in den Niederlanden (1350-1400), pp. 62-63, p. 23.

120. G. Groote, Epistolae, ed. J. G. R. Acquoy, pp. 20-32, 34-35.

121. Ibid., p. 38. — J. Busch, Chronicon Windeshemense, p. 261.

122. W. J. Kühler, Levensbeschrijvingen van devote zusters te Deventer, p. 46: "Qui eciam secundum consilium magistri Gerardi multa pauperibus distribuerat".

123. G. Groote, De simonia, p. 10.

124. Th. à Kempis, Vita Gerardi Magni, ch. XVIII, § 19.

125. G. Groote, Epistolae, ed. X. de Ram, p. 94: "Et non moveat vos, quod aliqui habeant propria".

126. G. Groote, Epistolae, ed. W. Preger, p. 41: "Indigeo pecuniis. Exhaustus, Deo gracias, pene sum". — P. 37: "Everardus noster in Domino in Campis receptus indiget pecunie, vestium, et re vera non habui, ut possem sibi sicut desiderarem succurrere". Therefore Groote asks Cele to help him.

127. G. Groote, Sermo de paupertate, pp. 434-436.

128. D. A. Brinkerink, Biographieën, 1901, p. 422. — Th. à Kempis, Vita Gerardi Magni, ch. XI, § 3.

129. These passages are: Matthew XIX, 10-12; Luke XIV, 20; I. Corinthians VII, 26, 27, 35; Augustine, Nona confessio: "Convertisti me ad Te, ut neque uxorem quaererem".

130. G. Groote, De simonia, p. 13.

131. G. Groote, De matrimonio, pp. 174, 169.

132. Ibid., pp. 231-233, 227.

133. G. Groote, Zed. toespraak, p. 306.

134. G. Groote, Epistolae, ed. X. de Ram, p. 108.

135. G. Groote, Zed. toespraak, p. 307.

136. Ibid., ed. G. Bonet-Maury, p. 96.

137. D. A. Brinkerink, Biographieën, 1901, p. 422. — Thomas à Kempis, Vita Gerardi Magni, ch. XIV, § 4.

138. G. Groote, Epistolae, ed. X. de Ram, p. 84.

139. G. Groote, Epistolae, ed. W. Preger, p. 41: "Nihil tantum proficit contra temptacionem dyaboli, sicut anime hilaritas et confidencia in Domino".

140. G. Groote, Zedelijke Toespraak, p. 301.

141. G. Groote, De simonia, p. 24: "Unde under desen drien is dat hoechste geistlike guet doechde unde mynne unde is vele geistliker, dan de andere, want se den menschen geistliker maken in em selven unde gode naer verenen in den geiste, dan de tekene der sacramente of miracles of prophecies".

142. Ibid., pp. 24-25: "Item de doechde syn boven doechden, de ene boven den anderen, na eren grade unde eren ambochten, unde al syn se um de mynne; unde in der mynne verenighen se uns mit gode unde mit den hilghen geiste. Als vele tilghen komen wt eenre wortelen also werden gheboren vele duechden wt eenre mynnen".

143. G. Groote, Zedelijke Toespraak, pp. 299-300.

144. Th. à Kempis, Vita Gerardi Magni, ch. XVIII, § 20.

145. G. Groote, Epistolae, ed. X. de Ram, p. 79.

146. G. Groote, Zed. toespraak, pp. 303-304. See also: G. Groote, Tractatus in divinitate super septem verba dominica, fol. 259°: "Dimittite et dimittetur nobis. Hec est doctrina novi testamenti. Hoc est quod Dominus in morte crucis quasi in testamenta nobis legavit ut dimittamus nobis iniuriantibus sicut ipse crucifixosibus".

147. G. Groote, Epistolae, ed. X. de Ram, p. 80: "Domine, omnia mea et me ipsum tibi obtuli et superioribus, et me ipsum abnegavi propter te; et hoc majus est omnibus aliis, quae in mundo potui facere".

148. Th. à Kempis, Vita Gerardi Magni, ch. XVIII, §§ 5-6.

149. G. Groote, Epistolae, ed. H. Nolte, p. 294.

150. Ibid., ed. J. G. R. Acquoy, pp. 98-99; ed. H. Nolte, pp. 291-293; ed. W. Preger, p. 35.

151. Copiarum literarum nostrarum, in: Ms. no. 70 H 75, Royal Library, The Hague, fol. 1ᵃ, 2ᵇ, 3ᵇ, 7ᵇ.

152. P. Horn, Vita Gerardi Magni, p. 355.

153. G. Groote, Epistolae, ed. H. Nolte, p. 283; ed. W. Preger, p. 35: "Semper sum inutilis, semper garrulus, semperque avarus et peravarus librorum".

NOTES 363

154. G. Groote, Epistolae, ed. H. Nolte, p. 296. — M. Schoengen, Die Schule von Zwolle, p. 25, p. 76.
155. M. Schoengen, Die Schule von Zwolle, p. 76.
156. G. Dumbar, Het kerkelyk en wereltlyk Deventer, p. 304.
— M. Schoengen, Die Schule von Zwolle, p. 26. — G. Groote, Epistolae, ed. H. Nolte, pp. 290-291, p. 302. — W. Preger, Beiträge zur Geschichte der religiösen Bewegung in den Niederlanden, p. 39, note 1.
157. Th. à Kempis, Vita Gerardi Magni, ch. X, § 1.
158. M. Schoengen, Die Schule von Zwolle, pp. 35-36.
159. G. Groote, Epistolae, ed. J. Clarisse, pp. 22-24: "Et quomodo quis coecus aliis ducatum praebeat? Si coecos coeci ducent, coecorum omnes coeci et duces in praecipitium cadunt. Quomodo curabit scientiam, qui non habet scientiam? .... Et quomodo quis docere potest illud, quod nunquam didicit? Et speculatores positi sunt Curati, quoniam tenentur omnia scire, quae ad eorum officium pertinent, tanquam mundiores oculos ad omnia et longiora et densiora discernenda, et ad praemuniendum et ad defendendum habentes".
160. See p. 27.
161. G. Groote, Epistolae, ed. J. G. R. Acquoy, p. 71; ed. W. Preger, pp. 38-39; ed. H. Nolte, pp. 290-291. — M. Schoengen, Die Schule von Zwolle, pp. 36-37.
162. See p. 15, note 44; the translation in our text is taken from: Th. à Kempis, Works, vol. III: The chronicle of the Canons Regular of Mount St. Agnes, edited by J. P. Arthur, p. 163.
163. The translation given in our text is found in: Th. à Kempis, Works, vol. III: The chronicle of the Canons Regular of Mount St. Agnes, ed. J. P. Arthur, pp. 213-217.
164. Th. à Kempis, Vita Gerardi Magni, ch. I, § 2.
165. J. Busch, Chronicon Windeshemense, p. 46.
166. J. Busch, Chronicon Windeshemense, pp. 41, 245.
167. H. Pomerio, De origine monasterii Viridis Vallis, p. 290.
168. D. A. Brinkerink, Biographieën, 1901, p. 412.
169. Memoryboek der oude Zusteren te Weesp, in: Archief voor Nederlandsche kerkgeschiedenis, vol. X, Leiden 1839, p. 188.

NOTES TO CHAPTER II

1. G. Dumbar, Het kerkelijk en wereltlyk Deventer, vol. I, pp. 548-549.
2. The document is found in: J. de Hullu, De statuten van het Meester-Geertshuis te Deventer, pp. 63-76; a shorter one in: G. Dumbar, Het kerkelyk en wereltlyk Deventer, vol. I, pp. 549-550.
3. D. de Man, Hier beginnen sommige stichtige punten, p. XXXVIII. — J. de Hullu, Statuten, p. 67.
4. J. de Hullu, Statuten, p. 67.
5. Ibid., pp. 67-68.
6. D. de Man, Stichtige punten, pp. XXIX, XXX, XXXVI, XLI.
7. J. de Hullu, Statuten, pp. 66, 73, 67, 70.
8. See p. 23.
9. D. de Man, Stichtige punten, pp. LVIII, LIX.
10. Th. à Kempis, Vita Flor., ch. IV, § 2.
11. Th. à Kempis, Chron. Mont. Agn., ch. XI. He died in 1400 at the age of 50; hence he was born in 1350.
12. M. Schoengen, Die Schule von Zwolle, p. 18.
13. Ibid., p. 18. — J. H. Gerretsen, Flor. Radewijns, p. 49.
14. J. H. Gerretsen, Flor. Radewijns, p. 49.
15. Th. à Kempis, Vita Flor., ch. VI, § 2. — D. A. Brinkerink, Biographieën, 1902, pp. 1, 23.
16. J. H. Gerretsen, Flor. Rad., p. 50.
17. Th. à Kempis, Vita Flor., ch. IV, § 1.
18. Ibid., ch. XI, § 1. — Dier de Muiden, Scriptum, p. 12.
19. See p. 15.
20. G. Bonet-Maury, Gérard de Groote, p. 57.
21. J. G. R. Acquoy, Het klooster te Windesheim, vol. I, p. 45.
22. J. H. Gerretsen, Flor. Radewijns, pp. 60-70.
23. E. Barnikol, Studien, p. 32.
24. D. A. Brinkerink, De vita venerabilis Ioannis Brinckerinck, p. 324: "Quorum XII illi familiarius adherebant, ita ut unanimi consensu, spe vite liberioris, voto se castitatis astringerent, licet unus ex illis postea iret post sathanem. — D. A. Brinkerink, Biographieën, 1902, p. 24: "Meyster Gerijt die hadde

vnt irste XII discipele, die onsen lieven Heren hoer reynicheid laveden ende alle vuerige manne woerden ende columpne der deuchden, behalve ene; die viel weder of en sterf quader doet".

25. P. Horn, Vita Gerardi Magni, p. 362.

26. A few cases are mentioned in the sources.

27. I do not see why we should have to reject the account by Busch. For nowhere is he so trustworthy as in his narrative relating to Groote's activities as founder of the new brotherhood. When Groote preached at Zwolle, it was his custom to stop at the house of Busch's grand-father (see: M. Schoengen, Jac. Voecht narratio, p. 6, note 6); Busch was one of Cele's best friends, while Groote's confessor, named Henry of Höxter, told him a great many details about Groote's last years: J. Busch, De ref. mon., p. 703: "Dominus Henricus Huxaria, qui fuerat eius confessor, hec mihi sepius enarravit et plura alia".

28. J. Busch, Chronicon Windeshemense, p. 254: "Predilecte magister! Quid noceret, quod ego et clerici isti scriptores bone iam voluntatis ea, que septimanatim habemus expendere, in unum reponentes in communi pariter viveremus? ....
Communia? Isti de ordine mendicancium id nullatenus sustinebunt, sed totis suis viribus resistere et omnino se opponere temptabunt".

29. J. Busch, Chron. Windeshemense, p. 254. — D. A. Brinkerink, Biographieën, 1901, p. 420: "Aldus mynlic ende gesellic plach hij te wesen mit sinen discipelen, mer sij en leyden noch gheen gemeen leven toe samen. Want dat en dorste meyster Gerijt niet bestaen, om dat hij soe vele wederstaens hadde; mer hij stercte sine discipele daer seer toe, ende sechde: wert dat sijs bestaen dorsten, hij wolde hem gerne een guet hoeft wesen".

30. J. Busch, Chronicon Windeshemense, p. 256. — W. J. Kühler, Johannes Brinckerinck, p. 19. — Frensweger handschrift, pp. 22-27.

31. J. Busch, Chronicon Windeshemense, p. 255.

32. P. Horn, Vita Gerardi Magni, p. 362: "Vitam tamen communem discipuli eius post mortem illius de consilio et beneplacito ipsius inceperunt". — D. A. Brinkerink, Biographieën, 1901, p. 420: "Ende na sijnre doet soe waert die eerweerdige meystere her florens die overste, ende doe weren sij daer allentelen wat toe gecomen". — R. Dier de Muiden, Scriptum, p. 13: "Dominus Florencius custodivit pecunias secum habitancium. Videns autem quod tam plene essent conversi ad Dominum et

tam tractabiles et flexibiles, fudit pecunias eorum in unum et fecit eas esse omnium, que fuerant per partes singulorum; et ita deinceps ceperunt vivere in communi". There is one other account which ought to be of some interest to us. In Ms. no. 75 G 58 of the Royal Library at the Hague we find a treatise by Gabriel Byel or Bael, rector of the Brethren of the Common Life at Butzbach near Mainz (see: G. Coeverincx, Analecta, part II, ed. G. van den Elsen and W. Hoevenaars, p. 128), called: Tractatus de communi vita clericorum. The rector tells his readers on fol. 11^b of this treatise that Groote was unable to find good monasteries for his followers. For that reason he withheld many of them from entering a monastery. Finally he resolved to follow Augustine's example by founding a society or congregation, instructing his followers to live the "common life".

33. J. Busch, Chronicon Windeshemense, pp. 263-264.

34. Th. à Kempis, Vita Ger. Magni, ch. XVI, §§ 2-3.

35. Thomas à Kempis very plainly states that Groote urged his disciples to build a monastery and join the Augustinian Canons Regular (Vita Ger. Magni, ch. XV, § 3). Acquoy overlooked this fact; see: W. J. Kühler, De prediking van Geert Groote, pp. 231-232.

36. D. A. Brinkerink, De vita venerabilis Ioannis Brinckerinck, p. 326.

37. D. A. Brinkerink, De vita ven. Ioannis Brinckerinck, p. 327: "In quottidianis igitur anxietatibus constituti magister Gerardus et sui, maturo et deliberato consilio concluserunt, se monasterium ordinis regularium S. Augustini velle construere, sub cuius alis et umbris ceteri sine approbata apostolica regula, sed in seculari habitu simplici aut clericali degentes protegerentur". — P. Horn, Vita Gerardi Magni, pp. 362-363: "Habuit eciam in proposito edificandi monasterium clericorum ordinis canonicorum regularium, volens quosdam de ydoneis clericis sibi adherentibus ad religionis habitum promovere, ut aliis devotis essent in exemplum et contra senientem mundum in refugii castrum religione munitum".

38. R. Dier de Muiden, Scriptum, p. 7. — D. A. Brinkerink, Biographieën, 1902, p. 3. — Th. à Kempis, Vita Flor., ch. X, § 2.

39. Th. à Kempis, Vita Flor., ch. XIV, § 1. — D. A. Brinkerink, Biogr., 1902, p. 9.

40. Th. à Kempis, Vita Flor., ch. XVI, §§ 2-4.

41. Ibid., ch. XIV, § 3.

42. Th. à Kempis, Vita Flor., ch. I, § 1.

43. D. A. Brinkerink, Biographieën, 1902, p. 9. — Th. a Kempis, Vita Flor., ch. XIII, § 1.

44. Th. à Kempis, Vita Flor., ch. XIV, § 3; ch. XV, § 3; ch. XVI, § 2.

45. Ibid., ch. XV, § 3.

46. R. Dier de Muiden, Scriptum, p. 22. — Th. à Kempis, Vita Flor., ch. XX, § 1.

47. J. H. Gerretsen, Flor. Rad., pp. 125-126.

48. Th. à Kempis, Vita Flor., ch. XI, § 2, § 1; ch. XXIV, § 3. — R. Dier de Muiden, Scriptum, p. 21.

49. Th. à Kempis, Vita Flor., ch. XXIV, § 3.

50. Ibid., ch. XVII, § 1.

51. Ibid., ch: XVII, § 1, ch. XI, § 2. — D. A. Brinkerink, Biographieën, 1902, p. 19.

52. Th. à Kempis, Vita Flor., ch. XVIII, § 3.

53. De magistro Everardo de Eza, in: Ms. no. 8849-8859, Royal Library, Brussels, fol. 80ᵃ.

54. Th. à Kempis, Vita Flor., ch. XVIII, § 3.

55. R. Dier de Muiden, Scriptum, p. 21.

56. Th. à Kempis, Vita Flor., ch. XI, § 2, § 3.

57. R. Dier de Muiden, Scriptum, p. 21: "Aliqui civium obloquentes devotis in Daventria excusabant tamen Fratres Domus domini Florencii. Aliqui vero omnes condemnantes solum dominum Florencium collaudabant".

58. J. H. Gerretsen, Flor. Rad., pp. 132-133.

59. Fl. Radewijns, Omnes inquit artes, fol. 1ᵃ: Item et vie nostre finis quidem est regnum Dei. Quid vero sit scopos debet diligenter inquiri......... Finis quidem nostre professionis ut diximus regnum celorum est; destinacio vero scilicet scopos puritas cordis sine qua ad illum finem impossible est quempiam pervenire".

60. Ibid., fol. 1ᵃ.

61. Fl. Radewijns, Omnes inquit artes, fol. 2ᵃ-3ᵃ.

62. Ibid., fol. 4ᵇ-5ᵃ.

63. Ibid., fol. 3ᵇ-4ᵇ.

64. Fl. Radewijns, Tractatulus de spiritualibus exercitiis, p. 384.

65. Ibid., p. 384: "Caritas autem vera non est nisi in corde puro a viciis, et ipsa in se omnem comprehendit virtutem".

66. Ibid., p. 384: "Porro quantum homo plus purgaverit cor suum a viciis et consupiscentiis inordinatis, tanto amplius impletur virtutibus seu caritate".

67. Ibid., p. 385.

68. Ibid., p. 386.

69. Fl. Radewijns, Omnes inquit artes, fol. 82ᵃ-83ᵇ.

70. Fl. Radewijns, Tract., p. 384.

71. Ibid., p. 387: "Et est recte simile in proposito de instrumento musico, cuius corde sunt indisposite, licet non destructe, quod non potest reddere bonam melodiam. Sic eciam **vires et affectiones** anime deordinate seu deformate sunt, licet non destructe".

72. Ibid., p. 387: "Et in hoc eciam consistit vera conversio et spiritualis, ut scilicet amor convertatur seu reformetur, ut nichil diligat nisi deum vel propter deum".

73. Ibid., pp. 392, 391, 397, 398.

74. Fl. Radewijns, Omnes inquit artes, fol. 18ᵃ: "Ecce caritas excellentissima via est que ducit ad celestem patriam et sine qua illuc nemo pervenire poterit".

75. Ibid., fol. 18ᵇ, 20ᵃ-23ᵃ.

76. Fl. Radewijns, Tractatulus, p. 413.

77. Fl. Radewijns, Omnes inquit artes, fol. 23ᵇ-28ᵇ.

78. Fl. Radewijns, Tractatulus, pp. 401-402. — Omnes inquit artes, fol. 26ᵃ⁻ᵇ.

79. Fl. Radewijns, Omnes inquit artes, fol. 26ᵃ: "Pro spiritualibus exerciis non omnia equaliter corporalia conveniunt, **sed** illa que cum spiritualibus maiorem habent convenienciam et sollicitudinem de quibus inter cetera est sacram scripturam scribere".

80. Fl. Radewijns, Tractatulus, p. 389. — Omnes inquit artes, fol. 23ᵇ.

81. Fl. Radewijns, Tractatulus, p. 389. — Omnes inquit artes, fol. 23ᵇ: "Tota sacra scriptura est propter virtutes; et si homo haberet virtutes et inconcusse servaret, non indigeret scriptura quantum ad se, ut dicunt Augustinus et Crysostomus, quia **multi** sine codicibus sancte vixerunt in solitudinibus".

82. Fl. Radewijns, Tractatulus, p. 389. — Omnes inquit **artes,** fol. 23ᵇ.

83. Fl. Radewijns, Tractatulus, p. 393.

84. Ibid., p. 395.

85. Ibid., pp. 396-399.

86. Fl. Radewijns, Omnes inquit artes, fol. 6ª-17ª. — Tractatulus, pp. 405-406, 409, 414.

87. Fl. Radewijns, Tractatulus, p. 404.

88. Fl. Radewijns, Tractatulus, p. 411.

89. Ibid., p. 412.

90. Ibid., p. 413.

91. Ibid., p. 415.

92. Ibid., p. 417.

93. Ibid., p. 421.

94. Ibid., p. 423.

95. About one half of the Omnes inquit artes is devoted to the life of Christ (fol. 28ᵇ-62ª, and also fol. 62ª-77ª).

96. See p. 46, note 32.

97. R. Dier de Muiden, Scriptum, p. 13.

98. W. J. Kühler, Johannes Brinckerinck, p. 13.

99. R. Dier de Muiden, Scriptum, pp. 7-8: "Ioannes de Huxaria fuit ordinatus presbiter, sed morte preventus non celebravit missam, sepultus est........ Erat autem idem Ioannes de Huxaria tante perfectionis, quod ad tempus dubitatur an ipse vel dominus Florencius fieret rector Fratrum in Daventria: tandem convenerunt in dominum Florencium".

100. Found in: G. Dumbar, Het kerkelyk en wereltlyk Deventer, vol. I, pp. 616-620.

101. G. Dumbar, Het kerkelyk en wereltlyk Deventer, vol. I, p. 616.

102. Much has already been written on this subject, but as has been the case with the foundation of the new brotherhood, we have hitherto been led astray by a spirit of negative criticism which distrusts all chronicle writers, even those men who lived themselves in the house at Deventer, as Thomas à Kempis did and Rudolf Dier de Muiden. Only the documents are to be trusted, these critics say, and then only a certain class of documents, — not the official ones, for these deliberately created titles of non-existing offices (see E. Barnikol, Studien, p. 32). Thus the whole reading public, both in Holland, Germany, and elsewhere, have been left in the dark concerning the early history of the Brethren of the Common Life. And yet the sources tell a very plain and simple story, which is in no way contradicted by a single document.

103. G. Dumbar, Het kerkelyk en wereltlyk Deventer, vol. I, pp. 603-610. — Analecta Daventria, vol. I, p. 224, p. 16.

104. G. Dumbar, Het kerkelyk en wereltlyk Deventer, vol. I, p. 629.

105. R. Dier de Muiden, Scriptum, pp. 38-39. — G. Dumbar, Analecta Daventria, vol. I, p. 238. — Ms. no. 70 H 75, Royal Library, The. Hague, fol. 13ᵇ-14ᵃ: "Nos Godfridus Toorn, Rodolphus de Muden et Otgerus Johannis presbyteri et custodes domus magistri Florencii in Daventria notum facimus........ empta est cum domibus in ipsa edificatis de pecuniis deputatis ad primum usum: ad hoc ut in ipsis habitent devoti clerici vel scolares".

106. D. A. Brinkerink, Biographieën, 1902, p. 8: "Onder desen schoelres waert soe grote dissepline gehoelden, oftet reliose cloesterlude hadden geweest, ende dat overmides die goddienstige insettinge here Florens ende sijnre devoeter bruders". See p. 45.

107. G. Dumbar, Analecta Daventria, vol. I, pp. 102-103.

108. Th. à Kempis, Vita Flor., ch. XV, § 2. — R. Dier de Muiden, Scriptum, p. 24.

109. R. Dier de Muiden, Scriptum, p. 24.

110. Ibid., p. 24.

111. Ibid., p. 24.

112. J. de Hullu, De Hervorming in Overijssel, p. 91.

113. This was at any rate the impression received by Thomas à Kempis (see: Th. à Kempis, Vita J. Gronde, ch. I, § 3).

114. R. Dier de Muiden, Scriptum, p. 14.

115. R. Dier de Muiden, Scriptum, p. 65. — D. A. Brinkerink, Biographieën, 1902, p. 11.

116. J. Badius Ascensius, Vita Thomae Malleoli, ch. IX. The translation given in our text is from: Th. à Kempis, Meditation on the incarnation of Christ, ed. D. V. Scully, pp. XXVII-XXVIII.

117. Thomas à Kempis, Vita Arn. Scoonhoviae, ch. II.

118. J. Lindeborn, Historia episcopatus Daventriensis, p. 98.

119. R. Dier de Muiden, Scriptum, p. 25.

120. W. J. Kühler, Joh. Brinckerinck, p. 21.

121. M. Schoengen, Jacobus Traiecti narratio, p. 500.

122. R. Dier de Muiden, Scriptum, pp. 34, 40.

123. Ibid., p. 42.

124. Ibid., p. 41.

125. See p. 110.

126. R. Dier de Muiden, Scriptum, p. 41.

127 Th à Kempis, Vita Florentii, ch. XXXV, § 1.

128. G. Dumbar, Analecta Daventria, vol. I, p. 99.

129. Ibid., pp. 95-97.

130. Ibid., p. 106: "Nescientes ad quid amplius optemus vivere, cum totiens vita nostra moriatur".

131. G. Dumbar, Analecta Daventria, vol. I, pp. 111-113.

132. See: G. H. J. W. J. Geesink, Gerard Zerbolt van Zutfen, p. 13.

133. Zerbolt died in 1398 at the age of thirty-one (see Th. à Kempis, Vita Ger. Sutph., § 8).

134. Th. à Kempis, Vita Ger. Sutph., § 2. — G. J. H. W. J. Geesink, Ger. Zerb., p. 6.

135. D. A. Brinkerink, Biographieën, 1902, pp. 336-337.

136. Th. à Kempis, Vita Ger. Sutph., § 4.

137. Th. à Kempis, Vita Ger. Sutphan., §§ 5-6.

138. See my article in the Ned. Arch. voor Kerkgesch., 1921, pp. 109-114; p. 118, note 7.

139. G. Zerbolt, Super modo vivendi, fol. 2ª.

140. Ibid., fol. 2ª-ᵇ: "Si autem premisse persone vivunt et cohabitant simul non collegialiter vel conventualiter sive per modum et ritum seu assumpcionem nove religionis sed pocius per modum simplicis societatis et unionem karitatis; sic extra religionem in una domo et societate convivere et cohabitare est omnino licitum. Et hoc modo simul convivere et cohabitare est in ecclesia Dei valde consuetum, dictis et auctoritatibus sanctorum et doctorum recommendatum et a sede apostolica specialiter licenciatum". Then he gives a great many proofs and concludes: "Quare multomagis causa devocionis et pietatis in modum simplicis societatis sive collegii vel corporis constitucione convivere et cohabitare est omnino licitum et meritorum". If it were prohibited, Zerbolt continues on folio 3ª, to live the common life in private homes, the whole world would be in a state of condemnation. On fol. 3ᵇ-4ª he shows that the common life has always been practised in the Christian Church, and approved by the pope. The common life is recommended in the Bible (Psalm 133, Job XXI, Genesis II), he finally remarks.

Ibid., fol. 6ª.

142. Ibid., fol. 7ª-8ᵇ. He plainly proves that to live in common sa the Brethren of the Common Life did, was quite distinct from monasticism, and he concludes by saying: "Unde patet quod sola professio faciat religiosum. Nec habitus sine professione

facit aliquum religiosum...... Unde propter hoc quod habitum deferunt humilem non sunt dicendi facere aliquam religionem".

143. Ibid., fol. 8[b].

144. Ibid., fol. 10[a]-11[b].

145. Ibid., fol. 10[a].

146. Zerbolt refers to the mind or reason of man before the fall, of which he still possesses a small remnant; see also p. 80.

147. G. Zerbolt, Super modo vivendi, fol. 10[b]-11[a].

148. Ibid., fol. 11[a]: "Ymmo maxima pax et quies fieret et optima rerum disposicio si tanta esset vel posset esse caritas hominum quod possent excludere proprietatem rerum, juxta illud Senece, 'De moribus' ".

149. G. Zerbolt, Super modo vivendi, fol. 11[a].

150. Ibid., fol. 12[a]: "Homo enim naturaliter est animal sociale ut dicit philosophus [Aristotle], primo Politice. Nullus enim homo solus sibi sufficit ad ea que sibi sunt necessaria procuranda ad victum acquirendum, coquendum, ad materiam vestitus faciendum et preparandum, etc.. Unde Stoyci dicere consueverunt quod homo esset hominum causa generatus, videlicet in adiutorium, sicut patet Genesis II[o] [verse 20]: 'Ade autem non erat adiutorium simile' ".

151. Ibid., fol. 12[a].

152. Ibid., fol. 12[a].

153. Ibid., fol. 12[a], 12[b].

154. Ibid., fol. 12[b]: "Hoc autem modo contingit quod homines communem vitam istis temporibus solum trahunt ad religiosos ac scripturas divinas de communi vita loquentes solum de religiosis capiendas arbitrantur. Quoniam hoc tempore insuetum aut rarum est extra religionem vivere in communi, quod tamen fuit usitatissimum in fervore ecclesie primitive et postmodum longo tempore. Sed eadem ratione posset forsitan videri inhibitum multis religiosis quibus nostris temporibus quibus refrigescente caritate iniquitas omnia occupavit, est vel fieri incipit insolitum in communi vivere sine omnini proprietate. Similiter hodie multa sancti ewangelii consilia non sunt multum consueta, nec tamen ideo ea facientibus sunt minus meritoria, quomodo quis ea inter malos Dei consilia non sategerit adimplere, secundum Gregorius, primo Moralium".

155. Ibid., fol. 12[b].

156. Ibid., fol. 12[b]-13[a].

157. Ibid., fol 13[a].

158. Ibid., fol. 13ᵃ. Zerbolt does not seem to have been aware of the fact that the Pythagoreans were not disciples of Pythagoras.

159. Ibid., fol. 13ᵃ.

160. Ibid., fol. 13ᵃ⁻ᵇ.

161. G. Zerbolt, Super modo vivendi, fol. 14ᵃ.

162. Ibid., fol. 14ᵃ-15ᵃ.

163. Ibid., fol. 15ᵇ-17ᵇ.

164. Ibid., fol. 17ᵇ-18ᵇ.

165. See my article on the Super modo vivendi in the Ned. Arch. voor Kerkgesch., 1921, p. 107, p. 115.

166. Ibid., pp. 115-116.

167. F. Jostes, Die Schriften des Gerhard Zerbolt van Zutphen, p. 7.

168. Revius gave a few extracts from this treatise (J. Revius, Daventria illustrata, pp. 41-58).

169. G. Zerbolt, Super modo vivendi, fol. 19ᵃ; see W. Preger, Beiträge, p. 55.

170. G. Zerbolt, Super modo vivendi, fol. 19ᵇ-21ᵃ. — W. Preger, Beiträge, pp. 55-57.

171. G. Zerbolt, Super modo vivendi, fol. 20ᵇ. — W. Preger, Beiträge, p. 56.

172. G. Zerbolt, Super modo vivendi, fol. 21ᵃ⁻ᵇ. — W. Preger, Beiträge, p. 58.

173. G. Zerbolt, Super modo vivendi, fol. 21ᵇ-22ᵃ. — W. Preger, Beiträge, p. 58.

174. G. Zerbolt, Super modo vivendi, fol. 22ᵃ⁻ᵇ. — W. Preger, Beiträge, pp. 58-59.

175. G. Zerbolt, Super modo vivendi, fol. 22ᵇ. — W. Preger, Beiträge, pp. 59-60.

176. G. Zerbolt, Super modo vivendi, fol. 22ᵇ-24ᵃ. — W. Preger, Beiträge, pp. 60-61.

177. G. Zerbolt, Super modo vivendi, fol. 24ᵇ.

178. Ibid., fol. 25ᵃ.

179. Ibid., fol. 25ᵃ.

180. Ibid., fol. 25ᵇ-26ᵃ.

181. Ibid., fol. 26ᵃ: "Ymmo sine hac obediencia non potest pax et concordia inter simul habitantes conservari".

182. Ibid., fol. 27ᵃ: "Primo cum quis confitetur in necessitate laico eciam peccata mortalia quod licitum est ut patet quarto

374 NOTES

Sentenciarum, distinctio XVII, cap. 7. Sed in hoc theologi et juriste sunt ei contrarii".

183. Ibid., fol. 27ª.
184. Ibid., fol. 27ª⁻ᵇ.
185. Ibid., fol. 27ᵇ.
186. Ibid., fol. 27ᵇ-28ª.
187. Ibid., fol. 28b: "Ex quo patet quod quantum ad hanc revelacionem peccatorum sive confessionem non sacramentalem non est necessarium requirere aliquem habentem auctoritatem clavium sed magis habentem discrecionem spirituum nec tam literatum quam expertum qui possit in omnibus temptacionibus et laqueis dyaboli hominem dirigere et premunire".
188. Ibid., fol. 28ᵇ.
189. Ibid., fol. 28ᵇ-29ª: "Et ista confessio non sacramentalis quondam apud viros spirituales erat valde consueta et laudata licet nunc sit rara et multis incognita et magis est dolendum a plerisque ut illicita impugnatur".
190. See p. 46.
191. See p. 60.
192. Dier of Muiden.
193. See p. 101.
194. G. Zerbolt, Super modo vivendi, fol. 29ª-31ª.
195. Ibid., fol. 32ᵇ.
196. Ibid., fol. 33ª.
197. Ch. VII.
198. G. Zerbolt, De spiritualibus ascensionibus, ch. III. — De reformatione virium animae, ch. I.
199. G. Zerbolt, De spir. ascens., ch. IV.
200. G. Zerbolt, De ref. vir. an., ch. II-III.
201. Ibid., ch. III: Cor autem purgare, nihil aliud est, quam cupiditates extinguere. Cupiditates et inordinatas concupiscentias extinguere, est vires animae reformare.
202. G. Zerbolt, De spir. ascens., ch. IV: "Ita homo anima tua rationalis, quae est dignior omnibus temporalibus creaturis, impuritatem et immunditiam contrahit ex hoc, quod rebus temporalibus subijcitur per amorem".
203. Ibid., ch. VI-VIII.
204. Ibid., ch. V.
205. G. Zerbolt, De ref. vir. an., ch. III.
206. G. Zerbolt, De spir. ascens, ch. XII.
207. Ibid., ch. XIII.

208. Ibid., ch. XVI.
209. Ibid., ch. XVI
210. Ibid., ch. XIX.
211. Ibid., ch. XX.
212. Ibid., ch. XXI.
213. Ibid., ch. XXII-XXIV.
214. Ibid., ch. XXVII.
215. Ibid.: "Per humanitatem Christi ad spiritualem affectum assurgere, et iam ipsum Deum per speculum in aenigmate mentalibus oculis intueri, et sic ex humanitate ad notitiam et amorem divinitatis pervenire".
216. F. Radewijns, Multes inquit artes, fol. 28ᵇ-61ᵃ: Extract from the gospel of St. John, chapter I (fol. 28ᵇ-29ᵃ), from Bonaventura's works (fol. 29ᵃ), from the prophecies (fol. 29ᵇ-30ᵃ), the annunciation (fol. 31ᵇ), the visit of Mary to Elisabeth (fol. 32ᵇ), the birth of Jesus (fol. 33ᵇ-34ᵇ), the visit of the wise men (fol. 36ᵃ⁻ᵇ), the presentation at Jerusalem (fol. 37ᵃ⁻ᵇ), the flight to Egypt (fol. 38ᵃ⁻ᵇ), the baptism (fol. 39ᵃ), the temptation in the desert (fol. 39ᵇ), the transfiguration (fol. 42ᵃ-43ᵃ), the parable of the lost sheep (fol. 43ᵃ), the entrance into Jerusalem on Palm-Sunday (fol. 44ᵇ), the Last Supper (fol. 49ᵇ-50ᵇ), Gethsemanéh (fol. 51ᵃ-52ᵃ), the capture of Christ (fol. 52ᵇ), Christ brought before Caiaphas (fol. 53ᵃ), Peter denies the Lord (fol. 53ᵇ), Pilate (fol. 54ᵃ-55ᵃ), on the way to Golgotha (fol. 55ᵇ-56ᵃ), Golgotha (fol. 56ᵃ-57ᵇ), the resurrection (fol. 59ᵃ), Christ appears to Mary and the disciples (fol. 59ᵇ-60ᵃ), and ascends (fol. 60ᵇ).
217. G. Zerbolt, De spir. ascens., ch. XXVIII-XL: The prophesies (ch. XXVIII), the annunciation (ch. XXIX), the life of Christ, and last supper (ch. XXX-XXXI), the passion of Christ (ch. XXXII-XXXVIII), the resurrection(ch. XXXIX), the ascension (ch. XL); see also: G. Zerbolt, De ref. vir. animae, ch. XXVI-XXXIII.
218. G. Zerbolt, De spir. ascens., ch. XI, ch. XLVIII.
219. See p. 54.
220. In ch. LXVII of the De spiritualibus ascensionibus and ch. XXXIX of the De reformatione virium animae the blessings of manual labor are extolled, and ch. LXVIII of the De spiritualibus ascensionibus deals with the relations with one's superiors, equals, and inferiors.
221. See p. 65.
222. R. Dier de Muiden, Scriptum, p. 48.

223. See pp. 46-49; and cf. W. J. Kühler, Johannes Brinckerinck, p. 21.

224. R. Dier de Muiden, Scriptum, p. 13: "Ista fuit causa movens ad instituendum religiosos, quia simplici communi vita timebant sustinere persecutiones ab emulis, ut sic, aliquibus existentibus religiosis, multi fratres devoti non professi religione tuerentur seu laterent sub professis religionem".

225. J. Busch, Chronicon Windeshemense, p. 267; cf. J. G. R. Acquoy, Het klooster te Windesheim, vol. I, pp. 64-65. The bishop, named Floris van Wevelinkhoven, signed his letter of permission on July 30, 1386; see J. G. R. Acquoy, Het klooster te Windesheim, vol. III, pp. 262-264.

226. J. Busch, Chronicon Windeshemense, pp. 274-275. The names of first six men were: Henry Klingebijl, Henry van Wilsem, Berthold ten Hove, William Keynkamp, John à Kempis, brother of Thomas à Kempis, and Henry de Wilde. The man who was sent ahead was Henry of Höxter. Cf. J. G. R. Acquoy, Het klooster te Windesheim, vol. I, p. 66.

227. J. G. R. Acquoy, Het klooster te Windesheim, vol. I, p. 66. — J. Busch, Chronicon Windeshemense, p. 16.

228. J. G. R. Acquoy, Het klooster te Windesheim, vol. I, p. 68, note 2.

229. Ibid., p. 66.

230. J. G. R. Acquoy, Het klooster te Windesheim, vol. I, pp. 67-68.

231. Privilegia et statuta capituli generali Windesemensis, in: Ms. no. 78 D 55, Royal Library, the Hague, pp. 105, 205.

232. J. Busch, Chronicon Windeshemense, pp. 280-281.

233. See: J. G. R. Acquoy, Het klooster te Windesheim, vol. I, p. 72.

234. J. Busch, Chronicon Windeshemense, p. 278.

235. J. Busch, Chron. Wind., p. 342: "In illa tempora [1392] tanta caritas erat inter illos, ut bona temporalia et spiritualis congregacionis Daventriensis monasterii in Windeshem et Fontis Beatae Mariae pene erant illis communia".

236. Ibid., pp. 342-343.

237. J. G. R. Acquoy, Het klooster te Windesheim, vol. I, p. 230.

238. J. Busch, Chron. Wind., p. 28: "Iste est homo, quem quesivi, cum quo multa bona in terra operabor".

239. Ibid., p. 28.

240.   Ibid., p. 59. For further particulars regarding this remarkable man, see J, Busch, Chron. Wind., pp. 35-37, 54-55, 226-244; as for the authorship of the course of religious exercises which is ascribed to him by Busch, see: J. G. R. Acquoy, Het klooster te Windesheim, vol. I, p. 161.

241.   J. Busch, Chron. Wind., p. 26.

242.   J. Busch, Chron. Wind., p. 94.

243.   Ibid., pp. 95-97; see also: J. G. R. Acquoy, Het klooster te Windesheim, vol. I, pp. 244-248.

244.   J. Busch, Chron. Wind., p. 62.

245.   J. Busch, Chron. Wind., p. 99.

246.   Ibid., pp. 101-102.

247.   Ibid., pp. 105-107.

248.   Ibid., pp. 189-191.

249.   Ibid., pp. 199-203.

250.   Th. à Kempis, Vita Ioannis Gronde, ch. II, §§ 1-2.

251.   See p. 47. Cf. W. J. Kühler, Johannes Brinckerinck, pp. 134-135.

252.   Th. à Kempis, Vita Ioannis Gronde, ch. II, § 3.

253.   He died May 7, 1392, and was buried in Groote's grave; see: Th. à Kempis, Vita Ioannis Gronde, ch. II, § 5.

254.   See: W. J. Kühler, Joh. Brinck., pp. 15-18.

255.   W. J. Kühler, Joh. Brinckerink, p. 11. Here he lived eight years (1384-1392). He helped to build the new brethren-house in 1391, for he was carpenter: D. A. Brinckerinck, Biographieën, 1902, p. 25. His character has been strikingly portrayed in the following passage from the pen of a modern Dutch historian: "Met rijke gaven toegerust, en onvermoeid deze te werk stellend tot heil van anderen; praktisch van aanleg, met een scherpen blik op menschen en toestanden; meester van het woord en indrukwekkend door zijn krachtige persoonlijkheid; streng zonder hardheid en in zijn ernst niet geheel zonder humor; godvruchtig bovenal, tegelijk van diepen ootmoed en kinderlijk vertrouwen vervuld — was hij boven velen de man om den vromen zin en den redelijken ernst te leiden en te versterken" (W. J. Kühler, John. Brinck., p. 7).

256.   W. J. Kühler, Joh. Brinck., p. 34.

257.   Ibid., pp. 34-36.

258.   D. A. Brinkerink, Biographieën, 1902, p. 30.

259.   W. J. Kühler, Joh. Brinck., p. 38.

260. See: D. de Man, Hier beginnen sommige stichtige punten, pp. LV-LX, 6, 11, 12, 225, 240, etc.

261. W. J. Kühler, Joh. Brinck., p. 37.

262. D. A. Brinkerink, Biographieën, 1902, p. 26: "Onder die heilige susteren toe Meyster-Gerijtshuys was alsoe groten vuer des Heiligen Geestes ontsteken, dat al dat lant hieromtrijnt daer warm van waert, ende dat overmides der leer ende anwisinge hoers vaders here Iohan Brynckerinck".

263. W. J. Kühler, Joh. Brinck., pp. 38-39.

264. W. J. Kühler, Joh. Brinck., p. 51.

265. Ibid., pp. 53-56.

266. Ibid., pp. 57-58.

267. On the 21st of January, 1408, the dedication took place, and in 1412 it joined the general chapter of Windesheim (W. J. Kühler, Joh. Brinck., p. 67, p. 72).

268. M. Schoengen, Die Schule von Zwolle, pp. 46, 47. — Jacobus Traiecti narratio, pp. 6, 17, 27.

269. M. Schoengen, Jacobus Traiecti narratio, p. 14.

270. Ibid., p. 6.

271. Ibid., pp. 7-8; p. 8, note 3.

272. Ibid., p. 9.

273. Ibid., p. 9, note 2; p. 280.

274. Ibid., p. 9. For a biography on John Ummen, see: W. J. Kühler, Joh. Brinck., p. 34. — M. Schoengen, Jac. Traiecti narratio, p. 7, note 2. — D. de Man, Stichtige punten, p. 196.

275. M. Schoengen, Jac. Traiecti narratio, pp. 22-23, 216-217.

276. Ibid., pp. 25, 219.

277. Ibid., pp. 28, 219, 293-294. The observation made here by Schoengen on p. 28, note 5 is not correct, for the document he refers to was not dated September 17, but August 9 (see pp. 293-294 of the same work, where the document itself is found).

278. M. Schoengen, Jacobus Traiecti narratio, pp. 219-220, and 28.

279. Ibid., p. 59, note 3.

280. See p. 37.

281. Ten letters, addressed by Groote to Cele, are still in existence. They were edited by W. Preger.

282. J. Busch, Chron. Wind., p. 209.

283. M. Schoengen, Die Schule von Zwolle, p. 83.

NOTES 379

284. J. Busch, Chron. Wind., p. 209. — M Schoengen, Die
Schule von Zwolle, p. 38.
285. See p. 12.
286. M. Schoengen, Die Schule von Zwolle, p. 97.
287. W. Preger, Beiträge, p. 14.
288. J. Busch, Chron. Wind., p. 213: "Ut autem exemplar
et formam bone vite et sancte conversacionis seipsum preberet
discipulis, incepit a seipso Christum in hoc imitatus non docens
sermone, que prius opere non fecisset".
289. J. Busch, Chron. Wind., p. 214.
290. Ibid., p. 214.
291. J. Busch, Chron. Wind., p. 217.
292. M. Schoengen, Die Schule von Zwolle, p. 70.
293. J. Busch, Chron. Wind., p. 220: "Et quia multos sacre
pagine libros sibi comparaverat dicens Dei testamentum in libris
sanctis consistere et sanctam matrem nostram ecclesiam fidem
catholicam spem futuri seculi celestis nostre patrie hucusque
per libros in esse conservatas et sine ipsis diu periclitatas".
294. W. Preger, Beiträge, p. 14.
295. M. Schoengen, Die Schule von Zwolle, p. 87.
296. J. Busch, Chron. Wind., p. 206.
291. J. Busch, Chron. Wind., p. 206.
298. Cele was not only a great friend and admirer of the
brethren, but he is to be regarded as one of the members of
the local institution, although he did not live in their house.
The following passage by John Busch, one of his teachers, is
significant: "In habitu exteriori moribus et conversacione
magistro Gerardo Magno domino Florencio et patribus congregacionum per omnia se fecit similem........ Qui et suos
discipulos similiter incedere verbo docuit et exemplo" (J. Busch,
Chron. Wind., p. 213). Furthermore, he was a sort of supervisor
of the brethren at Zwolle, or guardian, as appears from certain
documents: M. Schoengen, Jacobus Traiecti narratio, p. 294:
"Hier waren over ende an, doe dit gheschiede, meyster Johan
Cele, scoelmeyster to Zwolle, ende Albertus van Wynberghen".
— J. H. Hofman, De broeders van 't gemeene leven, in: Arch.
voor de gesch. van het aartsbisdom Utrecht, vol. II (1875),
pp. 243-244. — M. Schoengen, Jac. Voecht narr., p. 300.
299. J. Busch, Chron. Wind., p. 206.
300. See: M. Schoengen, Die Schule von Zwolle, p. 107.
301. Ibidem. As for the two other innovations, mentioned

by Schoengen, Cele's modern biographer (Dr. Schoengen is archivist at Zwolle), namely the special emphasis on religious instruction, particularly exegesis, and the improved course of instruction mapped out by Cele for future clergymen, I have made some mention of these in the text above. See also: M. Schoengen, Die Schule von Zwolle, p. 95.

302. J. Busch, Chron. Wind., p. 208.

303. M. Schoengen, Die Schule von Zwolle, pp. 75-76. — J. Busch, Chron. Wind., p. 207.

304. J. Busch, Chron. Wind., p. 207: "Et tunc eciam notabilia quedam dicta sanctorum in futurum clericis profutura per totam scolam pronunciavit singulis ad sua rapiaria cuncta scribentibus. Unde epistolas et evangelia in festis per annum occurencia omnes habere voluit et rapiarium theologicale, quo nucleum scripture sacre brevibus in verbis colligerent, et ita successive Dei noticiam timorem et sapienciam novis testis memorie facilius commendarent".

305. J. Busch, Chron. Widn., p. 206, p. 217.

306. Ibid., p. 220. — J. H. Hofman, De boekerij van St. Michiel te Zwolle, pp. 387-389.

NOTES TO CHAPTER III

1. See p. 60.
2. Ch. V.
3. R. Dier de Muiden, Scriptum, p. 60: "Perseveretis in statu nostro. Licet enim status Monachorum secundum ecclesiam est perfectior; tamen si quis in humili statu perfecte vixerit premium perfecti hominis recipiet".
4. Ibid., p. 55, p. 53.
5. See p. 61.
6. R. Dier de Muiden, Scriptum, p. 54.
7. See p. 111.
8. See p. 110.
9. R. Dier de Muiden, Scriptum, p. 52.
10. Ibid., p. 59, p. 61.
11. G. Dumbar, Analecta Daventria, vol. I, p. 117: "In libris placebat illi Fratrum studiositas, sed valde trahebat Fratres ad libros magis devotos et morales........ Felicis (inquit) memorie Frater Iohannes Vos, prior in Wyndesem, solebat Fratres suos refrenare a studio librorum sancti Thome et ceterorum similium modernorum scholastice de obedientia et materiis similibus tractantium, volens ut permanerent in simplicitate sua".
12. Ibid., p. 118.
13. Ibid., p. 114.
14. See my article in: Ned. Arch. voor Kerkgesch., 1921, p. 125, note 1.
15. G. Dumbar, Anal. Dav., vol. I, p. 114.
16. See Ch. VII.
17. G. Dumbar, Anal. Dav., vol. I, p. 173: "Ipse nempe Legatus commendavit statum, privilegia pro munimento obtulit, et Canonicatum cum privilegiis Fratribus dare voluit, sed dominus Egbertus simplicitatis amator acceptare rennuit, ne a primitivorum Patrum et Fratrum praeposito discederet, quorum vox esse consuevit: 'Quia in humilitate nostra memor fuit nostri, et redemit nos ab inimicis nostris' ".
18. Ibid., pp. 173-175.
19. At least this is the impression I have from the many times I heard that remark when a school boy there.

20. G. Dumbar, Analecta Daventria, vol. I, p. 177.
21. Ibid., p. 162.
22. A list of these rectors is found in: G. Dumbar, Het kerkelyk en wereltlyk Deventer, vol. I, p. 620.
23. G. Dumbar, Anal. Dav., vol. I, p. 238. In 1484 the brethren secured the "Antiqua Domus" in exchange for another. See: G. Dumbar, Het kerkelyk en wereltlyk Deventer, vol. I, pp. 611-612.
24. G. Dumbar, Het kerkelyk en wereltlyk Deventer, vol. I, pp. 610-614, pp. 631-633. — Anal. Dav., vol. I, pp. 40-41, p. 227.
25. G. Dumbar, Anal. Dav., vol. I, p. 167, p. 228. — Het kerkelyk en wereltlyk Deventer, vol. I, p. 610.
26. G. Dumbar, Het kerkelyk en wereltlyk Deventer, vol. I, pp. 631, 634, 636. — J. de Hullu, De Hervorming in Overijssel, p. 76, p. 93.
27. M. Schoengen, Jac. Voecht narr., pp. 49-51.
28. M. Schoengen, Jac. Voecht narr., p. 42.
29. See: M. Schoengen, Jac. Voecht narr., p. 233, n. 1, p. 64.
30. M. Schoengen, Jac Voecht narr., pp. 64, 69, 70, 72, 76, 78.
31. Ibid., p. 62, p. 58.
32. D. A. Brinkerink, Van den doechden der vuriger susteren, pp. 314-315.
33. M. Schoengen, Jac. Voecht narr., pp. 108-112, 428.
34. Ibid., p. 127: "Postea cum esset vir late caritatis et sicut Apostolus dicit, quantum in ipso fuit, cum omnibus amicitiam et pacem habere volens et providere bona, non solum coram Deo, sed et coram omnibus hominibus. Jam rector factus, invitavit scabinos ad prandium, semel puto omnes, sepius aliquos, quatinus essent amici et fautores nostri et domus nostre. Sed et omnes vicarios similiter invitavit ad prandium. Sed ut experiebatur et experti sumus omnes, nichil taliter profecimus, quia scabini exinde nobis magis favorabiles et fideliores fuerunt, et vicarii a nobis corrigi noluerunt".
35. Ibid., pp. CCXIII-CCXIV.
36. See p. 91.
37. M. Schoengen, Jac. Voecht narr., p. 639.
38. Ibid., p. 638. — M. Van Rhijn, Wessel Gansfort, pp. 32-34.
39. M. Schoengen, Jac. Voecht narr., p. 125.
40. Ibid., p. 640.
41. Ibid., pp. 279-404.
42. G. Dumbar, Het kerkelyk en wereltlyk Deventer, vol. I,

p. 626. — W. F. N. van Rootselaar, Amersfoort (777-1580), vol. I, p. 449. — Amersfoort, Geschiedkundige bijzonderheden, vol. II, pp. 7-8.

43. R. Dier de Muiden, Scriptum, pp. 54-55. — G. H. M. Delprat, Verhandeling over de broederschap van G. Groote, p. 120. — M. Schoengen, Jac. Voecht narr., p. 18, n. 5, where a bibliography for the history of this house is given.

44. G. H. M. Delprat, Verhandeling over de broederschap van G. Groote, pp. 119-120.

45. M. Schoengen, Jac. Voecht narr., pp. 482 and 32; on p. 32, n. 5, is a bibliography.

46. Ibid., p. 484, pp. 30-31; p. 30, n. 1 has a fairly good bibliography.

47. Ibid., pp. 78-79; p. 78, n. 3 has a bibliography.

48. M. Schoengen, Jac. Voecht narr., p. 84, n. 3.

49. M. Schoengen, Jac. Voecht narr., pp. 84-85, p. 84, n. 8. — R. Dier de Muiden, Scriptum, p. 76. — Chronicle of the brethren-house at Doesburg, p. 6.

50. H. O. Feith, Het klerkenhuis en het fraterhuis te Groningen, pp. 10-12. — M. Schoengen, Jac. Voecht narr., p. 101. — M. van Rhijn, Wessel Gansfort, p. 30, p. 30, n. 5. — E. H. Roelfsema, De fraters en het fraterhuis te Groningen, pp. 30-31.

51. M. Schoengen, Jac. Voecht narr., p. 485, p. 99, p. 99, n. 5.

52. H. Gysbertszoon, Kronyk van het fraterhuis te Gouda, pp. 10-13, 14, 16. The house was not recognized, however, till 1456: H. Gysbertszoon, Kronyk, p. 7, p. 22, p. 45.

53. J. J. Dodt van Flensburg, De stichtingsoorkonden van het Utrechtsche fraterhuis, pp. 90-92. — G. H. M. Delprat, Verhandeling over de broederschap van G. Groote, p. 151. — S. Muller, Catalogussen, Stads-archief, part I, p. 123.

54. H. D. J. van Schevichaven, Oud Nijmegens kerken, kloosters, gasthuizen, stichtingen en openbare gebouwen, p. 100. — G. H. M. Delprat, Verhandeling, p. 161.

55. R. Doebner, Annalen und Akten der Brüder des gemeinsamen Lebens im Lüchtenhofe zu Hildesheim, pp. 95, 98-100, 103, 105, 111, 115-116, 271.

56. R. Dier de Muiden, Scriptum, p. 54. — K. Loeffler, Neues über Heinrich von Ahaus, p. 234. — L. Schmitz-Kallenberg, Monasticon Westfaliae, p. 56.

57. K. Loeffler, Heinrich von Ahaus, 1909, p. 778. — Neues über Heinrich von Ahaus, p. 238. — Gedächtnisbuch Kölner

Brüderhaus, p. 5. — Das Fraterhaus Weidenbach zu Köln, pp. 104-105.

58. K. Loeffler, Heinrich von Ahaus, p. 782. — E. Barnikol, Studien zur Geschichte der Brüder vom gemeinsamen Leben, p. 47.

59. E. Barnikol, Studien, p. 63.

60. Ms. No. VII, 3305, Staatsarchiv, Münster, pp. 3-5, 69-71. — Ms. No. VII, 3307, Staatsarchiv, Münster, p. 130. — L. Schmitz-Kallenberg, Monasticon Westfaliae, p. 34. — E. Barnikol, Studien, p. 66.

61. E. Barnikol, Studien, p. 71. — A. Wolters, Reformationsgeschichte der Stadt Wesel, p. 13. — K. Loeffler, Heinrich von Ahaus, p. 780. — Neues über Heinrich von Ahaus, p. 239.

62. R. Doebner, Annalen, pp. 3 and 259. — J. Busch, De reformatione mon., p. 545. — E. Barnikol, Studien, p. 98.

63. K. Loeffler, Das Fraterhaus Weidenbach, p. 111.

64. G. C. F. Lisch, Geschichte der Buchdruckerei in Mecklenburg. — R. Doebner, Annalen, pp. 263, 264, 266, 281, 286, 307, 315. — A. Hulshof, Verslag van een onderzoek te Rostock, pp. 38-41.

65. R. Doebner, Annalen, pp. 192-193, 288, 292, 314, 317. — O. Scheel, Martin Luther, vol. I, pp. 70-97. — E. Barnikol, Luther in Magdeburg und die dortige Brüderschule, pp. 12-13.

66. R. Doebner, Annalen, pp. 267, 279-282.

67. Ibid., pp. 25, 166-171, 184, 188-190, 266, 317.

68. G. H. M. Delprat, Verhandeling, p. 183.

69. O. Meyer, Die Brüder vom gemeinsamen Leben in Würtemberg.

70. Thus we read in the Chronicle of the brethren-house at Doesburg on p. 104: "Sciendum est enim quod ex domo fratrum in Noviomago novella domus fratrum inchoata fuerat in Kempone" [Kempen].

71. M. Schoengen, Jac. Voecht narr., pp. 134-135.

72. G. H. M. Delprat, Verhandeling, p. 175.

73. J. Lindeborn, Historia sive notitia episcopatus Daventriensis, p. 115.

74. Letter by Pope Eugene IV, in: Ms. no. 16515, Royal Library, Brussels, fol. 2b. — G. H. M. Delprat, Verhandeling, p. 178.

75. G. H. M. Delprat, Verhandeling, p. 180.

76. Ibid., p. 180.

77. M. Godet, La congr. de Montaign, p, 114. — G. H. M. Delprat, Verhandeling, p 181.

78. Vita Joh. Hatten, in: An. Daventria, vol. I, p. 182.

79. J. G. R. Acquoy, Het klooster te Windesheim, vol. III, p. 101. — G. H. M. Delprat, Verhandeling, p 170.

80. G. H. M. Delprat, Verhandeling, p. 181.

81. The "House of Master Gerard"; see p. 43.

82. The "Lammenhuis", founded in 1390: H. F. Heussen and H. van Rijn, Oudheden en gestichten van het bisdom Deventer, vol. I, p. 305.

83. The "Buyskenshuis", founded in 1405: H. F. Heussen en H. van Rijn, Oudh. en gest. van Dev., vol. I, p. 309.

84. The "Kerstkenhuis"; for a bibliography on this house see: D. de Man, Hier beginnen sommige stichtige punten, p. 58, note d.

85. The "Brandeshuis"; for a bibliography on this house see: D. de Man, Hier beginnen sommige stichtige punten, p. 87, note a.

86. See: M. Schoengen, Jac. Voecht narr., p. XV.

87. H. F. Heussen en H. van Rijn, Oudheden en gestichten van Deventer, vol. II, pp. 196, 197, 480, 24, 517, 427, 574. — Oudheden van Utrecht, vol. II, pp. 443, 629. — W. Moll, Kerkgeschiedenis van Nederland, vol. II, part 2, p. 176. — M. Schoengen, Het Weduwenhuis te Doesburg, pp. 388-390. — Jac. Voecht narr., pp. XV, 69, 48, 77, 81, 82 n. 2, 89, 129, 145, 197, 208. — S. Muller, De moderne devotie te Utrecht, pp. 25-30. — R. Doebner, Annalen und Akten, pp. 263 (Ahlen), 258-260 (Borken), 264 (Büderich), 259 (Calcar), 260 (Coesfeld), 256-258 (Dinslaken), 76-78 (Eldagsen), 259 (Essen), 259 (Volkmarsen), 261 (Groll), 261 (Herford), 256 (Schüttorf), 259 (Wesel), etc. — L. Schulze, Brüder des gemeinsamen Lebens, (1897), p. 487; (1914), p. 262.

88. D. de. Man, Hier beginnen sommige stichtige punten, pp. LIII, 35, 45, 90.

89. Ibid., p. 56.

90. Ibid., p. 56.

91. Ibid., p. 85.

92. M. Schoengen, Jac. Voecht narr., p. XV.

93. See p. 90.

94. J. G. R. Acquoy, Het klooster te Windesheim, vol. III, p. 75. — W. F. N. Rootselaar, Amersfoort (777-1580), vol. I, p.

386 NOTES

451. — Amersfoort, Geschiedkundige bijzonderheden, vol. II, p. 9.

95. W. F. N. van Rootselaar, Amersfoort (777-1580), vol. I, p. 461.

96. Ibid., p. 477.

97. Ibid., p. 486.

98. H. F. van Heussen en H. van Rijn, Oudheden en gestichten van het bisdom Deventer, vol. I, p. 210.

99. M. Schoengen, Jac. Voecht narr., p. 18, note 5.

100. J. G. R. Acquoy, Het klooster te Windesheim, vol. III, p. 127. — M. Schoengen, Jac. Voecht narratio, p. 37. — Privilegia, capituli Windesemensis, fol. 320ᵃ-321ᵇ.

101. H. Gysbertszoon van Arnhem, Kronyk van het fraterhuis te Gouda, ed. A. H. L. Hensen, p. 27: "Eo quod pro paupertate et parvitate loci ipsis patribus animus non erat ad fundandam congregacionem clericorum".

102. See note 52.

103. M. Schoengen, Jac. Voecht narratio, pp. 134-138, pp. 493-496.

104. W. Moll, Kerkgeschiedenis van Nederland, vol. II, part 3, p. 96.

105. Constitution of the house at Zwolle, in: M. Schoengen, Jac. Voecht narr. pp. 240-241. — Constitution of the house at Deventer, in: Ms. no. 73 G 22, Royal library, the Hague, fol. 1ᵇ-2ᵇ.

106. Constitution of the house at Zwolle, pp. 241-242. — Constitution of the house at Deventer, fol. 2ᵇ-3ᵈ. The selection and arrangement of the subject matter was the work of Florentius Radewijns, for not only does the prologue of the constitution in use at Deventer explicitly state that the written rules of this constitution were the same as those practised in the house at Deventer before, but in the extracts we have of Radewijns' rules, the same subjects are arranged exactly in the same way as found in the written constitution. See: D. J. M. Wüstenhoff, Florentii parvum et simplex exercitium, p. 96. It was not Theodore Herxen, rector of the house at Zwolle, therefore, who composed the chapter on meditation, as Schoengen believes (M. Schoengen, Jac. Voecht narr., p. CXL), but Florentius Radewijns.

107. Constitution of the house at Zwolle, pp. 242-243. —

NOTES   387

Constitution of the house at Deventer, fol. 3ª-4ᵇ. — Hildesheim constitution, p. 241.

108. Zwolle const., p. 244: "Tunc enim per devotam meditationem, et compassionem Dominice passionis, et per pias affectiones, quasi ad spiritualem communionem nos debemus preparare".

109. Zwolle const., pp. 244-245. — Deventer const., fol. 6ᵇ-7ᵇ. — Cf. Hildesheim const., p. 241.

110. Zwolle const., p. 245. — Deventer const., fol. 7ᵇ-8ᵇ. — Cf. Hildesheim const., pp. 239-240.

111. Zwolle const., p. 246. — Deventer const., fol. 8ᵇ. — Cf. Hildesheim const., p. 241.

112. Zwolle const., pp. 246-247. — Dev. const., fol. 10ª-ᵇ. Theodore Herxen composed a series of Dutch sermons, filling two bulky volumes (see p. 106), made especially for the citizens of Zwolle. Of the brethren at Gouda we read that they frequently addressed the people in the vernacular. One of the brethren would read a passage from the Scriptures, while another would explain and comment upon this passage: H. Gysbertsz. van Arnhem, Kronyk van het fraterhuis te Gouda, p. 44.

113. Zwolle const., pp. 247-248. — Dev. const., fol. 10ᵇ-11ª.
114. Zwolle const., p. 248. — Dev. const., fol. 11ª-12ᵇ.
115. Zwolle const., pp. 248-250. — Dev. const., fol. 12ᵇ-14ᵇ.
116. Zwolle const., pp. 250-252. — Dev. const., fol. 14ᵇ-16ᵇ.
117. Zwolle const., pp. 252-255. — Dev. const., fol. 19ª-20ᵇ.
118. Zwolle const., pp. 255-257. — Dev. const., fol. 16ᵇ-18ᵇ.
119. Zwolle const., pp. 257-258. — Dev. const., fol. 20ᵇ-21ᵇ.
120. Zwolle const., pp. 258-259. — Dev. const., fol. 25ᵇ-26ª.

121. R. Doebner, Annalen und Akten, pp. 225-226, 227-231, 233-235. — G. Boerner, Die Annalen und Akten, pp. 76-86; and p. 87: "Das Generalkapitel oder die Union von Münster ist 1499 zustande gekommen, und deshalb sind auch die Unionsstatuten in diesem Jahre errichtet".

122. Zwolle constitution, pp. 259-260. — Deventer constitution, fol. 26ª-28ª. — M. Schoengen, Jac. Voecht narr., pp. LVI-LVIII. — M. A. G. Vorstman, Stukken betreffende de Broeders des Gemeenen Levens, pp. 79, 81, 115, 133.

123. R. Doebner, Annalen und Akten, pp. 214-215.

124. Zwolle const., pp. 260-261. — Dev. const., fol. 28ª-29ª. — Hildesheim const., pp. 243-245.

125. Zwolle const., pp. 262-263. — Dev. const., fol. 30ª-34ᵇ. —

See also: M. Schoengen, Jac. Voecht narr., p. CLXXXVII; for the German houses, see: R. Doebner, Annalen und Akten, pp. 218-222.

126. Zwolle const., pp. 263-264. — Dev. const., fol. 35ᵃ-36ᵃ. — Hildesheim const., pp. 222-223.

127. Zwolle const., pp. 264-265. — Dev. const., fol. 36ᵃ⁻ᵇ. — Hildesheim const., pp. 236-238.

128. Zwolle const., pp. 265-266, p. 268. — Dev. const., fol. 37ᵇ-38ᵃ, 40ᵃ⁻ᵇ. — Hildesheim const., pp. 235-236.

129. Zwolle const., p. 265. — Dev. const., fol. 36ᵇ-37ᵇ. In the rules laid down by the "Colloquium" of Münster, nothing is said about this subject, for in the year 1499 and after, more attention was paid to mechanical rules than the acquisition of virtues. This may at least be said of the constitutions drawn up by the Brethren of the Common Life in Germany.

130. Zwolle const., pp. 266-268. — Dev. const., fol. 38ᵃ-40ᵃ. — Cf. Hildesheim const., pp. 238-239.

131. The Sisters of the Common Life also had constitutions. The first one, drawn up by Groote in 1379, was followed in due time by more elaborate ones, among which the one used at Münster has recently been made more accessible in printed form (see: W. E. Schwarz, Studien zur Geschichte des Klosters Marienthal, pp. 112-126).

132. W. J. Kühler, Levensbeschrijvingen van devote zusters te Deventer, pp. 27, 53-54. — D. de Man, Stichtige punten, pp. L, 7, 12, 64, 225, 240. — Rector Peter Dieppurch's discourses, in: R. Doebner, Annalen und Akten, pp. 144, 145.

133. D. de Man, Stichtige punten, pp. 19, 88, 123, 63, 114, 133, 154, 186, p. 6, note b, p. 109, note c, p. 112, note c; pp. XLVIII, 52, 122, 160, 58, 151, 189. — Rector R. Dieppurch's discourses, in: R. Doebner, Annalen und Akten, p. 149.

134. D. de Man, Stichtige punten, p. 176.

135. That the Sisters of the Common Life were very fond of reading biographies is indicated in: D. de Man, Stichtige punten, p. LXXI.

136. D. de Man, Stichtige punten, pp. LXXIV, XLIX, 27, 90, 193, 199, 206, 233, 252-253.

137. M. Schoengen, Jac. Voecht narr., p. 277.

138. D. de Man, Stichtige punten, pp. 16-17.

139. See p. 105.

140. R. Dier de Muiden, Scriptum, p. 65. — D. de Man, Stichtige punten, p. LV, p. 129.

141. J. G. R. Acquoy, Het klooster te Windesheim, vol. II, pp. 301-302.

142. D. de Man, Stichtige punten, p. LV, p. 37, note b, p. 51, note a.

143. Th. à Kempis, Vita Luberti, § 36. — R. Dier, Scriptum, p. 64. — W. J. Kühler, Joh. Brinckerinck, pp. 34 and 36. — D. de Man, Stichtige punten, pp. LI-LII, p. LIV. — J. G. R. Acquoy, Het klooster te Windesheim, vol. II, p. 290, note 7.

144. D. de Man, Stichtige punten, p. 49, note d. — W. J. Kühler, Joh. Brinckerinck, p. 34. — R. Dier de Muiden, Scriptum, p. 64. — M. Schoengen, Jac. Voecht narr., p. 223.

145. R. Dier de Muiden, Scriptum, p. 28. — W. J. Kühler, Joh. Brinckerinck, p. 36. — D. de Man, Stichtige punten, p. 34, note b, p. LIV. — D. A. Brinkerink, De vita Joh. Brinckerinck, p. 344.

146. D. de Man, Stichtige punten, p. L.

147. See: Deventer constitution, fol. 16b-18b. — Zwolle const., pp. 255-257. — Hildesheim constitution, pp. 232.

148. Hildesheim constitution, pp. 234-235: "Sollicitus sit, ut debito tempore diligenter et munde coquenda praeparet et, ne quid crudum vel intemperatum fratribus offeratur, solerter caveat, hospitario etiam et infirmario benignum se exhibeat".

149. R. Dier, Scriptum, p. 70.

150. See p. 53.

151. See pp. 117-118.

152. See pp. 124-134.

153. To the negative criticism of Acquoy and Hirsche many theories have been added from time to time. Hence it has become very difficult to read modern Dutch, German, French, and English writers without getting one's views bemuddled by the opinions of authorities which were copied verbally by their followers, even in Holland.

154. According to a legend invented about a century ago it was Florentius Radewijns, the first rector of the Brethren of the Common Life at Deventer, who taught in the school of St. Lebwin's, wherefore his followers also were induced to imitate his example. It now is a well-known fact in Holland that Florentius Radewijns never taught school at all, nor did any one of the brethren at Deventer act as rectors of the cathedral

school or as assistants for a great many years after his death. And yet the legend is still believed in by many students in England and France, wherefore attention should be called to this side of the truth also. On the other hand the writer would warn against going to the other extreme of refusing to find any interest in education among Groote's disciples at Deventer. Radewijns had been too intimate a friend of Groote not to have felt the need of better teachers and better schools. See: M. Schoengen, Die Schule von Zwolle, pp. 24-25, and especially Th. à Kempis, Vita Florentii, ch. XXIV, § 2.

155. J. H. Gerretsen, Florentius Radewijns, pp. 67-70.

156. M. Schoengen, Die Schule von Zwolle, p. 19.

157. See p. 36; cf. M. Schoengen, Die Schule von Zwolle, p. 11, note 1, and p. 19.

158. M. Schoengen, Die Schule von Zwolle, pp. 17-18.

159. See pp. 92-97.

160. W. F. N. Rootselaar, Amersfoort, vol. II (1898), p. 12.

161. E. Barnikol, Luther in Magdeburg, p. 56.

162. See p. 114.

163. P. Opmerus, Martyrum Batavicorum, p. 152 (quoted in: D. van Bleysweyck, Delft, p. 520): "A duodecim ingenuis adolescentibus gratuito habitatur, qui severis constricti legibus ad perdiscendas liberales disciplinas Scholam publicam quae in proximo est, frequentant".

164. D. van Bleysweyck, Delft, p. 519: "Gelegen 't eynde de Schoolstraet achter aen Stads-wallen en recht tegen over 't voorbeschreve Oude Weduwenhuys van Charitaten, opgerecht om eenige Latijnsche Scholieren, die van geen middelen en nochtans van goede apparentie en naerstigheyt waren te alimenteren en in de Studie tot den Kercken-dienst op te trecken". — Speech made by Theodore Graviae, prior of Windesheim, in the brethren-house at Delft: "Insuper id quod studetis refundere potestis in iuvenibus, qui apta sunt vasa ad Dei graciam suscipiendam" (found in: J. G. R. Acquoy, Het klooster te Windesheim, vol. III, p. 331). — S. W. A. Drossaers, Archieven van de Delftsche statenkloosters, p. 322.

165. Chronicle of the Brethren-house at Doesburg, pp. 38, 46, 84.

166. Henric van Arnhem's Kronyk van het fraterhuis te Gouda, p. 40: "Et tunc dominus Cornelius suos retraxit fratres, excepto quod dominus Jacobus Naeldwijc usque in annum

sexagesimum permanére permissus est. Qui satis fideliter egit in omnibus pro ista domo, tanquam membrum hujus fuisset, et precipue in regendo scolas in domo, unde satis bonum lucrum habuimus et graciam atque amiciciam bonorum hominum quorum filios bene informavit in disciplinis scolasticis et bonis moribus........ In principio antequam scolas habebamus et sic favorem hominum acquirebamus........ fratres........ in multis deficiebant". P. 45: "Et alia pars subdivisionis erat camera, in qua unus erat lectus repositus pro hospitibus recipiendis, in qua, quia alius locus non fuit, scolas habebant scolares et commensales hic visitantes".

167. H. F. van Heussen and H. van Rhijn, Oudheden van Deventer, vol. I, p. 216.

168. J. van Waasberge, Beschrijving van Geraartsbergen, vol. II, p. 37.

169. Provincial archives, Groningen, 1511, no. 23. "Wy Borgemester en Raed in Groningen betugen mit desen openen brewe voer ons en onse nakomelingen dat wij tot vereweringhe vordernisse ende behulp der guder leringhe der scholers in onser stat ter eren Goedes puerlike om Goedes willen hebben opgedragen en overgegeven........ den pater en broders des convents des fraterhuses"........ (the Brethren of the Common Life are to get a part of the city wall on condition that they build a house on it and instruct children). — H. G. Feith, Het klerkenhuis en het fraterhuis te Groningen, appendix no. VI, p. 19: "De conventualen........ sullen altoes voer ogen hebben, dat selve huis, eersts geinstitueert ende de guederen daer to van beginne sint gegeven gewest, om de ioeget toe leeren, toe institueren ende te tuchtigen ende voorts in de wetenheit van kunsten unde disciplinen unde in de kentnisse Goedes Almachtich unde sine godtlijcke deensten geoeffent te worden, om aldaer een christelijck anvoetsel ende seminarii der heijlliger kercke op te richten".

170. H. F. van Heussen and H. van Rhijn, Oudheden van Deventer, vol. I, p. 215. Several references are given here, from one of which it appears that often more than 1200 pupils were attending the school of the Brethren of the Common Life in that city. Cf. J. Lindeborn, Historia episcopatus Daventriensis, p. 132; G. Bonet-Maury, De opera scholastica fratrum vitae communis, p. 80. See particularly: Gysberti Coeverincx, Analecta, part II, ed. by G. van den Elsen and W. Hoevenaars, p. 82.

171. L. Kückelhahn, Johannes Sturm, pp. 9, 10-13. — G. Bonet-Maury, De opera scholastica, p. 90.

172. E. Barnikol, Luther in Magdeburg, pp. 3-18, p. 60.

173. E. Wintzer, Die Schule der Kugelherren in Marburg, pp. 161-163. — E. Barnikol, Luther in Magdeburg, pp. 56-59.

174. H. D. J. van Schevichaven, Oud-Nijmegens kerken, pp. 101, 103-105.

175. G. C. F. Lisch, Geschichte der Buchdruckerkunst in Mecklenburg, p. 36. — B. Lesker, Die Rostocker Fraterherren, pp. 147-148.

176. A. Dekker, De Hieronymusschool te Utrecht, pp. 8-59. — W. Moll, Kerkgeschiedenis, vol., II, part II, p. 245. — S. Muller, Catalogussen, Stads-archief, part I (1913), p. 123.

177. M. Godet, La Congrégation de Montaigu, p. 3.

178. The Brethren of the Common Life conducted a very flourishing school at Hulsbergen, according to Dr. Moll (W. Moll, Kerkgeschiedenis, vol. II, part II, p. 244). At Harderwijk also they had a very good school: H. Bouman, Geschiedenis der voormalige Geldersche Hoogeschool, vol. I, pp. 6-11.

179. Consilium Joannis Sturmii, in: G. Bonet-Maury, De opera scholastica, p. 90: "Leodii, Daventriae, Zwollae, Vuasaliae literarum exercitationes habent, eisque unum assignatum locum, distributum suis ordinibus, atque ex illis ludis feliciora et plura plerumque prodeunt ingenia quam ex vicinis, ut vocant, Academiis".

180. I. J. van Doornink, Bouwstoffen voor een geschiedenis van het onderwijs in Overijssel, part IX (1888), p. 98. — M. Schoengen, Die Schule von Zwolle, pp. 110-111.

181. M. Schoengen, Die Schule von Zwolle, p. 116. — I. J. van Doornink, Bouwstoffen, part IX, p. 98.

182. M. Schoengen, Die Schule von Zwolle, p. 119.

183. Ibid., pp. 120-121.

184. M. van Rhijn, Wessel Gansfort, p. 37.

185. See p. 97.

186. W. Dillenberger, Al. Hegius, pp. 483-484. This village is situated in the "Kreis" of Ahaus, about four miles south-east of Gronau, and six miles from the present Dutch frontier.

187. H. E. J. Vandervelden, Agricola, p. 80.

188. P. S. Allen, Opus ep. Erasmi, vol. I, p. 580, n. 23.

189. Ibidem.

190. J. Butzbach, Auctarium, p. 231.

191. W. Dillenburg, Al. Hegius, p. 490.

192. W. Gansfort, Opera omnia, preface, where among other references this letter is found: Alexander Hegius doctissimo atque praestantissimo M. Wesselo Groningensi, qui Lux Mundi: "Mitto tibi, vir praestantissime, Homilias Ioannis Chrysostomi .... Non enim decet me quidquam habere quod tecum non communicem........ Sequutus sum consilium tuum, pernitiosa enim literatura est, quae enim jactura probitatis discitur. Vale, et siquid me facere voles, mihi significato, et factum putato. Ex Daventria". This letter is also found in the Dialogi of Hegius.

193. L. Geiger, Renaissance und Humanismus, pp. 391-392.

194. A. Hegius, Letter to Gansfort: "Fui, ut nosti, in Cusana bibliotheca. Illic reperi multos Hebraicos libros, mihi prorsus ignotos: ex Graecis autem pauciores inveni".

195. In one section of his Dialogi he includes a great many statements about grammatical constructions, written in the dialect of Westphalia and Overijssel.

196. D. Reichling, Murmellius, p. 11.

197. A. Hegius, Dialogi (1503), fol. 82^b.

198. D. Reichling, Murmellius, p. 13.

199. J. Butzbach, Auctarium, p. 238.

200. He died on December 27, 1498.

201. J. Butzbach, Auctarium, p. 239.

202. Ibid., p. 239. — Cf. L. Geiger, Renaissance, p. 393.

203. P. S. Allen, Opus ep. Erasmi, vol. I, p. 118. — J. Lindeboom, Bijb. humanisme, p. 77. — J. Lindeboom, Bijb. hum., p. 70. — H. E. J. Vandervelden, Agricola, p. 81, p. 144.

204. J. Butzbach, Auctarium, p. 220.

205. Ibid., p. 236.

206. J. Lindeboom, Bijb. hum., p. 70.

207. Cf. J. Lindeboom, Bijb. hum., p. 121. — W. Moll, J. Brugman, vol. II, p. 79: "En wat zag Brugman in deze Deventersche mannen, waarom hij hun zulk een veelbeteekenenden lof toezwaaide? De gansche inhoud van den brief leert het: hij zag in de discipelen van Meester Geert en Heer Florens trouwe dienaren van God, die met Christus riepen: 'Laat de kinderkens tot ons komen', opdat zij knapen en jongelingen onderwezen in hetgeen een godvruchtig mensch te doen en te laten heeft" (see: J. Brugman, Epistolae, ed. W. Moll, p. 216: "O fratres mei cordialissimi, de facili ab exerciis necessariis parvulis studentulis

averti nolite! A propagacione filiorum Christi cessare ne
velitis"!). — Frederic van Baden, bisbop of Utrecht, Epistola
(1514), ed. M. A. G. Vorstman, p. 126: "Sed palmites vestros in
decorem domus ejus in diversis ecclesiis et monasteriis extend-
atis, scholares de rudi saecula colligendo et bonis moribus et
Dei timore instituendo et fovendo, sicque religiosis domibus et
ecclesiis habilitando". — Philip of Burgundy, bishop of Utrecht,
Epistola (1517), ed. M. A. G. Vorstman, p. 130: "Odor boni
nominis vestri........ multiplexque fructus, quem in ecclesia
sua per vos efficit Dominus, nos hortantur et admonent, quo
favoribus vos prosequamur opportunis". — J. Butzbach, Auctarium, p. 237: "Ex quo [Hegius' "gymnasium"] maxime tamen
nostra in his Germaniae partibus in aptis litteratura personis ab
inicio reformationis suae, quae nondum ad centesimum in aliquo
pervenisse monasterio perhibetur annum, foveri et enutriri
meruit". — F. Jostes, Johannes Veghe, p. XXI: "Dabei tasten
Sie jedoch weder diese [use of indulgences] noch eine andere
kirchliche lehre im prinzip an, vielmehr suchen sie diese immer
nur von dem überwachsenden aberglauben zu befreien und die
damit getriebenen missbräuche zu beseitigen". — K. Loeffler,
Heinrich von Ahaus (1909), p. 763: "Der Geist der Brüderschaft
ist die innerliche Erneuerung und Vertiefung des christlichen
Lebens, die 'devotio moderna' ". — H. Hermelink, Die religiösen
Reformbestrebungen des deutschen Humanismus, p. 9: "Ihre
[Brethren of the Common Life] geschichtliche Aufgabe war
nicht nur die Schaffung einer kirchlichen Laienkultur auf
religiös-innerlichster Grundlage, sondern ihre von der Kirche
genehmigte und unterstützte Organisation diente gegen Ende
.... auch zur Verbreitung der eigentlich humanistischen
Bewegung in den Niederlanden und in Norddeutschland". —
P. Mestwerdt, Die Anfänge des Erasmus, p. 134.

208. D. Reichling, Murmellius, p. 9.

209. Cf. D. Reichling, Ortwin Gratius, pp. 60-81. — L. Geiger,
Renaissance und Humanismus, p. 429. — L. Geiger, Reuchlin,
pp. 248-252. — J. Lindeboom, Bijb. humanisme, pp. 106-108.

210. J. G. de Hoop Scheffer, Geschiedenis der Hervorming
in Nederland (1870), p. 28.

211. J. Geny, Geschichte der Stadtbibl. zu Schlettstadt, p. 18.

212. G. C. Knod. Aus der Bibl. des B. Rhenanus, p. 4. —
J. Knepper, Jacob Wimpfeling, p. 6.

213. Vol. I, p. XIV.

214. Aus der Bibl. des B. Rhen., pp. 3 6.
215. G. C. Knod, Aus der Bibl. des Beatus Rhenanus, p. 7.
216. L. Geiger, Ren. und Hum., p. 388.
217. G. C. Knod, Bibl. des Beat. Rhen., pp. 8-12.
218. Ibid., p. 4.
219. J. Knepper, Das Schulwesen in Elsass, p. 330: "Es sagt genug, dass sein erstes Schulbüchlein erbaulicher Natur war: eine Erklärung der sieben Busspsalmen nach Gregor dem Grossen". It may be of interest to note that the first selections from the Bible translated by Gerard Groote into the vernacular were those very same penitential psalms.
220. G. C. Knod, Bibl. des Beat. Rhen., p. 16, note 4.
221. See p. 99.
222. J. B. Nordhoff, Denkwürdigkeiten, p. 122.
223. D. Reichling, Murmellius, p. 27. — Die Reform der Domschule zu Münster, p. 32. — A. Parmet, Rudolf von Langen, pp. 67-69.
224. Cf. A. Bömer, Das lit. Leben in Münster, p. 43. See also: D. Reichling, Die Reform, p. 27.
225. See: K. Löffler, Das Fraterhaus Weidenbach in Köln, p. 101, p. 103.
226. See: D. Reichling, Die Reform, p. 20.
227. A. Bömer, Der Münstersche Domschulrektor Timann Kemner, p. 184.
228. D. Reichling, Murm., p. 1, p. 3.
229. Ibid., p. 45, p. 69.
230. J. Lindeboom, Bijb. hum., p. 92.
231. D. Reichling, Murmellius, p. 44.
232. Ibid., pp. 42-43.
233. See: D. Reichling, Die Reform, p. 65.
234. L. Geiger, Ren. und Hum., p. 397. — D. Reichling, Murmellius, p. 47.
235. See: D. Reichling, Murmellius, pp. 46, 48-69, 88-94, 98-115. On pp. 132-165 a list of his works is given.
236. L. Geiger, Ren. und Hum., p. 398.
237. D. Reichling, Murmellius, p. 101.
238. D. Reichling, Die Reform, p. 69-70.
239. Ibid., pp. 74-75. — D. Reichling, Die Humanisten J. Horlenius u. J. Montanus.
240. See: A. Egen, Der Einfluss der Münsterschen Domschule auf die Ausbreitung des Humanismus.

NOTES TO CHAPTER IV

1. J. Busch, Chronicon Wind., p. 43.
2. W. J. Kühler, Brinckerinck, pp. 23-24.
3. J. Busch, Chron. Wind., p. 44.
4. D. A. Brinkerink, Vita Brinck., p. 327.
5. J. Busch, Chron. Wind., p. 343.
6. See J. G. R. Acquoy, Windesheim, vol. II, pp. 7-10. Cf. M. Schoengen, Narratio, pp. LXIII-LXIV.
7. J. Busch, Chron. Wind., pp. 343-344; cf. J. G. R. Acquoy, Windesheim, vol. II, pp. 8-9.
8. J. Busch, Chron. Wind., p. 344.
9. J. G. R. Acquoy, Windesheim, vol. II, pp. 9-10.
10. J. G. R. Acquoy, Windesheim, vol. II, p. 10.
11. Ibid., pp. 11-13.
12. Ibid., vol. II, p. 13.
13. J. Busch, Chron. Wind., pp. 344-345. — J. G. R. Acquoy, Windesheim, vol. III, p. 26; vol. II, p. 13 n. 1.
14. J. Busch, Chron. Wind., p. 348. — J. G. R. Acquoy, Wind., vol. III, p. 34.
15. J. Busch, Chron. Wind., p. 345. — J. H. Richter, Frenswegen, p. 16.
16. J. Busch, Chron. Wind., p. 349. — J. G. R. Acquoy, Wind., vol. III, p. 38.
17. J. Busch, Chron. Wind., p. 350.
18. Ibid., p. 350.
19. Ibid., p. 351. — J. G. R. Acquoy, Wind., vol. III, p. 54.
20. J. Busch, Chron. Wind., p. 351. — J. G. R. Acquoy, Wind., vol. III, p. 62.
21. J. Busch, Chron. Wind., pp. 352-353. — J. G. R. Acquoy, Wind., vol. II, pp. 16-18.
22. J. Busch, Chron. Wind., pp. 365-366, p. 401. — C. Block, Chronicle, ed. J. G. C. Joosting, p. 48. — Ordinationes Windeshemense, pp. 15, 20.
23. J. Busch, Chron. Wind., p. 366.
24. Ibid., p. 366. — J. G. R. Acquoy, Wind., vol. III, p. 92.
25. J. Busch, Chron. Wind., p. 366. — J. G. R. Acquoy, Wind., vol. III, p. 94.

26. J. Busch, Chron. Wind., p. 482. — J. G. R. Acquoy, Wind., vol. III, p. 97.
27. B. P. Velthuysen, Twee onbekende conventen, p. 41.
28. Ibid., p. 41.
29. J. G. R. Acquoy, Wind., vol. II, p. 55.
30. Ioannis ab Horstmaria, Chronica, fol. 2ᵇ-3ᵃ.
31. Ibid., fol. 5ᵇ-6ᵃ.
32. J. H. Richter, Frenswegen, pp. 16-17.
33. J. Busch, Chron. Wind., pp. 165-172, 175-179. — Ioannis ab Horstmaria, Chronica, fol. 30ᵃ-33ᵇ. — J. H. Richter, Frenswegen, pp. 19-21.
34. V. Becker, Een onbekende kronijk, p. 388. — J. G. R Acquoy, Wind., vol. I, p. 291 n. 3.
35. J. Busch, Liber de ref. mon., p. 393.
36. Ibid., p. 395.
37. Ibid., pp. 396-397, 708.
38. Ibid., p. 402.
39. Ibid., p. 404.
40. Ibid., p. 406.
41. Ibid., p. 706; cf. p. XXXV.
42. Ibid., p. XXXV n. 1.
43. Ibid., p. 420.
44. Ibid., p. 432.
45. Ibid., p. 452.
46. Ibid., p. 433.
47. Ibid., pp. 452, 457.
48. Ibid., pp. 457-459.
49. Ibid., pp. 459-460.
50. Ibid., p. 455.
51. Ibid., pp. 555-568.
52. Ibid., p. 730. — Chron. Wind., p. 247.
53. J. Busch, De ref. mon., p. 784.
54. Ibid., p. 498.
55. Ibid., pp. 431-432.
56. Ibid., pp. 539-544, 613-615.
57. Ibid., pp. 562-565, 568-572, 588-597, 617-618, 629-632.
58. Ibid., pp. 505-507, 514-517.
59. K. Grube, Die Legationsreise des Cardinals Nikolaus von Cusa, p. 394.
60. See: P. E. Schatten, Kloster Böddiken. — L. Schmitz-Kallenberg, Monumenta Budicensa.

61. W. J. Kühler, Brinckerinck, p. 313.

62. See pp. 15, 48, 63-64, 88.

63. W. J. Kühler, Brinckerinck, pp. 313-316.

64. Ibid., pp. 317-318.

65. Ibid., p. 319.

66. Ibid., p. 334.

67. Ibid., pp. 326-335; here the whole story of the reform at Hilwartshausen is found.

68. Ibid., p. 335.

69. W. Moll, Kerkgeschiedenis, vol. II, part II, p. 227.

70. J. G. R. Acquoy, Windesheim, vol. I, pp. 205-206.

71. Ibid., pp. 207-211.

72. J. G. R. Acquoy, Windesheim, vol. II, p. 127.

73. Ibid., vol. II, pp. 300-301.

74. Ibid., vol. I, p. 190; vol. II, pp. 281-282.

75. Ibid., vol. I, pp. 187-188.

76. Ibid., vol. I, pp. 99-106.

77. Ibid., vol. I, pp. 186-189.

78. Ibid., vol. II, p. 280.

79. Ibid., vol. I, p. 184.

80. Ibid., vol. II, pp. 284-295.

81. Ibid., vol. I, p. 198.

82. Ibid., vol. II, pp. 204-207.

83. Ibid., vol. II, 198-199.

84. Ibid., vol. II, p. 195.

85. Ibid., vol. II, p. 143.

86. J. Busch, Chron. Wind., pp. 311-312.

87. Ibid., p. XIX n. 1.

88. Ibid., p. 312. — J. G. R. Acquoy, Windesheim, vol. II, p. 209, p. 214.

89. J. G. R. Acquoy, Windesheim, vol. II, pp. 229-230.

90. Ibid., vol. II, pp. 236-237.

91. Ibid., vol. II, p. 238.

92. Ibid., vol. I, p. 327.

93. Ibid., vol. II, pp. 258-262.

NOTES TO CHAPTER V

1. A. J. Thebaud, Who wrote the Imitation of Christ? in: American Cath. Quart. Rev., 1883, p. 650.

2. O. A. Spitzen, Thomas à Kempis, p. 2. — E. Waterton, Thomas à Kempis, p. 22.

3. K. Hirsche, Prologomena, vol. III, pp. 44-62.

4. Book I, ch. 22 (p. 43^{30-31} of Pohl's edition); book I, ch. 13 (p. 22^{15-19}); book III, ch. 55 (p. 250^{8-10}).

5. I, 25 (p. 53^{6-9}); III, 19 (p. 178^{6-7}); I, 3 (p. 10^{1-6}); III, 38 (p. 213^{26-28}); III, 53 (p. 244^{25-26}); I, 2 (p. 8^{8-10}).

6. I, 11 (p. 19^{7-15}); III, 5 (p. 151^{25-26}); I, 13 (p. 36^{24-29}); II, 9 (p. 76^{29-31}, p. 77^{3-14}); III, 35.

7. I, 3 (p. 10^{19-24}); IV, 7 (p. 109^{22-25}, p. $109^{27}-110^1$); II, 10 (p. 77^{26-27}); III, 4 (p. 150^{2-5}); III, 56 (p. $252^{27}-253^1$); I, 8; III, 45 (p. 225^{6-7}); III, 53 (p. 244^{10-11}).

8. I, 8 (p. 15^{24-27}); I, 10; I, 20 (p. $35^{18}-36^7$); III, 54, (p. 248^{24-31}); III, 58 (p. $256^{29}-257^{27}$); II, 6 (p. 69^{7-15}); I, 1 (p. 61^{17-18}); I, 1 (p. 6^{15-16}); I, 18 (p. 31^{2-3}); I, 25 (p. 55^{29-31}); II, 6 (p. 69^{20-22}); II, 7 (p. 70^{9-11}); II, 9; III, 26 (p. 194^{10-13}); III, 45 (p. 223^{9-11}).

9. I, 12 (p. 20^{25-26}); I, 17 (p. 29^{6-7}); I, 23 (p. $47^{31}-48^1$); II, 1 (p. 60^{23-30}); III, 53 (p. 244^{13-15}); III, 59 (p. 261^{23-24}); I, 21 (p. $39^{6, 13-16}$); III, 57.

10. II, 12 (p. 85^{9-11}, p. 87^{17-20}).

11. See p. 80.

12. III, 14, 13, 20, 51; IV, 15, 18.

13. I, 9; II, 11; III, 13.

14. I, 7; I, 12 (p. 21^{1-3}); I, 20 (p. 36^{12-18}); II, 10 (p. 78^{15-24}); III, 7 (p. 158^{11-30}).

15. I, 17 (p. 28^{29-31}); II, 12 (p. 82^{7-8}); III, 32, 37; III, 39 (p. 215^{19-22}); IV, 8.

16. I, 24 (p. $51^{3-4, 9-12}$); II, 12 (p. 88^{3-5}).

17. II, 12; IV, 8; II, 4, 6; III, 11, 15, 44, 53.

18. I, 17, 20; I, 5; I, 23 (p. 46^{12-13}); I, 19 (p. 34^{2-7}); I, 7 (p. 14^{15}).

19. I, 1 (p. 6^{11-13}); III, 34, 42, 46, 50; IV, 7, 8, 9, 15.

20. I, 17 (p. 29^{7-8}); II, 1, 7, 11; III, 6; IV, 1, 3, 11, 17.

21. I, 13 (p. $23^{3\text{-}5}$); I, 14, 15, 16, 25; II, 3 (p. $64^{17\text{-}23}$); III, 25 (p. 192); III, 45 (p. $225^{4\text{-}6}$).

22. III, 27 (p. $195^{8\text{-}10}$).

23. II, 1 (p. $59^{5\text{-}6,\,9\text{-}11,\,14\text{-}16}$); III, 2 (p. $144^{27}\text{-}145^{4}$); III, 40 (p. $216^{15\text{-}17}$); I, 3 (p. $9^{8\text{-}13}$).

24. III, 43 (p. $220^{20\text{-}22}$); I, 3 (p. $10^{12\text{-}14}$); I, 1 (p. $6^{2\text{-}11}$); I, 3 (p. $8^{25\text{-}28}$); III, 3 (p. $146^{5\text{-}7}$); III, 43; III, 44 (p. $149^{9\text{-}11}$).

25. See pp. 19-20, 54, 80.

26. See pp. 20-21, 34.

27. III, 4 (p. $150^{31}\text{-}151^{4}$); III, 5, 53, 54, 55.

28. III, 55 (p. $250^{15\text{-}17}$).

29. Epistle of James, ch. II, 14, 19-20.

30. III, 3 (p. $147^{27\text{-}29}$).

31. V. Becker, L'auteur de l'Imitation, p. 4.

32. K. Hirsche, Prologomena, vol. III, p. 264.

33. J. Mooren, Th. à Kempis, p. 113.

34. Ibid., p. 32, p. 227.

35. Ibid., pp. 230-231: "Wy Schepene van Kempen, doen kunt, ... Dis vurss. coepp is geschiet mit volkomen willen ind gehenkenysse her johan hemerkes priesters canonichs van den regulieren, die myt verteighen heit vur sich ind Thomaes synen witlichen broeder myt wytlichen vertyghenysse als vur uns recht ind gewoenlich is". In spite of this Puyol wrote as late as 1899: "Il y a incertitude sur son nom véritable".

36. See p. 86.

37. H. Rosweyden, Vindiciae, p. 123.

38. Th. à Kempis, Vita Joh. Gronde, ch. I, § 2.

39. Ibid.

40. Th. à Kempis, Vita Florentii, ch. XXIV.

41. Th. à Kempis, Vita Joh. Gronde, ch. I, § 2.

42. Th. à Kempis, Vita Arn. Schoonhoviae, § 3.

43. Ibid.

44. Th. à Kempis, Vita Joh. Gronde, ch. I, § 2.

45. Th. à Kempis, Vita Arn. Schoonh., § 3.

46. Th. à Kempis, Vita Flor., ch. XVI, § 4.

47. It should also be borne in mind that Thomas à Kempis was only one of the many boys who happened to be copying religious writings at Deventer. From far and near they had come to Deventer to attend school there, and, as happened with Thomas Hemerken of Kempen, to "learn to read and write the Holy Scriptures and books on moral subjects". Thus thousands

of manuscripts were written at Deventer, which as a rule were
taken home when the boys left the Yssel country, or, in case
they entered some monastery, these manuscripts were added to
the library of that monastery. It is a great pity that so few
writers have investigated this phase of the influence exerted by
the Brethren of the Common Life at Deventer, Zwolle, and
elsewhere. The only one who appears to have mentioned the
subject is Dr. M. Schoengen of Zwolle, who found three manuscripts in the Episcopal Seminary at Liège which expressly
mention the fact that they had been written at Deventer and
Zwolle. Schoengen even claims that in the library of this institution twenty-five unpublished treatises of Groote are found
(M. Schoengen, Nederlandica in Belgische archieven, p. 180).
But after a careful examination of the manuscripts in question
during the summer of the year 1920, the present writer noticed
that many of them were in all probability copied at Deventer,
but not a single unpublished treatise written by Groote is found
in any one of them. And still this subject is of such significance
that results cannot fail the serious student. A few examples
might illustrate the nature of this interesting problem. In the
"Stadt- und Landesbibliothek" at Düsseldorf a manuscript is
found, called Ms. B. 180, containing 171 folios. Some extracts
from Groote's writings were written in it and other material
by a certain "John Nijell at Deventer in the year 1458, when
seated in the 'Nova domo clericorum'", which was the building
constructed by the Brethren of the Common Life for the purpose
of accommodating poor school boys with proper board and
lodging (see p. 104). Manuscript G. B. 8°83 of the "Stadtbibliothek" at Cologne also contains a note stating that this
manuscript had been written at Deventer (fol. 90b: "Explicit
iste liber scriptus et completus per manus Wilhelmi Vos de
Ghiecen anno Domini 1416 in profesto Valentini Daventrie").
And on fol. 1a of Ms. G. B. 8°76 of the same library we read the
following statement: "Iste libellus pertinet fratribus s. Crucis in
Colonia et vocatur Farago ea quod in eo multa ac diversa raptim
undique collecta sint, et primo do servire Deo et multis aliis
ut patet in folio sequenti, ubi ponitur eciam per numerum
foliorum". This table of contents is found on fol. 2a-3a, while
on fol. 8b we read: "Sequuntur multa bona collecta Swollis
ante annos 30a, quorum tabula in principio huius habetur". On
fol. 12b we find the date 1412. Unfortunately it was not

customary in those days to write such notes in the manuscripts, wherefore it is difficult to estimate how many of them were written by pupils of the Brethren of the Common Life. Only incidentally do we find indications which lead to definite conclusions. One very interesting example is the following. Manuscript G. B. 4⁰ 249 of the City Library at Cologne was written at Deventer, though we would never have known about this, if a very curious accident had not impelled the copyist to mention the fact. He had already copied the Sermo de nativitate Domini in this manuscript under the title of Tractatus magistri Gerardi dicti Groet de Daventria de quatuor generibus meditabilium sive contemplacionum. We are very grateful to him for that, as until a few years ago the Sermo de nativitate Domini by Groote had been thought lost, and as it was believed that the Tractatus de quatuor generibus meditabilium was a separate work. Next he had copied a few extracts from Gregory (fol. 13ᵇ-15ᵇ), followed on fol. 22ᵃ by Groote's De locatione curae animarum and an excerpt from the Liber apum, called De pluritate beneficiorum, which he believed to be also a treatise composed by Groote (fol. 37ᵇ: "Expliciunt valde horribilia de pluritate beneficiorum visa a magistro Gerardi dicto Groet de Daventria"). The words: "visa a magistro Gerardi dicto Groet de Daventria" were scratched out by a later hand and the following note written on the margin: "Ex libro apum scripta". On fol. 38a he had begun a treatise on the ten commandments and had already come to the top of the second column of fol. 68, when his work was interrupted. A cat soiled the page on which he had been writing, wherefore the next morning he drew a picture there of the cat and added the following commentary: "Confound that wretched cat which soiled this page one night at Deventer. Care must be taken that no books are left open at night where cats are". On fol. 73b he finished the Commentum super decem precepta, and on fol. 73ᵇ-90ᵃ we find the Tractatus de peccatis capitalibus sive mortalibus.

48. See: H. Rosweyden, Vindiciae, p. 110.
49. Th. à Kempis, Vita Florentii, ch. XIII, § 2.
50. Ibid., ch. XVIII, § 3.
51. What is worse, even those who claim to be very much interested in the lives and writings of the Brethren of the Common Life have failed to give substantial evidence of their interest. In the meantime the works of a great many minor

reformers and less influential scholars have been published everywhere. Is it not a pity that nowhere in any Dutch library can one find — or could not in 1920 — the letters of Groote which Nolte published? And to think that Groote's Septem verba dicta a Domino, perhaps his best work, is practically unknown, even in Holland. And as for his "Sermo de nativitate Domini", what writer has ever made use of it? In Zerbolt's case the situation is still worse. Zerbolt was the greatest scholar and the most influential writer the Brethren of the Common Life at Deventer could ever boast of. But what do even the friends of Thomas à Kempis say about him? Professor F. Jostes of Münster, who rightly claims that the De Imitatione Christi is a sort of "rapiarium", and must have been the work of some follower of Gerard Groote (F. Jostes, Nieuwe bijzonderheden over de Navolging, p. 272) wrote something very strange about Zerbolt. Gerard Zerbolt of Zutphen, Jostes declared, could never have written the De libris teutonicalibus, or the Super modo vivendi (F. Jostes, Die Schriften des Gerhard Zerbolt van Zutfen, pp. 8-9). He uses about the same arguments that are brought forward by the antagonists of Thomas à Kempis. Now the fact is that Jostes had never seen the De libris teutonicalibus. And who has ever made intelligent use of the Super modo vivendi by Zerbolt? Next came Wüstenhoff and declared that Zerbolt also could not have written the "De preciosis vestibus", and certainly not his "Scriptum pro quodam" (D. J. M. Wüstenhoff, "Florentii parvum et simplex exercitum", p. 90). Nobody in Holland seems to have raised a voice against these critics, although the latter did not bring forward any positive evidence to prove their assumptions. Somebody must have written those four treatises. They were found in the library of the Brethren of the Common Life at Deventer by J. Revius, one of the best scholars of seventeenth century Holland. Zerbolt had been librarian there and somebody in that library had written a note in the manuscript to the effect that Zerbolt was the author of them all. None of the original sources give us any justification for doubting the veracity of Revius' report. And still a few unsound arguments have made nearly everybody in Holland believe the statements of a foreign scholar, who knew practically nothing about Zerbolt, rather than Revius, their own countryman, whose statements are supported by Rudolph Dier

of Muiden, next to Thomas à Kempis the best biographer of
Groote and his disciples at Deventer (see: A. Hyma, Is Gerard
Zerbolt of Zutphen the author of the "Super modo vivendi"?
p. 114). If Zerbolt could not have written the Super modo
vivendi, then Thomas à Kempis certainly was neither the author
nor the editor of the De Imitatione Christi. Hence one need
not be surprised to find so many modern writers who have
taken up arms against the friends of Thomas à Kempis.

52. According to Rosweyden he went to Mount St. Agnes
in 1399 (Vindiciae, p. 110), and his probation lasted for six years
(Vindiciae, p. 111), but according to the continuation of the
Chronicon Mt. St. Agnetis by an anonymous writer, he was
invested in 1406.

53. V. Becker, L'auteur de l'Imitation, p. 7.

54. K. Hirsche, Prologomena, vol. III, p. 267.

55. The above selection is taken from D. V. Scully's translation of the Sermons to the Novices Regular, pp. XXI-XXII.

56. See: Thomas à Kempis, Opera, Nuremberg 1494, fol.
84b-85a, where a biography is given by an anonymous writer.
This sketch is also found in a manuscript at The Hague, and
is edited in the edition of the "Imitation" by L. Peters, Leiden
1902, where on pp. XI-XV a list of the 38 works is given.
Since neither the Opera of the year 1494 are accessible to most
students, nor the other work mentioned here, a few excerpts
are inserted here from the latter: "Hic Thomas cognomento
Heymergijn [Hemerken], id est Malleus, qui vere malleus
existens in suis dictis et tractatibus, devotis et indevotis........
Multum affabilis et consolatorius fuit infirmis et tentatis iste
bonus et devotus pater, et valde zelosus pro salute animarum;
et omnes cupiebat salvos fieri sicut se ipsum........ Et quia
in juventute incepit congregare divitias, scilicet virtutum, ideo
sortitus est nomen bonorum........ Item adhuc multa alia
pluro audivi a fratribus illius conventus, qui adhuc vivunt, quod
vix millesimam partem enarravi scribendo. Sed quid dicam
amplius? Sicut alios docuit et instruxit dictando et scribendo,
sic ipse fecit vivendo: opera implevit quod sermonibus dixit
esse faciendum.......... Hic Thomas multum profecit in virtutibus, de die in diem proficiens, addens semper fervorem
fervori, devotionem devotioni, virtutem virtuti, ita ut omnes
mirabantur de ejus fervore et devotione; et quia multum humilis
fuit, ideo a Deo magnam et singularem gratiam meruit habere,
sicut patet ex ejus dictis".

57. See pp. 64-65.

58. The quotations are all from: Th. à Kempis, The founders of the New Devotion, ed. J. P. Arthur, pp. 59, 54, 67, 72-73, 153-160, 192-207, 238, 251, 260.

59. F. R. Cruise, Thomas à Kempis, pp. 159-160. Cf. E. Amort, Ded. crit., p. 50.

60. A. Loth, L'auteur de l'Im., pp. 531-537.

61. Ibid., p. 547: "Il est certain qu'en 1406 l'Imitation était non seulement composée, mais connue et propagée".

62. V. Becker, Thomas van Kempen (1892), p. 11.

63. Ibid., p. 14. That Holland is so poorly represented is due to the wholesale destruction of Catholic libraries by Dutch reformers.

64. See: J. E. G. De Montmorency, Th. à Kempis, p. XIX, pp. 110-112.

65. V. Becker, Thomas van Kempen (1892), p. 9.

66. K. Hirsche, Prologomena, vol. III, pp. 181-190.

67. O. A. Spitzen, Nouvelle défense, pp. 50-51. The manuscript in question contains the following note: "Notandum quod iste tractatus editus est a probo et egregrio viro magistro [master of the novices] Thoma de Monte sancte Agnetis...... descriptus ex manu autoris in Trajecto [in the bishopric of Utrecht] anno 1425". Hirsche, however, refuses to believe that this is the correct date (see his Prologomena, vol. III, pp. 167, 172).

68. O. A. Spitzen, Les Hollandismes, p. 74.

69. K. Hirsche, Prologomena, vol. III, pp. 174-181. — O. A. Spitzen, Les Hollandismes, p. 63.

70. O. A. Spitzen, Th. à Kempis gehandhaafd, pp. 58-60. On the last page of the manuscript in which Spitzen discovered this very important translation we read: "Item een boeken van gheesteliken vermaningen qui sequitur me". Hence book I was originally drawn up in Latin. This translation was made by John Scutken, the friend of Thomas à Kempis (see: O. A. Spitzen, Les Hollandismes, p. 61; Nouvelle défense, p. 42).

71. O. A. Spitzen, Nouv. déf., p. 110; Nalezing, p. 35.

72. K. Hirsche, Prologomena, vol. III, pp. 190-191.

73. O. A. Spitzen, Nouv. déf., p. 100.

74. K. Hirsche, Prologomena, vol. III, p. 194. — E. Barnikol, Studien, p. 64.

75. O. A. Spitzen, Les Hollandismes, p. 62.

76. O. A. Spitzen, Nouv. déf., pp. 58, 197-199.

77. 'L. Korth, Die älteste deutsche Uebersetzung der "Imitatio Christi", pp. 89-90: "Van Jhesus geboirt syn jair getzalt dusent ind vierhundert, vierinddrissich dar zu gestalt, wie seer mich des verwundert. Darumb eyn frunt van mynnen hait uns geschreven eyn bochelyn, der en woulde sich nyt nennen, dat ist ym eyn ewich gewyn. Dat bochlijn ist mir komen vur zu setzen uss dem latijne ind heist 'qui me sequitur'". See also p. 91, where the last word of line 80 of this poem is contracted with the last word of line 74, thus forming the name of the brethren-house at Cologne, of which the Weidenbach Strasse still reminds us to-day.

78. See: V. Becker, Thomas van Kempen (1892), pp. 16-19. Becker mentions copies of the years 1428, 1429, 1433, 1436, brought to Liège, Erfurt and other places.

79. J. Busch, Chron. Wind., p. 58: "......... qui plures devotos tractatulos composuit, videlicet 'qui sequitur' de imitacione Christi cum aliis".

80. "All that the supporters of Thomas à Kempis have left", triumphantly exclaimed Wolfsgruber in his well-known work on the abbot Gersen, "is the account by Busch and the autograph of Thomas à Kempis, finished in 1441" (C. Wolfsgruber, Gersen, p. 74). On one page he claims that Thomas à Kempis cannot have written the "Soliloquium animae" (p. 63), while a little further he points to the difference in style between the "Soliloquium animae" and the "Imitation". Thomas, being the author of the first work, could not very well have written the latter, he asserts (pp. 83-85)! G. Kentenich wrote an article in the Zeitschrift für Kirchengeschichte, called: Zum Imitatio Christi — Streit, in which he made some very interesting statements. John Busch, the celebrated missionary of Windesheim, was such a foolhardy liar, he asserts, that inasmuch as he calls Thomas à Kempis the author of the "Imitation", his testimonial simply proves that Thomas cannot be considered the author (see: pp. 468-469 of this article).

81. See: Ó. A. Spitzen, Nouvelle défense, p. 48.

82. See: V. Becker, L'auteur de l'Imitation, pp. 33-55. — J. B. Malou, Recherches, pp. 77-89. — V. Becker, Derniers travaux, pp. 49-51. — F. R. Cruise, Thomas à Kempis, pp. 149-157, 242-248. The best source on this question remains: E. Amort, Ded. critica, pp. 94-118. See also: O. A. Spitzen, Th. à Kempis

gehandhaafd, pp. 165-177.   H Watrigant, La genèse des Exerc. spirit., p. 104.

83. See: O. A. Spitzen, Nouv. déf., pp. 44-45.

84. K. Hirsche, Prologomena, vol. III, pp. 11-14. — A. Loth, L'Auteur de l'Imitation, pp. 581-585. — E. Renan, L'Auteur de l'Imitation de Jésus Christ, pp. 320-322.

85. De im. Christi, book I, ch. XXV.

86. E. Renan, L'Auteur de l'Im., pp. 323-334. — Wolfsgruber, J. Gersen, pp. 172-185 (the author is an Italian), 185-198 (written in the thirteenth century). Cf. W. Moll, Kerkgeschiedenis, vol II, part. II, p. 372: "De volslagen onbekendheid dezer geleerden [Renan and his followers] met onze litteratuur van de XIVe en XVe eeuw mag bij de waardeering van hunne kritiek niet voorbij gezien worden. Zoo Renan ook maar een enkel stuk van Gerlach Peters gelezen had, zou hij in zijn opstel L'auteur de l'Imitation zich onthouden hebben van redeneeringen wier oppervlakkigheid door den fraaijen stijl geenszins bedekt wordt".

87. K. Hirsche, Prologomena, vol. II, pp. 2-88.

88. See p. 19.

89. O. A. Spitzen, Nouvelle défense, 136-144.

90. Ibid., p. 162.

91. P. Hagen, De Navolging van Christus en Thomas van Kempen, p. 40.

92. J. F. Vregt, Eenige ascetische tractaten, p. 323, p. 330 They are chapters X and XIII.

93. Ibid., p. 325.

94. J. B. Malou, Recherches, pp. 119-120 (from a letter by John Vos of Heusden, prior of Windesheim), pp. 391-402 (from the Admonitiones of Florentius).

95. O. A. Spitzen, Thomas à Kempis gehandhaafd, pp. 71-82

96. V. Becker, L'auteur de l'Imitation, pp. 145-194.

97. G. Bonet-Maury, E quibus fontibus, pp. 15-37.

98. V. Becker, De Navolging Christi is een oorspronkelijk werk, p. 111.

99. Found on pages 27-40 of the issue of the year 1920.

100. This article has also appeared in the Zeitschrift für deutsches Altertum, vol. LIX, pp. 23-35.

101. Mss. theol. germ. 8° no. 43 and 4° no. 15.

102. Ms. theol. germ. 8° no. 54. On fol. 42b a prayer was written (ending on fol. 47a), which is not found in the "Imitation". It is called: "Dit is en innich gebeth alle tyd to lesende

deme mynschen", and it begins as follows: "Leve Here, ut der groten diepe myner sunde rope ick verlorene dochtere tho dy vader vul aller gnade".

103. On the history of this house see: J. Hartwig, Die Frauenfrage im mittelalterlichen Lübeck, in: Hansische Geschichtsblätter, vol. XIV (1908), pp. 85-88.

104. On fol 1ᵃ of the manuscript in question we read: "Anneken Poises op Sunte Johannes hort dyt bock". Cf. the article mentioned in the preceding note.

105. See the notices in: Sitzungsberichte der kön. preuss. Ak. der Wiss., for Jan. 1911, pp. 108-109, and in: Neue Jahrbücher für das klassische Altertum, Geschichte und deutsche Literatur, vol. XXXI (1913), p. 51.

106. The Latin equivalent of L has: "Domine, Domine Deus, Domine Deus meus, tu Deus Domine Jesu, Domine Deus inspirator et illuminator omnium prophetarum, Domine Deus meus aeterna veritas, O veritas mea et misericordia mea, Deus meus Trinitas beata, Domine Deus sancte Pater", and "tu clemens et misericors Deus". The "Imitation", however, has: "Domine, Domine Deus, Domine Deus meus, Deus meus, Deus, Domine Jesu, Veritas tue, aeterna Veritas, Pater sancte, Deus meus misericordia mea, Pater coelestis, Pater Domini mei Jesu Christi, O Pater misericordiarum et Deus totius consolationis, te cum unigenito filio tuo et Spiritu Sancto paraclito, Eia Domine Deus amator sancte meus, Deus meus amor meus, te dilectum meum, tu O dulcissime, O fons amoris perpetui, benignissime Jesu, fortissime Deus Israel, Zelator animarum fidelium, dulcissime et amantissime Jesu, O mi dilectissime sponse Jesu Christe amator purissime dominator universae creaturae, O Jesu splendor aeternae gloriae, solamen peregrinantis animae, tu Deus meus, spes mea, salus aeterna, O Patris sapientia, Jesu bone, piissime Deus meus, Deus meus dulcedo ineffabilis, Pater dilecte, O lux perpetua, cuncta creata transcendens lumina, Domine Deus judex juste fortis et patiens, Pater juste et semper laudande, Pater amande, Pater perpetue venerande, tu Domine Deus meus coelestis medicus animarum", and "Deus meus misericordiarum Pater".

NOTES TO CHAPTER VI

1. M. Luther, Letter of recommendation for Gansfort's letters, in: W. Gansfort, Opera, p. 854; the translation is found in: E. W. Miller and J. W. Scudder, Wessel Gansfort, vol. I, p. 232. — M. van Rhijn, Wessel Gansfort, p. 233.

2. The "parva domus" was for boys who paid for their lodging; see p. 109.

3. M. van Rhijn, Wessel Gansfort, pp. 23-39, 45, XXXVIII.

4. M. Schoengen, Narratio, p 156, "Cum ergo et ipse esset totus devotus et fervidus, et Rutgerus procurator devotissime de sero pro juvenibus faceret collationem adjuvit eum, et -ex conflatione mutua inflammabant juvenes ad virtutes et ad odium viciorum".

5. M. Schoengen, Narratio, p. 157.

6. See pp. 93, 120.

7. De Im. Christi, bk. I, ch. III.

8. M. van Rhijn, Wessel Gansfort, pp. 39-45.

9. Ibid., pp. 45-78.

10. A. Hardenberg, Vita Wesseli, in: Gansfort's Opera, p. X: "Itaque, utroque pede concessit in sententiam Nominalium, quos reperit aliquanto puriores, aut saltem subtiliores".

11. M. van Rhijn, Gansfort, p. 83.

12. For all these facts see: M. van Rhijn, Gansfort, pp. 87-100.

13. E. W. Miller and J. W. Scudder, Gansfort, vol. I, p. 331.

14. A. Hardenberg, Vita Wesseli, in: W. Gansfort, Opera, p. XII. — E. W. Miller and J. W. Scudder, Gansfort, vol. II, p. 325. Some modern writers have refused to believe this story, but the arguments brought forward by them are insufficient, as according to several witnesses, parts of Wessel's bible were seen at Groningen for more than a hundred years after his death. Cfr. M. van Rhijn, Gansfort, pp. 103-105.

15. W. Gansfort, Scala Meditationis, bk. I, ch. XIII (Opera, p. 212): "Videmus Florentinos posse: Zvvollenses non posse. Mallem ego istorum ignaviam, quam illorum acumen; adeo non interest quo ingenio sis; verum quo consilio utatis et dirigas in finem. Volenti tamen in bonum dirigere, grande quidpiam est

exercitatos habere sensus, et potentes ad discretionem boni ac mali".

16. M. van Rhijn, Gansfort, pp. 105-108.

17. W. Gansfort, De Sacramento Poenitentia, Opera, pp. 782, 788-789. — E. W. Miller and J. W. Scudder, Gansfort, vol. II, pp. 206, 214.

18. M. van Rhijn, Gansfort, p. 111.

19. Ibid., pp. 111-122. Cfr. J. G. C. Joosting, Wessel Gansfort lijfarts van bisschop David, pp. 123-124.

20. M. van Rhijn, Gansfort, pp. 122-132.

21. Ibid., pp. 135-142, 154-155.

22. W. Gansfort, Opera, pp. 920-921. — E. W. Miller and J. W. Scudder, Gansfort, vol. I, pp. 236-237.

23. He probably became acquainted with some wandering Greeks and one or more Jews.

24. M. van Rhijn, Gansfort, pp. 64-68.

25. Ibid., p. 67.

26. M. van Rhijn, Gansfort, pp. XLII-XLV.

27. See ch. V, note 47.

28. Wessel called his rapiarium "Mare magnum". Many passages of his "De Causis Incarnationis" and his "De Magnitudine Passionis Domini" had been taken by him out of his rapiarium, undoubtedly in the same manner that Thomas à Kempis copied much of the "De Imitatione Christi" from his rapiarium. The "Mare Magnum" of Wessel was lost together with some other works of his, due to the work of the Dominicans, who destroyed all the writings by Gansfort they could get hold of (see: M. van Rhijn, Gansfort, p. L). The following works were lost: 1. Liber notularum de scripturis sacris et variis scripturarum locis; de creaturis; de angelis; de daemonibus; de anima. 2. Liber alius magnus de dignitate et potestate ecclesiastica; de indulgentiis. 3. Libellus pro Nominalibus. 4. De triduo Christi in sepulcro pro Paulo Burgensi Contra Middelburgensem. 5. Duo libelli practici in medicina. 6. Mare Magnum. 7. Liber de futuro seculo. 8. Some letters (see: M. van Rhijn, Gansfort, pp. LII-LIII).

29. W. Gansfort, Opera, p. XXXI. — E. W. Miller and J. W. Scudder, Gansfort, vol. I, p. 333.

30. W. Gansfort, Opera, p. 720. — E. W. Miller and J. W. Scudder, Gansfort, vol. II, pp. 87-89.

31. G. Geldenhauer, Wesseli Gansfortii Frisii vita, in: W.

Gansfort, Opera, pp. XXVIII-XXIX. — E. W. Miller and
J. W. Scudder, Gansfort, vol. II, p. 345.

32. W. Gansfort, Opera, p. 722, p. 830. — E. W. Miller and
J. W. Scudder, Gansfort, vol. II, p. 90, pp. 282-283.

33. Ibid., p. 830 (vol. II, p. 283).

34. Ibid., pp. 676, 677, 699 (vol. II, pp. 28, 29-30, 60).

35. Ibid., p. 697 (vol. II, p. 57).

36. Ibid., p. 711: "Ex hoc jam facile liquet verbum Platonis,
volentis naturam nihil aliud esse quam voluntatem Dei regulariter volentem; et miraculum opus divinae voluntatis non regulariter ita volentis" (Scudder's transl., vol. II, p. 75).

37. Ibid., p. 716 (transl., vol. II, pp. 81-82).

38. Ibid., p. 713 (vol. II, p. 77).

39. W. Gansfort, De Magnitudine Passionis, ch. XLV
(Opera, p. 550): "Quomodo non adversum dicunt Paulus,
adserens, sola fide, sine operibus justificare credentes in
Christum per ejus improperium; et Iacobus, dicens fidem sine
operibus mortuam........ Diversum dicunt Apostolus Paulus
et Iacobus; verum non adversum. Communis utrique sententia
est: Iustum ex fide vivere; fide, inquam, per dilectionem
operante. Operibus enim vitae corpus docetur, quas nisi exercet
mortuum judicatur. Et si nullas vitales actiones exerceret in
corpore, uti sunt, halites et pulsus, et praecordiorum calor,
prorsus mortuum haberetur. His actionibus vivere judicatur:
non tamen his actionibus vivit, sed harum actionum fonte vivit,
anima videlicet".

40. Ibid., ch. XX (p. 493): "Hunc voluit ex obedientia impositi mandati adstruere, quemadmodum ipse discipulis in caena
pridem dixerat: 'Si me diligitis, mandata mea servate'. Quasi
dicat: Vestrae dilectionis argumenta erunt servata mea mandata,
et mensura servati mandati argumentum erit mensurans dilectionem". — De Providentia Dei (p. 713): "In majoribus
ergo salutis operibus operanti Deo credentes cooperantur, et
in hoc secula credendo, spectando, amando, ut verae cooperationes Deo simus; et in illa cooperatione Deus facit nos
cooperari; qui sine eo nihil possumus, et omnia possumus in eo
confortante nos" (based on John XIV, v. 12). — Scalae Meditationis liber IV, ch. XIX (p. 203): "Dominus Iesus amicos
diffinit, quibus omnia revelavit maxima sua bona" (in: John XV,
v. 15). — De Sacramento Eucharistiae, ch. IX (pp. 676-677):
"Neque formidet, qui sic manducat carnem Filii hominis, mortem

interioris hominis; quoniam vita illius hominis (quae vero Spiritus et vita est, ac tertia in Trinitate persona ac per hoc Deus aeternum) non sit 'volentis aut currentis hominis', quia Patris et Filii unus Spiritus est".

41. Ibid., pp. 732-733, 746-747, 548-549 (transl., vol. II, pp. 105-106, 142-145). The last propositions are based on Paul.

42. Ibid., p. 868 (transl., vol. I, p. 271).

43. See p. 30.

44. W. Gansfort, Opera, pp. 890-891, 772. — E. W. Miller and J. W. Scudder, Gansfort, vol. I, pp. 302-303; vol. II, pp. 187-189 (duplicate of vol. I, pp. 302-303), 193.

45. Ibid., pp. 773, 775-776 (Scudder's transl., vol. II, pp. 194, 197).

46. See p. 29.

47. W. Gansfort, Opera, pp. 748-749 (translation, vol. II, pp. 152-153).

48. Ibid., p. 751 (transl., vol. II, p. 156).

49. Ibid., p. 780 (transl., vol. II, p. 204).

50. "Miror autem, quae infelicitas obsteterit, quo minus in publico Christianissimus hic auctor versetur: nisi in causa fuerit, quod sine bello et sanguine vixerit, quia una re mihi dissimilis est; aut metus Judaeorum nostrorum eum oppresserit, qui suis impiis inquisitionibus in hoc nati videntur, ut optimos quosque libros faciant haereticos, quo suos Aristotelicos et plus quam haereticos nobis statuant Christianos, quorum finis Deo vindice jam desinit in confusionem". (Luther's letter of recommendation, in: Gansfort, Opera, p. 854).

51. Ibid., p. 921 (transl., vol. I, p. 237).

52. Ibid., p. 886: "Doctores antiqui nihil expresse scripserunt; quia talis abusus nondum temporibus Augustini, Ambrosii, Hieronymi, Gregorii irrepsat".

53. M. van Rhijn, Gansfort, pp. 257-262.

54. See: M. van Rhijn, Gansfort, p. 233. The German writer is O. Clemen. Cfr. M. van Rhijn, Gansfort, p. 233.

55. E. Barnikol, Luther in Magdeburg, pp. 3-15.

56. Vatican Library, Ms. no. 4927; Nationalbibliothek, Vienna, Mss. nos. 4923, 13708, 15262; University Library, Innsbruck, Ms. no. 669.

57. D. J. M. Wüstenhoff, Het Traktaat "De pretiosis vestibus", pp. 16-17. This library is now called Preussische Staats-

NOTES 413

bibliothek, and the manuscript is no. 240 (quarto, theol. lat.). On fol. 1ᵃ we read: "Liber sancti Petri in Erfordia".

58. He refers to the "Spiritual Ascensions" by Gerard Zerbolt.

59. M. Luther, Dictata super Psalterium (1513-1516); in his Werke, Weimar ed., vol. III, p. 648: "Unde est quidam tractatus super istu versu Gerardi Zutphaniensis".

60. Ibid., p. 380: "Et sic idem opus vel totum corpus potest esse omnia sacrificia, ut Roset. [Basel 1504], fol. 155.

61. E. W. Miller and J. W. Scudder, Gansfort, vol. I, p. 130.

62. W. Gansfort, Opera, p. 892 (transl., vol. I, pp. 304-305; vol. II, p. 190).

63. G. Groote, Epistolae (Paris manuscript), fol. 61ᵃ: "Unde Abacuc III: 'Iustus ex fide vivit'".

64. W. Gansfort, Opera, p. 553. — E. W. Miller and J. W. Scudder, Gansfort, vol. I, p. 131. The quotation is from the De Magnitudine Passionis, ch. XLVI.

65. M. van Rhijn, Wessel Gansfort, p. 232: "Volgens Wessel is de menschelijke wil vrij".

66. Bk. III, ch. LVIII.

67. W. Gansfort, Opera, p. 713, p. 714 (transl., vol. II, p. 78, p. 80).

68. See p. 135.

69. M. van Rhijn, Gansfort, p. 73. — H. Hermelink, Theol. Fakultät Tübingen, pp. 80, 195, 200.

70. R. H. Murray, Erasmus and Luther, London and New York 1920, p. 49.

71. W. Gansfort, Opera, pp. 779-780 (translation, vol. II, pp. 202-203). Cfr. M. Luther, Assertio omnium articulorum per Bullam Leonis V, 1520, in his Werke, Weimar ed., vol. VII, p. 127: "Romanus pontifex, Petri successor, non est Christi vicarius super omnes totius mundi Ecclesias ab ipso Christo in beato Petro institutus. Numquam enim fuit super omnes Ecclesias totius mundi Romanus pontifex........ Neque enim super Ecclesias Graeciae, Indiae, Persidis, Aegypti et Affricae unquam fuit neque adhuc est". And Gansfort adds: "Dico item Latinorum fidelium, quia tot linguae fidelium ultra fontes Nili, trans Indum Hydaspen, et extra Gangen, quo Latina decreta perringere non possunt".

72. W. Gansfort, Opera, p. 775 (transl., vol. II, p. 196).

73. See pp. 309-326.

74. P. S. Allen, Opus Ep. Erasmi, vol. I, p. 584. — Still we

are not at all certain about these dates. Erasmus probably was born in 1469, and left Deventer in 1483, according to H. Kronenberg, Wanneer is Alexander Hegius te Deventer aangekomen? in: Verslagen en Mededeelingen der Vereeniging tot beoefening van Overijsselsch Recht en Geschiedenis, 2nd series, part 29, Deventer 1913, p. 6.

75. See for example P. S. Allen, The Age of Erasmus, ch. I (pp. 7-32): The Adwert Academy.

76. H. Brugmans, De kroniek van het klooster te Aduard, pp. 69-70.

77. M. van Rhijn, Gansfort, pp. 132-135.

78. Erasmus' remarks about the brethren, for example, are wholly misleading. See: P. Mestwerdt, Die Anfänge des Erasmus, pp. 182-195.

79. M. Schoengen, Narratio, p. 254.

80. M. van Rhijn, Gansfort, p. 141.

81. J. Lindeboom, Bijbelsch Humanisme, p. 115.

82. A. Tilley, Dawn of the French Renaissance, p. 291.

83. P. Mestwerdt, Die Anfänge des Erasmus, pp. 224-225.

84. D. Erasmus, Opera, ed Le Clerc, vol. X, col. 1622: 'Doctor Wesselus multa habet cum Luthero communia, sed quanto Christianius ac modestius ille proponit sua dogmata quam istorum plerique faciunt".

85. D. Erasmus, Opera, vol. V, col. 56: "Nec alia est flamma, in qua cruciatur dives ille comessator Evangelicus, nec alia supplicia inferorum quam perpetua mentis anxietas, quae peccandi consuetudinem comitatur".

86. See p. 285.

87. P. S. Allen, Opus Ep. Erasmi, vol. I, pp. 200-201.

88. Fol. 7^b-13^a.

89. Fol. 13^b-19^b.

90. Fol. 19^b. Renaudet, in discussing the genesis of Erasmus' mind, says: "Indifférents à la théologie et à la scolastique, aux querelles des réalistes et des nominaux qui, à Paris comme à Cologne, à Bâle comme à Vienne, mettaient aux prises ceux qu'on appelait les anciens et les modernes, l'acceptation muette de la parole du prêtre, la froide pratique des sacrements et des oeuvres ne leur suffisaient pas. Ils lisaient le Nouveau Testament, les Évangiles, les Épitres, les Pères qui avaient le mieux pénétré les secrets de la vie intérieure, saint Augustin et saint Bernard. Des maisons de la Vie-Commune et des couvents des

chanoines, qu'unissait la même pensée, étaient sortis d'innombrables et prolixes ouvrages, inspirés de cette piété intime, contemplative et cependant agissante, qu'on appelait la dévotion moderne, et qui, dès les vingt premières années du XVe siècle, avait trouvé dans les quatre livres de l'Imitation son expression la plus efficace et la plus humaine". (Érasme, pp. 232-233).

91. Gabriel Byel, Tractatus de communi vita clericorum, in Ms. No. 75 G58, Royal Library, The Hague, fol. 11b-13a.

92. See p. 205.

93. R. H. Murray, Erasmus and Luther, p. 74. Cfr. P. Smith, Luther's correspondence, vol. I, Philadelphia 1913, pp. 243-244 (incomplete).

94. W. Gansfort, Opera, p. 876 (transl., vol. I, p. 286).

95. R. H. Murray, Erasmus and Luther, p. 75. — P. Smith, Luther's correspondence, p. 180, where we also read: "The more hateful to Christian ears is the name of heresy, the less rashly ought we to charge anyone with it. Every error is not heresy, nor is he forthwith a heretic who may displease this man or that........ The best part of Christianity is a life worthy of Christ. When this is found we ought not easily to suspect heresy".

96. From: R. H. Murray, Erasmus and Luther, p. 79.

97. Ibid., pp. 79-80.

NOTES TO CHAPTER VII

1. A. Renaudet, Préréforme et Humanisme à Paris (1494-1517), p. 174. — Jean Standonk, pp. 7-13.

2. In a manuscript at Zwolle, the "Cartularium of the Heer Florenshuis and the new dormitory", copies are found of documents stating the amount and purposes of the donations. An extract from one of these reads as follows: "Van tyen mudde roggen uyt Vrouwenberch to Raelte in der buerscap van Lundertten gegeven 'pauperibus in Nova Domo. Ic Seygher van Rechteren ende van Voerst, in der tyt amptman in Sallandt, do kont ende bekenne mit desen openen brieve, dat vor my in enen ghehegeden gherichte ende gespannen banck ende vor gherichtes lude heer na bescreven, ghekomen sint Geert Kreync ende Wobbe syn echte wyf; ende Wobbe mit Geerde vors. alse wit horen echten man ende ghekoren momber, den sy koes mit mit hande ende mit monde ende oer in desen saken gegeven wart alse ordel ende recht wysde, ende hebben al daer vor my in den gherichte vor hen ende vor oere erfghen. mit oren gansen vrien willen overgheven ende geven mit desen selven breve vor een erflick testament vor oere beyder older sele slecht vanderhant den Armen Klerken ofte Schoellers to Deventer in dat Nye Fraterhuys tyen mudde guedes drughen claren wynter roggen iaerlik erfrenthen erfliken ende eweliken alse uyt onsen alingen erve en guede ter Vrouwenberch........ Ende heer sollen erflicken ende ewelike verwarers van wesen de priesters ter Florenshuys binnen Deventer ter behoef des huses ende der Armer Scoelers........ Gegeven in den iaer ons Heren Dusent veerhondert drie ende tachtentich op sunte Iohans avent Baptisten (fol. 8ᵇ-9ᵇ).

3. See p. 113.

4. See p. 90.

5. Cele had earned a handsome fortune with his school at Zwolle, and the Brethren of the Common Life in that city were so prosperous that their house became known as the "rich brethren-house".

6. A. Renaudet, Jean Standonk, p. 13.

7. M. Godet, La Congrégation de Montaigu, p. 4.

8. A. Renaudet, Jean Standonk, pp. 14-22.
9. Ibid., p. 21.
10. See pp. 117-118.
11. A. Renaudet, Jean Standonk, p. 21, note 3: "Durius ibidem invehebat contra concubinarios et aliqs notorios peccatores". Standonk probably knew the "Sermo contra focaristas" by Groote.
12. A. Renaudet, Préréforme, p. 176, note 5.
13. A. Renaudet, Standonk, pp. 23-26.
14. E. Barnikol, Luther in Magdeburg, p. 23: "Da stand da plötzlich der junge Luther, sah und sah mit weiten Augen auf das seltsame, auffallende Bild, auf den erbarmungswürdigen müden Mönch, dem alle bedeutungsvoll nachblickten, dessen Namen und Stand durch alle Reihen lief". — Pp. 61-62: "Ja, dann ist es auch nicht zu kühn, über Köhler und Scheel und deren Ansätze hinausgehend, zu vermuten, dass, als wenige Monate danach, bei Stotternheim an jenem 2. Juli 1507 der fordernde Gott seines Glaubens den jungen Martin im Blitz überfiel, als ihm Angst und Not das Gelübde auspressten: 'Hielff die liebe S. Anna, ich will ein Mönch werden!', dass da dieses ihm als Ziel und Rettung vor Augen stehende Mönchsbild die Erinnerungs- und Heiligkeitszüge des Magdeburger Mönches von der Breiten Strasse her getragen hat".
15. A. Renaudet, Jean Standonk, pp. 26-27.
16. A. Renaudet, Préréforme, pp. 178-182.
17. Ibid., p. 179, note 8.
18. M. Godet, La Congrégation de Montaigu, p. 10, note 3: "'Insuper, certis temporibus, capitulum eis tenebatur, cum sermone aliquo de contemptu mundi, de virtutibus, de fructu religionis praemisso, deinde sequibatur proclamatio et correctio erratorum'. Standonck empruntait ces pratiques particulières à ses maîtres, les Frères de la Vie commune".
19. Ibid., page 11, note 1: "Omnium animos inflammabat ad Christi amorem ac aemulationem virtutum, quoniam tempore videri poterat, quia quasi greges caprarum festinantium ad lavatrum cunctatim studentes ad religionem convolare non tantum ex ejus paedagogio verum ex aliis, tam magistri quam studentes, tanquam patrem piissimum quaerebant, quos laetissimo blandoque vultu suscipiebat, eos instruens de regno Deo et de justitia ejus".
20. Ibid., p. 11.

21. Ibid., pp. 11-16.

22. Ibid., pp. 23-25. Several extracts from this rule are published on pp. 144-145, 146, 146-151, 153-154, 160, 166.

23. A. Renaudet, Standonk, pp. 56-63.

24. M. Godet, La Congrégation de Montaigu, pp. 29-31, pp. 109-130.

25. A. Renaudet, Préréforme, pp. 196-198, 311-312.

26. M. Godet, La Congr. de Mont., pp. 31-32.

27. Ibid., pp. 32-38, 197-199, 208-209.

28. Ibid., pp. 39-40.

29. Ibid., pp. 43-44. On pp. 198-197 of the same work is published the act by which the brethren of Ghent secured the management of the institution at Cambray. It is a very important domument, showing that: (1) The brethren at Ghent and Brussels taught school: "Considerantes quam utile, necessarium, quamque laudabile sit sensus hominum ab adolescentia sua ad malum nedum pronos verum etiam a sua natura inertes penitus et inscios dirigi facere et instrui ad morum probitatem et litterarum scientiam, providaque attentione attendentes quantum Gandavi, Bruxelle necnon in diversis aliis partibus fructum afferat tam in scientiarum instructione, quam etiam in bonorum ac proborum morum diligenti scolarium in formatione ac virtutum plantatione". (2) The brethren consciously and conscientiously strove to imitate the primitive church: "........ laudabilis honesta et exemplaris vita conversatio ac residentia fratrum quorundam, tam presbyterorum quam clericorum et aliorum de communi vita seu in communi viventium, secundum institutionem primitive ecclesie, qui sub evangelicis ac sanctorum patrum ...... preceptis et salutaribus monitus ...... viventes". (3) They preferred to see their pupils enter the ranks of the clergy, not only regular, but both: "........ ut exinde undecumque monasteria et loca ecclesiastica felicia admodum incrementa ...... susceperunt". (4) The brethren at Ghent were going to found a brethren-house at Cambray: "........ vocare ad nos decrevimus fratrem Jacobum pro tempore Rectorem domus fratrum ...... in Gandavio ...... ab eodem expetendo quatenus de suis fratribus mittere vellet in loco eisdem designando ...... tandem ...... ex suis adducere decrevit nonnullos viros probos, presbyteros et clericos, ex sua prefata domo Gandensi". (5) They were to conduct school there: "Et primo quod dicti fratres et eorum successores non poterunt eandem

domum ypotecare vel obligare ...... quam ad dictas scolas tenendas applicare vel convertere ...... Item possit idem Rector per se et suos substitutos in forma qua supra audire confessiones scolarium in civitate Cameracensis vel foris manentium, scolas dictorum fratrum frequentantium". (6) The Brethren of the Common Life at Cambray were permitted to preach simple sermons on Sundays and holidays: "Item possint fratres dicte domus omnibus ipsorum scolaribus aut intus vel foris manentibus ac etiam aliis secularibus ...... domonicis et festivis diebus ...... facere collationem non quidem per modum solemnis predicationis sed simplicis exhortationis".

30. It is indeed very interesting to note in this connection that the first written constitution, or in other words, the original constitution of the first brethren-house mentions the names of only two daughter institutions: the one at Delft, founded by the Deventer house, and the one at Gouda, founded by the brethren of Delft.

31. M. Godet, La Congr. de Mont., p. 45.

32. Ibid., p. 45: "Leurs écoles étaient les séminaires où se recrutaient ...... comme plus tard à Montaigu ...... les ordres mendiants".

33. M. Godet, Montaigu, pp. 45-47.

34. Th. à Kempis, Chronicon Montis Sanctae Agnetis, ch. XXIX (ed. H. Rosweyden, p. 130).

35. A. Renaudet, Standonk, pp. 40-42.

36. J. Mombaer, Venatorium Sanctorum ordinis Canonici, in Ms. no. 14662 Bibl. Nat., Paris, fol. 162ª: "Et frater Thomas Kempis in Monte dive Agnetis ...... Composuit libellum Qui sequitur me, quem falso quidam domino Gerson attribuunt".

37. A. Renaudet, Standonk, pp. 42-45.

38. Ibid., pp. 45-47.

39. P. C. Molhuysen, Cornelius Aurelius. Korte schets van zijn leven en werken, in: Nederlandsch Archief voor Kerkgeschiedenis (1902), pp. 1-35. — Cornelius Aurelius. Nieuwe bescheiden, in: Ned. Arch. v. Kerkgesch. (1905), pp. 54-73. — P. S. Allen, Erasmi Epistolae, vol. I, pp. 92-122, 135-136, 143, 205, 586-687, 610.

40. A. Renaudet, Standonk, pp. 47-51. — Érasme (I), pp. 242-244.

41. A. Renaudet, Standonk, pp. 51-53.

42. P. S. Allen, Erasmi Epistolae, vol. I, pp. 200-201: "Con-

sultationem nobis iniunctam Domino Praesidenti de Hacqueville dudum dedimus in praesentia Domini de Emery ...... Reverendum magistrum nostrum Standonck saepius commonui ut de his et aliis iniunctis vos certos efficeret, praesertim quid patribus scribendum putaret; quod et fecit. Expectavimus et adhuc expectamus reverendum in Christo patrem vestrum, quem admonendum et adhortandum diligenter curabimus per amicos vestros, viros utique gravissimos".

43. A. Renaudet, Standonk, pp. 53-55, 75-77. — Préréforme, pp. 338-341, 446-452.

44. J. Mombaer, Rosetum, prologue: "Exercitabar et scopebam a Hierusale et in Hiericho de lapsum originali iusticia, dignitate, puritate spoliatum resculpere, reformare atque in priorem restituere gradum opere precium erit purgativis primum exercitiis exemplo clarissimi prophete David a viciis et corruptis affectibus eundem spiritum scopere, purgare, castigare".

45. W. Gansfort, De. Providentia Dei, in: Opera, p. 716 (translation, vol. II, pp. 82-83).

46. J. Mombaer, Rosetum (Zwolle 1494), fol. 1ᵇ: "Duo enim iuxta magistrum Gerardum Groot in exercitiis sunt praecavenda: nimia afflictio et occupatio immoderata".

47. P. S. Allen, Erasmi epistolae, vol. I, p. 166.

48. Fol. 59ᵇ-62ᵇ.

49. J. Mombaer, Rosetum, fol. 1ᵇ: "Sit purus, spernens, fervens, moderatus ...... Concors, consultum, moderatum, congruat et stet". Fol. 2ᵃ: "Si vis fervere debes hec mente tenere: Dignus, fert, mandat, donavit multa, spospondit, hostes, iudicium, pene, mirabile, spectant". Fol. 2ᵇ: "Exemplum scriptum, mala, peccatum, rea, stultum". Fol. 3ᵃ: "Ordo, locus, tempus, socius, provisio, votum".

50. Ibid., fol. 10ᵃ: "Labor autem rusticanus vel labor messis non est respuendus a religioso, sed devote amplexandus, quemadmodum docet Magister Gherardus Groot super illo verbo Eccles. VIIᵒ: 'Non oderis opera laboriosa et rusticitatem a Deo creatam', dicens: 'Generosos animos labor nutrit' ".

51. Watrigant has shown that Mombaer copies from Zerbolt.

52. P. S. Allen, Erasmi epistolae, vol. I, p. 166.

53. A. Renaudet, Standonk, p. 44. Since the leaders were so fond of the work, we may safely infer that a considerable number of their followers also studied it. Moreover, it was printed at Paris in 1510.

54. A. Renaudet, Érasme (I), pp. 232-233.

55. A. Tilley, Dawn of the French Ren., p. 242.

56. Statuten der Bursa Cusana zu Deventer, in: J. Marx, Nikolaus von Cues, pp. 241-243. While all the early sources inform us that Cusa was educated at Deventer, they do not tell why he went there. It seems that he had been influenced by the monks of the Carthusian monastery near Coblenz, whom Groote had befriended, and to whom Cusa later entrusted the supervision of the dormitory at Deventer. See: G. Groote, Epistolae (Hague m.s.), fol. 122a: "Pulcher lapis Hermannus, pulcrumque monasterium Confluencie, pulcriorque tota cartusia sancta religio". Groote had lived in a Carthusian monastery himself, and later wrote a letter of recommendation for Radewijns to the Carthusian monks of Coblenz.

57. See pp. 102, 230.

58. Fol. 8a: "Ideo nullem est iudicium humanum certum de membris ecclesiae".

59. See p. 30. Cusa wrote: "Unde sicut ecclesia universalis est corpus Christi mysticum" (fol. 10a).

60. Fol. 13a.

61. Fol. 23b: "Sed scimus quod Petrus nihil plus potestatis a Christo recepit aliis apostolis........ Et quamquam Petro dictum est: 'Tu es Petrus et super hanc petram', tamen per petram Christum quem confessus est intelligimus, et si Petrus per petram tanquam lapis fundamenti ecclesiae intelligi deberet: tunc secundum sanctum Hieronymum ita similiter alii apostoli fuerunt lapides fundamenti ecclesiae........ Et si Petro dictum est: 'Pasce oves', tamen manifestum est quod illa pascentia est verbo et exemplo. Ideo recte dicimus omnes apostolos in potestate cum Petro aequales". Fol. 25a: "Papa non est universalis episcopus sed super alios primus".

62. Book III commences with the mystical body of Christ, and mentions various subjects of little importance for us, though all connected with the reform of the church. In vol. II of the Opera we find various works, some on theological, some on mathematical subjects. In part of these Cusa expresses his philosophical views, which transcended the worldly wisdom of Groote's disciples at Deventer. This is particularly true of book I of the Exercitationum libri X, in which he quotes chiefly from Plato, Procul, Parmenides, Zeno, and Melissus. Nevertheless, even in this book he devotes most of his attention to

theology (fol. 11ᵇ-21ᵃ, and partly on fol. 7ᵃ-11ᵃ), while the other nine deal almost entirely with theological subjects. Some of the things he says remind us of Groote's disciples: "Homo huius saeculi ad hunc finem ut habeat divitias vitae temporales ...... Filii lucis seu aeternitatis: pro aeterna vita adipiscenda non habent talem prudentiam aliquo modo" (fol. 23ᵃ). "Quando in nobis loquitur Christus sive sapientia: tunc illa loquitur in ratione nostra. Nam Christus est sapientia et ratio infinita. Praecepta rationis sunt praecepta aeterna legis, quae est sapientia patris" (fol. 24ᵃ). "Nisi Christus ostendat se: est invisibilis, corpus eius qui de morte ad vitam resurrexit: est eo modo spirituale quod nisi seipsum ostendat et revelet sive cognitioni sensibili ingerat non sentitur" (fol. 133ᵃ). "Doctrina illa Christi Domini nostri non consistit in verbo sed in imitatione. Si quis enim ·sciret omnia evangelia mente: non esset propterea perfectus, sed requiritur quod per imitationem induat forman filii Dei [fol. 174ᵇ; cfr. De im. Chr., bk. I, ch. I: "Qui sequitur me non ambulat in tenebris ...... Si scires totam bibliam exterius et omnium philosophorum dicta, quid totum prodesset sine caritate Dei et gratia?] ...... "Vivit vero in me Christus. Nam vitiis per vivam hostiam extirpatis" (fol. 175ᵃ). Cusa was opposed to the acceptance of money for indulgences: "Dum essem legatus et ponerem confessores: primo non bene attendens ad hoc evangelium inhibui confessoribus ne pecuniam sumerent ...... Demum mandavi confitentibus ne quicquam darent: alioqui non absolverentur et profeci" (Excitationum Liber V, fol. 78ᵃ).

63. N. Cusa, Excitationum liber VI, fol. 98ᵃ: "Omnis peccator servus est peccati. Servus autem: seipsum a servitute liberare et haeredem facere nequit. Sed si opera legi et facta iustificarent: tunc posset per facta seipsum iustificare. Hoc autem impossiblie est: immo contradictio".

64. A. Renaudet, Préréforme, p. 597.

65. Ibid., p. 600.

66. Ibid., pp. 600, 603, 621. — A. Tilley, Dawn of the French Ren., p. 243.

67. A. Renaudet, Préréforme, p. 622: "Loin de le blâmer d'avoir écrit en flamand, il affirme qu'un lettré peut composer en langue vulgaire des ouvrages précieux. Peut-être en 1510, à Cologne, chez les Frères de la Vie Commune, avait-il compris l'efficacité des livres de propagande, rédigés, selon la

pensée de Gérard Groote, pour l' édification des simples. Et déjà Lefèvre commençait à regretter que les fidèles ne pussent comprendre les prières latines du culte catholique, l' Évangile ou l' Épitre dont le prêtre, à la messe, récite le texte mystérieux".

68. A. Tilley, Dawn of French Ren., pp. 591-592.

69. Ibid., p. 593.

70. Ibid., p. 230. Cfr. A. Renaudet, Préréforme, p. 409.

71. A. Renaudet, Préréforme, p. 409.

72. See pp. 61-62.

73. "Neque ob hoc aspernemini quam eruditionis bonae pleniores ipsi edere potestis". See: A. Roersch, L'humanisme belge, p. 13.

74. P. H. Watrigant, S. J., La genèse des Exercitia Spiritualia, p. 29.

75. Ibid., p. 30.

76. Ibid., pp. 56-57, 59.

77. Ibid., p. 58; p. 54: "On peut dire que presque toutes les directions pratiques, presque tout ce qui se rapporte à la méthode générale des exercices spirituels, dans les deux traités de l' abbé de Montserrat, est extrait du Rosetum".

78. Ibid., pp. 28-44. — H. Böhmer, Studien, vol. I: Loyola, pp. 34-45.

79. Ign. Loyola, Exercitia Spiritualia, ed. J. Roothaan, S: J., II. Hebdomada. De Incarnatione (p. 132): "Pro secunda hebdomada et ita deinceps, valde prodest legere subinde [aliquid] ex libris de Imitatione Christi vel Evangeliorum et vitarum Sanctorum".

80. Ibid., note 9: "Notandum, primo loco poni lectionem aliquam ex libris de Imitatione Christi; haec enim planior, facilior, neque talis, quae mentem avertere a praecipuo contemplationum argumento posset, sed potius ad practicas conclusiones inter meditandum conceptas magis confirmandas aptissima est" (this note is by Roothaan).

81. H. Böhmer, Studien, vol. I, p. 46.

82. Ibid., p. 47.

83. Ibid., p. 64: "Sein originellstes Werk, die exercitia spiritualia, ist im Grunde nur eine letzte Frucht der 'devotio moderna'".

84. P. H. Watrigant, S. J., La genèse des Exercitia Spiritualia, p. 59. Cfr. M. Godet, La Congrégation de Montaigu,

p. 93: "Mais les véritables précurseurs des 'Exercises' se trouvent au XIVe et XVe siècle dans les Pays-Bas. Ce sont les écrivains mystiques de l' école de Windesheim, les Frères de la Vie Commune, Gérard Groote, Florent Radjevins, Jean Mombaer et surtout Gérard de Zutphen". — H. Böhmer, Studien, vol. I, p. 64, note 1. Gothein in his Ignatius von Loyola (Halle 1895) gives a long account of Spanish mysticism of which Loyola was a sort of representative and missionary, according to this writer. His whole story has been ably criticized by Böhmer (p. 64, note 2).

85. M. Godet, Montaigu, pp. 98-99: "La bibliothèque mystique formée par Standonck en 1499 contenait, sans contredit, les oeuvres de l' école de Windesheim".

86. Ibid., p. 99.

87. See p. 228.

88. M. Godet, Montaigu, pp. 103-106.

89. P. H. Watrigant, La génèse, pp. 103-106.

90. Quoted in M. Godet, Montaigu, p. 106, note 1: "Fratrum porro exemplo, Societas Jesu per orbem universum scholas aperit"?

91. H. Böhmer, Studien, vol. I, pp. 150-157.

92. See pp. 130-132.

93. E. Doumergue, Jean Calvin, vol. I, p. 78.

94. Ibid., p. 81.

95. Ibid., pp. 81-84.

96. A. Renaudet, Préréforme, p. 623, note 4.

97. Ibid., p. 622.

98. This is the De libris teutonicalibus, or An liceat libros divinos transferre in vulgare, which the present writer discovered at Nuremberg.

99. Ibid., pp. 87-111.

100. Ibid., pp. 64-75, 125.

101. A. Lang, Die Bekehrung Johannes Calvins, pp. 5-37.

102. E. Doumergue, Jean Calvin, vol. I, pp. 331-336.

103. G. Groote, Sermo super septem verba, fol. 258c: "Unde in Iohanne querit cecus a Iudeis: 'Num quid et vos vultis discipuli eius fieri'? Et ipsi responderunt: 'Tu discipulus illius sis, nos discipuli Moysi sumus'. Heu! quam plures discipulos habet Moyses quam Christus! Christus enim docet humilitatem et mansuetudinem, dicens: 'Beati pauperes spiritu. Discite a me, quia mitis sum et humilis corde' ".

104. W. Gansfort, Opera, p. 761 (translation by Scudder, vol. II, p. 169).

105. See p. 322.

106. A. Lang, Die Bekehrung Johannes Calvins, pp. 25-30.

107. That is, till 1520.

108. E. Doumergue, Jean Calvin, vol. I, pp. 589-595.

109. The first edition was a very small work, and contained no real Protestant beliefs. Calvin speaks of it as follows in the Preface of the edition of 1559: "In the first edition of this work, not expecting that success which the Lord ...... hath given, I handled the subject for the most part in a superficial manner, as is usual in small treatises".

110. See pp. 130-132.

111. See p. 218.

112. A. Eekhof, De avondmaalsbrief van Cornelis Hoen, p. XV. The visit occurred in the house of Cratander the printer. "If Rode wishes that the works of Wessel be printed, Cratander will do so", he writes to his friend Hedio: "Rodio Traiectensi parum hoc vesperi loquutus sum, cras ad prandium Cratandri vocabo ...... Wesselum, si volet Rodius, imprimet Cratander".

113. G. Anrich, Martin Bucer, p. 47.

114. He had been taught by Erasmus, according to Melanchton (Ph. Melanchton, Opera, in: Corpus Reformatorum, vol. IV, col. 970); and Erasmus derived some of the new views from Gansfort. However, Zwingli and Melanchton exaggerated the influence of Erasmus in this respect. Erasmus never accepted the symbolical interpretation. See: J. Lindeboom, De Theologie van Erasmus, Leiden 1909, pp. 137-146. The present writer also received some very helpful suggestions from Professor Preserved Smith, the author of a biography of Erasmus (New York 1923). Professor Smith discusses the subject very ably on pp. 378ff. of his new book.

115. A. Eekhof, De avondmaalsbrief van Cornelis Hoen, p. XVI. On October 23, 1525, Zwingli wrote to Bugenhagen: Ibi dei munere factum est, ut duo quidam et pii et docti homines, quorum etiamnum tacebo nomina, ad Leonum nostrum et me, conferendi de hoc argumento causa venirent; cumque nostram hac in re sententiam audirent, gratias egerunt Deo, suam enim ipse celabant, quod tum non erat tutum cuique communicare, quod in hac re sentires, ac epistolam istam cuiusdam et docti et pii Batavi, quae iam excusa est anonyma, soluta sarcina commun-

icarunt. In ea foelicem hanc margaritam 'Est' pro 'significat' hic accipi inveni. Cumque hanc sententiam cogeremur in Commentario palam exponere, consultius videbatur, ipsam vocem, in qua tropus latet, adperire sua ista clave, quam solummodo dicere: Tropus est. Sic igitur docuimus, 'est' pro 'symbolum est, figura est, significat' hic positum esse; neque nos piget huius expositionis. Sexcenties enim dicas: Tropus est, nec tropum adperias, infractam nucem puero praebueris".

116. A. Lang, Johannes Calvin. Ein Lebensbild, p. 57.

117. A. Lang. Der Evangelienkommentar Martin Butzers, p. 14.

118. Ibid., p. 8.

119. Ibid., pp. 365-366, 372.

120. N. Weiss, Guillaume Farel, p. 197.

121. Ibid., p. 179.

122. Ibid., p. 196. — Le premier traité protestant en langue française, pp. 71, 73, 76. — A. Lang, Johannes Calvin, p. 57: "Butzer, das Haupt der oberdeutschen Theologen, der Vermittler der Wittenberger Konkordie und Freund des Landgrafen Philipp, war neben Melanchton der Führer der Protestanten: er zog Calvin hinter sich her".

123. G. Anrich, Martin Bucer, p. 143.

124. Ch. Schmidt, Histoire littéraire de l' Alsace, vol. I, p. 4.

125. L. Kückelhahn, J. Sturm, Strassburgs erster Schulrektor, p. 23.

126. Ibid., pp. 9-14. — W. Sohm, Die Schule Johann Sturms, pp. 26-27.

127. See notes 126 and 130.

128. W. Sohm, Die Schule Johann Sturms, p. 29.

129. Ibid., p. 25.

130. Consilium Joannis Sturmii curatoribus scholarum Argentorati propositum: "Itaque nisi multitudo tanta sit, ut locus unus non satis sit, utilius est coacta esse quam dissipata studia. Leodii, Daventriae, Zwollae, Vuasaliae literarum exercitationes habent, eisqué unum assignatum locum, distributum suis ordinibus, atque ex illis ludis feliciora et plura plerumque prodeunt ingenia quam ex vicinis, ut vocant, Academiis. Saepe fit ut qui ibi docte et pie informati sint, in illis artificum maiorum gymnasiis corrumpantur ...... Leodii cum essem dissensio orta erat inter magistros, et quidam separatim docere instituerunt,

quibus si successissent consilia, perditum esset illud Hieronymitanum Gymnasium"!

131. E. Doumergue, Jean Calvin, vol. I, pp. 58-63.

132. A. Lang, Johannes Calvin, p. 49: "An der Spitze der Schule stand Johannes Sturm, geboren 1507 in Schleiden, nächst Melanchton zweifellos der bedeutendste evangelische Pädagoge, der wie Mathurin Cordier aus dem Studium der Alten und aus der Schule der Brüder des gemeinsamen Lebens neue und fruchtbare pädagogische Grundsätze geschöpft hatte".

133. F. Pijper, De invloed van de Broeders des Gemeenen Levens op de schoolstichting van Calvijn, pp. 116-117.

134. Ibid., 118-120. The present writer had already mentioned most of the facts narrated above in chapters II and III; see pp. 91-97, 122-135.

135. F. Pijper, De invloed, pp. 120-122.

136. The whole book contains the "De duplici copia verborum, ac rerum commentarii duo", the "De ratione studii", and some letters and poems. The "De ratione studii" is found on pp. 253-279. Here we read: "Nihil autem facilius discitur [p. 255] quam quod rectum et verum est. At prava si semel inhaeserint ingenio, dictu mirum, quam non possint revelli. Primum igitur locum grammatica sibi vendicat, eaque protinus duplex tradendum pueris, Graeca videlicet, ac Latina. [p. 256] Ergo parata sermonis facultate, si non luxuriosa, certe casta, mos ad rerum intelligentiam conferendus est animus [p. 257] Nam unde nam haurias vel purius, vel citius, vel iucundius quam ab istis fontibus? [p. 260] Sed in primis ad fontes ipsos properandum, id est, Graecos et antiquos. Philosophiam optime docebit Plato et Aristoteles, atque huius discipulus, Theophrastus, tum utrinque mixtus Plotinus. Ex theologis secundum divinas literas, nemo melius Origene, nemo subtilius, aut iucundius Chrysostomo, nemo sanctius Basilio, inter Latinos duo duntaxat insignes in hoc genere, Ambrosius mirus in allusionibus et Hieronymus in arcanis literis exercitatissimus. [p. 261] Eadem debet esse cura in arborum, herbarum, animantium, instrumentorum, vestium, gemmarum nominibus, in quibus, incredibile dictu, quam nihil intelligat literatorum vulgus. Horum noticia partim e diversis autoribus, quae de re rustica, de re militari, de arhitectura, de re culinaria, de gemnis, de plantis, de naturis animantium conscripserunt, colligitur. [p. 263] Hinc iam thematiis exerceri debent, quibus illud in

primis cavendum, ne (quod fieri solet) aut sensu sint inepto, aut sermone insulso ...... quae tamen ab ingenio puerili non nimium abhorreat, ut interim aliud agentes, simul ex aliquid discant, in gravioribus studiis usui futurum".

137. F. Pijper, De invloed van de Broeders, pp. 123-126. Professor Pijper thinks that Sturm made an improvement on the method of the brethren by assembling all the pupils in one building. He evidently mistakes the dormitories at Deventer and Zwolle for the school of Hegius and Cele: "Hadden nog de Broeders des gemeenen levens de klassen eener zelfde school soms in verschillende gebouwen van de stad ondergebracht, Sturmius toont aan, dat het noodzakelijk is ze alle in één gebouw te vergaderen" (p. 124). Almost all modern writers have confused the schools at Deventer and Zwolle with the different dormitories erected for the school boys in these two cities by the Brethren of the Common Life. Although one may speak of schools conducted by the brethren, particularly after 1500, it is not quite correct to call Cele's school a "school of the Brethren of the Common Life" Moreover, Sturm, instead of improving on Cele's method, told his employers at Strasbourg that he wanted to imitate it, as was indicated above in the text. See also: K. Engel, Das Gründungsjahr des Strassburger Gymnasiums, pp. 116-117.

138. F. Pijper, De invloed van de Broeders, pp. 126-128. L. Kückelhahn, J. Sturm, Strassburgs erster Schulrektor, pp. 9-13, 74-75.

139. Fr. Meyer, Der Ursprung des Jesuitischen Schulwesens, p. 54.

140. See also: H. Veil, Zum Gedächtnis Johannes Sturms, pp. 38-69.

141. E. Doumergue, Jean Calvin, vol. II, p. 462.

NOTES TO CHAPTER VIII

1. C. Ullmann, Reformers before the Reformation, vol. II, pp. 176-177. The originals are found in Luther's Letters, edited by E. L. Enders, vol. IX, pp. 146-147; Erlangen ed., no. 386.

2. Th. à Kempis, Vita Gerardi Magni, appendix (the translation is from J. P. Arthur's ed., pp. 74-75).

3. It should be noted, however, that Thomas compares the labors of Radewijns with those of Christ himself.

4. Th. à Kempis, Vita Florentii, ch. I-III (translation in Arthur's ed., pp. 85, 87, 88).

5. Scriptum, pp. 22-28, 31-33.

6. Th. à Kempis, Vita Gerardi Sutph., § 1 (transl. in Arthur's ed., p. 220).

7. See for example: S. Kettlewell, The authorship of the De Imitatione Christi, pp. 11-20.

8. H. Denifle, Luther und Luthertum, vol. I, pp. 423-479. — H. Grisar, Luther, vol. I, pp. 146-212. See also: Review by Smith, of Strohl, L'Évolution religieuse de Luther jusqu'en 1515, in: American Hist. Rev., July 1922, p. 819.

9. See: H. C. Vedder, The Reformation in Germany, p. 125. — H. Wace and C. A. Buchheim, First principles of the Reformation, p. XXI: "In fact, it presents the most complete view of 'Luther's theology, alike in its principles and in its practice, almost entirely disembarrassed of the controversial elements by which his other works, and especially those of a later date, were disturbed".

10. M. Luther, Vorlesung über den Römerbrief, ed. J. Ficker, p. 144.

11. It is printed in M. Schoengen, Jacobus Voecht narratio, pp. 501-503.

12. D. J. M. Wüstenhoff, Florentii parvum et simplex exercitium, p. 105.

13. M. Luther, The Babylonish captivity, ed. H. Wace and C. A. Buchheim, pp. 155-156. The original: Weimar ed., vol. VI, p. 508.

14. H. Denifle, Luther und Luthertum, vol. I, pp. 535-536. — H. Grisar, Luther, vol. I, pp. 112-113; p. 124, note 1.

15. H. Denifle, Luther und Luthertum, vol. I, pp. 591-612.
16. See pp. 211-215.
17. M. Luther, The Babylonish captivity, ed. H. Wace and C. A. Buchheim, p. 141. The original: Weimar ed., vol. VI, p. 497.
18. P. Smith, The life and letters of Martin Luther, p. 4.
19. M. Van Rhijn, Wessel Gansfort, p. 231: "Gansfort heeft een geheel andere opvatting van den arbeid en bestrijdt het monnikenwezen niet".
20. W. Gansfort, Opera, pp. 656-657 (transl. by J. W. Scudder, vol. I, pp. 243-245).
21. See pp. 218-226.
22. F. Radewijns, Tractatulus, p. 384.
23. S. Kettlewell, The authorship of the De im. Christi, p. 34.
24. G. Zerbolt, De spiritualibus ascensionibus, ch. III.
25. H. Grisar, Luther, vol. I, p. 168.
26. Ibid., p. 170.
27. See p. 314.
28. H. Grisar, Luther, vol. I, pp. 172-179.
29. Ibid., pp. 246-253.
30. M. Luther, Address to the German nobility, pp. 58, 56 (the original in Weimar ed., vol. VI, pp. 439, 438).
31. M. Luther, Concerning Christian liberty, pp. 110-111 (Weimar ed., vol. VII, p. 25).
32. C. Ullmann, Reformers before the Reformation, vol. II, p. 416; cfr. W. Gansfort, Opera, p. 571.
33. Ibid., p. 417. — Opera, p. 559.
34. Ibid., p. 485. — Opera, p. 759.
35. Ibid., p. 579.
36. M. Luther, Address to the German nobility, pp. 20-30 (Weimar ed., vol. VI, pp. 406-415). — W. Gansfort, Opera, p. 771.
37. See p. 313. Cfr. M. Luther, Address to German nob., pp. 31-49 (Weimar ed., pp. 415-432).
38. M. Luther, Address to nob., pp. 58-59, 66 (Weimar ed., pp. 442, 447). — W. Gansfort, Opera, pp. 772-773.
39. See p. 201. — M. Luther, Address to nob., p. 78 (Weimar ed., p. 457).
40. M. van Rhijn, Gansfort, p. 233.
41. See p. 321.

42. W. Gansfort, Opera, pp. 817, 819, 941 (transl., vol. II, pp. 260, 264, 299).

43. See pp. 211-216.

44. M. Luther, Concerning Christian liberty, pp. 126, 127 (Weimar ed., p. 65).

45. Cfr. H. Denifle, Luther und Luthertum, vol. I, pp. 658-771.

46. Quoted in: R. H. Murray, Erasmus and Luther, pp. 294, 295.

47. Ibid., pp. 291, 284.

48. This quotation is from: C. Ullmann, Reformers before the Reformation, vol. II, pp. 519-521.

49. W. Gansfort, Opera, p. 703 (transl. by J. W. Scudder, pp. 67-68).

50. He refers to the Dominicans who had attempted to destroy Gansfort's works.

51. C. Ullman, Reformers before the Reformation, vol. II, pp. 580-581.

52. Ibid., vol. II, p. 521.

53. H. C. Vedder, The Reformation in Germany, pp. 304-305.

54. A. M. Hunter, The teaching of Calvin, p. 94.

55. W. Gansfort, Opera, p. 714 (transl., vol. II, pp. 79-80).

56. J. L. Motley, History of the United Netherlands, vol. IV, New York 1870, p. 548.

57. A. Egen, Der Einfluss der Münsterschen Domschule, pp. 16-18.

58. H. E. J. M. van der Velden, Rodolphus Agricola, pp. 99-100, 206-207.

59. M. Ch. A. Thudichum, Calvin als Pädagoge, Geneva 1915, p. 27. On p. 26 Thudichum makes this remark: "Das Gymnasium der Hieronymianer zu Lüttich, das von den 'Brüdern des gemeinschaftlichen Lebens' geführt wurde, hatte die grosse Schulreform inauguriert".

60. See for example Dr. Köhler's contribution in: Ulrich Zwingle. Zum Gedächtnis der Zürcher Reformation (1519-1919), Zürich 1919.

61. Edinburgh and London 1904.

62. Pp. X, XI, 12.

63. J. C. van Slee, Necrologium Diepenveen, p. 354.

64. See: C. Burrage, The early English dissenters, 2 vols., Cambridge 1912.

65. Ibid., vol. I, p. 33.

66. Ibid., p. 293.
67. Ibid., p. 293, n. 1.
68. A. F. Pollard, Thomas Cranmer, New York 1904, p. 272.
— H. W. Clark, History of English Nonconformity, vol. I, London 1911, p. 135.
69. N. Pocock, The restoration settlement of the English church, in: Engl. hist. review, vol. I, pp. 677-698.
70. C. Burrage, l. c., vol. I, p. 121. Nearly all the English Anabaptists in the Netherlands were converts of the Mennonites, followers of Menno Simons (1496-1561). A good biography of this reformer is: K. Vos, Menno Simons, Leiden 1914.

APPENDIX A

THE REFERENCES CITED BY GROOTE

On page 17 a list is found of the writings to which Groote refers in his various works. This same list is given here again, provided with a number of notes. The references in question are the writings of Albert Magnus[1], Ambrose[2], Anselm[3], Antony[4], Apuleius[5], Aristides[6], Aristotle[7], Augustine[8], Bede[9], Bernard[10], Boethius[11], Bonaventura[12], Cassianus[13], Cato[14], Chrysostom[15], Cicero[16], Climacus[17], Cyprian[18], Demosthenes[19], Diogenes[20], Dionysius[21], Eusebius[22], Fabricius[23], Francis of Assisi[24], Gregory[25], Gregory of Nianza[26], Henry of Ghent[27], Hippocrates[28], Isidor[29], Jerome[30], Juvenal[31], Lucan[32], Lyra[33], Nepos[34], Permenianus Donatista[35], Peter of Damiani[36], Plato[37], Pliny[38], Seneca[39], Socrates[40], Suetonius[41], Suso[42], Theophrastus[43], Thomas Aquinas[44], Valerius[45], Vegetius[46], Virgil[47], and the Canon Law with many commentaries[48].

1. G. Groote, Sermo contra focaristas, 3rd part, p. 55.

2. G. Groote, De locatione ecclesiarum, p. 128. — Tractatus de matrimonio, p. 214. — Epistolae, ed. H. Nolte, p. 291. — Septem verba dominica, fol 263 c.

3. G. Groote, Epistolae, ed. X. de Ram, p. 75.

4. G. Groote, Tractatus de matrimonio, p. 180. — Epistolae, ed. X. de Ram, p. 72.

5. G. Groote, Sermo de paupertate, p. 463.

6. G. Groote, De locatione ecclesiarum, p. 143.

7. G. Groote, Tractatus de matrimonio, pp. 199, 211, 224, 230, 236, 245. — De simonia, p. 8, p. 10. — Epistolae, ed. W. Preger, p. 35.

8. G. Groote, Sermo contra focaristas, 1st part, p. 366, 3rd part, pp. 7, 8, 17, 28, 38, 58, 77, 78, 79, 97. — Tractatus de matrimonio, pp. 167, 170, 171, 177. — De locatione ecclesiarum, p. 130. — De simonia, pp. 14, 20, 24. — Epistolae, ed. X. de Ram, p. 84; ed. H. Nolte, pp. 291, 292, etc. — Tractatus super septem verba dominca, fol. 262a, 263c, 265a, 266a, 266b, 268a. — De nativitate Domini, fol. 113b, 117b, 119b.

9. G. Groote, De simonia, pp. 21, 22. — Epistolae, ed. W. Preger, p. 49. — Tractatus super septem verba dominica, fol. 267a.

10. G. Groote, Sermo contra focaristas, 3rd part, pp. 13, 20,

21, 22, 46, 56, 57, 58, 70; 1st part, pp. 373, 376. — Tractatus de matrimonio, pp. 164, 239. — Epistolae, ed. J. Clarisse, pp. 9, 23, 25, 27. — Tractatus super septem verba dominica, fol. 112ᵃ, 128ᵃ, 131ᵇ. — De nativitate Domini, fol. 264ᵈ, 265ᶜ, 266ᵃ⁻ᵇ, 267ᵇ⁻ᶜ.

11. G. Groote, Sermo contra focaristas, 1st part, p. 368; 3rd part, pp. 29, 30, 34. — Tractatus de matrimonio, p. 183, p. 208.

12. G. Groote, De nativitate Domini, fol. 112ᵃ.

13. G. Groote, Tractatus de matrimonio, p. 194.

14. G. Groote, Tractatus de matrimonio, p. 170. — De locatione ecclesiarum, p. 143.

15. G. Groote, Sermo contra focaristas, 3rd part, pp. 30, 34, 35. — Tractatus de matrimonio, p. 179. — De simonia, p. 22.

16. G. Groote, Tractatus de matrimonio, p. 237.

17. G. Groote, Epistolae, ed. X. de Ram, p. 75.

18. G. Groote, Sermo contra focaristas, 3rd part, p. 104.

19. G. Groote, Tractatus de matrimonio, p. 246.

20. G. Groote, Tractatus de matrimonio, p. 213.

21. G. Groote, Sermo contra focaristas, 3rd part, p. 56. — De locatione ecclesiarum, p. 121. — Epistolae, ed. J. Clarisse, pp. 19, 23, 24; ed. X. de Ram, p. 73. — De nativitate Domini, fol. 111ᵇ, 127ᵃ, 129ᵃ, 130ᵇ.

22. G. Groote, Sermo contra focaristas, 3rd part, p. 47.

23. G. Groote, De locatione ecclesiarum, p. 143.

24. G. Groote, Sermo contra focaristas, 1st part, p. 378. — Tract. de matrimonio, p. 191.

25. G. Groote, Sermo contra focaristas, 3rd part, pp. 7, 10, 20. — Tractatus de matrimonio, p. 161. — De simonia, pp. 14, 20, 25. — Epistolae, ed. X. de Ram, p. 72; ed. W. Preger, p. 51; ed. J. Clarisse, pp. 22, 25. — G. Groote, Tractatus super septem verba dominica, fol. 263ᵇ, 264ᵃ.

26. G. Groote, Tractatus de matrimonio, p. 230.

27. G. Groote, Epistolae, ed. W. Preger, p. 42.

28. G. Groote, Epistolae, ed. X. de Ram, p. 73; ed. W. Preger, p. 41.

29. G. Groote, Epistolae, ed. H. Nolte, p. 291.

30. G. Groote, Sermo contra focaristas, 3rd part, pp. 9, 45, 46, 55, 67, 68, 69, 78. — Tractatus de matrimonio, pp. 161, 202. — Epistolae, ed. J. Clarisse, p. 8; ed. W. Preger, p. 43. — De simonia, p. 22. — De nativitate Domini, fol. 131ᵇ. — Tractatus de septem verba dominica, fol. 266ᵃ, 260ᵇ, 261ᵈ.

31. G. Groote, Tractatus de septem verba dominica, fol. 266ᵃ.

32. J. Clarisse, Over den geest en de denkwijze van Geert Groete, in: Archief voor Ned. Kerkgesch., vol. VIII, p. 368.

33. G. Groote, Epistolae, ed. W. Preger, p. 43.

34. J. H. Gerretsen, Florentius Radewijns, p. 40.

35. G. Groote, Sermo contra focaristas, 3rd part, pp. 73, 99.

36. G. Groote, Sermo contra focaristas, 3rd part, p. 101.

37. G. Groote, De locatione ecclesiarum, p. 143.

38. J. H. Gerretsen, Florentius Radewijns, p. 40.

39. G. Groote, Tractatus de matrimonio, p. 218, p. 239, p. 240. — Sermo contra focaristas, 3rd part, p. 7. — De locatione ecclesiarum, p. 143. — Epistolae, ed. X. de Ram, p. 81; ed. H. Nolte, p. 291.

40. G. Groote, Tractatus de matrimonio, p. 213, p. 236. — De locatione ecclesiarum, p. 143.

41. G. Groote, Sermo de paupertate, p. 463.

42. G. Groote, Epistolae, ed. W. Preger, p. 35; ed. X. de Ram, p. 106.

43. G. Groote, Tractatus de matrimonio, pp. 170, 232, 244.

44. G. Groote, Sermo contra focaristas, 3rd part, p. 54, p. 80. — Epistolae, ed. X. de Ram, p. 74. — De simonia, p. 4.

45. G. Groote, Tractatus de matrimonio, p. 170. — De locatione ecclesiarum, p. 143.

46. G. Groote, Epistolae, ed. X. de Ram, p. 71.

47. G. Groote, Sermo contra focaristas, 3rd part, p. 50.

48. J. Clarisse, Over den geest en de denkwijze van Geert Groete, in: Archief voor Ned. Kerkgesch., vol. III, pp. 60-84.

APPENDIX B
GROOTE'S LETTERS

Since many of these letters have remained unpublished, and the others were edited mostly in a haphazard way, a list is given here, showing how many were published, and where they can be found. This list was prepared chiefly by Reverend Mr. A. Karthon, a Roman Catholic pastor at Heusden, Holland, with whom the author had the pleasure to become intimately acquainted. Mr. Karthon had intended to edit all of Groote's unpublished works, but death claimed him in the summer of 1921. And although the author now has a copy of these unprinted works, it may take one or two years before they will appear in print. The following list, therefore, may prove helpful to many readers.

EPISTOLAE COGNITAE GERARDI MAGNI

A. In Codice Hagae Comitis no. 78 J 55 et alibi (Leodii, Hannoverani, Wolfenbüttel, Vindebonensis, Coloniae Agrippinae, Romae, Bruxellis, etc.).

Praenotamen. Series manuscripti Hagae Comitis hic ut norma habetur. In Bibliotheca Universitatis Leodii simile manuscriptum (no. 366) invenitur. Numeratio epistolarum paululum differt.

Numerus	Destinatio vel contentum breve	Folia	Edita per scriptorem	Non edita	Annotationes
	Protestatio Gerardi Magni	113a—113b	Th. a Kempis (ed. Sommalii, Duaci 1635) p. 914.	—	
1.	Ad Guilhelmum Salvarvillam	113b—117b		I	
2.	Ad Bertholdum ten Hove	117b—118b	Clarisse A. V. K. G. VIII 285-287 sed Valde incomplete.	—	Etiam per Bonet-Maury MSum Hannoveranum secutus. Valde incorrecte edita.
3.	Ad Abbatissam S. Clarae in Colonia	118b—119b	....	2	Hae tres epistolae agunt de eodem objecto etiam epistola 29.
4.	Ad Dominum Henricum de Lippia, cantorem S. Severini in Colonia	119b—120b	....	3	
5.	Litterae recommendationis pro ingressu alicujus sororis nobilis in monasterio				
6.	Ad Carthusianos in Confluentia	120b—121a	....	4	
7.	Ad Fratres in Campen	121a—122a	....	5	De ordinando aliquem (Flor. Radewijns?) in presbyterum.
8.	Ad Abbatem in Campen	122a—122b	Acquoy, Ep. V.	—	
9.	Ad Fratres in Campen	122b—123b	....	6	
10.	Ad Abbatem in Campen	123b—124a	....	7	
		124a—125b	....	8	Cfr. Ep. 53; contentum hic compendiose pro parte idem.
11.	Ad Guilhelmum Vroede	126a—129b	Nolte, Ep. III.	—	Theol. Quartalschrift Tübingen 1870.
12.	„ „ „	129b—131a	Preger 7.	—	Abhandlungen der bayr. Akademie 1894 Abt. I.
13.	„ „ „	131a—132b	Nolte Ep. IV valde incorrecte.	—	

14 De beneficio curati minori non de-

Numerus	Destinatio vel contentum breve	Folia	Edita per scriptorem	Non edita	Annotationes
15.	Ad Praepositum de Eemsteyn pro Bertholdo ten Hove	134b—135b	Clarisse l. c. VIII p. 287-289. Incorrecte.	—	
16.	Ad Patres in Groenendaal	135b—136b	Preger 15.	—	
17.	Ad Wernerum Keynkamp	136b—137b	Acquoy Ep. VI.	—	
18.	Ad Stephanum pro tunc curatum in Lochem	137b—139a	Acquoy Ep. VII.	—	
19.	Epistola Salvarvillae Urbano Papae de Gerardo Magno	139a—140a	Thomas a Kempis p. 926. Acquoy Epistolae p. 59.	—	Hae duae epistolae non sunt Gerardi, sed agunt de eo.
20.	Testimonium Salvarvillae	140a—140b	Thomas a Kempis p. 913.	—	
21.	Ad Johannem Cele	140b—141b	Preger 12, Nolte VII.	—	
22.	Ad episcopum Florentium	141b—142b	Acquoy Ep. III.	—	Ut ep. 7 et hae duae agunt de
23.	Ad Florentii Vicarium	142b—143a	Acquoy Ep. VI.	—	fratre Bartholomeo haereseos suspecto.
24.	Ad Fratres Harderovicenses contra Johannem Heyden	143a—144a	Acquoy Ep. VIII.	—	
25.	Ad Fratrem Carthusianum infirmum in capite, etc.	144a—147b	Clarisse l. c. III, Aant I, p. 1-4.	—	
25.[a]	Responsum cuidam juveni volenti accipere beneficium	148a—154b	Clarisse l. c. III, Aant 3, p. 13-27.	—	Numerus 25 in Ms. Hag. Com. per errorem bis cccurrit.
26.	Ad Praepositum in Eemsteyn	155a—155b	Nolte VII.	—	
27.	De Oppugnando errorem (tenebras) et spargendo veritatem (lumen)	156a—156a	....	9	
28.	Ad quendam Lapsum (Gherlacum)	156a—161a	....	10	
29.	Ad Arnoldum de Celarem	161a—162a		11	De eodem objecto (ac epistolae 3, 4, 5).
30.	Ad Dominum Bernardum	162a—164a	Acquoy Ep. VIII.	—	
31.	Ad Salvarvillam	164a—166a	Preger 16.	—	
32.	Ad Ruysbroec	166a—168a	Preger 1.	—	
33.	De Correptione Auditorum	168a—171a	Acquoy Ep. IX.	—	

Numerus	Destinatio vel contentum breve	Folia	Edita per scriptorem	Non edita	Annotationes
34.	Litterae recommendationis ad quoddam monasterium pro Magistro Ricoldo	171a—172a	....	12	
35.	Ad Dominum Johannem Stiefvader in Campen	172a—173b	....	13	
36.	Ad Guilhelmum Oude Scute, etc.	173b—175b	Preger 13.	—	
37.	Ad Dominum Johannem de Gronde	175b—180a	Acquoy Ep. X.	—	
38.	Nobilis ep. excitans ad patientiam et imitationem Christi	180a—187a	De Ram. In Compte Rendu de la Commission Royale d'Histoire 1861 Ep. IV.	—	Exemplare hujus epistolae invenitur in permultis Europae bibliothecis, ob praeclaram doctrinam saepe transcripta.
39.	Ad Guilhelmum Salvarvillam	187a—198a	....	14	
40.	Ad Dominum Henricum Clingibile de Huxaria	198a—201a	Busch Chron. etc. C. 30 Clarisse l. c. III, Aant 2, pp. 5-11; VIII p. 277-281.	—	
41.	Ad novum Monachum	201a—204b	De Ram l. c. Ep. III.	—	
42.	Ad quendam Magistrum Canonicum pro fratribus de Eemsteyn	205a—205b	....	15	Cfr. ep. 26. Verosimilius agitur de eadem re.
43.	Ad Johannem de Gronde	205b—207a	Preger 14.	—	Cfr. Nolte p. 294.
44.	Ad Dominum Johannem de Gronde	207a—208b	....	16	
45.	Ad Johannem calumniantem	208b—209b	Acquoy Ep. I.	—	
46.	Ad Regnerum Curatum Swollensem de Bartholomaeo	210a—211a	Acquoy Ep. II.	—	
47.	Ad Dominum Henricum de Scoenhove de Gouda	211a—215b	Acquoy XI.	—	
48.	Ad quendam Beneficiatum de restitutione ei facienda	215b—216a	....	17	

rus	Destinatio vel contentum breve	Folia	Edita per scriptorem	edita	Annotationes
50.	Ad Guilhelmum Salvarvillam de Schismate	221a—230	......	18	Haec epistola etiam invenitur Viennae in bibliotheca olim regia dicta: n. 4923, fol. 192a-196a; etiam Romae.
51.	Responsum ad Fratres quoad quaedam dubia circa proprietarios	230a—233a	......	19	
52.	Ad Abbatum in Campen	233a—239a	De Ram, l. c. Ep. VII.	—	Bibl. Vat. lat. n. 4927, fol. 137a-143a.
53.	Ad quandam sororem in Christo de proprietate monialium	239a—243a	......	20	Idem contentum ac ep. 10 sed magis fuse.
54.	Exhortatio ad quendam olim valde et adhuc multum dilectum ad fugiendum peccatum et aemulandum virtutem.	243a—248a	De Ram, l. c. Ep. VIII.	—	
55.	Suo novitio Mathiae de Tyle	248a—249a	De Ram, l. c. Ep. V.	—	
56.	Exhortatio ad quendam monachum ut firmus in votis permaneat	249a—250b	De Ram, l. c. Ep. VI.	—	
57.	Ad Johannem de Cele	250b—252a	Preger 9.	—	
58.	" " "	252a—254a	" 3.	—	
59.	" " "	254a—257b	" 5.	—	
60.	" " "	257a—258b	" 11.	—	
61.	" " "	259a—259b	" 2, De Ram, Ep. II.	—	
62.	" " "	259b—259b	" 4, Nolte V.	—	
63.	" " "	259b—260a	" 8, Nolte p. 295.	—	
64.	" " "	260a—260b	" 6.	—	64 et 65 — Leodii 65.
65.	" " "	261a—262a	" 10, Nolte p. 295.	—	

B. Epistolae non in Codice Hagae Comitis, sed alicubi nempe Parisiis, Bibl. Nat. Nouveles acquisitions Latines, M. S. no. 1250.

	Destinatio vel contentum breve	Folia	Edita per scriptorem	edita	Annotationes
	Ad quendam multipliciter temptatum.	59c—63a	......	21	In quantum scio, solum Parisiis invenitur haec epistola.
	Ad quendam, qui praeest monialibus contra detractionem.	63a—65a	......	22	Invenitur etiam Leodii, in Bibliotheca Universitatis no.191 (390); Liber Conventus Sanctae Crucis Leodiensis fol. 222a-224a. Ultima verba vero hic desiderantur,

APPENDIX C

THE ORIGINAL CONSTITUTION OF THE BRETHREN OF THE COMMON LIFE AT DEVENTER

This constitution is found in Ms. no. 73 G 22 of the Royal Library at the Hague. It may seem strange that no one has ever thought of examining it carefully. Schoengen calls it the constitution of a house founded by the brethren at Zwolle (M. Schoengen, Jac. Voecht narr., p. CXXVII, p. CXLIX), and suggests that the one found in Ms. no. 70 H 79 of the Royal Library at the Hague, which contains but a few brief and incomplete rules, was written and used by the brethren at Deventer (M. Schoengen, Jac. Voecht narr., p. 59, note 3). But why should the men who founded all the other houses, either directly or indirectly, have had to be content with only a small fragment of the constitution in use at Zwolle, which had been copied after their own constitution, as Schoengen himself admits (M. Schoengen, Jac. Voecht narr., pp. CXXXIV—CXL)? Moreover, it is not very difficult to prove that Ms. no. 73 G 22, Royal Library, The Hague, contains the constitution of the "Domus domini Florentii" at Deventer, for: (1) On fol. 43ᵇ we find that the brethren were to pray for their friends at Delft, where in 1403 a house had been founded by the "Domus domini Florentii". (2) The only other houses which could be expected to offer such prayers were those of Gouda and Utrecht, but on the same page of our manuscript the word Gouda was added in a later hand, while the house at Utrecht was founded as late as the year 1474, long after this constitution was written. (3) The prologue refers to Pierre d'Ailly's letter of recognition, which was given in 1413, for in that same year the cardinal visited the Yssel valley as papal legate, and granted some privileges to the Sisters of the Common Life at Deventer; this letter of approbation encouraged them, they said, to draw up their rules in writing, as practised in their house before; in the cardinal's letter of approbation only the houses of Deventer, Zwolle, and Münster are mentioned by name, and even if they all had been enumerated there, only one of them would be found to have direct relationship with the house at Delft. (4) The brethren at Deventer prayed for their friends at Delft, simply because these friends were members of their own house.

Noma modq vuedi riete...

sme mrgs i roi i capstitate et...

mutua et laboe manuu dno...

no dutipat a lege duua et huana...

nerno p sunos pontifes i seuagutibj...

est arennatq Insip et per quuia Colomen...

per legatu sedis et aplice ad quuia Colomen...

et alias missu dmi petzu de eyaro Cardma...

lem Cancarensem Auite Sedis aplice et su...

legatiois hic modus vuuendi est confirmatq...

et appbatq Dmno sedm uia oes pbri debent...

uuuere i roi ut patet i de uita et honestate...

tcleroru Igitur aspuate dno ihu et pia mre...

eius p ytercessione beissimi yg domui ygfesso...

zib adiuuate quter hic modus uiuedi p bonas...

et stus tosuetu nes i moribus et disciplina...

seruai debeat est pfequendu et hic i scriptis...

redigedu ne a memoia ura sine successou...

nrozu per obluuone excidat vel p teposem...

dissuetut sed fequt renouulade ad rustadi...

am disciplme et bonozu mozu attendant...

Cu em sedm augustiu bom tosistit i modo...

et spene et ordme ut ait m libzo de ura bo...

The rector of the brethren at Delft had been procurator of the "Nova domus" at Deventer (see: R. Dier de Muiden, Scriptum p. 54). So close were the relations between Deventer and Delft that in 1458, when R. Dier de Muiden wrote his Scriptum, he said, in speaking of the house at Delft: "Cornelius is rector there" (see: R. Dier de Muiden, Scriptum, p. 55). No other houses were mentioned by name in the constitution, except the one at Delft, hence this constitution certainly could never have been drawn up in a daughter-institution of the house at Zwolle. (5) Of Petrus Horn, a member of the house at Deventer, we read that he never had to ask forgiveness for having fallen asleep beside his candle; our constitution explicitly demands the asking of forgiveness in such cases, which clause is not found in other constitutions known to us (see: G. Dumbar, Anal. Dav., vol. I, p. 152, and the constitution, fol. 47[a]).

[Q]uoniam modus vivendi clericorum et presbiterorum sine propriis in communi, in castitate, et caritate mutua et labore manuum Domino serviencium non dumtaxat a lege divina et humana approbatur, necnon per summos pontifices in extravagantibus variis est licenciatus; insuper et per provinciam Coloniensem per legatum sedis et apostolice ad provinciam Coloniensem et alias missum dominum Petrum de Elyaco, cardinalem Cameracensem, auctoritate sedis apostolice et sue legacionis hic modus vivendi est confirmatus et approbatus; ymmo secundum iura omnes presbiteri deberent vivere in communi, ut patet in: "De vita et honestate clericorum"[1], igitur aspirante Domino Ihesu et pia matre eius per intercessionem beatissimi Iheronimi confessoris adiuvante, qualiter hic modus vivendi per bonas et sanctas consuetudines in moribus et disciplina servari debeat, est prosequendum et hic in scriptis redigendum, ne a memoria nostra sive successorum nostrorum per oblivionem excidant vel per teporem dissuescant, sed frequenti renovacione ad custodiam discipline et bonorum morum accendant.

Cum enim secundum Augustinum bonum consistit in modo et specie et ordine, ut ait in libro "De Natura Boni" [fol. 1[b]] .... est ordinare. Unumquodque naturam quantum habet de ordine, tantum habet de bonitate. Unde idem Augustinus in libro "De Opere Monachorum": "Optima", inquit, "est gubernacio, ut omnia suis temporibus distributa gerantur ex ordine, ne animum humanum turbilentis implicacionibus involuta perturbent". Sicut eciam ait Hugo de Sancto Victore: "Virtus non alio modo apprehenditur, nisi disciplina virtutis non negligenter custodiatur". Licet ergo non obligamus nos

voto vel professione ad observanciam istarum consuetudinum
vel alicuius religionis, non est tamen sine culpa in huiusmodi
negligens vel inobediens inveniri, turbare pacem domesticam
et occasionem dare vite remissioris.

De fundacione domus Capit. I

[D]omus hec nostra a quadam devota matrona ad hoc
fundata et paucis redditibus et bonis parvis dotata est, ut ad
exemplum ecclesie primitive devoti presbiteri et clerici cum
nonnullis paucis laicis in ea vivant in communi de labore
manuum, videlicet opere scripture, et de redditibus sive bonis
ecclesiasticis vitam transigant mediocrem, prelatis suis reverenter
obediant, humilem habitum et [fol. 2ª] simplicem statui tamen
clericali competentem deferant, canones et decreta sanctorum
patrum diligenter custodiant, virtutum et devocionum studiis
sollerter insistant, et non solum irreprehensibiles, verum eciam
exemplares se aliis exhibeant, ut sic possint Deo gratum et
acceptabile servicium exhibere, non solum de bona conversacione
sua, sed eciam de aliorum quorum Deus corda per eorum
monita et exempla conpungere dignabitur, conversione et salute.
Quia igitur verus profectus vite spiritualis consistit in cordis
puritate, qua neglecta frustra ad perfectionem nitimur, que
est in caritate; sit igitur summum et quotidianum studium et
excercicium nostrum proficere in cordis puritate, ut videlicet
primo omnium discamus nos ipsos cognoscere, vicia et passiones
anime sine dissimulacione diiudicare et eas totis viribus niti
extirpare, gulam domare, concupiscencias refrenare, superbiam
deprimere, temporalia conte[m]pnere, proprias voluntates fran-
gere, et alia quelibet vicia impugnancia expugnare, et inter
hec pro veris virtutibus acquirendis summum studium adhibere,
ut videlicet humilitatem, caritatem, castitatem, pacienciam,
obedienciam, ac alias virtutes, in quibus beneplacitum est
Domino Deo, possimus [fol. 2ᵇ] obtinere. Ista est verior et
tucior via et modus proficiendi in vita spirituali, prout sancti
patres determinaverunt, et habetur inde notabiliter in "Colla-
cionibus Patrum", in prima collacione abbatis Moysi et in
"Profectibus Religiosorum", ubi dicitur de Caathitis, quos
optimos iudicat de triplici genere religiosorum. Ad istum modum
proficiendi debemus omnia nostra excercicia dirigere: oracionem,
meditacionem, lectionem, opus manuum, vigilias, ieiunia, exer-
citaciones, composicionem tam interioris quam exterioris
hominis, ut sic directa via ad caritatem Dei, ad gustum eterne
sapiencie possimus pervenire.

[De materiis meditandi]

Quia vero timor Domini necessarius est proficere volentibus,
— qui enim sine timore est non poterit iustificari, — idcirco
expedit cuique nostrum indefesse ruminare materias illas que
provocant hominem ad timorem Dei, ut est materia de peccatis,
de morte, de iudicio, de inferno. Sed ne timor continuatus
mentem deiectam et desperatam faciat, si non in spe divine

misericordie respiret, [fol. 3ª] idcirco intermiscere expedit
materias ad spem et amorem Dei provocantes, videlicet de
regno celorum, de beneficiis divinis, de vita Ihesu Cristi et
passione eius. Quas materias sic solemus dividere et alternare,
ut meditemur sabbatis de peccatis, dominica die de regno
celorum, feriis secundis de morte, feriis terciis de beneficiis
Dei, feriis quartis de iudicio, feriis quintis de penis inferni,
feriis sextis de passione Domini, de qua singulis feriis eciam
infra missam convenit meditari, incipiendo a vita Domini
dominica die, et consequenter singulis diebus aliquem passûm
passionis, prout habemus signatum. Circa festivitates vero
precipuas conformamus nos ecclesie catholice, formando medita-
ciones et exercicia nostra de materia festi. De hiis materiis pro
innovacione memorie solemus aliquem punctum perlegere mane,
vespere et de sero.

De hora surgendi et preparacione ad oracionem

De mane infra terciam et quartam media hora, quando non
cantamus, ad signum excitacionis surgimus simul omnes per
singulos dies ad matutinas, alacriter quidem et vivaciter,
excucientes [fol. 3ᵇ] sompnum ab oculis nostris iuxta illud
Ieremie: "Consurge, lauda in nocte in principio vigiliarum
tuarum, effunde sicut aquam cor tuum ante conspectum Domini,
leva ad eum manus tuas". Protunc enim primicias cogitacionum
debemus offerre Domino Deo in aliqua bona cogitacione, vel
oracione, cordis intencionem ad Dominum convertentes. Quales
enim in oracione inveniri volumus, tales nos ante oracionis
tempus debemus preparare. Convenientes ergo quantocius in
ecclesiam ad dicendum sive cantandum divina officia et oraciones
ac horas canonicas, habebimus nos composite in membris, in
motibus secundum motum in ordinario domus expressum,
sedendo sive stando vivaciter, sequentes exemplum sanctorum
patrum in Egipto, de quibus ita dicit Cassianus in "Institutis
Patrum", libro secundo: "Cum Sinaxes celebraturi conveniunt,
tantum prebetur a cunctis silencium, ut, cum in unum tam
numerosa fratrum multitudo conveniat, preter illum, qui con-
surgens psalmum decantat in medium, nullus homini putetur
penitus adesse". Ac precipue, cum consummatur oracio, id est
collecta, in qua non [fol. 4ª] sputum emittitur non excreacio
obstrepit non tussis intersonat non ossitacio sompnolenta dissutis malis et hiantibus trahitur. Illum vero, qui constitutus
in tempore mentis aliquid horum, que predixi, e faucibus suis
emittit ac precipue ossitacionibus prevenitur, dupliciter peccare
pronunciant. Primo quod oracionis sue reus sit, quod eam
videlicet negligenter offerat, secundo quod indisciplinato strepitu
alterius quoque qui forsitan intencius orare potuit, intercipit
sensum. Non eciam multitudine versuum, sed mentis intelligencia
delectantur, illud tota virtute sectantes: psallam spiritu, psallam
et mente. Menbru² eciam nostra decet nos ab inquietudine et
superfluis occupacionibus frenare, ne vel nos vel alios ab
intencione psalmorum et aliorum que in divino officio recitantur

distrahant vel avertant. Insuper et folia vertere, vel alia sine necessitate pervidere cavendum est, maxime cum oracionem dominicam vel Credo silenter dicimus, vel quando lectio vel collecta vel aliquid aliud recitatur, quod ab uno solo singulariter dicitur, propter quod iuvenes et indigentes [fol. 4ᵇ] . . . . quantum commode possunt de . . . . esse provisi, ne se ipsos et alios per inquietudinem vel confusionem ab interiori intencione abstrahere possint. Persolvendo autem horas legemus vel cantabimus modeste et moderate, non nimis cursorie, nec nimis tractim, facientes pausam modicam in medio versus, solliciti uniformiter legere et cantare sine confusione, ut devocioni et maturitati et exultacioni deserviat. Semper autem presbiteri et clerici de mane dicunt matutinas et primas de tempore simul in ecclesia et alias horas sequentes postea eciam in ecclesia similiter suis temporibus, excepto quod ferialibus diebus tantum terciam et ˌsextam seorsum servamus. Omni eciam tempore legunt qui sacerdotes non sunt, omnes simul matutinas et primas de Sancta Cruce et de Domina extra ecclesiam cum psalmo pro defunctis, ut consuetum est[3] post primas de primas[4] de tempore. Addentes tunc particulam de materia conpunctionum aut alias, ut tempus exigit. Simili modo eciam post vesperas de tempore in choro fi- [fol. 5ᵃ] nitas dicent vesperas de sancta . . . . cum alliis ut supra de matutinis et . . . . dicitur. Die autem precedente communionem fratrum legent de mane loco conpunctionum materiam de preparando ad sacram communionem et eciam septem psalmos cum letaniis et collectis consuetis. Dicitur a singulis fratrum omni die responsorium "Benedic Domine" cum collectam, ut consuetum est, pro animabus eorum qui nobis in intercenariis et missis commissi sunt, ac eciam fratrum et parentum nostrorum, benefactorum, amicorum, et omnium fidelium defunctorum de bone consuetudine. Dicimus pariter in ecclesia per totum annum vigilias feriis secundis et quartis, dum in eis nec festum sit nec profestum, excepto quod per quadragesimam hora tercia post meridiem eas dicimus omni die preter in dominica in choro, sed in aliis festis vel profestis tunc occurrentibus in privato. Preter hoc dicet quisque fratrum per se ad minus semel vigilias in privato pro eis quibus supra[5].

De studio sacre scripture

Quia sacra scriptura a sanctis doctoribus [fol. 5ᵇ] conscripta salubriter instruit nos, quomodo in via Dei ambulare debemus, movetque affectum et voluntatem ad amorem virtutum et fugam viciorum simul eciam memoriam nostram, seclusis vanis et nocivis cogitacionibus, occupat fructuosis et utilibus. Simus ergo diligentes et continui in studio sacre scripture, habentes singuli penes nos aliquem librum de canonica aut alias autentica vel probata scriptura, quem librum elegamus de consilio confessoris nostri, perlegentes in eo singulis diebus aliquem passum pro spirituali refectione anime. Et ad hoc deputatam habemus specialiter unam horam de mane post lectionem horarum; qua

hora vitabimus inutiles discursus et negocia inpeditiva, quibus
abstrahamur a studio, nisi utilitas maior incumbat, aut obediencia
caritatis aliud iniungit.

De missa audienda   Cap. V

Et quia missam cotidie consuevimus audire, studeant se
sacerdotes sollicite preparare, ut hora sexta simul et uniformiter
possint celebrare, ita ut quasi simul incipi [fol. 6ª] simul
incipiant et quasi .... Ad quam missam audiendam
.... signo tempestive convenimus in ecclesia nostra.
In qua non solemus ad populum conversi stare vel sedere,
ne distrahamur mente, sed magis ab impedimentis liberum,
prout oportunius valemus, locum querere. Quapropter clerici
audientes missam maneant in choro vel loco secreto semper
prostati et a populo segregati, ut eo intencius possint cor suum
ad Deum dirigere et memoriam dominice passionis agere et
per pias affectiones quasi ad spiritualem communionem nos
debemus preparare. Si enim secundum Bernardum omni tempore et in omni loco, precipue tamen illo in tempore et illo
loco rem misterii illius eo modo, quo traditum est, hoc est
devoto pietatis affectu agere, tractare et sumere sibi in salutem,
omnibus in promptu est⁶. Omnes ergo missa finita cum silencio
revertimur ad cellas, agentes in eis opus quod pro tempore
expediens est. Sequitur

De labore

[fol. 6ᵇ] Quoniam humana fragilitas non permittit, ut homo
in mentalibus exerciciis continue totus occupetur, idcirco prout
multipliciter persuasum habemus, quotidie aliquid manibus
laboramus. Qui enim non est contentus quotidie aliquid manibus
operari, non potest in cella diucius perdurare, ut dicitur in
institutis sanctorum patrum, de quibus beatus Bernardus in
epistula ad fratres de monte Dei: "Patres nostri in Egipto
et Thebaida, sancte huius vite ardentissimi emulatores, labora-
bant manibus suis, et de labore suo pauperes pascebant, viventes
de labore manuum suarum". Opus eciam manuum reddit nos
liberos, ne habeamus necesse inhiare pro donativis aliorum.
Que causa promovit beatissimum Paulum, cum scribit ad
Thessalonicenses: "Nec panem gratis manducamus ab aliquo,
sed in labore et fatigacione, ne quem vestrum gravaremus"⁷.
Inter opera manuum precipue consuluntur illa que cum
spiritualibus propriorem videntur habere similitudinem, ut est
opus scripture [fol. 7ª] cui operi insistebat eciam gloriosus
.... fratribus suis, discipuli .... sicut dicit
beatus Bernardus: "Serius tamen et prudens animus ad omnem
se comparat laborem". Sic autem consuevimus dividere tempora,
ut tribus⁸ horis ante prandium ferialis diebus qui clerici sunt
laboribus insistamus, presbiteri vero duabus, decima hora ante
prandium cessantes. Post prandium vero a duodecima hora
usque ad terciam iterum operi manuum insistimus dicturi
vesperas; quarta hora ad opus redimus. Si fuerit tamen dies

ieiunii, laboramus ante prandium usque undecimam et post prandium incipimus hora prima. In opere manuum debemus esse fideles et ferventes: maledictus enim qui facit opus Domini negligenter. Et licet debeamus esse continui, non tamen nimii vel importunii, ne spiritum extinguamus; ymmo debemus niti manere, si non in continua bona meditacione, saltim in bona affectione, sepius erigendo cor nostrum ad Deum per breves oraciones, quas iaculatorias vocat beatus Augustinus. Item debemus in silencio operari, brevius [fol. 7ᵇ] protunc expediendo ad nos venientes, nisi evidens utilitas persuadeat maturius loqui cum alio. Sequitur

De commestione

Officium preparandi mensam noviciis vel iunioribus committitur, ut consuetum est, ad quos pertinet statuto tempore ad prandium sive ad cenam mensas preparare; panem, potum, et alia necessaria apportare, aquam eciam ad lavatorium haurire et pro eo sollicitari, ut numquam canale sine aqua inveniatur, preterquam in hyeme, quando gelu constringit aquam, quia tunc semper ad prandium et cenam recens aqua in vase aliquo apportatur, et propter gelu removetur postea. Anforas eciam lavare debent precipue in estate sepius et post cenam et prandium vacuas et interdum ablutas ad sua loca reponendo. Et in hoc debet quisque noviciorum sive iuniorum suam ebdomadam custodire et in fine ebdomade refectorium, transitum et alia necessaria scobis purgare, ut moris est.

Ad mensam ergo sic paratam [fol. 8ª] debemus omnes simul mature tempestive in pulsu convenire, ut intersit unusquisque, cum legitur "Benedicite". Euntes autem ad mensam .... silencium in via, nihil loquendo et precipue apud lavatorium. Similiter servantes silencium redeuntes ad ecclesiam, usque dum post exitum ecclesie quisque venerit ad cameram suam. Sedentes autem ad mensam debemus cum silencio sedere, cavendo ab omni strepitu, ut possimus eo quiecius et attencius sacram scripturam, que ibi legitur, auscultare. Item debemus visum continere, ne circumspiciamus, quid in mensa fiat, nisi alicui ex officio hoc incumberet. Et non debemus esse exquisiti et singulares in quantitate vel modo percipiendi cibum vel potum. Si habunde nobis fuerit amministratum, debemus cum graciarum actione percipere; si vero parcius, nichilominus debemus sine murmure contenti esse, cogitantes de penuria et frugalitate multorum, eciam secularium, qui multo minoribus et vilioribus sunt contenti. Non debent eciam fratres sedentes ad mensam [fol. 8ᵇ] .... priusquam rectorem premissa mo .... lectionis attingere viderint .... aliquid modice inclinamus et ipse in nobis. Bibentes, sicut moris est, duabus manibus amphoram vel ciphum teneamus, mensalia non convoluimus, donec rector suum convoluat. In estate ab octava Pasche usque ad festum Exaltacionis Sancte Crucis⁹ consuevimus dormire post prandium, lectis nonis quousque per lectorem mense, prandio suo facto, fuerimus suscitati. Et dum fratres

matutinas cantaverint, datur eciam sompnus meridianus, quocumque tempore anni fuerit, et excitabuntur per lectorem, sicut
in estate consuevit fieri. Eo tempore erit domus clausa et
cavebit sibi quisque a strepitu, ne impediat quiescentes. In
hyeme vero, si post prandium sompno gravaremur, solemus
sedentes modice inclinare caput per Miserere vel duo. Sequitur

De lectore mense Capit. VIII

[fol. 9ᵃ]. Lector autem mense .... dere libros, in
quibus lege .... loca ubi incipiendum et ut legenda
per .... refectionem sufficiant. Aperte autem et distincte
leget omnia et attente sine festinacione et importunitate, ita
ut perfecte possint intelligi, et tali voce, ita ut ab omnibus
possit audiri. Solet autem unusquisque de presbiteris et clericis
habere unam integram ebdomadam legendi ad mensam, incipiendo a senioribus sabbato de sero. Sed a feria quarta, que
est in capite ieiunii, usque ad diem Pasche quotidie succedunt
sibi in ordine, non legentes nisi per unum diem. Quod si lector
absens fuerit, precedens eum locum eius supplebit, nisi, qui
lector erit, omnino per totam ebdomadam vel quasi non
venerit, quia tunc sequens eum succedit, ipse vero, qui per
absenciam ebdomadam suam non custodivit, postea supplebit.
Lectori eciam licitum est aliquid gustare, priusquam fratres ad
refectionem intrent et sero ante collacionem bibere, si necesse
fuerit. Et dum [fol. 9ᵇ] .... accommodare et oculum
cor .... emendaverit intelligere possit ....
ebet inchoare lectionem, donec strepitus .... conquie-
scat. Item lector et qui post commedunt cum eo silencium
tenent.

Quid post cenam fiet Capit. IX

Cena facta et dicto completorio, facit unusquisque in camera
sua quid convenit sibi, vel pumicat, vel lineat, vel studet, vel
loquitur cum aliquo de edificacione anime usque ad octavam
horam. Qua signata sine mora dimittemus a nobis, si qui assint
alieni, et claudetur domus et vocabit unusquisque sibi servando
silencium ex tunc usque ad sextam horam de mane. Et tunc
precipue convenit quod beatus Bernardus ait: "Fidelis servus
Ihesu Christi post completorium singulis diebus capitulum sibi
teneat et convocatis cogitacionibus, ponat cum eis racionem",
et cetera. Et sic media hora infra octavam et nonam habito
prius devoto exercicio et examine sui, ut dictum est, solemus
simul ire dormitum.

[De collacione]

Sed quia per collacionem [fol. 10ᵃ] mutuam, ubi de aliqua
materia sacre scripture fit caritativum colloquium, non solum
instruimur ad scienciam, sed eciam accendimur ad fervorem
et precipue nutritur ex hoc caritas fraterna. Dicit enim beatus
Anthonius optimum esse, si se fratres mutuis consolentur
sermonibus. Idcirco consuevimus festivis diebus, dum per

rectorem aut procuratorem in eius absencia signum factum
fuerit, de sero post completorium convenire et colloqui de
materia edificatoria, occasionem conferendi sumentes ex libro
qui collacionale dicitur, ex quo passus designatus illi diei vel
tempori per rectorem aut procuratorem in eius absencia legetur.
Sed valde necessarium est, ut fratres solliciti sint, ut de materia
proposita uniformiter loquantur non adducentes vana vel
extranea. Nec fiant inter nos disputaciones vel argumentaciones
infructuose, sed unusquisque cum modestia proponit quid pro
materia deseruit. Item pro maiori iuvenum consulitur, ut novicii
illi collacioni disciplina, verecundia, et reverencia ad fratres
servanda non intersint, sed seorsum per se loquantur de materia
bona et edificatoria; et ad mensem aut sex ebdomadas aut
quomodocumque placet rectori mittatur ad eos instructor
noviciorum aut alius seniorum, priusquam lecta est materia
collacionis[10]. Diebus eciam festivis finitis vesperis in ecclesia
parochiali [fol. 10b] .... nostris per rectorem ad
hoc .... emet rector pro communi populo facere
collacionem in ecclesia nostra. In qua collacione studebit
quisque secundum datam sibi graciam verbis edificatoriis
populum commovere, non quidem per modum predicacionis,
sed simplicis exhortacionis. Et hoc faciet quidem ferventer et
efficaciter, attendens quod non est Deo gracius sacrificium quam
zelus animarum. In quo opere non studebit ornatis locucionibus,
vel magistralibus allegacionibus, que pascunt tantummodo aures
audiencium, sed magis motivis et compunctivis verbis corda et
voluntates audiencium tangere. Collacione igitur huiusmodi
completa non stent fratres in omni via, neque misceant cum
secularibus et extraneis multos sermones, sed ibit quisque ad
cameram suam, revolvens et ruminans in corde suo quid audierit
aptabitque profectui sue spirituali. [fol. 11a] Et eciam clericis
vel .... quod ipsis conveniat ad emenda ....
Et si qui a nobis consilium pecierint, possumus eis humiliter
et mature quod bonum videtur suggerere. In arduis tamen
casibus consulendis et in confessionalibus ad eum qui preest
domui nostre eos dirigere. Quando eciam ad cameras nostras
tunc vel aliquo alio tempore locuturi nobiscum veniunt, non debemus eos diucius et ad longius ultra dimidiam horam apud nos
tenere, nec de inutilibus aut rumoribus seculi cum eis colloquium
habere, sed magis de hiis que pro salute animarum suarum eis
necessaria videntur efficaciter eos instruere, precipue exhortantes,
ut in revelandis temptacionibus et passionibus suis sint aperti
et ad acquiescendum sanis consiliis prompti et voluntarii.
Sequitur

De correpcione Capitulum X

Quoniam correpcio, prout est actus caritatis fraterne,
necessaria videtur pro conservacione discipline, dicit enim
Crisostomus: "Bonus, nisi correptus perit fuerit"[11]. Idcirco
proposuimus nos invicem ex caritate corripere secundum modum
nobis a Salvatore propositum: [fol. 11b] "............... est

te sciente frater tuus corripe eum inter te et ipsum solum",
et cetera[12]. In remis .... peccatorum et, ut passiones
et vicia nostra vincere possimus, debemus interdum ad hoc
convenire ad invicem ammonendum et corripiendum, dum
rectori bonum visum fuerit. Sic autem congregati post lectionem
prius fratrum surgat iunior omnium primo et dicat in genibus:
"Karissimi fratres est culpa mea quod male conversando non
tam bene servavi consuetudines domus, ut debui, prebens aliis
malum exemplum". Et precipue dicet in duobus vel in tribus
suis propriis defectibus culpam suam, subiungens: "Et quod
ulterius in me notastis, rogo ut propter Deum michi in caritate
dicatis, quia libenter volo me emendare". Et tunc dicent ad
nutum rectoris duo vel tres vel plures, quid in ipso notaverint,
qui ad singula humiliter dicet, Mea culpa. Et quando sic dicta
sunt, tunc ulterius dicet cum omni humilitate: "Indulgeatis
michi propter Deum quod tam male me habui, libenter me
emendabo et rogo eciam, [fol. 12ª] ut sitis semper liberi ad
me .... nendum, ut oretis Deum pro me ....
emendandi post hoc osculando res .... Et antiqua
consuetudine servatum est, ut .... cepti fratres et layci
et clerici ad aliquos annos vel ad sacerdocium[13] et si qui alii
sunt, quibus hoc commissum est, exeant post ammonicionem
ipsis factam. Igitur in hoc tempore et in aliis locis et temporibus
debet esse ammonicio dulcis, humilis; et supplicatoria a fratribus
porrecta. Rigorosa aliquando spectat ad rectorem, cum duricia
vel cecitas superba alicuius vel alia causa requirit. Secundum
Bernardum attendere debemus tria in correpcione, scilicet
compassionis affectum, zelum rectitudinis, spiritum discrecionis.
Item debemus invicem corripere de apertis negligenciis et
excessibus contra bonos mores et pias consuetudines, maxime
quas habemus in scriptis; item de verbis duris, clamorosis,
iocosis, de excusso risu, de verbis ociosis, de multiloquio infra
tempus cuiuslibet operis, de guerris aut rumoribus seculi, que
ad nos non spectant, cum hospitibus sive inter nos, de silencio
post commedencium infra comestionem post octavam in coquina
[fol. 12ᵇ] .... rasure et apud ignem, prout melius
teneri potest, non servato, de negligenciis in officiis commissis,
de partinacia in propria voluntate et proprio consilio, sive
excusando sive defendendo, de moribus et gestibus incompositis
et inconsuetis, et sic de similibus aliis viciis apertis. Istud
omnino visum est sic expedire, nec per minima non correpta,
successive vicia in domo pullulent et fervor paulatim pereat.
Et ideo, ut liberiores ad corripiendum nos mutuo faciamus,
quilibet ibit semel in quindena ad aliquem de fratribus, petendo,
ut non vereatur eum corripere, cum in aliquo excessu ab eo
fuerit deprehensus. Si autem predicta collacio defectuum nobis
proficiet, oportet, ut fratres de correptis studeant se emendare.
Et quod rector domus super omnia attendat, an ea fratres opere
perficiant, de quibus correpti sunt, et eciam sepius requirat,
si omnes per quindenam pro defectibus et ante festa communicabilia ad II aut III fratres pro venia sua vadant, ut vigilanter
ammoneat transgressores.

De rectore

Quia in magna et in parva qualibet republica, [fol. 13ᵃ] si conservari debeat, necesse est esse unum presidentem, — dicit enim beatus Iheronimus: "Non civitas, non regnum, non minima domuncula diu maneret in rure, si cuius voluntati pareretur, deesset". Idcirco de communi consilio fratrum et aliorum patrum nostrorum visitatorum consuevimus unum presbiterum ad hoc deputare, qui patrisfamilias loco personarum domus et rerum ad eam pertinencium principalem curam gerat. Huic, licet nullam iurisdictionalem auctoritatem super fratres habeat, tamen propter profectum suum et meritum obediencie et propter pacem domesticam et conservacionem rerum et status nostri ex caritate subiecti esse non gravabuntur. Huic precipue incumbit fratres de excessibus corripere et redarguere, confessiones personarum domus de licencia prelatorum suorum audire, et ad meliora queque verbo et exemplo provocare. Huic fratres in corde caritatem, in verbis fidelitatem, et in exhibicione reverenciam studeant conservare. Et licet ubique, tamen maxime in presencia eius observare fratres debent, ut modeste et verecunde se habeant. Sine huius scitu et licencia nemo presumat literas alicubi mittere, aut missas aperire vel legere. Similiter fiat [fol. 13ᵇ] .... ulis aut sine literis nun .... posito rectori occultetur animo .... Sine huius licencia nemo domum exeat, nisi propter commissionem aliquam de hoc licenciam generalem habeat, ut cocus vel aliter in exterius deputatus. Item sine eius licencia, dum presens fuerit, nullus fratrum hospites invitet, et in eius absencia, qui invitandus videtur, de licencia procuratoris invitetur. Item si aliquid de maioribus negociis domus nostre vel alias grave tractandum fuerit, ipse fratres in unum faciat convenire, ibique cum omnes quid senserint libere pronunciant, quod maiori et saniori parti visum fuerit expedire, per eum ulterius concludatur; in minoribus vero negociis, que consilium et deliberacionem fratrum requirant, cum procuratore domus vel tribus de senioribus colloquium habens, quod sanius et racionabilius inventum fuerit, sine dissencione aut partinacia cuiusquam pacifice determinetur. Quodsi propter aliquid intricatum vel alias, quod absit, inter se expedire non poterunt, ad omnes fratres referatur, et quod [m]aiori et saniori parti visum fuerit, sine replicacione concludatur. [fol. 14ᵃ] Ceterum studebit rector domus nostre aliis fratribus se conformare in cibo et potu, et humilitate habitus, et ceteris consuetudinibus, que convenienter servare poterit. Nec concesso sibi abutatur officio, sed sciat eo magis debere irreprehensibilem se gerere, quantum humana permittit fragilitas, tam coram extraneis quam coram domesticis; et videat sibi, ne querat que sua sunt, sed que Ihesu Christi. In fratribus suis sic persequatur vicia aliena, ut non palpet sua, nec dominum se attendat, sed servum fratrum suorum, quibus si vere superior vult inveniri, omnium servum et minimum studeat se in veritate estimare. Nitatur ipse precipue esse affabilis et dulciter seriosus, in ammonicionibus fervidus, in consiliis providus et in promocione omnis boni sollicitus. Fugiat perplexitates et distractiones secularium negociorum et precipue execuciones testamentatorum, ubi racionabiliter recusare poterit. Sit semper paratus et voluntarius cedere officio suo, si fratribus et patribus visitatoribus nostris videatur alteri iniungendum. Et non debent fratres proni esse ad iudicandum sive sinistre [fol. 14ᵇ] interpretandum facta vel dicta rectoris sui, si humanum aliquod in eo notaverint. Quodsi ammonere eum vel premuniri utile videatur, fiat hoc servata debita humilitate et verecundia. Et quia interdum cum latere contingit, tam de se quam de aliis que expediret sibi notificari, bonum est quod ad hoc deputet unum de fratribus qui de talibus eum habeat ammonitum et premunitum. Salvo quod unusquisque in specie cor suum interdum eidem libere debet aperire et preter ista precipue quater in anno, ut inferius dicetur. Sequitur

De procuratore

Pro speciali cura temporalium nostrorum rector domus de consilio fratrum, vel maioris et sanioris partis eorum, eligere consuevit unum procuratorem, cuius officium est redditus nostros et alia que debentur nobis, per se vel per alium monere et tollere, quecumque pro victu et vestitu legata et donata levare et, que nos tenemur solvere indigemus, tempestive procurare, quecumque emenda, vendenda, vel coquenda sunt, ordinare. Item sollicitabitur, ne res domus pereant et annullentur, sive in victualibus, [fol. 15ᵃ] sive in utensilibus, sive in edificiis, et que curanda vel reparanda sunt, per se vel per alium studeat'reparare. Non tamen advocabit alienum operarium sine consilio rectoris. Cum aliquid edificandum est, ei incumbit providere de singulis, salvo quod structura ordinetur de consilio rectoris et fratrum. Item ipse consuevit ad mensam ministrare. Item potest fratres advocare indifferenter ad communes labores in domo, et potest coquum et alium ad externa deputatum mittere pro negociis suis extra domum, sed non alios fratres sine licencia rectoris et ipse, quando exire habet, loquatur prius rectori antequam exeat, dum presens est, in eius tamen absencia debet hoc intimare seniori de fratribus. Item omnia recepta, concessa, legata, vel donata sollicite et sine dilacione ponat in scriptis. Similiter debita soluta deleat sine mora. Alias enim notabile incommodum vel eciam disceptacio cum extraneis inde possit evenire. Item non concedat ab aliquo ultra libram grossorum sine scitu rectoris et consensu vel duorum discretorum fratrum, si rector absens fuerit. Nec eciam concedet ultra dimidium florenum uni persone sine scitu ut supra. [fol. 15ᵇ] Item nulli aliquid sive in pecuniis sive in aliis rebus, ultra valorem dimidii stuferi al .... sepius dabit. Nec eciam concedet aliquibus utensilia domus, videlicet lectos, lintheamina, ollas, et cetera, ad quartalle anni sive ultra sine scitu rectoris. Item de elemosinis dandis pauperibus ipse sollicitabitur, sed non excedet notabiliter modum consuetum elemosinarum sine scitu rectoris. Item non presumat absente rectore alique attemptare vel imponere que non faceret per se presente rectore, sed si alique cause necessarie occurrerent, in huiusmodi faciat de consilio duorum vel trium discretorum fratrum. Item non presumat per se annullare vel immutare aliqua hactenus consueta, sive in vestibus, sive in victualibus, sive in aliis consuetudinibus, nec in agendis querat pascere propriam voluntatem, sed nitatur omnia facere secundum velle rectoris et fratrum. Item studeat expedite facere facienda et non ociose huc illucque discurrere, quasi sub pallio officii sui, sed semper quo cicius recurrere ad laborem manuum, si hora [fol. 16ᵃ] est, vel ad spirituale excercicium in camera sua. Et precipue de mane et de vespera nitatur se abstrahere ab occupacionibus, recolligendo mentem suam, ne distractiones externe penitus eviscerent eum a desiderio eternorum et faciant secularem. Item laboratoribus nostris et precipue pauperibus qui laborant nobis solvat plenam mercedem operis sui, ne habeant de nobis conqueri. Item nitatur proinde tractare et facere pacta sua cum secularibus, ne contingat cum eis habere dissenciones et rixas. Item videat sibi quod inveniatur verax in verbis suis et non permittat debita nostra que tenemur diu insoluta, maxime ubi creditores nostri non sunt contenti de mora solucionis. Item non permittet que debentur nobis inveterare, ne debitores nostri oblivioni tradant et postea recusent solvere. Si in huiusmodi negligens repertus fuerit, sciat se increpacione dignum, eo quod non fuerit in commisso fidelis. Item diligenter custodiat cedulas et registra reddituum nostrorum et pactorum cum colonis nostris, cum quibus ipse habet computare et tractare tractanda; sed non elocabit aliquam terram ad annos sine scitu rectoris. [fol. 16ᵇ] Item semel in anno, circa tempus inicii, registri sui vide .... sicionis faciet de omnibus coram rectore et fratribus computacionem planam, resignans bursam, claves, registrum, et officium suum, quantum in ipso est, et petens humiliter absolucionem. Item fratribus qui debent ambulare extra civitatem dabit bursam cum pecuniis, secundum quod reysa brevior vel longior sibi videbitur expedire. Qui eciam revertentes reddant sibi bursam et pecuniam, si que superfuit. Item salvis premissis sit ille qui habet officium procuratore, sicut ceteri fratres, et videat sibi, quod utiliter, humiliter et pacienter habet se cum fratribus. Et ipsi fratres humiliter, benigne, et caritative se habeant cum omnibus, maxime tamen cum eo. Sic enim decet, ut eis qui presunt in sollicitudine non onerosos sed graciosos se exhibeant.

De vestiario XIII

Licet procuratori incumbat providere fratribus de vestitu, consuevit tamen a rectore in sublevamen procuratoris uni de fratribus committi specialis cura de vestibus laneis et lineis, calceis, et calopodiis. Iste respectum habebit, ne fratres [fol. 17ᵃ]

defectum in aliquo horum paciantur; unde rupta faciat quo
ricius reçartiro, que vero attricione soluta resartiri decenter
non possunt, novis studeat commutare. Non tamen fiat alicui
nova toga, sive tunica sine scitu rectoris, cui vestiarius hoc
debet intimare. De preciositate panni servetur modus noster
consuetus, videlicet pro togis et tunicis quatuor ulne non
excedant valorem duorum florenorum Renensium ad omne
magis, sed pro capuciis una ulna duodecim stuferos vel circa
constabit. Item ipse dicet procuratori, ut pannum satis tempestive provideat. Item pannum ipse custodiat. Item proxima
feria post festum Exaltacionis Sancte Crucis ipse circueat
cameras fratrum cum rectore et provideat lectos et lectisternia,
lintheamina et suppellectilia fratrum, similiter cussinos et vestes
inferiores, ut qui in aliquo horum superhabundat, quo carere
potest, resignet. Qui vero deficit, per providenciam vestiarii, quo
indiget, oportuno tempore accipiat. Habeat quilibet pellicium
et duas subtunicas, unam simplam et unam duplam. [fol. 17ᵇ]
Pellicia fratrum ante festum Sancte Crucis aliqua serena die
simul in ortum ventilanda et excucienda ipse deferat, et que
reparacione vel innovacione indigent, ipse pervideat. In figura
vestimentorum nostrorum, latitudine videlicet et longitudine,
servetur modus humilis, qui humiles et devotos clericos decet;
presbiteri habent tunicas longas usque ad talos, clerici vero ad
latitudinem manus supra talos, laici nostri adhuc breviores.
Clausa sint desuper vestimenta nostra. Provideat vestiarius ut
duo vel tres sint tabbardi de nigro panno et similiter toge due
vel tres. Vel loco nigrorum[14] tria sint vel quatuor[15] capucia
grisea, que portabunt layci nostri sicut tabbardi nigri, et toge
distribuantur iuxta videre rectoris[16]. Item pervideat vestiarius
circa festum Exaltacionis Sancte Crucis, an alique tunice
inferiores indigent, ut laventur. Item pannum lineum ad
femoralia[17] et alia necessaria ipse habet procurare, et ut camisie
fratrum, que de laneo panno preter infirmos erunt[18], et femoralia
linea laventur et camisie, si que [fol. 18ᵃ] linee sint[19], laventur,
quociens fuerit oportunum, et ut lota distribuantur fratribus,
in qua distribucione nulla fiat specificacio, nisi quod respiciatur
quantitas stature fratrum. Et quia de lavandis ipse habet se
intromittere, eciam de mappis mensalibus et manutergiis lavandis
et innovandis eidem cura commissa est. Item circa inicium
mensis Octobris ipse dabit fratribus capucia duplicia circa
hyemem futuram, que precedente hyeme ab unoquoque
receperat. Que si satis attrita fuerint, commutabit in nova et
recipiat ab eis simplicia in suam custodiam procurando, ut
laventur et curentur. Eodem quoque tempore dabunter fratribus
calige et socci et alia quibus indigent circa hyemem. Item circa
finem mensis Aprilis recipiet a fratribus capucia duplicia et
restituet eis simplicia. Item fratres debent humiliter et cum
graciarum actione recipere quod eis fuerit amministratum, nec
conqueri [fol. 18ᵇ] super vilitate alicuius vestimenti, attendentes
quod qui preciosis et mollibus vestiuntur in domibus regum
sunt: num enim celesti sed terreno regno militant, qui pro Deo

perpeti adversa fugiunt, sed solis exterioribus dediti presentis
vite molliciem et venustatem querunt. Item si aliquis frater
pateretur defectum aliquem scissuram vel rupturam in vesti-
mento, qui ad extra non deprehenderetur, hoc deberet cum
debita humilitate referre vestiario. Ipse vero vestiarius sollicitus
sit, quantum paupertas nostra sustinet, omnibus moderate
procurare, nec permittat aliquem in dissutis et attritis diucius
incedere, nisi forte ex industria de voluntate rectoris ob humilitatis excercicium aliquis vetera solito tardius permitteretur
commutare. Item vestiarius pie corripiat eos qui negligencius
vestes suas custodiunt. Item provideat quod habeantur teristra
pro laborantibus in externis et calcei et pillei pro itinerantibus.
Sequitur

De cura scribendorum Capit. XIV

[fol. 19ᵃ] Uni de fratribus .... committi cura
scribendorum et parandorum et custodia pergameni ....
quantum poterit, ut omnes fratres sufficienter habeant ad
scribendum et exemplaria correcta. Et si fieri poterit, omnibus
procuret Latinum scribere. Et non· facile remittat aliquem
petentem sibi unum bonum librum scribi, quamvis pro tempore
nullus vacaverit, sed inducat, ut exspectet modico tempore.
Cum aliquis pecierit sibi scribi librum, pro quo habet scriptorem,
ostendat ei manum scriptoris et conveniat cum eo de quaterno
in quaternum; de notabilibus tamen libris non conveniat cum
aliquo, nisi de consilio rectoris. Item faciat contractus suos
plane et, si necesse est, per cedulas, ne postea cum aliquo
altercari necesse habeat. Et ubi non presumitur propta²⁰ solucio,
non resignet librum ante solucionem vel fideiussionem cope-
tentem²¹, maxime apud ignotos. Et in magnis libris accipiat
[fol. 19ᵇ] .... libri pro emendo pergameno
.... habebit curam de incausto braxando
quod semper bonum incaustum sit pro scriptoribus nostris.
Circa custodiam pergameni et franceni et aliorum scribentibus
necessariorum sollicitabit tempestive. Item sit sollicitus plane
et distincte omnia debita et recepta signare in registro suo.
Et quod de pecuniis ad manus eius venerit, tradet procuratori.
Iste debet ammonicionem facere tempore collacionis dierum
festorum post completorium, ut in cuiuslibet mensis solaris
secunda die, si ferialis sit, quisque fratrum cum socio sibi
deputato corrigat et inscribat scripturam correcture, antequam
ulterius scribatur. Sequitur

De armario Cap. XV

Armarius omnes libros domus ad officium divinum non
spectantes in custodia sua habet, quos eciam propriis nominibus
singillatim annotatos habere debet et diligenter prospicere, ne
in eis tinea vel alia quelibet corruptela infectum quid vel exesum
sit. [fol. 20ᵃ] Et signabit omnes libros .... domum
accommodantur et nomina .... et terminum concessionis
et sit .... repetere per internuncium, si qui libri diu

profixe concessionis non reportantur. Et non debet aliquem
librum concedere alicui extra opidum sine scitu rectoris. Sed
nec aliquis fratrum presumat quemcumque librorum extra domum
concedere sine scitu librarii. Libris autem quos pro studio
accipiunt fratres omnem diligenciam curamque prebere monentur, ne vel pulvere vel alia qualibet sorde maculentur. Armarius
eciam ostendat legentibus ad mensam quid et quando debeant
legere. Omelie sanctorum in festis et hiis diebus qui eas
proprias habent primo omnium legantur, deinde biblia ad
prandium et alii sermones et passiones sanctorum, ut moris est,
eciam ad vesperum, ubi semper pronunciabitur, in martirologio
pro die sequenti, preter quam in triduo ante Pascha quibus in
martirologio non recitatur. Semel in anno in estate colligat
armarius [fol. 20ᵇ] .... debita vocati fratres presente
.... et mundare et examinare .... armarius
rectori cedulam librorum .... tunc vel alias possit
numerum librorum. Sequitur

De infirmario   XVI

Infirmorum cura uni de fratribus solet committi. Hunc precipue convenit esse compassivum et obsequiosum. Iste postquam
per rectorem vel procuratorem ad alicuius infirmi nostri
servicium vocatus fuerit, de cetero frequencius secundum quod
infirmitas plus vel minus videtur exigere, ad eum debet accedere,
eique sedule ministrare, lectum eius preparare et ea quibus
circa lectum pro infirmitate indiguerit procurare. Cibum ipse
habet apponere et que commedenti superfuerint asportare et
de coquendis pro infirmo apud procuratorem providere. Si pro
medicina aliqua facienda videntur, habet ipse rectori vel procuratori intimare. Si circa infirmum vigilari necesse fuerit, alii
fratres de licencia rectoris petant infirmarium supportare. Item
si infirmitas invaluerit, de communione et unctione [fol. 21ᵃ]
debet rectorem ammonere. Et debet diligenter ea que circa
officia sacre communionis et unctionis requiruntur preparare.
De quibus pro consuetudine ecclesie servanda habeat cedulam,
in qua premissa et ea que circa officium defunctorum pertinent
sint inscripta. Item infirmarius secundum quod infirmo notaverit
expedire, debet eum dulciter ammonere ad pacienciam et ad
graciarum actionem, ad invocacionem Dei et sanctorum, ad
spem, ad fidem, et cetera, que saluti eius putaverit deservire.
Et si qui per longas confabulaciones et crebras visitaciones
infirmo onerosi fuerint, eos debet ab infirmo cohibere. Si vero
sine visitacione, que sibi grata sive necessaria est, relinquitur,
hoc debet aliquibus intimare. Et licet infirmarius pro posse
suo in omnibus que racionabiliter petit infirmus, debet ei
graciose condescendere et servire. Caveat tamen infirmus nimiis
et immoderatis serviciis infirmarium onerare, sive eciam in
diversis petendis et requirendis, que minus necessaria videntur,
ipsum et alios inquietare sive eciam querulosus [fol. 21ᵇ]
insistere, sed pacienciam, quam tempore sanitatis habuit in
proposito, tempore infirmitatis studeat habere in facto. Studeat

in omnibus Deo gracias agere, ne infirmitas, que data est ei ad
purgacionem anime, vertatur in augmentum culpe. Item caveat
infirmarius, ne tempus quod sibi suppetit sub pallio servicii sui
ocio vel negligencia deducat, sed quando vacare poterit ad
laborem manuum et alia consueta excercicia recurrat.

De rasura, minucione, et locione

Officium radendi vel ad id necessaria preparandi, dum barbi-
tonsor in domo non est, unus de fratribus infirmario vel alteri
cuique debet committi, qui, dum tempus rasure fuerit, aquam
calidam et alia debet disponere, et videant fratres ne rasurem
vocatus mora sua molestet, sed expedite festinabit adesse.
Quando eciam raduntur fratres, caveant clamores et strepitum
in loco rasure et, si que necessaria fuerint loqui, indicant paucis
verbis et submissis. Omni septimana radi debent tonsure
presbiterorum et barbe aliorum, vel barbe clericorum, tonsure
circa quindenam. [fol. 22ᵃ] Istius officii est eciam preparare
.... in omni mense semel, ut fratres pedes abluunt
nisi gelaret et ad hoc habetur in sua custodia vasa loture apta
et mappulas vel alia ad tergendum. Item lixivium et alia ad
lavandum capita procurare omni feria sexta quatuor temporum
vel sabbato, si ferialis dies sit. Hic eciam cum minucionis
tempus, quod quater in anno observatur, advenerit, debet omnia
ad minucionem necessaria preparare. Die ergo illa qua minuendi
sunt fratres tempore debito construatur ignis in loco deputato
et omnibus ad minucionem requisitis preparatis in signo
conveniant omnes et non minuti eisdem, quibus minuti par-
ticipant beneficiis. Et primam quidem diem totam in communi
iocunditate fraterne socialitatis deducimus tempore refectionis
premissa aliqua lectione cum modestia invicem colloquentes.
Observetur, ut omnia in recreacione fiant sine notabili tumultu
et effusione spiritus, ita ut laxamenta illa sint plena honestatis
et si careant nimio pondere, non tamen careant edificacione.
Secunda die post vesperas hora quarta de licencia rectoris
[fol. 22ᵇ] .... eadem gracia ad signum convenire
.... ac sub cena ut prius dicitur ....
colloquium exercere. Sequitur

De custode   Cap. XVIII

Solet eciam rector domus uni fideli devoto et accepto clerico
domus nostre committere claves et custodiam ecclesie nostre
et curam omnium que in ecclesia sunt, videlicet albas, casulas,
calices quoque et omnes libros et reliqua omnia ad divinum
officium pertinencia. Ipse igitur custos omnia que habet sub
sua custodia cum magna reverencia et diligencia servare debet
et frequenter inspicere, ne quid forte ex sua negligencia in rebus
quotidie necessariis desit, vel ne ornamenta ecclesie aliqua
corrupcio vermium aut humorum destruat. Et ideo, si qua in
ornamentis aut in ceteris que ad ministerium ecclesie pertinent
scissa vel contrita, aut quolibet alio modo reparanda fuerint,
debet curare ut cicius reparentur, omnia queque munda custodire

et immunda queque, ut cicius abluantur, procurare, [fol. 23ᵃ] et diligenter precavere ne un .... quelibet alin consecrata seu benedicta .... nerint ad alios usus extra sacrum ministerium.

Et ideo debet distinguere per signa vel scriptam appositam consecrata a non consecratis, sive nova fuerint sive vetera, ne eciam ex errore vel negligencia prophana et non consecrata in sacrum ministerium veniant loco sacrorum. Quocienscumque autem ablui debent corporalia vel calicum lintheolam, debet hoc congruo tempore providere et similiter de aliis quibuscumque lavandis. Ad cuius eciam officium pertinet habere curam horologii, oblata quoque et vinum ad missas, oleum et cereos et eciam alias candelas ad usum ecclesie pertinentes tempestive procurare et servare. Prunas quoque ad thurificacionem in missa et utrisque vesperis in solempnibus festis per se vel per alium procurabit, similiter et lampadem et campanam, cum necesse fuerit, mundare debet et inungere. Ecclesiam totam a summo usque deorsum bis mundabit in anno, pavimentum vero ecclesie et precipue ipsius chori et sanctuarii [fol. 23ᵇ] .... mundare debet cum opu .... pertinet debita tempora, quando ad .... endum est custodire et signa pulsare et alia ad sanctum ministerium necessaria preparare. Tempore estivo debet interdum, dum serena dies fuerit, ornamenta ecclesie excutere et ventilare. Item triduo ante Pascha calices lavabit, vel lavari procurabit, lavaturas in piscinam proiciendo. Eodem tempore per sacerdotem cum reverencia comburetur sacrum oleum, combustionem in piscinam similiter fundendo. Candelabra et alia vasa ecclesie, quociens opportunum fuerit, debet mundare per se vel per alium. Item registrabit custos omnes libros ecclesie et ornamenta et albas et mappas et candebra²² et cetera notabilia utensilia ecclesie, ut semel in anno presente rectore et fratribus pervideri possint²³. Hec igitur sunt que custodis sollicitudini commissa sunt, in quibus debet niti fidelis et diligens inveniri, ut mercedem a Domino Deo tam pii laboris in celesti templo ergo recipere mereatur. Sequitur

De hospitario Cap. XIX

Hospitarius unus eligatur per rectorem de fratribus acceptis in bonis moribus et disciplina, quantum fieri potest, eruditus [fol. 24ᵃ] qui super venientes hospites .... recipiens et omnibus honorem .... reverenciam impedens maxime religiosis et devotis singulis, sicut caritas exigit, et humanitatem exhibere et obsequium curat impendere. Caveantur autem colloquia vel interrogaciones cum hospitibus de rumoribus seculi, sed magis exhortentur ad emendacionem vite et contemptum mundi, si seculares sint. Provideat semper pro hospitibus aliquem librum, ex quo legere possunt aliquam particulam pro refectione ipsius anime, qua detur occasio et materia loquendi de Deo et edificacione et salute anime, quem quidem librum semper super mensam debet ponere, antequam ipsis primum ferculum amministraverit. Debet eciam hospitarius hospitum pedes lavare, vel facere lavari, dum de longa via pedestres venerint, vel alias opus fuerit, maxime si religiosi et devoti fuerint, vel tantum aquam calidam eis apponere, ut lavent [fol. 24ᵇ] .... non permiserint, providebit .... mentibus lumen de mane. Ipse .... sternere et in hyeme eciam ipsis ignem construere. Ad ipsum eciam pertinet mensalia et manutergia, lectos et cussinos et omnia necessaria et requisita pro hospitibus impetrare et conservare. Sollicitetur ut hospites suos de sero tempestive cenare faciat et similiter ad requiem eos deducat tempestive, specialiter quando sunt religiosi et devoti, nec faciliter eos permittat sine causa diu ultra octavam expectare, ut et ipse sibi ipsi vacare possit. Et ideo consuescat queque agenda cum tranquillitate, hilaritate, et maturitate sic expedite perficere, ut et ipse operi manuum cum ceteris possit insistere, ne sub pallio officii fabulacionibus ociose tempus suum perdat.

De portario XX

Unus de fratribus acceptis, per rectorem designatus, custodit portam, qui, quantum fieri poterit, probatus sit moribus, benignus et affabilis. [fol. 25ᵃ] Hic portam omni tempore .... teneat. Ergo apud portam .... nec longam moram facturus inde .... alium vice sua relinquat. Huic magnopere .... dum est, ne advenientes de foris aliquo modo contristet. Vagos et mendicos seculi nequaquam intromittat ad hospitandum, nec eciam religiosos vagos non observantes, sine socio venientes sine evidenti necessitate absque licencia rectoris inducat, sed eos maxime quorum specialis noticia non habetur. Portam anteriorem claudere debet in hyeme secundum plus vel minus, prout tenebre diem obscuraverint, in longioribus autem diebus et in estate semper hora octava, nisi legitimo impedimento aliud intervenerit. Mane autem aperiendi tempus erit in hyeme, quando clarum mane illucessit, in estate vero et in longioribus diebus circa quintam horam, nisi eciam aliud intervenerit. Temporibus meridianis, quando fratres dormiunt, manente porta tunc precipue clausa neminem sine evidenti [fol. 25ᵇ] necessitate intromittet. Feminas autem quocumque .... de causa sine speciali licencia rectoris nequaquam ingredi permittat. Ista et alia non expressa domus nostre officia possunt per rectorem unum, duo vel pluria alicui uni ydoneo committi, secundum quod noverit expedire. Officiales proinde fratres, secundum quod eis a rectore iniungitur, debent humiliter et fideliter sua officia exequi et ex caritate servire fratribus, sperantes, se maiorem tanto apud Deum mercedem habituros, quanto eorum ministerium laboriosius et humilius comprobatur. Qui ut eo melius officia sua iuxta consuetum in domo modum exsequi possint, cedulas per quas in opere suo dirigantur sibi dari et ordinari petant et procurent. Isti, si de negociis suis in aliquo dubitant, habebunt recursum ad procuratorem, cui

eciam ex caritate debent humiliter obedire. Et licet illis qui
humiliorem in domo nostra commissionem habuerint conveniat
voluntarium sacrificium [fol. 26ª] suum fratribus exhibere cum
omni humilitate, ipsos tamen fratres alios non decet inferiores
suos estimare, qui pari caritate cum eis ad communiter et
socialiter convivendum sunt assumpti. Et ideo, si aliquis eorum
opere indiguerit, non debet preceptorie exigere, sed humiliter
postulare. Nec eciam alii fratres qui non habent commissionem
de officiis eorum se debent intromittere, nisi quod si negligenciam
aliquam notaverint, possunt eos sicut alios ammonere.

De visitacione

Visum est nobis expedire pro domo nostra, ut semel in anno
advocemus presbiteros duos rectores congregacionum, qui nobis
in colloquio patrum designati fuerint, de quibus presumimus
specialem fidelitatem ad domum et statum nostrum, qui loquantur
cum rectore et fratribus nostris de hiis que concernunt pacem,
concordiam, et profectum nostrum. Cum quibus eciam capiemus
consilium, si que occurrent negocia ardua, in quibus consilio
indigemus. Quot si rector domus fortasse [fol. 26ᵇ] deponendus
sit et alter in loco eius ordinandus eorum ....
et consilio. Ad primum ergo, cum advenerint, convocent omnes
fratres simul, intimando eis causam adventus sui, quoniam
vocati in caritate venerint, parati, si quid possent pro utilitate
et profectu fratrum, habentes ammonitos fratres, ut unusquisque
libere aperiat cor suum et respondeat ad ea de quibus fuerit
requisitus, prout sibi constat. Loquantur deinde primum cum
rectore de pace sua, de statu domus et fratrum, et an sit
gravatus alicuius nimia insolencia vel rebellione, et an sit domus
gravata debitis. Consequenter loquantur cum fratribus singillatim, incipiendo a senioribus, investigantes quoniam sint in
pace in semetipsis cum rectore et cum fratribus, et an constet
eis de alicuius notabili pertinacia vel insolencia, vel de discordia
aliqua in domo, an ne res et excercicia domus excedant in nimia
laxacione vel in rigore nimio et sic de similibus. [fol. 27ª] Et
videtur expedire quod permittatur unusquisque libere dicere que
videntur ad dicendum necessaria vel utilia, nec multum res-
pondeatur unicuique super motivis suis, nisi ad plenum omnibus
auditis, et signentur motiva uniuscuiusque, que sunt alicuius
ponderis. Caveant tamen fratres, ne ex passione aliquid pro-
ponant, ne per motiva sua magis turbacionem excitent quam
profectum. Ipsi eciam patres caucius hoc discernant; alias enim
contingeret, vicia magis foveri quam deleri. Preterea omnibus
auditis iterum advocent illos qui in singulari ammonendi vel
corripiendi videntur. Post hoc omnes simul convocent faciendo
eis ammonicionem aliquam salubrem in genere de hiis que
notate sunt profectui fratrum convenire, ut post istam caritativam
visitacionem remaneat maior pax et concordia inter fratres,
maior obediencia et promptitudo uniuscuiusque ad profectum
suum. Sed ne minus quam iustum sit fratres ponderent actus
et excercicia visitacionis [fol. 27ᵇ] .... diligencius

et sollicicius custo .... per patres inserimus hic
et .... clausulam de auctoritate visitatorum inter
privilegia domini Episcopi Traiectensis domui nostre indulta,
que sequitur in hec verba: "Preterea, ut virtutes inter vos
floreant et vicia suppremantur, tenore presencium committimus
ac concedimus auctoritate nostra ordinaria visitatoribus domus
vestre presentibus et futuris plenariam potestatem, vos et domum
vestram visitandi, excessus personarum tam in capite quam in
membris corrigendi ac penitenciam salutarem pro commissis
aut ex causa legitima, quociens oportunum fuerit, iniungendi
omniaque et singula faciendi que ad officium visitacionis per-
tinerent, dinoscuntur, quorum visitatorum consilio statuta et
consuetudines statui et domui vestris deservientes condere,
illam seu illas in toto vel in parte tollere et [fol. 28ᵃ] loco
sublatorum vel sublat .... edere
sive statuere, illis que adde .... cipere.
Transgressores que consuetudin .... iuxta perpetrati
delicti exigenciam nostra auctoritate ordinaria corrigere".
Sequitur

De colloquio mensurno XXII

In principio cuiuslibet mensis, quando primum ad hoc vacare
possumus, solent fratres qui acceptati sunt, vel alias a communi
colloquio non segregati, convenire aliqua hora, quam rector
ipsis designat et colloqui de hiis que deserviunt domui et statui
nostris; pro tunc enim movet unusquisque siggillatim quod pro
utilitate domus et status nostri dignum mocione excogitavit,
specialiter si circa aliquas consuetudines domus observandas
fratres sunt negligentes, ut in hiis ammoneantur, vel si res
domus nostre neglici vel deperire videantur, ut ad hoc respectus
adhibeatur, vel si rector domus nostre minus circa exercicia
fratrum invigilat, ut puta in humiliando eos, [fol. 28ᵇ] vel
frangendo eorum voluntates, vel increpando eos de defectibus
et similia excercendo, per que proficere possent in extirpacione
viciorum, ut si quacumque causa hoc intermiserit, fiat eorum
mocione et desiderio ad hoc liberior et diligencior in hiis et
similibus movendis, servetur debita disciplina et modestia, ne
alique dissenciones insurgant, et caveat quilibet, ne in sensu suo
habundans vicium partinacie vel proprii sensus incurrat, ne
collacio, que profectui nostro deservire debuerat, in profectus
nostri detrimentum cedat. In ista collacione potest rector domus
ad motiva fratrum per se respondere secundum quod sibi videbitur, ut fiat, nisi idem secundo et tercio motum fuerit, tunc enim
debet scrutari vota fratrum, et quid faciendum videbitur eorum
agere consilio. Si eciam pro tunc aliquid de principalioribus
negociis domus motum fuerit, fiat [fol. 29ᵃ] quod maiori et
saniori parti fratrum videbitur expedire. Sequitur

De consiliis et principalioribus negociis

Quia premissum est quod rector principalia negocia domus
faciet de consilio fratrum vel maioris et sanioris partis eorum,

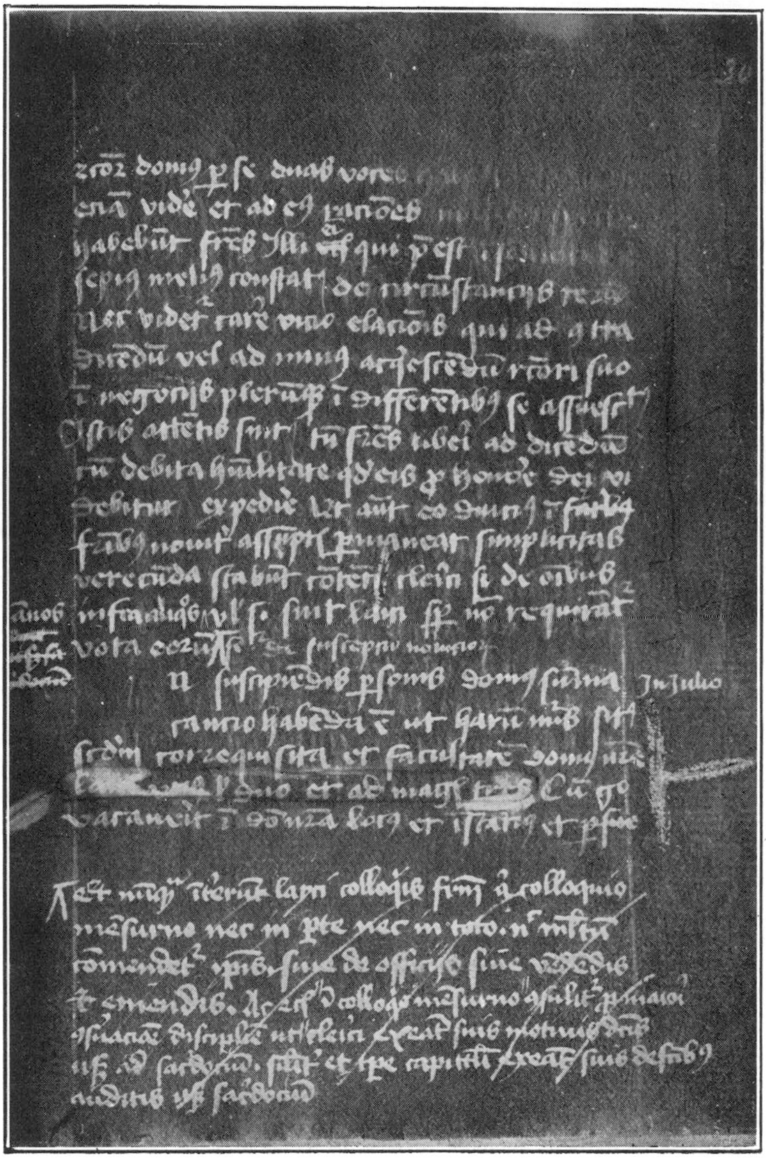

ount ergo ista que habemus pro principalibus negociis domus nostre. In primis, si rector domus nostre est apponendus vel deponendus, quod fiat per modum superius tactum. Item si aliquis acceptandus est ad manendum nobiscum in domo perpetue, vel qui acceptatus est videtur perpetue expellendus. Item si predia redditus, vel alie res immobiles emende vel vendende sunt. Item si aliquis procurator constituendus est vel constitutus deponendus. Item si aliqua res immobilis ultra valorem quatuor scudatorum alicui danda est. Item si aliquid ultra unam libram grossorum edificandum est. Item si que sunt alie cause notabilem permanentem [fol. 29ᵇ] utilitatem vel inutilitatem tangentes consimili modo fiant de consilio rectoris et fratrum, vel maioris et sanioris partis eorum. Sed ex quo sepissime incertum est et dubiosum, que causa notabilem utilitatem vel inutilitatem in se habent, cum ex parvis occasionibus aliquando magna et permanens utilitas vel inutilitas originem trahat, et unus res levius ponderat et alter gravius, ergo volumus pro maiori certitudine et utilitate hoc ponere in discrecione rectoris, ut ipse discernat de hiis rebus vel causis emergentibus et secundum suum videre de hiis loquatur vel supersedeat, ut utilitas promoveatur et inutilitas precaveatur. Consulcius eciam videtur quod non leviter per voces certatim aliquid concludamus, pocius si negocium dilacionem patitur, cum vota fratrum sibi non concordant, ad deliberacionem maturiorem differatur. Si tamen aliquo tempore necessarium fuerit per voces aliquid concludi, tunc [fol. 30ᵃ] rector domus per se duas voces habeat, ad cuius eciam videre et ad eius raciones notabilem respectum habebunt fratres. Illi enim qui preest in sollicitudine sepius melius constat de circumstanciis rerum, nec videtur carere vicio elacionis, qui ad contradicendum vel ad minus acquiescendum rectori suo in negociis plerumque in differentibus se assuescit. Istis attentis sint tamen fratres liberi ad dicendum cum debita humilitate, quod eis pro honore Dei videbitur expedire. Ut autem eo diucius in fratribus noviter assumptis permaneat simplicitas verecunda, stabunt contenti clerici, si de omnibus infra aliquos annos, vel si sint laici semper non requirantur vota eorum²⁴ et nunquam intererunt layci colloquiis fratrum aut colloquio mensurno nec in parte, nec in toto, nec multum commendetur ipsis sive de officiis sive vendendis et emendis. Ac eciam consulitur de colloquio mensurno pro maiori conservacione discipline, ut clerici exeant suis motivis dictis usque ad sacerdocium; similiter et tempore capituli exeant suis defectibus auditis usque sacerdocium²⁴. Sequitur

De suscepcio noviciorum

In suscipiendis personis domus summa caucio habenda est, ut harum numerus sit secundum correquisita et facultatem domus nostre, laici unus vel duo et ad magis tres. Cum ergo vacaverit in domo nostra locus et instancius et persue²⁵ [fol. 30ᵇ] . . . . pecierit aliquis nobiscum habitare, considerentur primo diligencius circumstancie persone, si sit virtuosus, dicibilis, competentis litterature, ad minus congruus, si sit facetus in moribus, satis fortis capitis et pectoris, an sciat et possit scribere, cuius fervoris et conversacionis in ante acta vita sua, an sit aptus ad communia exercicia domus nostre et ad hec voluntarius et promptus, an sit gravatus cura parentum suorum debilium vel pauperum. Secundo quod super omnia caveatur a symonia et turpi lucro, ne corde aut ore aut quoquomodo aliquid temporale a quocumque vel pro quocumque assumendo petatur aut exigatur, sed pure propter Deum recipiatur, sive pauper sive dives fuerit²⁶. Cum de hiis fuerimus mundi et de predictis aliis et similibus condicionibus habuerimus probabilem coniecturam, possumus eum admittere ad nostram societatem et hospicium et probare per duos menses aut tres. Si vero infra illud tempus [fol. 31ᵃ] eius conversacionem considerantes verisimiliter putaverimus eum non convenire sibi et nobis, statim remittatur ad locum suum, vel promoveatur, si in nobis est, ad locum magis sibi congruentem, quia utilius et minus confusivum tam sibi quam nobis quod recessurus ad primum recedat. Et ideo, qui difficiliter amonibilis putaretur ab hospicio, non leviter admittatur. Si vero conversacio eius placuerit fratribus, nichilominus non recipiatur ad communem vitam nostram, nisi prius per decem vel duodecim menses laudabiliter nobiscum fuerit conversatus, infra quod tempus considerent eum fratres diligenter, an propositum eius sit firmum et ad anteriora extentum probetur, an possit et velit suffere correpciones et humiliaciones, an sit promptus ad obediendum in quibuscumque vilibus et humilibus et sic de aliis bonis moribus vite nostre premissis, demum si eciam sit apertus in revelandis temptacionibus suis et per silencium quietus. Sequitur

De institucione noviciorum XXXV

Ut autem de predictis plenius innotescat [fol. 31ᵇ] ....
.... uni e fratribus boni testimonii ....
eum instruat de incessu inclinacio .... statu et omni gestu suo, quomodo debeat oculos dimissos et custoditos habere, submisse, verecunde, et non festinanter loqui et reverenciam maxime rectori exhibere. Precipue ammonebit eum frequenter, ut mores et consuetudines seculares studeat dediscere, propriam quoque voluntatem et proprium consilium propter bonum obediencie mortificare, humilia queque et viliora et quosque labores libenter amplectendo, quod ut perfectius consequi valeat, tamquam mortuus mundo et sibi ipsi; de multis rebus forensibus seu negociis domus privatim aut publice se aliquo modo intromittat. Soli Deo vivere, querens celle et quietis sue studiosus observator, ocio torpere refugiat, lectionibus sacris et oracionibus et compunctioni cordis et meditacionibus sanctis vel eciam laboribus manuum in cella seu foris, prout fuerit, sibi innittum, secundum modum vite nostre et consuetudines domus insistendo seu ea discendo. [fol. 32ᵃ] Et ut salubrius sibi .... quascumque et secreta cordis sui

.... suam sepius rectori sive magistro suo
.... debet. Nec quitquam habeat quod rectori vel
magistro .... velit esse occultum, nec debat colloquiis
aliorum aut operibus se ultro ingerere, sed omnibus honorem
deferendo, vix audeat aliquid coram aliis proferre et ad interro-
gata respondere et hoc paucis verbis fiat. Ad communes vero
conventus ubi ipsum oportet presentem existere maxime ad
officium divinum die noctuque tota alacritate et fervore spiritus
assuescat devotus et tempestive occurrere. Debet eciam magister
suus quotidianam eius conversacionem et, si quid magis vel
minus quam oportet egerit, frequenter considerare, ut eum
secrete coripiat et instruat humiliter suam culpam confiteri, ut
oportet. Diligenter proinde eum instruat modum vite nostre et
mores ad hoc deservientes tenere et negligencias cavere et pro
eis venias et penitencias, uc moris est, cum prompta humilitate
[fol. 32ᵇ] .... alicui fratri. Ymmo quicumque
frater al .... silencio aut dicendo Deo ....
humiliter et caritative caput discat inclinare cum serenitate.
Cum eciam ipse novicius vel quicumque alius frater cellam
intraverit alterius, debet, quicumque sit intrans, dicere Ihesus
et bonum punctum aliquem de materia diei et hoc diligenter
observetur et exiens petat similiter oracionem. Sequitur

De acceptacione noviciorum

Cum igitur novus aliquis ad probam susceptus, ut premissum
est, probatus inventus fuerit et desideraverit instancius ad domum
nostram et societatem acceptari, debet ad videre rectoris per
eum aut magistrum suum informari, ut ipsi rectori et singulis
fratribus singillatim in privato provolutus in genibus petat
humiliter, et graciam ei et misericordiam velit facere dando sibi
locum in hac domo nostra et quamvis non meruerit, promittens
se cum adiutorio Dei valde emendaturum. Ammonendus est
eciam talis acceptandus, ut antequam accepteter promittat²⁷
[fol. 33ª] in privato omnipotenti Deo beatissim ....
sancto Paulo apostolo et omnibus sanctis ....
continenciam carnis non quod cogere vol ....
obligari ad hoc, sed ut servetur bona consuetudo de hoc ab
inicio in domo hac servata, neminem scilicet posse per nos
acceptari ad domum istam, qui hanc continenciam, ut prefertur,
non promiserit. Et cum ista fecerit advenienti oportuno tempore,
quo fratres in unum convenerint, fiet primo inquisicio de
consensu et voluntate fratrum de huiusmodi acceptando, et ut
singuli quod noverint dicant, ipsi ea que notabilia sunt ammo-
nenda et tunc, si rectori et fratribus, vel maiori et saniori parti
eorum super hoc requisitis videatur ammiendum, debet acceptandus vocari, ut veniat in medium fratrum prostratus ad
genua. Cui cum rector dixerit: "Quid est frater, quod petis?"
Respondebit: "Postulo misericordiam Dei et vestram fraternitatem michi dari". Ad quod poterit rector dicere: "Bonum erit
forsan diucius et melius vos deliberari". Si tunc constanter
[fol. 33ᵇ] .... Tunc per rectorem

464 APPENDIX

predicetur .... et quod secundum eundem oportebit eum abne .... Domini ewangelicum se ipsum propriam voluntatem et proprium consilium in obediencia caritatis secundum voluntatem rectoris et fratrum, sine tamen voto obedire ex consilio, nec aliquid proprium more primitive ecclesie habere, in castitate et ceteris virtutibus studere vivere, et sic de aliis similibus. Fiet ei eciam tunc per rectorem talis ammonicio, que ei pro futura summa[28] emendacione possit proficere, et dicatur sibi precipue id quod fratribus tunc prius super hoc interrogatis ammonendum videatur. Demum interrogetur per rectorem, si sit liber et non servus, si de aliqua congregacione vel conventu exierit, si alicui mulieri fidem sposponderit, si aliquo voto sit obligatus et absque aliquo morbo incurabili et occulto, si sit absolutus de querelis et debitis universis, si sit legitimus, et ad omnes sacros ordines qui clericus est possit promoveri, demum si velit in hoc consentire quod [fol. 34ª] post hanc horam absque rectore .... votum emittet, si forsan quod abs .... hoc nullum sit et irritum ad videre .... Requiratur insuper, si paratus sit deinceps, ut supra dicitur, sine propriis vivere et propterea infra mensen facere recognicionem coram notario et testibus quod nichil proprietatis vel dominii habeat in domo vel in rebus domus et quod, si recesserit aut expulsus propter legitimas causas in sequenti capitulo dicendas aut iussus fuerit exire, quod non debeat repetere aliquid eorum, que ex parte eius domui provenerunt, nichil secum auferendo, vel repetendo nisi vestimenta sua quotidiana, quoniam tunc cum pace discedat. Et facere velit talem donacionem quod heredes sui non habeant ius vexandi fratres aut ipse vel quelibet persona ex parte sui post eius recessum vel obitum; propterea ergo debet per instrumentum coram notario et testibus resignare et donare donacionem, que dicitur, inter vivos omnia, que habet aut habiturus est aliquando per hereditatem testamentum [fol. 34ᵇ] .... sive per modum possibilem quemcumque .... ad hoc nos excitet consilium .... ewangelicum sed et sancta paupertas, qua nichil fratres proprii iuvet et fortificet nos secundum secundum sancti apostoli dictum manere in vocacione qua vocati sumus in hac domo nostra et instabiles nullum commodum temporalium comperiant societatem nostram devotam deserendo. Item ad videre rectoris possunt queri in acceptacione tam clerici quam layci cui vel quibus resignare intendunt sua bona et sumantur fratres assistentes in testes responsionum suorum .... liberam voluntatem resignandi bona .... voluerit propter symoniam vitandam .... gratitudinem debitam exhibere fratribus pro eo quod ad .... acceptati sint et sustentandi ab ipsis quamdiu inibi vixerint[29]. Deinde interrogetur et proponat sibi rector sequens capitulum singillatim, scilicet propter que reiciendus sit, si ad hec omnia pronus consenciat, et si sit laycus, quod ultra hec predicta contentari

...libera voluntate resistendi no[n]
...voluerit p[ro]pt[er] symonia[m] vita[n]da[m]
...lendib[us] debita exhibe[re] fr[atr]ib[us] q[ui] eo v[e]l ad
...p[er]fecti s[un]t [et] sustentati ab ip[s]is q[uan]d[a]m ...
...su[n]t p[er] modu[m] possibile q[uon]d[...]
...ad hoc nos exposet i[n] s[...]
...scire s[ed] et s[ecundu]m paup[er]tas q[ui] nich[i]l
...q[ui] a[n]i[m]et et fortifi[...] nob[is] s[ecundu]m
s[ecundu]m s[an]c[t]i ap[osto]li i[n]stitu man[er]e i[n] vocat[i]o[n]e
q[ua] vocati su[mus] i[n] hac s[e]d[e] n[ost]ra et i[n]stabiles n[on]
commoveri i[n] p[er]iculu[m] r[e]pella[n]t s[er]u[et]ate ma[n]u[m]
devot[us] p[er]s[e]v[er]ando. Dei[n]de r[...]oget et p[ro]p[ter]
sibi ur[t]o[r] sequeb[us] ex p[ar]tis fragilitatis s[ed] p[ro]pt[er] q[uo]s
remedia[n]b[us] s[i]t [si] ad hoc o[m]ia p[ro]nus co[n]se[n]tiat
Et si s[i]t laycus q[ui] ur[...] q[uod] p[er] se[ip]s[u]m r[ati]o[n]i velit q[uo]d
nu[n]q[uam] habeat voce[m] i[n] fr[atr]es q[ui] au[...]b[us] voc[et]
ut mo[r]is est. Q[uo]d si ad i[s]t[u]d alia se p[ro]pone[re] d[ie]
h[uiusmod]i a[n]i[m]ate[m] viderit se si[n]e difficultate ult[ra]
libent[er] obte[m]p[er]abu[n]t, et p[er] dei gr[ati]a[m]
et ad[i]utoriu[m] fr[atru]m gratu[it]e exequit[ur] [...]
fr[atr]es ad ge[n]u[s] p[ro]lut[...] legat[...] su[...] Vere i[n]t[...]
aut i[n] v[er]i sp[iritu] sit[...] i[n] v[er]o [...]lo. Cop[...] hoc s[...]
d[...] Cui[us] o[mn]i pat[...] de [...]oz et q[ui] mult[...] h[...]
s[er]vore p[...]sor[um] p[ro]fusione s[an]c[t]i sp[iritu]s cogita
redd[...]tu[r] ut p[ro]sse te dilige[re] et digne laude[re] val[...]

Accepta[n]t[ur] s[ecundu]m forma[m] cedule[...] h[...] p[ro]posita[m].

velit, quod numquam habeat vocem inter fratres aut alias[30] ubi vocetur, ut moris est. Quod si ad hec et alia sibi proponenda bene animatus responderit, se sine difficultate ultimo libenter obtemperaturum et per Dei graciam et adiutorium fratrum gratuite executurum et humiliter dando manum rectori si rectori placet, se miser [?] ad singulare [?][31]. Tunc fratres ad genua provoluti legant ymnum "Veni creator", aut antiphona "Veni sancte spiritus", cum versiculo "Confirma hoc Deus": "Deus, cui patet omne cor et quem nullum latet secretum, purifica per infusionem sancti spiritus cogitaciones cordis nostri, ut perfecte te diligere et digne laudare valeamus". Acceptentur secundum formam cedularem hic impositarum: [fol. 35ᵃ].

"Porrige nobis Domine Deus .... et per intercessionem sanctissime Dei genitricis .... auxilium nobis superne virtutis impende. Excita, quesumus, Domine, in nobis spiritum, cui beatissimus apostolus tuus Paulus[32] servivit, ut eodem nos replente studeamus amare quod amavit, et opere exercere quod docuit. Da, quesumus, Domine, perseverantem in tua nobis voluntatem famulatum, ut in diebus nostris populus tibi serviens et numero et merito augeatur, per Christum Dominum nostrum. Amen". Post residentibus fratribus ipsi adhuc in genibus persistenti dicat rector: "Ad honorem omnipotentis Dei, beatissime virginis Marie, sanctissimi Pauli[33], patroni nostri, et omnium sanctorum recipimus te de hospite in fratrem et membrum domus et damus tibi locum in hac domo nostra et societate devota, ac participacionem omnium bonorum nostrorum temporalium et spiritualium. In nomine patris et filii et spiritus sancti. Amen". Nunc videat sic acceptus quod pro gratitudine gracie sibi facte et nunc et semper gratus sit fratribus opere et verbo. Sequitur

Propter que videtur aliquis reiciendus

[fol. 35ᵇ] Non est dicendus prudens pastor qui pocius totum gregem infectionis periculo vult exponere, quam unam ovem morbidam a grege seperare; nec est dicendus misericors qui in tocius congregacionis detrimentum sustineri vult fratrem quantumlibet viciosum. Debemus enim, ut ait beatus Gregorius, districtionem viciis compassionem nature. Hac de causa pro pena carcereali, quam non habemus, deliberavimus inter nos, quod si aliquis frater domus nostre, quod absit, a bono proposito suo averteretur et interpesceret, quod circa emendacionem vite sue et consuetudines domus omnino negligens existeret, vel si aliquis contra rectorem et fratres rebellere et obstinacem sine notabili emenda se exhiberet, et in hoc perduraret, vel si aliquis proprietatis infidelitate societatem nostram maculare presumeret, ille secundo ac tercio a rectore in presencia fratrum ammoneri et corripi seriose deberet, et si nullam emendacionem efficacem promitteret, a societate nostra per rectorem et fratres reiciendus [fol. 36ᵃ] esset. Si vero aliquis, quod absit, in lapsum carnis incideret, vel si conatus ad hoc perpetrandum exquireret, vel alia manifesta et scandalosa malefacta perpetraret, ex quibus totam congregacionem nostram confusionem et derogacionem notabilem sustinere contingeret, vel si personalibus debitis vel fideiussionibus se et domum nostram sine scitu et consensu rectoris et fratrum gravaret, maxime non habens officium, vel si societatem deserens nostram ad alia loca se transferret, ille statim omne ius, quod in domo et societate nostra habuisset, amitteret. Sequitur

De caritate XXVIII

Licet cum omnibus hominibus, quantum in nobis est, pacem et caritatem servare teneamur, precipue tamen ad invicem inter nos studebimus, habere cor unum et animam unam, unum velle et unum nolle in bono. Et ergo ut pax, caritas, et concordia inter nos inviolate permaneant, nitemur ad illa, per que servari et nutriri possit [fol. 36ᵇ] concordia caritatis, studebimus honore invicem prevenire, alter alterius onora portare, cum gaudentibus gaudere et cum flentibus flere, infirmitates aliorum, tam morum quam corporum, pacienter ferre, vitabimus mutuas offensas, derisiones, detractiones, et pertinaces contradictiones. In quibus, si aliquis alium offenderit, debet humiliter indulgenciam postulare. Sola enim humilitas, ut ait Bernardus, est reparacio lese caritatis. Expedit eciam vitare singulares continuas familiaritates vel personarum accepciones, que interdum suspicione carnalis affectionis non carent, sed vigeat et servetur inter nos una communis caritas, que persuadet aliquando hiis qui nobis aliquo modo contrarii putantur, se magis affabilem et obsequiosum exhibere.

[De humilitate XXIX]

De humilitate dicit Bernardus: "Hec est via et non est alia preter eam. Qui aliter vadit, cadit pocius quam ascendit, [fol. 37ᵃ] quia sola humilitas est que exaltat, sola que ducit ad vitam". Quia igitur humiliacio via est ad humilitatem, sicut lectio ad scienciam, idcirco proposuimus humilem ducere vitam in habitu, in gestibus, in moribus, in edificiis, in suppellectili domus nostre, ut, licet habeamus illa ut decent et conveniunt, absit tamen curiositas atque venustas. Eligant semper fratres, quantum in ipsis est, humiliorem statum tamquam tuciorem, scientes quod non in altitudine status, sed in puritate mentis acquiritur regnum Dei. Non solum autem in statu, sed eciam in quibuslibet aliis, videlicet in cameris, in utensilibus, in officiis, eligat et requirat unusquisque quod vilius et humilius est, ut sic per humiliacionem corporis introducatur humilitas cordis. Consuevimus eciam pro humiliacione habere aliqua excercicia humilitatis, videlicet per vices quisque debet lavare vasa coquine, ut moris est, et cetera. Item petere veniam, cum nostra negligencia aliquid fuerit destructum, [fol. 37ᵃ] vel amissum, quod excedit valorem quartali de .... stufero, vel cum negligentes fuerimus in observancia alicuius bone consuetudinis, que sub pena alicuius venie nobis fuerit imposita, vel commissa, ut eciam postea in fine libri patebit.

[De obediencia XXX]

Ne vero illius virtutis merito et premio fraudari nos contingat, cuius in se formam fidelibus Unigenitus Dei exhibuit, qui factus est obediens usque ad mortem et dixit: "Non veni facere voluntatem meam, sed eius qui misit me"; idcirco proponimus iura obediencie sollicite observare, in primis Dei preceptis et ecclesie nec non prelatorum nostrorum ac eciam sacris canonibus pro posse et nosse humiliter obedire. Insuper presbiteri nostri qui patrisfamilias loco regimen domus habet commissum monitis et consilliis voluntarie acquiescere, iuxta consilium beati Petri: "Castificantes corda nostra in obediencia caritatis", de cuius consilio convenit unumquemque nostrum in ordinacione vite sue pendere, eius ammoniciones libenter audire, [fol. 38a] eius correpciones paciencer sufferre. Ei nec parvum nec magnum quod inter nos geritur debemus velle esse occultum. Ad eum in temptacionibus, perplexitatibus, et adversatitibus[34] nostris continuum debemus habere recursum. Et licet nichil speciale occurrat, quater tamen in anno habet quilibet fratrum cum rectore singulare colloquium de passionibus anime sue, petendo ab eo, ut liber sit ad corripiendum vel eciam exercitandum eum, prout notaverit sibi pro profectu suo spirituali expedire. Sequitur

De communi vita et paupertate XXXI

Quoniam dicit Augustinus quod inter familiares amicos debet esse communitas eventuum, non enim debet esse dispar eventus, quorum est compar affectus, nec diversa fortuna, quorum una est anima; idcirco pro exhibicione et conservacione mutue caritatis, nec non pro exoneracione quotidiane sollicitudinis, simul eciam pro adimplecione illius consilii ewangelici de abrenunciandis omnibus que [fol. 38b] possidemus, ad honorem Dei proposuimus in domo nostra abdicare omnem proprietatem, ita quod nullus nostrum proprium aliquid possideat, sed sint nobis omnia communia. Sit communis bursa, sit communis archa, sit mensa et provisio communis, nisi quod provideatur unicuique, prout cuique opus existit. Quod autem communis vita extra religionem non solum licita, sed eciam meritoria et expediens sit proficere volentibus in via Dei, de hoc habemus scripta sufficiencia diversorum doctorum, qui hoc probant per iura, per raciones, per autoritates sanctorum, maxime cum presbiteri et clerici secundum iura deberent vivere in communi, intendimus igitur ex hoc et deinceps libera et plena voluntate hoc observare et temporalia in commune proferre, contenti de provisione nobis facienda, nec murmurare, si non habuerimus omnia nostra comoda[35], ut non simus de illis pauperibus de quibus tangit Bernardus: "Sunt aliqui qui volunt esse pauperes; eo tamen pacto, ut nichil eis desit; et sic diligunt paupertatem, [fol. 39a] ut nullam inopiam paciantur". Cavere eciam debemus, ne illis rebus quorum nobis usus est concessum, pertinaci affectu alligati simus; sed ita studebimus ab amore rei familiaris affectum nostrum suspendere, ut si aliquis a rectore missus fuerit mutare cameram suam, statim prompte hoc faciat, nichil secum exportando, nisi que ab eo sibi fuerint designata. Ob hanc eciam causam rector domus consuevit semel in anno, videlicet in capite ieiunii, circuire cameras fratrum et videre que et qualia habeamus in libris, utensilibus, et aliis quibuscumque, que omnia producemus coram eo, ut, si sibi placuerit aliqua tollere, tollat et que placuerit relinquere, relinquat. Nemo habebit clausuram in qua res ponuntur, exceptis rectore et procuratore et forte librario, si expedit et rectori nichil abscondatur. Et si quid datur vel offertur alicui a parentibus aut aliis caris quibuscumque, scilicet vestis species vel quodcumque aliud, primo rectori offeratur in cuius potestate sit ipsi reddere vel non [fol. 39ᵇ] .... vel eciam alteri dare. Item nullus fratrum qui non habuerit ex officio permittet aliquas pecunias pernoctare apud se in camera sua, sed si ad manus alicuius venerint, deferat ad illum cui ex officio incumbit levare easdem. Preterea quia fragilitas et miseria nostra videtur exigere competentem provisionem victualium et aliorum necessariorum, ne tamen nos vel posteri nostri mensuram sufficiencie excedant et tot redditus sibi accumulent, ut non necesse habeant manuum suarum adiumento victum querere et ab hoc ociositatis et vagacitatis pericula contingat incidere, idcirco proponimus firmiter quod nobis et posteris nostris, quod in annuis perpetuis redditibus summam centum nobilium pro personis domus nostre nequaquam volumus excedere. Sed si contingat post hoc aliqua bona ad nos devolvi, possumus unam terciam partem de hiis ad librariam nostram deputare, cetera pauperibus volumus erogare. Quod si propter frequenciam hospitum, vel eciam propter casum alicuius infortunii contingat, nos debitis notabilibus pregravari, [fol. 40ᵃ] vel eciam defectum pateremur in congrua necessaria structura aliqua, si quid tunc de bonis ad nos devolvendis in illos usus deputandum est, fiat cum bono moderamine pauperes Christi non tamen obliviscendo in parte saltim alique bona. Sequitur

De castitate XXXII

Ut perpetuam continenciam, que a nobis exigatur, semper inviolatam custodiamus, et ne umquam sinistra de aliquo nostrum suspicio oriatur, pro custodia castitatis volumus, ut sicut hactenus sic et semper omnem mulierem de domo nostra arceamus et eas ad nos intrare non sinamus; sed si cum aliqua loquendum est, ante portam fiat cum licencia rectoris, vel si alias aliqua femina nos allocuta fuerit, caveamus, ne intente aliquam inspiciamus, vel nimis blande in colloquiis cum ipsis non habeamus sed quanto brevius nos expediamus. Nam iuxta verbum beati Augustini, "cum mulieribus brevis sermo et rigidus habendus est". Quot si fratrem aliquem existentem extra domum aliqua femina alloquatur, cum paucis verbis satisfaciat alloquenti, et postea accedat ad rectorem et dicat ei, quod illa talis eum allocuta fuit, et si requisierit rector, quid cum eo tractaverit, dicat ei [fol. 40ᵇ] nichil ex proposito occultando. Si vero tale

sit negocium, quod solum respiciat officium alicuius fratris, tunc
sufficit eidem referre. Rectore vero absente, vicem eius in hac
parte tenebit procurator vel senior presbiter domus nostre.
Ante portam loquentes cum aliqua non sedeant, sed stantes
loquantur, excepto cum matre vel sorore, nisi de hoc speciale
licenciam tunc habeant, quando causa necessaria sive digna
requirit, et semper brevitati studeant. Pro maiori eciam cautela
proposuimus et volumus quod nemo ....
scolares sive iuvenes visitantes seu non visi ....
plures apud se clausis ianuis³⁶.

De sobrietate XXXIII

Qui castus esse desiderat studeat sobrietati. Caveamus ergo,
ne metas sobrietatis excedamus et voluptatibus gule inserviamus,
sed magis, quantum valitudo permittit, corpus nostrum discrete
castigemus et in servitutem redigamus, et ideo a vino et
assaturis, necnon exquisitis et sumptuosis condimentis ciborum
abstineamus. In aliquibus tamen summis festivitatibus et
tempore minucionis, vel quando nobis ob graciam aliquam
propinatur vinum, possumus habere et assaturos; pro hospitibus
providebimus eadem que pro fratribus, quia ex hoc magis
edificantur; quod si utile videatur alia providere, fiat de scitu
rectoris servata debita simplicitate, que nos decet. Circa festa
communicabilia volumus nos per aliquam ab- [fol. 41ᵃ] stinen-
ciam preparare, ita quod non commedamus carnes ad minus
per tres dies, nisi forte festum Epiphanie, vel Marie Magdalene
in quarta feria venerit, ut tunc propter dominicam diem carnes
commedamus, vel eciam circa festum Visitacionis fuerit nobis
concessum commedere carnes in die apostolorum propter festum.
Aut quod rector eciam aliter circa talia festa cum esu carnium
pie dispensaverit. Item preter vigiliam diei communicabilis adhuc una die illius tridui erimus sine cena, nisi propter aliquam
racionabilem causam fuerit nobis concessa cena de licencia
rectoris. Item circa festum Penthecostes a feria secunda usque
diem sanctum erimus sine carnibus. Item circa festum Assumpcionis et Omnium Sanctorum abstinebimus a carnibus per
quatuor dies et post dominicam quinquagesime abstinebimus a
carnibus. Item in quatuor temporibus et vigiliis sanctorum et
in profestis beate Virginis non commedemus butirum exceptis
profestis purificacionis et visitacionis eiusdem³⁷. Item in adventu
Domini non commedemus carnes et ieiunabimus sine cena tribus
diebus in septimana. Item in feria sexta non soluamus ieiunium,
nisi moveat causa satis digna, ut loco specierum aliquid
gustemus [fol. 41ᵇ] de licencia rectoris. Preterea quoniam a
medio virtutis facile contingit deviare, si fuerit aliquis frater
sibi nimis rigidus et inpercipiendis alimentis singulariter parcus,
ille debet ab eo qui considerat ammoneri; et si se non correxerit,
debet rectori intimari ut ipse habeat eum ammonitum, ne se
destruat et ad spiritualia et corporalia exercicia se impotentem
efficiat. Sequitur

De silencio [XXXIV]

Silencium ab inutilibus et ociosis sermonibus et maxime a rumoribus seculi detractione et derisione ubique et semper servare nos convenit. Quod si de secularibus rebus aliquid refertur vel auditur, ad pietatem studeamus referre, sed non in talibus ociose tempus expendere. Ceterum aliquibus temporibus et locis eciam ab utilibus sermonibus temperare proposuimus, videlicet de vespere post octavam horam usque ad sextam horam de mane. Omni tempore fratres silencium teneant apud ignem, similiter in loco et tempore rasure, quod si necessario aliquid dicendum fuerit, pauci et submissa voce fiat. Eciam ante et post commede[n]tes in refectorio vitabunt summe confabulaciones. In refectorio similiter vitabimus quocumque tempore [fol. 42ª] colloquia non necessaria. Item precipue in coquina vitabimus colloquia, quam eciam non intremus sine licencia rectoris, procuratoris vel coci, si alter eorum fuerit presens. Ut eciam Domino Deo devociores occurramus et conceptam devocionem diucius conservare valeamus, erit silencium servandum a tempore, quo pulsatur eundum ad ecclesiam, usque dum post divina quisque redierit ad cameram suam, et maxime ne ad ecclesiam euntes vel inde revertentes in via quitquam sine magna necessitate loquamur, cum gravitate et maturitate incendentes de bona et laudabili consuetudine. Similiter servamus silencium, quando pulsatum est ad refectionem, et cavebimus sumopere in via ad mensam aliquid loqui et precipue apud lavatorium, dum fratres abluant manus. Dum eciam fratres in pistrino convocati panes coagulant, ut silencium melius servetur, solemus legere vigilias, septem psalmos et horas de Domina prout occurrit, ubi servabitur talis ordo in prelegendo vel alias, ut in choro per ebdomadarium vel in horis de Domina fieri consuetum est. Postremo servabimus similiter silencium in tempore et loco quo locio pedum et cetera. [fol. 42ᵇ]

[De oracione XXXV]

Debemus semper ad manum habere tutissimum oracionis refugium, et non solum pro nostris, sed eciam pro aliorum necessitatibus devotas preces effundere. Et ideo, quando desideratur a nobis, ut oremus pro aliqua causa pia, puta pro aliquo defuncto, vel infirmo, vel temptato, vel pro aliqua alia causa instante vel urgente, tunc non debemus hoc negligenter permittere excidere a memoria, nec eciam profunctorie et superficialiter perficere, sed diligenter, instanter, cordialiter et efficaciter pro posse nostro succurrere apud Deum precibus nostris hiis, qui tribulato sunt corde, attendentes necessitudinem illius, qui gravatus est, et quomodo nos vellemus nobis fieri in consimili angustia constitutis. Item quando aliquis fratrum nostrorum tam infirmatur, quod non possit visitare ecclesiam, tunc quotidie in horis de Domina tam ad matutunas[38] quam ad vesperas legemus pro eo collectam "Deus infirmitatis humane", et cetera. Item tempore communionis et sacre inunctionis alicuius infirmi fratris nostri debent adesse cum devocione omnes fratres, nisi fuerit tempore pestilenciali. Et post inunctionem huiusmodi legent fratres pro infirmo cotidie septem psalmos. [fol. 43ª] Sed si diu duraverit infirmitas sine certa spe convalescencie, possunt una die legere psalmos, alia die letanias. Et dum aliquis fratrum fuerit in agone constitutus, nisi utsupra tempore pestilenciali, ubicumque tunc fratres fuerint, dum tabula percussa fuerit, sine mora debent omnes simul convenire legentes in via "Credo in Deum" et manebunt iuxta infirmum, donec spiritum ex[h]alaverit, dicendo interim septem psalmos cum letaniis, et si longa fuerit mora obitus sui, psalterium sine gloria. Et post obitum legemus statim commedacionis, ut in libro commedacionis habetur, item per octavam legemus pariter vigilias novem lectionum et ulterius usque ad triginta dies ab obitu quotidie vigias³⁹ trium lectionum et per annum quotidie tam ad vesperas quam ad matitunas³⁸ de Domina collectam pro defuncto fratre. Statim post obitum, quando primo poterit ad hoc vacari, recipiet quilibet fratrum ex pietate disciplinam a rectore pro defuncto fratre. Item de ordinacione rectoris cicius, quo fieri poterit, legatur psalterium et terminetur sive in choro sive in privato, [fol. 43ᵇ] ut ipsi videbitur. Et dicent (compleant) singuli presbiteri nostri simul unum tricenarium, quo primum poterint, pro defuncto fratre. Item in primo anniversario fratris nostri defuncti legemus vigilias IX lectionum et in sequentibus anniversariis eorum trium lectionum. Item in obitu alicuius parentum nostrorum legemus vigilias IX lectionum et per octavam trium lectionum et presbiteri compleant simul tricenarium missarum et in primo anniversario parentum nostrorum vigilias trium lectionum. Item pro laycis nostris in infirmitate et eciam in obitu eorum faciemus tantum sicut pro parentibus fratrum nostrorum⁴⁰. Item pro fratribus nostris in Delf et in Gouda⁴¹ defunctis legemus vigilias trium lectionum et per octavam trium lectionum et complebunt sacerdotes nostri simul tricenarium. Item pro fratribus et sororibus congregacionum nostrarum legemus semel vigilias; item pro familiaribus et benefactoribus et pro devotis aliorum locorum faciemus sicut videbitur ei qui habet curam domus.

[De cummunione XXXVI]

Circa festa communicabilia volumus nos preparare per abstinenciam, ut premissum est. Item ordinabimus, prout melius possumus, ut ante maiora festa communicabilia per diem vel duos simus quieti a notabilibus occupacionibus sive distractio- [fol. 44ª] nibus, que convenienter differi possunt. Et sunt hec consueta festa communionis fratrum: Festum Pasche, Ascensionis, Penthecostes, Sacramenti, Visitacionis Marie, Marie Magdalene, Assumpcionis Marie, Dedicacionis ecclesie nostre, sive Nativitatis Marie, Michaelis, Omnium Sanctorum, Katherine, Concepcionis Marie, Nativitatis Christi, Epiphanie, Conversionis sancti Pauli, Agnetis vel Purificacionis Marie, Petri ad cathedram, si venerit in ieiunio, si non venerit in ieiunio, tunc prima

472 APPENDIX

dominica in quadragesima, et deinceps singulis dominicis usque Pascha, computando inter eos Annunciacionem Dominicam et alias, cum apparuerit rectori domus pro temporis congruitate expedire. In quibus festis nemo nostrum omittat communionem sine scitu et licencia rectoris. Item circa ista festa, vel ad longius circa mensem, persuadebimus clericis et aliis hominibus bone voluntatis, qui consueverunt ad nos venire pro consiliis, quo'd faciant confessionem; et qui ydonei sunt, preparent [fol. 44ᵇ] se ad communionem, maxime in summis festis.

[De ambulantibus XXXVII]

Fons et origo omnium malorum sunt inutiles discursus. Idcirco proposuimus difficiles esse ad reisas excepta causa magna necessitatis vel utilitatis. Non permittantur fratres assumere reisas extra oppidum et super omnia iuniores et precipue ad amicos et cognatos, quia ex talibus frequenter spiritualis profectus tam interioris propositi quam devotorum morum accipit detrimentum. Quod tamen cum necesse fuerit, detur illi socius vie ydoneus et spiritualis, et quocumque pro negociis fuerint vel transierint, nitantur pariter ambulare et omnia negocia mutuo revelare. Summe autem caveamus, ne foris existentes inedificatorie et seculari modo nos habeamus, ne cibum vel potum exquisitum requiramus, ne hincinde diversa, que ad negocium nostrum non spectant, circumlustremus, ne oculis, auribus et lingue frena laxemus, ut non effusi vani, vacui et consciencia gravati et ob hoc minus festivi ad domum redeamus. Item semper, quando vacat nobis [fol. 45ᵃ] hospicium apud devotos vel religiosos, ad eos accedamus. Extra eciam hospicium non commedemus sive quoquam, ubi necesse non fuerit, ire debemus sine licencia patris sive rectoris loci. Consuetudines domus nostre in horis legendis et materiam diei et edificativos mores observare, prout possumus, debemus tam in hospiciis quam in plateis et viis. Nec cuiusquam fratris imperfectionem domus nostre extra domum devotis vel secularibus recitabimus. Similiter si in reisa fratres vel foris existentes aliquorum devotorum vel secularium perceperint aut notaverint defectus, cum domum redierint, fratribus domus nostre non enarrabunt; et reverti festinabunt attendentes illud ex vitis patrum: "Sicut piscis ex aqua eductus statim moritur, ita monachus perit, si foras cellam suam tardare voluerit". Postquam vero domum redierint, racionem reddent negociorum peractorum rectori vel procuratori in eius absencia, resignantes bursam cum pecuniis, que superfuerunt. Et solent post hoc rectori confiteri omnia peccata in reisa [fol. 45ᵇ] perpetrata non obstante quod habita licencia in remotis ydoneo sacerdoti eo confessi sint, nisi ipse rector contentus esse velit de confessione foris facta. Fratres, qui in via diriguntur, secundum doctrinam sancti Epictici benedictionem spiritualis patris requirant flexis genibus ante eum, que talis est: "Benedictio Dei patris et Filii et Spiritus Sancti descendat super vos et maneat semper. Amen". Et illud Thobie: "Sit Dominus in itinere

vestro et angelus Domini bonus comitetur vobiscum. Amen".
Dolent eciam **fratres** per totum tempus reise pro in itinere
existentibus bis in die orare, ut moris est, legendo collacionem:
"Adesto Domine supplicacionibus nostris'. Sine magna necessitate non debent fratres reisas facere in festivis diebus, et
monentur a foris revertens rumores seculi, ubi audierunt,
dimittere et fratribus domi non recitare. In arbitrio eciam
rectoris stabit, coquum vel aliquem alium solum emittere sine
socio. Preterea visitaciones et negocia ad domos opidi, sive
sint nobis alieni sive cognati vel noti, vitabimus, prout salvis
salvandis possumus, ne multum simus molesti rectori domus super
huiusmodi licencia. [fol. 46ᵃ]. Et si in heremo cum patribus
non sumus, faciamus nobis ipsis in nostro habitaculo cum beato
Ambrosio, celesti doctore, heremum. Et ubi necessitas vel
utilitas exegerit, cum licencia exire debemus caute et sancte in
moribus nos custodientes. Dissolutus enim exitus est frequenter
ab intencione animi concepta peremptorius et mortalis secundum
Theodorum collacione octava. Ceterum nemo exibit sine speciali
licencia rectoris et socio sibi ab ipso deputato preter coquum et
alium ad negocia deputatum et nominetur locus, quo eundum
sit, et tota causa et nullibi aliorsum transeatur, quod postea
rectori non dicatur. Item quando mittimur pro negociis in
opidum, debemus expedite facere facta nostra et redire non
circumspiciendo hincinde in platea, vel inspiciendo domos et
salutando matronas. Item in opido missi non commedemus
parum vel multum in domibus, ad quas venimus sine licencia
eius, qui preest, nec potabimus ultra semel. Quod si sine
offensa amicorum nostrorum non possemus [fol. 46ᵇ] hoc pro
tempore observare, tunc postea debemus super hoc a rectore
licenciam postulare. Item exire in plateam vel stare in porta
ad plateam non debemus, exceptis quibus hoc ex officio in-
dulgetur causa necessitatis. Ceterum cavenda est fratribus
decepcio dyabolica, qua quidam mundum relinquentes iterum
sub specie bona revertuntur corde in Egyptum, occasionem
frequentis exitus ad domos vel parentum vel consanguineorum
sibi facientes, curam domus parentum ex proprio consilio
assumendo, gaudentes et dolentes cum eis in mundanis, non-
numquam ut veri mundani. Isti sunt similes litori salsi maris
a fructu alieni, quia cor eorum et tota conversacio alienantur
a vero proposito sui profectus et mundo conformantur. Amen.
[fol. 47ᵃ]
Qui tarde venerit ad legendum "Benedicite" ad mensam,
faciat veniam suam ibidem, postquam lectum est, osculando
terram. Qui venerit ad matutinas et ad omnes alias horas,
postquam inceptum fuerit, faciat ibidem veniam osculando terram. Et qui venerit ad matutinas post "Venite" et ad minores
horas post ympnum et ad vesperas et completorium post primum
psalmum, faciet ibidem veniam osculando terram, et post
"Benedicite" in refectorio eciam petens veniam dicat culpam
suam osculando similiter terram. Qui ex toto non venerit ad
aliquam horarum, nisi licencia habuerit, petens veniam dicet

culpam suam post lectum "Benedicite". Qui correptus vel
ammonitus se excusaverit, infra "Benedicite" iacebit pronus in
terra super genua et cubitos confitendo culpam eciam addendo
quociens hoc fecerit. Qui dormierit apud candelam, petet
veniam cum candela, postquam "Benedicite" fuerit lectum,
sedendo in genibus, donec iubeatur surgere per rectorem, si
presens est. Si vero rector non affuerit, cum lector lectionem
inchoaverit, surgat. Qui annichilaverit ultra valorem oert-
kini[?], similiter faciet tenendo partem rei annichilate, si
commodo potest. Qui fratrem verbo vel facto offenderit, petet
veniam, ipso die coram eo flexis genibus et eciam coram hiis,
quibus presentibus hoc fecit [fol. 47ᵇ] vel partem anfore ad
hoc ibidem reservate. Qui correptus fuerit a rectore in presencia
fratrum, statim genua flectet, donec iubeatur surgere, osculando
terram. Qui non paraverit lectum ante octavam horam,
osculabitur terram post "Benedicite". Qui infra quindenam non
merit pro defectibus, petet veniam in collacione, postquam
lectus est punctus. Qui notabiliter male cantaverit, vel alias
confusiones fecerit in ridendo vel similibus precipue in
ecclesia, petet veniam post "Benedicite", confitendo culpam.
Qui post ammonicionem statim defectum non emendaverit,
scilicet ammonitus tenere silencium vel simile quid, petet veniam
super genua et cubitos confitendo eciam culpam suam. Qui
inobediens fuerit officiantibus in causis sibi attinentibus, petet
veniam confitendo culpam post "Benedicite". Qui sine causa
et licencia prehabita subtraxerit se a laboribus communibus,
vel nimis tarde advenerit, petet eciam veniam post "Benedicite",
confitendo culpam. Qui cum alio litigaverit vel excesserit in
verbis duris, petet veniam confitendo culpam et commedet
super terram et hoc faciet cum scitu rectoris. Qui tempus suum
male expenderit sive laboris sive aliud, dicet culpam suam post
"Benedicite", subinferendo quomodo et quantum temporis expenderit. [fol. 48ᵃ] Qui inobediens fuerit rectori, vel qui se ei
pertinater[42] opposuerit, petet veniam confitendo culpam et
osculando fratrum pedes commedet super terram. Qui non
officians sine licencia rectoris vel, si ille non affuerit, procuratoris, exierit domum, faciet similiter, ut predictum est. Qui ex
negligencia habuerit scolares sive iuvenes apud se clausis ianuis,
unum aut plures, dicet culpam suam postquam "Benedicite"
est lectum. Qui sepius in hoc excesserit aut longas moras sic
cum ipsis fecerit, huius penitencia stabit ad arbitrium rectoris[43].
Qui in aliis notabilibus et scandulosis casibus excesserit, huius
penitencia pendet eciam ad arbitrium rectoris. Has penitencias
et eis similes non facient fratres in festis communionis sed
proximo sequentibus, nisi alicui rector aliter innuerit. Qui
eciam in predictis et similibus veniis confitetur suam culpam,
tam alta voce dicet dicenda, ut ab omnibus possit faciliter
audiri cum humilitate cordis et magno proposito se emendandi.
Amen.

NOTES TO APPENDIX C

1. Corpus Juris Canonici, Decretalium Greg. IX, Lib. III, tit. 1, cap. 9.
2. For Membra.
3. The last seven words were struck out later.
4. The last two words were struck out later.
5. This sentence was struck out later.
6. On the margin was added: Item festivis diebus consuevimus eciam omnes audire primam missam.
7. II Thessalonians III, 8.
8. The word duabus was written later above the word tribus.
9. September 14.
10. This whole sentence was inserted. written on the lower margin, but later struck out.
11. Should read: Bonus, nisi correptus fuerit, perit.
12. Matthew XVIII, 15.
13. The last ten words were inserted, written on the left margin, but the last six words were struck out later.
14. The last fifteen words were struck out later.
15. Vel quattuor was struck out later.
16. The last twelve words were struck out later.
17. Ad femoralia was struck out later.
18. The last two words were struck out later.
19. The last eight words were struck out later.
20. For prompta.
21. For competentem.
22. For candelabra.
23. This sentence was inserted, written on the lower margin, but struck out later.
24. Et nunquam .... usque sacerdocium was added on the lower margin, and struck out later.
25. These two syllables were struck out later.
26. The last five words were inserted on the right margin.
27. There is a note on the lower margin which reads: Item de acceptacione laicorum quere in fine libri infra.
28. The word summa was written on the margin.

475

29. Item ad videre .... devotam deserendo was added on the lower margin of fol. 34ª and the upper margin of fol. 34ᵇ.

30. For alios.

31. The last twelve words were added on the right margin.

32. Apostolus tuus Paulus was changed later into: tuus levita Laurencius.

33. Pauli was changed later into Iheronimi. The house appears therefore to have been dedicated originally to the Apostle Paul. All other sources are silent on this point, merely stating that Jerome was the patron. This passage gives additional evidence that here we have to do with the original constitution of the house at Deventer.

34. For adversitatibus.

35. For commoda.

36. This sentence was added on the upper margin and struck out later.

37. This whole sentence was underlined.

38. For matutinas.

39. For vigilias.

40. This sentence was added on the upper margin.

41. The last three words were added later, inserted above Delf.

42. For pertinaciter.

43. The last two lines were added at the bottom of the page.

BIBLIOGRAPHY

I. UNPUBLISHED SOURCES

The Hague

Koninklijke Bibliotheek (Royal Library)

Ms. no. 70 H. 75. Copia literarum nostrarum de redditibus nostris, sive diplomatarium sive codex traditionum, privilegiorum, aliorumque documentorum fratribus domus Florentii in Daventria concessorum.

Ms. no. 70 H. 78. Scripta doctorum de congregacionibus. On fol. 1ᵃ-33ᵃ: G. Zerbolt of Zutphen, Super modo vivendi devotorum hominum simul commorancium.

Ms. no. 70 H 79. Consuetudines domus nostre. 1564. Rules followed in a brethren-house, belonging to a vicar at Deventer. They do not form a real constitution, however, but were adopted for the vicar's personal needs.

Ms. no. 73 G. 22. The original constitution of the brethrenhouse at Deventer. It was written between 1413 and 1419. A few additions were made afterwards.

Ms. no. 75. G. 58. On fol. 1ᵃ-21ᵃ: Gabriel Byell (Biel), Tractatus de communi vita clericorum.

Ms. no. 78 D. 32. Privilegia et statuta capituli generali Windesemensis.

Ms. 78 I. 55. Epistolae Gerardi Magni (on fol. 112ᶜ-262ᵃ).

Ms. 133 C. 2. Decreta (ordinationes) capitulorum generalium congregationis Windeshemensis 1395-1795 (on fol. 8ᵃ-184ᵃ).

Deventer

Athenaem — bibliotheek

Ms. no. 61 (formerly no. 1718). Fl. Radewijns, Omnes inquit artes (on fol. 1ᵃ-84ᵃ).

Ms. no. 101 G. 13. Frensweger handschrift.

Zwolle

Provincial Archives

Cartularium of the "House of Florentius" and the "House of Poor Clerks" at Deventer. A recent acquisition, not mentioned in the catalogues.

478   BIBLIOGRAPHY

Bibliotheek der vereeniging tot Overijsselsch Regt
en Geschiedenis

Ms. no. 147. Liber monasterii Nemoris Beate Marie virginis
prope Northorn (Frenswegen). On fol. 126ᵇ-127ᵇ: G.
Groote, Cautele confessorum circa magnos peccatores
adhibendi.

Utrecht

University Library

Ms. no. 1585. G. Groote, Sermo de nativitate Domini (on fol.
108ᵃ-132ᵇ).

Arnhem

Provincial Archives

Chronicle of the brethren-house at Doesburg.

Brussels

Bibliothèque Royale des Ducs de Bourgogne (Royal Library)

Ms. no. 8849-8859. On fol. 79ᵇ-81ᵇ: De magistro Everardo
de Eza.

Liège

University Library

Ms. no. 229 (366). Incipit tractatus magistri Gerardi in divinitate super septem verba dicta a Domino Ihesu Christo
pendente in cruce (on fol. 258ᵃ-268ᶜ).

Münster

Library of the Verein für Geschichte und
Altertumskunde Westfalens

Ms. no. 103. Chronica monasterii Nemoris Beate Marie Virginis
vulgo Frenswegen prope civitatem Nordhornensem, by
Ioannis ab Horstmaria.

Cologne

Stadtbibliothek, or rather: Stadtarchiv

(The archives of the city are in the library building)

Ms. no. G. B. 4⁰. 249. Tractatus magistri Gerardi dicti Groet de Daventria de quatuor generibus meditabilium sive contemplacionum (fol. 1ᵃ-13ᵃ). This is the work which is known as the Sermo de nativitate Domini.

Nuremberg

Stadtbibliothek (City Library)

Ms. Cent. II, No. 10. G. Zerbolt of Zutphen, De libris teutonicalibus, or An liceat libros divinos transferre in vulgare (on fol. 335ᵃ-341⁹).

Lübeck

Stadtbibliothek

Ms. theol. germ., no. 15. Manynghe de dar theen to bynnenwendighen dinghen (on fol. 156-242).

Ms. theol. germ., no. 43. Vormanynge de dar theyn to bynnenwendighen dinghen.

Ms. theol. germ., no. 54. Wo men sick hebben schal vor der missen (on fol. 36ᵃ-58ᵇ).

Paris

Bibliothèque Nationale

Mss. latins, no. 14662. J. Mombaer, Venatorium sanctorum ordinis canonici.

Nouv. acq. latines, no. 1250, fol. 59ᵇ-63ᵃ: Epistola magistri Gerardi Groot (Magni) ad quemdam sibi dilecto in Christo multipliciter temptatum. Fol. 63ᵃ-65ᵃ: Epistola eiusdem ad quemdam qui preest monialibus contra detractionem.

II. PRINTED SOURCES

Acquoy, J. G. R., Het klooster te Windesheim en zijn invloed, 3 vols., Utrecht 1875-1880.

Allen P. S., Opus Epistolarum Desiderii Erasmi Roterodami, vol. I, Oxford 1906.

............The age of Erasmus, Oxford 1914.

Amort, E., Deductio critica qua juxta saniores criticae leges moraliter certum redditur ven. Thomam Kempensem librorum de imitatione christi authorem esse, Augsburg 1761.

Anrich, G., Martin Bucer, Strasbourg 1914.

Auger, A., Étude sur les mystiques des Pays-Bas au Moyen-Age, in: Mémoires couronnés et autres mémoires de l'académie royale de Belgique, Brussels 1891 (1902).

Barnikol, E., Luther in Magdeburg und die dortige Brüderschule, in: Theologische Arbeiten aus dem rheinischen wissenschaftlichen Predigerverein, Neue Folge, vol. XVII (Heft 17), Tübingen 1917, pp. 1-62.

............Studien zur Geschichte der Brüder vom gemeinsamen Leben; extra issue of (Ergänzungsheft zur): Zeitschrift für Theologie und Kunst, Tübingen 1917.

Becker, V., L'auteur de l'Imitation et les documents néerlandais, The Hague 1882.

............Een brief van Johannes van Schoonhoven, in: De katholiek, nieuwe reeks, vol. XX, Leiden 1884, pp. 199-210, 352-361; vol. XXI, Leiden 1885, pp. 126-141.

............Eenige meditaties uit den Windesheimer kring, in: De katholiek, niewe reeks, vol. XIX, Leiden 1884, pp. 29-47, 101-116.

............Het "Système de monsieur Loth" en de schrijver der Navolging, in: De katholiek, nieuwe reeks, vol. XIX, Leiden 1884, pp. 230-266.

............Een onbekende kronyk van het klooster te Windesheim, in: Bijdragen en mededeelingen van het hist. gen. te Utrecht, Utrecht 1887, pp. 376-445.

............Thomas van Kempen, jongste ontdekkingen, in: Dietsche warande, vol. V (1892), pp. 5-28, 162-168, 237-246.

............De Navolging Christi is een oorspronkelijk werk, in: Dietsche warande, vol. X (1897), pp. 45-59, 93-115.

Bleyswyck, D. van, Beschrijvinge der stadt Delft, Delft 1667.

Block, C., Chronicle of an Augustinian monastery at Utrecht

(Latin), ed, by J. G. C. Joosting, in: Bijdragen en mededeelingen van het historisch genootschap te Utrecht, The Hague 1895.

Böhmer, H., Studien zur Geschichte der Gesellschaft Jesu, vol. I, Bonn 1914.

Bömer, A., Ausgewählte Werke des münsterschen Humanisten Johannes Murmellius, Münster i. W. 1892-1895.

............Das literarische Leben in Münster bis zur entgültigen Rezeption des Humanismus, Münster i. W. 1906.

Boerner, H., Die Annalen und Akten der Brüder des gemeinsamen Lebens im Lüchtenhofe zu Hildesheim, Fürstenwald 1905.

Bonet-Maury, G., Quaeritur e quibus nederlandicis fontibus hauserit scriptor libri cui titules est De imitatione Christi (1384-1464), Paris 1878.

............Gérard de Groote. Un précurseur de la Réforme au quatorzième siècle d'après des documents inédits, Paris 1878.

............De opera scholastica fratrum vitae communnis in Neerlandia, Paris 1889.

Bouwmeester, W. L., Het klooster Bethlehem bij Doetinchem, Doetinchem 1903.

Brecht, W., Die Verfasser der Epistolae obscurorum virorum, in: Quellen und Forschungen zur Sprach- und Culturgeschichte der germanischen Völker, vol. XCIII, Strasbourg 1904.

Brinkerink, D. A., Van den doechden der vuriger ende stichtiger susteren van Diepen Veen, Leiden 1902.

............Devote epistelen, in: Ned. arch. v. kerkgesch., n.s., vol. IV, pp. 312-338, 388-409.

............Biographieën van beroemde mannen uit den Deventer kring, in: Arch. voor de gesch. v. h. aarsb. Utr., vol. XXVII, pp. 400-423; vol. XXVIII, pp. 225-276, 321-343; vol. XXIX, pp. 1-37.

............De "Vita venerabilis Ioannis Brinckerinck", in: Ned. arch. v. kerkgesch., 1901, pp. 314-354.

Brugman, J., Epistola, in: W. Moll, Johannes Brugman, vol. I, pp. 198-217.

............Epistola directed to Egbert ter Beek, rector of the brethren-house at Deventer, in: W. Moll, Joh. Brugman, vol. I, pp. 218-221.

Brugmans, H., De kroniek van het klooster te Utrecht, in: Bijdragen en mededeelingen van het historisch genootschap te Utrecht, Amsterdam 1902.

Busch, J., Chronicon Windeshemense, and Liber de reformatione monasteriorum, ed. by K. Grube, in: Geschichtsquellen der Provinz Sachsen und angrenzender Gebiete, vol. XIX, Halle 1886.

Butzbach, J., Auctarium de scriptoribus ecclesiasticis, ed. by C. Kraft and W. Crecelius, in: Zeitschrift des bergischen Geschichtsvereins, vol. VII (1871), pp. 224-281.

Clarisse, A. and J., Over den geest en de denkwijze van Geert Groete, kenbaar uit zijne schriften, in: Arch. voor kerk gesch., vol. I (1829), pp. 355-398; vol. II (1830), pp. 245-395; vol. III (1831), pp. 1-90; vol. VIII (1837), pp. 1-384.

Coeverincx, G., Analecta, ed. by G. van den Elsen and W. Hoevenaars, and publ. by: Provinciaal genootschap van kunsten en wetenschappen in Noord-Brabant ('s-Hertogenbosch 1905).

Cruise, F. R., Thomas à Kempis, notes of a visit to the scenes in which his life was spent, London 1887.

Delprat, G. H. M., De broederschap van G. Groote, 2nd ed., Arnhem 1856.

Denifle, H., Cartularium universitatis Parisiensis, vol. III, Paris 1894.

..........Luther und das Luthertum, vol. I, Mainz 1906.

Dier de Muden (Muiden), R., Scriptum de magistro Gherardo Grote, domino Florencio et multis aliis devotis fratribus, in: G. Dumbar, Analecta Daventria, vol. I, pp. 1-87.

Diest Lorgion, E. J., Bijdrage tot de geschiedenis van het fraterhuis te Groningen, in: Groningsche volksalmanak, Groningen 1851, pp. 105-118.

Dillenburger, W., Geschichte des Gymnasiums zu Emmerich, in: Jahresbericht über den Schulcursus 1845-1846 an dem königlichen Gymnasium zu Emmerich, Emmerich (1846), pp. 1-56.

..........Zur Geschichte des deutschen Humanismus; Alexander Hegius und Rudolf von Langen, in: Zeitschrift für das Gymnasialwesen, vol. XXIV, Berlin 1870, pp. 481-502.

Dodt van Flensburg, J. J., De stichtings oorkonden van het Utrechtsche fraterhuis, in: Archief voor kerkelijke en wereldlijke geschiedenissen, inzonderheid van Utrecht, vol. I, Utrecht 1838, pp. 89-95.

Doebner, R., Annalen und Akten der Brüder des gemeinsamen Lebens im Lüchtenhofe zu Hildesheim, in: Quellen und Darstellungen zur Geschichte Niedersachsens, Hanover 1903.

Doorninck, J. I. van, Bouwstoffen voor een geschiedenis van het onderwijs in Overijssel, in: Bijdragen tot de geschiedenis van Overijssel, vol. IV, Zwolle 1877, pp. 67-83, 140-157, 233-249; vol. IX (1888), pp. 97-110.

Doumergue, E., Jean Calvin, vols. I and II, Lausanne 1899, 1902.

Drossaers, S. W. A., De archieven van de Delftsche staten-kloosters, The Hague 1917.

Dumbar G., Analecta Daventria, vol. I, Deventer 1719.

............Het kerkelyk en wereltlyk Deventer, 2 vols., Deventer 1732-1788.

Eekhof, A., De avondmaalsbrief van Cornelius Hoen (1525), The Hague 1917.

Egen, A., Der Einfluss der münsterschen Domschule auf die Ausbreitung des Humanismus, in: Festschrift zur Feier der Einweihung des Paulinischen Gymnasiums, Münster i. W. 1898, pp. 15-48.

Ekker, A. De Hieronymusschool te Utrecht (1474-1636), Utrecht 1863.

Engel, K., Das Gründungsjahr des Strassburger Gymnasiums (1538-1539), in: Festschrift zur Feier des 350 jährigen Bestehens des Protestantischen Gymnasiums zu Strassburg, Strasbourg 1888, pp. 112-142.

Erasmus, D., Opera, ed. Leclercq, Leiden 1703-1706.

Evelt, J., Die Anfänge der Bursfelder Benedictiner-Congregation, in: Zeitschrift für vaterländische Geschichte und Alterthumskunde (Westfalens), vol. XXV, Münster i. W. 1865, pp. 121-180.

Erhard, H. A., Gedächtniss-Buch des Frater-Hauses zu Münster, in: Zeitschrift für vaterländische Geschichte und Alterthumskunde (Westfalens), vol. VI, Münster i. W. 1843, pp. 89-126.

Feith, H. O., Het klerkenhuis en het fraterhuis te Groningen, in: Bijdragen tot de geschiedenis en oudheidskunde inzonderheid van de provincie Groningen, vol. VI, Groningen 1869, pp. 1-24.

Fredericq, P., Corpus documentorum inquisitionis haereticae pravitatis neerlandicae, vol. II, Ghent and the Hague 1896

Gallee, J. H., Middeleeuwsche kloosterregels: I. De regel der Windesheimsche vrouwenkloosters; II. Het boek der statuten van het klooster Bethlehem bij Hoorn, in: Ned. arch. v. kerkgesch., vol. V (1895), pp. 250-322, 345-420.

Gansfort, W., Opera, Groningen 1614.

Gantesweiler, P. T. A., Chronik der Stadt Wesel, Wesel 1881.

Geesink, G. H. J. W. J., Gerard Zerbolt van Zutfen, Amsterdam 1879.

Geiger, L., Johann Reuchlin, sein Leben und seine Werke, Leipsic 1871.

..........Renaissance und Humanismus in Italien und Deutschland, in: Allgemeine Geschichte, ed. by W. Oncken, Part II, vol. VIII.

Gelder, H. E. van, De Latijnsche school te Alkmaar, vol. I, Alkmaar 1905.

Geny, J. and G. C. Knod, Die Stadtbibliothek zu Schlettstadt: I. Geny, J., Geschichte der Stadtbibliothek zu Schlettstadt; II. Knod, G. C., Aus der Bibliothek des Beatus Rhenanus, Strasbourg 1889.

Gerretsen, J. H., Florentius Radewijns, Nijmegen 1891.

Godet, M., La congrégation de Montaigu (1490-1580), Paris 1912.

Grisar, H., Martin Luther, vol. I, Freiburg i. Br. 1911.

Groote, G., Cautele confessorum circa magnos peccatores adhibendi; see under: Unpublished sources, Zwolle.

............Epistolae, ed. J. G. R. Acquoy: Gerardi Magni epistolae XIV, Amsterdam 1857.

............Epistolae, ed. G. Bonet-Maury, in: Gérard de Groote, un précurseur de la Réforme, Paris 1878, pp. 99-100.

............Epistolae, ed. J. Clarisse, in: Archief voor kerkgesch., vol. III (1831), pp. 5-27.

............Epistolae, ed. H. Nolte, in: Tübinger theol. Quartalschrift, 1870, pp. 280ff.

............Epistolae, ed. W. Preger, in his Beiträge zur Geschichte der religiösen Bewegung in den Niederlanden, pp. 29-61.

............Epistolae, ed. X. de Ram: Venerabilis Gerardi Magni de Daventria epistolae VIII, in: Comptes rendus d'histoire de Belgique, vol. II (1861), pp. 66-110.

BIBLIOGRAPHY 485

..........Conclusa et proposita non vota, in; Thomas à Kempis, Opera omnia, Antwerp 1615, pp. 915-921, and in: Archief voor kerkgesch., vol. III (1831), pp. 371-383.

..........Defense and explanation of his Sermo contra focaristas, ed. J. Clarisse, in: Archief voor kerkgesch., vol. VIII (1837), pp. 108-117.

..........Dicta quaedam, in: Th. à Kempis, Vita Gerardi Magni, ch. XVIII.

..........Dit sijn de vijf poente, die meester Geert de Groote in den volke 't Uutrecht predicte, ed. W. Moll, in: Studien en bijdragen op 't gebied der theologie, vol. I, pp. 409-411.

..........Een goede leer, ed. W. Moll; see under Moll.

..........De locatione ecclesiarum, ed. J. Clarisse, in: Arch. voor kerkgesch., vol. VIII (1837), pp. 119-152.

..........De matrimonio, ed. J. Clarisse, in: Arch. voor kerkgesch., vol. VIII, pp. 159-249.

..........Protestatio de veridica Evangelia praedicatione, in: Th. à Kempis, Opera, Antwerp 1615, pp. 914-915; also in: G. Bonet-Maury, Groote, pp. 95-96, and in: Arch. voor kerkgesch., vol. I (1829), pp. 359-360.

..........Sermo contra focaristas, ed. A. and J. Clarisse, in: Arch. voor kerkgesch., vol. I, pp. 364-379; vol. II, pp. 307-395; vol. VIII, pp. 5-107.

..........Sermo de paupertate, in: W. Moll, Geert Groote's sermoen voor Palmzondag over de vrijwillige armoede, in: Studien en bijdragen op 't gebied der theologie, vol. II, pp. 425-469 (the sermon itself: pp. 432-469).

..........Sermo de nativitate Domini; see under: Unpublished sources, Utrecht.

..........Sermo de septem verbis; see under: Unpublished sources, Liège.

..........De simonia ad beguttas, in: R. Langenberg, Quellen und Forschungen zur Geschichte der deutschen Mystik, Bonn 1902, pp. 3-33.

..........Tractatus de quatuor generibus meditabilium sive contemplacionum. See: Unpublished sources, Cologne.

..........Zedelijke toespraak, ed. J. Van Vloten, in: Nieuw arch. voor kerkgesch., vol. II (1854), pp. 295-307.

..........Zedelijke toespraak, in: G. Monet-Maury, Gérard Groote, pp. 96-98.

Gysbertszoon, H. van Arnhem, Kronyk van het fraterhuis te

Gouda, in: Bijdragen en mededeelingen van het historisch genootschap te Utrecht, vol. XX, Amsterdam 1898.

Hegius, A., Dialogi, Deventer 1503.

Heussen, H. F. van, and Ryn, H. van, Oudheden en gestichten van Deventer, Leiden 1725.

Hirsche, K., Prologomena zu einer neuen Ausgabe der Imitatio Christi, 3 vols., Berlin 1873-1894.

Hölscher, 'L., Geschichte des Gymnasiums in Herford, Programm Herf. Gymnasium, 1869, 1872, 1874.

..........Reformationsgeschichte der Stadt Herford, Gütersloh 1888.

Hofman, J. H., De boekerij van St. Michiel te Zwolle, in: Arch. v. d. gesch. v. h. aartsh. Utr., vol. IV (1877), pp. 387-389.

............De broeders van 't Gemeene Leven en de Windesheimsche kloostervereeniging, in: Arch. v. d. gesch. v. h. aartsb. Utr., vol. II (1875), pp. 217-275; vol. V (1878), pp. 80-152.

Hoogeweg, H., Verzeichnis der Stifter und Klöster Niedersachsens vor der Reformation, Halle and Leipsic 1908.

Hoop Scheffer, J. G. de, Geschiedenis der Hervorming in Nederland van haar ontstaan tot 1531, in: Studien en Bijdragen, vol. I (1870), pp. 1-142, 169-257, 413-576; vol. II (1872), pp. 129-360.

Horn, P., Vita Gerardi Magni, ed. by W. J. Kühler, in: Ned. arch. voor kerkgesch., n. s. (1909), pp. 325-370.

Hullu, J. de, Bescheiden betreffende de Hervorming in Overijssel, vol. I (1522-1546), Deventer 1899.

Hulshof, A., Verslag van een onderzoek te Rostock naar handschriften, drukwerken en bescheiden belangrijk voor de geschiedenis van Nederland, The Hague 1909.

Joosting, J. G. C., Wessel Gansfort lijfarts van bisschop David in: Gron. volksalmanak, vol. XXIX, Groningen 1917, pp. 121-124.

Jostes, F., Johannes Veghe, ein deutscher prediger des 15ten jahrhunderts, Halle 1883.

...........:Het Nederduitsch proza omtrent 1500; nieuwe bijzonderheden over de "Navolging", in: Dietsche warande, nieuwe reeks, vol. VI (1893), pp. 265-279.

...........Twee-en-tachtig zinnespreuken uit een handschrift der 15e eeuw, in: Dietsche warande, nieuwe reeks, vol. VII (1894), pp. 69-75.

............Die Schriften des Gerhard Zerbolt van Zutphen, "De libris teutonicalibus", in: Historiches Jahrbuch der Görres-Gesellschaft, vol. XI, Munich 1890, pp. 1-22, 709-717.

Kempis, Th. à, Opera, Nuremberg 1494. Contains biographical notices called by Rosweyden: Vita Thomae à Kempis Canonici Regularis auctore incerto paene coaevo (the Stadtbibliothek at Cologne has a copy, which was consulted by the author).

............Opera, ed. J. Badius Ascensius, Paris 1523. Contains: Vita beati Thomae Malleoli.

............Opera omnia, ed. R. P. Henrici Sommalii, S. J., Antwerp 1615.

............Chronicon Montis S. Agnetis, una cum vindiciis Kempensibus Heriberti Rosweydi pro libro De imitatione Christi, Antwerp 1621. On p. 137 this chronicle is continued by another writer.

............Opera omnia, ed. J. Pohl, 7 vols., Freiburg 1902-1921.

............Works, vol. I: Prayers and meditations on the life of Christ, ed. W. Duthoit, London 1908; vol. II: The founders of the New Devotion, ed. J. P. Arthur, London 1905; vol. III: The chronicle of the Canons Regular of Mount St. Agnes, ed. J. P. Arthur, London 1906; vol. IV: Sermons to the Novices Regular, ed. V. Scully, London 1907; vol. V: The incarnation, life, and passion of our Lord, ed. V. Scully, London 1907.

Kentenich, G., Noch einmal "Die Handschriften der Imitatio Christi und die Autorschaft des Thomas", in: Zeitschrift für Kirchengeschichte, vol. XXIV, Gotha 1903, pp. 594-604.

............Zum Imitatio Christi-Streit, in: Zeitschrift für Kirchengeschichte, vol. XXVI, Gotha 1905, pp. 467-470.

Kettlewell, S., The authorship of the De Imitatione Christi, London 1877.

Keussen, H., Die Matrikel der Universität Köln (1389-1559), vol. I (1389-1466), Bonn 1892.

............Der Dominikaner Matthäus Grabow und die Brüder des gemeinsamen Lebens, in: Mittheilungen aus dem Stadt-archiv Köln, vol. XIII, Cologne 1887, pp. 29-47.

Knepper, J., Jakob Wimpfeling (1450-1528), in: Erläuterungen und Ergänzungen zu Janssens Geschichte des deutschen Volkes, vol. III, parts 2-4, Freiburg i. Br. 1902.

Korth, L., Die älteste deutsche Uebersetzung der "Imitatio

Christi", in: Mittheilungen aus dem Stadtarchiv Köln, vol. XIII, Cologne 1887, pp. 88-92.

Kraft, C. and Crecelius, W., Mittheilungen über Alexander Hegius und seine Schüler, in: Zeitschrift des Bergischen Geschichtvereins, vol. VII, Bonn 1871, pp. 213-286. On pp. 224-281: Auctarium Joannis Boutzbachii de scriptoris ecclesiasticis.

Kronenberg, H., Wanneer is Alexander Hegius te Deventer aangekomen, in: Verslagen en mededeelingen der vereeniging tot beoefening van Overijsselsch regt en geschiedenis, vol. XXIX of 2nd series, Deventer 1913, p. 5.

Kronenberg, M. E., De bibliotheek van het Heer-Florenshuis te Deventer, in: Ned. archief voor kerkgeschiedenis, nieuwe serie, vol. IX (1912), pp. 150-164, 252-300, 313-322.

Kückelhahn, L., Sturm, Strassburgs erster Schulrektor, Leipzig 1872.

Kühler, W. J., Johannes Brinckerinck en zijn klooster te Diepenveen, Rotterdam 1908.

............Levensbeschijvingen van devote zusters te Deventer, in: Archief voor de gesch. v. h. aartsb. Utrecht, 1910, pp. 1-68.

............De vita Gerardi Magni. See under: Horn, P.

Lang, A., Der Evangelienkommentar Martin Butzers und die Grundzüge seiner Theologie, in: Studien zur Geschichte der Theologie und der Kirche, vol. II², Leipzig 1900.

............Johannes Calvin. Ein Lebensbild zu seinem 400. Geburtstag am 10. Juli 1909, in: Schriften des Vereins für Reformationsgeschichte, vol. XCIX, Leipzig 1909.

............Die Bekehrung Johannes Calvins, in: Studien zur Geschichte der Theologie und der Kirche, vol. III, Leipzig 1897.

Lesker, B., Die Rostocker Fraterherren, Frankfurt 1887.

Lindeboom, J., Het Bijbelsch humanisme in Nederland, Leiden 1913.

Lindeborn, J., Historia sive notitia episcopatus Daventriensis, Cologne 1670.

Lisch, G. C. F., Geschichte der Buchdruckerkunst in Mecklenburg, bis zum Jahre 1540, in: Jahrbücher des Vereins für mecklenb. Gesch. und Alterthumskunde, vol. IV (1839), part I (pp. 1-62): Buchdruckerei der Brüder vom gemeinsamen Leben zu St. Michael in Rostock; vol. VI, pp.

209-281: Urkunden-Sammlung. Urkunden der Brüder vom gemeinsamen Leben zu Rostock.

Löffler, K., Heinrich von Ahaus und die Brüder vom gemeinsamen Leben in Deutschland, in: Hist. Jahrbuch der Görres-Gesellschaft, vol. XXX, München 1909, pp. 762-798.

............Neues über Heinrich von Ahaus, in: Zeitsch. für Gesch. und Altertumskunde Westfalens, vol. LXXIV (1916), pp. 229-240.

............Das Fraterhaus Weidenbach in Köln, in: Annalen des historischen Vereins für den Niederrhein, vol. CII, Cologne 1918, pp. 99-128.

............Das Gedächtnisbuch des Kölner Fraterhauses Weidenbach, in: Ann. des hist. Ver. f. d. Niederrhein, vol. CIII (1919), pp. 1-47.

Loth, A., L'Auteur de l'Imitation. Nouvel examen de la question d'après un manuscrit de 1406, in: Revue des questions historiques, 1873, pp. 527-616.

Malou, J. B., Recherches historiques et critiques sur le véritable auteur du livre de l'Imitation de Jésus-Christ, Paris and Tournai 1858.

Man, D. de, Hier beginnen sommige stichtege punten van onsen oelden zusteren, The Hague 1919.

Mande, H., Hoe dat wij wt selen doen den ouden mensche mit sinen werken ende ons mit cristo overmids warachtige doechden sellen verenighen, in: G. Visser, Hendrik Mande, Appendix, pp. 1-17.

............Boexken vanden binnensten ons liefs heren ihesu christi, in: G. Visser, Mande, Appendix, pp. 18-43.

............Een spiegel der waerheit, in: G. Visser, Mande, App., pp. 90-107.

............Boecskijn van drien staten eens bekierden mensche, dairin begrepen is een volcomen geestlic leven, in: W. Moll, Johannes Brugman, vol. I, pp. 263-292.

............Een devoet boecskyn van der bereydinghe ende vercieringhe onser inwendingher woeninghen, in: W. Moll, Joh. Brugman, vol. I, pp. 293-309.

Marx, J., Festschrift zum Bischofs-Jubiläum 1906, Trier 1907; pp. 129-243: Nikolaus von Cues und seine Stiftungen zu Cues und Deventer.

Massaeus, Chr., Chronicorum multiplicis historiae libri XX, Antwerp 1540.

Mestwerdt, P., Die Anfänge des Erasmus. Humanismus und "Devotio Moderna", Leipzig 1917.

Meyer, F., Der Ursprung des Jesuitischen Schulwesens. Ein Beitrag zur Lebensgeschichte des heiligen Ignatius, Gräfenhainichen 1904.

Meyer, O., Die Brüder des gemeinsamen Lebens in Würtemberg, Tübingen 1913.

Miller, E. W., and Scudder, J. W., Wessel Gansfort, New York 1917.

Molhuysen, J. C., Cornelius Aurelius, in: Nederlandsch Archief voor kerkgeschiedenis, vol. II (1903), pp. 1-35; vol. IV (1907), pp. 54-73.

Moll, W., Geert Groote de ketterhamer, in: Studien en Bijdragen, ed. Moll and De Hoop Scheffer, vol. I (1870), pp. 343-346.

..........Geert Groote's dietsche vertalingen beschreven en toegelicht, in: Verhandelingen der koninklijke akademie van wetenschappen, afdeeling letterkunde, vol. XIII, Amsterdam 1880.

..........Geert Groote's raadgevingen aan een kluizenaarster, in: Studien en bijdragen op 't gebied der theologie, ed. W. Moll and J. G. de Hoop Scheffer, vol. III (1876), pp. 430-437.

..........Een goede leer van meester Gherit die Groot, in: Kerkhistorisch archief, vol. III (1862), p. 320.

..........Geert Groote's verklaringen aangaande den inhoud zijner prediking te Utrecht, in: Studien en bijdagen, vol. I (1870), pp. 404-411.

..........Gerlach Peters en zijne schriften, in: Kerkhistorisch archief, vol. II, Amsterdam 1859, pp. 147-256.

..........Johannes Brugman en het Godsdienstig leven onzer vaderen in de vijftiende eeuw, 2 vols., Amsterdam 1854.

Mooren, J., Nachrichten über Thomas à Kempis, Crefeld 1855.

Müller, H., Les origines de la Compagnie de Jésus; Ignace et Lainez, Paris 1898.

Muller, S., Openbare verzamelingen der gemeente Utrecht. Catalogussen van de bij het Stads-archief bewaarde archieven. Eerste afdeeling: De aan de stad Utrecht behoorende archieven, Utrecht 1913.

..........De Moderne Devotie te Utrecht, in: Ned. archief voor kerkgeschiedenis, nieuwe serie, vol. XII (1915), pp. 16-34.

Nordhoff, J. B., Denkwürdigkeiten aus dem Münsterschen Humanismus, Münster 1874.

Parmet, A., Rudolf von Langen. Leben und gesammelte gedichte des ersten münsterschen humanisten. Münster 1869.

Paulsen, F., Geschichte des gelehrten Unterrichts auf den deutschen Schulen und Universitäten vom Ausgang des Mittelalters, vol. I, Leipzig 1896.

Peters, G., Soliloquium, Cologne 1616.

............Breviloquium, in: W. Moll, Gerlach Peters, pp. 174-199.

............De eerste brief aan Lubbe Peters (first letter to his sister Lubbe), in: W. Moll, l. c., pp. 202-214.

............De tweede brief aan Lubbe Peters (second letter to his sister Lubbe), in: W. Moll, l. c., pp. 218-229.

Pomerius, H., De origine monasterii Viridisvallis una cum vitis b. Joannis Rusbrochii primi prioris huius monasterii et aliquot coaeterneorum ejus, in: Analecta Bollandia, vol. IV, Paris, Brussels, and Geneva 1885, pp. 263-322.

Preger, W., Beiträge zur Geschichte der religiösen Bewegung in den Niederlanden in der 2. Hälfte des 14. Jahrhunderts, in: Abhandlungen der kön. bayer. Akademie der Wissenschaften, III Cl., vol. XXI, Munich 1894, pp. 1-64.

Puyol, P. E., L'Auteur du livre de Imitatione Christi, 2 vols., Paris 1899-1900.

Pijper, F., Een nonnenklooster onder den invloed van Windesheim, in: Ned. Arch. voor kerkgesch., vol. V (1895), pp. 229-249.

............De invloed van de broeders des Gemeenen Levens op de schoolstichting van Calvijn, in: Kerkhistorische opstellen van het gezelschap S. S. S., The Hague 1914, pp. 115-129.

Radewijns, F., Omnes inquit artes. See: Unpubl. sources, under Deventer.

............Tractatulus de spiritualibus exercitiis, in: Vregt, J. F., Eenige ascetische tractaten, pp. 383-427.

Reichling, D., Ortwin Gratius; sein Leben und Werken; eine Ehrenrettung, Heiligenstadt 1884.

............Johannes Murmellius; sein Leben und seine Werke, Freiburg i. Br. 1880.

............Die Reform der Domschule zu Münster im Jahre 1500, Berlin 1900.

492   BIBLIOGRAPHY

............Joseph Horlenius und Jacob Montanus, in: Zeitsch.
für Geschichte und Alterthumskunde Westfalens, vol.
XXXVI, Münster 1878, pp. 3-32.

............Zur Geschichte der Münsterschen Domschule in der
Blütezeit des Humanismus, in: Festschrift zur Feier der
Einweihung des neuen Gymnasialgebäudes am 27 April
1898, Münster 1898, pp. 3-12.

Renan, E., L'Auteur de l'Imitation de Jésus-Christ, in: Études
d' histoire religieuse, Paris 1880, pp. 317-336.

Renaudet, A., Érasme, sa vie et son oeuvre jusqu'en 1517
d'après sa correspondance, in: Revue historique, vol. CXI,
pp. 225-262; vol. CXII, pp. 241-274.

............Jean Standonk, un Réformateur Catholique avant
la Réforme, in: Bulletin de la société de l'histoire du Protestantisme français, Paris 1908, pp. 5-81.

............Préréforme et Humanisme à Paris (1494-1517),
Paris 1916.

Richter, J. H., Geschichte des Augustinerklosters Frenswegen in
der Grafschaft Bentheim, Hildesheim 1913.

Rhijn, M. van, Wessel Gansfort, The Hague 1917.

Roelfsema, E. H., De Fraters en het Fraterhuis te Groningen,
in: Gron. volksalmanak, 1920, pp. 28-39.

Roersch, A., L'humanisme belge à l'époque de la renaissance,
Brussels 1910.

Rogge, H. C., Gerardus Listrius, in: Ned. arch. voor kerkgesch., vol. VII (1897), pp. 207-220.

Rootselaar, W. F. N., Amersfoort, geschiedkundige bijzonderheden, Amersfoort 1897.

............Amersfoort (777-1580), 2 vols., Amersfoort 1878.

Rosweyden, H., Vindiciae Kempenses, Antwerp 1583.

............Vita Thomae à Kempis ex variis auctoribus con-
cinnata, in his Vindiciae.

Scheel, O., Martin Luther. Vom Katholizismus zur Reformation, vol. I: Auf der Schule und Universität, Tübingen 1917.

Schevichaven, H. D. J. van, Oud-Nijmegens kerken, kloosters,
gasthuizen, stichtingen en openbare gebouwen, Nijmegen
1909.

Schmidt, Ch., Histoire litteraire de l'Alsace à la fin du XVe et
au commencement du XVIe siècle, 2 vols., Paris 1879.

Schoengen, M., Die Schule von Zwolle von ihren Anfängen bis
zu dem Auftreten des Humanismus, Freiburg i. Br. 1898.

BIBLIOGRAPHY 493

............Nederlandica in Belgische aichievan, in: Nederlandsch archievenblad, vol. XVII, pp. 177ff.

............Jacobus Traiecti alias de Voecht narratio de inchoatione domus clericorum in Zwollis, Amsterdam 1908.

Schmitz-Kallenberg, L., Monasticon Westfaliae, Münster 1909.

Schwarz, W. E., Studien zur Geschichte des Klosters Marienthal, in: Zeitschrift für Geschichte und Altertumskunde
Westfalens, vol. LXXII, Münster 1914, pp. 48-151.

Slee, J. C. van, Het necrologium en cartularium van het convent
der reguliere kanunikessen te Diepenveen, in: Arch. voor
de gesch. v. h. aartsb. Utrecht, vol. XXXIII (1908), pp.
318-485.

Smith, P., The life and letters of Martin Luther, Boston and
New York 1914.

Sohm, W., Die Schule Johann Sturms und die Kirche Strassburgs in ihrem gegenseitigen Verhältnis (1503-1581),
Munich, Berlin 1912.

Spitzen, O. A., Thomas à Kempis als schrijver der Navolging
van Christus gehandhaafd, Utrecht 1880.

............Nalezing op mijn Thomas à Kempis als schrijver
der Navolging van Christus gehandhaafd, Utrecht 1881.

............Les Hollandismes de l'Imitation de Jésus-Christ et
trois anciennes versions du livre. Réponse à M. le Chevalier
B. Veratti, Utrecht 1884.

Sturm, Joh., Consilium curatoribus scholarum Argentorati propositum VI. die Kal. Martii 1538, in: G. Bonet-Maury, De
opera scholastica fratrum vitae communis in Neerlandia,
p. 90.

Tilley, A., The dawn of the French Renaissance, Cambridge
1918.

Tolensis, F., Vita Thomae Malleoli à Kempis, in: Th. à Kempis,
Opera, ed. H. Sommalius, Antwerp 1615, pp. 27-31.

Ullman, C., Reformers before the Reformation, vol. II, Edinburgh 1855.

Vedder, H. C., The Reformation in Germany, New York 1914.

Veil, H., Zum Gedächtnis Johannes Sturms. Eine Studie über
J. Sturms Unterrichtsziele und Schuleinrichtungen mit
besonderer Berücksichtigung seiner Beziehungen zu dem
niederländischen Humanismus, in: Festschrift zur Feier des
350 jährigen Bestehens des Protestantischen Gymnasiums
zu Strassburg, Strasbourg 1888, pp. 1-[132].

Velden, H. E. J. M. van der, Rodolphus Agricola (Roelof Huusman), Leiden 1909.

Velthuijsen, B. P., Twee tot nog toe onbekende conventen der kloostervereeniging van Windesheim, in: Verslagen en mededeelingen der vereeniging tot beoefening van Overijselsch regt en geschiedenis, vol. XVIII, Zwolle 1891, pp. 39-56.

Vregt, J. F., Eenige ascetische tractaten, afkomstig van de Deventersche broederschap van het gemeene leven, in verband gebracht met het boek van Thomas à Kempis, de Navolging van Christus, in: Archief voor de geschiedenis van het aartsbisdom Utrecht, vol. X, Utrecht 1882, pp. 321-498.

Wace, H., and Buchheim, C. A., First principles of the Reformation, London 1883.

Waterton, E., Thomas à Kempis and the Imitation of Christ, London 1883.

Watrigant, P. H., La genèse des Exercitia spiritualia, Amiens 1897.

Weiss, N., Le premier traité protestant en langue française: La summe de l'Escripture Saincte 1523, in: Bulletin de la société de l'histoire du Protestantisme français, 1919, pp. 63-79.

Wiese, J., Der Pädagoge Alexander Hegius und seine Schüler, Berlin 1892.

Whitney, J. P., Erasmus, in: English historical review, vol. XXXV (1920), pp. 1-25.

Wolters, A., Reformationsgeschichte der Stadt Wesel, Bonn 1868.

Wüstenhoff, D. J. M., "Florentii parvum et simplex exercitium", naar een Berlijnsch handschrift medegedeeld, in: Nederlandsch Archief voor kerkgeschiedenis, vol. V (1895), pp. 89-105.

Zerbolt, G., Opuscula duo ad vitam corrigendam recteque instituendam quibusvis accomodo. — I. — De reformatione interiori seu virium animae. — II. — De spiritualibus ascensionibus, Cologne 1539.

............Super modo vivendi devotorum hominum simul commorancium. See: Unpubl. sources, under The Hague.

............De libris teutonicalibus, or An liceat libros divinos transferre in vulgare. See: Unpubl. sources, under Nuremberg.

INDEX

Acquoy, 84, 155.
Adrian, Floriszoon, Pope Adrian VI, 247.
Adwert, 202, 203, 227.
Aelius, 341.
Agnes, Mount St., 138, 168, 176, 189, 202, 203, 207, 251, 339.
Agnietenberg, or Mount St. Agnes, 171, 194, 236.
Agricola, Rudolph, 40, 126-128, 203, 204, 228, 241.
Ahaus, Henry of, 111.
Ailly, Cardinal Pierre d', 101, 197, 206, 231, 311.
Alanus, 203.
Alexander VI, Pope, 247.
Ambrose, Church Father, 164, 206, 210, 248.
Amilius van Buren, 99, 173, 175.
Anna of Brittany, 247.
Anrich, 287.
Anselm, 17,301.
Anthony, 226.
Apuleius, 17.
Aquinas, Thomas, 17, 19, 53, 67, 68, 77, 164, 169, 181, 206, 233, 235, 295, 301, 319.
Aristotle, 17, 68, 172, 206-208, 295, 338.
Arius, 234.
Arsenius, 78.
Ascensius, Badius, 61, 264, 265, 279.

Assisi, Francis of, 3, 17.
Athanasius, 206.
Augustine, 11, 15, 17, 19, 46, 70, ' 73, 77, 86, 143, 164, 200, 206, 207, 214, 225, 229, 230, 234, 238, 321.
Aurelius, Cornelius Gerard of Gouda, 253, 254.

Badius, see Ascensius.
Baduelle, 342.
Bailly, 252.
Balthasar, 113.
Barrowists, 348.
Bartholomew, 30, 31, 46, 65.
Basil, 191.
Basselen, Heylwig van der, 9.
Becker, 177, 182.
Béda, 247, 252, 279.
Bede, 17, 68.
Beiaard, 183.
Beek, Egbert ter, 102-103.
Benedictine, monastic order, 144, 145, 147.
Bergen, Henry of, 247.
Bernard, 3, 17, 158, 164, 172, 200, 206, 207, 338.
Berner, Lubbert, 173.
Bessarion, 197.
Bethlehem, 155, 178-179.
Biel, Gabriel, 221, 312.
Blankenheim, Frederick van, 90, 101.

495

THE CHRISTIAN RENAISSANCE
Part II

AUTHOR'S NOTE

Since the publication of *The Christian Renaissance* in 1924 a vast number of books and essays have been written about the "Devotio Moderna." The author has himself published twenty-three letters by Gerard Groote, three books by Gerard Zerbolt, and one book by Groote. Moreover, he has contributed numerous critiques and reviews which have received wide attention. In some cases he has shown where he was mistaken in drawing certain conclusions because the original sources had not been accessible to him. For this reason he has decided to add five new sections to the original edition. Part of this material has been published before and some of it is entirely new.

THE INFLUENCE OF THE "DEVOTIO MODERNA"

In the period before 1924 the career of Gerard Groote and the three institutions he founded were seldom studied with proper attention by European and American historians. Even the great scholars in the Netherlands paid very little attention to the Devotio Moderna. But during the past two decades a marked change has occurred in several countries. One reason why Groote has finally come into his own is that in 1942 a large biography was published by Professor J. van Ginneken, S.J. This highly influential scholar indicated that Groote had spent eight years at the University of Paris studying law. As a result of his legal training the government of his native city, Deventer, dispatched him to the papal court at Avignon, where he successfully negotiated problems concerning tolls and other dues. The present writer has mentioned some of the details in his book, *The Brethren of the Common Life* (pp. 16-18), while further evidence has been presented to show how much Groote contributed to the Northern Renaissance and the Reformation (pp. 38-39). The contents are here reproduced.

Until the third decade of the twentieth century Gerard Groote did not appear as a prominent figure in the history of the Netherlands. Outstanding historians like Professor Robert Fruin and Professor P. J. Blok paid very little attention to him and the movement he inaugurated. In the courses devoted to Dutch history few pupils ever heard much about his preaching or his books, not to mention the Brotherhood of the Common Life. But in recent years it has become fashionable among Dutch scholars of note to reserve for him a modest place beside the great admirals, governor-generals, scientists, and painters who hitherto nearly monopolized all space in the hall of fame. The man who dared to defy the scribes and pharisees of his time and suffered a mental crucifixion for his boldness has finally come into his own. We may henceforth speak of him as the founder of two powerful institutions which rank with others of far greater fame but of much less influence in the modern world.

Gerard Groote was born at Deventer in the year 1340. His father, Werner Groote, was a prominent member of the municipal government, being a *schepen*, or alderman. He had married Heilwich van der Basselen, who according to our only original source still extant gave birth to the boy in the month of October. Werner Groote belonged to a prominent merchant guild which engaged in the purchase and sale of cloth. The city of Deventer was a member of the celebrated Hanseatic League; during the fourteenth century it flourished mightily, together with the great cities of northern Germany, such as Hamburg, Bremen, and Lübeck. The Groote family occupied a pretentious home in the Bagijnestraat, or Street of the Beguines. Here little Gerard grew up to be a handsome boy, and later a highly intellectual youth.[1]

Unfortunately the father did not long survive the arrival of the dreaded Black Death in the city of Deventer; he passed away about the year 1350, while his wife died on July 24, 1350. Those years of pestilence must have made a terrible impression upon Gerard's mind. He had no brother or sister except one of illegitimate birth called Bernard, who succeeded Werner Groote in the merchant guild. But Gerard found a worthy guardian in Johannes Groote, or Ockenbroeck, who seems to have married a sister of Werner Groote. This uncle lived on the street called Brink, which in the region of the Yssel Valley usually was the square in the center of the city. This may once have been the house belonging to Gerard's mother, for in one of the original sources we read that he was born in this particular house.[2]

Gerard attended for several years the excellent school attached to the venerable church called St. Lebwin, the same school in which more than a century later the famous Erasmus studied. We know very little about this period in Gerard's life, but it appears that he received some education in the ancient German cities of Aachen and Cologne. In 1355 he matriculated in the University of Paris, where he stayed three years, obtaining the degree of Master of Arts in 1358.[3] He also studied magic at that time, a fact which caused him much regret in later years. At Prague also he sought to improve his knowledge.[4] But here he did not remain long. He devoted about eight years at the University of Paris to the study of law, after having received his degree just mentioned. In some of the university documents dating from the years 1363 and 1366 he is mentioned as a student in the faculty of law.[5]

Formerly the historians of the Netherlands completely ignored the legal studies of Groote in Paris. The chroniclers in the Yssel Valley had known nothing about those eight fruitful years spent by Groote in the law school. As a result his importance in the history of the Dutch Reformation was seldom fully understood. He could never have accomplished the task he set out to perform if he had not been thoroughly familiar with the Canon Law and the *Corpus Juris Civilis*. His appearance before the higher clergy in the Bishopric of Utrecht during the summer of 1383, when he himself was but a mere deacon, would seem preposterous if it had not been for his tremendous learning.

How are we to account for the honors bestowed upon him by the government of his native city if we overlook his legal training in France? The municipal council of Deventer dispatched him to the court of Pope Urban V at Avignon, where he negotiated successfully problems concerning tolls and other dues. In 1359 he had returned to Deventer, and there he had distinguished himself as a capable scholar.[6] It is doubtful that he spent much time there in this particular period; for various reasons he preferred Paris above Deventer. He admitted later that he was one of those "wandering students" who could not long be satisfied with one school, or home, or woman. He made love to women "in every green woods and upon every mountain," so he frankly stated in one of his letters.[7] When many years later he composed a learned work on the married life, he was in a position to discuss the subject not merely from a religious but also from a medical standpoint.[8] His escapades kept him away from Deventer, as we suggested, for more than one reason. No wonder that later he was so profoundly impressed by the experiences of St. Augustine, who had also "wasted his substance" and dabbled in heresies and black magic before he turned from the ways "of this world."

About Groote's mission to Avignon the sources present little concrete information. From the beginning of January to the end of August 1365 he was being consulted by the municipal council of Deventer. It offered him a handsome sum of money to defray his expenses, but to the surprise of the aldermen he refused to accept it, and at the end of the year 1365 he traveled at his own expense from Paris to Avignon. On February 7, 1366, he requested that the papal court appoint him pastor of a congregation at Ouderkerk in the Bishopric of Utrecht. He did not by any means, however, neglect the affairs of his native town, for we read in the documents that on August 20, 1366, and on January 14, 1367, Henricus van Rijpen arrived from Avignon with letters from Gerard Groote.[9]

Although his parents had left him a fortune from which he earned about two hundred gold- pounds a year, he was not satisfied with this income. As early as 1362 he was promised a prebend in the ancient city of Aachen (Aix-la-Chapelle), which he finally received during the winter of 1368-69, while he was suffering from a serious illness. He spent some time in that city, but soon removed to Cologne, where he lived in great luxury, having obtained a second prebend in the city of Utrecht. All the chronicles devoted to his life mention his wayward life, for the contrast between the period before and after his conversion was most striking. Thomas à Kempis aptly remarked that "he walked in the ways of this world."[10]

His significance as a reformer in the fourteenth century has seldom been properly analyzed. Not until the year 1942 did a comprehensive biography of Groote make its appearance, and before 1938 only scattered works of no great scope were devoted to his life and writings. But in 1940 and 1941 extensive publications attested the rising interest in his life and teachings. In the Netherlands a society was founded which is now actively engaged in preparing an edition of his *Opera Omnia*. This is the *Geert Groote Vereeniging*, which recently published a Dutch translation of the biography of Groote by Thomas à Kempis. It was published as No. 155 of the publications issued by this society, and in the near future we may look for some remarkable developments. At the same time some useful work is being done in the United States. One notable book is the admirable dissertation by Professor William Spoelhof, which deals with the development of religious toleration by Groote and his followers.

What made Groote so important in the history of western Europe was his successful attempt to revive the primitive Christian Church. Contrary to the opinion of hostile critics, he paid very little attention to the many heretical beliefs current in his day. But he did consider seriously the evil of heretics. When a learned friend named Salvarvilla wondered why he did not care to help heal the Great Schism in the Western Church, he told this scholar that outward schisms were caused by lack of inner power and love. We must first heal the schism in our hearts, so he reasoned. His main theme always was the acquisition of spiritual power rather than the building of concrete structures. What could he accomplish in Rome or Avignon if ordinary members of the Church were being lost because of sinful living?[11]

There is a hidden power in the famous book entitled the *Imitation of Christ* which has made it the most widely read work ever composed in Europe. It flowed from the pens of Groote's disciples as easily and as logically as did the books of the New Testament in the Near East. A man of tremendous spiritual power gathered around him twelve chosen disciples, of whom one became a traitor. He founded two institutions which reminded thoughtful men and women of the first church in Jerusalem. The scribes and pharisees of his day he unmercifully flayed and was promptly silenced by them, as had happened in a similar case at the Holy City. After his death his sayings were jotted down and his program was executed. From the Yssel Valley in all directions his influence spread, largely unseen but most powerful just the same. George Eliot knew something about this phenomenon when in the famous novel, *The Mill on the Floss,* she portrayed the tremendous change that came over the young woman in the story who found in her attic a copy of the *Imitation.* Thousands of such cases could have been recorded from actual facts.

Groote established a Christian Renaissance, not an inquisition. He wanted to instill personal religion rather than mere doctrines. In that respect he resembled Erasmus, who at times was a faithful child of the Devotio Moderna. What did he care if a certain man or woman erred in matters of doctrine as long as one tried to imitate the life of Christ? Seeing how corrupt a large number of clergymen were, he hoped to rally all laymen to his side, which was also a characteristic of Christ in Palestine. The Netherlands was much like the Holy Land. A small country, devoid of great natural resources, lay on the western shore of a huge continent. The route of trade traversed it as did the Oriental arteries of commerce in the days of the Apostles. "From all nations under the sun" the merchants and tourists came to the Low Countries. The travelers brought with them many new ideas, and upon their return they took to their respective communities a message of hope and cheer for a wicked world. Before long some of the most venerable monasteries in France, Germany, and the southern Netherlands bowed before the spiritual scepter of Windesheim, which began its humble existence two years after Groote's death, but soon saw its reformers carry the new gospel to hundreds of older institutions. In this manner did Groote operate long after his death. Those who still insist in looking upon him as an inquisitor must examine him anew. Then they will understand why he spent so much energy in reforming both clergy and laity.

Another reason why Groote's reputation has become greatly enhanced is that in the year 1955 an illuminating book was published by G. A. van Asseldonk, m.s.f., entitled, *De Nederlanden en het Westers Schisma* (Utrecht and Nijmegen: Dekker & van de Vegt). The author has devoted pp. 154-219 to the views of Groote and Salvarvilla on the papal schism. He shows that Salvarvilla was not merely a cantor in Paris (in the cathedral of Notre Dame and not at the University of Paris, as the present writer had stated) but also for many years a professor of theology in the local university, besides a canon in Paris and in Rouen. Salvarvilla's eulogy of Groote has been reproduced in *The Christian Renaissance* (pp. 37-38), and no doubt many readers have wondered why an insignificant person received so much space. Largely as the result of his influence in Rome, Pope Urban VI granted his request to let Groote preach again, which was not known to the present writer in 1924. By the year 1950, when his book on the Brethren of the Common Life appeared, he had discovered that Groote was accorded the right to resume his preaching (pp. 22-23), but by the time the papal message reached Deventer, Groote was dead.

Not only had Groote made far greater contributions to the Northern Renaissance and the Reformation than the great historians in Europe and America believed, but the same was true of Gerard Zerbolt. Particularly important was the latter's essay on the reading of the Bible in the vernacular, of which only one copy has survived. In the year 1947 the principal of the Geert Groote School in Deventer (the author of the first comprehensive biography of Zerbolt: J. van Rooij, *Gerard Zerbolt van Zutphen*) told the writer that he had written to about 400 libraries and had been unable to find another copy than that which the writer had published in 1924. The writer was also the first person to publish the brilliant work of Gerard Groote entitled, *Tractatus de Quattuor Generibus Meditationum,* and also *Sermo de Nativitate Domini.* It had not been known that the two titles referred to the same work.

Zerbolt copied some important statements made by Groote. For example, on p. 10 of the edition published in 1925, we find this: "Quid profuit vel Herodi vel Pylato vel Iudeis vidisse Christum oculo non sequebantur precepta?" Zerbolt in his famous book entitled, *Spiritual Ascensions,* has the following, as quoted in *The Brethren of the Common Life:* "Quod profuit inde Pilato, Herodi, vel Pharisais, quod Christi mores vel gestus, aut praesentiam corporalem viderunt, qui eum imitari noluerunt?" It is interesting that Groote and Thomas à Kempis talked merely about following Christ, whereas the highly gifted Zerbolt had the courage to insist upon imitation.

Another champion of the Devotio Moderna was Gabriel Biel, the rector of the house operated by the Brethren of the Common Life in Butzbach. Professor William Landeen in his illuminating treatise, *Gabriel Biel and the Devotio Moderna in Germany* (1960), has proved that his position in the brotherhood was far more important than had been realized by German scholars, while some American historians and theologians referred to Biel as a Franciscan monk, rather than a Brother of the Common Life. Moreover, Luther's dependence upon the brotherhood has been described properly by both Landeen and Professor Julia Henkel of Malone College. The latter wrote a fine dissertation entitled, *An Historical Study of the Educational Contributions of the Brethren of the Common Life* (University of Pittsburgh, 1962).

It is not surprising that the periodical *Renaissance News* in its Winter 1963 issue published the following statement by Professor Robert G. Collmer: "The idealism and concern for the minutiae of Northern European Humanism, associated with Hyma since the mid-1920's when he published his studies on the Low Countries Brotherhood of the Common Life, reappear in these essays." He refers to the fourteen contributions by former students and close friends, published by Kenneth Strand in his valuable book, *The Dawn of Modern Civilization* (1962).

The change in the opinions regarding the Devotio Moderna entertained from 1948 to 1963 by both European and American experts may be seen reflected in various books dealing with the bibliography of the Renaissance. In the year 1948 two important bibliographies were published which deserve some attention here. Professor Wallace K. Ferguson issued his well-known work, entitled, *The Renaissance in Historical Thought* (Houghton Mifflin). On p. 313 he devoted only seven lines to *The Christian Renaissance*. Next he mentioned a book by Heinz Heimsoeth, who "had made even more sweeping claims for the mystics of his own country." The Dutch mystics, according to the present writer, "owed nothing to Eckhart or the other German mystics, and very little to the Italians, but their influence was decisive for the thought of the northern humanists and of such varied religious reformers as Luther, Zwingli, Calvin, and Loyola." Even more ridiculous was the verdict of H. Schulte Nordholt in his book, *Het Beeld der Renaissance* (Amsterdam: Querido). On p. 58 he said that "Hyma described the Devotio Moderna as the source not only of the whole of Northern Humanism in the Netherlands, England, France, and Germany; but also of the Reformation."

In the first place it should be noted that there were many Dutch mystics who were not connected with the Devotio Moderna, while the others owed extremely little to Eckhardt, as we have seen. Zerbolt took great pains to treat Eckhardt as had been done by the Archbishop of Cologne and Pope John XXII. As for other German mystics, both Groote and Zerbolt expressed much respect for Suso. Gerlach Peters, who was somewhat neglected by the present writer, owed a few ideas and phrases to both Suso and Tauler, according to a splendid dissertation by Jacobus J. Mak, published by him in 1936: *De Dietse Vertaling van Gerlach Peters' Soliloqium* (p. 87). Worth noting here also is the excellent introduction to the *Soliloqium* of Peters in the Italian language by Arrigo Levasti, whose book carries no date, but his note inscribed in the copy he sent to the writer is dated by him November 1938. He, like Mak, has much to say about Ruysbroek but little about the German mystics. On p. 33 he mentions Eckhardt and says that Ruysbroek was strongly affected by Eckhardt, which does not mean that Peters showed the same influence by Eckhardt. Upon the whole we may say that the Devotio Moderna owed very little to the German mystics, while the latter after 1500 were greatly indebted to the Devotio Moderna. The present writer has never claimed that the Dutch mystics owed nothing to the German mystics. They owed much to the Italians, for the latter made numerous contributions to Dutch civilization ever since the days of Emperor Augustus. Groote quoted from Ambrose, Francis of Assisi, Gregory the Great, and Thomas Aquinas, as the writer has shown.

It is remarkable that many scholars have accused the writer of having made extravagant claims about the influence of the Devotio Moderna upon Luther, Zwingli, Calvin, and Loyola. To speak of "decisive influence" is of course plain nonsense. And as for the humanists in England and Germany, those scholars were subject to many currents of thought coming from all sorts of directions, both in time and place. Perhaps it may prove useful to many readers to reproduce here a short article by the writer entitled, "The Influence of the 'Devotio Moderna,'" in *Nederlandsch Archief voor Kerkgeschiedenis,* published in 1925.

The author of "The Christian Renaissance", having read a considerable number of reviews of his book, has come to the conclusion that many readers do not understand the general aim of the work. In "The Methodist Review" of March-April, 1925, for example, the writer was surprised to find this astonishing statement: "All modern church history is quite largely a river that flows from those modest, holy, self-sacrificing, non-monastic brother-houses,[12] . . . a river flowing from the Yssel valley in Holland down over the fields of all churches to-day." Several critics in fact claim that the writer has overestimated the influence of Groote's two institutions.

The title of the book itself requires an explanation. To use the term "Devotio Moderna" frequently, makes one's book difficult to read, while the English equivalent "New Devotion" is lacking in color and effect. It was not at first the writer's aim to use a substitute at all, but later, when he became anxious to improve the literary form of his book, he chose the term "Christian Renaissance." In using this term he did not wish to intimate that the "Devotio Moderna" was the antithesis of the Italian Renaissance, nor that it was the only revival of Christianity, nor even the greatest.

The writer also made use of what he considered effective summaries, such as the last paragraph in the first chapter. That paragraph, as interpreted by him, in reality means: "To conclude, Gerard Groote . . . *became in a certain sense a* spiritual father of all the men educated by the Brethren," etc.

The relation between Luther and the Brethren of the Common Life should also be interpreted by the writer. Many Protestant and Catholic theologians maintain that there is a world of difference between the views of Luther and Zerbolt on original sin. They say that the writer should have known that. He is supposed to have made the mistake of confounding modern Protestantism with Luther's Protestantism. Luther, they add, must not be taken seriously. He was greatly mistaken in seeing so much resemblance between his view and that of Zerbolt,[13] although Groote's school and Luther agree that man in his present state can do absolutely nothing on his own initiative. In the "Imitation of Christ" we read that without grace, or the Holy Spirit, man is but a piece of withered wood, lifeless, impotent.[14]

Another important doctrine is that of predestination. It is well known that this doctrine teaches the following. God has ordained that a certain number of human beings shall be saved, and that the rest shall be damned. God selects a certain few, who are called the elect. The writer was educated for a period of ten years by men who support this doctrine. It was not ignorance, therefore, which made him say so little about it. The Brethren of the Common Life were not primarily theologians; even Groote was not. There are two kinds of predestination: the limited form as taught by Luther and Calvin, which includes only man's salvation; and the complete form, commonly named providence, which Christ himself taught. The second includes the first; it was held by Groote and Gansfort, and was accepted by Luther and Calvin.

Much could also be written about the doctrines of free will and justification by faith alone, which are closely connected with those on original sin and predestination. Groote's followers held that man possesses a very small remnant of free will; Luther on the other hand thought man had nothing left. In the last analysis, however, the small remnant amounted to nothing of any value in itself, since man could do nothing without God's aid.

It is true that Luther often indulged in the use of exaggerations. When he said that Gansfort and he had much in common, he meant to be taken seriously, but was thinking only of ideas uppermost in his mind. If he had stopped to search for differences, he would undoubtedly have found some. The writer knew that and assumed that such was taken for granted. He also knew that Luther got married, often used abusive language, and even encouraged bigamy at one time. In all this Luther differed from Groote's followers. The writer could have spoken of the lies told by Erasmus; of his love for temporal gain, his heartless mockery, and his selfishness, but he deemed this beyond the scope of his book. Erasmus was influenced by many religious movements; so were Luther, Calvin, and Loyola. Even Thomas à Kempis was, although he never left the Yssel-valley. The "Devotio Moderna" itself was subject to change. Gansfort went further than Groote; Hoen went beyond the limits of the movement, but still Gansfort and Hoen were loyal pupils of the Brethren of the Common Life.

The writer has suggested the channels through which the influence of the "Devotio Moderna" was exerted upon the heroes of the Reformation. It is impossible to measure this influence and compare it with that of the Italian Renaissance, the "saints" of medieval Europe, the great universities, the "heretics" condemned by the Church, and of a number of other movements which have as yet received no name.

The Brethren had much in common with Luther, but they were not precursors of the Reformation; they had much in common with Loyola, but were not precursors of the Counter-Reformation. Erasmus was saturated in their thoughts, and was also steeped in the learning of the Italian humanists. Standonck's library in Paris furnished a considerable part of the material Calvin needed for his famous "Institutes," for here he unquestionably found the Bible and Augustine. However, he later found much the same material in other places. Luther was influenced directly by Zerbolt and Biel, but also by a host of other writers. Rode and Hoen exerted much influence on Bucer and Zwingli; so did Carlstadt.[15]

Whereas a well-known Catholic editor accuses the present writer of making Groote's followers appear as precursors of the Reformation,[16] another prominent Catholic reviewer takes exactly the opposite view. He shows how thoroughly he understands the writer's opinion when he writes: "For, though some of the reformers looked upon certain phases of it with admiration, the Devotio Moderna was an essentially Catholic movement, and, as Dr. Hyma points out, there can be no doubt as to the unswerving Catholic loyalty of Groote and his followers."[17]

Many critics have refused to change their opinions in spite of the attitude adopted by all sorts of authorities. This has been the case in particular of those who have written textbooks dealing with the history of civilization. Professor Wallace K. Ferguson, for example, has repeated his former allegations in the textbook written by him and Geoffrey Bruun: *A Survey of European Civilization.* In Vol. I, dated 1955, we read this on p. 380: "The new mysticism began in Germany. Its creator was a German Dominican friar, Master Eckhart (1260-1327), and to him the movement owed its philosophy." The section in which the statement appears is called "The Waning of the Middle Ages and the Renaissance of the North." The reader gets the impression that during the fifteenth century medieval civilization declined, whereas in the Transalpine countries there was a great increase in learning and much wholesome progress in the field of religion and ethics. On p. 382 we read that "these northern humanists had all the reverence for antiquity, and all the scorn for the Middle Ages, that was characteristic of their Italian brethren." We also note this title on p. 380: "The Renaissance Crosses the Alps." In other words, the North had no innate powers in the field of learning. Practically all the inventions and new ideas were borrowed from Italy.

Equally disappointing is the account in Vol. I of the book by Crane Brinton and two colleagues entitled, A History of Civilization. Published by Prentice-Hall, it made a veritable sensation at first. In the edition of 1955 we read nothing about the Brethren of the Common Life. On p. 280 the Imitation receives two sentences. On p. 454 we read this about Erasmus: "He studied, taught, and lived at Oxford, Cambridge, and Paris, and in Italy, Switzerland, and Germany." True, he "was Dutch by birth." Although he spent the first 25 years of his life in the Netherlands, he studied elsewhere. The fact that he studied with the Brethren from 1475 to 1486 was totally ignored, while the seven years at the monastery of Steyn also escaped the attention of the authors. He "lived in Oxford," so we learn, but unfortunately his stay there was not what the famous A. Renaudet concluded, namely, the winter of 1499-1500, but only six weeks. Brinton undoubtedly envisioned several years spent at Oxford. We have an inspiring book entitled, Erasmus en Leuven, by Olaf Hendriks (Brussels and Bruges, De Kinkhoren, 1946). Here we find that Erasmus spent much more time in Louvain than in Oxford.

In general we may conclude that the textbooks dealing with the history of civilization have become so poorly organized that finally in the summer of 1963 the American Association of University Professors was forced to publish a comprehensive report about the big sellers. The top men said: "We do not like the course, for it is impossible to teach; it is impossible to maintain a continuity in the course." Not only the Renaissance and the Reformation but also the whole of ancient and medieval civilization are as a rule so badly distorted that the students have become rebellious. But no doubt no field has been so incompetently discussed as the civilization in the Netherlands from 1400 to 1700. Here follow a few pages on the subject.

ERRONEOUS OPINIONS EXPRESSED BEFORE THE YEAR 1959. The part played by the Low Countries in the shaping of modern civilization is often distorted beyond recognition. The average historian seems to feel with Professor Johan Huizinga of the University of Leyden that the civilization of the Renaissance in the Netherlands and what is now Belgium was strongly affected by pessimism and superstition. His famous book, *The Waning of the Middle Ages*, deals chiefly with the culture of northern France and the Low Countries, and it gives the impression that medieval civilization during the fifteenth century suffered from ascetic tendencies accompanied by morbid inclinations. The Middle Ages were thought to have faded away into a tailspin, especially in the Netherlands, where according to Henri Pirenne, the renowned Belgian historian, there was a tremendous outburst of commercial and industrial activity, together with a great flowering of art and learning. Who then was right, Pirenne or Huizinga?

THE SLAUGHTER OF THE RENAISSANCE BY CERTAIN HISTORIANS. In the United States a number of influential historians vied with Huizinga and his followers to slaughter the

Renaissance. In one widely used textbook much was said about the Medieval Renaissance and the Medieval Reformation, but the real Renaissance was almost entirely ignored. In several other textbooks a similar trend was revealed. It appeared as if the fourteenth and fifteenth centuries ushered in an age of intellectual decline. There was one scholar, however, E. P. Cheyney, who produced for the House of Harper a charming volume: *The Dawn of a New Era*. It was the first in the series of books depicting the history of modern Europe. Cheyney assumed that there was actually a dawn of modern civilization, with the Middle Ages leading into modern times with a marvelous display of energy, enlightenment, and empire building. Cheyney stood for the hallowed tradition, according to which Italy experienced a stimulating revival of learning correctly known as the Renaissance, or rebirth of classical scholarship and art. In 1952 appeared the volume covering the period from 1453 to 1517: *The World of Humanism*, by Myron P. Gilmore. The latter shared with Huizinga the concept of decline up to 1453, followed by a period of progress and advancement by the European states in general. Once more we might ask a question: Who then was right, Cheyney or Gilmore?

THE HARVARD THEORY.   Gilmore reflects his environment at Harvard University. He sees very little in the Northern Renaissance, and his section on German humanism is very disappointing. As a matter of fact, he does not take up humanism at all until he has reached p. 204 of his text, which ends on p. 270. The title of his book is therefore misleading. He is merely giving us a history of Europe from the fall of Constantinople to Luther's Ninety-five Theses, with little emphasis on the history of ideas. For the Italian Renaissance he has extremely little respect, considering its real importance in the development of modern civilization.

The Northern Renaissance, particularly the phase in the Low Countries, is treated with scorn.

ANOTHER FALSE CONCEPTION OF RECENT DATE. As we turn to the bibliography of the Renaissance by Wallace K. Ferguson, we note a strange attempt to divide nearly all Renaissance experts into two classes: pro-Burckhardt and anti-Burckhardt. He must assume that before Burckhardt there was only a limited understanding of the Italian Renaissance, and after his great work appeared in 1860 (*The Civilization of the Renaissance in Italy*) it became an almost universal fashion to go with or against the Burckhardt thesis. The vast multitude of scholars who continued to travel their own way were overlooked. [This was demonstrated very well by a Belgian scholar, whose large book on the same subject is much more comprehensive than that by Ferguson, largely because he has covered the art of the Renaissance, which Ferguson unfortunately chose to overlook: Herman Baeyens, *Begrip en probleem van de Renaissance* (Louvain, 1952). But Ferguson and Baeyens agree in their treatment of the Northern Renaissance. They surmise that the latter had very little to compare with the work of Lorenzo Valla, Leonardo da Vinci, Machiavelli, Petrarch, Boccaccio, and Michelangelo. They both conclude that the present writer was mistaken in his attempt to give the Low Countries their share in the whole Renaissance movement.]

RESULTS OF MISUNDERSTANDING AMONG CERTAIN HISTORIANS. When the art of the Low Countries is completely ignored and when the scholarship of Desiderius Erasmus and the finest teachers employed by the Brotherhood of the Common Life is conveniently passed by in silence, how are we to grasp the rise of the Dutch Republic and its enormous wealth and sea power? What shall we do then with the Dutch scientists of the seventeenth century, with the Reformation in Germany, with the rise of the British Empire? What will become of the growth of capitalistic enterprises, the expansion of Europe, the introduction of democratic institutions in the modern world? Is all of this to come out of the darkness of the fifteenth century or only out of the Italian Renaissance? The fishermen of Holland during the fifteenth century would have been very much amused if they had been accused of lethargy and pessimism. And the merchants of Amsterdam who in the fifteenth century almost entirely destroyed the Hanseatic League would have sniffed with scorn had they been told that they were too superstitious and ascetic for their own good. When Sir Thomas More observed the thriving industries of Flanders, he did not suggest that the rising tide of capitalism must be suppressed in England. On the contrary, he told the old speaker at the end of *Utopia* that capitalism was most welcome to him and his friends in England. He envied the high degree of civilization attained by the inhabitants of Flanders and Brabant.

THE FALSE THESIS OF FANFANI, THE FAMOUS ITALIAN STATESMAN. The present writer has indicated elsewhere that he does not favor the contention of A. Fanfani expressed in his book on Christianity and capitalism to the effect that when the Venetian galleys ceased to trade with Flanders as in former times, this was because the area around the North Sea was declining in economic power. On the contrary, by 1550 the Low Countries were surpassing Italy in both the field of commerce and of scholarship. We must not lightly assume that printing with movable type was introduced by mere chance in the Rhine Valley rather than in Italy, or that the tremendous upheaval called the Reformation in Germany was a mere coincidence. The patrons of learning and art have first grown rich before they give their patronage to professors, painters, musicians, and literary apostles. That has happened not only in the thirteenth century but also in the sixteenth, not merely in Italy but also in the Transalpine countries. Along the south shores of the North Sea and adjoining regions the world has witnessed until this day a fascinating sight. The languages and political institutions of England, France, and Germany spread into the remotest regions of Asia and Africa, not to mention North America. This was but the natural consequence of age-old laws governing the human race from its earliest infancy to the middle of the twentieth century. Who is there today in India or in China that despises the English language? And who dares to deny the splendors of the great cities along the river Rhine?

INFLUENCE OF THE NORTHERN RENAISSANCE. The Northern Renaissance and its contributions to the making of the Protestant Reformation as well as the Catholic Reformation need no longer suffer from the neglect of prominent historians. Again, the growth of Dutch and English sea power after 1450 is no freak affair without significance. We must remember that the fall of Constantinople in 1453 was bad for Italy but good for the Low Countries. Dutch sea power in 1453 matched the Flemish industries, and the invention of printing (which was partly caused by Laurent Coster in Haarlem) gave evidence of a thirst for knowledge not known in Europe for a thousand years. More's *Utopia* was naturally first published in the Low Countries, where a hundred years earlier a great school of art was born, and where Wessel Gansfort in 1475 enunciated daring political and religious maxims, surpassing those by Rousseau in 1775. Moreover, Gerard Groote, the founder of the Brotherhood of the Common Life, in 1383 fore-shadowed the learning of his brotherhood, so that Luther in

1498 could imbibe the practical wisdom of the brothers in Magdeburg, while Erasmus in 1483 had seen Hegius at work in Deventer.[18]

EVENTS FROM 1453 TO 1529. To return for a moment to the Turks who in 1453 had taken Constantinople. Their followers in 1516 did not inspire the Germans with glad tidings as they marched across the northern mountains of the Balkan Peninsula. And when in 1529 they stood before the very gates of Vienna, few Italians were delighted with the progress made by the Turks. After all of Hungary had fallen, Erasmus and Luther were both extremely pessimistic about the future of central Europe. Luther uttered endless tales of woe as late as 1545. But at the same time the merchants in Amsterdam and Rotterdam were well pleased with their expanding business establishments. Long before Calvin was born, the Dutch controlled more than half of the Baltic trade, which according to many historians was the result of Calvinism. Calvin must have been very active before he appeared in the flesh! Luther, on the other hand, was responsible for the poverty of the German people, for his peasant mind could not appreciate the blessings of capitalism, even after he had become one of the most successful capitalists in Germany. But there is such a thing as the spirit of capitalism, and that stems from Calvinism, so we are told by many prophets of enlightenment. It would seem, however, that where the spirit is, there the influence upon the body must be. The Dutch could hardly have been expected to get anywhere with their sea power until they accepted Calvinism. Strange to say, though, the Italians and the Portuguese, whom they sedulously imitated, were not much in favor of Calvinism. Furthermore, they could hardly have foreseen in 1454 what Calvin would do to them.

SEA POWER OF THE DUTCH BEFORE 1550. Contrary to the opinions of certain scholars, the Dutch and the Frisians were masters of the North Sea and the Baltic Sea as early as the Norman Conquest of England in 1066. It was they who gave us the name for their sea: North Sea, in contrast with the South Sea (Zuiderzee). The English had done very well with their trade to the East up to the Norman Conquest. But this conquest by French noblemen deflected their principal interests from the countries around the Baltic Sea. As a direct result, the Frisians and the Dutch were encouraged to enter the Polish and the Russian markets, way up the northern reaches of the Volga River. During the fifteenth century they were even so bold as to catch fish along the coasts of England and Scotland. This they continued to do until the time of Oliver Cromwell, who passed the Navigation Act of 1651, because his merchants and fishermen were still unable to compete with the Dutch. As we shall see below, the Navigation Act did not reduce the commerce of the Dutch in the East, again contrary to the opinion of many influential educators.

COMMERCIAL SUCCESS OF THE DUTCH BEFORE 1550. The Dutch finally operated as many merchant and fishing vessels as all other European peoples together, and Colbert warned King Louis XIV in 1667 that "of every ten parts of our foreign commerce the Dutch control nine." This was merely an extension of similar developments in the fifteenth century, when the Frisians were highly successful with their merchant fleets. In the days of Erasmus the Dutch shared with the Italians the wealth accruing from lucrative business interests. Financial success brought with it the patronage of scholars and artists, as can readily be seen in the United States of America. Consequently, the civilization of the Renaissance in the Low Countries found a counterpart in Italy, and vice versa.

DUTCH SCHOLARSHIP AND ART NEGLECTED BEFORE 1959. Now the curious thing about contemporary scholarship is that the wealth and learning in the Low Countries at the beginning of the modern period has consistently been ignored, partly by the Dutch and the Belgians themselves. If Professor Johan Huizinga had been aware of the Frisian sea power during the Middle Ages, he could not have spoken of the "autumn of the Middle Ages" and referred to the morbid mentalities of the people in the Low Countries from 1330 to 1500. And if Gilmore and Ferguson had been aware of the environment that helped Erasmus master Greek and Latin to perfection and fathom the minds of all the multitudes around him, they would have written a different account of the Northern Renaissance. Erasmus did not merely reflect the teachings of the scholars at Deventer, for he had at his disposal other sources of knowledge. Erasmus and his teachers gathered information outside of the schools conducted by the Brethren of the Common Life. The latter in turn did not neglect to take advantage of their good fortune. So did the professors at the University of Louvain, as will appear.

FLEMISH ART. A sound historiography of the Renaissance must take cognizance of the superb music and painting produced in Flanders. The absence of titles dealing with these subjects in the book by Ferguson does not make that music and painting lose its value. Similarly, the deliberate silence on the part of other historians when discussing the Northern Renaissance in the Low Countries does not cause the school of the Brotherhood of the Common Life to disappear. In Liége and Brussels around the year 1500 the Brethren of the Common Life obtained control of all teaching above the sixth grade, which also happened in Utrecht. Both Brussels and Liége by the year 1500 were cities of considerable wealth and importance. That the only printing press in Brussels during the fifteenth century was owned by the Brethren of the Common Life must have been a matter of interest to Belgian scholars. This interest, however, was not expressed in printed form.

THE COLLEGE OF THE THREE LANGUAGES AT LOUVAIN. Fortunately the College of the Three Languages founded upon the campus at the University of Louvain in 1517 has recently attracted proper attention. Professor Henry De Vocht has published his four-volume work entitled, *History of the Foundation and the Rise of the Collegium Trilingue Lovaniense 1517-1550*. The founding process was discussed in great detail by the author in his first volume, while the next two cover the later events. In the third volume the "full growth" is depicted (1954). Here some remarkable events are mentioned which throw much new light upon the civilization of the Renaissance in the Low Countries. On p. 13 we read:

> That room, which, in 1520, was constructed to contain three hundred hearers, had become too small within a few years, so that John Stercke had bought on January 28, 1524, part of the premises of a neighbour, . . . at any rate, Erasmus could refer, already on April 8, 1525, to the six hundred hearers who regularly gathered in the magnificently constructed room. Three years later, the auditory had become too small again, for Glocenius was obliged to double his lessons, as he announced to Erasmus on May 10, 1528.

MORE ON FLEMISH ART.   Now let us for a moment listen to the voice of two eminent authorities on art: David M. Robb and J. J. Garrison, whose illuminating textbook (*Art in the Western World*) was published by the House of Harper (3rd. ed. 1953). Chapter XXVII is entitled, "Renaissance Painting in the North." More important still is Chapter XXV, which is devoted to late medieval painting and starts with the Franco-Flemish tradition. The two authors are much impressed by the patronage of the Burgundian Court. They speak with respect of the work done under the supervision of the Duke of Burgundy who had become the Count of Flanders and had established in the famous port of Bruges a splendid center of political administration. The Flemish masters were called *primitive,* meaning the first of a new school in the North: "It has been termed decadent, for it marks the end of the mediaeval epoch, but this is to ignore its amazing vigor in the hands of a few masters." Although the ages of faith were ending now, the modern age "had the vitality to establish firmly a tradition of naturalism which, fused with the Renaissance tradition of Italy, was to create an integrated style."

GREAT FLEMISH ARTISTS. Proper attention is paid to Rogier van der Weyden, who died in 1464, but seemed of little importance to Gilmore for the period starting with the year 1453. His famous masterpiece, "Descent From the Cross," should be mentioned in any work dealing extensively with European civilization in the period from 1453 to 1517. Moreover, Memling, his pupil, was only one of many painters in the Low Countries who were strongly affected by him. Significant is this statement on p. 619: "The presence of a large and notable northern painting in Florence created one more of the many incidents of contact between northern Europe and Italy. The impact of Flemish art upon Italian and of Italian upon Flemish continued increasingly during the next two hundred ·years." What the average American historian has almost never visualized is the impact of the North upon the Italian scene. It was not always a one-way street affair, influence being exerted by Italy upon the North. On the contrary, the time was not very distant when the Low Countries would surpass Italy as a great center of art and science. As for Hans Memling, we are told that he was perhaps the best loved of all the Flemish masters. Although he died as late as 1494, Gilmore has only eight words for him over against more than a whole page for Hieronymus Bosch. W. K. Ferguson does not even list the name of Flanders in his Index. But Robb and Garrison give pp. 609-627 to Flanders, and pp. 627-638 to Italy in their chapter dealing with late medieval painting.

MUSIC IN THE LOW COUNTRIES. In the history of music the Low Countries also made notable contributions. Only during the past three decades has the music of the Low Countries been recognized for what it was at the close of the Middle Ages. Most helpful is the chapter on music in the book entitled, *The Netherlands,* published in 1943 by the University of California Press. The book mentions the admirable work done by four Dutch schools in succession: (1) that of Guillaume Dufay (1400-1474) and his followers, (2) that of Johannes Okeghem (1420-1495) and the celebrated Jacob Obrecht (1430-1505), (3) that by Josquin des Prez (1450-1521), and (4) that by Lupus Hellinck and Jacob Clemens (1510-1556). On p. 286 we read this illuminating statement: "A combination of Renaissance and Gothic elements was characteristic of the fifth, and last, generation of these fifteenth- and sixteenth-century Dutch masters. At this time the center of music shifted more and more to Italy, where the great figure of the Maestro Palestrina began to show itself on the horizon." And on p. 287: "Dutch leadership of European music ended in this period." The book here refers to the fifth school, which flourished under the leadership of Roland de Lassus (1532-1594). This was the last group which kept the Low Countries at the top of the list from about 1450 to 1575. It must seem strange that before the Golden Age of Dutch Civilization began about the year 1625, there were Dutch musicians who were putting the very best Italian masters in the shade. Their work must definitely be considered a part of the Northern Renaissance. Furthermore, these Dutch musicians indicated plainly that the northern Netherlands could do some wonderful things in the field of art. This was partly the result of the great progress made by the merchants and fishermen in the provinces of Holland and Friesland.

TYPICAL FALSIFICATION OF MEDIEVAL WRITINGS. Professor Johan Huizinga was highly regarded in Europe and America, with the result that his errors in judgment, like those of Toynbee, caused numerous students of history to make erroneous conclusions. One notorious example will suffice here. On p. 215 of the edition of the *Waning of the Middle Ages,* published in 1924 (London: Edward Arnold & Co.), we read this strange remark: "What are we to say, lastly, of the curious levity of the authors of the close of the Middle Ages, which often impresses us as an absolute lack of mental power?" We are told that "superficial description of outward circumstances – that is all we get from writers like Froissart and Monstrelet." When compared with Herodotus "their narrative is disjointed, empty, without pith or meaning." But Photios, as we saw, said correctly that Herodotus was fond of telling old woman's tales. Another remark also needs improvement: "In general the mental attitude towards supernatural facts was a vacillating one." That all depends upon the kind of writers we examine. Huizinga made dangerous generalizations without having read enough good and sound authors. He should· have found time to quote from the following brilliant writers: Cardinal Cusa, Wessel Gansfort, Rudolph Agricola, Gerard Zerbolt of Zupthen, and Gerard Groote.

CONTRIBUTIONS BY GERARD GROOTE, FOUNDER OF THE

BROTHERHOOD OF THE COMMON LIFE.   His remarks about
asceticism, material poverty, the power of the sacraments,
and the virtue of humility are edifying:

Asceticism is often very harmful, for the devil will
frequently use it as a tool, telling the person in question that it is a very helpful method for the religious
student, and yet all this watching, praying, and fasting will often cause mental diseases, anger, or pride.
Man is prone to think that he can do good on his own
initiative, thus taking too much pride in his own work,
which if really good, is not his work, but that of God.
Hence there are many people who pray much and inflict physical hardships upon themselves, while within
they are unrighteous and avaricious. . . .

O Lord of all riches why didst thou elect such humble garments? Why didst thou choose to sit on an ass
which was found tied to a gate near a public road,
upon which even the humblest man was free to ride,
and worse, on a colt upon whose back no man had ever
sat, as it had thus far been used for the meanest sorts
of employment? Rejoice, ye poor ones, for this seeming poverty is but a guise, since he, though poor in
earthly goods, was master of all, magnificent, royal,
divine! Follow in his footsteps, ascend the road which
leads from ignominy to glory, from toil and strife to
peace and rest, to heights sublime. . . .

If the pope should command you, or a bishop, or
any other superior, under whatever form of penalty,
even that of excommunication, suspension, deposition,
or privation, to administer the Holy Supper, and you
have not repented of certain mortal sins, no human
law of obedience can compel you to do it; on the

other hand, you should refuse to administer the sacrament in question, heedless of all temporal loss or calumny. For the laws and regulations of the Church are on the same level with those enacted by all human agencies. . . . The sacraments, have power independent of the priest who administers them, and his sins have no effect on the nature of the sacrament; all one's pollutions are taken away by one's faith in Christ, nor can any sinner pollute the divine sacraments. . . .

The more we realize our own imperfections, the nearer we approach perfection. Before all things, and in all things study specially to become humble inwardly. For it is far better to do but little good out of obedience to God's will than to do a great deal more on one's own account, since the lesser becomes the greater before God. "Good will" means to acquiesce in God's will. God speaks to us through his acts. Blessed is he who obeys God's voice and bears in mind that everything which befalls him is predestined by God, even the wrongs done by others. False accusations and slander he ought to bear in peace, for God knows best. Let him say to his Creator: "Lord, all that is mine and my own self I surrender to thee; I renounce my will for thy sake. This is the greatest thing I have been able to do in this world."

OPINIONS OF RUDOLPH AGRICOLA.   This scholar was often called the Petrarch of Germany, for he was noted for his labors in behalf of the restoration of classical Greek and Latin learning. His textbook on rhetoric replaced that of Aristotle in Paris. During the last year of his life he taught at the University of Heidelberg (1484). He made the following comments on (1) his native Friesland, (2) barbarous mediovel Latin, and (3) the revival of learning in the Holy Roman Empire:

What is more wonderful than that you, O Frisia, have produced men the like of which Liguria scarcely knows? No, Frisia, no longer does the name of "barbarian" disgrace you, now that the Attic elegance and the language of Latium temper the harshness of your pronunciation and the mellow sound of poetry refines your uncouth manners. . . .

You know that I cannot bear the corruption of language by the barbarians who are everywhere in power — that terrible Latin of theirs! But you also know their disposition: how they rage and fume and denounce whenever someone dares attack their opinions and dares assert that they as boys learned superfluous, corrupted rules, which they now, at an advanced age, will have to unlearn. They may do what they can to force me, but they cannot compel me to give up mine. . . .

I cannot easily tell you how much pleasure your epistle has given me, partly because it was from you, my dearest friend, and partly because I notice that you grow daily more careful and tasteful in your language, and I cherish the fond hope that through your guidance and your exhortations . . . the refined letters will penetrate into German lands and will some day capture that fortress.

THE RELIGIOUS AND POLITICAL IDEAS OF WESSEL GANSFORT (1419-1489). This writer is unfortunately neglected by many historians. His works reflect a tremendous amount of study and traveling. Luther in particular was amazed at his great learning. Here are some of his profound comments:

You have heard of the peril of that venerable man, Master John of Wesel. Now, although — as you have heard me say repeatedly — I do not like his absurdities, which deviate from the truth and are a stumbling block to the people; yet his learning.and unusually keen faculties are such that I cannot help loving the man and sympathizing with him in his misfortune. Oh, what an advantage it would have been to him, as I often said inter nos at Paris, if he had first been trained thoroughly, as we were, in the studies both of the Realists and the Formalists! For in that case he would not have been incautious and off his guard, but as if from a citadel and watch-tower he would have foreseen the coming assault. . . . I have often feared his inconsiderate and rash manner of speech. For although his teaching had some scholastic subtlety and possibly at times contained some catholic truth, yet to make such statements as he did to the unlearned crowd and to those who were incapable of understanding them caused serious scandal to simple-minded people and was altogether odious. . . .

Therefore what Aristotle calls the active intellect I call the light of God's countenance. What he says concerning conscience and reason pleading for the best things, I ascribe, not to any power of the soul or to the natural state of the soul, but rather to the breath of life breathed into man by divine power, and to divine assistance not only for the will but also for intelligence. When it is said that man was made in the image and likeness of God, this applies only to the inward man. . . . The image of God, the likeness of

God, Is not perfected unless perfect union is attained, so that the soul holding fast to its prototype, the living God, becomes one in spirit with him.

Faith is not the cause of our justification, but its proof. . . . "The just shall live by faith". . . . Hence in unbelievers, their unbelief separates them from life. But "he that believeth on him hath eternal life." Therefore our good works nourish and strengthen the bond of life, namely our faith. For only Christ and the Spirit quicken us, and Christ's sacrifice sanctifies us, and we are more strongly bound to this life by the stronger bond of our faith. But nothing strengthens this bond more than love; for love is strong as death. When indeed faith works through love, it is firm and the beginning of our confidence is firm. . . . By the works of the law shall no flesh be justified before him; even if one fulfil the chief commandment by his work, he will not because of this be righteous in God's sight. . . . Hence it is not our faith — whether it be in Christ or in God who delivered Christ over to be a sacrifice — nor is it the sacrifice of Christ that constitutes our righteousness; but it is the purpose of God, who accepteth the sacrifice of Christ, and who through Christ accepteth the sacrifice of Christians.

You, therefore, cautiously take refuge behind a condition as though behind an impregnable wall, declaring that only that will stand unshaken which the pope in matters of this sort shall decide, "if his key is not in error and Christ does not reject it." What, I ask, is the meaning of this indispensable condition, "if his key is not in error?" What is this key of the kingdom of heaven? And what is the error of this key? You are obviously assuming a key that may err and at the same time be the effectual and lawful key of the kingdom of heaven. O dreadful kingdom, if its gates, bars, bolts, and keys are such that through them error, falsehood, and ignorance can creep stealthily within! The key, as Augustine explains, is love diffused through the Holy Spirit in the hearts of the children of the kingdom. The Lord Jesus before his resurrection promised these two keys to Peter when he said: "I will give unto thee the keys of the kingdom of heaven: and whatsoever thou shalt loose on earth shall be loosed in heaven." In like manner he presented these keys after the resurrection — not to one — but to all unitedly, when he breathed on them, saying: "Receive ye the Holy Spirit: whose soever sins ye forgive, they are forgiven unto them; whose soever sins ye retain, they are retained." These two keys, in Augustine's opinion, are never rejected by Christ, nor does it ever happen that they are in error. For he defines the keys of the kingdom as being: (1) love diffused through the Holy Spirit in the hearts of the children of God, and (2) the Holy Spirit. And he says that to loose and to bind is to receive into fellowship because of the similitude of love or to exclude from fellowship because of dissimilitude. . . . When the Lord Jesus promised Peter the keys of the kingdom of heaven so that whatsoever he bound on earth would be bound in heaven, he promised nothing else than the Holy Spirit, and through the Holy Spirit the diffusion of love in the heart of Peter.

Indulgences and excommunications are on the same plane with the authority of power of the keys. The pope has no more power in reconciling souls to God than in alienating them from him. Indeed in excommunicating he has no power except, through an ecclesiastical court, publicly to exclude a person from the privileges of the the Church. Similarly, in indulgences he can only free a person from the bond of the canons and from censure. . . . In absolution before a court of penance, special considerations must be given to the fact that it is not the priest that binds the chain by which the sinner is held. For it is sin alone that separates the sinner from God. Nevertheless by this I do not mean that confession ought not to be made when it can be done to advantage, that is, so that those who are quickened and see may have a wider vision.

In every well organized republic the highest magistrate should be restrained from arrogance by fixing a limit either to his term or his authority; so that he can rule for one year or by a consensus of votes, For what is the meaning of an election unless the voter is free to choose? Inasmuch as obedience is due the better man, election should point to him. In so far as the election fails to secure such a man, in so far he is not to be obeyed. . . . On this ground kings should not be obeyed in evil measures; besides, they may be justly driven from their thrones, unless there is danger that still greater evils would result.

HUIZINGA'S GREATEST ERROR. Huizinga was a liberal Baptist, and his contempt for Catholicism, Lutheranism, and Calvinism caused him to write the following nonsense.

The credulity and the lack of critical spirit are too generally and too well known to make it necessary to cite examples. . . . In general the mental attitude towards supernatural facts was a vacillating one. Rational interpretation, timid credulity, or the suspicion of diabolical ruses, have the upper hand by turns. . . . So towards the end of the Middle Ages this dark system of delusion and cruelty grew slowly to completion.

All the deficiencies of medieval thinking and its inherent tendencies to gross error had contributed to its building. The fifteenth century transmitted it to the coming age like a horrible disease, which for a long time neither classical culture nor Protestant reformation nor the Catholic revival were able or even willing to cure.

THE ORIGINAL VERSION OF THE "IMITATION OF CHRIST"

Protestants in general would have been much more friendly to the *Imitation* if it had come out at once in the garb which Zerbolt originally gave to it. He not only composed Book I but also the treatise upon which the second and third books were based. This treatise the present writer published in English translation in his edition of the *Imitation* (1927). It was the first English translation of this powerful piece of mystical literature. The *Imitation* received its title and most of its appeal from Book I. In its original form it reflected perfectly the attitude of the Brethren of the Common Life toward the duty of the average Christian in the world of affairs. These pious men did not condemn monasticism but preferred to live in semi-monastic institutions. They kept the three monastic vows and they were very friendly with the monastic orders, especially after Zerbolt had convinced the Franciscans and the Dominicans that they were thoroughly orthodox. At the Council of Constance (1414-1418) they were ably and successfully defended by Gerson, the Chancellor of the University of Paris. Moreover, from Pope Eugene IV they received valuable privileges. Again, Cardinal Cusa was so impressed by their useful labors that near the end of his life he left a large sum of money for the founding of a home for twenty young men, who were to study with the Brethren of the Common Life at Deventer. This house survived the storms of the Reformation.[1]

Nevertheless, the Brotherhood of the Common Life, as

Zerbolt showed in his brilliant treatise, *On the Common Life*, had a tendency to side with those who favored a reduction of asceticism in all directions. Thomas à Kempis, as we shall see, frowned upon Zerbolt's bold ideas in the realm of politics. He naturally did not have much interest in legal studies, but Zerbolt was an expert in those. Consequently, Chapter II of the *Imitation* mentioned a person who knew less about the law than others did. Thomas à Kempis retained this interesting passage. Neither he nor Zerbol showed heretical inclinations. They freely utilized the works of medieval saints and doctors, and praised them for their work. Luther and Calvin, on the other hand, showed little respect for them.

It has recently been demonstrated that Radewijns and Zerbolt were deeply interested in a mystical treatise by the Franciscan friar, David of Augsburg, entitled, *Profectus Religiosorum*. Radewijns strongly urged his disciples to read that inspiring book, and it is mentioned in the introduction to the original constitution of the brethren-house at Deventer.[2] The two famous works by Zerbolt contain large sections copied almost verbally from this treatise. In the *Treatise of Spiritual Exercises* by Radewijns numerous quotations have also been found.[3]

About the year 1840 a teacher at the Gymnasium in Eutin, in what was once known as Oldenburg, found an interesting manuscript containing the Eutin Copy of Book I of the *Imitation*. This book is after all the only one of the four in the *Imitation* which deserves the title subsequently given to the four books collectively. The German instructor in question was fascinated by the fifteen chapters which follow the first book of the *Imitation*. There are altogether forty chapters, of which the first twenty-five form Book I of the *Imitation*. In 1845 he published a treatise on the subject, in which he stated that here we have the original version of Book I of the *Imitation*.[4] He was absolutely right, but later authorities disowned his claim, which led to the neglect of the manuscript until 1927.

Now we know that Chapter XXIX in the composite work was largely copied from Chapter LXI of Book III of the *Profectus Religiosorum* by David of Augsburg, and that all of the forty chapters owe much to the same writer, though still more to Radewijns and Zerbolt. According to one learned professor in the University of Nijmegen, the first twenty-five chapters were copied from an earlier treatise by Gerard Groote. Zerbolt was the copyist.[5] But other writers in the Netherlands made different assertions, pointing to errors of judgment in the numerous articles by this admirer of Groote.[6] The latter, however, had done an immense amount of research work, and we are greatly indebted to him for the publication of four versions in parallel columns, including Book I of the *Imitation* as it appeared in the autograph of Thomas à Kempis. These four versions clearly reveal the influence of Radewijns and Zerbolt upon Thomas à Kempis.

The Eutin Copy deserves careful study. Its first twenty-five chapters form a mystical treatise far superior to Book I of the *Imitation* as the literary world has known it ever since the middle of the fifteenth century. This composition may well be considered the finest flower of Christian mysticism, and it ranks next only to the New Testament in the Bible. Here indeed we find the very heart, the Gospel, of the Devotio Moderna. It was written in the brethren-house at Deventer, either by or under the influence of Radewijns and Zerbolt. Why a work of such immense religious power should have lain neglected so long in a German monastery and later in an insignificant high school at Eutin may seem a veritable mystery. Its superiority to the poor copy by Thomas à Kempis can be seen in the following comparison:

Verse 3 in Chapter I cannot fail to arrest the eye of the observer: While Thomas à Kempis asks to meditate upon the life of Christ, the Eutin Copy insists that the reader do not stray from his subject, which is the imitation of Christ. As we have seen, Thomas very often wandered away from his theme, and he delighted in fanciful discursions, interrupting God or Christ at inopportune moments. He was the author of a book entitled, *Meditations on the Life of Christ*. Consequently, he changed the third verse in the *Imitation* to suit his own taste. He liked meditation better than action.

In the fourth verse of the Eutin Copy, unlike that by Thomas, we are told that "he who has the spirit of Christ will find the hidden manna." Thomas speaks of having the spirit, and other copies of the spirit of God, whereas the subject introduced is the doctrine of Christ. Consequently, the reader of Christ's words is expected to have His spirit in order to understand these words.

The tenth verse contains a sensational revelation. In the Eutin Copy we find the correct Latin phrase: "*Si scires totam bibliam*," while Thomas à Kempis, unlearned as he was in the Latin tongue, inserted a Germanic phrase: "*Si scires totam bibliam exterius*." That is a literal translation of the Dutch idiom, so well known to Thomas. Another version reads: "*Si scires totam bibliam corde*." That corresponds to our own English: "If you knew the whole Bible by heart."

In the nineteenth verse Thomas refers to a proverb, which is not mentioned in the Eutin Copy. In the next verse the latter adds a lengthy statement about the main theme in the *Imitation*, which Thomas chose not to copy here: "Conform yourself to the invisible things and the better life, and thus you will imitate Christ, for every action of His is for us an instruction." Then follows a text from the Book of Job, which is to be found also in the Lübeck edition of 1489. This is most significant, for it was in the home of the Sisters of the Common Life in Lübeck that Book II and Book III of the *Imitation* were read in the original version, though in Low German translation. Eutin is not far from Lübeck, and the whole region between the Yssel Valley and Lübeck was thoroughly affected by the spirit of the Devotio Moderna.

In the first verse of Chapter II the Eutin Copy contains another important statement not accepted by Thomas. In the fourth verse Thomas talks about a person who knows all things in this world but does not possess love, while the Eutin Copy mentions only the knowledge about Christ. The title above Chapter II is here: *"De Cognitione sui."* Thomas, on the other hand, has *"De Humili Sentire sui ipsius."* He again has strayed from his subject in the fourth verse of this chapter, while the author of the Eutin Copy continues to adhere to his chosen task: the imitation of Christ. The latter has nothing to correspond to verses 7-10, but adds material later on in the chapter that is missing in the printed version. It is becoming clear to us now why Thomas could have been so bold as to assert that he wrote the *Imitation.* He certainly made numerous far-reaching changes in Book I. Both versions, however, have the famous and characteristic phrase: *"Ama nescire,"* or *"Ama nesciri."* Thomas has the latter, which seems more to the point. Yet the Eutin Copy is not without merit, for it reads: *"Ama nescire ad quae non teneris et gaude pro nihilo reputari."*

As a matter of fact, we note a tremendous difference between the view of Zerbolt and that of his pupil, Thomas à Kempis. The former wrote: "If you wish to know or learn anything profitable, then love to know nothing about those things that do not concern you, and rejoice in being considered of little value." The pupil was more drastic and less sensible. He changed Zerbolt's profound words into these: "Love to be unknown." Zerbolt would hear of no such thing, for he was a scholar and recognized the hand of God in all forms of scholarship. In the fourteenth century there were indeed numerous mystics who took pride in the fact that they were dealing with things unknown. One work was entitled, *The Cloud of Unknowing,* and the House of Harper in recent years published an English version of this remarkable book. It was not the type that Zerbolt and Groote were recommending for their lay pupils.

In Chapter III Thomas added verses 3-6, in which he discussed topics studied in the schools. Since he himself attended none of the higher institutions of learning, he spoke disparagingly about "genus and species." The author of the Eutin Copy, on the other hand, was a real scholar, such as Zerbolt was, and he did not wish to belittle the work done in the universities. Very well known are these words of Thomas à Kempis in verses 3 and 4: "What does it avail to cavil much about dark and hidden things, concerning which we shall not be reproved in the day of judgment, because we did not know them? It is a great folly . . . to give our minds to things that are curious."

Zerbolt was too great a scholar to argue that his readers should not be interested in "things that are curious." He had naturally heard certain fearful clergymen talk about the need of avoiding the study of scientific subjects. The latter were of the opinion, as was Thomas à Kempis, that laymen must not pry into God's secrets. Zerbolt also was not the author of verses 10-22 in Chapter III, where Thomas à Kempis wanted all things reduced to one. The latter favored the process of generalization, so appealing to simple minds. He praised those who did not exhibit "deep search after learning." No wonder, for Thomas had never attended a university and was afraid of science. What is still worse, Thomas wrote in verse 14: "Quanto aliquis magis sibi unitus et interius simplificatus fuerit." As has been pointed out by Professor J. van Ginneken of the Catholic University at Nijmegen, and repeated in the handsome volume entitled, *The Following of Christ: The Spiritual Diary of Gerard Groote*,[7] Thomas wrote "sibi" for "tibi," and he mistook "simplificatus" for "similatus." He also missed the words "de te."

Even more startling is the absence in the Eutin Copy of these famous remarks by Thomas: "Tell me where are all those doctors and masters with whom you were well acquainted while they lived and flourished in learning?" Zerbolt had too much respect for these men with doctor's and master's degrees to treat them with such words of scorn. Thomas writes in verse 30: "Oh, how quickly passes the glory of this world." That is strictly Biblical and respectable, but Zerbolt had to utilize the services of doctors and masters in the affairs of his brotherhood. We know of one learned Benedictine abbot, who aided him in his work.[8] And how could Zerbolt have talked so glibly about learned abbots as did Thomas when he wrote in verse 28: "Now others possess their prebends"? Thomas showed much concern over the fate of those who "perish through their vain learning in this world," but the Eutin Copy maintains a discreet silence here (verse 32).

In this connection it might be noted that in verse 11 of Chapter II Thomas suggested that nobody be puffed up because of great knowledge in some art of science, while Gerard Zerbolt warned against pride without complaining about having accomplished something great in art or science. The title of Chapter II is equally revealing. While

Zerbolt speaks of self-knowledge as being the main topic, and makes much of studying a person's own thoughts and character, the humble Thomas shows his dislike for the idea of obtaining knowledge, even of the person himself.

The title of Chapter V is in itself enough to prove that Gerard Zerbolt was the author of the original version as found in the Eutin Copy. There he copied the exact words he had used in a separate treatise devoted to the same subject. His title was "De Lectione Sacrae Scripturae." Thomas changed these words into the following: "De Lectione Sanctuarum Scripturarum." Zerbolt was the author of an interesting pamphlet - entitled, *An Liceat Libros Divinos Transferre in Vulgare.* Only one copy of this composition escaped the destruction of the sixteenth and seventeenth centuries. This copy was discovered by the present writer in the year 1920. He was the first to publish it.[9] The first sentence in this treatise begins with these words: "Quoniam sunt nonnulli minus sacram scripturam intelligentes."

The first verse in the copy in Eutin reads: "Veritas in sacris scripturis inquirenda est, non eloquentia." The corresponding verse by Thomas à Kempis has: "Veritas est in scripturis sanctis quaerenda: non eloquentia." Here again we note the contrast between the words "sancta" and "sacra." The third and fourth verses by Thomas discuss the problem of preferring useful ideas above profound thoughts, while the reader is advised to read "devout books" rather than profound literature. That is in keeping with the pious mind of Thomas à Kempis. Gerard Zerbolt, on the other hand, has nothing to say about these matters. In verse 5 Zerbolt says that the reader must not be offended by the simplicity of the author or the book he reads, while Thomas speaks of the authority of the writer. In verse 10 Zerbolt again has the telling phrase "sacra scriptura," and this time

Thomas does not mention the sacred writings at all. Thomas in verse 11 refers to the "words of the saints." Zerbolt shows no interest here in saints. Over against "lectione sacrae scripturae" by Zerbolt in verse 9 Thomas has "lectione scriptuarum." Moreover, Zerbolt does not have the two verses (7 and 8) in which Thomas says that human beings will pass on while the truth of God remains forever.

It was of course perfectly natural for Zerbolt to devote a whole chapter to the subject of reading sacred literature. He had said in his treatise on the reading of sacred books in the vernacular that laymen ought not to read books that were too difficult or obscure. That is why in the present book he told the reader not to complain if his reading material seemed too simple to him. He also made much of the fact that the truth is more important than the style of a book. Again, he spoke eloquently about the need of reading a book in the same spirit as that in which it was written. Thomas à Kempis would probably have seen no need at all of writing a chapter on the reading of sacred books, but, having been provided with such a chapter by Zerbolt, he kept and changed it to suit his own tastes. It is also interesting to note the title of Chapter IV in the Constitution of the Brethren of the Common Life at Deventer, published for the first time by the present author: "De Studio Sacrae Scripturae." This title is almost identical with that of Chapter V in the *Imitation* by Zerbolt.

Chapter VI is of great importance, as it urges the reader not to become too familiar with other persons. In recent years a number of Dutch historians have overlooked this feature in the Devotio Moderna. For example, a learned Dutch scholar at the University of Leiden went so far as to say that when Erasmus indulged in neurotic friendships with other monks, he resembled the leaders of the Devotio Moderna. Since he had nothing else of importance to say about the Devotio Moderna in his study of Erasmus, he certainly left us a sad picture about the influence of this great movement upon the mind of the famous Dutch humanist.[10] Zerbolt and Radewijns, as well as Thomas à Kempis, would have resented such thoughtless interpretation on the part of a modernistic professor. In the Eutin Copy we read the same sentiments as those presented by Thomas. Even more convincing are the verses in Chapter VIII: "On Shunning too much Familiarity." Erasmus must have paid little heed to that chapter when he was a monk.

It is not clear why the author of the Eutin Copy in Chapter VII did not discuss, as Thomas did, the fate of those who are considered "poor in this life." Thomas told them not to be ashamed of their condition, while the original version ignored the poor people. In the latter work there is also no reference to the desirability of loving only God and the angels, rather than human beings. Zerbolt no doubt felt that a person should love his neighbor as himself, as Christ had stated. In his opinion it would not do to go so far as Thomas and condemn all forms of human affection (Chapter VIII, verse 6).

Most interesting is the plagiarism indulged in by the author of the Eutin Copy in verse 5 of Chapter VIII. While he copied literally from David of Augsburg, as the scribe did also in Chapter XXIX, that is the fourth chapter added by a scribe to the first twenty-five, Thomas carefully revised the original version. Thomas said that a man should merely commend all women to God. Zerbolt was not so inhumane, and he suggested that one should either love all women equally or else keep at a distance from all of them.

It is interesting to note the difference in the word order adopted by the two writers in question. Thomas often follows an arrangement that resembles somewhat the order in Dutch sentences. He puts the verbs farther to the end of the sentence, while Zerbolt has another type of sentence structure. For example, the first verse in Chapter VIII reads in the copy at Eutin: "Ne revele cor tuum omni homini." Thomas, on the other hand, has: "Non omni homini revele cor tuum." In Zerbolt's treatise on the reading of the Bible in the vernacular we find this statement: "Quam si illud expenderent in rebus terrenis." Thomas would probably have put the verb at the end of the sentence.

Another difference between Thomas and Zerbolt is the way in which Thomas wanders away from his subject while Zerbolt meticulously goes right on with his theme. This is a matter of great importance, since we are now dealing with the book which caused the great fame of the four put together in the form of the *Imitation* as we now know it. The first book begins with these words: "He who follows me shall not walk in darkness, says the Lord." Zerbolt, who was very consistent and scholarly, stuck to his subject and at the end of Book I he wrote these significant words: "Follow the Lord." Thomas, on the other hand, rambled on with no thought about literary perfection. He ended the first book in this manner: "The more violence you do to yourself, the more, also, you will grow in virtue."

The title of Chapter IX shows that Thomas was not satisfied with a discussion of obedience but had to add to the original version these two words: "And Subjection." In verse 4 he wrote: "Go where you will, you will find no rest save in humble subjection to the rule of a superior." That sentiment was too strong for Zerbolt and Radewijns, who had refused to accept monasticism for themselves. Consequently, the Eutin Copy does not contain this verse. The same is true of verses 7-10, which mention the desirability of excessive obedience and humility. Instead of this we have the important political theory of the rights of the individual, not brought up by Thomas: "If you have an opinion which is better than the yoke of your prelate, nevertheless for the sake of obedience relinquish your idea and accept the order of your superior, in so far as it is good. But if the commands of the prelates are contrary to the precepts of God, we are not obliged to obey them but rather those of God." Such bold language naturally did not appeal to the humble monk, but Zerbolt had written in this *Treatise on the Common Life* that he and his associates were free to carry on as they saw fit regardless of the criticism leveled against them by venerable prelates. Groote had used almost exactly the same words as those we have just quoted. He had gone so far as to say that it was not necessary to obey the Pope unless the latter were in the right.[11]

In Chapter XI Thomas inserted his eighth verse, which reads: "If we were perfectly dead to ourselves, and not entangled within our own breasts; then should we be able to taste divine things, and to have experience of heavenly contemplation." In the brethren-house at Deventer this sentiment was not entirely overlooked, but the scholarly mind of Zerbolt was too much immersed in legal affairs to ignore the value of worldly wisdom. Extreme forms of asceticism were not nearly so popular in Deventer as they were at Windesheim. Deventer was the home of practical mysticism, but Thomas felt more at home in his monastery than in the brethren-house. To the original version of the *Imitation* he added statements that seem logical to a monk but not fashionable in great Hanseatic cities. He also added verse 13, in which he spoke of *"religio,"* the Latin for monasticism. On the other hand, he eliminated the references made in the Eutin Copy to the devil who is going around and roaring like a lion, seeking whom he may devour. He also refused to copy the phrase so familiar in the brethren-house: *"bona exercitia."* Futhermore, he left out the reference to those who welcome temptations in order to achieve new victories (Chapter XIII, verses 3 and 9).

The title of Chapter XII in Zerbolt's version reads this way: "De Adversitate." But Thomas has "De Utilitate Adversitatis." We see here a difference in the respective attitudes toward the suffering of adversity. While the Brother of the Common Life is less ascetically inclined than the average monk, he must give expression to his own state of mind by leaving out the idea that adversities are in themselves useful. At the end of Chapter XII Zerbolt adds two significant verses, which Thomas must have disliked. Zerbolt says that temptations force us to know ourselves better. In his famous book on spiritual ascensions he made much of self-knowledge, and here in his first book of the *Imitation* he again emphasized the need of studying our inner selves and our thoughts.

In verse 8 of Chapter XIII Zerbolt presented some interesting observations about certain monks. He knew that Groote had at one time entered a Carthusian monastery, but that at the end of his life he had cautioned his followers against adopting severe rules, like those of the Carthusians. Now Zerbolt was sitting in the house of the Brothers of the Common Life in Deventer. He was thinking about the Carthusians and he wrote: "The more saintly a man is or the place in which he resides, the stronger will be the temptations he will have to deal with: The Carthusians and the cloistered folks and the real monks sustain the greatest temptations." He was pointing toward the monks as a bystander; he was not one of them himself. Now what did Thomas do with this passage? He wrote: "There is no order so saintly nor a place so secluded that there are no temptations nor adversities."

The fourteenth chapter adds further contrasts between

the two versions under discussion. While the Eutin Copy in verse 3 presents a famous text from the Gospel about a man who out of the good treasure of his heart produces good works, Thomas omits the quotation and establishes for himself a greater degree of independence. In his ninth verse he refers to differences of opinion which lead to discussions. Again he speaks of "religious persons," meaning monks, and again the Eutin Copy ignores the monks. The title of Chapter XV makes us wonder why Thomas wishes to increase the gap between the two versions. Whereas he speaks of works done out of love, the other version is entirely negative in referring to evils to be avoided. Once more we must point to Thomas' habit of wandering from his subject. He adopted a new title for the chapter, though the old one conformed absolutely to the contents of the opening verse which begins as follows: "For no worldly thing, and for the love of no man, is any evil to be done." In this chapter the older version mentions "fraternal love" and "fraternal charity," for a brother was known as a "*frater.*" He was not a "*religiosus.*" Thomas omitted both phrases, as might have been expected of a man who was once a "*frater*" and later a "*religiosus.*"

The "*frater*" who wrote Chapters XV and XVI had much to say about going out to help the poor and afflicted: he quoted the Apostle who wrote: "Bear each other's burdens." That verse was not literally copied by Thomas who ascribed it to God directly. The title of his seventeenth chapter reads significantly: "Of the Monastic Life." The Eutin Copy could not very well carry such a heading, and here we read: "Of the Life of the Congregation." In the second verse Thomas referred only to monks, but the older version has at the end of the first verse the phrase, "discordia fratrum," meaning discords among the Brethren of the Common Life, and in the next verse it discusses a congregation which may live either in a spiritual or a secular atmosphere. Thomas of course had to drop the remark about the secular environment, for that was the realm in which the Brethren of the Common Life labored by preference. However, in verse 3 the Eutin Copy has one reference to the monastic life. Verses 9-12 by Thomas are not to be found in the Eutin Copy. Here we read: "You came to serve, not to rule. You must know that you were called to suffer and to labor, not to be idle and gossip. Here therefore are men tried as gold in the furnace." That was true of the monastery, but the Brethren were too busy helping people in the cities to devote themselves to suffering and to the serving of a monastic superior.

Whereas the title of Chapter XVIII in the Eutin Copy has simply, "Of the Examples of the Fathers," Thomas wrote, "Of the Examples of the Saintly Fathers." In verse 5 the former begins thus: "The elect of God all hated the worldly things." Thomas said nothing about the elect of God but merely mentioned the fact that "they hated their lives in this world." In verse 12 he remarked that the saints were poor in things of this world, which statement is missing in the other version. The latter also lacks verses 18-24, in which the typical expressions of Thomas appear four times: "*O quantus,*" "*O quanta,*" "*Och teporis*" and "*Utinam.*" It was exactly this type of literature, as we saw, that he added to the second and third books of the *Imitation.* Moreover, the word "*Och*" is Dutch, not Latin. Zerbolt would have scorned to use it.

Thomas took far more liberties with the first book than with the others, for after his departure from the "fraterhuis" at Deventer he sensed the profound difference between the Brotherhood of the Common Life and the monastic orders. Consequently, when he came to Chapter XIX with its simple title of, "On the Good Life," he felt impelled to change it into these words, "On the Exercises of a Good Monk." In the first verse the "good man" became the "religious man," meaning the monk. Verses 19-26 do not appear in the Eutin Copy, for Thomas wanted to add some remarks about exercises fitted for monks. Similarly, he added verses 38-43 to Chapter XX, which are devoted to a depreciation of worldly things. Again, in Chapter XXII he inserted verses 9-11, 19-20, and 24-29. His favorable opinion of asceticism was neatly expressed in two verses (35 and 36) of Chapter XXIII, where he wrote: "Chastise your body now with penitence, that then you may have a sure confidence."

Near the end of Chapter XXIV Thomas presented this new material (verses 40 and 41): "If until this day you had always lived in honors and delights, what would all that profit you, if you were to die this moment? All is therefore vanity, except to love God and to serve Him only." Verses 31-35 are also his original work. In the last chapter we note further revisions. Verses 11-24 are all by Thomas and missing in the Eutin Copy. This section begins with these words: "Nor did he have a mind to search curiously any further, to know what would befall him." Thomas was again urging the reader not to become too much interested in secular things. In verses 29-31 he referred twice to monks, but both statements are missing in the older version. Gradually he was leading up to a very important remark that has caused much misunderstanding among the European authorities.

We must carefully weigh his words in verse 35, for the whole paragraph is wanting in the Eutin Copy, as is perfectly natural: Thomas was an Augustinian monk, and he remembered the words of Groote in connection with the founding of the new monastic organization. Groote's disciples had been asking him what order they should join, and he replied, "Not the Carthusians, nor the Cistercians, for their rules are too strict for you." But as for the Augustinian Canons Regular, that was another matter. They formed a highly venerable order, and their asceticism was very mild. Consequently, we are not a bit surprised to hear Thomas remark: "Observe the Carthusians, the Cistercians, and the monks and nuns of various orders, how they do every night rise to sing psalms to the Lord!" Yes indeed, they were used to rigorous discipline and mortification of their bodies, which elicited the admiration of Thomas à Kempis. If he had been in Groote's place, he might well have told the men and women to become Carthusians. Groote had spent a few years himself in a Carthusian monastery, and he knew what was expected of his associates. Naturally he could not have composed the verse just quoted, although one Dutch writer has repeatedly asserted that he wrote the whole of Book I of the *Imitation*. Why should a Carthusian monk say to his colleagues, "Look at those Carthusians"?

In short, the original version of Book I of the *Imitation*, published for the first time in the year 1940, reveals the intellectual and religious climate in which its author labored. What the present writer surmised in 1919 was proved to be a fact in 1940. The momentous years at Deventer when Zerbolt and Radewijns instructed Thomas à Kempis were fruitful in many ways. Zerbolt saved the Brotherhood of the Common Life through his brilliant treatise on the nature of his congregation. His two mystical treatises were just being acclaimed as masterpieces. He was the leading scholar in his brotherhood for a period of fifty years, and until the *Imitation* was finally put together, his *Spiritual Ascensions* was the outstanding book of spiritual exercises in the Devotio Moderna. He combined sound scholarship with religious fervor, and he cautioned his

colleagues against excessive mortification of the flesh. Radewijns agreed with him in setting the brotherhood apart
from the monastic world, while maintaining the highest
moral standards possible. In this manner these two instructors of Thomas à Kempis provided him with choice material
which he saw fit to adjust to the monastic ideal. The immortal work would have reflected the Christian philosophy
far more successfully if he had not tampered with the
ideals of his great teachers. But when the original text has
become available in modern languages it may be expected
that the Gospel of the Devotio Moderna shall illuminate
the world as its diluted copy never could have done.

Conclusive proof for the authorship of Book I of the
Imitation by Gerard Zerbolt of Zutphen may be found in
the very first chapter. Thomas à Kempis has the following
statement known as verse 20: "Endeavor therefore to withdraw your heart from the love of visible things and turn
to the invisible things." The version in the Eutin Copy
reads: "Endeavor therefore to withdraw your heart from
all love of visible things. . . . and thus you will imitate
Christ, for every act of His is an instruction for us." In
the treatise which Zerbolt wrote for the Brethren of the
Common Life entitled, *Super Modo Vivendi,* he wrote:
"Every act of Christ is an instruction for us, as St. Augustine
says." The Latin text is given here for the convenience of
the reader: Book I of the *Imitation:* Ut sic Christum
imiteris, quia omnis actio (eius) nostra est instructio. *Super
Modo Vivendi:* Sexto omnis Christi accio nostra est instructio secundum Agustinum.[12]

These few words quoted above contain a wealth of illu-
mination. In the first place, they indicate what is the correct
title of the whole book in the English translation. In recent
years a number of scholars have hit upon the following
title, borrowed from the opening words of the first chapter:

The Following of Christ. If they had been acquainted with the version by Zerbolt, they would have noted his reading, *imiteris*. The whole idea of Book I is an actual imitation of Christ, which is more than a mere following. It is a great pity that Thomas à Kempis saw fit to eliminate the beautiful passage by Zerbolt, as quoted from St. Augustine. He was nearing the end of the first chapter. There was but one verse left. Why could he have been so blind as not to realize that Zerbolt was building up a powerful argument for the imitation of Christ? Zerbolt suggested that every action of Christ was an example and an instruction. Christ's disciples should imitate every action insofar as it was humanly possible.

Illuminating also is the difference between the versions of Zerbolt and Thomas à Kempis near the beginning of Chapter I. Once more we shall give the Latin originals:

THOMAS à KEMPIS	ZERBOLT
Summum igitur studium nostrum sit in vita Iesu Christi meditari. Doctrina Christi omnes doctrinas sanctorum praecellit et qui spiritum haberet. . . .	*Summum igitur nostrum studium sit in vita Iesum imitari, quia eius doctrina omnes instructiones sanctorum praecellit et qui eius spiritum haberet. . . .*

What do we find here? Once more we have the Latin word for imitating Christ, and once more Thomas à Kempis refuses to use it. Zerbolt is very meticulous with his style, and he does not want to confuse his readers. He speaks again about the instruction we get from Christ, but Thomas à Kempis again omits this thought. Zerbolt emphasizes the imitation of Christ, as he should. He has only reached the third verse of the first chapter. Why should he wander away from his main theme? Poor Thomas was not so wise and so learned as Zerbolt. He did not want to copy everything as he had found it in the library of the brethren-house at Deventer. He no doubt was under the impression that he was making some sort of an improvement. Unfortunately that was not the case. And so it happened that the first six thousand editions of the *Imitation* were marred by his amateurish meddling. It seems almost incredible that scholars in Europe failed to note the incongruities in the work by Thomas à Kempis. When in the year 1845, a German writer of no mean ability made the contents of the Eutin Copy known to the world and told the truth about Book I of the *Imitation,* he could get no hearing. For more than another hundred years the imperfect rendering was printed and read by millions of devout Christians, who would have been edified far more had they read the powerful version by Gerard Zerbolt.

In the year 1927, the present writer published in the *Nederlandsch Archief voor Kerkgeschiedenis* a remarkable work by Gerard Zerbolt. It is entitled, *Scriptum pro Quodam Inordinate Gradus Ecclesiasticos et Praedicationis Officium Affectante.* Chapter III has the following heading: "De Vicioso et Inordinate Appetitu ad Sacerdocium." What was more natural for Zerbolt than to prepare a similar title for a chapter in the *Imitation?* That he certainly did. Chapter VI of the *Imitation* has this heading: "De Inordinatis Affectionibus." The first verse corresponds neatly to the chapter heading: "Quandocumque homo inordinate aliquid appetit. . . ." Here we have two typical concepts of Zerbolt. In the first place, the idea of a person's having excessive desires to possess something. In the second place, we note that the sinner has a bad appetite. Both of these phrases Thomas à Kempis took over from Zerbolt.

Very interesting is the contrast between Zerbolt's discussion of predestination in Chapter XIII of Book I of the

Imitation and that by Thomas à Kompis (verse 27), Zerbolt merely says that a person's whole life is ordained according to the foreknowledge of God. Thomas à Kempis presents here the full-fledged Calvinistic doctrine of predestination, which led Father Joseph Malaise in his edition of the *Imitation* to write (p. 271): "The third of the three verses, interpolated by à Kempis after verse 23, has left him open to the accusation of holding the heretical doctrine of Predestination." On the other hand, Zerbolt, in his version of Chapter XVIII, has plain references to predestination which Thomas à Kempis omits. Zerbolt also favors some belief in predestination near the end of his treatise, *Scriptum pro Quodam* (p. 231 in the version published by the present writer). He says that God equips each person with talents he needs for his vocation, just as He endows all animals with certain faculties. His argument reminds us of the theories expressed by him in Chapter XVIII of the *Imitation*.

Another curious development is the voluminous writing by J. van Ginneken. Being a brilliant speaker and linguist, and at one time the Rector of the Roman Catholic University at Nijmegen, he attracted much attention with his thesis that Gerard Groote was the author of the *Imitation*. He admitted that the Eutin Copy was the work of Zerbolt, who had merely acted as a copyist. He felt that Zerbolt had not only copied Book I, but also the next two books.[13] There is much similarity between the Eutin version of Book I and the version of Books II and III as discovered by Paul Hagen in Lübeck. Van Ginneken noted that himself, and he was right. But he was unable to convince his own colleagues that his main thesis was correct. They continued to believe that the present writer had come closer to the truth in the year 1921, when he paid a visit to Paul Hagen's home in Lübeck and spent a week there studying the manuscripts left by the Sisters of the Common Life in that city and their neighbors across the street. In the year 1489, a copy of the *Imitation* was published in that city which contains the same rendering of the last passages of Chapter I as those by Zerbolt and to be found in the Eutin manuscript copy. There is a good reason for this similarity.

Van Ginneken even went so far as to publish a Dutch translation of Book I of the *Imitation* as based upon a Latin version he ascribed to Gerard Groote. This work was subsidized by the famous institute in Amsterdam known as the *Koninklijke Nederlandsche Akademie van Wetenschappen*, thus showing the high reputation Van Ginneken enjoyed. A new edition appeared in the year 1945, which was used by the present writer. The latter feels called upon to make a few remarks which indicate how a person may be led by a false theory to draw strange conclusions.

Van Ginneken's thesis was that Groote had written a diary, as the original sources indicate. This diary is the *Imitation of Christ*. Now we happen to know that Groote burned his diary, and it is very doubtful that he had two copies at his disposal. The *Imitation* is a composite work, and certainly not a diary. The first book was issued under its proper title. The four do not form a book that corresponds to the title intended for only the first book. Neither Zerbolt nor Thomas à Kempis realized that some day the four books would be bound together and called the *Imitation of Christ*. Thomas actually placed Book IV in front of Book III, showing his own ignorance of the fact that Book II and III have very much in common and differ very much from Book.IV.

Van Ginneken got himself into some difficulties with his thesis. The copy of Book I which he ascribed to Groote does not contain the fourth chapter. Nevertheless, Van Ginneken provided one which he borrowed from Thomas à Kempis. He also did not worry much about a passage in Chapter XIII quoted from St. Gregory, who is mentioned there by name (verse 28). This passage was taken over by the editor of the translation, published in 1937, by the America Press. It should be noted, however, that Book I of the *Imitation,* as originally composed, did not carry the names of any of the Church Fathers. Thomas à Kempis did not go that far, either. Zerbolt did mention such names in his other works, but the *Imitation* was a special kind of book.

Another difficulty is caused by verse 35 in Chapter XXV of Book I. Van Ginneken reasoned that Groote wrote that book while doing penitence and penance in a Carthusian monastery. Verse 35 starts as follows: "Look at the Carthusians, the Cistercians." Thomas à Kempis no doubt added that passage, since the Eutin Copy does not contain it. He himself was an Augustinian monk and could well exclaim about the holiness of the Carthusians. But how could Groote have composed it? The manuscript which Van Ginneken used has a note at the top, stating that it was written in a Carthusian monastery in the Rhine Valley. Van Ginneken should have noted that this was proof of copying, not the original authorship of Book I. In short, a monk in a Carthusian monastery in the Rhine Valley made the particular copy of the version which Van Ginneken erroneously ascribed to Gerard Groote.[14]

We must conclude that the Eutin Copy of Book I of the *Imitation* and the Low German version of Books II and III as found by Paul Hagen in the City Library of Lübeck point definitely to Gerard Zerbolt as the author. The version by Thomas à Kempis contains too many errors to be considered the original of much better compositions. Gerard Zerbolt was the only writer, in the movement called the Devotio Moderna, before 1450, who had produced "big sellers" in a class with the *Imitation*. Gerard Groote was not the type of a writer who could stir the hearts of millions the way Zerbolt could. We have in Book I of the *Imitation* as written originally by Zerbolt a number of typical phrases to be found in other works by Zerbolt. The latter was the librarian in the brethren-house at Deventer when Thomas à Kempis lived in the same city and joined the brotherhood.

Thomas à Kempis wrote about his teacher, Gerard Zerbolt: "He was our librarian at Deventer. . . . He loved sacred books above all the riches of the world. . . . He said that we cannot do without them any more than without the sacraments of the Church. . . . He collected from the writings of the doctors various aromatic spices, to be used against the diseases of vices and for the curing of the languors of the souls: as appears particularly in two of his books which begin respectively with, 'A certain man,' and 'Blessed is the man.'" Those are the two great mystical treatises we have discussed above.

Dier de Muden, who used to wear the tunic left by Zerbolt and wrote a fine account of Zerbolt's life, made this startling remark: "He gathered from the sacred writings those which were useful for our House and other persons: for he composed or dictated numerous books." In other words, the two most reliable sources plainly indicate that Zerbolt wrote much more than just those two books generally ascribed to him. Moreover, the Sisters of the Common Life in Lübeck had in their library a translation of the book by Zerbolt entitled, *Spiritual Ascensions*. The dialect used for this purpose was the same as that employed in the translation of Books II and III of the *Imitation*. It should be noted here that both translations were made from the original Latin of Zerbolt, and that no great liberties were taken in either case. Those who have seen and read these interesting manuscripts in the dialect of Lübeck know exactly how this work was performed. Dr. Paul Hagen, the city librarian, did not labor in vain.

In short, the facile pen of Gerard Zerbolt, gave to the *Imitation* such power that his assistant now known as Thomas à Kempis could not reduce it to the level of mediocrity. Today the world is once more in a state of flux, similar to the transition witnessed in the period from 1375 to 1525: the Age of the Renaissance. No doubt the *Imitation* as originally composed by Zerbolt will calm the hearts of many devout Christians who are puzzled by the evils of wars, strikes, divorces, and all manner of personal crimes.[15]

In the year 1952 the Editorial Board of the *Archief voor de Geschiedenis van het Aartsbisdom Utrecht* published a lengthy article by the present writer entitled, "The Original Version of 'De Imitatione Christi' by Gerard Zerbolt of Zutphen." The members said that they were glad to publish this article, for the writer was thoroughly familiar with the most important sources. But there were two reasons why they did not accept the thesis that Gerard Zerbolt had written the original version: In the first place, it was doubtful that Zerbolt had composed the learned treatise entitled, *Super Modo Vivendi Devotorum Hominum Simul Commorantium*. And in the second place, Zerbolt was not the only author who had quoted this statement: "Ut sic Christum imiteris, quia actio (ejus) nostra est instructio." For example, Everard Foec and an anonymous writer had done the same, as shown in the famous work by P. Fredericq, *Corpus Documentorum Haereticae Pravitatis*, Vol. II, pp. 160 and 172.

It is surprising that these men still wanted to uphold the old and wornout thesis to the effect that Zerbolt had not written the admirable treatise which the present writer had published in the same periodical, filling 100 pages, and having been accepted with great satisfaction by His Eminence Johannes Cardinal de Jong (1926). Moreover, they also erred sadly in their remark about Everard Foec and an anonymous author who had used the same phrase as Zerbolt. The latter in the year 1398 had persuaded the two writers to issue a defense of the Brotherhood of the Common Life, as indicated by the present writer in his first publication, "Is Gerard Zerbolt of Zutphen the Author of the 'Super Modo Vivendi'?" Here follow the pertinent pages.

From the letters of deacon Foec of Utrecht, abbot Arnold of Dickeninge in Drenthe, the bishop of Utrecht,[16] and cardinal Pierre d'Ailly[17] we gather some more particulars regarding the author of our "Super modo vivendi," and his negotiations with these church officials. Zerbolt knew deacon Foec personally; he refers to one of his visits to the deacon in his letter addressed to Radewijns.[18] With abbot Arnold he was very well acquainted, as we have seen, while the bishop of Utrecht was the object of one of his intended visits to Dickeninge.[19] If we now read once more manuscript no. 70 H 78 of the Royal Library, and compare the "Super modo vivendi" with the first treatise by Foec, with the treatise by Arnold, the letter of approbation by the bishop of Utrecht, and the letters of the Cologne jurists, we shall find so much similarity in thought, style and arrangement of the subject matter that we can't help thinking of a certain close relationship between all these pieces. They seem to have a common source. The person who wrote our manuscript evidently knew all about this relationship or common source. Each chapter of the "Super modo vivendi" he divided into two or more sub divisions. The elaborate table of contents he thus had prepared was written on the first folio of the manuscript we have been discussing. Behind each sub-division was placed a sort of arrow to indicate on which pages the subject in question was found. If Jostes had only known what these arrows meant on folio 1, he would have seen at once that the title below this table of contents refers only to the first treatise and not to the collection as a whole. The written catalogue of the manuscripts of the Royal Library at the Hague also gives the title of the "Super modo vivendi" as the title of the whole manuscript, while the information on manuscript no. 70 H 78 in this written catalogue is far from reliable, and in certain respects wholly misleading.

All the treatises found in Ms. no. 70 H 78 of the Royal Library at the Hague seem to be based on the labors of that person who asked deacon Foec, abbot Arnold, and the Cologne jurists to approve the "modus vivendi" practised by the Brethren of the Common Life. Was that person a member of that new brotherhood? He must have been, else the writer of our manuscript would only have been too glad to mention his name, a fact which never seems to have occurred to Jostes.[20] This one consideration might suffice, but fortunately we have found a witness in the bishop of Utrecht: "Let it be known to you," he says, "that several men and women, moved by the zeal of devotion and the love of divine worship, told me concerning their way of living that they had on several occasions asked many learned men of high station, doctors of theology and law, to examine and discuss their mode of life, for which purpose they had drawn up their statements in writing, and had presented these writings to the doctors of theology and

570   THE CHRISTIAN RENAISSANCE

law. Then these doctors, having found nothing objectionable or illicit in their writings, wrote and sealed their approbations."²¹ There are many sentences in the bishop's letter which verbally agree with the "Super modo vivendi,"²² as also is the case with the letters and treatises by deacon Foec, abbot Arnold, and the Cologne jurists. But if the "Super modo vivendi," and the letters addressed to Foec, Arnold, and the jurists of the university of Cologne proceeded from the Brethren of the Common Life as a whole, who can have been the composer, except Gerard Zerbolt of Zutphen? It was Zerbolt who collected sayings from "sacred writings" for the protection of his brotherhood. He wrote and dictated several books for this purpose, and it was he also who took care of the transactions with deacon Foec, with abbott Arnold, and directly or indirectly with the bishop of Utrecht during the summer of the year 1398, when Florentius Radewijns had secretly forsaken him. Yes, Radewijns had actually fled from Amersfoort, and that at a time, when the brotherhood was being attacked, when the pest was raging at Deventer! Radewijns was discouraged, he wanted to go home to the quiet circle of beloved friends at Deventer, where he would not have to fight those enervating battles which had to be carried on at Amersfoort, Utrecht, and Amsterdam. From Zerbolt's letter to Radewijns we learn how disappointed our Zerbolt was, when he found his master gone: "I fear," he writes, "that you are going to stay too long; to all our friends it seems that you have fled . . . if you were all here, we would still be unable to manage this enormous undertaking . . . and now I am here all alone."²³

Gerard Zerbolt of Zutphen was *the* scholar among the Brethren of the Common Life. More clearly than his own master did he see the signs of the times. He was constantly on the look-out for more privileges, and greater protection for his brotherhood. This was the reason why he so diligently searched the books on Canon Law of his time.[24] Soon he became famous for his knowledge of legal problems, so that even his own master would often ask him for advice. With the help of other scholars he finally drew up a collection of arguments for the protection of his brotherhood, which was then being attacked by enemies of various kinds. Revius saw such a collection of arguments and called it: "Super modo vivendi devotorum hominum simul commorantium," which reminds us of the title of our "Super modo vivendi": "Incipiunt quedam scripta ex dictis sanctorum et determinacionibus doctorum in unum collecta *super modo vivendi devotorum hominum simul commorancium.*" Revius used the same or nearly the same treatise as the one found in Ms. 70 H 78 of the Royal Library.[25] Who then is right, Revius or Jostes? Whom shall we believe, Dier de Muiden or Jostes? And who knew more about the "Super modo vivendi," the bishop of Utrecht, who was personally acquainted with Zerbolt[26] or Jostes, who only built his arguments upon the shifting sands of negative criticism? It is true, we can trace the influence of De Groote on every page of the "Super modo vivendi"; some of the soundest and most learned arguments were undoubtedly the outcome of frequent consultations with deacon Foec and abbot Arnold. Zerbolt therefore was no author in our sense of the word. But he possessed "that something" which made Loyola the author of the "Spiritual Exercises," and Calvin the writer of the "Institutes," both of which works were also original in part, and partly based on the literary gems of the "Devotio Moderna" or "Christian Renaissance."

It should be noted here that Zerbolt was presenting a number of arguments to show that the Brethren of the Common Life were fully justified in living their particular kind of life. The Bishop of Utrecht copied directly from Zerbolt's treatise when he took up the problem of having laymen read sacred writings in their own language, as we saw. On p. 32 of the treatise published by the present writer we note that Zerbolt listed the imitation of Christ as the sixth point. He wrote as follows: "Sexto omnis accio nostra est instructio secundum Augustinum. Sed Christus in communi vixit et, si quid habuit, in communi habuit, secundum doctores. Igitur et cetera." It is obvious that this important point was taken up by Foec and the other protectors of the new brotherhood, for which reason they gladly copied the significant remark by Zerbolt. Thomas à Kempis unfortunately refused to copy this particular statement in Chapter I of *The Imitation of Christ*, where he differed from the learned men consulted by Zerbolt. Since he had never attended any grades above elementary ones, he did not appreciate higher education, thus doing immense damage to the original version by Zerbolt. Thousands of scholars in many foreign countries were to wonder about his strange contempt of higher learning, drawing the conclusion that the Brethren of the Common Life were antagonistic to the best type of scholarship. The same thing has often been said about the New Testament, as well as about Professor Martin Luther. It is high time that the vast difference between the version of Zerbolt and that of the ignorant Thomas à Kempis be recognized at last by all discerning critics.

Zerbolt not only stated with much authority that every action of Christ was an instruction for His followers, but in his seventh point he said this: "Septimo, sicut dicit Beda in quadam omelia, perfectum vite magisterium est semper

ecclesie primitive actus imitari." In other words, the perfect
way of life is to imitate the Primitive Church. Zerbolt goes
on as follows: "Status enim ecclesie primitive fuit status
perfectissimus christianitatis." He refers to the verdict of
Thomas Aquinas, who also believed that the status of the
Primitive Church was the most perfect status of Christianity. Consequently it behooved all good Christians to imitate the early Church of the Apostles. Here we have the
chief purpose enunciated by the Brotherhood of the Common Life, as stated in the opening paragraph of the original constitution in Deventer. The imitation of Christ went
hand in hand with the imitation of the Primitive Church.
Thomas à Kempis merely advised meditation on the life
of Christ, whereas Zerbolt said in verse 3 of the first chapter in *The Imitation of Christ:* "Let therefore our chief
endeavor be to imitate Jesus in our life." He recommended
action above meditation: "Every action of Christ is an
instruction for us." Everard Foec and the Bishop of Utrecht
were well aware of Zerbolt's message. They eagerly copied
his words at his own request. The same may be said about
the anonymous writer mentioned above. Professor R. R.
Post rendered a useful service to all earnest scholars by
telling them about the action taken by Foec and the anonymous author.

Perhaps it might be helpful to add some more information about the career of Everard Foec. We have a list of
provosts of the Church of St. Salvator in Utrecht, published
in Vol. I of *Historie ofte Beschryving van't Utrechtsche
Bisdom,* translated from the Latin version with many notes
added by a scholar listed on the title-page as H.V.R. It was
published at Leiden in 1719. On p. 193 the list of provosts
comes to an end, and here we read that now follows the
list of important deans. Only four names are given, namely,
Gerardus Foek, who died in 1383; Everardus Foek, dean in

the year 1390, being the son of Gerardus Foek's sister; Henricus Houbergh, dean in 1425; and Gerardus de Suggerode, who died in 1533.

Very interesting is the will made by Everard Foec on February 8, 1397, or one year before he carried on negotiations with Gerard Zerbolt. It was written on a large sheet. Here we read that he bequeathed certain sums of money to a "natural son" and a "natural daughter." We observe that he was permitted to retain his exalted position in spite of this embarrassing situation. In the year 1383 Gerard Groote had denounced all the members of the higher clergy who had been guilty of similar misdemeanors. This happened in the city of Utrecht!

Dean Foec was a great benefactor of the Church of St. Salvator, so says the Dutch source we have just mentioned; and his friendship with Gerard Zerbolt is highly significant to those who wish to understand how Zerbolt was able to use Foec's influence to the advantage of his brotherhood. One of the most important statements made by Foec naturally was to the effect that all actions of Christ are a source of instruction for His followers. He knew as well as Zerbolt that following Christ was not nearly so effective as imitating Him. Thomas à Kempis had no conception of what actual imitation implied, but Zerbolt was fully aware of it.

We have seen that Professor R. R. Post failed to understand the relation between Foec and Zerbolt, while he also failed to realize the significance of Zerbolt's reference to the imitation of the Primitive Church. Another Dutch scholar who has misrepresented the facts in connection with the authorship of the *Imitation* is Dr. P. Grootens, S.J., who made light of the present writer's article on the subject which was edited by Post. His comments were published in *Ons Geestelijk Erf,* Vol. XXV (1951). On p. 301 he repeats the faulty arguments of Post, claiming that Zerbolt's authorship of *Super Modo Vivendi* has never been proved, and that the phrase concerning Christ's actions being an instruction for His followers was also quoted by others, meaning of course Foec and the anonymous author mentioned above. Grootens did not realize that this fact supports rather than damages the writer's arguments. Members of the clergy in the Roman Catholic Church naturally favor the work of Thomas à Kempis, regardless of the latter's poor style and contempt of higher education. Zerbolt, on the other hand, remained with the brotherhood until the end, but strongly aided by distinguished clergymen. The Jesuits owe more to him than to Thomas à Kempis.

The Jesuits no doubt will be delighted with the following statement by Zerbolt in his *Spiritual Ascensions*, near the end of Chapter I: "Debes sursum manus extendere ad dominum qui est innixus parti scale et clamare: 'Trahe me post te,' et ita beatus eris." Here the reader is exhorted to extend his hands and say to the Savior: "Draw me behind Thee." Then will he be blessed. Moreover, Zerbolt also recommended the following of Christ in Chapter XXX, where he said: "Nota hic et attende quomodo (or quod) frequenter sequebatur Christum multitudo maxima . . . usque ad heremum. Sequere et tu et esto circa Iesum ut verba eius audias: faciem Christi et apostolorum inspicias et colloquia et miracula videas." The reader must observe that often a very large multitude followed Jesus, even into the desert. The reader must also follow Jesus and listen to His message. He must look into Christ's features and examine His miracles. Here we have only the following, not the actual imitation, but nevertheless, Zerbolt has in mind both of them rather than just one, where Thomas à Kempis was weak. Zerbolt's book just mentioned was a powerful force for good in Spain as well as in Italy. The great Cisneros, as we saw, was powerfully affected by this book, which was also true of Luther when he was a devout Roman Catholic professor of Biblical studies (1515-1516).

As we now turn to an examination on Book IV, we must express regret that Thomas à Kempis saw fit to insert it between the second and third books of the Imitation, for the latter two show a close affinity, while Book IV is of an entirely different nature. In L, the second and third books form one unit, which is not strange. How Thomas à Kempis in his autograph of 1441 could have shown himself so unaware of these matters must ever remain a dense mystery. It does make us wonder about the admirers of his who go on from year to year ignoring his errors and the merits of his teachers in Deventer. It is generally agreed upon that a book of great significance must have sources, but in the case of the autograph by Thomas à Kempis a large number of scholars with fine reputations stubbornly maintain that he, unlike all other writers of similar books, must have had before him none of the works of his own teachers. When he arrived in Deventer he was an ignorant boy, wholly unprepared to compose the most famous book ever produced in Europe. How could such a person have done the impossible?

Some new light may now be shed upon his literary labors by an examination of Book IV in Dutch translation to be found in an old manuscript that was thought to have perished in the closing months of World War II. The ms. was the property of the Canisius Institute in Nijmegen, which was destroyed in the year 1944. Fortunately, the Dutch ms. in question survived the holocaust. It starts with the customary title, followed by the familiar words of Jesus, divided into five verses. But a marked contrast between the version of Thomas à Kempis and that in the Nijmegen ms.

is seen at the very beginning. After the first four verses the latter, which will be referred to as N, continues at some length and as follows: "Come to my table. You are called and shall commune. Come now unto me and do not despise me, lest hereafter you shall be despised by me and must hear these words 'Depart from me.' Come unto me who loves you dearly, and out of love have paid for the food. It is good to go into my tavern; it has all been paid for and prepared. Be joyful and glad to go at my expense; so you go freely; and not you alone but come all, the spiritually inclined and the worldly, good and bad, poor and rich. Whoever you are come in the same way.

"Come unto me all that labor with penitence and are laden with temptation. Come and I shall relieve you and I shall take away the burden of temptation. I shall provide you with my body and blood, and give you joy, that you may forget all your affliction and sorrow.

"Come unto me particularly who are laboring in sin and are burdened with great guilt. Be converted and come with all your heart unto me. My father did not send me into the world to judge it but that through me it shall be redeemed. Do not therefore fear me but come altogether without exception.

"I shall gladly forgive the sins; I shall remit the guilt of pain. My father has inflicted upon me all the guilt. Come then to me: I shall enrich you with myself. My holy body I shall give unto you, and my holy blood I shall present to you.

"Eat and drink and be filled with the best I have to offer, open your ears and hear me and receive me. Forsake your people and your father's house. Forsake the world; leave behind you everything in the world. Give up your old sinful life and join me, that you may entrust me with your faith, consolation and love.

"Then shall I, your Lord and God and your bridegroom, desire your beauty and unite yourself with me. Hear the voice of your Lord today, not tomorrow, and do not harden your heart. Hear your redeemer who has placed himself at your disposal that you might make use of him forever. He has bought you at a great price that he might possess you. Come and I shall give you myself for food and an eternal reward."

At this point N goes on exactly as does the version of Thomas à Kempis, which we shall again name T. The fifth verse of the introduction is missing in N, but the first chapter of the text itself is the same in both versions. On the other hand, Ch. II is very different in places. In N there is no such thing as the voice of the disciple, and even in Ch. I there is no statement to the effect that here we have the voice of the disciple. Only in a short opening paragraph does the sinner speak to Christ. Then Christ himself begins to address the communicant. He says that the words of the sinner are true, for he is indeed unworthy to participate in divine blessings. Nevertheless, divine grace will make him worthy. God is truly omnipotent. Everything in the universe belongs to him.

"What glory and wealth are in my house! Where I dwell there is a great abundance. If you have received me in your tavern what else will you need? Not one thing that I have created may satisfy you. You must be encumbered with these temporal things but not satisfied. What do you want outside of me; to whom do you wish to go that is better than I? Who can make you richer than I who will give myself to you?"

Such a message was not suited to the ascetic taste of Thomas à Kempis, who refused to copy any of this. Moreover, N goes on some more in the same vein, much to the

displeasure of those who could not fathom the words in Ch.
I in N. These words remind us of a verse in Book I which
was quoted above. The reader was informed that if he
would let Jesus enter his heart he would have within him
all things, for Christ was the creator of all things. Here we
have again the same line of thought: "It must be an avaricious creature who refuses to be satisfied with me, the rich,
generous God." Christ was the living bread which had been
sent down from heaven in order that sinners might obtain
spiritual food. He did not offer the kind of bread which the
Hebrews ate in the desert. Christ's bread was his holy body,
and he who eats that will live forever. No liquid can quench
thirst as can the cup with Christ's holy blood; that was the
same blood which ran out of his side when he hung on the
cross. It becomes a fountain of life in the body of the
converted sinner.

Illuminating also is the following exhortation: "Come
then freely to me and eat my bread and drink my wine
which I have prepared and poured. If it be that you should
feel yourself unworthy to partake because you are sinful
and impure, be reassured of me, for I am the merciful God
who came into the world to purify you in my wounds.
Since you are ill as you have correctly stated, hasten to
come unto me, for nowhere else can you find better medicine. Nothing will make you stronger than the living bread
that came down from heaven. If you are naked and devoid
of all virtue and for that reason ashamed to be in my
presence, come to me with a penitent heart. I am the
fountain of all virtues and shall cover your nakedness with
the garment of eternal salvation, and shall adorn you with
my holy blood. Although you are blind and because of sin
in darkness, come unto me. I am the clarity of eternal light.
I am the light that illuminates all men. Adorn the bedroom

of your heart and the bed of your conscience. I am pleased to dwell in you and with you. Prepare yourself with great humility."

All of this amazing material seems to have escaped the attention of the great experts for some four or five hundred years. Every sentence was rejected by Thomas à Kempis, who was quite willing to accept some pantheistic teachings of Eckhart and Ruysbroeck but lacked the courage to strike out for individual and personal power. To him the imitation of Christ involved little action. What he favored was meditation and contemplation. To let his own personality disappear in the universal soul or spirit called God suited him perfectly. For that reason he added a number of verses to the first three chapters in the *Imitation* which clearly betrayed his anti-intellectual attitude.

According to N the message by Christ quoted above was the end of Ch. I of Book IV. On fol. 79r, we note that Ch. II begins exactly as does Ch. II in T, but there is no reference to the voice of the disciple. The same is true of Ch. III and of Ch. V. In T, Ch. V begins with these words: "Voice of the Soul." But N does not have this chapter at all, probably because it is a glorification of the priestly office in the church here upon earth. It would seem that the voice of the soul should have chosen a more worthy subject, since the main theme of Book IV is obviously the participation of the sinner in the sacrament and his communion with Christ in person. Ch. V of N, which corresponds to Ch. VI in T, begins with the word "Disciple." In the next chapter we meet with this title: "The Voice of Christ." Thomas has "Voice of the Beloved." The contents of these chapters do not require further discussions here. The same is true of the next three. It should be noted, however, that Ch. XI is not to be found in N, this being again a piece of literature most pleasing to priests and monks but not to all

Christians in general. The office of the priest is here eulogized to such an extent that the reader can distinguish the hand of Thomas à Kempis.

Since Chs. XIII, XIV, XV, XVII, and XVIII are also missing in N, we must come to the conclusion that this version consists in only eleven chapters. In the year 1927, the present writer published an edition of the *Imitation* in which Book IV had only eight chapters, and these did not follow the same order as that of T. At that time the writer was not yet familiar with N and had to rely upon the Low German version in Lübeck. It would seem to him now that N is much closer to the original version than the others. He hopes that in the near future more attention will be paid to N, as well as to the manuscript in Eutin.

THE ORIGINAL CONSTITUTION OF
THE SISTERS OF THE COMMON LIFE

In the year 1952 Professor R. R. Post published two versions of the original constitution prepared by Gerard Groote for the Sisters of the Common Life living in his ancestral home at Deventer. The copy issued by Professor J. van Ginneken in his biography of Groote (1942) is not reliable, as Post has shown; while his publication of the first book of The *Imitation of Christ* as found in the famous Eutin Manuscript contains at least 100 errors. We are fortunate to have the excellent edition in two columns of both versions side by side as given by Post. But we regret to add that Post is completely mistaken in reporting that the long version dated July 13, 1379, is a forged piece of work, made by the municipal government in Deventer. The original copy is available in the *Olde Copienboek*, preserved in the City Archives of Deventer, No. 1607, fol. 192-194. There is no longer in existence the original copy of the short version, dated July 16, 1379. It was published by D. Dumbar in his valuable work, *Het kerkelyk en wereltlyk Deventer*, Vol. I (1732), p. 548. Post says on the last page of his article (p. 46) that the long version was made after Groote's death, and that the Sisters of the Common Life did not appear before the Brethren of the Common Life. This is an astonishing assumption, since all the experts have always known that Groote tèn years before his death (1374) deeded his house to some older women and gave them an order to lead what is called "the common life." He obviously issued explicit instructions to them concerning their manner of living together without monastic vows and yet forced to follow their contents: chastity, poverty, and obedience.

Thus far it has been customary to ignore to a great extent the Sisters of the Common Life, although they had more houses than the brothers. Partly because of this fact the original constitution has seldom been studied with proper care. It certainly has great historical significance, since it was formulated by Groote himself and became a model for the more elaborate constitution prepared by the brothers in Deventer. The latter was published for the first time by the present writer in his first book, *The Christian Renaissance.*

Although the short version is dated July 16, 1379; and the other July 13, 1379, the first was probably drawn up before the second. In the first it is stated that there will be a mother superior chosen each year on St. Gregory's Day or Evening, while in the other we are informed that there will be two to choose (Article 8 as numbered by Post). No doubt the original number of women living in Groote's house was so small that one mother would be deemed sufficent. We must assume that Groote at first gave oral instructions, which later on were drawn up in writing. In the first article the opening sentences are almost identical: The women may not found a monastic order nor become beguines (the latter are not mentioned in the short version). Next they are informed that they are not permitted to be attached to men nor to monastic orders, for they are always free to leave the house, on condition that they may never come back. They must not join the clergy (art. 3). After Groote's death the aldermen shall govern the house, as is done with the Stappen House. The women may not wear the monastic garb, though they shall be careful not to attract men through display of finery (art. 6). In the short version we read that there is one house with one mother, while the long version mentions both the Stone House and the Rear House. Each house is to have its own mother, as stated in art. 9. This means that at first there was one house and later two involved.

Articles 14 to 20 are present only in the long version. They mention heresies to be avoided. The women may not discuss matters that are above their comprehension. Here Groote uses exactly the same language as in a work of his that was considered lost but retrieved in the year 1952 by the present writer when he bought two Dutch manuscripts mentioned by him in an article published in *Archief voor Nederlandsche Kerkgeschiedēnis* (Vol. 40, 1954), entitled, "Een vergeten werk van Geert Groote." Groote warned the sisters against the writings of Eckhardt, just as Gerard Zerbolt did in 1397 and 1398. He also insisted that they must perform certain tasks that will keep them out of mischief and will produce some income for the house (art. 21). Only in the long version does Groote say that in the Rear House there will not be more than eight beds and eight rooms, and upstairs in the Stone House not more than seven, while downstairs one bed or person in the kitchen (art. 22). Groote has retained two rooms, and above each there shall be one person. Two persons shall have beds in the rooms with stone walls, one where Groote sleeps and one in his study, for after Groote's death there will be some changes. Those who die in the house must leave there all clothes, bed, tools, ornaments, plus some things they owned outside of the house (art. 24). In the long version was added a stipulation about silver and gold being exempt, besides interest on capital, cows, sheep, etc. But interest or income for one year must be left behind for the house. In the next article of the long version we read about the possessions left by deceased members. Those must be used for repairs and improvement of the house, and they may not be distributed for expenses incurred by members.

Both versions order the women to pay proper respect to the memory of Groote's father and mother, besides some other relatives (art. 34). In the last article we are informed that all details have been submitted to the aldermen of the city, who were pleased with everything. They did not object to a single point. In the longer version alone it is stated that Gerard Groote has placed his personal seal on three copies (art. 36). No doubt his acquaintance with the members of the municipal council and his endeavors to assist them in obtaining special favors from the papal court at Avignon endeared him to them all. Since Groote in the year 1379 started his preaching and very soon gained numerous converts, it is not surprising that in the same year he formulated his constitution for the sisters, who did indeed live "the common life" after that, although Post refused to believe this (p. 40). He continually returns to his idea of a forgery on the part of the aldermen. The latter were for the most part businessmen, who had no idea who Eckhardt was, nor what was done at the Council of Vienne about so-called heresies. In short, we owe both versions to the pen of Gerard Groote.

Another important point raised by Professor R. R. Post is the fact that Groote did not say: "I have placed my seal on this document." On another occasion he had indeed made such a statement. But in the year 1379 he did not write in the first person. All the way through the long version allusions are made to him in the third person, for which reason the last sentence must agree with all the others, as was actually the case. Here then we do not have proof of forgery on the part of the aldermen, contrary to Post's allegation. The same thing happened when Everardus Foec, Dean of St. Salvator's Church in Utrecht, issued his will on February 8, 1397. He was a protector of Groote's successor in Deventer. This will says that "Venerabilis dominus Everardus Foec, Canonicus Traiecten, compos per Dei gratiam mentis, corpis, et racione . . . ordinavit." Then follow the terms, and at the bottom of the document there is a seal with a statement by a notary public in the first person: "Et ego, Adolpus de Goch, Clericus Colonien. dioc. publicus," etc. This sort of thing has always been very common, for which reason we must be careful not to read into the documents issued by Gerard Groote any sign of forgery merely because Groote did not say: "And I, Gerardus Groote," etc.

It seems strange that highly honored authorities in the Netherlands when writing about Gerard Groote often make astonishing errors. Post has indicated in his article that both Professor J. van Ginneken, S.J., and D. de Man, who published a chronicle about the house founded by Gerard Groote, erred in concluding that the short version of the documentary grant was composed later than the longer version. Similarly, many curious statements were made by Dutch experts about the original constitution of the Brethren at Deventer. The original document was available to competent scholars for more than 400 years, and yet nobody had surmised its significance until the year 1920. It slumbered peacefully in the Royal Library at The Hague, where in the catalogue of manuscripts a vague statement was presented, making it difficult for the average reader to determine just what had happened in the famous *Fraterhuis*. Is it then surprising that the constitution for the Sisters of the Common Life in Groote's own home was the subject of misleading calculations?

Even more remarkable has been the critique dealing with the present writer's publication of the original constitution of the Brethren in Deventer. On p. 257 of the *Archiv für Reformationsgeschichte*, Vol. 54, dated 1963, we read this about the Festschrift issued by Kenneth A. Strand: "Auf die Kritik, die diese Deutung gefunden hat, hätte hingewiesen werden müssen." The reviewer was referring to "den Abdruck der von A. Hyma 1924 veröffentlichen Constitutiones von Deventer." Strand should have discussed the critique, according to Robert Stupperich in Münster. In the first place, A. Schoengen tried unsuccessfully to overthrow the writer's thesis to the effect that he had found and published the original constitution of the Brethren in Deventer. Moreover, in Vol. XXV of *Ons Geestelijk Erf* (September 1951), M. van Woerkum, S.C.J. says on p. 240 that the writer was mistaken in thinking that he had published the original version, although he did admit that the constitution published was indeed used in Deventer, which Schoengen denied. It was not until 1495 that the Brethren received permission to have a public church of their own. How then could they have had one in 1415 or 1420? Van Woerkum refers to pp. 443 and 456-457 in the writer's first book, *The Christian Renaissance*, where the pertinent passages read as follows: "Convenientes ergo quantocius in ecclesiam ad dicendum sive cantandum divina officia. . . . Et ideo, si qua in ornamentis aut in ceteris que ad ministerium ecclesie pertinent." These words do not imply that the Brethren had their own public church.

The most important references to the church attended by the Brethren are to be found on p. 448. Here we find mention of the "parochial church" and also of "our church." The Brethren were instructed to deliver speeches to the people of the town: "Diebus festivis finitis vesperis in ecclesia parochiali . . . emet rector pro communi populo facere collacionem in ecclesia nostra." In the chapter entitled, "De Custode," it is stated that the Rector must entrust a reliable brother with the key of "ecclesie nostre," together with all the portable utensils, plus the books and the relics (p. 456). This shows that they did have a church building of their own, but nowhere is it stated that the building was a public church. The phrase used by Van Woerkum is "publieke kerk." Moreover, the constitution could not possibly have been issued as late as 1495, for we read in the first paragraph about the recent protection by Pierre d'Ailly, Bishop of Cambray, effected in the year 1413. It would not have made much sense to mention this 80 years after it had occurred. It should also be noted that the Brothers were to pray for those in the house at Gouda, which name was added in a later hand. It was founded in the year 1425, partly by the house at Delft, and that in turn began its existence in 1403 when some men from Deventer started it going. These facts indicate clearly that the house in Deventer was provided with its constitution before 1425. By that time a little church or chapel had been provided, as was perfectly natural.

It seems almost incredible that Post on p. 44 of his article had the temerity to consider both versions of the constitution dated 1379 pure forgeries. The aldermen had gone so far, he thinks, as to make it appear that the documents were drafted while Groote was still alive. "Still worse was their declaration that Groote had drawn them up himself, whereas they had actually done this between 1393 and 1398, long after Groote's death. By putting the date 1379 on both of them and reporting that Groote had placed his seal on them, they made a forgery." They even forged his personal seal, and they made Groote say that he did not want any women in his home who accepted the 28 articles of Eckhardt which were condemned by the ecclesiastical authorities. "This conclusion will support the thesis by Miss

M. A. Lücker to the effect that Groote's works show a great deal of influence exerted by Eckhardt."

At this point Post goes beyond the limits of scholarly documentation. Sister Lücker went way too far in her allegation, as was indicated by Professor L. Reypens in his review of the book by her entitled, *Meister Eckhart und die Devotio Moderna.* This review appeared in *Ons Geestelijk Erf,* Vol. XXV (1951), pp. 215-220. Groote, like Zerbolt after him, strongly disapproved of Eckhardt's errors in doctrine. For that reason he took great pains in his constitution for the Sisters to warn them against his writings. In the United States of America there are also historians who do not understand Eckhardt's position in the Roman Catholic Church. In one textbook dealing with the history of civilization we actually read that Eckhardt was regarded by the highest authorities as a saintly person, hence declared blessed. This type of historiography is very common in the most widely used textbooks, because their authors do not grasp the theology of the most famous mystics in medieval Europe, nor that of the leaders in the Protestant Reformation. But it is truly pathetic that distinguished professors in Europe also have begun to fail in this important field of study.

THE "DEVOTIO MODERNA" AND
THE REFORMATION

On November 6, 1925, Professor Johannes de Jong wrote a long letter to the present writer. He had just published a 33-page review of *The Christian Renaissance,* and he hoped he would receive by the middle of February 1926 the 23 letters of Gerard Groote which were to be published in Vol. 53 of the *Archief voor de Geschiedenis van het Aartsbisdom Utrecht* (1927). About one-half of them appeared in 1929, however. The professor was still a young man, and he had no idea that eventually he would become the Cardinal of the Netherlands. He had been reading the proof sheets of the lengthy treatise by Gerard Zerbolt entitled, *Super Modo Vivendi,* which he said was "very important." He had received from the writer a copy of the review of *The Christian Renaissance* in *The Commonweal* of September 2, 1925; and he wrote that a favorable review had also appeared in the Roman Catholic periodical *Revue des Sciences Théologiques et Philosophiques.* But he did not want to admit that there had been in the Devotio Moderna any ideas that were specifically Protestant:

My objection to your book, as I have indicated on p. 41 of my review, is that you claim to have found in the Devotio Moderna rudiments of both the Protestant and Catholic Reformations. I agree with you naturally that Luther and Calvin were influenced by the Devotio Moderna, just as both Protestantism and Roman Catholicism have taken over thoughts from the

590

Gospel and the piety of the Church Fathers and the Fathers of the Middle Ages. Both confessions have much in common, and in both there are elements which are also found in the Devotio Moderna. However, I believe that you claim to have found in the Devotio Moderna specifically Protestant concepts that are not accepted by Roman Catholics. In my opinion you have not proved that. Afterward some of the houses of the Brethren of the Common Life joined the Protestants, but in my opinion they then broke with the original doctrines of the Devotio Moderna, and of Gerard Groote. It would be an interesting problem to investigate and prove this point, but you have not discussed it. I do agree with you that you did say in your book that the Devotio Moderna was a Roman Catholic movement, and I gladly believe that you meant it. Nevertheless, you still say that there were specifically Protestant concepts in the Devotio Moderna. On p. 50 of my review I have discussed the doctrine of total depravity. You have answered me by saying that Zerbolt believed in nearly total depravity, and Luther in total depravity. You argue that there is not much difference between 99 and 100 percent depravity. But that is exactly the issue I am taking up with you. We Roman Catholics say that man is almost totally corrupt, but he has retained some powers, with which he can cooperate with God. In this way God does not do everything. Luther says that man is totally corrupt, and so he cannot do anything and God does everything. That is the big point of difference.

You write in your letter that Groote, Radewijns, Cele, Zerbolt, and Thomas à Kempis were 100 percent Roman Catholic. This means then that Luther and Calvin in some of their doctrines swerved from the Devotio Moderna. This was the only point I wanted to refute. And I thought that this was your belief: Where Luther and Calvin broke with Roman Catholicism they were under the influence of the Devotio Moderna. I objected to this. If we accept the fact that the Devotio Moderna was essentially Roman Catholic, it affected Luther and Calvin only in the Roman Catholic views they received from it. Later on some of the men connected with the Devotio Moderna may have exerted influence in shaping specifically Protestant points of view. If you meant that, I shall agree with you completely.

The reason why I objected to your title, *The Christian Renaissance,* is that the Roman Catholic authorities in using the term have in mind a much broader movement than the Devotio Moderna. For example, Pastor in his *Geschichte der Päpste,* includes also the Roman Catholic currents of the Renaissance, or of humanism, in Italy, Germany, and France. Your book would have been much more valuable if you had indicated just what was the scope of the Devotio Moderna in the midst of all those currents of religious thought, both Roman Catholic and Protestant. You write as follows in your letter: "I have written only the history of the Devotio Moderna." But since you think so highly of this movement, where I agree with you, you give the impression that you ascribe too great an influence to it. You should have indicated how Gansfort and Erasmus deviated from the Devotio Moderna, and in this manner they exerted great influence upon Luther and Calvin.

During the past forty years the present writer has often wondered what he should have done with the title of his first book. A great many distinguished writers in Europe have used the term "Christian Renaissance." In numerous instances they have discussed religious and intellectual movements that were not genuine rebirths of the Primitive Church. Zerbolt was the greatest writer among the Brethren of the Common Life and in the whole of the Devotio Moderna. He said, as we saw, that in his house at Deventer he and his colleagues were deliberately imitating the Church of the Apostles. That was his seventh point in the argument to show that the Brotherhood of the Common Life was justified in having set up its mode of living. In the sixth point he stated that every action of Christ was an instruction for mankind. He referred to Thomas Aquinas in arguing that the Primitive Church was the most nearly perfect church there ever was. If we can find an institution at the end of the Middle Ages that came closest to a rebirth of the Primitive Church, we shall have seen an actual Christian Renaissance. The word "Renaissance" simply means rebirth, does it not? Then why should we now wish to object to the term "Christian Renaissance" in depicting a real rebirth of the Apostolic Church?

What Ludwig Pastor and others termed the Christian Renaissance was certainly not a rebirth of primitive Christianity. The Apostle Paul in Ch. XII of his famous Epistle to the Romans said that a genuine Christian must not "become conformed to this world." That statement was accepted literally by Groote and Zerbolt, but not by the great humanists in Italy, Germany, and France. Erasmus certainly was a "man of this world." And so was Pope Leo X. Those who have argued with Professor Douglas Bush of Harvard that "the classical humanism of the Italian Renaissance was thoroughly medieval and thoroughly Christian," simply do not know what Christianity is. Bush was so fortunate as to deliver the Alexander Lectures at the University of Toronto in 1939. The general title of these

lectures was "The Renaissance and English Humanism."
They were published under that title by the University of
Toronto Press. The author, like Erasmus and Pope Leo X,
also was "a man of this world." On p. 68 we have his exact
statement: "The classical humanism of the Renaissance was
fundamentally medieval and fundamentally Christian."

Bush also says on the same page that continental humanism "reveals a creed and a programme in which the major
articles remain constant." He includes all humanism in
Continental Europe "from the twelfth century to the early
sixteenth." On p. 62 we read a startling confession about
the meaning of Christianity, which is shared unfortunately
by many other so-called experts in the field of European
civilization. Bush says that he must add the comment by
Erasmus on Plato's account of the death of Socrates, "for
nothing in Renaissance writing is closer to the heart of
Christian humanism." Erasmus wrote as follows: "I can
scarce forbear, when I read such things, of such men, but
cry out: 'Sancte Socrates, ora pro nobis.' " Here we are supposed to find the most faithful representation of Christian
humanism. If the Christian Renaissance is such a thing,
then we can only conclude that the men who have drawn
this conclusion must have been suffering from a strange
hallucination. Here we certainly do not witness a rebirth
of Christianity. But we do find one in the house where
Zerbolt acted as the librarian and told many things to
Thomas à Kempis.

As for the doctrine of human depravity, on p. 21 of
The Christian Renaissance we have the following statement by Groote: "God is the 'summum bonum'; if we have
him, we have all goodness; if we lose him, nothing but
evil is left unto us." The Latin original appears on p. 357.
Groote explains his declaration in the following words:
"Because that part of us which is divine cannot exist with-

out the life-giving contact with Him who alone can sustain life and nourish our inner selves." This illuminating interpretation is well worth serious study, for here Groote sets forth perfectly sound theology. He means that it is preposterous for man to initiate the process of sanctification in his own power. Although Zerbolt said that man's powers were not totally destroyed by the fall of man in paradise, and Luther held to the doctrine of total depravity, there was a common platform for both upon which to build a Christian Renaissance. Jesus, although the only begotten Son of God, said: "I of myself can do nothing; it is the Father within Me that does all the work." For that reason both Zerbolt and Luther had to imitate Christ here as well as elsewhere. *The Imitation of Christ* as composed originally by Zerbolt said in verse 3: "Let therefore our chief endeavor be to imitate Jesus in our life." Luther confessed that nowhere had he read such a reliable description of human depravity as in the book by Zerbolt entitled, *Spiritual Ascensions.* Are we to assume that Luther had misunderstood Zerbolt?

Christianity obviously includes both Roman Catholicism and Protestantism, and *The Imitation of Christ* transcends both of them. Christ rises above Zerbolt and Luther. In the year 1957 two scholars (Jacques Huijben and Pierre Debongnie) published a book in which they sought to minimize the labors and influence of Zerbolt: *L'Auteur ou les Auteurs de L'Imitation* (Louvain: Bibliothèque de la Revue d'histoire ecclésiastique, Fascicle 30). They had suddenly been confronted by the discovery of two copies of Zerbolt's version of the *Imitation,* Books II and III, dated respectively 1450 and 1452. Their theory had been that the version of Book I in the Eutin Manuscript and that of Books II and III in the Lübeck Manuscript had been drawn up after the middle of the fifteenth century. On pp. 256-272 of their book they try in vain to rescue themselves from their unpleasant situation, made all the more perilous after L.M.J. Delaissé in 1956 published the copy of all four books as autographed by Thomas à Kempis in 1441. The editor was greatly impressed by the fact that the ignorant Thomas had placed Book IV between Book II and Book III, and as a result he became dubious about the theory advanced by the two scholars just mentioned (see pp. 114-132 in his book). Zerbolt continues to emerge as the outstanding scholar in the Devotio Moderna.

Let us then copy some statements made by Zerbolt in his widely read book entitled, *On the Reformation of the Powers of the Soul.* Of the edition published in 1492 Van Rooij found 38 copies still extant in Europe, while there were also editions issued in 1493, 1539, 1579, 1618, 1624, 1632, 1644, 1654, 1672, 1677, and 1688. A Dutch edition was published in 1951 (Amsterdam: Holland), with a valuable introduction by Dr. S. van der Woude, who tells on p. 8 that Zerbolt was the author of six books, three of which were published for the first time by the present writer. He also states correctly that Zerbolt remained within the limits of the Roman Catholic religion. It is significant that the editor found traces of influence exerted upon Zerbolt by David of Augsburg. We have indicated elsewhere in our discussion of the authorship of the *Imitation* that Zerbolt copied many a statement from David's book, *Profectus Religiosorum.* Radewijns was also greatly indebted to the same German mystic. Thomas à Kempis in his *Vita Gerardi Zutphania* said that Zerbolt read many books, including two by David of Augsburg. The latter died in 1272. Those who agree with Professor Wallace K. Ferguson in that Eckhardt was the "creator of German mysticism" should read the book entitled, *Bruder David von Augsburg. Ein deutscher Mystiker aus dem Franziskanerorden* (Munich,

1914), Before the *Imitation* became the most widely read book in Europe outside of the Bible, the *Profectus* had that honor in Northern Europe. In the Netherlands alone there were some 150 copies in manuscript form.

Zerbolt devotes his first chapter to the fall of Adam. He starts with a quotation from Luke X, 30; which says that "a certain man descended from Jerusalem to Jericho." Figuratively spoken, this man was Adam, who fell from a status of perfection (Jerusalem) to that of vacillation and misery (Jericho). Man once was equipped with great powers: intellect, reason, and others, with which he could clearly view and comprehend God. He also had at his disposal his will, with which he could control all feelings and emotions. But the moment he became disobedient, he lost those powers, and now he is the prey of evil desires and sinful inclinations. His only hope is to return to the original state of innocence and virtuous living. In the second chapter the reader is advised to concentrate upon his study of man's original state under God's guidance and his present condition of servitude to sin. Here we have plain Christianity at work, not merely Roman Catholicism.

In addition to the astonishing errors of Wallace K. Ferguson we shall have to reckon with those of Roland H. Bainton, who in the year 1959 published a review of the present writer's book entitled, *New Light on Martin Luther* (Eerdmans, 1958). It appeared in *The American Historical Review*, pp. 380-381. He misrepresented the use of indulgences during the Middle Ages, thinking that papal bulls forgave all sins, and not merely provided a substitute for penance. He unfortunately misunderstood the following phrase in the bull of 1513: "Plenariam omnium peccatorum suorum, ac cum Altissimo reconciliationem, indulgentiam et remissionem." He added that the instructions of Albert of Mainz promised "plenaria remissio omnium peccatorum."

True, in all cases forgiveness of sins was promised, but only after confession, contrition, and absolution. Nowhere was it said that the indulgence did the trick for the sinner. The long Latin quotation merely says that there will be absolution plus an indulgence: "reconciliationem, indulgentiam et remissionem." When Luther attacked the instructions given by the Archbishop of Mainz to Tetzel, "Leo X commissioned the Master of the Sacred Palace to draft a reply, which he did, branding Luther as a heretic." Bainton thought that this statement proved heresy on the part of Professor Luther. It did nothing of the sort, for Luther merely stated the orthodox Roman Catholic position. Bainton says that this conclusion by the present writer in the book on Luther was false, but it was true nevertheless. Pope Leo X, as we have just stated, was "a man of this world." He had no idea what heresy was in this particular case. Bainton is correct in saying that "back of Albert stood Leo X." But the latter did not fathom the nature of Luther's attack, although some historians say that he led the Christian Renaissance.

In short, there are many European and American scholars with great reputations who simply have no idea of what Luther was trying to do in the year 1517. Take, for example, the most highly touted historian in the world, Arnold J. Toynbee. In his widely read book, A Study of History, he says this on p. 383: "Luther, for example, attacked the sale of indulgences as practised by the Roman Church in his day as being the substitution of a commercial transaction, disguised under ritual forms, for Christian repentance." This statement appears in the section dealing with the Japanese internal proletariat. Not only are we having a difficult time finding out where the Japanese external proletariat was, but we also have to wonder about the difference between repentance and penance. The Roman

Catholic Church has never offered indulgences as a substitute for repentance. Toynbee did not know what penance was, while Bainton also ignored its existence. Is it then surprising that in the summer of 1963 the American Association of University Professors issued a sad report about the manner in which the big sellers dealing with the history of civilization caused immense confusion in the survey courses all over the country? Hundreds of hallucinations are thrown each year at our freshmen in both public schools and Christian colleges. Their instructors seldom have time to figure out what the prima donnas mean in their pontifical textbooks. We hear that Eckhardt created German mysticism long after thousands of German mystics had been fully indoctrinated by David of Augsburg and other authors. We also hear that the Devotio Moderna made no contribution to Protestantism. Finally, we hear that Erasmus came to Oxford to study Greek, after having been taught that language in the Netherlands and Paris.

Perhaps the most important contribution made by the Devotio Moderna to the development of orthodox Protestanism was the doctrine fashioned by Groote and Zerbolt concerning the fall of Adam and the extent of human depravity. Johannes Cardinal de Jong was not aware of the view presented by Groote in his far-famed *Book Of Litanies* in the Dutch language. About 800 copies were circulating in many libraries during the fifteenth century. Professor N. van Wijk in 1940 published a version in the dialect of Deventer and vicinity (*Het Getijdenboek van Geert Grote*, Leiden: Brill). On pp. 150 and 151 there appear some sentences that were composed by Groote himself or else changed into a new form. The present writer in the year 1952 purchased a manuscript that has a better version of this section. In the printed version we have this: "Van den dat wi ons trecken over onse gheliken ende gheliken ons den hoghen." In the manuscript on fol. 88r we read: "Van den dat wi ons trecken over onse ghelike of gheliken ons den hoghen." In English translation the first reads as follows: "From that we consider ourselves above our equals and equals." The second makes more sense: "From that we consider ourselves above our equal or equals." Here follow some statements that are certainly identical with the Protestant views of Luther and Calvin:

> From all evil satisfaction with ourselves and our good works free us. From thinking that we have anything good in ourselves free us. From that we give ourselves more credit for good and less for evil than we have free us. From that we consider ourselves above our equal or equals and that we hold ourselves equal to a person in virtues free us.

What struck Groote and Zerbolt was that many of their acquaintances thought they could in their own power assist God in the process of salvation. On fol. 69v in the manuscript just mentioned Psalm 32 (31) starts as follows: "Salich sint die ghene die verdienen dat hem hore sonden vergheven werden." Here is the embarrassing translation: "Blessed are those who have earned their forgiveness of sins." Or perhaps this is a better translation: "Blessed are those who have earned that their sins be forgiven." In other words, here we have the idea of good works carried to an extreme. In another manuscript bought by the writer in 1952 the psalm starts as follows: "Salich sijn die ghene die har sonden vergeven sijn over mits rouwe, ende die hair sonden bedect sijn mits biechte ende penitentie." Blessed are those whose sins have been forgiven on condition of repentance, and whose sins are covered on condition of confession and penitence. One of these versions was written down in the monastery occupied by Thomas à Kempis until 1471.

Groote says definitely that those who think they have anything good in themselves are in the wrong. This is exactly what the former Dutch cardinal had in mind. He felt that a Christian has enough good in his own nature to assist God. His own words are clear enough: "We Roman Catholics say that man is almost totally corrupt, but he has retained some powers, with which he can co-operate with God." Groote entertained a different opinion. Since he was the founder of the Devotio Moderna and Zerbolt often copied verbally from his writings, we must conclude that he entertained a doctrine of great historical importance, identical with that of Luther and Calvin. Zerbolt seems to have modified it, and yet Luther was very enthusiastic in praise of his opinion on the subject.

Now the question arises as to what Groote himself did with his translation of Psalm 32 (31). Unfortunately the present writer in the period from 1919 to 1952 paid practically no attention to this important problem. He did not realize the significance of Groote's far-reaching labors in the field of Bible translation. No doubt he overlooked the greatest task performed by Groote in creating an increasing demand for the translation of the whole Bible. It is not at all surprising that only one copy of Zerbolt's treatise on this subject has survived, for many clergymen during the fifteenth century looked with disfavor upon the newly awakened desire on the part of ignorant laymen to study the Bible for themselves and exercise what in their opinion was their right to interpret the Bible on their own initiative. The manuscript in which the false translation of Psalm 32 (31) appeared concerning a Christian's privilege to earn the forgiveness of sins has also on fol. 95r an entirely different version than that on fol. 69r. And as for the manuscript used by Professor N. van Wijk for his publication of the psalm as translated by Groote, he has on pp. 139-144 the Seven Penitential Psalms. The first verse in Psalm 32 (31) reads as follows: "Salich sijn die ghene dien hoer boesheiden sijn vergheven ende hoer sunden bedect sijn." So here we have the proper translation made by Groote himself. The two false translations reproduced above were made long after his death, and one probably in the presence of Thomas à Kempis, whose version of the *Imitation* did immense harm to the Roman Catholic Church.

The King James version of the Bible has this translation: "Blessed is he whose transgréssion is forgiven, whose sin is covered." Groote has this: "Blessed are those whose transgressions have been forgiven, and whose sins have been covered." He is not accurate here, for he did not have at his disposal the most reliable manuscripts. Moreover, the writer committed another error when in his chapter on the Congregation of Windesheim (p. 155) he made the following statement: "One of the most remarkable achievements Windesheim could boast of was the correction of the Vulgate." Father Matthias Goossens, O.F.M., the author of a brilliant dissertation entitled, *De Meditatie in de Eerste Tijd van de Moderne Devotie* (Haarlem and Antwerp: Gottmer, n.d.), explained to the present writer in the autumn of 1952 that the latter had magnified the task performed by the Congregation of Windesheim. They carefully consulted a valuable book on the subject entitled, *De Windesheimse Vulgaatrevisie in de Vijftiende Eeuw* by Professor N. Greitemann (Hilversum: Brand, 1937). This author has shown that there was a revision made, but it was not nearly so thorough as the present writer had carelessly assumed in following the opinion of the famous Professor J.G.R. Acquoy. Furthermore, the writer's statement about the influence of the revision exerted upon the commission appointed by Pope Sixtus V was entirely misleading. It did not become "the basis for the Vulgate adopted officially by the Church at the close of the fifteenth century." Here K. Hirsche had acted as a poor guide to the writer. We shall have to accept the conclusion made by Greitemann on pp. 80-88.

It is regrettable that such great experts as Acquoy and Hirsche in trying to magnify the contributions of their compatriots during the fifteenth century, did not take proper pains in studying the original sources in Rome, Vienna, and Munich. During the period from 1919 to 1924 the present writer stood in such awe of those men that he never checked up on their research while he spent twelve months in Italy, Austria, and Bavaria. Obviously the papal scribes and their colleagues had at their disposal many ancient manuscripts which the monks of the Windesheim Congregation in the Netherlands had never consulted. Furthermore, Thomas à Kempis and his companions were not eminent scholars. Let us examine, for example, the following statement on p. 188 of *The Christian Renaissance:* "Semper enim debetur gratia digne gratias referenti." The present writer concluded that the word "debetur" could not be correct, for grace was always freely bestowed, and never earned by any mortal being. Such was his personal opinion, not being aware of the fact that Thomas à Kempis actually entertained another opinion of his own. Unlike Groote and Zerbolt, he believed that grace could be earned by human beings. He had found an abbreviation of "dabitur" and made it to read "debetur." Zerbolt knew enough about the Bible to quote it correctly (see Matthew XIII, 12). Unfortunately Thomas à Kempis has been supported for five hundred years now by Roman Catholic scholars who simply did not want to admit the theological and grammatical errors committed by him.

Before Martin Luther became a Protestant (1515-1516), he sided with Groote and Zerbolt over against Eckhardt and Thomas à Kempis. Afterwards he and Calvin continued to follow the same course of action, together with many Roman Catholic pastors and professors.

THE EDUCATIONAL CONTRIBUTIONS BY
THE BRETHREN OF THE COMMON LIFE

The most important phase of the Devotio Moderna was the work done by the Brethren of the Common Life in the schools. In the year 1954 the present writer published in *Medievalia et Humanistica* an article which had resulted from research done in Europe in 1952 and 1953. He had been inspired by an article on the Renaissance in Germany written by a distinguished scholar named Hans Baron, who afterward came to the United States to live. Baron devoted several pages to *The Christian Renaissance,* and the editors of the *Historische Zeitschrift* sent two copies of the issue in which the article appeared to the writer. The latter was not surprised to note that Baron did not want to accept the actual figures given by a number of German and Dutch humanists and reformers concerning the enrollment in the schools operated by Hegius in Deventer and other scholars employed by the Brethren of the Common Life. When in April 1956 the writer came to his library in Chicago to read a paper on Erasmus in England, he was amused to note Baron's first remarks about his article of 1925. He thought that the writer was peeved by his refusal to take the facts reported by contemporary authors at face value. On the contrary, the writer said that he had greatly appreciated the publicity given to him by that famous German periodical. Baron was not the only German scholar in 1925 who did not want to believe the account by Johannes Busch in his famous book, *Chronicon Windeshemense,* in which he mentioned the size of Cele's school in

606   THE CHRISTIAN RENAISSANCE

Zwolle. The same was true about other schools. Here follow a few paragraphs from the article of 1954.

In the year 1925 Hans Baron published in the *Historische Zeitschrift* an article entitled, "Zur Frage des Ursprungs des deutschen Humanismus und seine religiösen Reformbestrebungen." He was intrigued by the fact that the Northern Renaissance, unlike Italian humanism, tended to generate religious reform. He devoted several pages to the present writer's first book, *The Christian Renaissance: A History of the "Devotio Moderna,"* observing that at the close of the Middle Ages the Low Countries shared with Italy the honor of being more opulent and more blessed with artistic and scholarly progress than any other regions in Europe.

In the same year 1925 Professor Johannes de Jong, who afterward was appointed Cardinal of the Netherlands, devoted an article of 32 pages to the *Devotio Moderna.*[1] In his opinion the civilization of the Renaissance in the Low Countries was largely the result of widespread prosperity and individual liberty. At the same time there originated in the Netherlands a popular demand for religious fervor. De Jong remarked: "Among the movements aimed at reform during the fourteenth and fifteenth centuries one of the most important was the 'Devotio Moderna.' Starting at Deventer and Zwolle, it exerted its wholesome influence upon the whole of the Netherlands, Belgium, north and west Germany, even into Poland and France. The movement is not only remarkable in itself, but it was the first time that our country influenced to a considerable extent the religious and intellectual life of neighboring countries, and more than it has probably done ever since."

In the period from 1925 to 1952 an immense amount of research was conducted by European and American scholars, in order to determine the relation between *Devotio Moderna* and humanism. It was revealed that in the career of Erasmus both movements were almost constantly reflected. Erasmus personified the leading characteristics of the Northern Renaissance. He represented a school of thought that combined personal piety with a thirst for learning. In the midst of terrific intolerance and unnecessary bloodshed he rose far above the wild passions of the multitudes, pleading for the exercise of charity and sound reasoning. His knowledge of human nature was such that he readily detected all symptoms of folly. Unfortunately his vast learning was not widely appreciated in his own age, and even today the church leaders who despised him are generally applauded above him.

When Erasmus was about six years old his mother took him to the city of Deventer, a long distance from his native Rotterdam. The question has very seldom been asked why she chose Deventer above Utrecht or Leiden or Amsterdam. It has often been said that the Brethren of the Common Life at Deventer and Zwolle, whose fame had reached the ears of many parents in Holland, were not interested in secular learning, and that poor Erasmus was sadly bored by his ignorant teachers. But when we study the original sources of the period we obtain an entirely different picture of his early education. The history of the printing press in the Low Countries is one of the most enlightening guides for us in this field. According to the first comprehensive list of incunabula compiled for this area we learn the startling fact that not in mighty Antwerp and Brussels, nor in the great ports' and industrial centers of Holland, but in Deventer the demand for new books was most strongly expressed.

We shall list for each city the total number of books printed in the fifteenth century, followed by the number of books containing classical works, Greek or Latin: Utrecht, 67, 12; Zwolle, 102, 14; Louvain, 251, 24; Leiden, 32, 0; Haarlem, 20, 0; Gouda, 86, 1; Ghent, 11, 1; Deventer, 508, 90; Delft, 138, 4; Brussels, 38, 1; Bruges, 30, 1; Antwerp, 350, 29; Alost, 19, 0; grand total, 1,705, 177.[2] Although Louvain had its university, founded in 1425, while the second university in the Low Countries was not founded until 1575 at Leiden, it was greatly surpassed by Deventer. Even the famous industrial cities of Flanders lagged far behind Deventer, and Zwolle outclassed Utrecht, seat of the only bishopric in the northern Netherlands. It must seem remarkable that those scholars who were so certain of the bad luck experienced by Erasmus in Deventer did not stop to look around for their proof.

Equally remarkable are the figures for England, a country not seldom depicted as a shining example of great admiration for classical learning during the fifteenth century. Frederic Seebohm's book, *The Oxford Reformers*, continues to appear in new editions, faithfully reproducing the old legend to the effect that Erasmus went to England in 1499 to study Greek. Moreover, Margaret Mann Phillips informs us that Italian humanism was more deeply appreciated in England than in Paris.[3] But the actual situation was very different from that imagined by these two writers.

We shall list the leading centers of printing in the same manner as above: Westminster, 93, 8 for the famous Caxton, 103, 3 for Wynkyn de Worde, with 4 others for men of lesser note; London, 101, 10; Oxford, 14, 4; St. Albans, 8, 0; grand total for England, 364, 29. As for the city of Paris, we find some interesting figures in the *Catalogue of Books Printed in the XVth Century Now in the British Museum*, Part VIII (1949), dealing with France and French-speaking Switzerland. The total for this large area is smaller than that in the Low Countries; Paris has 677, 66; Geneva, 20, 0; the grand total for the whole region outside of Paris is 390, 32. Illuminating also is the information presented in the work by Konrad Haebler, *Bibliografía Ibérica*, in two volumes (Leipzig, 1903, 1917). The grand total for Spain and Portugal is 833, 41. The number of classical books printed in Paris is probably smaller than that for the little town of Deventer, while Salamanca in Spain, in spite of its great fame as a university center, could boast of only 5 classical books.

In *The Christian Renaissance* the writer did not do proper justice to the educational contributions by the Brethren of the Common Life. For example, he did not mention the fact that the Brethren in Deventer had a school of their own from 1534 to 1538. He wrote as follows on p. 122: "In the first place, let it be understood that the brothers in Deventer never had a real school of there own there." Subsequent research revealed how great the influence exerted by the Brethren in Deventer actually was. Consequently, Julia Henkel in her brilliant dissertation entitled, *An Historical Study of the Educational Contributions of the Brethren of the Common Life* (Pittsburgh, 1962), has on page 163 this significant remark:

"Actually, in 1534, the municipal council tried to break the monopoly of the clergy, and were pleased to have the Brethren of the Common Life conduct a school of their own in Deventer. But the clergy prevailed upon the governor ('stadhouder') of Overijsel and the provincial estates to intervene in their behalf; so, in 1538 an official decree stated that from then on the situation would remain as it had been before."

In Amersfoort, the Brethren also did far more than had previously been assumed by the present writer, who spent five months at Bilthoven near Amersfoort during the academic year 1952-1953. At that time he also made a careful study of Everardus Foec's career, who has been discussed in another section of this book. Professor Julia Henkel has devoted pp. 171-177 to the school in Amersfoort. Moreover, Professor R. R. Post has shown that the Brethren in Brussels and Liége around the year 1500 obtained control of the junior and senior grades, as they did also in Utrecht. Even more interesting has been the study of the school operated by the Brethren in Magdeburg, which was located in their own house. Here Martin Luther spent one year.

NOTES

THE INFLUENCE OF THE "DEVOTIO MODERNA"

1. J. van Ginneken, *Geert Groote's Levensbeeld*, pp. 80-83. This writer devoted many years of study to the life of Groote and the institutions founded by him. He made useful suggestions for which all scholars will be very grateful, but unfortunately he was never able to produce a well-organized history of the Devotio Moderna. His scattered articles on the *Imitation of Christ* and his biography of Groote leave much to be desired. Nevertheless, we shall frequently refer to those passages of his which contain trustworthy information. At the present time the chief sources for the life of Groote are still the same four which the present writer mentioned so often in his first book, *The Christian Renaissance,* namely, the story by Thomas à Kempis, the narrative by Dier de Muden, the first chapters in John Busch's *Chronicle of Windesheim,* and the work by Petrus Horn. Although we do possess an older account on Groote, composed in rhymed verse in 1421, and still another dated somewhat later, these two are too vague to be considered on a par with the four just mentioned, notwithstanding Van Ginneken's arguments to the contrary. We shall refer to these poetical works as the *Frenswegen Hymnus* and the *Windesheim Hymnus.* They were both published in 1942 by Professor T. Brandsma in *Ons Geestelijk Erf,* pp. 5-51. On these six sources see R. Post, "De onderlinge verhouding van de vier oude vitae Gerardi Magni en haar betrouwbaarheid," in *Studia Catholica,* XIX (1943), 9-20. Post is absolutely justified in defending Thomas à Kempis against both Van Ginneken and Professor W. J. Kühler. The latter devoted two articles to these old sources, mentioned in our Bibliography.

2. J. van Ginneken, *op. cit.,* pp. 80-88.

3. J. van Ginneken, *op. cit.,* pp. 94-96.

4. P. Horn, *Vita Gerardi Magni,* pp. 333-334. — J. Badius Ascensius, *Vita Thom. Malleoli,* Ch. VIII.

5. R. R. Post, *De Moderne Devotie*, p. 11. — J. van Ginneken, *op. cit.*, pp. 108-109.

6. P. Horn, *Vita*, p. 334.

7. G. Groote, *Epistolae, ed. W. Mulder*, No. 23, pp. 105-106.

8. J. van Ginneken, *op. cit.*, pp. 99-100. — G. Groote, *De Matrimonia*, Ch. XVIII, ed. M. H. Mulders, pp. 74-76. The editor in pp. 98-107 of his admirable work, *Geert Groote en het huwelijk*, presents a useful discussion of Groote's views on matrimony. In his opinion Groote was mistaken in following the Apostle Paul and St. Augustine. The present writer is of the opinion that Groote knew something about the value of continence that was not fully appreciated by Mulders.

9. J. D. van Doorninck, *De Cameraarsrekeningen van Deventer*, Vol. III, Part I (Deventer, 1888), nos. 339, 541, 615, 625, 636. — J. van Ginneken, *op. cit.*, pp. 110-111.

10. G. Dumbar, *Kerkelyk en Wereltlyk Deventer*, Vol. I, p. 548. — R. Dier de Muden, *Scriptum*, p. 3. — Thomas à Kempis, *Vita Gerardi Magni*, Ch. II.

11. G. Groote, *Epistolae*, ed. W. Mulder, No. 20, pp. 74-75. The first adequate treatment of Groote's attitude toward heretics appears in the doctoral dissertation of William Spoelhof: *Concepts of Religious Toleration as Developed by the Brethren of the Common Life, 1374-1489*, Ch. II and Ch. III. Dr. Spoelhof has shown that several authorities in the Netherlands have signally failed to comprehend the cardinal features of Groote's message.

12. The houses of the Brethren of the Common Life.

13. J. de Jong, *Het karakter en de invloed van de "Moderne Devotie,"* in: *Historisch Tijdschrift*, 1925, blz. 47-53.

14. Book III, Ch. LV: Quid sum sine ea nisi aridum lignum; et stips inutilis ad ejiciendum?

15. The writer does maintain, however, that Hoen's influence is more significant than that of Carlstadt. Those who have not read Professor A. Eekhof's *De Avondmaalsbrief van Cornelius Hoen*, 's-Gravenhage, 1917, may easily assume that Rode did not go to Wittenberg in 1521. Zwingli in 1525 wrote on the title-page of Hoen's celebrated letter: "Epistola Christiana admodum ab annis quatuor ad quendam . . . ex Bathavismissa." This "quendam" is Luther, as Eekhof shows, and Rode must have visited him before April, 1521. Dr. H. Eells of Princeton claims that Bucer derived his view on the eucharist from Carlstadt (see: *The Methodist Review*, March, 1925,

NOTES 613

p. 325). But now we may ask: Who was the first to teach the new view in Wittenberg/ Was it not Rode (see: P. Smith, *The Age of the Reformation*, New York, 1920, p. 401)?

16. J. de Jong, *l.c.*, blz. 56.

17. Brother Leo, in: The Commonweal, New York, September 2, 1925, p. 401.

18. On the work of Laurent Coster see Vol. III of *Histoire Générale des Civilisations*, ed. by E. Perroy (Paris: Presses Universitaires de France, 1955), p. 574.

THE ORIGINAL VERSION OF THE "IMITATION OF CHRIST"

1. See Jakob Marx, "Nicolaus von Cues und seine Stiftungen zu Cues und Deventer," in *Festschrift zum Bischofs-Jubileum* (Trier, 1906), pp. 210-22.

2. C. Smits, "David van Augsburg en de invloed van zijn Profectus op de Moderne Devotie," in *Collectanea Franciscana Neerlandica I* ('s-Hertogenbosch, 1927), pp. 171-203.

3. C. Smits, *op. cit.*, pp. 192-198.

4. J. F. Meyer, *Thomae à Kempis Capita quindecim inedita* (Lübeck, 1845).

5. J. van Ginneken, *Trois textes pré-Kemistes du premier livre de l'Imitation*. Published in *Verhandelingen der Kon. Ned. Akad. van Wet. Afd. Lett.*, Vol. XLIV (Amsterdam, 1940), pp. 5-12.

6. R. R. Post, *De Moderne Devotie* (Amsterdam, 1940), pp. 151-154.

7. Edited and translated by Joseph Malaise, S. J. Published by the America Press, New York, 1937. See p. 271.

8. See J. van Rooij, *Gerard Zerbolt*, p. 41.

9. See A. Hyma, *The "De Teutonicalibus" by Gerard Zerbolt of Zutphen*, The Hague, 1923.

10. J. Huizinga, *Erasmus* (Haarlem, 1925), pp. 15-17.

11. W. Mulder, "Ter Chronologie van het leven van Geert Groote," in *Historisch Tijdschrift*, Vol. XII (1933), pp. 349-357. Mulder found in Groote's words an almost revolutionary message, but we

must bear in mind that Groote wrote his letter on the Papal Schism, in which he enunciated his remarkable view, during a time in which two popes were reigning simultaneously, one in Rome and one at Avignon. People generally had little respect for the Pope. Nevertheless, Groote did not mince words, and Zerbolt also was not afraid to put his finger on certain sore spots in the hierarchy.

12. See the first printed version published by the present writer in *Archief voor de geschiedenis van het Aartsbisdom Utrecht* (1926), p. 32. The treatise fills one hundred pages, and it is a brilliant defense of the brotherhood by the greatest scholar among its members from 1384 to 1460. It is inconceivable that such a person would have bothered to take a work by Gerard Groote and change it into a composition of his own, as Professor J. van Ginneken claimed.

13. J. van Ginneken, *Trois textes pré-Kempistes du second livre de l'Imitation* (Amsterdam, 1941), p. 32.

14. One of the most devastating attacks upon the Van Ginneken thesis appeared in R. R. Post, "Hendrik van Kalkar en Geert Groote?" in *Studia Catholica*, Vol. XXI (1946), pp. 88-92. Here we discover that Groote never mentioned in his correspondence Hendrik Eger van Kalkar, who induced him to enter a Carthusian monastery and who, according to Van Ginneken, assisted Gerard Groote in the composition of *De Imitatione Christi*. Moreover, Hendrik Eger never mentioned Groote in any of his works.

Van Ginneken makes much of the fact that Groote's biography by P. Horn mentions Groote's friendship with Henry Eger, the Carthusian monk. He also indicates that in the *Conclusa et Proposita* of Groote there is a section with this title, "De Sacris Libris Studendis," while the title of Chapter V in the *Imitation* reads "De Lectione Sacrae Scripturae." The resemblance is less striking than that we mentioned above in the text, where we compared Zerbolt's phrase with that heading Chapter V in the *Imitation*. In the great treatise by Zerbolt entitled *De Reformatione Virium Animae*, we find this chapter heading (Ch. XV); "De Reformatione Intellectus per Sacram Lectionem." Zerbolt emphasizes the reading of the sacred writings, while Groote talked more about studying. In Chapter XXVII of *De Spiritualibus Ascensionibus* Zerbolt made some telling remarks about the imitation of Christ: "Et tu etiam primo hoc modo sequere Christum, esto in eius comitatu . . . Attende eius sermones et dulcissimam doctrinam .et attende modum quo Christus se in omnibus habuit, quam dulciter et benigne verba illa melliflua protulit. Attende modi quo interius se habuit . . . Quod profuit inde Pilato, Herodi, vel Pharisais, quod Christi mores vel gestus, aut praesentiam corporalem viderunt, qui eum imitari noluerunt?" In Chapter XXXII we read: "Et cogita semper quasi Christus dicat tibi: 'Haec feci ut sequaris me.'"

15. In December, 1948, an excellent article on Van Ginneken's thesis appeared in the Belgian periodical, *Ons Geestelijk Erf*. The author is B. Spaapen, S. J. He reviews two Swiss publications dealing with the original version of the *Imitation*. He concludes, on the basis of these two contributions (though he had made up his mind long before they appeared in print), that Gerard Groote certainly did not write any part of the *Imitation* in the Dutch language, although Van Ginneken stated in one of his bigger works on the subject (*Op zoek naar den oudsten teskst en den waren schrijver van het eerste boek der Navolging van Christus*, Wetteren, 1929) that Groote had written the whole of the work in Dutch. The present writer, on several occasions, has discussed this question with colleagues of Van Ginneken, and the latter presented him with a copy of the interesting volume just mentioned. But he said from the beginning that Van Ginneken's main thesis was all wrong, namely, that Groote wrote the original version of the *Imitation*. Spaapen on October 24, 1948, wrote on p. 377 of his article: "Haar *Bemerkungen* slaan cnkel op de vraag naar den Oertekst der Navolging, die door P. v. Ginneken niet bevredigend is opgelost." His Emminence, Johannes Cardinal de Jong, in Vol. II of the fourth edition (p. 431) of his magisterial work, *Handboek der Kerkgeschiedenis* (1947) expresses the same opinion. Moreover, Professor J. Tesser, S.J., wrote a frank statement in his study of the city of Rome, which was published in *Ons Geestelijk Erf* for May, 1949 (p. 169): "Het staat voor ons vast dat professor van Ginneken zijn thesis historisch niet heeft bewezen." The same opinion is shared by the outstanding Roman Catholic educators in the Netherlands, including Professor R. R. Post at Nijmegen. Significant also is the rejection of Van Ginneken's thesis in the admirable study by J. Tiecke: *De Werken van Geert Groote* (Nijmegen, 1941).

16. Found in: M. Schoengen, *Jacobus Trajecti alias de Voecht narratio* blz. 512-514.

17. Found in: M. Schoengen, *Jacobus Trajecti alias de Voecht narratio*, blz. 501-511.

18. G. Dumbar, *Analecta*, Tom. I, p. 88. "Carissime pater, feria secunda precedente ivi Traiectum, ubi maneo adhuc propter nego-

616   THE CHRISTIAN RENAISSANCE

tium, expectens adhuc responsum finale a Decano sancti Salvatoris."

19. G. Dumbar, *Analecta,* Tom. I, p. 88. "Credo quod adhuc oportet negotium agitari trans Iselam coram Episcopo per Abbatem de Dickeninghe, vel alios amicos."

20. Jostes suggests for example that deacon Foec might have written the "Super modo vivendi." If this were true, the writer of our manuscript would certainly have indicated this fact, as he did with the two compositions which Foec did write. But Jostes was encouraged by the catalogue of the manuscripts of the Royal Library at Brussels (*Catalogue des Manuscrits de la Bibliothèque Royale des ducs de Bourgogne,* Tom. I, Bruxelles 1842, p. 46), where Foec is called the author of the various chapters or articles contained in the "Super modo vivendi." Now it happens that neither the author of this catalogue (the new catalogue fails to correct the older one here) nor Jostes himself had any right to infer from the manuscript in question (no. 2285-2289, or rather Ms. no. 2285-2301, fol. 1a-42a), that Foec is the author. The Augustinian monk who wrote this manuscript knew quite well that Foec did not write the "Super modo vivendi," for he says, after having copied the "Super modo vivendi," on fol. 32b: "Magister Everardus Foec decanus ecclesie sancti salvatoris Traiectensis licenciatus in utroque iure de infra positis dubus ita reperitur dixisse: 'Queritur utrum sine offensa iuris aliquibus extra religionem de suis temporalibus ac de laboribus manuum suorum viventibus cohabitare liceat et in communi vivere.' Et quia iam decanus magister respondens ad hanc questionem plura dicit eorum qui supra tacta sunt." Nor is any one justified in saying that Foec wrote these treatises in 1419, for all our monk said about the year 1419 is that in this year Grabow was defeated by the Council of Constance.

21. M. Schoengen, Jacobus Trajecti alias de Voecht narratio, blz. 512.

22. The bishop treats for example the question of reading "sacred writings" in the vernacular, though this question had been completely ignored by the Cologne jurists. His conclusions seem· to have been suggested to him by the author of the "Super modo vivendi": Frequenter Sacram Scripturam et libros sanctorum approbatos, in Latino seu etiam in vulgari editos legunt, dummodo tamen haeresin non contineant, sed de materia plana pertractant"; this sentence we also find on fol. 19 *a* of the "Super modo vivendi."

23. G. Dumbar, *Analecta,* Tom. I, pp. 88-89.

24. That the books on theology and law were accessible in the Low Countries is evident from a note by Fredericq placed below his edition of deacon Foec's first treatise: P. Fredericq, *Corpus documentorum Inquisitionis*, Dl. II, blz. 166-167: "Koninklijke Bibliotheek te 's-Gravenhage, H. S. X. 101 (Th. 355): *Scripta doctorum de congregacionibus*, fol. 68-78. — Op dit stuk en op de vier volgende werd ik opmerkzaam gemaakt door de zeer beknopte ontleding ervan bij Delprat, *Verhandeling over de broederschap van G. Groote*, 2de uitgave, blz. 50-53, die naar het Haagsche handschrift verzendt. De godgeleerde schriften, waarvan, in dit stuk en in de volgende, aanhalingen en bewijsplaatsen worden gebruikt, waren op het einde der 14de eeuw algemeen bekend, zooals blijkt uit het testament van Henricus de Suderlande, canonicus Leodiensis et scholasticus sancti Gereonis Coloniensis ecclesiarum (20 December 1390), die al zijne handschriften aan de hoofdkerk van Luik schonk. Daaronder vermeldt hij: 'Andream de Barule super tres libros crodicis, decretum, decretales, sextum librum decretalium, Clementinas, summam Ostiensis, Innocentium, Ostiensem in duobus voluminibus, Bernardum Compostulanensem, Henricum Boyc super decretales in duobus voluminibus, Archydyaconum et Johannem monachi et novellam Johannis Andree super sextum librum decretalium, Dynum et novellam Johannis Andree super regulas juris libri sexti' (S. Borman, *La librairie de la Collegiale de St. Paul à Liège au XVe siècle*, in den *Bibliophile belge*, deel I, 1866)."

25. This fact has already been explained by Jostes.

26. In Ms. No. 70 H. 75 of the Royal Library at the Hague we find the copy of a document, signed or rather sealed by Frederic of Blankenheim at Deventer on 15 April 1398 on behalf of the Brethren of the Common Life living in the "Heer-Florenshuis," where Zerbolt was then busy at work (see fol. 10 *b*—11 *a* of this important manuscript).

THE EDUCATIONAL CONTRIBUTIONS OF THE BRETHREN OF COMMON LIFE

1. J. de Jong, "Het karakter en de invloed van de 'Moderne Devotie', in *Historisch Tijdschrift,* IV (1925), 26-58.

2. M.F.H.G. Campbell, *Annales de la typographie néerlandaise* (The Hague, 1870).

3. M. M. Phillips, *Erasmus and the Northern Renaissance* (London, 1949), p. 43.